Readings in
Management Control
in Nonprofit Organizations

READINGS IN MANAGEMENT CONTROL IN NONPROFIT ORGANIZATIONS

Kavasseri V. Ramanathan
University of Washington

Larry P. Hegstad
Pacific Lutheran University

1807 1982
175 YEARS OF PUBLISHING

John Wiley & Sons, Inc.
New York   Chichester   Brisbane   Toronto   Singapore

Copyright © 1982, by John Wiley & Sons, Inc.

All rights reserved. Published simultaneously in Canada.

Reproduction or translation of any part of
this work beyond that permitted by Sections
107 and 108 of the 1976 United States Copyright
Act without the permission of the copyright
owner is unlawful. Requests for permission
or further information should be addressed to
the Permissions Department, John Wiley & Sons.

Library of Congress Cataloging in Publication Data:

Readings in management control in nonprofit
   organizations

   Bibliography: p.
   1. Social work administration—Addresses,
essays, lectures.   2. Associations, institutions,
etc.—Management.   I. Ramanathan, Kavasseri V.
II. Hegstad, L. P.
HV41.R39   658´.048   82-20525
ISBN 0-471-86974-0   (cloth)   AACR2
ISBN 0-471-05883-1   (paper)

Printed in the United States of America

10 9 8 7 6 5 4 3 2 1

831553

LIBRARY
ALMA COLLEGE
ALMA, MICHIGAN

Preface

Nonprofit organizations share the management problems usually associated with large industrial complexes. These organizations are as concerned with motivation, goal congruence, and achievement of results as the more frequently considered profit-seeking ones.

For more than 50 years, the behavior of individuals in large industrial organizations has been the subject of intensive research. This research effort has yielded many of the concepts of modern management such as motivation, decentralized organizations, participation, responsibility centers, budgeting, planning, programming, management by objective, and management control.

Recent changes in public attitudes toward government expenditures, the fiscal problems of many large American cities, and new methods for financing public expenditures have increased interest in applying advanced management techniques to the nonprofit sector. Two primary and conflicting views initially emerged. In the first view, the absence of the profit motive made few, if any, of the management concepts employed in the industrial sector applicable to the typical nonprofit organization. The second view held that there were no fundamental differences between the two sectors of the economy and, therefore, management principles applied successfully in one sector could be transferred without modification to the other. Today we see a more mature attitude. This attitude recognizes differences between the two sectors, and proceeds to adapt some of the concepts applied in industry to the nonprofit sector.

Management control is one such concept. It is effectively applied in the private sector, and today many types of not-for-profit organizations also utilize some of its elements. Management control is a motivational process, involving formal and informal procedures, communication, performance reviews, and planning; it seeks to motivate members of an organization to take actions that are in its best interests. Thus, management control attempts to achieve congruence between the personal goals of individuals, the goals of their departments, and the goals of the entire

v

organization. It is a dynamic process recognizing the ever-changing goals of organizations and individuals.

Our discussions are particularly relevant for the larger organizations where top management is incapable of making all decisions and is thereby forced to delegate some decision making to lower-level managers. The larger the organization and the more layers of management there are, the greater is the need for management control. Ideally, the decisions made by the operating managers are exactly the same as those top management would have made if it actually had acted.

The increased emphasis on the management problems of nonprofit organizations has had a major impact on education. Management courses are being developed and added to the curriculum of such professional programs as hospital administration, public administration, social work, public health administration, and policy analysis. In addition, the traditional business schools are recognizing the need for courses concerned with the public sector. Accounting courses for government and not-for-profit organizations are increasingly common. Many MBA programs now offer a public administration emphasis also.

Such changes pose major challenges to both educators and students. The number of journals covering the various areas of the nonprofit sector is large. In addition, there are the traditional accounting and management journals. The practical intent of this book of readings is to make readily available a varied selection of articles covering the full range of management control topics as applied to the nonprofit sector. Approximately 200 journals representing a 15-year period were reviewed in the selection process. The articles represent a wide range of disciplines, encouraging readers to look beyond the traditional journals in their own fields.

Conceptually the book seeks to establish in a variety of nonprofit settings the linkages between elements of management control, its theory, and its application. The first three chapters introduce the reader to the nonprofit environment and to basic accounting techniques relevant for control. Chapter 4 develops the concepts of a general model of management control, which has technical and behavioral dimensions. These are explored further in Chapters 5 through 11. These chapters consider the various components of management control and, more important, the relationships among these components.

This book can be used as the basis for class discussions in seminars or case-oriented courses, or it can serve in lecture courses as a companion to a main text when more extensive coverage is desired. This book blends particularly well with K. V. Ramanathan's *Management Control in Nonprofit Organizations: Text and Cases.* (New York: Wiley, 1982) since they share the same organizational content. We also have class tested the reading material using the following companion texts at the University of Washington and Pacific Lutheran University:

1 Anthony, Robert N., and Herzlinger, Regina E. *Management Control in Nonprofit Organizations,* revised edition. Homewood, Illinois: Richard D. Irwin, 1980.

2 Hay, Leon E. *Accounting for Governmental and Nonprofit Entities,* sixth edition. Homewood, Illinois: Richard D. Irwin, 1980.

3 Henke, Emerson O. *Introduction to Nonprofit Organization Accounting.* Boston, Massachusetts: Kent Publishing Company, 1980.

4 Lynn, Edward S., and Freeman, Robert J. *Fund Accounting: Theory and Practice.* Englewood Cliffs, New Jersey: Prentice-Hall, Inc., 1974.

The following table suggests one way of matching the articles in this book to the chapters in the four texts above.

Chapters In

Reading No.	Anthony/Herzlinger	Hay	Henke	Lynn/Freeman	Ramanathan
1	1	1	5,14,15	1,2	1
2	2,7	1	5,14,15	1,2	1
3	1	1	14,15	1	1
4	4	21	1,2,3,6	17,18	2
5	4	18	11	21	2
6	4	21	14	17,18	2
7	4	21	14	17,18	2
8	5	—	16	15	3
9	5	—	16	15	3
10	11	—	16	15	3
11	4,5	—	16	15	3
12	1	—	15	—	4
13	6	—	15	—	4
14	6	—	5,14,15	—	4
15	2	—	1	1	5
16	2,4	—	11,14,15	—	5
17	2	—	—	—	5
18	3,8	2	15	—	6
19	3,8	2	15	—	6
20	9	—	15	—	6
21	7	—	15	—	6
22	7	—	12,15	—	7
23	7	—	15	—	7
24	6,12	—	14	—	7
25	2	—	—	—	7
26	6	—	5,14,15	—	8
27	6	—	14,15	—	8
28	6	—	5,14,15	—	8
29	1,6,11	—	5,14,15	—	9
30	7	—	5	3	9
31	8	—	5	—	9
32	8	2	5,15	3	10
33	7	2	5,15	3	10

Chapters In

Reading No.	Anthony/Herzlinger	Hay	Henke	Lynn/Freeman	Ramanathan
34	7,8	2	5,15	3	10
35	7,8	2	5,15	3,16	10
36	8	2,15	5,15	3,16	10
37	10,11	2	5,15	3	10
38	11	—	15,16	15	11
39	10	—	15,16	15	11
40	11	—	15,16	15	11

Throughout the text the terms *nonprofit, not-for-profit, public sector,* and *human resource agency* are used interchangeably despite slight shadings of meaning when used in other contexts. The intent is that these terms represent ideas that may be used in different ways by organizations, whether private or governmental, that are not part of the for-profit sector.

This book would not be possible without the generous cooperation of the article authors and publishers. We extend our sincere thanks to them for authorization to reprint their articles. Professors E. James Burton and Walter L. Johnson, who reviewed the book, offered many helpful suggestions and brought additional articles to our attention. They deserve a special note of appreciation. We would also like to acknowledge the contribution of Surendra Avasare for his efforts in library research.

K.V. Ramanathan

L.P. Hegstad

Seattle, Washington
February, 1982

Contents

Readings in
Management Control
in Nonprofit Organizations

CHAPTER 1

Introduction: Control in the Nonprofit Sector

If the New York Stock Exchange listed not-for-profit organizations, they would be considered the growth industry of the last decade. Their rate of increase has been nothing short of phenomenal. Federal spending, for example, grew at an annual rate of almost 30 percent during the 1970s and now accounts for 23 percent of Gross National Product. Since 1960 governmental outlays for welfare services alone have grown by more than 20 percent annually, with attendant increases occurring in the private sector. One estimate postulated that in 1973 one of every four Americans received services from one of the several thousand private agencies in the welfare sector.

Accompanying the growth in nonprofit services and number of agencies providing them is deep concern on the part of many citizens and government officials about the value of socially useful services obtained for each dollar spent. Recent withdrawals of open-ended federal grants and the demand by lawmakers for more accountability over expenditures reflect a change in mood. Previously the attitude of many nonprofit organizations' management was to request as much money as they could possibly get, since it was believed that they were servicing basic human needs and, therefore, could efficiently utilize all resources received.

Scarce resources, competition from other nonprofit organizations, and changing public attitudes about nonprofit programs have put pressure on many nonprofit agencies to seek ways to improve both their effectiveness and their accountability. While the need to allocate finite resources is a problem common to all organizations, profit-seeking and not-for-profit alike, it is compounded in the case of the nonprofit sector by the lack of a profit motive to guide and assist investment and operating decisions. Also frequently lacking is any type of outside market pricing mechanism to measure the value of output. Such absence increases the difficulty of measuring the effectiveness and efficiency of various agencies and thereby of allocating resources to competing users. The question becomes not only that of determining the amount of total resources to be allocated to the nonprofit sector but also, and equally important, how this total should be divided among competing agencies.

Off-the-shelf adoption of management control techniques of profit-seeking enterprises by not-for-profit organizations is not always possible nor in the best interests of the agency. Private industry has not been motivated to provide these social services in a quantity demanded by society, casting doubt on the extent to which management techniques from the private sector can be applied in the public sector. Indeed, the major motivating force of the private sector, that is, profit maximization, is absent from public sector thinking.

The articles in this book explore the applications of sound management accounting techniques in a wide variety of not-for-profit organizations. Museums, hospitals, adoption agencies, drug rehabilitation programs, educational institutions and public libraries, as well as other nonprofit organizations, share many management problems. Successful application of management techniques in one area may provide useful insights to managers in other nonprofit areas.

The readings in Chapter 1 offer hope that accounting and management control devices can be applied to the nonprofit sector. It is not the intent of these articles, however, to provide quick solutions to the problems of nonprofit organizations. Indeed, if such solutions did exist, the management problems facing administrators today would be instead a thing of the past.

The articles collected here provide insights into the fiscal problems of many different types of not-for-profit organizations. A careful reading of the articles will demonstrate the vast amount of overlap in the management concerns of all nonprofit organizations. By way of example, successful application of a management concept to child welfare agencies may provide assistance to administrators of dance companies or model-city programs.

The first article, entitled "The City: Management by Crisis or Crisis Management?," has as its subject city government, which is a major type of not-for-profit activity. Coppie explores some of the major reasons for the fiscal decline of American cities. Contending that the "resource management" tools employed have not keep pace with the growth in size and complexity of the cities, Coppie reviews five management techniques and gives a prognosis for the future. In his view, many of the potential advantages of such sophisticated planning techniques as PPBS and zero-base budgeting have been limited by the lack of reliable cost and performance data.

The second article, entitled "Selected International Trends in Financial Planning and Control in the Public Sector," lends an international perspective to the problems of resource management at the national level. Campfield's review of budget history in the United States, the Soviet Union, Great Britain, Sweden, and South America reveals a general change in the role of budgets from a device for formulating policy to a device for measuring effectiveness. Campfield presents a strong case for the role that management accounting can perform in the support of economic planning in developing nations.

The desirability of transferring management control techniques successfully employed in profit-oriented organizations to not-for-profit ones has not gone without debate. In "Toward Defining the Accountant's Role in the Evaluation of Social Programs," Birnberg and Gandhi provide insight into this discussion. By carefully identifying the two types of evaluation decisions, that is, effectiveness and efficiency, the authors demonstrate the role that the accounting system (management control techniques) can perform.

THE CITY: MANAGEMENT BY CRISIS OR CRISIS MANAGEMENT?

Comer S. Coppie

Urban fiscal crunch. Central city decline. Buzz words used to describe a deterioration that has been a subject of national discussion for the last two decades.

Many observers single out the failure to apply proven management technology as the underlying cause of the central cities' agony. Improve management, the argument goes, and many urban fiscal problems will be overcome. Like most superficial answers to the problems of cities, however, this analysis fails to define the forces at work in the urban fiscal crisis and to explain how better management can help deal with them.

While he was serving as Under Secretary of HUD, Robert Wood once remarked that we must first "complexify" the problems of cities if we are to deal more effectively with them. In other words, we must attempt to understand their full complexity rather than base policy actions on overly simplistic notions of cause and effect relationships that only partially explain the dynamics of urban growth and decay. The financial metabolism of cities is clearly far more complicated, and to a large extent much less understood, than the simple "improve management" prescription would suggest. Nevertheless, there is an important element of truth in this prescription. Improved resource management will be an essential, if not a totally sufficient, condition for relieving the financial pressures cities now face.

Source. Copyright © 1978 by National Association of Accountants, 919 Third Ave., New York, N.Y. Reprinted wih permission from *Management Accountint* (November, 1978), pp. 13–21.

This article is intended to "complexify" the relationship between the urban fiscal crisis and several management techniques frequently listed among the basic tools for urban financial survival. In it we will explore some of the major reasons for the fiscal decline of cities by using the District of Columbia as an illustration of the impact these forces have had on the underlying structure of the urban economy. We will then follow with a brief review of five management techniques that have been developed by government and private industry to stretch the most out of a given financial base. Finally, we will assess the prospects for successfully applying these techniques in city government along with the probable impact their implementation will have on the problem of urban finance.

THE GROWING FISCAL GAP

Most major cities today face an ever-widening gap between expenditures and revenues. This directly results from annual revenue growth being far outstripped by annual increases in expenditure demands. These demands are not caused by new or improved services, but simply by the cost of maintaining ongoing program commitments.

In the District of Columbia, Mayor Walter E. Washington coined a term to describe this phenomenon of urban finance: the "15-5 Rule." In any given year, expenditures can be expected to increase on the order of 15%, but revenues from existing taxes add only 5% through natural growth in the revenue base. This means mayors and city councils across the country begin each new budget cycle with a 10% gap between spending requirements and available revenues, a gap that must be closed during the budget process through a combination of tax increases and expenditure cuts. Of course, the actual gap varies from year to year and from city to city, but the parameters underlying the fiscal structure of most large cities are remarkably consistent.

The "15-5 Rule" has left a significant mark on the financial statements of most large cities. Total spending by all municipalities has jumped at an annual rate of 12% since 1969. And state governments were not far behind the city average. Direct state expenditures increased 11.5% yearly from 1969 to 1973. Even the federal government has fallen victim in that its budget has not been in balance at any point during the current decade, and cumulative deficits of $185 billion were recorded from 1970 to 1976.

Unlike the federal government, cities must balance expenditures with revenues. The urban fiscal gap has been closed through a combination of spending cutbacks and revenue increases in the form of higher taxes and charges as well as new taxing instruments. For example, the District of Columbia has held expenditure growth to an average of 11% per year between 1969 and 1976. To help balance city spending over the period, however, substantial local tax increases were necessary—$35 million in the individual income tax, $6 million added to sales and excise tax receipts, four increases totaling $16 million in property tax, and several increases in business taxes. Together, these levies bring an additional $65 million into the city treasury. But fiscal projections for the District show no sign of dramatic improvement in basic financial outlook. Although the size of the gap ultimately depends on future economic conditions and fiscal policies, by 1982, the city would probably need

another $300 million in new taxing authority to finance today's program commitments.

UNDERLYING CAUSE OF THE FISCAL GAP

In order to recognize the fiscal realities most major cities face today, it is critical to understand some of the primary forces behind urban expenditure and revenue trends and to diagnose the principal causes of the fiscal disparities that lie at the heart of the urban crisis.

Demographic Shifts and Suburbanization

During the 1950s and 1960s, central cities absorbed large influxes of relatively poor migrants from rural areas. At the same time, suburban developments sprang up to house relatively more affluent city residents who were moving out of the inner core. The effects of these population shifts have been dramatic in terms of urban expenditures and revenues.

Significant changes in the demographic profile of urbanized areas over the years accompanied the flows of residents in and out of central cities. Middle-income families, for example, have followed a consistent pattern of settling in suburban communities, lured by such attractions as homeownership and better-quality housing, modern schools, lighter tax burdens, less congestion and crime, and the like. As a result, cities have increasingly become the domicile mainly of rich and poor, with large commuting populations entering the city each day to work and returning to the suburbs at the close of business hours.

The District's experience in demographic change is not unlike many other large cities. Census data show the total population remained relatively stable from 1960 to 1970, dropping only 1% over the ten-year period. At the same time, however, the city experienced population increases of 44% in the number of youth aged 5–24 and 2% in the senior citizen ranks. These increases were offset by a sharp 40% drop in the number of persons in the primary working years, aged 25–64.

Central cities, therefore, have much heavier concentrations of people highly dependent on public services to meet their basic needs, especially the poor, the aged, and those most affected by discrimination in housing and employment. This dependency has led to mushrooming workload increases and service demands in such areas as social services, health programs, and education. In the District of Columbia, nearly one out of every two dollars added to the budget since 1969 has gone to meet costs in the broad program categories of human resources and education.

Economic Fluctuations: Inflation and Recession

Coupled with the population movement, many of the older industrial cities have been crippled by depression-like conditions in their local economies. Simultaneous inflationary and recessionary forces tend to widen the fiscal gap because the impact on expenditures is much greater than any off-setting increase in revenue. In general, most city revenues, such as property taxes, are much less sensitive to inflation than expenditures for personal services, materials, and construction. Thus, the urban economic slump has significantly altered both sides of the fiscal ledger by decreasing potential revenues while increasing service delivery costs and overall governmental expenditures.

A lagging economy usually means a loss of jobs, and with a reduction in the number of jobs available comes higher public assistance and unemployment compensation caseloads, greater dependency on public health and welfare services, and increases in criminal activity. Each of these results in higher costs of service

delivery and greater pressure on governmental budgets.

Inflation brings with it additional financial stresses that most people can understand from their own experiences. But price levels for governmental purchases of goods and services have actually increased more rapidly than general consumer prices because government spends a proportionately larger amount on such items as durable equipment, fuel, medical supplies, and utilities. In 1975 alone, prices for District government purchases increased an estimated 16% compared with an 8% growth in consumer prices.

Wage Comparability and Municipal Unionism

The decade of the 1960s saw an unprecedented growth both in public-sector salaries and union membership. Sparked by the Federal Pay Comparability Act of 1962, which firmly established at the federal level the principle of salary comparability with the private sector, states and local governments increased wages to provide competitive salaries. At the same time, public employee unions have grown to the point where today 50% of all public employees are organized, twice the rate of union membership in the private sector.

Together, these forces have combined to push up personal services costs in central cities, an especially significant factor, as city governments are primarily labor-intensive, service-oriented institutions. In the District, for instance, about half the city's work force is unionized. Since the start of this decade, average salaries have increased 40% (compared with 38% growth in CPI), in line with increases in federal pay, to which we are currently tied. In this respect, the District fares better than cities that formally negotiate wages for most public employees. Salaries for about two-thirds of our work force are linked with federal pay scales and, thus, are not subject to collective bargaining. Indicative of the power of municipal unions, salary increases since 1970 for the remaining third of the city work force—whose wages are set through negotiations—averaged six to sixteen percentage points above federal white-collar pay raises.

Federal Programs and Regulations

Through policies, programs, and regulations it has pursued over the decade, the federal government, perhaps unwittingly, has contributed to the problems cities face today. Some federal programs—Federal Housing Administration (FHA) mortgage guarantees and highway construction programs are notable examples—have spurred the flight of higher-income families from the central cities and thereby reduced the urban revenue base. Other categorical programs—Model Cities, mental health grants, and OEO projects—created constituencies who are now looking to city hall for assistance as federal funding sources dry up. This places greater pressure on the municipal budget because many more interest groups are competing for a share of the public purse.

Apart from grant programs, in which to a certain extent cities have the option of not participating, federal statutes also require substantial new commitments on the part of state and local governments. Too frequently, however, such regulations do not provide sufficient funding to meet the cost of federally mandated services. Water pollution control is a case in point. The District estimates it will cost an additional $50 million annually to meet federal water-quality standards. Although capital funds are available from federal programs to construct sewage-treatment facilities, no

federal operating subsidies are in sight. Moreover, because the federal government has failed to overhaul outmoded programs—such as public assistance and medicaid—state and local government are forced to share half the cost for problems that are truly national in scope.

Finally, the proliferation of federal assistance grants in the '60s and early '70s acted as a powerful inducement to cities to apply for the federal funds available regardless of their actual needs. The trend toward block grants and revenue sharing is a change in the right direction because they allow local officials to determine how such funds might be best used to meet community needs.

Rising Expectations of Municipal Government

A less-publicized reason for growing demands on public services has been the decline of alternative service institutions such as the extended family, community groups, religious and voluntary agencies, and other private-sector organizations. Many of the functions once performed entirely by such agencies have now become the responsibility of local government, contributing to perhaps unrealistic expectations concerning government's ability to solve all manner of human problems.

Prior to 1973, bus service in the Washington metropolitan area was provided by four private bus companies. These bus companies were purchased in 1973 by a regional transit authority, which now operates the bus system at a loss. A portion of the resulting deficit is allocated to each local jurisdiction. Since public ownership began, the District's annual payment to subsidize bus operations has grown to an annual rate of about $20 million. And prospects are good for even larger deficits in the future with the opening of the 100-mile Metro system that will gradually be completed over the next ten years.

Another service category that has exhibited a sharp increase in public-sector responsibility is the care of neglected and dependent children. When parents were unable to care properly for children in the past, there was usually an ample supply of persons willing to take them in—relatives, friends, private adoption agencies, church groups, and so forth. But as the problems of the inner-city intensified, and the strong, closely knit fabric of urban society gradually weakened, government was called upon to play an increasing role in the care of dependent children. We have experienced a dramatic rise in the cost of dependent child care in the District. During the last decade, the cost of public foster care services has shot up over 400%, reflecting both more children in need of care and the difficulty in locating parents in the community to provide these services. In a related area, ten years ago, the city did not provide day-care services, but today this program is a $10 million-a-year operation.

Counterproductive Tax Policies

Inordinately heavy reliance on tax systems that discourage, rather than encourage, residential and commercial location is the final major factor underlying the weakening fiscal structure of central cities. Because geographical boundaries of cities typically do not coincide with boundaries for economic activity or service needs and benefits, cities are not in a position to redistribute wealth from higher- to lower-income individuals. The reason is obvious even if the solutions are not: higher taxes simply encourage taxpayers to move outside the city's limits, leaving proportionately fewer taxpayers in the city to carry the burden of meeting the cost of public services. Many municipal services benefit persons living beyond the city's borders (e.g., commuters), yet city taxing authority is typically severely limited beyond its geographical limits.

The population of the District of Columbia, for example, expands about 50% on a typical workday as a result of the tremendous influx of commuters, students, and tourists who cross the city's boundaries each day. In fact, the District has earned the dubious distinction of having the highest percentage of total public and private employment held by nonresidents of any large city in the country, a phenomenon that adds significantly to the cost of service delivery in such areas as traffic control, street and highway maintenance, police and fire protection, sanitation, and the like. Yet the District is without legal authority to tax commuter incomes, a restriction shared by two out of every three cities of over 500,000 population. Some cities get around the tax jurisdiction problem through annexation of outlying areas, but this option, like commuter taxation, is not open to the District.

POTENTIAL MANAGEMENT CURES

Since World War II, local government in this country has emerged from small-scale institutions of the "mom and pop" variety to major organizations whose annual balance sheets can often be measured in the hundreds of millions or even billions of dollars. Have resource management tools that have come along in recent years kept pace with the enormous growth in size and complexity of city government? Not completely, although some steps have been taken by the District of Columbia and other local governments to improve resource management.

Because of the severe pressures described above, the quest for better management in local government has accelerated, especially during the past decade. Some of the techniques that have been used recently are discussed below.

Planning-Programming-Budget System

The PPBS approach to public-sector budgeting was applied in the Department of Defense in the early '60s and then extended to the rest of the federal government by presidential order in 1965. As a result of the highly publicized claims associated with this budgetary technique, many state and local governments launched PPBS efforts throughout the remainder of that decade.

PPBS represented a departure from the traditional budgetary practice of focusing on line items or objects of expenditure (i.e., what government buys). Instead, this analytical planning approach emphasized the end purposes of government (i.e., what government produces), multi-year rather than annual time horizons, and systematic comparison of program alternatives in terms of their costs and benefits. Although the initials PPBS are no longer widely used to denote budget modernization activities, the concept had a visible impact on the budget processes of many state and local governments (Commonwealth of Pennsylvania and the city of Charlotte, North Carolina, are notable examples). The positive effects of PPBS implementation experiences reported by jurisdictions included a sharper focus on the objectives of the jurisdiction, a more easily understood budget as a result of casting it in a programmatic rather than line-item/organizational format, and increased recognition of the need to identify and examine alternatives within the context of budget decision-making.

Despite some positive results, PPBS implementation in state and local governments was hampered by a wide range of technical and behahavioral impediments:

1 Operating managers had relatively limited involvement in what essentially is a top-down approach to budgeting.
2 Mechanisms usually were not available, or developed, to ensure effective implementation of programs and policy decisions.
3 System designs tended to produce mountainous paperwork exercises in many governments, the costs of which far outweighed the benefits.
4 Legislative bodies exhibited disinterest, skepticism, or even outright hostility to the concept. Because of legislative opposition to changing appropriation account structures, the executive branch in many jurisdictions was forced to operate a dual budget system: the program budget for executive decision-making and the traditional line-item/organizational format for legislative review.
5 A dearth of cost and performance data as well as trained analytical staff limited the volume and quality of cost-effectiveness analyses that could be undertaken.

When measured both against its basic objectives and the claims made by a number of its proponents, the overall impact of PPBS on resource management in the public sector has been marginal at best. PPBS undoubtedly suffered from massive overselling as the answer to the resource allocation needs of public officials. Perhaps its overriding conceptual weakness was its lack of focus on examining the existing resource base available to agencies and programs. This lack of emphasis on examining the base is not altogether surprising when one considers the era in which PPBS was introduced. It came into vogue during the economic expansion of the '60s and was primarily used as a planning tool to allocate the increased discretionary resources available to state and local governments during that period.

Productivity Measurement and Improvement

Accelerating fiscal pressures during the first half of the '70s renewed local government interest and activity in the area of productivity improvement. For example, the District of Columbia recently installed a system to measure program productivity on a monthly and quarterly basis. To date, some 63 programs in 13 major departments have been included in this system, which currently keeps track of 425 productivity measures. By means of a review process involving managers at all levels up through agency heads and the mayor, the extent of progress toward productivity goals is assessed. Service improvement opportunities are identified in this process, and after action is initiated to increase service performance, the results are monitored.

The most important actions initiated in the process are special productivity improvement projects undertaken by personnel in line service agencies and the Office of Budget and Management Systems. These projects are designed to implement changes in management procedures at the service-delivery level, which will improve service quality and productivity. The results of recent projects include:

1 A 42% improvement in refuse collection productivity by instituting work measurement and methods improvements.
2 Redeployment and rescheduling of ambulances so that more are available to respond during peak workload periods.
3 A 19% improvement in the discovery of apartment units with housing code viola-

tions by implementing new scheduling procedures and standardized work methods. These operational improvements now allow a constant number of inspectors to survey buildings in poor and fair condition twice rather than just once a year.
4 A 95% increase in employee shuttle bus utilization and a 14% improvement in driver productivity through the redesign of shuttle bus routes.
5 A 115% revenue gain in parking meter operations by implementing improved methods in collection, maintenance, and security functions.
6 Removal of legislative barriers to efficient work force utilization and timely service in the areas of motor vehicle registration and business licensing.

The results achieved by the District of Columbia—and the impressive gains made elsewhere—have demonstrated that productivity improvement is a valid and effective technique for better utilizing existing resources and maintaining the level and quality of local services in the face of rising cost pressures. Realistically speaking, however, we cannot expect productivity improvement in the short term to resolve the immediate urban fiscal dilemma.

Management Auditing

The U.S. General Accounting Office and the International City Management Association joined forces several years ago in helping local governments expand the audit function to embrace the efficiency and effectiveness of public expenditures as well as the more traditional legal dimension of financial audits. In the District of Columbia, we have incorporated the executive audit function within a broader budget and management setting so that audit teams composed of persons with operations analysis and financial management skills can participate in joint projects (e.g., billing system for solid waste disposal).

Management auditing as a technique for improving the efficiency and effectiveness of government operations has two serious limitations, however. First, local governments typically have very little in the way of substantive information available for conducting a meaningful audit of managerial performance because work standards and reliable costs and performance data systems are not in place. Thus, audit reports time and again wind up identifying these as deficiencies and conclude by recommending the implementation of work measurement and reporting systems. Even where analyses of efficiency and effectiveness are attempted, the softness of the data leads to heavy reliance on guesstimates of conditions or results. From a management viewpoint, such findings are extremely unreliable and represent a superficial basis for effective corrective action.

Second, the primary mission of the audit function is to perform an independent, objective appraisal of an operation. This function typically does not have an *implementation* role or responsibility with respect to improved management practices. The absence of this latter support at the operating program level has been the single greatest impediment to improved efficiency and effectiveness. Thus, from a practical standpoint, the most we can expect from the audit function is greater external pressure for change.

Multi-year Fiscal Planning

Although often considered a part of the overall PPBS thrust, long-range fiscal planning is one of the key elements of modern resource management. Many of the fiscal problems cities are

facing today could have been avoided, or substantially lessened, had cities been able to anticipate them.

The District of Columbia has built a sophisticated fiscal planning system which the Municipal Finance Officers Association recently honored with its Louisville Award for outstanding achievement in public financial management. The multi-year financial planning system is a computerized budget planning model designed to forecast operating cost implications of current program commitments and propose changes over a five-year period. The system can also store up to five years of historical data to compare past and future expenditure trends. Two other key features of the system are its capability to show a variety of different profiles of the budget over time (e.g., by cost factor, agency, program, clientele group, and direct vs. indirect expense), and to project the impact of capital budget decisions on future operating budget requirements (debt service, new facility staffing, and maintenance costs).

The District uses its multi-year financial planning system as a tool for program and fiscal policymaking at the front end of the budget cycle. Rather than waiting until all the numbers are in to determine the true dimensions of the problem and to make tough fiscal and program decisions during the budget crunch period, the data provided by this system give District policymakers sufficient lead time to:

1 Determine the size of the gap between expenditures and revenues in the upcoming budget year and four succeeding fiscal years,

2 Compare the current and projected mix of program resource investments against emerging needs and priorities,

3 Identify the cost factors and programs that

are growing faster than the budget and the reasons underlying these trends,

4   Gauge the impact of current and proposed capital projects on future operating budget requirements and revenues, and

5   Develop strategies for holding down cost factors and program expenditures that exhibit unacceptable patterns of growth.

The multi-year financial planning system has proven to be a powerful tool for strengthening financial management in the District of Columbia. For, in order to correct problems effectively, or to avoid costly mistakes, data must be routinely available to top-level policymakers on the future cost implications of current and proposed commitments.

Zero-Base Budgeting

A growing number of state and local jurisdictions—and most recently the federal government under presidential directive—have undertaken ambitious efforts to implement a different budgeting approach aimed at breaking the endless cycle of adding incrementally to the previous year's budget base. "Zero-Base Budgeting" forces each program manager to re-examine the cost and effectiveness of current activities being performed. Instead of applying the pure zero-base model and beginning "de novo," the methodology being widely used starts with a minimum, or survival, level of funding (i.e., below current resource availability) and builds up a series of decision packages that can be ranked in priority order. Based on resources available and the priority ranking of decision packages throughout the organization, ZBB has the potential of cutting back, or even eliminating, previously funded activities.

The ZBB approach puts to rest the notion that the budget base is sacred and inviolate. In contrast to PPBS, which was used primarily to

allocate discretionary resources available during the economic expansion of the '60s, ZBB has been referred to by Allen Schick and others as budgeting for an "era of retrenchment." The upsurge of interest in ZBB, among politicians and practitioners alike, clearly has been sparked by growing taxpayer resistance to the burgeoning costs of government at all levels as well as the "anti-bureaucracy" wave that came into vogue several years ago. Government expenditures now constitute roughly one-third of our nation's GNP, with much of the growth over the past two decades occurring in the state and local sectors. In addition to the enlarged role government is playing in our national economy, rising state and local taxes have been taking larger bites out of the taxpayer's pocketbook. The response has been to demand a leveling off of budget growth and the elimination of government's past spending habits.

ZBB has two major advantages over other budgeting approaches. Primary emphasis is placed on the re-examination of base resources, and all levels of management throughout the organization are involved in the budgetary process. Like PPBS, however, ZBB implementation will be hampered by the widespread lack of reliable cost and performance data at the responsibility center level of most public agencies. In addition, the dearth of analytical talent in the public sector presents a major roadblock to full realization of ZBB's potential benefits because, as a budgetary technique, it is more analytically demanding than PPBS.

Perhaps the most prevalent criticisms leveled against ZBB to date have been the monumental paperwork it creates and the enormous development and review energy required to complete a ZBB cycle. Some critics warn that government runs the risk of not focusing sufficient attention and staff work on the really strategic fiscal and programmatic issues to be resolved in the upcoming fiscal year because of the ten-fold increase in paper and thousands of hours consumed in support of ZBB-related activities. The cost vs. payoff issue in ZBB has already started a noticeable trend toward simplification of the process among jurisdictions that have gone through several ZBB cycles. As the process of making the system more manageable moves forward, it will become increasingly difficult to distinguish ZBB from incrementalism packaged in program terms.

The District government is testing the ZBB approach in several of its major agencies. While awaiting an objective evaluation of this demonstration, many questions remain unanswered. Can ZBB match the costs and benefits of a well-managed cost-reduction program? Will the data and analysis generated by ZBB be sufficiently powerful to increase the prospects of executive budget proposals winning approval in the political marketplace? After years of experience with program and budget reviews, audits and special studies, many budget executives have built up substantial documentation on inefficient and ineffective programs. Despite years of budget bloodletting and reams of justification and testimony, however, the track record on cost reduction in the public sector does not hold out much promise—outmoded and inefficient programs continue to prevail. Rather than another tool for identifying inefficiency, perhaps what is needed most is an effective way to mold political consensus on "who gets what, and how much."

IMPACT OF IMPROVED MANAGEMENT TECHNIQUES

Although resource management innovations recently applied to local governments have been helpful, they have failed to provide a comprehensive solution to cities' fiscal problems. For several reasons, resource management techniques are not sufficient to do the job alone.

Resource management techniques do nothing about the irrational revenue structures and intergovernmental fiscal relationships that cripple central cities.

All of the resource management improvement approaches highlighted above deal with the expenditure side of the budget. In effect, they try to squeeze the most out of the resources we have. They do not help rationalize the revenue side of the fiscal balance sheet, so cities are forced into the position of driving out middle-income residents in order to provide for the needs of the urban poor.

For central cities to achieve success in extricating themselves from perennial fiscal crises, deliberate steps will have to be taken at the federal level to alleviate some of the problems that previous national actions and policies have created for central cities. The first priority: assign fiscal responsibility to the level of government that can best internalize the costs and benefits of public services. Many public finance experts have long recognized that cities are not appropriate institutions for financing the substantial costs of public assistance, medical services, and education because the causes of poverty and the benefits of a healthier and better-educated society are attributed to the nation as a whole. Cities thereby become irrational mechanisms for income redistribution within the federal structure. Nationalization of programs such as public assistance and medical insurance may become a reality in the coming years as the federal government accepts responsibilities that are truly national in scope.

Another needed change has already begun: the shift in federal and state aid to broad block grants from a myriad of narrow program categories. This approach allows local governments to tailor their programs to their particular needs while, at the same time, it assures those who provide the funding that high-priority objectives are being pursued. In addition, the block grant or revenue-sharing concept reduces the need for large bureaucracies at all levels of government to prepare and review complex grant applications. Under this approach, federal agencies can concentrate their efforts on auditing the results of programs initiated at the local level.

The two federal initiatives cited above—nationalization of certain program responsibilities and expanded use of the block grant concept—will require the development of a broad consensus in the executive and legislative branches of the federal government, plus considerable legislative and implementation lead time. Because of this, they probably lie outside the fiscal planning horizon of most cities.

Resource management techniques do not address thorny political questions that will have to be resolved concerning governmental priorities.

Elected leaders will be called upon to forge the competing demands of special interest groups—whether they be employee unions or vocal constituent groups—into a consensus that represents the "public interest."

As one objective of the political process, governments will have to decide which program commitments should be decreased or eliminated entirely. Throughout the 1960s, many lively public debates over spending priorities occurred when it came to deciding how additional funds were to be allocated. The problem over the balance of this decade, however, will be that of deciding which activities can no longer receive the level of public financial support they enjoyed in prior fiscal years. Although good analytic work can provide a source of objective evidence for this discus-

sion, the judgments on governmental priorities must ultimately be formulated in the political arena. Such process will necessarily require a delicate balance across a wide spectrum of competing demands.

Resource management techniques are primarily designed and installed at the staff level, and staff personnel cannot single-handedly correct our underlying management deficiencies.

The emphasis on assembling a critical mass of analytical talent has had demonstrable payoffs in terms of public policy decisions, but one of the critical weaknesses still to be overcome is effective policy implementation at the program level. Fundamental changes in the way resources are expended will not occur until line program managers make them.

Local government has not had a strong management tradition. Nor has it done a great job of building a managerial cadre within the municipal bureaucracy. Training in management techniques has not received high priority, even though most public program managers come from a professional service background—teaching, medicine, social work, law enforcement—rather than from a background in basic management skills. As a result, not enough is known about actual performance and effectiveness of programs, more productive methods of service delivery, and other critical aspects of modern management. This problem is exacerbated by the long-standing tradition of financial centralization in the public sector, which has left individual program managers with minimal accountability for obtaining the most efficient use of personnel and material resources assigned to them.

Turning from program management to top management, the nature of political executive leadership often has been cited as the single greatest impediment to successful application of management techniques in the public sector. Unlike their private-sector counterparts, whose management behavior is governed by easily understood measures of profit and loss and degrees of market penetration, the nature of the political environment forces elected chief executives to look outward rather than inward in discharging their administrative responsibilities. The bottom line for the political chief executive is most often viewed in terms of his or her ability to be re-elected. As a consequence, it is not surprising to find disproportionate weight being placed on political, rather than purely economic, criteria in the decision-making process. In fact, many would claim this is the essence of democratic forms of government.

A further institutional impediment associated with the political process involves the qualifications and experience of chief executives in the public sector. The presence of substantive management training and experience traditionally has not been a prerequisite for advancement along the career path to top public office. In fact, like program managers, the overwhelming proportion of chief executives in government have come from backgrounds other than management (e.g., law). Therefore, professional staff in the public sector, as compared to their counterparts in the private sector, have had to carry added burdens because they must educate chief executives on the importance of applying long-established and widely used management tools.

Greater attention must be devoted to increasing productivity in the public sector and driving management responsibility and accountability down from the policymaking level to the point of service delivery.

Rather than continually paying lip service to the latest management fad or administering government by acronym, we must get back to the basics. As a first step, program managers at every level must be given far greater voice in the budgetary process and must be provided with the tools and staff resources needed to stay within budgetary allocations. This means that training programs for public managers will have to be expanded, and city government must attract managers with proven expertise and track records in productivity improvement. Civil service systems also should be modernized to eliminate excessively restrictive personnel practices and to provide incentives for better management.

TAKING THE GAP SERIOUSLY

Cities will not quickly regain the confidence of the investment community, nor will they achieve wider political consensus on solutions to urban problems until they establish a sense of credibility in the way the business of local government is conducted. The "management gap" must be closed before we take the fiscal gap seriously.

SELECTED INTERNATIONAL TRENDS IN FINANCIAL PLANNING AND CONTROL IN THE PUBLIC SECTOR*

William L. Campfield

Planning and Control—the key ingredients of management in any endeavor of life—in the public sector take place in an environment of scarcity. Scientific analyses can point up the relative benefits and costs of various prospective programs. Also, conclusions may very well be drawn that there are many worthwhile programs that should be undertaken. But rarely are there enough resources to allocate to the fulfillment of all worthwhile programs. *Planning,* in particular, and *control,* as the eternal complement to planning, become matters of trying to best proportion or strike a balance between the many demands for services by a society and the inevitable short supply of resources to allocate toward satisfaction of the demands.

One of the transparent weaknesses of trying to discuss a subject such as the one above is the tendency to generalize over a vast and complicated subject area. Time has not allowed for the kind of interviewing and other empiricism which would establish greater insights and seasonality to this article. The limitation is all the more regrettable inasmuch as economic and financial decision-making and control in the public sector have not been subject to

nearly enough comprehension and study in depth.

Notwithstanding the limitations, the writer will try to present a picture of some attempts by selected governments to make significant improvements in their financial management practices. The presentation will be directed to four areas: (1) Benchmarks for Planning and Control, (2) Selected Developments in Performance Budgeting, (3) The Decision-Facilitating Role of Accounting, and (4) Audit as a Surveillance and Evaluation Instrumentality.

BENCHMARKS FOR PLANNING AND CONTROL IN GOVERNMENT

The increasing role of government, the growth of public expenditures, and arguments about the proper content and level of public activities are certainly not newly developed phenomena. In Britain, France, and other European countries, the mid-nineteenth century and forward was a period of ferment about fiscal theories and public management. We are told by one economist that in the United States the forty-year period 1880 to 1920 was one in which debate about the role of government and public expenditure policy occupied the center stage of economic controversy.[1] The argument has indeed had a long history.

Source. William L. Campfield, "Selected International Trends in Financial Planning and Control in the Public Sector," *The International Journal of Accounting Education and Research,* Vol. 5, No. 1 (Fall 1969), pp. 123–151 (Urbana, Ill.: Center for International Education and Research in Accounting, 1969).
*The views expressed in this paper are the sole responsibility of the author and not intended to state official position or policy of any organization with which he is associated.

[1]William Habacivch, *Congressional Preferences for Expenditure Proposals: Some Theoretical and Empirical Considerations,* unpublished Ph.D. dissertation, University of Illinois, Urbana, 1967, p. 1.

And now the arguments have been stoked with added coals and furies. In almost every country the share of the public sector of the economy has grown spectacularly, especially during the period following World War II. It makes little difference whether the measure is public employment, government's share of total capital employed, or total current government expenditure. The magnitude and importance (both quantitatively and qualitatively) of the public sector in any country on the lives of its inhabitants is unmistakable.

Why then the increasing shift of interest and emphasis in the public sector as the thermostatic control of the welfare of a nation? These are a few of the major reasons:[2]

1 The increasing incidence of war (both hot and cold), with the attendent rise in military spending and economic sanctions and directions for the private sector.
2 The rapid shifts of populations with a tendency toward increasing problems of urban housing decay, welfare payments, transportation congestion, and the like, which are not solvable by the private sector.
3 The growing social interdependence of individuals and institutions, and hence a need for the government to serve as coordinator and perhaps even arbitrator.
4 The growth of special interest or pressure groups in society for whom countervailing powers must be balanced and harmonized by the government. Examples are representatives of managements, labor union, associations and institutes of various professional groups.

Governments the world over have evolved in response to the collective will of the communities they serve. In the long run they will do whatever the consensus of the communities dictates should be done with the authority granted by the people. Professor William Andrews has noted that the inert, sometimes passive, relationships of government are dimensioned differently in so-called democratic governments and so-called totalitarian governments. In the former, governments evolve in response to the will of the people, and as an instrumentality in which the people participate in some way in the management of their government, thus both identifying with the instrumentality and accepting responsibility for it. Per contra, the totalitarian governments are characterized by the absence of active participation by the people in the instrumentality, although at various points of time the government may very well function in general accord with the popular will.[3] We shall try to ascertain as we progress whether these differences in *people participation* have any substantive effect upon the efficiency in financial management in the public sector.

In every country, management of the public sector involves budgeting in one form or another. Government budgeting is one of the processes by which a nation's scarce resources are allocated among competing needs and effectively controlled in use. A study of the formulation and execution of a government budget can be said to be a study in the applied economics of a country.[4] To the extent that budgetary planning and control is performed competently, government programs will respond to the needs of the people, enhancing both their material and their psychic well-being.

A brief diversion into the origin and early

[2]Ibid., p. 5. Habacivch's bare framework has been expanded in this paper to include fuller descriptive terminology by the present writer.

[3]William G. Andrews, *European Political Institutions: A Comparative Government Reader*, D. Van Nostrand, Inc., New York, 1962, p. 3.
[4]B. N. Gupta, *Government Budgeting*, Asia Publishing House, New York, 1967, p. 1.

development of budgeting may be instructive. The word *budget* is derived from the French word *bougette,* meaning a small bag or pouch. The word was first used in England to describe the white leather bag or pouch that held the seal of the medieval court of the Exchequer. Later the Minister's bag containing his proposals for financing government expenditures also become known as his *budget.* When he presented his proposals to Parliament he was therefore said to "open his budget"—a phrase first used in 1733. Gradually the word *budget* came to be used for the proposals themselves, and hence for any statement of plans and expectations for a future period—whether of governments, other public bodies, private enterprises, or private individuals.[5]

The national budget system came into being in England as a means of asserting parliamentary control over the executive portion of government. During the nineteenth century and early portions of the twentieth other governments followed the British lead and established budgetary systems as one of the fundamental safeguards of constitutional government. Another entirely new approach to budgetary planning and control, occasioned by the revolution in economic theory, opened up in the 1930s. The new school of economists (popularly referred to as Keynesian) directed attention to the previously not considered possibilities of using government fiscal measures to control the level of employment, the role of the national budget as an instrument of economic planning and for regulating the volume of taxation and government expenditures to offset threats of either economic inflation or recession.[6]

In recent years, particularly beginning with the 1950s, yet another dimension of

budgets has emerged, i.e., the managerial or administrative use of budgets not only as a means of formulating policy but as a means for checking on the *efficiency* with which government programs and activities are carried out. The term *efficiency* in this context is used as descriptive of a state of best or relatively high output or yield in relation to some planned input of resources.

Modern systems of financial management for a government must possess considerable flexibility just as there would be the need for flexibility in the various systems employed by large-scale private enterprises. Accordingly, in every country the prevailing systems of financial management need periodic reexamination and updating to make them respond to the changing requirements of governmental administration.

In the United States, Great Britain, France, Sweden, and the Netherlands, where national fiscal techniques have been employed for many years, a continual examination, readaptation, and modification of governmental techniques is generally performed as a matter of standing policy. During the past two decades, with the United Nations serving as coordinator, recently emerging or underdeveloped nations have made considerable efforts to install or to improve their systems of government financial management.

Beginning in the 1950s governments in the emergent countries started developing meaningful information on government transactions with a view to facilitating macroeconomic analysis and better decisions over the whole range of fiscal affairs. One of the first tasks was to devise useful classifications of data. After a series of workshops on budget classification and management held in Asia, Africa, and South America, the United Nations published in 1958 *A Manual for Economic and Functional Classification of Government Transactions.* Concurrently, a number of the more mature nations as well as several of the developing

---

[5]*Budgeting in Public Authorities,* Study Group of the Royal Institute of Public Administration, George Allen and Unwin, Ltd., London, 1959, p. 13.
[6]Ibid., p. 14.

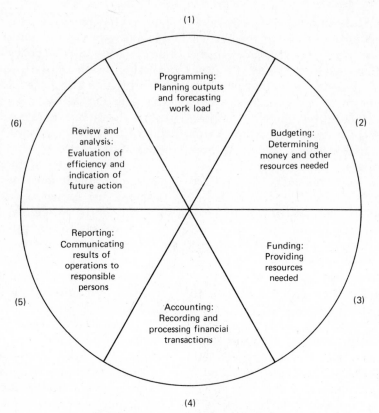

(1)

Programming:
Planning outputs
and forecasting
work load

(6)

Review and
analysis:
Evaluation of
efficiency and
indication of
future action

(2)

Budgeting:
Determining
money and other
resources needed

Reporting:
Communicating
results of
operations to
responsible
persons

Funding:
Providing
resources
needed

(5)

Accounting:
Recording and
processing financial
transactions

(3)

(4)

FIGURE 1   *Financial management cycle*

nations began to experiment with refinements in program and performance budgeting. New techniques and methods for budget forecasting and evaluation of budget execution were devised. The following are the interrelated features of program and performance budgeting:[7]

1 Meaningful programs and activities are set up to show precisely the work objectives or outputs of each agency or department of a government.
2 Systems of accounts and financial management are brought in line with the classifications.

3 Each program and activity is appropriately subdivided, and schedules, work measures, and standards are established as guides for performance.
4 Performance is evaluated in the light of predetermined goals or outputs and related quantitative and qualitative measures of efficiency.

In consequence of the foregoing features, it is proper to say that a performance budget, now considered the sine qua non of public financial management, presents the twin inseparable and invaluable components of effective management, namely, a clear-cut explanation and detailing of *why an action(s) is undertaken,* and *the money cost* of the action.

The financial management function de-

[7]*A Manual for Programme and Performance Budgeting,* Department of Economic and Social Affairs, United Nations, New York, 1965, p. 2.

scribed as a continuous cycle of actions supporting required management decisions can be presented schematically as indicated in Figure 1.[8]

And now, having established our planning and control touchstones, let us examine some recent performance budgeting developments around the world.

In determining where to start we might well be reminded of the story of a chance meeting between two industrialists. The German industrialist said: "Today, Germany is the strongest nation in Europe." The Japanese industrialist said: "Today, Japan is the strongest nation in Asia." The German thought for a moment, and said: "I wonder how the winners are doing?" The so-called winners, the United States and the Soviet Union, have for about a half-century represented the polar extremes in management of the economy. The former places great stress on participation of the populace and the operation of the free market as means of allocating economic resources. The Soviet Union has over the years placed emphasis on central political authority and central planning.

We are told that during the past twenty years the so-called uncommitted countries have closely watched the actions of the giants and meticulously compared the more visible performance indexes of the two economic and political systems.[9]

SELECTED DEVELOPMENTS IN PERFORMANCE BUDGETING

The United States

Perhaps the most significant thing about the American way of public management is that formulation of broad national goals emerges from a consensus that is patiently extracted from a complex of differing goals and differing emphases on the part of the numerous regional, social, economic, and political groups that comprise the United States.[10] A factor of corollary significance is that the U.S. federal budgetary system which we know today has evolved in response to fundamental changes in the size and character of the basic economic, political, and social institutions in the nation.

During the approximate first 150 years of the nation's history, financial planning and control procedures of the federal government were very simple. Prior to 1921 there was no one agency responsible for preparation of an organized budget for the government as a whole. Each agency prepared an annual estimate of funds required, and these were brought together by the Secretary of the Treasury in a "book of estimates" and presented directly to the House of Representatives.

As a result of administrative abuses in government during the early twentieth century, the impact of public expenditures during World War I, the successful use of an *execute budget* by some American cities and states, and the use of advanced budgetary methods by some European governments, the United States government was ripe for reform by 1921. Hence, the Budget and Accounting Act of 1921, which placed direct responsibility upon the President for preparing the federal budget, was a landmark in making possible, for the first time, a unified national budget.[11] It is of interest to note along this period of history that although World War I called forth heavy public expenditures by the standards of that day, the magnitude of federal funds in that era was trivial compared to the funding of today. For example, in fiscal year 1930 the federal debt was

---

[8]Ibid., p. 29. The diagram in this paper has been modified slightly from that set forth in the cited reference.

[9]Robert W. Campbell, *Soviet Economic Power: Its Organization, Growth, and Challenge,* 2nd Edition, Houghton Mifflin Company, Boston, 1966, p. v.

[10]*Budgeting for National Objectives: Executive and Congressional Roles in Program Planning and Performance,* Committee for Economic Development, New York, 1966, p. 58.

[11]Ibid., p. 17.

about $16 billion and the expenditures for the year about $3 billion.[12] Forty years later the budget for fiscal year 1970 shows the federal debt estimate for June 30, 1969, to be approximately seventeen times as large at $277 billion, and annual expenditures sixty-five times as large at $195 billion.[13]

Between 1921 and 1965 there were but few milestones in reforming financial management in the federal sector. Perhaps the most noteworthy happenings were the following: (1) the transfer in 1939 of the Bureau of the Budget from the Department of the Treasury to the Executive Office of the President, thus permitting improvement and strengthening of fiscal control by the President over the executive branch of the government, (2) enactment by Congress of the Government Corporation Control Act of 1945, which required the President to include in his annual budget document *business-type* budget estimates for all wholly-owned government corporations and which mandated the Comptroller General of the United States to perform annual audits of the financial activities of these corporations, (3) enactment of the Budget and Accounting Procedures Act of 1950 which restated the principles and responsibilities for improving accounting, financial reporting, and auditing and authorized for the first time the preparation of a performance budget with information in terms of functions and activities of the government, and (4) enactment of legislation in 1956 which required federal agencies to develop cost-based budgets and establish accrual-basis accounting in accordance with principles and standards by the Comptroller General.[14]

This brief sweep through the history of budgetary reform in the United States brings us to significant developments of the past four years, namely: (1) the 1965 government-wide adoption of planning-programming-budgeting (PPB) of the type that had been initiated by the Defense Department in 1961 and used successfully by that department since inception, and (2) the adoption of budget reforms and recommendations presented in October 1967 by the Presidential Commission on Budget Concepts.

The essential characteristics of the PPB system are: (1) development of more concrete and precise identification of program objectives, (2) systematic consideration of alternative means of reaching those objectives most efficiently, and (3) determination of the total lifetime costs of present decisions.[15]

PPB systems stress the use of modern analytical techniques to provide both a firmer basis for choice among alternative program proposals and clear-cut standards for later measurement of actual accomplishments. Alain Enthoven, one of the architects of PPB applications to national defense planning, states that in order to obtain optimal results from systems analysis and related studies, an agency must: (1) perform open and explicit analysis in which all assumptions, factors, calculations, and judgments supporting alternative programs are clearly disclosed for all interested parties, and key issues (especially when there are differences between program administrators) are highlighted and calculations made to show the results of each differing assumption, and (2) responsive cost/benefit or cost/effectiveness analysis is made which seeks to identify the alternative(s) which yields best output or result from the resources available.[16]

[12]Jesse Burkhead, *Governmental Budgeting,* John A. Wiley & Sons, New York, 1955, p. 21.

[13]*The Budget in Brief: Fiscal Year 1970,* Executive Office of the President, Bureau of the Budget, U.S. Government Printing Office, Washington, D.C., 1969, pp. 6–7.

[14]*Budget Reform and Overall Executive Management,* unpublished address by the Comptroller General of the United States at the Institute for Budget Management Training, Lexington, Kentucky, July 10, 1968.

[15]*The Budget in Brief,* loc. cit., p. 62.

[16]Alain Enthoven, "What Systems Analysis Is and Is Not," *Defense Management Journal,* Winter 1967–68, pp. 11–13. In respect to drawing precise specifications in support of the differing assumptions, Dr. Enthoven describes a situation in which he and the Secretary of the Army were in conflict on estimates of the probable damage to the United States

While PPB is not significantly new or different in concept from earlier performance budgeting philosophy, it does involve some fundamental changes in traditional budgeting which will take several years to perfect. In recent testimony before congressional committees it was deduced that PPB has engendered these major circumstances:[17]

Advantages

Departments and agencies can now determine their program goals and objectives with greater precision and comprehensiveness.

Decision-makers are furnished better data for ordering goals and program priorities, and in choosing between alternative ways of achieving program objectives.

Disadvantages

The PPB system has been applied differently and unevenly under similar circumstances in various agencies and departments, and this has caused difficulties in evaluating multiagency programs. For example, the Army Corps of Engineers does not include in its programming the secondary returns or benefits relating to its construction projects, e.g., improvement of highway access contiguous to, say, a constructed bridge. Per contra, the Bureau of Reclamation, Department of Interior includes all measurable direct and indirect benefits in its analyses of construction projects similar to those of the Army. There has also been evidence of use by differing agencies of widely varying discount rates for cost/benefit analyses applicable to similar programs.[18]

Agencies and departments have found in many instances that they could not obtain current essential data. For example, population-type statistics were available only by reference to the 1960 census data.

Programs are not currently structured on a broad cross-agency basis; hence there is clear and present danger of program duplication and conflict.

The second major recent development in federal budgetary planning and control improvements pertains to reform in budget concepts as adopted in the 1969 budget in accordance with recommendations made by the Presidential Budget Commission of 1967. The primary thrust of the basic recommendations was adoption of the concept of a unified summary budget statement to replace the multibudgets heretofore used. The procedural implementation of the recommended unified budget is not difficult since it involves largely a mere rearranging of tables prepared by the

---

and the Soviet Union which would result from various possible thermonuclear wars, with alternative antiballistic missile defense systems. At the reqest of the Secretary of Defense, Enthoven and the Secretary of the Army prepared a joint memorandum which made explicit the assumptions of each party, the points of agreement and disagreement, rules for computations, and tables of results under each set of stated assumptions. In this way the Secretary of Defense, the Joint Chiefs of Staff, the military department officials, and others were furnished sufficient information to bring their respective judgments to the determination of which assumptions and related estimates were most realistic. As an oversimplified example of the second point, the cost/benefit analysis in terms of seeking military effectiveness might alternatively seek an answer to: (1) Given $1 billion available, how much bombing (assuming the present state of the arts, assuming specified material and equipment, and assuming various reactions and interactions vis-á-vis the enemy) of enemy targets is attainable? or (2) given a specified degree of military effectiveness (e.g., destroy X number of enemy targets at Y locations) what is the least cost for each of a set of assumed material/ troup/ aircraft/ missile combinations or postures?

[17]*The Planning-Programming-Budgeting System: Progress and Potentials.* Hearings before the Subcommittee on Economy in Government of the Joint Economic Committee, Congress of the United States, 90th Congress, 1st Session. U.S. Government Printing Office, Washington, D.C., 1967, pp. 1–4.

[18]For example, the Agency for International Development has used discount rates ranging from 8 percent on a power plant project to a rate as high as 12 percent in evaluating certain highway projects. On the other hand, the Department of Interior has used a 6 percent discount rate on certain utility type programs, and the Department of Transporrtation has used a zero rate in evaluating many highway projects involving federal funds. For further examples refer to: *Interest Rate Guidelines for Federal Decision-making,* Hearing before the Subcommittee on Economy in Government of the Joint Economic Committee, Congress of the United States, 90th Congress, 2nd Session. U.S. Government Printing Office, Washington, D.C., 1968, pp. 4–7.

Bureau of the Budget and the Treasury Department. However, as revealed by several critiques of the Commission's Report,[19] the new focus upon all inclusive or consolidated totals of current and proposed government financial activity may well call forth as many new controversies as the new emphasis dispels old fears of proliferation and manipulation of budgets.

It will probably be useful to just tick off the key recommendations by the Commission, and then discuss briefly some of the things that particularly concern budget people and accounting personnel. In essence, the Commission's key recommendations were that:[20]

1   A single federal budget concept should be used.
2   The budget should include all programs of the federal government and its agencies.
3   Budget revenues and expenditures should be stated on an accrual basis, i.e., respectively as earned and as incurred rather than on the cash basis used in the past.
4   Federal loans, after deduction of any subsidy elements, should be differentiated in the budget from all other expenditures.
5   Sales of participation certificates in loan pools should be treated as a method of financing rather than as a deduction from expenditures.

[19]For example, refer to *The New Federal Budget Concept: An Explanation and Evaluation*, Tax Foundation, Inc., New York, 1968, pp. 10–11; and Samuel B. Chase Jr., "Federal Budget Concepts: A Critique of the Report of the President's Commission," *Proceedings of a Symposium on The Federal Budget in a Dynamic Economy*, The American Bankers Association, New York, April 2, 1968, pp. 24–25. Each of the cited references points up sins of commission, e.g., combining loan and credit activities of the government with conventional receipt-expenditure activities in order to measure the budget surplus (deficit) and sins of omission, e.g., excluding some lending programs such as federal land banks and federal home loan banks.
[20]*Report of the President's Commission on Budget Concepts*, U.S. Printing Office, Washington, D.C., 1967, pp. 6–10.

6   Revenues from agency activities which are enterprise- or market-oriented should be treated as offsets to the expenditures to which they are related.

Of considerable interest to all persons concerned with budget theory and practice is the fact that the Commission, in explaining its recommendations, took great care in underscoring the role and importance of the Congressional appropriations review and authorization process as the focal point in the actual allocation of resources among the various federal programs. Also of significance was the Commission's emphasis on effective use by agencies of the PPB system approach to budget preparation and review. At the risk of being accused of laboring the obvious, the Commission in effect endorsed the idea that agencies needed to ensure that adequate disclosure would be made of all information needed for sound program decisions, initially in presentations by the agencies to the Bureau of the Budget and subsequently during hearings before the legislative and appropriations committees of the Congress.

Good financial management also requires proper organizational arrangements and overt efforts to seek out and apply measures that result in maximum output at least commensurable cost. In respect to the former, many fundamental organizational changes have been made by the federal government during the past five years to adapt its structure to changing program requirements. Some of the more significant changes follow: (1) In 1964, the Office of Economic Opportunity was established to be the central agency for the planning, coordination, and operation of the national antipoverty program; (2) in 1965, the Department of Housing and Urban Development was created to provide overall coordination of programs designed to improve urban areas; and (3) in 1966, the Department of Transportation was formed, bringing together a number of major transpor-

TABLE 1
Changing Structure of Federal Budget Outlays (in Billions of Dollars)

Program	1964 Actual	1968 Actual	1969 Estimate	1970 Estimate
National Defense	$ 53.6	$ 80.5	$ 81.0	$ 81.5
(Special S.E. Asia support)	—	(26.5)	(28.8)	(25.4)
Major social programs:				
Social Insurance (excluding Medicare)	22.7	30.2	33.3	37.2
Welfare payments and service	3.4	4.6	5.3	6.1
Education and Manpower Training	1.6	6.4	6.5	7.2
Health (including Medicare)	1.8	9.7	11.4	13.0
Housing and community development	0.8	2.7	3.3	4.4
Subtotal major social programs	30.4	53.7	59.8	67.8
Interest	9.8	13.7	15.2	16.0
Veterans benefits and service	5.7	6.9	7.7	7.7
All others	19.2	24.0	20.0	22.4
Grand Total	$118.6	$178.9	$183.7	$195.3

tation programs previously administered in separate agencies.[21]

In order to achieve maximum cost consciousness in the financial affairs of the federal government, the Bureau of the Budget initiated in 1965 a government-wide systematic, formal cost-reduction program. Under this new effort, the head of each federal agency and department was required to: (1) assume direct supervision of a formal cost reduction program; (2) establish specific dollar cost reduction goals; (3) subject every major proposed expenditure to searching scrutiny in terms of costs and benefits; (4) employ independent means to verify savings; and (5) recommend high-priority use of savings achieved.[22] In order to strengthen the effort, an Advisory Council on Cost Reduction, which was established in 1967, has consulted continuously with leaders in the private sector to benefit from their experience and ideas for reducing costs.

The United States budget significantly influences the economic activity of the country, and in turn is greatly influenced by the changing needs of the American people. The changing composition of the budget, disclosed in Table 1, reveals much about the nation's priorities.[23]

Between 1964 and 1970 annual budget outlays will have increased about $77 billion or about 65 percent. Of the increase, $28 billion ($25 billion for special Southeast Asia support) is attributable to increased spending for national defense, but spending for major social programs has similarly increased. As the nation has intensified efforts to widen the opportunities for the disadvantaged and improve the quality of life for all Americans, the expenditures in these areas have more than doubled since 1964, increasing by approximately $37 billion, or 123 percent.

While the demand for public services has grown dramatically during the decade of the 1960s, so has the nation's ability to pay for these services. The estimated $195 billion of expenditures for 1970 is roughly one-fifth of the estimated gross national product (GNP) for

[21]*The Budget in Brief,* loc. cit., p. 61.
[22]Ibid., p. 62.

[23]Ibid., p. 19.

that year, and the estimated outlays for the Vietnam engagement will amount to less than 3 percent of GNP. The increase in the United States' GNP since 1960 has been about $400 billion, which is larger than the total output of the six countries of the European Economic Community (Germany, France, Italy, Holland, Belgium, and Luxembourg), or roughly comparable to the total GNP of the Soviet Union in 1968.[24]

The Union of Soviet Socialist Republics (USSR)

Perhaps the most timely observation we can make about economic planning and control in the Soviet Union is that the idyllic socialist state of Marx–Engel design is being rapidly transformed into a benevolent people's capitalism. Between 1960 and 1966 Soviet leaders have brought about considerable changes in economic thought and applications as they groped with ways to counter the substantial deterioration that has occurred in the Soviet Union's economic performance since the late 1950s. A revolution in economic theory spearheaded mostly by economists V. V. Novozhilov and L. V. Kantorovich has brought about a retreat by Soviet leaders from the previous high degree of centralized planning and a movement from the principle of administrative guidance in the allocation of resources to that of price guidance.[25]

To obtain better perspective on the shape and depth of change in Soviet economic planning it is well to note some of the circumstances underlying the development of the USSR's eighth five-year plan, covering the period 1966–70. The plan, which was ratified by the Twenty-third Congress of the Communist Party in March–April 1966, was set up

in an environment influenced largely by the troublesome problems and unfilled promises of the ambitious seven-year plan, 1959–65, formulated by former Chairman Nikita Krushchev. Some of the inherited results that had to be overcome by the new Soviet leadership, L. Brezhnev, the General Secretary of the Communist Party, and A. Kosygin, the Chairman of the Council of Ministers of the USSR were:[26]

1   Failure of the agricultural sector to come up to announced official expectations; e.g., the average annual growth rate during the 7-year period was only 1.6 percent compared to the planned yearly rate of 7.0 percent. This was a deviation from standard of 77 percent.
2   An overall slowdown in the economic growth rate averaging a minus 27 percent.
3   A decline of 45 percent in the rate of per capita consumption.
4   A decline of 17 percent in the planned rate of investment.
5   A decline of 14 percent in the planned rate of urban housing new development.

After much backing and filling among Soviet leaders in trying to strike an appropriate balance in allocating resources among the competing uses—investment, comsumption, and national defense—the evidence, though sketchy in detail, seems to support the belief that the following are the emphases for resource allocation during 1969 and probably continuing into 1970:[27]

1   A marked increase in outlays for military and space programs, which also would

---

[24]Ibid., p. 52.
[25]Robert W. Campbell, *Soviet Economic Power: Its Organization, Growth and Challenge,* 2nd edition. Houghton Mifflin Co., Boston, 1966, p. vii.

[26]*Soviet Economic Performance 1966–67.* Materials perpared for the Subcommittee on Foreign Economic Policy of the Joint Economic Committee, Congress of the United States, U.S. Government Printing Office, Washington, D.C., 1968, p. 2.
[27]Ibid., p. 4.

constitute an increase in the share of GNP allocated to these programs.

2 Immediate and large additions to consumer money incomes through adjustments in base wages and in incentives and bonuses. Largely as a result of two good crop years, consumption of goods and services expanded during 1966–67 at about twice the rate recorded during the previous five years. The Soviet leaders were hopeful that maintaining this momentum would go a long way toward satisfying consumers' desires for greater diversity and better quality of food and other consumer goods.

3 A slowdown to deceleration in the rate of growth of investment, especially for producer goods.

4 A cutback from earlier plans to allocate large amounts of additional resources to agriculture during the period 1966–70.

Perhaps even more significant than the changed emphasis on the proportioning of resource allocation was a change or modification in the philosophy of resource allocation initiated in the fall of 1965. Among the key modifications were: (1) individual enterprise managers were given more authority to make decisions of the kind previously made at high central-authority levels. For example, a shoe manufacturing and distribution outlet could determine its production quotas, payroll requirements, inventories, etc., as a consequence of consumer demand schedules, as contrasted with previously centrally determined production and other quotas for the enterprise, and (2) criteria and guides for decision as well as evaluation of operating results were to be based upon such measures as volume of sales, profits, and rate of return on capital employed. During 1966 there were 704 enterprises comprising about 8 percent of the total industrial production of the Soviet Union that adopted to this new form of planning and

control. At the end of 1967 about 6,000 enterprises were under the new system, and the Soviets expected that the total transfer of enterprises would be completed prior to the conclusion of the 1966–70 plan.[28]

Additional light can be shed on what is happening in the way of economic planning by taking a look at the Soviet State Budget. This budget is much broader than national budgets for Western countries because in addition to encompassing the conventional national, republic, and local government activities, it includes, for example, funds for financing many kinds of investments that normally are financed by the private sector in capitalist countries. In rubles, the Soviet annual expenditures are about half as large as the Soviet gross national product. Compared to the United States, this proportion is about twice as great as that for U.S. budgets at all levels of government combined.[29]

Earlier we showed that comparative U.S. public expenditures over a period of time revealed shifts and emphases in priorities of public planning. A similar result can be obtained by examining the trend of Soviet expenditures, as summarized in Table 2.[30]

It is always dangerous to make comparison of somewhat dissimilar circumstances, particularly since the Soviet State budget includes so many things that the U.S. federal budget does not. Notwithstanding, we call attention to the fact that the 41 percent increase in expenditures for the eight-year period 1960–68 is somewhat smaller than the approximately 65 percent rate of increase in the public expenditures of the U.S. government for the period 1964–1970. It is also interesting to note that in the USSR the increases in expenditures for defense were 80 percent and also 80 percent for social-cultural measures. In the United

[28]Ibid., pp. 8–9.
[29]Ibid., p. 45.
[30]Ibid., p. 47.

TABLE 2
USSR Expenditures of the State Budget (in Billions of Current Rubles)

	1960	1965	1966	Plan 1967	Actual 1967	Plan 1968
Financing the national economy	34.13	44.92	45.18	46.92	49.9	50.19
Industry & construction	15.59	20.99	21.06	21.87	[a]	23.9
State agriculture and procurement	4.75	6.77	6.30	6.35	[a]	9.0
Trade (foreign & domestic)	3.59	2.27	2.84	3.17	[a]	4.0
Transportation and communications	2.81	2.83	2.61	2.67	[a]	2.3
Municipal economy and housing	3.22	4.23	4.53	4.08	[a]	[a]
Residual	4.17	7.83	7.84	8.78	[a]	[a]
Social-cultural measures	24.94	38.16	40.76	42.92	43.4	45.81
Education, science, and culture	10.31	17.51	18.73	19.67	19.9	21.0
Health and physical culture	4.84	6.67	7.10	7.40	7.4	7.6
Social welfare measures	9.79	13.98	14.93	15.85	16.1	17.1
Defense	9.30	12.78	13.40	14.50	14.5	16.7
Administration	1.09	1.28	1.41	1.44	1.5	1.53
Loan service	.70	.10	.10	.20	[b](.2)	[b](.2)
Budgetary expenditures residual	2.97	4.38	4.73	4.04	[b](5.0)	[b][c](9.17)
Total expenditures	73.13	101.62	105.58	110.02	114.5	123.60

[a] Not available.
[b] Estimated.
[c] Including reserve funds of the Councils of Ministers.

States the increase in defense expenditures for the shorter time span was only 52 percent, but the increase in expenditures for major social programs was a huge 123 percent.

Although there have been substantial changes in the Soviet economic system during the past decades, the leaders of the Soviets give every appearance of maintaining a deep faith in the value of the deterministic process of central planning. It has been aptly noted by a close student of Soviet fiscal planning that a factor that tends to aggravate difficulties in that country is the bureaucratization not only of the direction which the economy takes but also of the productive processes themselves.[31] In spite

of the decentralization of decision-making initiated by the Brezhnev−Kosygin team in 1966, there is still a belief extant in the western countries that the complicated Soviet scheme of wages and bonuses does not augur well for efficiency. The pay or incentive system requires complicated accounting and such a large percent of personnel engaged in control activities tends to impede rather than enhance overall worker productivity.

Two Democratic Monarchies

We have spent some time discussing the two political and economic monoliths of our times. It may serve our discourse well to examine the public planning carried on in two smaller nations, Great Britain and Sweden because: (1)

[31] Luca Pietromarchi, *The Soviet World*, A. S. Barnes & Co., Inc., New York, 1965, p. 232.

both nations rely heavily on free enterprise, comparable to the United States, but both also do welfare programming comparable to the socialist objectives of the Soviet Union, and (2) these two nations, as democratic monarchies, operate legislatively and administratively in a highly comparable manner.

Great Britain. Planning in an economy which, like that of the United States, is based upon open, competitive enterprise must take the form primarily of a voluntary coordination of the plans for expansion of both the public sector and the private sector of the economy. To improve the process of coordination, Great Britain has been experimenting in recent years with what has been termed *indicative planning*. For this purpose there was created in 1962 a body known as the National Economic Development Council, which in effect constituted a partnership between government, private management, and labor unions. The primary objective was obtaining better economic performance in Great Britain. Among the most important duties of the Council was studying the plans and prospects of the principal industries in Britain and correlating these plans with one another and then with the plans of the British government for the public sector, including the nationalized industries.[32]

However, in 1964 the British established a new government department, the Department of Economic Affairs, in order to give the national government a more positive lead in planning. The National Economic Development Council then became mostly a forum for discussing the economic plan of the government at various stages of its formulation. Linked with the main council are separate councils for each of the different industries which serve as channels for communication between the government and industry.[33]

TABLE 3
Public Expenditures in the United Kingdom (Millions of pounds at 1958 Prices)

	1950	1953	1955	1960	1966
Defense	1395	2221	1901	1507	1688
Domestic-civil	4396	4419	4524	5331	7245
Other	220	92	138	174	268
Total	6011	6732	6563	7012	9201

It may again be instructive, as we have done earlier in respect to the U.S.A. and USSR, to read out of national public expenditures over time some indications of reordering of priorities and change in emphases on allocations of resources. Table 3 discloses the trend of approximately two decades.[34]

If we use the period, 1960–66, a seven-year measurement which would approximate the scale of measurement applied in this paper to public expenditure changes in the U.S.A. and USSR, we find that the respective percent increases in total expenditures, 17 percent, defense expenditures, 12 percent, and major social programs, 36 percent, are significantly smaller than the indicators of change for the U.S.A. and USSR over a somewhat comparable unit of time.

The foregoing picture of a slowdown in priming of the public sector was an early predictor of the current difficulties of Britain's economy. *Time* magazine, in discussing recent tax increases in Britain, pointed out some current doubts about the vigor of public management of Britain's economy, namely: (1) the long-promised economic recovery is moving a lot slower than the government had hoped, and (2) for a substantial part of the past two decades Britain has ceased to make optimal use of its resources or technological know-how.[35]

[32]Noel Branton, *Economic Organization of Modern Britain,* The English Universities Press, Ltd., London, 1966, p. 6.
[33]Ibid., p. 8.

[34]E. A. Holmans, *The Growth of Public Expenditures in the United Kingdom Since 1950,* Manchester School of Economic and Social Studies, Manchester, England, 1968, p. 321.
[35]"Britain's Resistance to Painful Cures," *Time,* April 25, 1969, p. 104.

Among the various techniques and methods used by Britain's leaders to reverse the down trend in political and economic effectiveness have been some major governmental organization changes or the creation of new organizations. The following include some of the more significant events:[36]

1 Reduction of the size of the Cabinet from twenty-three to twenty-one.
2 Redistribution of major duties of the Foreign Office, the Department of Economic Affairs, and the Ministry of Defense. In the Ministry of Defense greater interservice coordination and more unified management planning and control was encouraged by giving the three senior Ministers of Defense special spheres of responsibility cutting across service lines.[37]
3 The Ministry of Land and Natural Resources was dissolved after three years of ineffective operations and its functions transferred to the Ministry of Housing and Local Government.
4 A Parliamentary Commissioner for Administration (popularly known as the Ombudsman) was established to facilitate control of administration and the investigation of citizens' complaints.
5 Establishment of the Industrial Reorganization Corporation (IRC) to bring about modernization in United Kingdom industry through promotion of socially desira-

ble mergers. The IRC would act as "good fairy" in bringing about "marriages" between private firms without retaining a controlling interest, or in the long run without retaining any financial interest.

Sweden.   Sweden is a very small nation (about eight million people) heavily dependent upon export trade, and hence an ardent advocate of free international trade, and a country extremely sensitive to economic developments and movements of the business cycle in other countries. Consequently, the shape and scope of economic planning is influenced more heavily by foreign trade considerations than is the case in most of the Western democracies.[38]

Constitutionally, the Swedish Parliament has an important position in economic policymaking. Much in the fashion of the British Parliament, it shares the formulation of legislation with the executive arm of government. Also in comparable fashion to Britain's Chancellor of the Exchequer, the Swedish Minister of Finance is the key executive officer in initiating and in applying national budgetary policy and control.

But perhaps unlike other countries, there has been an increasing emergence and influence by labor and other "pressure groups" during the past two decades in shaping public policy in Sweden. This circumstance is attributable in no small measure to the manner in which legislative proposals are initiated and presented to the Swedish Parliament. Royal Commissions, comprised of members of the government's Central Administrative Boards (CAB), politicians, and representatives of various groups of labor and other citizens, study any matter referred to it by the Government. The Commission reports to the Swedish Cab-

---

[36]B. C. Smith and J. Stanyer "Administrative Developments (Great Britain) in 1967: A Survey," *Public Administration*, Autumn 1968, pp. 239–46.
[37]Ibid., pp. 240–41. For example, the Minister of State for Army was given responsibility for all international policies relating to defense; the Minister for Navy was answerable for all personnel and logistics policies; and, the Minister for Air Force was responsible for the defense budget as a whole as well as for coordinating research and development for all three services.

[38]Hans B. Thorelli, *Overall Planning and Management in Sweden*, The Industrial Council for Social and Economic Studies, Stockholm, 1957, p. 23.

inet which, prior to submitting a proposal for legislation to Parliament, solicits comments from the government's administrative agencies as well as from private institutions and from various pressure groups.

The following examples of participation by royal commissions gives a fairly good indication of their role in the preliminary stages of political and economic planning in Sweden:[39]

1 A Commission on Post-War Economic Planning submitted to the Swedish Cabinet a series of reports dealing with industrial capacity and employment problems, and proposals for a broad range of public and private supported projects that might be initiated during any economic crisis.

2 A commission studying the problems of capital investment for the late 1950s and the 1960s called for acceleration of public investment in numerous areas and activities that had been held back during World War II and in the early postwar years.

3 A commission operated in the late 1950s to study the possibilities of preserving a stable currency in Sweden.

All of the foregoing suggests that the political process in Sweden, described as constitutional, parliamentary democracy, is one of widespread and active participation by Swedish citizenry.[40]

Before passing on to other matters it is pertinent to note that although the influence of the Swedish government permeates heavily all economic planning in the country, Sweden is properly categorized as a free-enterprise or capitalistic country. The following figures, set

TABLE 4

Expenditure and Investment in the Public and Private Sectors of Swedish Economy (in Millions of Kroner)

Sector	Expenditure		Investment	
	Amount	Percent	Amount	Percent
Public				
Central government	7,800	10.0	7,700	20.0
Local &regional government	10,700	13.0	6,400	17.0
Private	62,500	77.0	24,000	63.0
Total	81,000	100.0	38,000	100.0

forth in the Swedish National Budget for 1967—68, point up vividly the extent of influence by the private sector.[41]

South America—A Developing Region. Recent indicators of relative stability in the economic and political structures in South America have revived the interest of students of public management in that continent. Generally, the governments of most of the countries have taken on a hue of calm and reason; national currencies have been put on sounder bases; industrialization has taken hold and a trained work force is emerging. And several countries, previously noted for their protectionist attitudes, are offering significant economic inducements to draw foreign investment into vast undeveloped areas.[42]

Although the countries in South America taken as a geographic unit are considered to be less developed economically than most other nations in the so-called Western world, there are considerable differences in stages of political and economic development in the various countries. Accordingly, in discoursing on our central theme of international trends in public

[39]Ibid., p. 19.
[40]Albert H. Rosenthal, *The Social Programs of Sweden*, University of Minnesota Press, Minneapolis, 1967, pp. 92—96.

[41]Ibid., p. 160.
[42]Michael P. Sampson, "Economic Planning—a Key to the New Promise of South America," *The Lybrand Journal*, Vol. 49, No. 4, 1968, p. 23.

management we will perforce generalize most circumstances but cite specific country conditions as warranted.

Professor Edward L. Elliot, who has spent considerable time in South America, tells us that the following features of undeveloped and underdeveloped countries are present in most of South America:[43] (1) a high ratio of population to capital, (2) a relatively high dependence on primary production of one kind or another, (3) a low level of income and well-being as compared to other parts of the Western world, and (4) rapidly growing populations.

Professor R. E. Seiler, also a veteran of many years in South America, points up the need to accelerate the improvement of fiscal planning by giving us these two vignettes which underscore the need:[44]

1 In one country, the Minister of Public Works budgeted on amount for construction and paving of roads without obtaining information on: (1) the number of miles of paved or unpaved roads existing at the time, (2) traffic density, and (3) reasonably accurate estimates of costs of construction. The predictable result was that all kinds of "bottlenecks" occurred, and the nation's critically inadequate transportation system was not improved to any appreciable extent.

2 In another country, a $26 million chemical fertilizer manufacturing plant was constructed. The fertilizer was sorely needed to improve the nation's agricultural productivity. Upon completion of the plant and during the early period of operation it

was discovered that the cost of production was considerably higher than the cost to import the fertilizer. The plant, which had operated only a few months, was closed and the capital invested in the plant was for the most part irretrievable.

On the brighter side of public management in Latin America, there has been a trend in the countries, spurred by the Alliance for Progress, to simplify existing fiscal structures and increase tax-law enforcement efficiency. The U.S. Internal Revenue Service has sent teams of tax advisers to aid the local authorities in several countries. Also there has been considerable assistance furnished by the Inter-American Development Bank and other public and private financial institutions.[45]

Because inflation is a serious burden to improving economic planning in South America, it has been necessary for most countries to establish procedures for revaluing properties in terms of current monetary values. Revaluation systems are now in force in Argentina, Brazil, Chile, and Uruguay. Peru has recently established a partial revaluation system relating to equipment.[46]

It should also be noted that considerable tax-reform legislation has been going on in recent years. Changes have ranged from the completely revised and restated income tax codes of Brazil (in 1966) and Venezuela (in 1967) to important structural changes in Chile and Colombia and to lesser revisions in the laws of Peru and Argentina.[47]

Public planning and optimal allocation of resources in lesser developed countries become a difficult task of proportioning and interbalanc-

---

[43]Edward L. Elliot, *The Nature and Stages of Accounting Development in Latin America*, Center for International Education and Research in Accounting, Urbana, Illinois, 1968, p. 4.

[44]Robert E. Seiler, "Accounting, Information Systems, and Underdeveloped Nations," *The Accounting Review*, October 1966, p. 653.

[45]Michael P. Sampson, loc. cit., pp. 23–24. The success of tax enforcement programs is evidenced by these increases in tax collections during the 1961–65 year: Brazil, 39 percent; Chile, 31 percent; and Peru, 29 percent.

[46]Ibid., p. 26.

[47]Ibid., p. 35.

ing investment and consumption, production and distribution, exports and imports, and also interlarding economic considerations with needed cultural and spiritual considerations.

The progress made by most South American countries in getting their economic planning and development machinery harmonized and in high gear is harbinger of new hopes and promise for this segment of the world.

SELECTED OBSERVATIONS ON THE DECISION-FACILITATING ROLE OF ACCOUNTING

The role of accounting during the past two decades in facilitating the allocation-of-resources decisions in the Western world has been widely publicized. In the United States, intensive efforts have been made to make accounting in the public sector fulfill its role as a service to management. As a matter of record, the President's Commission on Budget Concepts commended this trend in its October 1967 report, commenting in part:

[in view of] the importance of program costs as an important tool for program management and for agency budget formulation and execution, the development of modern accounting systems makes it possible to adopt a much better method of measuring and reporting Government expenditures than was previously possible.[48]

In the Soviet Union, the economic planning reforms about which we have discoursed earlier have set in motion serious reexaminations of the role of cost accounting, in particular, in aiding Soviet planners. Professor Y. V. Novozhilov, one of the chief architects of the new economic conceptualization, says that improving and coordinating cost accounting with economic planning will be of inestimable value

to Soviet leaders in (1) making the choice of the best projects for commitment of resources and (2) assisting in production planning, product pricing, and evaluation of performance of enterprise and project managers.[49] It is noted by two Americans, professors Mills and Brown, that although cost accounting is all important in the Soviet's scheme of prices and costs, there are significant defects in Soviet accounting for depreciation and allocation of indirect costs to projects.[50] They further point out that if accounting is to be useful to the various levels of Soviet planners under the new economic planning philosophy, then considerable improvements in accounting systems design and operation will be necessary to support: (1) Preparation and reviews at appropriate management levels of both fixed and flexible budgets, and (2) better cost accounting and reporting by cost and responsibility centers, by units of production, by processes, and by projects.[51]

Managerial accounting can and does have its finest hours in supporting economic planning in the developing nations. Relevant to our earlier discussion of public planning in South America, we are informed by Professor Elliot that management-type accounting, even in its embryonic stages in some countries, is most useful to government in: (1) Origination, evaluation, and revision of national economic plans (budgeting, cost accounting, cash flow analysis, forecasting are all accounting-type contributions which are significant to the planning process), (2) national income accounts construction and reporting, (3) improving the construction and reporting aspects of tax systems, and (4) constructing performance standards data, thus facilitating audit and other

---

[48]*Joint Financial Management Improvement Program—20th Annual Report*, U.S. Government Printing Office, Washington, D.C., 1969, p. 4.

[49]*Soviet Economic Performance, 1966−67*, loc. cit., pp. 212−14.

[50]Robert H. Mills and Abbot L. Brown, "Soviet Economic Developments and Accounting," *The Journal of Accountancy*, June 1966, pp. 41−44.

[51]Ibid., p. 46.

evaluation of performance by various agencies and programs.[52]

Although there is a marked increase in the rise of management accounting and the participation of professional accountants in the planning of developing nations, there are some bothersome areas that need added attention. One of these areas of needed improvement is that of development within the affected countries of uniform, qualitative educational systems for turning out competent accountants.[53] Another problem area is that of obtaining sufficient cross-cultural understanding, communication, and cooperation among the accountants of a developing nation and those of assisting nations like the United States, Great Britain, et al. Of critical importance in this regard is the need for a common understanding of the role of accounting in a society, the assumptions upon which economic activity rests, the validity and usefulness of common methods of measuring economic activity, and the like.[54]

SOME NOTIONS ABOUT AUDIT SURVEILLANCE AND EVALUATION

E. L. Normanton, author of perhaps the most recent definitive book on international auditing in governments, refers to auditing as an inescapable response to the need for continuing assessment or public accountability by governments.[55] The need and the response have been accepted as articles of faith in most of the countries of the world.

In the United States, it is the view of most knowledgeable students of government that internal auditing has become an increasingly large and important factor in facilitating planning and control by federal agencies. It is also well established that the General Accounting Office (GAO), in performing its overview responsibilities for the Congress of the United States, is continually broadening the scope and depth of its review of the activities of the Executive Branch. Exemplary of the increasing participation by the GAO in *management efficiency* type audits is its recent completion of a comprehensive review of the poverty programs authorized by the Economic Opportunity Act of 1964.

The GAO's March 1969 report to Congress as a result of the review responded to that body's request that the GAO determine: (1) the efficiency of the administration of programs conducted under the Economic Opportunity Act, and (2) the extent to which the programs achieve the objectives of the enabling Act.[56]

Very little of consequence can be found either in the available Soviet literature or in the Western literature about the role of auditing in the decision evaluation process in the USSR. Perhaps we can surmise, in comparable fashion to Professor Robert W. Campbell's comments regarding Soviet accounting, that the auditing function is a sacrificial lamb on the altar of Marx–Lenin doctrine. Professor Campbell notes that the Marxist bias that value is created only by labor, hence that costs and value are mere expost summations of expenditures for labor, is itself the main source of trouble underlying all stages of Soviet planning and control.[57]

Author Normanton, referred to previously and himself a Briton, is quite critical of the way

---

[52]*Edward L. Elliot*, loc. cit., p. 183.

[53]Ibid., p. 179.

[54]Many writers have stressed these points. However, refer especially to: Garnett F. Beazley, Jr.m "An International Implication for Accounting," *The International Journal of Accounting*, Spring 1968, pp. 4–9; and Washington Sycip, "Professional Practice in Developing Economics," *The Journal of Accountancy*, January 1967, pp. 41–45.

[55]E. L. Normanton, *The Accountability and Audit of Governments*, Frederick A. Praeger, New York, 1966, p. 1.

[56]*GAO Newsletter*, April 15, 1969, p. 1.

[57]Robert W. Campbell, *Accounting in Soviet Planning and Management*, Harvard University Press, Cambridge, Massachusetts, 1963, pp. 255–57.

in which the audit function is employed in Great Britain. He states that the post of Comptroller and Auditor General, together with related staff in the Exchequer and Audit Department, established by Lord William E. Gladstone in 1866, has not changed in any fundamental respect during the approximate one hundred years of existence of the audit function in Britain. Additionally, he is caustic about: (1) the relatively low educational and experience requirements used as standards for selection of auditors, and (2) the excessive attention by auditors to the minutiae of accounts. Normanton makes rather pointed reference to the need for Britain to produce real reforms in the field of accountability and audit similar to those in the United States in 1921, 1945, and 1950 and those in France in 1946—48.[58]

Our review of the literature in respect to use of the auditing function in public administration in South America leads us to believe that this evaluative instrument has a very low effectiveness yield in this part of the world. Most of the current writing about financial management in the public sector in the southern continent stresses the great needs to significantly improve the education, training, and testing mechanisms for obtaining qualified auditors, and for the auditors' associations in the Latin countries to adopt sound accounting principles and auditing standards, and to establish the machinery to ensure that the principles and standards are complied with. A few years ago, the *Journal of Accountancy* editors pointed cheerfully to action by the Mexican Institute (Instituto Mexicano de Contadores Públicos) of Public Accountants in publishing a booklet on *Auditing Standards and Procedures*, patterned after the works of the American Institute of CPAs.[59] Hopefully, in the view of American officials, pioneer efforts in Latin America like the one cited will accelerate very swiftly and bring auditing into an acceptable and highly beneficial role of contributing to economic planning and development by the various governments.

CONCLUSIONS AND EXHORTATIONS

Perhaps second in importance only to the problem of achieving a just and lasting peace is the problem of bringing the vast, unwieldy machineries of governments the world over into some kind of timely and constructive response to the major needs of the universal people. There is a notion aloft that organized public management is the best way to allocate resources to meet those needs of the people which cannot be satisfied adequately and economically through the free and open operations of the marketplace.

In trying to assess the progress made in improving public management we could perhaps follow the admonition of James Thurber to "better ask some of the questions than to try to know all the answers." Consequently, we ask:

1 Will Planning-Programming-Budgeting (PPB) blossom first in one country and another, and then fade like other so-called management fads because of failure to synchronize it with the other essentials of planning and performing?
2 Is the Soviet experimentation with decentralized planning and with market-oriented decisions and techniques likely to become a permanent way of economic life in the Soviet Union? Will the changes in direction confirm the alleged latter-day cry of Karl Marx that "I am not a Marxist"?
3 Will, in fact, the sun set on the tradition of British innovativeness and enterpreneurship?

[58]E. L. Normanton, loc. cit., pp. 410, 422, 425.
[59]"Auditing in Latin America," *The Journal of Accountancy*, November 1965, pp. 34—35.

4 Can the Latins (South American version) demonstrate that their early momentum will ensure steady progress in economic planning and development?

The writer wishes he could either peer into the minds of the international leaders and confide in you what miracles they would wrought, or construct the infallible, normative planning model which no self-respecting nation could reject. Rather than valor, he has opted for a more discretionary commentary on some innovations here and some refinements there by governments in their efforts to make public programs and activities yield the best economic and social fruits for their people.

In thinking broadly about achievements in the public realm we should be reminded of the statement of James A. Garfield, twentieth President of the United States, that "All representative governments are managed by the combined wisdom and folly of the people." In this sense, we must be compelled to the long view that on balance there is persuasive evidence of significant progress in the universal public sector in achieving better management of resources, rending more and better services, and above all in bridging the gulf which often separates little citizens from the big administrators and staff in the governmental bureaucracies.

TOWARD DEFINING THE ACCOUNTANT'S ROLE IN THE EVALUATION OF SOCIAL PROGRAMS

Jacob G. Birnberg and Natwar M. Gandhi

Currently a debate is surging on in the accounting literature concerning the extension of the accountant's functions into the area of assessment of social programs. On one side of the debate we have enthusiastic accountants who have declared that

as it has done for the private sector of the economy, the accounting profession can help significantly to enhance efficiency in the public sector. . . . For CPAs to participate in this aspect of our rapidly evolving social structure, we should aggressively seek out the

challenges. By so doing, we will demonstrate our ability to make significant contributions to social measurement [Linowes, 1968, p. 42].

They also contend that

the American accounting profession and business management—working in tandem for the first time with the social scientists—have all the know-how needed to begin a "turn-around" for the public sector. Together they can create social investments that can finally begin showing desperately needed profits: improving the quality of life in the United States [Linowes, 1971, p. 14].

On the other side of the debate, however, there are those who take a different and dim view of the accountant's role in the evaluation

Source. Copyright © 1976 by *Accounting, Organizations and Society*. All rights reserved. Reprinted by permission from *Accounting, Organizations, and Society.* (Vol. 1, No. 1), pp. 5–10.

of social programs. For example, Francis (1973) contends that the accountant has no professional training or acknowledged expertise to understand social ills. He therefore will be a poor guide in the processes of planning as well as of evaluation of social programs designed to eradicate these ills. Further, he has too limited a stock of statistical skills to attest professionally to the veracity of data collected in conjunction with the evaluation of social programs. Thus, Francis (1973, p. 250) concludes that "the question is, given that independent auditing bodies should be established, does the accountant possess the training or experience to qualify him over others to audit in the social arena? The evidence seems to indicate that the answer to this question is negative."

Such a position predictably led to a series of comments from accountants (see Granof & Smith, 1974; McRae, 1973). They for their turn enumerated the strengths of accountants and after the rejoinder by Sobel and Francis (1974) we are at an impasse. The basic issue in this debate concerning the accountant's role in evaluation of the social programs is a very simple one: How well can we transplant the well-tested accounting evaluation techniques of the profit-oriented business entities into the environment of the not-for-profit social programs? Is there anything sufficiently unique about social programs such that the accounting evaluation process which flourishes in a profit-oriented business environment would necessarily languish in them?

In this paper we intend to clarify the issues and assess the appropriateness of various views so that the benefits of such an interdisciplinary exchange are not lost in partisan rancor. To do this we will return in the first section to some of the earlier literature on evaluation research and place arguments in perspective. In the second section we will review the current issues, and in the final section we will suggest that evaluation research and the management of social programs require the combined talents of all parties to the discussion.

A BRIEF REVIEW OF EVALUATION RESEARCH

The literature concerned with the evaluation of social programs considers two types of evaluation decisions. One is the program's *effectiveness* wherein the primary question is: Did the program achieve its goals? The other is the program's *efficiency* wherein the primary question is: At what economic costs were the program goals achieved? (For a discussion see Rossi & Williams, 1972.) It is therefore of significance that at the outset we separate any evaluation discussion into its two components—effectiveness and efficiency. These are separable issues measurable in different ways and in different dimensions.

Evaluation Problems

It is also instructive to note what the evaluation literature does *not* discuss. The authors in that area have little concern for the fiduciary aspects inherent in the funding of any social program (see for example, Perloff et al., 1976). Moreover, once the activity is no longer classified as a program—something that is experimental or tentative in nature—the evaluation researchers are not likely to find it of much interest. Their interests are primarily in research evaluation and not in administrative evaluation where the focus is primarily retrospective and the assessment is in terms of specific practices and decisions, operating costs and immediate pay-offs, and statutory compliance and efficiency. In research evaluation, however, the focus is on the future and primary emphasis is on the generalizable knowledge. Thus for the social scientists-researchers the administration of the programs is something of an inconvenience that they must tolerate. As Nelson (1975, p. 707) complains of the psychologist-researchers, they assume "an arrogant, distant, and academic stance, involving themselves with occupying nonadministrative functions.''

Further, even in research evaluation the social scientists have yet to solve certain fundamental problems whose solutions are crucial to the evaluation of the effectiveness of any social programs. Gorham (1967) has identified these problems, and we summarize them below:

1. Problem of Definition of the Objectives.

In many programs, from their broad social objectives mandated in the enabling legislation it is not clear *what* precisely should be the outcome of the programs and *what* precisely should an evaluator measure as benefits of the programs. The identification of the specific program benefits is a prerequisite both to the program administration as well as to the program evaluation.

2. Problem of Measurement of the Results.

Even if we were able to specify what specific benefits a program should strive for, the problem of their measurement still remains. The measurement problem is two-fold: (a) Many of these programs are wide in scope and diversity. They reach a variety of people in different socioeconomic segments in various geographic locations. Each recipient segment has a different utility function for the program benefits. Thus, there is a need for devising a measurement scheme which would attach different weights to the benefits accruing to different groups. (b) In the social arena we have a variety of programs dealing in such diverse fields as health, education, welfare, housing, etc. Even though they all have to compete against each other for funding, their benefits are in different dimensions and inherently incommensurable. "The incommensurability of the benefits makes it difficult for cost–benefit analysis to contribute greatly to the choices that must be made . . ." (Gorham, 1967, p. 7).

3. Problem of the Lack of Follow-up Information.

Even if we were to solve the problems identified in (1) and (2) above, there is just not enough relevant information now available concerning the effects of the social programs to conduct an effective evaluation process. Even in case of certain programs which are several years old by now, there is no relevant data-base available from which the evaluation indicators can be derived. As Drew (1967, p. 11) puts it so well: "Whatever the files and computers do contain, there is precious little in them about how many and whom the programs are reaching, and whether they are doing what they are supposed to do."

Evaluation Activities

It would appear that there are four evaluation activities which are ongoing in the not-for-profit sector as social programs are developed, implemented, evaluated, rejected, or continued on a relatively permanent basis. These are:

1 Assessing program *effectiveness*. Measuring the discrepancy, positive or negative, between the program's broad social objectives and its accomplishments. This is a macro-level analysis.

2 Assessing program *efficiency*. Measuring the operating performance by which the program utilized its resources in pursuing the objectives discussed in (1). This is a micro-level analysis.

3 Assessing program *compliance* with statutory requirements. Checking whether the program is carried out in accordance with the legislative mandate and guidelines.

4 Assessing administrative *efficiency*. Evaluating the administrative performance with a concern for the behavior of personnel rather than a program as discussed in (2). This is also a micro-level analysis.

As Wholey (1972) suggests, the evaluative activities are generally carried on at two levels in the hierarchy: (1) From the perspective of the policymakers, i.e., top-administrators and/or legislators, who are concerned with the legislative changes and budget levels; and (2) from the perspective of the program managers who are concerned with the immediate planning-management-control processes.

From the perspective of the policymakers the evaluation generally concentrates on both assessing the total impact of the existing programs and analyzing the results of field experiments and demonstration projects which may be the forerunners of new programs. This evaluation is holistic in nature, and what impact it has on the actual administration of these programs is purely a matter of conjecture. For example, in the case of the Labor Department, according to Wholey (1972, p. 363), evaluation of the impact of national programs plays almost no part in their day-to-day administration. Worse yet,

even if reliable and valid data were being generated in the national program impact studies being done, such studies are not appropriate support for the types of decisions actually made within the Labor Department. National program impact evaluation studies circulate from office to office in the Labor Department without being acted upon or in most cases even read, because Labor Department administrators do not make the types of decisions which these studies are designed to support.

The most salient point emerging from the literature is that even the most relevant evaluation studies conducted to assess the effectiveness of the social programs are quite seriously limited in their impact on the crucial decisions concerning resource allocation. There are powerful political as well as structural forces which bear heavily on these decisions when they are being deliberated upon in the legislative as well

as administrative bodies. In general the aims of a social policy or well-documented warnings of an appropriate evaluation are subordinated to the exigencies of political considerations. Thus the real enemy of even the most valuable evaluation studies is the very nature of American political process. As Coleman (1973) points out: "Probably because of the fragmentation of power, the principal deliberations in the formulation of policy are often deliberations about what strategies will generate enough support to enable passage of legislation, rather than deliberations about social consequences of the legislation."

THE ACCOUNTANT AND VARIOUS EVALUATION ACTIVITIES

It is clear from the outset that Francis (1973, pp. 249–250) is concerned with the first evaluation activity—assessing the program effectiveness as a social experiment at the macro-level. Her interests are in research evaluation and not in administrative evaluation. Her stressing of the limitations of the accountant as a social scientist and statistician are most telling on this point and would appear to carry the point to even the most reluctant critic. Significantly, even Granof and Smith (1974, pp. 824–825) carefully qualify conditions under which the accountant could assist. These qualifications deal with data certification, not data analysis, and the latter is an important problem in the evaluation of any social experiment.

In the second evaluation activity—program efficiency—there appears to be a question of definition. When does a social program of an experimental nature end and a social program on a relatively permanent basis begin? If, for purposes of discussion, we suppose that program efficiency refers to the period during which the macro-level statistical analysis of the program effectiveness is ongoing, then Francis (1973) is correct and the accountants have little part in evaluating the efficiency of the programs. The accountant's function is at best fiduciary and this is quite different from assessing the efficiency of the program. However, it must be noted that judging from the past records even the social scientist is in a blind alley too when it comes to the evaluation of the experimental programs.

The third evaluative activity—assessing program compliance with the statutory requirements—is fiduciary in nature and clearly the province of accountants and lawyers. This is an area where accounting expertise is needed. As Thomas (1975, pp. 8–10) quite correctly points out, in the conduct of social programs the higher social goals should be obtained not by ignoring the requirements specified in the enabling legislation but only within the statutory guidelines provided. The fiduciary reporting and financial controls are important parts of the evaluation process. This is particularly so when Federal funds are involved but the actual expenditure of funds is in the local hands. For example,

the best that can be said for the manpower programs that engaged private employers is that the performance record is mediocre. The firms that accepted performance contracts to teach the hard-to-teach have folded their tents and slipped away. There are many reports of sharp practices, shoddy workmanship, and outright fraud involving real estate brokers and builders working with federal funds to provide housing for poor families [Ginzberg & Solow, 1974, p. 218].

Given the decentralized nature of so many social programs, the assessing of statutory compliance is important to the proper management of social programs. Funding authorities must encourage the proper utilization of resources and take the necessary steps to ensure this. Toward this end the Federal government typically provides funds and sets forth basic guidelines as to how these funds are to be used. The funds and guidelines are disseminated to the operating units and the management of the program is generally left in the hands of local officials. Thus to make a social program operationally viable requires not only the cooperation of the local beneficiary population but also of the local authorities, for it may be the latter who actually operate the programs.

Further, the local authorities operating the program may have a different perception of the social ills and of the goals of the program designed to eradicate the ills than the Federal government who originated, designed, and funded the program. This critical delegation of responsibility between the design stage and the implementation stage may be a fatal blow to the original purposes of the program unless the strong fiduciary controls exist to ensure the statutory compliance. Here the accounting function can provide regular feedback information concerning the actual administration of the program and assure its adherence to the statutory guidelines.

The fourth evaluative activity—assessing the administrative efficiency—is usually ignored by the social scientist-researchers. It is realistic to assume that the managerial accountant is in a position to assist the program managers. Indeed a significant literature has already evolved in this area as accountants identified with "for-profit" firms shift their attention in varying degrees to the not-for-profit agencies (e.g., Anthony & Herzlinger, 1975; Livingstone & Gunn, 1974). It would appear to belabor the obvious to argue in favor of the role of the accountant in this area.

TOWARD A COOPERATIVE VIEW OF THE EVALUATION PROCESS

What then is the essence of the exchanges? First, that the accountant's role is not in assessing the effectiveness of the social programs is clear. This is the province, as Francis (1973, pp.

249–250) has noted, of a particular subset of social scientists who are adequately trained in *both* the social sciences and the appropriate statistical techniques. The resource allocation issue to which Francis (1973, p. 245) alludes is not a measurement of program effectiveness. Rather, it is a question of social policy and politics where the issues are complex and there is little firm knowledge available on which to base policy.

Granof and Smith (1974, pp. 824–825) are correct in stressing the relevance of the accountants in the compliance function when the goals can be stated operationally. This can create a potential conflict between the researchers for whom the efficacy of the program is open to question and the auditor for whom compliance is of essence. This conflict, which is stressed by Sobel & Francis (1974, pp. 829–830), is the crux of the difference between the evaluation of a program's effectiveness as a social experiment and a compliance audit by the GAO. Perhaps it is on this point that the orientation of the two groups may never be reconcilable.

In the arena of social programs at this juncture, given the state of evaluation art and the overwhelming political nature of decision-making, we contend that the evaluation process should be reoriented. There should *also* be a major emphasis on the micro-level analysis and statutory compliances as identified in the evaluation activities (2), (4), and (3) respectively. We believe that the accountant can contribute most to these evaluation activities which together form what may be described as "administrative evaluation" as distinguished from "research evaluation."

However, as Granof and Smith (1974, p. 825) point out, "the accountant can make a substantial contribution to the evaluation of social programs so long as their goals are stated operationally." Thus there is an operational bias in the accountant's view of the

evaluation. His evaluation role will be at the operating level and primarily for the program managers, who as Wholey (1972) points out, can use detailed information concerning what works best and under what conditions. We consider this a significant contribution because even many social scientist-researchers (e.g., Binner, 1973; Wholey, 1972) now believe that it is this kind of evaluation which provides the primary payoff in terms of decisions actually influenced.

Finally, all of the discussants have viewed the accountant as a potential social auditor. Yet it is as an assistor of management that he can do his most useful work. As resources for social programs become more scarce, their efficient utilization becomes even more important. It is in the area of efficient utilization of resources that the accountant can help the not-for-profit social programs and agencies.

SOME CONCLUDING OBSERVATIONS

Figure 1 provides a general evaluation scheme that could be applied in the evaluation of social programs. As it can be seen from the figure, we view the whole process of social programs in two phases. In the first phase the primary emphasis is on the formulation of social policy where politics plays a dominant role in deciding which social objectives are to be achieved, how much of national resources are to be devoted to their achievement, and what legislative mandate and guidelines are to be provided. The accountant's role at this stage in social programs is minimal and indirect at best.

The second phase of the process is operational and deals with the actual administration and evaluation of the programs. The transition from the first to the second phase, that is the reduction of the broad social objectives into operating program goals, is a function of social planners and is very crucial both to the program administrators as well as to the program

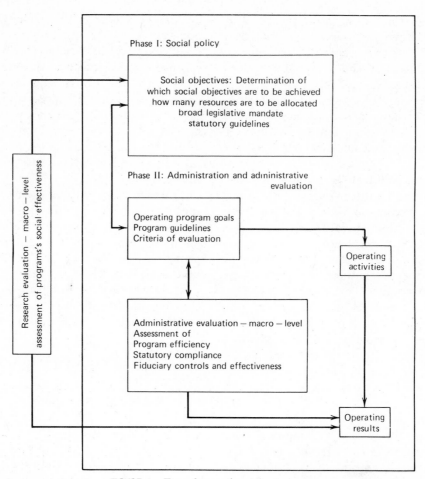

FIGURE 1   *Two phases of social programs*

evaluators. This is also a very frustrating function because there is no guarantee that a successful completion of the program goals would necessarily lead to the achievement of mandated social objectives.

It should be noted that this is quite in contrast with the profit-oriented business enterprises. In the business organizations most operating activities are well-structured, meaning that there are identifiable and measurable objectives as well as operational goals and activities. The causal linkage among all these is

more clearly defined and also is so perceived by those who are concerned with it. Thus we have a structure of established relationships in the profit-oriented businesses. What is more important, these objectives, goals, and activities can be measured on the accountant's unidimensional monetary scale. An established structure of causal relationships and its amenability to the unidimensional measurement scale are what make the accountant's evaluation task most effective in the profit-oriented business enterprises.

However, the accountant's unidimensional monetary measurement is quite inoperative when it comes to the measurement of a multidimensional phenomenon like a social objective (Gandhi, 1975). That is why "operationalization" of the social program—reduction of a broad social objective into measureable and verifiable operating goals, activities, and evaluation criteria—is a crucial prerequisite to the accountant's entry into the evaluation of a social program. In this regard Granof and Smith (1974, p. 824) correctly point out that "accountants should avoid becoming involved in evaluating social programs until policy-makers are able to establish operational objectives."

BIBLIOGRAPHY

Anthony, Robert N. & Herzlinger, Regina, *Management Control in Nonprofit Organizations* (Richard D. Irwin, Inc., 1975).

"Coleman cites NIMH, OE, NIH waste of Policy Research Funds." *APA Monitor* (February, 1973), p. 6.

Drew, Elizabeth B., HEW Grapples with PPBS. *The Public Interest* (Summer, 1967), pp. 9–29.

Francis, M. E., Accounting and the Evaluation of Social Programs: A Critical Comment. *The Accounting Review* (April, 1973), pp. 245–257.

Gandhi, Natwar, The Emergence of the Post-Industrial Society and the Future of the Accounting Function. Working Paper 110, Graduate School of Business, University of Pittsburgh, 1975.

Ginzberg, Eli & Solow, Robert M., Some Lessons of the 1960's. *The Public Interest* (Winter, 1974), pp. 210–220.

Gorham, William, Notes of a Practitioner. *The Public Interest* (Summer, 1967), pp. 4–8.

Granof, Michael H. & Smith, Charles, H., Accounting and the Evaluation of Social Programs: A Comment. *The Accounting Review* (October, 1974), pp. 822–825.

Linowes, David F., Accounting for Social Progress. *The New York Times*, (March 14, 1971) Section 3, p. 14.

——————, Socio-Economic Accounting. *The Journal of Accountancy* (November, 1968), pp. 37–42.

Livingstone, John Leslie & Gunn, Sanford E., *Accounting for Social Goals: Budgeting and Analysis of Nonmarket Projects* (Harper & Row, Publishers, 1974).

McRae, Thomas, Social Auditing Questioned. *The Journal of Accountancy* (December, 1973), pp. 92–94.

Nelson, Ronald H., Psychologists in Administrative Evaluation. *American Psychologist* (June, 1975), pp. 707–708.

Perloff, Robert, Perloff, Evelyn & Sussna, Edward, Program Evaluation. *Annual Review of Psychology*, 1976, in press.

Rossi, P. H., & Williams, W., eds., *Evaluating Social Programs* (Seminar, 1972).

Sobel, E. L., & Francis, M. E., Accounting and the Evaluation of Social Programs: A Reply. *The Accounting Review* (October, 1974), pp. 826–830.

Thomas, Arthur L., The EESP Debate: What's Really at Issue, unpublished paper.

Wholey, Joseph S., What Can We Actually Get From Program Evaluation? *Policy Sciences* (3, 1972), pp. 361–369.

CHAPTER 2

Financial Accounting Concepts

The use of public monies by governmental units or by hospitals, public schools, voluntary groups, and welfare organizations involves a relationship based upon trust. The contribution of resources may be either involuntary (taxes) or voluntary, but in either case the public in contemporary society demands the right to know how those resources are used. When a governmental unit contracts with a private organization such as a private welfare agency to perform certain services, the same expectation exists.

In each case there is an obligation on the part of the organization using the resources to account for all assets received. This type of reporting is referred to as financial reporting, which is distinct from managerial reporting. The latter refers to information used by management for making resource-allocation decisions within the organization; it is the major emphasis of the articles in the book. Financial reporting, in contrast, refers to reports prepared for individuals and agencies outside the organization. For example, a voluntary organization receiving financial support from United Way is required to file financial information with that agency.

There is, of course, tremendous variety both in the types of information that can be included in the financial reports and in the manner in which the data are presented. Quite frequently the funding source will require that the reports be verified (audited) by an accountant independent of the agency whose financial status and performance is being measured. The accountant may be the United States General Accounting Office (GAO), the audit agency of individual states, or a certified public accountant.

Both the accountant and the organization being audited should be familiar with the reporting requirements that apply to it, for different types of organizations also have different reporting requirements. These are prescribed by various agencies, primarily the American Institute of Certified Public Accountants (AICPA), state legislation, and industry trade groups.

A number of associations have been involved in promulgating accounting rules (principles) and reporting requirements for nonprofit activities. In addition to the AICPA, these include the Financial Accounting Standards Board (FASB), the National Council on Governmental Accounting, the American Hospital Association, the National Health Council, the National Assembly of National Voluntary Health and Welfare Organizations, and the United Way of America. Many states also have defined reporting rules for municipalities and agencies filing reports with state government, and the federal government requires many organizations to file reports meeting its requirements.

One of the difficulties encountered by certified public accountants when auditing nonprofit organizations has been the lack of guidance in determining what constitutes generally accepted accounting principles for a given type of nonprofit organization. Recent publications by the AICPA have resolved many of the issues and further work in this area is in progress by the Institute, the Financial Accounting Standards Board, and other agencies.

In the early 1970s the AICPA published industry audit guides for hospitals, colleges and universities, voluntary health and welfare organizations, and state and local governmental units. These were followed in 1979 by the Institute's *Statement of Position 78-10*, which sets forth recommended accounting principles for nonprofit organizations not covered by a specific industry audit guide.

In "Nonprofit Accounting: A Revolution in Process," Gross reviews three of the AICPA audit guides for nonprofit organizations and highlights the major changes that are likely to occur as a result of their publication. Of particular importance are the reporting requirements for unrestricted contributions and the classification of revenues and expenses by program. These two changes, which were designed to make it easier for an individual outside of the agency to determine its financial status and performance, promise to have the greatest impact on the agency's bookkeeping system.

Traditional financial reporting used by many municipalities and nonprofit organizations is frequently criticized because it treats each of the organization's funds as a separate accounting entity. As a consequence of this fragmentation process it is difficult to identify the financial status of the whole organization as opposed to that of a single fund. One alternative is to provide consolidated statements in addition to fund-by-fund reports. Advocating consolidation in "How to Succeed in Nonbusiness Without Really Trying: A University Case Study," Ramanathan and Weis present an interesting laboratory experiment in which subjects were asked to evaluate the financial performance of a university. Those receiving only traditional fund-by-fund financial reports were much more likely to misinterpret the organization's financial performance than were the subjects receiving both consolidated reports and fund-by-fund reports.

Interest in setting accounting rules, that is, generally accepted accounting principles (GAAP), for the public sector gained already tremendous momentum during the 1970s. Since accounting rules are not derived from any natural laws but are the result of manmade decisions, the approach taken in developing them is of critical importance. The Financial Accounting Standards Board (FASB), which sets accounting rules for the business sector, is currently exploring the role it should take in the nonbusiness or public sector as well. Its publication *Statement of Financial Accounting Concepts No. 4: Objectives of Financial Reporting by Nonbusiness Organizations* (December 1980) establishes the objectives of general-purpose external financial reporting by nonbusiness organizations. The Statement exempts state and local governmental reporting requirements until the issue of the appropriate mechanism for setting accounting rules in that sector is resolved.[1]

An FASB Research Report *Financial Accounting in Nonbusiness Organizations* which preceded Concept No. 4 provides the background for Engstrom's article "Setting Accounting Standards in the Public Sector." Approaching the subject of accounting rule making from a theoretical viewpoint, Engstrom presents a perceptive discussion on the issues that must be resolved before effective rules can be developed. The steps he outlines would result in a framework of assumptions and goals from which accounting rules could be derived in a logical fashion. Answers to the questions Engstrom raises are not self-evident and will require the full participation of the FASB, users of nonbusiness financial statements, and industry associations including the AICPA.

In addition to the theoretical issues raised by Engstrom, there is also debate regarding who the ultimate accounting rule-making authority should be. For municipalities the situation is particularly complex, as is well described in "Who's Watching the Books?" The article demonstrates the economic value of accounting information by estimating the interest penalty the bond market imposes upon municipalities with substandard accounting systems. Penalties in the form of higher interest costs may be incurred by any type of nonprofit organization with an inadequate accounting system, providing important incentives to adopt generally accepted accounting rules.

---

[1]A recent proposal suggests establishing an independent governmental accounting standards board to set accounting and reporting standards for governmental units. See *Report of The Governmental Accounting Standards Board Organization Committee* (October 13, 1981).

NONPROFIT ACCOUNTING: A REVOLUTION IN PROCESS

Malvern J. Gross, Jr.

"Anything goes!" That seems to have been the rule for nonprofit organizations in the past—for until recently there were relatively few "rules." But now, in less than 18 months, the accounting profession has laid down some very specific rules for the three most important sectors of the broad category referred to as nonprofit organizations. As a result, nonprofit organizations suddenly find themselves catapulted from an era of permissiveness to an era where the accounting and reporting requirements are spelled out in great detail. For them, it's a period of revolutionary change.

The nonprofit organizations category includes colleges and universities, hospitals, voluntary health and social welfare organizations, museums, membership associations, country clubs, and the like. As a group, they have tremendous influence on our society and on the way we solve the problems of our times.

Why then have there been so few accounting rules for these organizations? Basically, the answer is that only recently has the accounting profession devoted any significant attention to the accounting and reporting procedures these groups follow. Historically, their procedures were tied to the stewardship concept (that is, the accountability for funds received and disbursed). This type of accounting is usually referred to as fund accounting. Unfortunately, fund accounting can get very complicated—not because the underlying principles are complicated but because of the dozens of different "funds" some organizations tend to set up. Typically, each fund is accounted for as though it were a separate entity. As a result, it is usually hard to get an overall picture of an organization's activity.

THREE AUDIT GUIDES

About 18 months ago the American Institute of Certified Public Accountants (AICPA) issued the first of three audit guides. It dealt with hospitals. The second guide, issued last summer, pertained to colleges and universities. The third, issued last fall, applied to voluntary health and welfare organizations. Obviously, these guides have affected the specific organizations to which they were addressed. But their cumulative effect is also being felt by all other types of nonprofit organizations because the guides express opinions about appropriate accounting and reporting principles for transactions that are common to most nonprofit groups.

WHAT IS AN AUDIT GUIDE?

Audit guides provide direction to AICPA members in examining and reporting on financial statements. They set forth the considered opinion of knowledgeable accountants and, as such, represent the best thoughts of the accounting profession. The guides deal not only with the actual conduct of the audit but also the appropriate accounting and reporting principles. It is in the discussion of these principles that the guides will have the most impact on nonprofit organizations. A CPA who deviates from the

Source. Copyright © 1973 by Price Waterhouse & Co., 1251 Avenue of the Americas, New York, N.Y. Reprinted with permission from *Price Waterhouse Review* (No. 3, 1973), pp. 43–50.

EXHIBIT 1

Comparison of Accounting and Reporting Principles Prescribed in the New Audit Guides

		Hospitals	Colleges	Voluntary Health and Welfare
1	Accrual basis accounting required	Yes	Yes	Yes
2	Use of separate board-designated funds allowed in the income statement	No	Yes	No
3	Unrestricted contributions must be reported in income statement	Yes	Yes	Yes
4	Current restricted contributions reported in full in year received rather than in year expended	No	No	Yes
5	Pledges *must* be recorded if material	Yes	No	Yes
6	Contributed services must be recorded under certain circumstances	Yes	No	Yes
7	Unrestricted dividend and interest income must be reported in the income statement	Yes	Yes	Yes
8	Capital gains on legally unrestricted investment funds must be reported in the income statement	Yes	No	Yes
9	Transfers between funds reported in the income statement	No	Yes	Yes*
10	Use of a separate fixed asset or plant fund allowed	No	Yes	Yes
11	Fixed assets must be capitalized	Yes	Yes	Yes
12	Fixed assets must be depreciated and the depreciation charge reported in the income statement	Yes	No	Yes
13	Appropriations or encumbrances can be charged against expenses	No	No	No
14	Appropriations or encumbrances can be reported as a liability on the balance sheet	No	No	No
15	Transfers under the "total return" concept of reporting endowment fund gains must be reported as a transfer after the excess of income caption	Not discussed	Yes	Yes

*But only after the caption, "excess of income over expenses."

principles outlined in these guides may very well be forced to justify such departures. Effectively, then, the guides constitute an authoritative pronouncement on appropriate accounting and reporting principles.

CONSISTENCY AMONG THE GUIDES

Three separate committees were involved in writing these guides. Some attempt was made for conformity among them but differing industry practices and customs and the differing perspectives of the committees resulted in a number of principles that are not completely consistent. On some points, however, the guides are in agreement, therefore suggesting how a particular issue is likely to be resolved eventually. Exhibit 1 summarizes the major accounting and reporting principles and the position taken in each guide.

There are six areas where the guides will have particular significance for all nonprofit organizations. I will discuss each of these. I will also highlight the several inconsistent areas which will affect many types of organizations.

1. ALL LEGALLY UNRESTRICTED CONTRIBUTIONS REPORTED IN A SINGLE "INCOME" STATEMENT

The most important and far-reaching change is that each of the three guides now requires nonprofit organizations to record all legally unrestricted contributions in a single income statement so that the reader can see the total amounts received. Previously, it was common for boards of trustees to "designate" certain categories of legally unrestricted contributions for some specific purpose and then disclose them only in separate income statements for the "designated" funds. As a result, the casual reader who was unaware of this bookkeeping maneuver would see a bleak picture when he looked at what passed for an income statement. In fact, the organization may very well have

received substantial amounts which the board had designated for some other purpose and thus not included in the main income statement. Now, all unrestricted contributions must be reported in the general fund income statement.

Of course, if a donor designates in a legal fashion that he wants his contribution used only for an endowment fund or for some other restrictive purpose, these amounts will be recorded directly in that particular fund. But the board cannot assume this is the donor's intention. It has to be a legally binding action of the donor.

2. SUMMARIZING ALL OTHER UNRESTRICTED ACTIVITY ON ONE STATEMENT

Each of the three guides also requires that all other unrestricted income and expenses be reflected in this single income statement. There are three different styles of statement formats but each attempts to tell the reader what the excess of unrestricted income (revenues) over expenditures was for the year.[1]

Perhaps it is not so obvious, but in including all categories of unrestricted income, these guides are saying that investment income (dividends and interest) must also be reported in this "income" statement. In the case of hospitals and voluntary health and welfare organizations, capital gains arising from unrestricted investments must be included too. This will be a significant departure from past practices for many organizations.

---

[1]In the hospital audit guide, the statement comes down to the caption, "excess of revenues over expenses." In the voluntary health and welfare guide, the caption reads, "excess of public support and revenue over expenses." The college audit guide is not quite as clear cut because the accounting principles are still basically a stewardship type of reporting. Nevertheless, even in the college guide there seems to be a trend toward telling the reader what the net results of operation were for the year.

3. FIXED ASSETS AND DEPRECIATION ACCOUNTING

The recording of fixed assets in the financial statements and the taking of depreciation have stirred up controversy in nonprofit accounting for years. All three guides now require that fixed assets be recorded and reported in the balance sheet, and two of the guides (hospitals and voluntary health and welfare organizations) require that fixed assets be depreciated over their useful lives. The college guide requires capitalization of fixed assets but does not require depreciation. Even in this guide, however, there is permissive language allowing depreciation in the plant fund column of the statement of changes in fund balances. The acceptance of depreciation accounting by two of the guides and the emphasis on cost of services (discussed below) will put increased pressure on colleges to follow depreciation accounting in the future.

4. CARRYING INVESTMENTS AT MARKET

Significantly, both the college and the voluntary health and welfare guides state that investments may now be carried at market or fair value. This is not a mandatory requirement but rather an acceptable alternative to carrying investments at historical cost. Many institutions with large endowment funds may find carrying

---

EXHIBIT 2

National Association of Environmentalists Statement of Income and Expenses for the Year Ended December 31, 1973

Income:		
Membership dues	$233,550	
Research projects	127,900	
Contributions and bequests	91,500	
Advertising income	33,500	
Subscriptions to nonmembers	18,901	
Investment income	14,607	
Gains on sales of investments	33,025	
Total income		$552,983
Expenses:		
Program services		
"National Environment" magazine	110,500	
Clean-up month campaign	126,617	
Lake Erie project	115,065	
Total program services		352,182
Supporting services		
Management and general	33,516	
Fund raising	5,969	
Total supporting services		39,485
Total expenses		391,667
Excess of income over expenses		$161,316

National Association of Environmentalists Analysis of Functional Expenses for the Year Ended December 31, 1973

EXHIBIT 3

	Total All Expenses	Program Services				Supporting Services		
		"National Environment" Magazine	Clean-up Month Campaign	Lake Erie Project	Total Program	Management and General	Fund Raising	Total Supporting
Salaries	$170,773	$ 24,000	$ 68,140	$ 60,633	$152,773	$15,000	$3,000	$18,000
Payroll taxes and employee benefits	22,199	3,120	8,857	7,882	19,859	1,950	390	2,340
Total compensation	192,972	27,120	76,997	68,515	172,632	16,950	3,390	20,340
Printing	84,071	63,191	18,954	515	82,660	1,161	250	1,411
Mailing, postage, and shipping	14,225	10,754	1,188	817	12,759	411	1,055	1,466
Rent	19,000	3,000	6,800	5,600	15,400	3,000	600	3,600
Telephone	5,615	895	400	1,953	3,248	2,151	216	2,367
Outside art	14,865	3,165	11,700	—	14,865	—	—	—
Local travel	1,741	—	165	915	1,080	661	—	661
Conferences and conventions	6,328	—	1,895	2,618	4,513	1,815	—	1,815
Depreciation	13,596	2,260	2,309	5,616	10,185	3,161	250	3,411
Legal and audit	2,000	—	—	—	—	2,000	—	2,000
Supplies	31,227	—	1,831	28,516	30,347	761	119	880
Miscellaneous	6,027	115	4,378	—	4,493	1,445	89	1,534
Total	$391,667	$110,500	$126,617	$115,065	$352,182	$33,516	$5,969	$39,485

investments at market value is more meaning-ful than cost. The hospital guide does not pro-vide for carrying investments at market value. However, the subsequent release of the other two guides would seem to give the green light to hospitals (as well as other nonprofit organi-zations) to do so too.

5. AN INCREASED EMPHASIS ON PROGRAMS OF THE ORGANIZATION

Traditionally, nonprofit organizations have re-ported in terms of the amounts spent for salaries, rent, supplies, etc. The voluntary health and welfare guide takes a major step forward when it states that the organization exists to perform services and programs and therefore should be reporting principally in terms of its individual program activities or functions. Exhibit 2 is an example of an organi-zation reporting on a functional basis. This type of presentation forces management to tell the statement reader how much of its funds were expended for each program category and the amount spent in supporting services, including fund raising.

In addition to this statement, these organi-zations are encouraged to prepare a statement of functional expenses, which analyzes the costs of each program category. Exhibit 3 is an example of this kind of statement. Between these two statements, the reader is given a great deal of information.

Neither the hospital guide nor the college guide requires this reporting on a program (functional) basis. But because of the large number of voluntary health and welfare or-ganizations, the requirement for functional re-porting will have wide impact. Also, once the effective date of this guide passes (for years beginning after July 1, 1974), organizations re-quiring a CPA's opinion will have to follow this format if they want an unqualified opinion from

their CPA.[2] For many organizations, this ex-panded format will require significant changes in bookkeeping procedures in order for them to know how much of their costs relate to each program.

6. INTERNAL CONTROL OVER CONTRIBUTIONS

A little noticed (but very important) section of the voluntary health and welfare guide is a statement about the organization's responsibil-ity to take all practical steps to assure adequate internal control over contributions. For exam-ple, the guide observes that, when an organiza-tion solicits funds through a direct mail cam-paign, two employees should be assigned the function of jointly controlling incoming mail and preparing a record of amounts received. The guide also discusses the appropriate level of internal control over door-to-door solicita-tion. Many organizations—particularly smaller ones—do not provide the appropriate control. In the absence of adequate internal control, the CPA must qualify his opinion.

SIGNIFICANCE OF THESE CHANGES

All of these major accounting and reporting changes give recognition to the importance of nonprofit organizations in our society. At a time when their influence was relatively narrow and the principal persons concerned were usually knowledgeable contributors, the reporting and accounting principles they followed were of less importance. Today, an increasing portion of society's activities are carried out by non-profit organizations, and both the accounting profession and the leaders of these organiza-tions recognize that, if their role is going to

[2]The laws of New York, Pennsylvania, Georgia, Connecti-cut, Illinois, Wisconsin, and Minnesota have reporting re-quirements for organizations soliciting funds within these states. These requirements include an opinion by a CPA.

continue to expand, complete and straightforward reporting must take place. These three guides—which were the result of joint efforts by CPAs and the leaders of each type of organization—are designed in large part to help eliminate the credibility gap that many feel now exists.

These objectives are relatively clear—but implementing them is not going to be easy. The past permissiveness in accounting allowed some organizations effectively to conceal part of their assets. The new changes will result in full disclosure and will cause many organizations to reexamine their objectives and needs. Boards of trustees may have a hard time justifying a request for increased contributions if their financial statements show a surplus. But this is probably as it should be. If an organization cannot justify continued support or an increased level of support, then under our system the organization should not be able to raise these funds. Society gives nonprofit organizations a significant advantage in tax concessions and society has a right to insist that these organizations do, in fact, respond to public needs.

Many organizations are going to find that their bookkeeping costs will grow, as will their professional fees for auditing. The increased level of reporting along with an increased level of internal control over contributions will be expensive.

I believe these changes and the trend they indicate are clearly in the public interest. For many, greater disclosure will be a traumatic experience, and for some it may have an immediate negative financial impact. But where this happens board members will have to face up to the fundamental question: Is the organization providing a service which is needed by the public at a cost which is appropriate? The accounting and reporting principles in the new audit guides will help the public make an informed judgment. For this reason, the guides are a major contribution.

HOW TO SUCCEED IN NONBUSINESS WITHOUT REALLY TRYING: A UNIVERSITY CASE STUDY*

Kavasseri V. Ramanathan and William L. Weis

The following dialogue takes place in the office of the president of Smallendowment University. The time is two weeks before the end of the fiscal year.

President: George, this year will be the first that we include our audited financial statements in the annual report to friends and benefactors. How do you think this will affect the level of contributions?

George Moneyraiser, vice-president of development: That depends on the figures. In my opinion, an

*We would like to thank Professors R. N. Anthony, C. J. Casey, Jr., W. W. Cooper, R. Herzlinger, K. A. Merchant, and R. F. Vancil at the Harvard Graduate School of Business Administation and the participants at the Masschusetts Institute of Technology Sloan School Research Colloquium or their comments and suggestions.

Source. Copyright © 1980 by the America Institute of Certified Public Accounts, Inc. Reported with permission from *The Journal of Accountancy* (October, 1980), pp. 46–48, 51–52.

operating surplus would give potential donors confidence in our ability to survive the troublesome days ahead and would reflect favorably on our administration of the university's resources. However, too great a surplus might dissuade some donors from giving to a college that they believe really doesn't need the money. I would think that a modest surplus would stimulate the greatest donor performance. People will give to a viable, ongoing institution that both needs the money and shows that it will use it wisely.

President: Martha, what do you think about this?

Martha Goodnews, vice-president of public relations: I would expect greater giving to an institution that is showing a marginal operating deficit. A small deficit would suggest a need for additional donations—offering the promise that with a little more generosity we could be operating in the black. But why all the discussion about what operating results would produce the greatest donor stimulation? We can't do much about that, can we?

President: Harry, do we have any options at this point on our reporting for the year?

Harry Anynumber, treasurer: We certainly do. Would you prefer a small or large surplus or a small or large deficit? Just give me the word.

President: Aren't these statements going to be audited by an independent CPA firm? Don't the statements have to conform to standards or guidelines?

Harry: Just tell me what you'd prefer, and I'll fix everything.

The above dialogue may raise the following questions: Is Harry Anynumber

a   Underestimating the competence of the auditors?
b   Overestimating the flexibility of the reporting standards?
c   Both a and b?
d   Neither a nor b?

The answer is d. Readers who thought the answer was either a b, or c should review the accounting practices for collegiate organiza-

tions. Recommended readings include the American Institute of CPAs industry audit guide entitled *Audits of Colleges and Universities*[1] and the American Council on Education's *College and University Business Administration.*[2]

A LANGUAGE PROBLEM

The terms that Samallendowment University's administrative staff is using in the president's office—specifically, "operating surplus" and "operating deficit"—are not precisely defined in accounting. However, in the sphere of nonbusiness accounting (of which accounting for colleges and universities is a subset), well-defined terms for measures of operating effectiveness do not really exist. When referring to an operating surplus or deficit for a private university, what exactly is meant?

Numerous critics of nonbusiness reporting practices—and collegiate reporting practices in particular—have asserted that the change in the current fund balance is taken by readers of nonbusiness financial statements to be a measure of operating results for the period.[3] For example, the popular press uses terms like operating surplus and operating deficit in reporting on the release of a private university's financial statements for a given fiscal year, but the number identified with those terms, according to critics, is nothing more than the year's change in the current fund balance—a number that can be manipulated at the discretion of university administrators.

[1]Committee on College and University Accounting and Auditing, *Audits of Colleges and Universities,* 2d ed. (New York: AICPA, 1975).
[2]National Association of College and University Business Officers, *College and University Business Administration,* 3rd ed. (Washington, D.C.: NACUBO, 1974).
[3]See, for example, C. W. Bastable, "Collegiate Accounting Needs Re-evaluation," JofA, Dec. 73, pp. 51–57, and K. Schipper, "Evaluating Financial Statements of Private Colleges" (Ph.D. diss., University of Chicago, 1977).

We are faced with a language problem. There is nothing inherently sinister about providing a financial statement that merely details inflows and outflows of the current fund for a period and that concludes with a "bottom line" representing the net change in the current fund balance for the period. Such a bottom-line figure is a relatively meaningless number. However, in the absence of a statement of operating performance, users of collegiate financial statements may be assigning a performance-measure value to the bottom line of the statement of current funds revenues, expenditures, and other changes. Because that figure is substantially arbitrary, misunderstanding and misuse of the number could have unfortunate consequences.

An example of how this bottom-line manipulation can be effected may be helpful at this point. Imagine that you are the president of Smallendowment University and that you are sympathetic to George Moneyraiser's view that a marginal surplus would induce the most favorable donor behavior. However, as the end of the fiscal year approaches, it is becoming clear that some maneuvering will be needed to turn, say, a $250,000 decrease in the current fund balance into a modest $50,000 increase. Harry Anynumber, the university treasurer, describes his methodology for a solution to the problem: "There are several especially vulnerable items on the statement of current funds revenues, expenditures, and transfers. The timing of these items, in terms of their flow through the current fund, is largely at the discretion of management. I could effect an additional $300,000 increase in the fund balance by reducing the planned nonmandatory transfer from the current fund to the plant fund for debt retirement by $100,000, increasing the in-transfer from the quasi-endowment fund by $100,000, and postponing the transfer of $100,000 of unrestricted gifts to quasi-endowment until some future

period. These actions would produce the desired $50,000 'surplus' in the current fund."

According to critics of nonbusiness reporting practices, what is troublesome about this type of• finagling in the current funds statement is that users of the financial statements are likely to believe that the change in the current fund balance is a measure of operating results. Defenders of the conventional fund-by-fund reporting model for nonbusiness organizations, led by the National Committee on Governmental Accounting,[4] argue that this contention is unfounded.

TWO EXPERIMENTS

Recent evidence from two experiments tends to support the contention of critics of the fund-by-fund model. Specifically, these experiments suggest that

- Readers of fund-by-fund statements are prone to misuse the current fund balance when the statements are separated into component parts by funds (which is the traditional presentation).
- Across-fund, consolidated presentations tend to significantly reduce this misleading potential of the current funds statement.

The experiments, one using M.B.A. students and the other using commercial loan officers at three major commercial banks, were conducted in order to examine possible user effects from supplementing conventional fund-by-fund collegiate financial statements with organizationwide, across-fund consolidations.[5] In each experiment subjects were ran-

[4]National Council on Governmental Accounting, *Governmental Accounting and Financial Reporting Principles* (Chicago, Ill.: MFOA, March 1979).
[5]William L. Weis, "An Experimental Investigation of Some Effects of Consolidating Collegiate Financial Reports" (Ph.D. diss., University of Washington, 1979.

domly divided into two groups. Half of the subjects were given a conventional set of financial statements for a hypothetical private university for a two-year period. The other half received exactly the same statements, except that supplemental columns and schedules were included to present consolidated information for the whole organization. These supplements simply aggregated the data across the several fund groups so that readers could detect more easily the relationship between total "revenues" and "expenditures" for the whole university as well as its consolidated financial position.

Subjects were given questionnaires designed to measure perceptions about the financial condition and performance of the hypothetical university over the two-year period and were given sufficient time to respond to the questionnaire items based on their analyses of the financial statements provided. What the subjects were not told was that the financial statements were representative of a collegiate institution suffering severe financial distress, with the financial condition deteriorating during both years at an accelerating rate.

The results of the experiments were unsettling. In the M.B.A. experiment, 67.3 percent of those receiving only the fund-by-fund statements responded that the financial condition had improved rather than deteriorated during the two-year period, and 71.2 percent responded that the second year was the more favorable, financially, for the university. Of those receiving the consolidated supplements, the above percentages dropped to 42.3 percent and 52 percent, respectively, showing a significant improvement in performance in the presence of consolidated data.[6]

In the experiment using commercial loan officers, presumably a relatively sophisticated group of financial-statement analysts, 54 percent of those given only fund-by-fund statements thought the financial condition had improved over the two-year period, and 65.3 percent thought the second year was the better one, financially, for the institution. Again, those who were given across-fund consolidations fared much better, with only 18 percent misjudging the direction of change in the university's financial condition and 25 percent misjudging the relative financial performance between the two years.[7]

Is there a logical explanation for these results? One of the questionnaire items asked the respondents to rate the three basic statements contained within the reporting package in terms of their relative importance to analyzing the financial condition of the institution. Those three basic statements included the balance sheet, the statement of changes in fund balances, and the statement of current funds revenues, expenditures, and other changes. The consolidated supplements included a consolidated balance sheet as well as a consolidated column on the statement of changes in fund balances. The current funds statement was, of course, identical for both groups of subjects.

This question revealed that the statement of current funds revenues, expenditures, and other changes was rated as much more important than the other two statements by those who received only fund-by-fund financial information. The relative importance of this statement dropped off considerably when subjects were presented with across-fund consolidations. These findings strengthen the arguments of the proponents of consolidated reporting, who maintain that such consolidations are better matched with the entity base of

---

[6]Statistical significance at the .02 level and .05 level, respectively.

[7]Statistical significance at the .001 level in both cases.

interest to the users—in this case, the entire university, not one or more "funds."

The connection between the respondents' generally poor performance in analyzing the university's financial situation and their greater reliance on the current funds statement may be explained by the way the financial statements were developed. While the financial statements clearly depicted an institution in failing health, the change in the current fund balance was positive for both years, showing a greater increase in the second year than in the first. As pointed out earlier, the size and direction of this change is "manageable" to a large extent.

Therefore, those who received only the fund-by-fund statements demonstrated a greater propensity to rank high in importance the current funds statement and to misjudge the actual financial performance of the hypothetical university. This may be a coincidence, but the curious consistency between the responses and the change in the current fund balance for both years certainly raises a strong possibility that users of collegiate financial statements seize on the change in the current fund balance and use it as though it were something that it definitely is not—a reliable measure of operating performance.

CONCLUSIONS AND IMPLICATIONS

The fund-by-fund accounting model for nonbusiness organizations has been criticized as being arcane to most financial-statement users, who are trained to read "business" financial statements, and for failing to offer a readily discernible basis for evaluating operating performance. Defenders of the status quo point to dubious, if not irrelevant, distinctions between business and nonbusiness entities and assert that special stewardship legalities and segregations, unique to nonbusiness entities, demand the fund-by-fund reporting format. Further,

they argue that changing the current reporting model would have no user effects anyway. However, the statistically significant findings from our experiments lend further evidence to dispute the contention that no user effects would be forthcoming from consolidating nonbusiness financial statements.

In summary, critics of nonbusiness accounting statements have contended that users of such statements, primarily creditors and overseers, do indeed want a measure of performance for the organization as a whole. Such a measure is not being provided by conventional nonbusiness financial reports. In its absence users are searching for a substitute; too often, that substitute is the change in the current fund balance for the period. As we have seen, the size and direction of that change is substantially manipulable by management, and it is clearly unreliable and irrelevant as an entitywide performance measure.

The arguments against reporting reform are no longer convincing in light of recent research. Generally accepted accounting principles for nonbusiness organizations should mandate the consolidation of funds so that users can glean from the financial statements an organizationwide performance perspective.[8] Until this is done, users will continue to misinterpret the information, to their detriment and to the detriment of the public.

We hope that the next time Martha Goodnews, the public relations vice-president, asks, "We can't do much about that, can we?" the university president will reply, "No, not a thing." Perceptions of improvement in operating performance should come from actual improvement, not merely from juggling numbers.

[8]Price Waterhouse & Co., Position Paper on College and University Reporting, *A Proposal to Restructure and Simplify College and University Financial Statements to Communicate Better to College Trustees* (New York: Price Waterhouse & Co., 1975).

SETTING ACCOUNTING STANDARDS IN THE PUBLIC SECTOR

John H. Engstrom

On June 15, 1978, the Financial Accounting Standards Board issued a discussion memorandum (DM) entitled *An Analysis of Issues Related to Conceptual Framework for Financial Accounting and Reporting: Objectives of Financial Reporting by Nonbusiness Organizations.* Based on a research report by Robert N. Anthony,[1] the DM symbolizes and formalizes the increasing interest of the accounting profession in public sector accounting.

BACKGROUND

Until recently, the standard-setting process of the accounting profession did not specifically address governmental and not-for-profit organizations. Therefore, accountants and others working through professional organizations developed accounting principles and reporting formats that seemed to meet their needs. Organizations such as the National Committee (now Council) on Governmental Accounting, the American Hospital Association, and the National Association of College and University Business Officers promulgated accounting standards. During the past few years, the American Institute of CPAs has issued audit guides for colleges and universities, hospitals,

state and local governments, and voluntary health and welfare organizations, but those audit guides differ little from the accounting principles issued by the professional organizations.

As a result, the CPA engaged in audits of public sector organizations has been faced with a great deal of research to determine appropriate, generally accepted accounting principles (GAAP). Moreover, the independent development of GAAP for each type of public sector organization means that CPAs have been forced to redefine accounting principles when looking at each new type of organization. For example, a CPA would require depreciation for all assets in hospitals and for enterprise, internal service, and some trust fund assets in local governments but for none of the assets in a college. Exhibit 1 lists the sources of GAAP that have been used by CPAs when auditing in the public sector.

EXHIBIT 1

Some Present Sources of Nonbusiness GAAP (Including Some Pending Approval)

Federal government
Comptroller General of the United States. "Accounting Principles and Standards for Federal Agencies." Title 2 to the *General Accounting Office Manual for Guidance of Federal Agencies.* Washington, D.C.: General Accounting Office, 1972.

Source. Copyright © 1979 by the American Institute of Certified Public Accountants, Inc. Reprinted with permission from *The Journal of Accountancy* (March, 1979), pp. 83–87.
[1]Robert N. Anthony, *Financial Accounting in Nonbusiness Organizations: An Exploratory Study of Conceptual Issues* (Stamford, Conn.: Financial Accounting Standards Board, 1978).

State and local government

Committee on Governmental Accounting and Auditing. *Audits of State and Local Governmental Units.* New York: AICPA, 1975.

National Committee on Governmental Accounting. *Governmental Accounting, Auditing, and Financial Reporting.* Chicago, Ill.: Municipal Finance Officers Association, 1968.

National Council on Governmental Accounting. *NCGA Exposure Draft: GAAFR Restatement Principles.* Chicago, Ill.: MFOA, 1978.

Colleges and universities

Committee on College and University Accounting and Auditing. *Audits of Colleges and Universities.* New York: AICPA, 1975.

National Association of College and University Business Officers. *College and University Business Administration.* 3d ed. Washington, D.C.: NACUBO, 1974.

Hospitals

Subcommittee on Health Care Matters. *Hospital Audit Guide.* 2d ed. New York: AICPA, 1978.

American Hospital Association. *Chart of Accounts for Hospitals.* Chicago, Ill.: AHA, 1976.

Public schools

U.S. Department of Health, Education and Welfare, Office of Education. *Financial Accounting: Classifications and Standard Terminology for Local and State School Systems.* Handbook II rev. Washington, D.C.: Government Printing Office, 1973 (DHEW Publication no. OE 73-11800).

Voluntary health and welfare organizations

Voluntary Health and Welfare Organizations Committee. *Audits of Voluntary Health and Welfare Organizations.* New York: AICPA, 1974.

Other

Accounting Standards Division. *Statement of Position on Accounting Principles and Reporting Practices for Certain Nonprofit Organizations.* New York: AICPA, 1979.

RECENT DEVELOPMENTS

Recently, some accountants have questioned not only the diversity of accounting principles in the public sector but also the differences between public and private sector accounting. The interested reader can find examples of this questioning for the federal government,[2] state and local governments,[3] colleges and universities,[4] and all nongovernmental public sector organizations.[5] Arguments have been made (1) to use the corporate full accrual accounting model in the public sector, (2) to consolidate all funds into a single report, and (3) to use the same principles for all nongovernmental units.

As a result of this increased interest, the FASB commissioned the research study by

---

EXHIBIT 2

List of Issues Raised in FASB Discussion Memorandum*

1 Is the following list of primary users of financial report information adequate for the purpose of identifying needs for such information: governing bodies, investors and creditors, resource providers, oversight bodies, and constituents?

(Continued)

---

[2]*Sound Financial Reporting in the Public Sector: A Prerequisite to Fiscal Responsibility* (Chicago, Ill.: Arthur Andersen & Co., 1975).

[3]Sidney Davidson, David O. Green, Walter Hellenstein, Albert Madansky, and Roman L. Weil, *Financial Reporting by State and Local Government Units* (Chicago, Ill.: University of Chicago, 1977), and Coopers & Lybrand and the University of Michigan, *Financial Disclosure Practices of the American Cities: A Public Report* (New York: Coopers & Lybrand, 1976).

[4]*Position Paper on College and University Reporting* (New York: Price Waterhouse & Co., 1975).

[5]Malvern J. Gross, Jr., "Report on Nonprofit Accounting," JofA, June 75, pp. 55–9.

EXHIBIT 2 *(Continued)*

2 Is the following list of the types of financial report information needed by users adequate as a basis for deciding how best to meet these needs: financial viability, fiscal compliance, management performance, and cost of services provided?

3 Do users need a report of operating flows that is separate from a report of capital flows?

4 Do users need an operating statement?

5 Do users need a report of cost of services performed?

6 Should financial flow statements report encumbrances as well as, or instead of, expenditures?

7 Do users need a single, aggregated set of financial statements for the organization rather than separate financial statements for each fund group? If the latter, what criteria should determine the composition of fund groups?

8 Are there conceptual issues related to the balance sheet?

14 How, if at all, should business organizations be distinguished from other organizations for the purpose of developing accounting concepts?

15 Should the federal government and/or the state governments be excluded from the applicability of financial accounting concepts for nonbusiness organizations?

16 Should a single set of concepts apply to all types of nonbusiness organizations, or should there be one set for governmental organizations and one or more additional sets for nongovernmental nonbusiness organizations?

Source. Discussion Memorandum, An Analysis of Issues Related to Conceptual Framework for Financial Accounting and Reporting: Objectives of Financial Reporting by Nonbusiness Organizations (Stamford, Conn.: FASB, 1978). (Issues 9–13 of the Anthony study were not included in the DM.)

Anthony, issued the DM, and held three public hearings to discuss the major issues involved. Exhibit 2 lists the issues raised in the DM.

The purposes of this article are (1) to suggest a criterion that might be used to evaluate the issues, (2) to outline the order in which the issues might be resolved, and (3) to point out some of the complexities involved in some of the issues.

A SUGGESTED CRITERION

Financial reports are designed primarily so persons outside a business can make informed investment decisions. A business with a history of earnings and growth, a sound cash position, and freedom from excessive debt presumably should be able to sell stocks and bonds more easily than one with a poor performance record. Facilitating efficient resource allocation, then, could be said to be the aim of GAAP in the private sector.

An argument can be made that facilitating efficient resource allocation should also be the aim of GAAP for the public sector. Whereas resource allocation decisions for businesses are made largely by investors and creditors, such decisions are more widespread in the public sector. Resource allocation decisions should be made at two levels in the public sector. The first concerns how much should be transmitted to the public sector from the private sector. Decisions made at this level include whether to invest in city bonds, the appropriate level of taxation (proposition 13 falls in this level), how much should be given to the United Way, and which member of Congress with particular spending proposals and habits will be elected.

The second level involves the allocation of resources to various spending programs within the public sector. This refers to the budget and the product or service of the governmental or other nonbusiness entity. The budget process of an entity in the public sector, especially if it's a governmental unit, is not a private matter that need concern only management and management accounting. This is public business, and accounting principles that fail to report resource allocation decisions to the public in a meaningful way fall short of full disclosure.

The selection of objectives and GAAP for nonbusiness organizations should therefore be guided by whether a rational, reasonably informed person would be given the information necessary to make decisions that would allocate resources, at both levels described above, in an efficient way. In this case, "efficient" would be defined by each decision maker. For example, at budget time, a city council member might find it helpful to know how much it costs to collect garbage for businesses and whether charges exceed or are less than the costs. If the council member knows costs exceed charges, he or she could decide whether to subsidize business garbage pickup through the general property tax levy. Without such information, a rational choice cannot be made.

Using the criterion of facilitating rational resource allocation for nonbusiness entities would move the discussion away from arguments that might be more parochial. For example, arguments such as "investors understand the business model; therefore, let's use it" or "we know what's best for our nonbusiness entity because we work there every day" would not be the major determining factors.

SUGGESTED MODEL FOR DECISION MAKING

The order in which a person evaluates the issues presented in the DM may have an influence on the outcome. Exhibit 3 shows my suggested approach. If rational and informed resource allocation is accepted as a goal, the next step is to identify the decision makers who would have the most influence on that goal. Once the decision makers have been

identified, their needs for information would be explored. Finally, an investigation would be conducted to find out which financial reports, aggregated in the most meaningful way and based on the most appropriate accounting methods, would meet those needs. It is only then that questions should be raised as to whether nonbusiness reporting should be similar to that of businesses and whether all nonbusiness reporting should be uniform. Each step in the decisionmaking process has implications for each of the succeeding steps.

EXHIBIT 3

Suggested Model for Evaluating Issues

Adopt criterion

(Resource allocation)
1 To organization
2 Within organization

Determine users

1 Governing bodies
2 Investors and creditors
3 Resource providers
4 Oversight bodies
5 Constituents

Determine needs

1 Financial viability
2 Fiscal compliance
3 Management performance
4 Cost of service provided

Determine how to meet users' needs

1 Levels of consolidation
2 Reporting format
3 Accounting method(s)

Uniformity of principles

1 Same as business entities?
2 Federal and/or states included?
3 Government v. nonprofit?
4 Uniformity of nonprofits?

SOME COMPLEXITIES

Determining Users

There is a need to distinguish between (1) those who are current users and (2) those who should be users. The current receivers of information can be determined by reviewing the distribution lists of financial reports. Perhaps questionnaires and personal interviews might provide some insight as to who actually use the reports and in which ways.

It will be even more difficult to determine who "should" be users. Which decision makers have an impact on resource allocation to and within nonbusiness entities? If the decision makers can be identified, it will still be necessary to ask two questions: Would they use the information if it is available? Would the information alter their decisions?

Other questions must also be asked: Is there a priority listing of classes of users? Is this listing the same for all types of nonbusiness organizations? How compatible are the needs of these users both within and across types of organizations? In order to be more specific, exhibit 4 lists some of the users, assuming that the FASB grouping of users is adopted.

Determining Needs

Once a list of users is defined (and not before), it is important to define their informational needs when making resource allocation decisions. A glance at Exhibit 4 reveals a broad spectrum of users both within and between organization types. Within each organization type, the FASB will need to determine if the users' needs are compatible enough to justify general-purpose financial statements. If not, it will need to determine which users are the most important.

Meeting Users' Needs

The levels of consolidation, reporting format, and accounting methods should be considered as means toward the objective of providing resource allocation information, not as ends in themselves. How does a governmental unit or nonprofit organization best show its overall financial condition? By grouping all funds and groups, regardless of restrictions? By showing each fund separately? Does fund accounting help external users or is it merely a device for management control? Another question involves the consolidation of reporting units. Should all boards, commissions, etc., that are part of a governmental unit be reported with a governmental unit even though some fiscal independence may exist? What about school boards that are funded by county taxes but otherwise have autonomy? Should national offices of churches, health and welfare organizations, and membership associations be combined with or reported separately from local units?

How can the reporting format and accounting procedures serve the resource allocation needs of both budgeters and bondholders? Budgeters are helped by a system that reflects the cash needs of a fiscal year (including pension requirements), but they do not budget depreciation or accrued interest payable. Bondholders might be more interested in the overall financial health of the governmental unit, including the degree to which the fixed assets have been amortized.

What is the significance of a "bottom line" in an operating statement of a nonbusiness entity, especially if it includes a deduction for depreciation? Presumably, it would mean that the overall capital of the entity has been increased, decreased, or maintained. A high proportion of expenditures on capital assets as opposed to current services would increase the

EXHIBIT 4

Some Important Users of Nonbusiness Financial Accounting Information

Organization Type	Governing Bodies	Investors and Creditors	Resource Providers	Oversight Bodies	Constituents
			Classes of Users		
Federal government	Congress	Holders of bonds and notes, suppliers	Taxpayers, users of services, creditors	Legislative committees	Receivers of funds and services
State governments	Legislatures	Holders of bonds and notes, suppliers	Taxpayers, users of services, creditors, federal governmental grants	Legislative commissions	Receivers of funds and services
Local governments	Councils/commissions	Holders of bonds and notes, suppliers	Taxpayers, users of services, creditors, state and federal governmental grants	State and local committees, commissions	Receivers of funds and services
Hospitals	Boards of directors	Holders of bonds and notes, suppliers	Constituents, physicians, creditors, governmental grants, insurance companies	Governmental agencies, insurance companies	Patients

(Continued)

EXHIBIT 4 (Continued)

Organization Type	Classes of Users				
	Governing Bodies	Investors and Creditors	Resource Providers	Oversight Bodies	Constituents
Colleges and universities	Boards of trustees, legislatures	Holders of bonds and notes, suppliers	Constituents, creditors, taxpayers	State governments, federal agencies	Students, alumni
Public schools	School boards	Holders of bonds and notes, suppliers	Taxpayers, creditors, constituents	State boards of education	Students
Voluntary health and welfare organizations	Boards of directors	Suppliers	Contributors (not constituents)	National organizations	Recipients of service
Religious organizations	Vestries, boards of deacons, etc.	Members, suppliers	Contributors (constituents)	National organizations	Members
Membership organizations	Boards of directors, officers	Members, suppliers	Contributors (constituents)	National organizations	Members

bottom line. If nonbusiness managers were to be evaluated on the bottom line, an incentive toward greater size would be introduced. Is this desirable?

Uniformity of Principles

Two opposing forces seem to be active. On the one hand, the desire for simplicity, order, and user understanding results in as few differences as possible. On the other hand, past practice, differing users, and some genuine differing user needs result in differing principles.

At the conceptual level, it can be stated that all users have one need—information that will make efficient resource allocation possible. But the context in which resource allocation decisions are made may be quite different. At the reporting level, then, certain differences may be necessary. For example, a restricted-—unrestricted classification might be based on whether an amount is related to the entity's general taxing or fund-raising power. Two bottom lines may be shown: one for budgeters and another for bondholders.

Accounting principles lie between the conceptual level and the reporting level, and it may not be necessary to engage in extended debate over them if they can be solved at the reporting level. For example, if depreciation is useful for some purposes and not for others, it might be included in some parts of the report and not in other parts.

CONCLUSIONS

This article has attempted to publicize and suggest the importance of the issues in nonbusiness reporting facing the accounting profession. A model is suggested for approaching the issues, with the argument that efficient resource allocation in the nonbusiness sector of our economy should be adopted as the criterion for evaluating the issues.

With the growth of public sector expenditures and the increasing level of public concern about tax rates, the accounting profession is in a unique position to help provide financial input for public sector economic and political decisions. It is apparent that the profession is about to make some fundamental decisions in nonbusiness accounting, reconciling viewpoints that are often far apart. The FASB should use the best of accounting thought in both the business and nonbusiness sectors of our economy so that rational choices will be made.

WHO'S WATCHING THE BOOKS?

Standard & Poor's Corporation

Five years have passed since budgetary gimmicks led the nation's largest city to the brink of bankruptcy. Yet governmental accounting is

Source. Copyright © 1980 by Standard & Poor's Corporation. Reprinted with permission from the *Standard & Poor's Perspective* (November 26, 1980), pp. 1–5.

still undergoing major structural change. Concepts and standards are under debate. Special interest groups vie for authority to make the rules. States and cities, worried over the specter of federal controls, attempt to police themselves, creating the perception of progress. Much still needs to be done. Says the SEC:

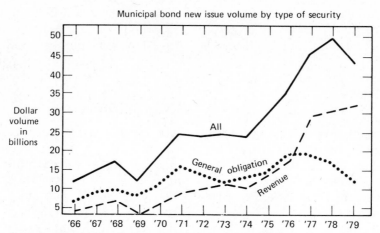

Municipal bond new issue volume by type of security

General obligation bonds have declined in recent years as a percent of total tax-exempt issues. Source: Public Securities Association.

"The market for municipal securities provides investors only limited protection compared with corporate, government or other types of issuers."

In the regulated corporate market, accounting must meet stringent standards. The unregulated market for municipal bonds has no effective way to enforce uniform rules of financial reporting. Investor protection depends on voluntary practices of states and each state makes its own rules.

While corporate bond investors may reasonably compare finances of one company with another, municipal accounting often leaves buyers in a quandary. Investors have become wary of general obligation bonds backed solely by a government's taxing power, while showing a preference for revenue bonds, with proven cash flows and more "business like" accounting. See Chart 1.

In another development, the market may be penalizing issuers for deficiencies in financial reporting. Poor accounting may be costing taxpayers many millions of dollars in higher interest costs, according to research recently undertaken by Standard & Poor's.

ACCOUNTING REFORMS

Recent attempts to improve accounting have produced results. Investors have access to more information. Financials include items previously omitted, like pension and sick leave liabilities and tax refunds owed but unpaid. Reports begin to reflect generally accepted accounting principles (GAAP) allowing comparison of bond issuers. Data is more reliable with the emergence of independent audits.

Efforts to improve the municipal market's credibility have drawn a dozen groups into a power play for ultimate rule-making supremacy. Driving them is the prospect of a takeover by Washington. Several bills linger in Congress for a federal agency to set reporting standards—which is anathema to state and local governments.

Equally abhorrent to some of them is a project to develop governmental accounting concepts by the Financial Accounting Standards Board, which makes rules for corporations and nonbusiness entities. Many fear this could lead to domination by the FASB, which allegedly lacks experience in the public sector.

As a compromise, a Governmental Accounting Standards Board has been proposed. This nonfederal body would set standards and seek compliance under the aegis of state and local governments, the accounting profession, municipal securities dealers, and users of financial statements.

There is no shortage of existing accounting rules. The industry bible is Governmental Accounting, Auditing and Financial Reporting (GAAFR), written by the National Council of Governmental Accounting and published by the Municipal Finance Officers Association. Statement No. 1 restated GAAFR last year. An implementation of it soon will be released by MFOA. There's also the industry audit guide by the American Institute of Certified Public Accountants, pronouncements by FASB, state legal codes, and academic texts.

S&P's ACCOUNTING POLICY

A bond rating implies the existence of adequate information to make a credit judgment. While S&P does not and cannot perform an audit function, the quality of financial reporting and accounting has long been considered in analyzing applications for bond ratings.

S&P has rejected applications and lowered or withdrawn ratings where reporting was inadequate. Last spring, that practice was formalized with publication of an S&P statement on municipal accounting and financial reporting. Accounting is one of many factors to be evaluated in the rating process on a case-by-case basis. The policy requests that financials:

Conform to generally accepted accounting principles

Be independently audited within six months of the fiscal year end

Be stated on a modified accrual, rather than cash basis, so that revenues are reported when they become measurable and available to pay expenses

Contain an auditor's opinion and disclosure notes, and cite any variance from GAAP which impact the results.

A cash-basis system shows revenues and expenditures only when cash is received or spent. Since many transactions may go unreported until payments are made, a cash system may not accurately represent a government's true financial condition.

Earlier this year, San Francisco's bond rating was withdrawn because of the lack of timely financial reporting. Bonds may be downgraded because of poor accounting plus deteriorating fiscal or economic factors, as with Massachusetts last May, and Toledo, Ohio, in June. Elsewhere, reporting weaknesses may be cited while bond ratings are maintained, as with New York State and Puerto Rico this year. Both say they are converting to GAAP.

As each issuer applies for a bond rating, compliance with S&P's accounting policy is evaluated and entered into a data bank. Ultimately, a substantial body of information will be available through this source.

S&P currently has a project team studying the question of whether S&P should simply withdraw from the business of rating issuers that utilize cash-basis accounting.

MARKET PENALTIES

This fall, S&P asked the research firm of Goldstein/Krall Marketing Resources Inc. to do a market survey on municipal accounting. Interviews were conducted among 200 underwriters, dealers, dealer banks, and institutional investors. Results show the market may already be imposing penalties in the form of higher interest costs where accounting and financial reporting are substandard.

To assess the size of the penalty, S&P looked to one of its units which regularly prices about $20 billion of tax-exempt bonds for investment trusts. Based on views obtained there, plus contact with underwriters and market makers who set interest costs on new issues, research shows penalties may average 0.125 to 0.25 percentage point.

On a typical $100 million issue of bonds with a 10-year average life, that equals a penalty of $1,250,000 to $2,500,000 over the issue's average life. The market for new general obligation bonds totals about $12 billion annually. Based on estimates that half of them don't comply with GAAP, taxpayers could be penalized from $75 million to $150 million over a 10-year average life of the bonds. This penalty would be repeated annually as more new bonds are issued in future years.

Of those polled by Goldstein/Krall on generally accepted accounting principles (GAAP) and the municipal bond market:

Fifty-four percent (54%) said they think the marketplace now imposes interest rate penalties on issuers who don't conform to accounting and reporting standards. Seventy-six percent (76%) of them think the penalties will increase in the future

Seventy-eight percent (78%) said they think issuers who ignore GAAP will have a harder time selling general obligation bonds in the future

Sixty-five percent (65%) said they think the market feels less comfortable now with general obligation bonds than five years ago

Ninety-five percent (95%) said in their opinion municipal accounting standards are important. Eighty-nine percent (89%) said they feel accounting practices as a bond rating consideration is "desirable."

The research also found critics among those interviewed. Among sample comments:

Municipal issuers may not decide to change accounting procedures for the sole purpose of getting an S&P rating

The accounting profession is trying to impose corporate standards on governments

It is not S&P's responsibility to make rules but to analyze what is given to them

So long as municipalities can get bids on bonds, they won't do more than they have to.

STATES MOVE TO GAAP

Many states are taking the initiative in moving to GAAP. New York State Comptroller Edward V. Regan, in a September memo to Governor Hugh Carey, said activities of his office are "moving the State from an archaic checkbook, or cash basis, for running government to a system conforming with generally accepted accounting principles." The conversion is expected to take several years.

Similarly, Puerto Rico has begun to convert a cash system to modified accrual as a more accurate measure of its fiscal condition. Under its timetable, the Commonwealth will have in place:

A computerized general ledger by fiscal 1981

An accounts payable and encumbrance system by fiscal 1982

Procedures to account for fixed assets by fiscal 1983

Final implementation of its central government accounting system by fiscal 1984.

Maryland, one of the first states to adopt GAAP, began in 1975. Last year, the project was operational. Did anyone notice? Officials in Annapolis say the bond market did. Last January, Maryland and a state with cash-basis accounting each sold more than $100 million of AAA-rated bonds on consecutive days. Maryland's interest rate was 0.15 percentage point lower, equal to $600,000 saving, in part reflecting conversion to GAAP, said Maryland's Comptroller Louis V. Goldstein. The saving paid the cost of the new accounting system, plus independent audits for 1979 and 1980, according to a report to the legislature.

Under GAAP, Maryland's financials now show all revenues when measurable and available instead of when cash is received, and all expenditures when the liability is incurred rather than when the payment is made. Also reported are contractual obligations incurred, and all other liabilities which exist at the close of the fiscal year. Omission of any of these could cloud the state's true fiscal condition. Under the cash-basis system used prior to 1979, for example, about $150 million of unpaid liabilities or uncollected receivables may have gone unreported.

NEW YORK CITY

Events have a way of coming full circle. New York City, where it all started, now wants back into the bond market. Mayor Edward Koch told a Wall Street group last month: "New York has eliminated all budgetary and accounting abuses that characterized its practices prior to 1975."

Recently, the city unveiled its integrated financial management system. Called IFMS, it centralizes budgeting, accounting, purchasing, and payroll in a single data-base computer network. "It's among the most sophisticated financial control systems of any government entity in the United States," says the mayor. From IFMS comes detailed monthly reports tracking $13.5 billion of annual revenues and expenditures within 30 days of the close of each month.

Previously considered unauditable, the city is now audited by a "Big Eight" accounting firm. That data is being examined by S&P as part of a request by the city to have its suspended rating reviewed relative to New York City's proposed reentry into the bond market.

INDEPENDENT AUDITS

If New York City can bring order out of its chaos, can any governmental unit credibly claim an inability to comply with accounting and auditing standards?

An indicator of local government compliance is the U.S. Comptroller General's report to Congress last May. To qualify for $25,000 or more under federal revenue sharing, 11,000 governments are asked for independent audits every three years. (Congress may amend that to annually.) Of the total reports submitted 63% met audit requirements, 26% partially complied, and about 11% were unacceptable.

At the state level the Council of State Governments is developing accounting practices for states under a National Science Foundation grant. Its survey of 50 states shows most of them audit agencies and departments. Few audit the entire state. That's as though General Motors Corp. had its divisions audited but not the parent company. Among states polled only 20 said they did annual audits. Others said audits were done every two, three, or four years, or were vague as to frequency and scope.

The credibility of an audit depends on the auditor's independence. Questions arise when audits are performed by the person who also keeps accounting records or who serves at the will of a governor or mayor. An auditor is considered independent if he:

Is elected to a term of office

Is appointed by a chief executive but reports to the legislature or city council which confirms the appointment

Is named by the legislature or city council to whom he reports

Is a state official auditing local government

Is an outside auditor who is a certified public accountant.

OPINION AND COMMENT

"General obligation bonds are suffering from an erosion in confidence—a credibility gap," said Brenton W. Harries, president of S&P, at a meeting of state auditors, comptrollers, and treasurers. Can the trend be reversed?

There's been a structural change in the municipal bond market and in the way investors look at debt backed by an issuer's "full faith and credit." Investors believed what they read in a state constitution that general obligation meant the issuer would raise taxes in whatever amount necessary in the event of default. With such assurances, there was little interest in financial statements, full disclosure, or independent audits. The experience of New York City and Cleveland shattered those illusions.

A general obligation pledge is not a key to unlock a city's assets. Nor can investors rely on interpretations of passages in a state constitution, which through legal maneuvers may be put aside under a state's police powers to protect the health, welfare, and safety of its citizens. The antidote to moratoriums is fiscal discipline scrutinized under full disclosure, standardized accounting, and timely auditing. From what we see at S&P, the message is getting across. But it is a slow, agonizing process, muddled in politics, legalities, and the desire of states to reject any tampering with sovereign rights and powers.

Because of their considerable political clout, governments may be able to forestall a federal legislative solution to this problem. However, they cannot defeat the forces at work in the financial markets. Investors have too many other bond issues to choose from, and may continue to penalize general obligation issuers using archaic accounting systems. "This decade will require accounting and financial reporting be brought up to snuff," said Mr. Harries. "Cash-basis accounting may well be the dinosaur of the 1980s."

CHAPTER 3

Management Accounting Concepts

The accounting system of the organization must be capable of providing the information needed for financial reporting requirements as well as for management decisions. The issues in setting principles for financial reporting are presented in Chapter 2. The present chapter examines both the information needs of management in its attempt to maximize the effectiveness and efficiency of resource allocation within the nonprofit agency and the techniques for identifying that information.

In order for management to be able to control costs, it must be able to compare planned costs with actual ones. Variances between the two may indicate the need for intervention by management. A simple comparison between the original budget amounts and actual costs, however, may be misleading. Unless the actual activity level of the organization is the same as that budgeted, comparisons of planned costs with actual costs will provide a minimum of useful information. The reason lies in the way costs vary with changes in activity level. While variable costs fluctuate in direct proportion to activity changes, fixed costs remain constant.

Knowledge of which costs are variable and which are fixed is essential for effective planning and control. In the planning process, management first estimates the volume of activity expected during the budget period. The activity level multiplied by the variable cost per unit of activity results in the total estimated variable costs for that period. Total estimated costs are obtained by simply adding the total estimated variable costs to the total estimated fixed costs.

At the end of the budget period, the actual activity level is known. It (actual activity) multiplied by the estimated variable cost per unit gives a figure representing what the variable costs *should* have been given the actual level of activity. By comparing actual variable costs with those estimated, management can determine how well the organization has controlled variable costs during the budget period.

Four techniques that can be used to estimate fixed and variable costs appear in Rowley's "Which Is Best to Find Cost Behavior?" Exemplified through a hospital setting, the author gives an excellent discussion of cost behavior applicable to any type of activity.

One important assumption that Rowley makes but does not spell out is that the organization's accounting system must be capable of measuring costs and revenues in "proper" time periods. That is to say, all costs and revenues for a given time period must be identifiable with that time period. An accounting system that matches costs and revenues within such a time frame is called an accrual accounting system. Many nonprofit organizations today remain on a cash-basis accounting system; they would need to change to accrual accounting before the techniques described by Rowley could be applied successfully.

In the chapter's second article, "Break-even Analysis for Higher Education," Larimore utilizes knowledge of cost behavior to formulate a technique for analyzing the interrelationships between costs and revenues. The tools he suggests are useful in any nonprofit organization where revenues received vary with the number of clients served, due either to user fees or to government payments based on activity level.

Larimore constructs a breakeven chart, which facilitates identification of the minimum activity level generating sufficient revenues to cover total costs. In addition to the organization-wide breakeven point, the author advocates using the same approach for each program. He recommends that programs in which total revenues do not meet at least the variable costs be carefully reviewed by management.

Gruber in "The High Cost of Delivering Services" proposes a technique quite different from those of Rowley and Larimore. Instead of basing his analysis on variable and fixed costs, Gruber examines the relationships of various costs to one another and draws conclusions about cost control from the resultant ratios. The author utilizes actual field data to illustrate his approach to costing, effectively overcoming several common objections to transferring this method of cost analysis from industry to the nonprofit sector.

While Gruber ignores the fact that costs include both fixed and variable ones, Rowley and Larimore in their articles do not extend their techniques to ratio analysis. Combining Gruber's approach with separation of fixed and variable costs would result in cost ratios for both fixed and variable costs. Such ratios would be unaffected by changes in activity level and may result in more useful information for agency management.

The chapter's final reading, "The Voluntary Agency as Vender of Social Services," shows that use of more sophisticated accounting techniques by nonprofit agencies implies negligible incremental costs. This relates to the fact that the growing reporting requirements of governments necessitates that much of the information useful for management control already be generated.

In this context, Vorwaller discusses the major recent trend of governmentally purchased social services from voluntary agencies. The resultant need for cost reimbursement accountability has a profound effect on what is considered an acceptable accounting system. As more cost information is generated to meet this need, it can be productively utilized for internal management decision making.

WHICH IS BEST TO FIND COST BEHAVIOR?

C. Stevenson Rowley

How costs behave must be known before financial forecasts and budgets can be drawn up. While cost containment has emphasized the importance of forecasting and budgeting, determining cost behavior patterns is still the first step. This article describes four basic methods for the first step—account analysis, graphic analysis, high-low analysis, and least squares regression analysis—and examines the reliability of each.

INTRODUCTION

Determining cost behavior patterns is not unique to the health care industry. All elements of business and government are concerned with this question and have developed successful methods for attacking it. Because not all health care financial managers are familiar with these methods, we will analyze them here in the context of the health care industry.

The behavior of a cost element can fall into four patterns: (1) completely variable with changes in activity, (2) completely fixed with changes in activity, (3) both fixed and variable, and (4) fixed over a small range of activity (often identified as semi-fixed). These four patterns are shown graphically in Figure 1. The pattern analysis methods suggested in this article are directed to the first three patterns.

GENERAL METHODS OF ANALYSIS

The two general approaches to determining cost behavior are *engineering analysis* and *analysis of historical data*. For engineering

Source. Copyright © 1976 by the Hospital Financial Management Association. Reprinted with permission from *Hospital Financial Management* (April, 1976), pp 18–22, 24–26, 28.

analysis, an activity is examined by industrial engineers, who determine what inputs of labor and capital should be required to perform the activity and estimate the costs that should be incurred. This approach is frequently used when a new activity is undertaken or when historical data are unreliable. But it is very expensive and should be used only when the anticipated benefits outweigh the costs.

A less expensive and more frequently used approach is the analysis of historical financial data; it is on this that the article will focus.

The following example will be used throughout the article to explain the four alternative methods of analyzing historical data.

A 150-bed hospital wishes to forecast its costs in the dietary department. It is assumed that the hospital wishes to use past financial information to forecast dietary costs and to gain some insight into the behavior of those costs.

Specifically, the hospital has accumulated weekly department costs for the quarter most recently ended (13 weeks). The hospital financial staff believes that if there is a variation in dietary department costs with hospital activity, the measure that should best explain that variation is patient days. Figure 2 shows the costs of the dietary department for the 13-week period with total patient days for each week. (At 80 percent occupancy, a 150-bed hospital would provide 840 patient days of service in a week.)

METHOD 1: ACCOUNT ANALYSIS

A common and uncomplicated method of analyzing past data to determine cost behavior is account analysis. Accounts for which cost behavior information is desired are identified, and the cost behavior of each classified as fixed

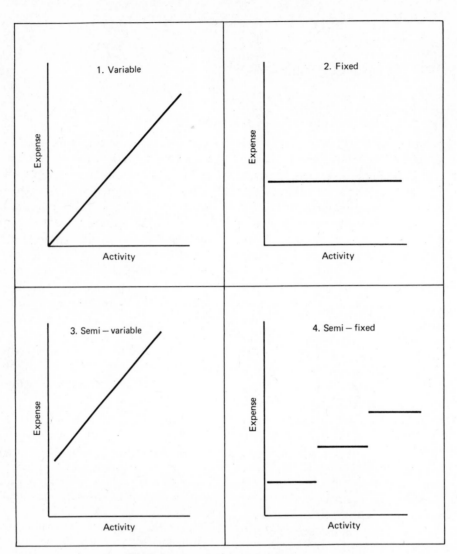

FIGURE 1   *Possible cost behavior patterns*

or variable. The behavior of each account, therefore, is assumed to follow pattern 1 or 2 in Figure 1. If an account seems to more closely follow pattern 3 or 4, it is nevertheless classified as variable or fixed, depending on which better identifies the relationship.

In Figure 2, for purposes of explanation, assume that the original classification of the account is fixed cost. Assume further that the

hospital expects to provide 850 patient days of service in the 14th week. What should be budgeted for the costs of the dietary department in the 14th week? The total dietary department costs for the 13-week period were $140,200; the average was $10,785 per week. If costs are classified as fixed, the estimated cost per week in the dietary department is $10,785 and this is the amount that will be budgeted

FIGURE 2   *Weekly dietary department expense and patient days of service*

Week	Dietary Department Expense	Patient Days of Service
1	$ 7,000	420
2	9,800	510
3	9,200	600
4	13,100	750
5	14,000	900
6	11,500	825
7	10,400	700
8	12,900	840
9	11,400	630
10	10,200	560
11	8,000	520
12	10,900	650
13	11,800	720
	$140,200	8,625

for the 14th week. Note that this estimate is not dependent on the information that 850 patient days of service will be provided in the 14th week. Because dietary department costs have been classified as fixed, the estimate is independent of information about patient days of service and would be unchanged if the patient day estimate were 800 or 900.

After analyzing the information in Figure 2, however, it seems more likely that the dietary department account is variable. The historical financial data indicate that the average expense per patient day during the past 13 weeks was $16.26. At this rate, the cost to provide dietary service for 850 patient days should be $13,821. Note here that the information about estimated patient days of service in the 14th week is used, and that the estimate will differ if the estimated patient days of service is 800 or 900.

RELIABILITY OF ACCOUNT ANALYSIS

If the dietary department account is classified as fixed, the budget estimate is $10,785 per week; if the account is classified as variable,

the budget estimate is $16.26 per patient day. How reliable are these estimates? One way to examine their reliability is to assume that they were used during the past 13 weeks and to calculate the error in the estimates for each of those weeks. This is done in Figure 3.

If the fixed estimate had been used during each of the past 13 weeks, the estimate would have differed from actual expense incurred by the amount in column 4 of Figure 3. If the variable estimate had been used, the estimate would have differed from the actual expense by the amount in column 6. The range in variation under the fixed classification is −$3,785 +$3,215, and −$1,910 to +$1,510 under the variable classification— approximately half of the variation range under the fixed classification. If a smaller variation between the estimate and the actual value is the criterion of a good estimate, then classifying dietary expense as a variable cost produces a better budgetary estimate than classifying it as a fixed cost.

METHOD 2: GRAPHIC ANALYSIS

Four possible cost behavior patterns were depicted in Figure 1. One method of determining the behavior pattern of an account is to graph the cost against the measure of activity that is believed to cause it to vary. A pattern similar to one of those in Figure 1 should appear. Figure 4 shows the data on weekly dietary department expense reported in Figure 2. The graph suggests a positive relationship between dietary department expense and patient days of service—that is, as the number of patient days of service increases, the dietary department expense increases, and vice versa. The relationship can be represented with a straight line.

The reader is asked to draw a straight line in Figure 4 to represent the behavior pattern of the points on the graph. This line should suggest that the costs of the dietary depart-

FIGURE 3 *Reliability of account analysis of estimates of dietary department expense*

Week (1)	Actual Dietary Department Expense (2)	Fixed Classification[1]		Variable Classification[2]	
		Expense Estimate (3)	Actual−Fixed Estimate (4)	Expense Estimate (5)	Actual−Variable Estimate (6)
1	$ 7,000.00	$ 10,784.61	−$3,784.61	$ 6,827.13	$ 172.87
2	9,800.00	10,784.62	− 984.62	8,290.09	1,509.91
3	9,200.00	10,784.61	− 1,584.61	9,753.04	− 553.04
4	13,100.00	10,784.62	2,315.38	12,191.30	908.70
5	14,000.00	10,784.61	3,215.39	14,629.56	− 629.56
6	11,500.00	10,784.62	715.38	13,410.43	− 1,910.43
7	10,400.00	10,784.61	− 384.61	11,378.55	− 978.55
8	12,900.00	10,784.62	2,115.38	13,654.26	− 754.26
9	11,400.00	10,784.61	615.39	10,240.70	1,159.30
10	10,200.00	10,784.62	− 584.62	9,102.84	1,097.16
11	8,000.00	10,784.61	− 2,784.61	8,452.64	− 452.64
12	10,900.00	10,784.62	115.38	10,565.80	− 334.20
13	11,800.00	10,784.61	1,015.39	11,703.65	− 96.35
	$140,200.00	$140,199.99	$ 0.01	$140,199.99	$ 0.01

[1]Fixed estimate calculated to the nearest cent for accuracy. Total for column 3 should sum to $140,200; consequently, total for column 4 should sum to zero. Difference caused by rounding.

[2]Calculations based on variable estimate of $16.255072 per patient day for accuracy. Total of column (5) should sum to $140,200; consequently, total for column (6) should sum to zero. Difference caused by rounding.

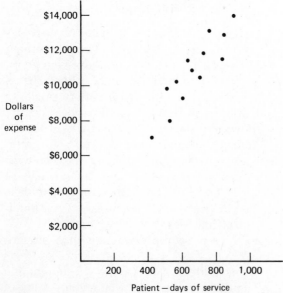

FIGURE 4 *Graphic analysis of dietary department expense (per week)*

ment contain both a fixed and a variable component. This conclusion differs from the assumption implicit in account analysis, where the alternatives were to classify the account as either completely fixed or completely variable.

Graphic analysis enables the user to identify the general behavior pattern of a particular cost. It is less useful for specifying exactly how the cost will vary with a change in activity. Use the straight line that you drew in Figure 4 to estimate the weekly fixed costs in the dietary department and the amount by which dietary department costs vary per patient day of service. Other readers will no doubt have drawn different lines, each to the reader's eye apparently reflecting the behavior pattern of the expense item. Each different line will, of course, indicate a different fixed cost component and, consequently, a different rate of variation in expense per patient day.

METHOD 3: HIGH–LOW ANALYSIS

Graphic analysis does not allow the user to identify the fixed and variable components of an account because no two readers of the graph are likely to draw identical lines to represent the behavior pattern of all of the points on the graph. If the analysis were limited to two points, however, most readers would draw identical straight lines through these two points. The high–low method of analysis insures comparability between readers by limiting the data points in the analysis to two: the highest and the lowest value of the activity variable. In the example of the weekly expenses of the dietary department, the activity variable is patient days of service, and the high and low values for this variable are 900 and 420 patient days per week respectively. Figure 5 shows a high–low analysis of the data in Figure 2.

In Figure 5, the change in patient days per week between the high and the low levels of activity is calculated, together with the related change in dietary department expense. The rate of change per patient day is $14.58. The variable rate is used to calculate the total variable component in dietary department expense for the high and low weeks of activity, and this total variable component is deducted from the total reported expense for each of these two weeks to determine the fixed component of expense: $875 per week. This behavior pattern is graphed in Figure 6. Compare the line in Figure 6 with the one that you drew in Figure 4.

The high–low method is subject to several criticisms; one is that it ignores available information. The more information available and used in estimating the pattern of a particular cost, the more likely that a reliable estimate will be obtained. In the example in Figure 5, data for 13 weeks were available, but eleven weeks' were ignored. A second criticism of the high–low method is that the two pieces of information used, the high and low values, may be the most atypical. For example, during

FIGURE 5 *Computations for high–low analysis of dietary department expense*

	Week	Patient Days of Service	Dietary Department Expense
High	5	900	$14,000
Low	1	420	7,000
Difference		480	$ 7,000

Rate of Variation in Expense per Patient Day $= \dfrac{\$7,000}{480} = \$14.58$

	Level of Activity	
	High	Low
Patient days of service	900	420
Total dietary expense	$14,000	$7,000
Variable dietary expense[1]	13,125	6,125
Fixed dietary expense	$ 875	$ 875

[1]Calculations based on $14.5833 per patient day.

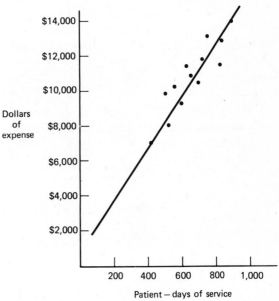

FIGURE 6 *High–low analysis of dietary department expense (per week)*

11 of the 13 weeks, conditions may have been relatively normal. However, during one week a very high level of activity was experienced while during another week a very low level of activity occurred. In both cases, these unusual levels of activity may have distorted the normal relationship between the activity variable and the related cost. The high−low method will ignore the normal relationship of the 11 weeks and concentrate on the abnormal relationship that occurred during the two weeks of abnormal activity.

RELIABILITY OF HIGH−LOW ANALYSIS

High−low analysis identified the fixed and variable components as $8.75 per week and $14.50 per patient day. Are these estimates better than the completely variable assumption—$16.26 per patient day—chosen for the account analysis method? Once again we can examine the reliability of the results with the estimation formula to predict dietary department expense for each of the past 13 weeks, and comparing these predictions with the actual data. These computations are presented in Figure 7. The range in variation of estimated values from actual values is −$1,406 +$1,488. This may be compared with the previously noted range for variable account analysis of −$1,910 to +$1,510. The use of high−low analysis, in the case of the dietary department expense account, appears to produce a smaller range of variation than the account analysis method which classified the account as completely variable.

METHOD 4: LEAST-SQUARES REGRESSION ANALYSIS

Graphic analysis and high−low analysis enable the user to separate a cost into its fixed and variable components. The results obtained from graphic analysis depend on the eye of the user, and those obtained from high−low

FIGURE 7 *Reliability of high−low estimates of dietary department expense*

Week	Actual Dietary Department Expense	High−low Estimate of Expense	Difference: Actual − Estimate
1	$ 7,000.00	$ 7,000.00	$ 0.00
2	9,800.00	8,312.50	1,487.50
3	9,200.00	9,625.00	− 425.00
4	13,100.00	11,812.50	1,287.50
5	14,000.00	14,000.00	0.00
6	11,500.00	12,906.25	−1,406.25
7	10,400.00	11,083.33	− 683.33
8	12,900.00	13,125.00	− 225.00
9	11,400.00	10,062.50	1,337.50
10	10,200.00	9,041.67	1,158.33
11	8,000.00	8,458.33	− 458.33
12	10,900.00	10,354.17	545.83
13	11,800.00	11,375.00	425.00
	$140,200.00	$137,156.25	$3,043.75

analysis depend on only two pieces of information. The objective of *statistical estimate* methods is to find the "best" line to draw through all of the points on the graph.

What is the "best" line? If the relationship between a particular cost and the activity variable is perfectly linear, then the best line will pass straight through all of the points on the graph. Extremely rarely, however, is the relationship between actual cost and actual activity data perfectly linear. As in the case of the data in Figure 4, most relationships approximate linearity. If no straight line will pass through all of the points in Figure 4, what is the best straight line to represent the approximately linear relationship depicted there? One might reasonably assume that the definition of *best* has something to do with the distance of the data points on the graph from the line selected. The definition most commonly used is that the sum of the square of the distance between each data point and the line selected should be less than it would be for any other line.

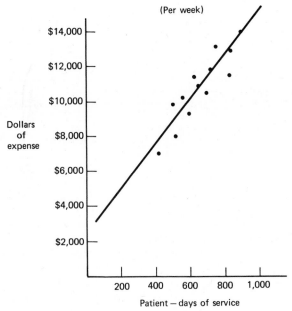

(Per week)

FIGURE 8 *Least-squares regression analysis of dietary department expense (per week)*

FIGURE 9 *Reliability of least-squares regression estimate of dietary department expense*

Week	Actual Dietary Department Expense	Regression Estimate of Expense	Difference: Actual − Estimate
1	$ 7,000.00	$ 7,695.75	−$ 695.75
2	9,800.00	8,837.60	962.40
3	9,200.00	9,979.46	− 779.46
4	13,100.00	11,882.55	1,217.45
5	14,000.00	13,785.65	214.35
6	11,500.00	12,834.10	− 1,334.10
7	10,400.00	11,248.19	− 848.19
8	12,900.00	13,024.41	− 124.41
9	11,400.00	10,360.08	1,039.92
10	10,200.00	9,471.97	728.03
11	8,000.00	8,964.48	− 964.48
12	10,900.00	10,613.82	286.18
13	11,800.00	11,501.94	298.06
	$140,200.00	$140,200.00	$ 0

This *least-squares regression analysis* is the most common method of statistical estimation.

Calculus formulas can be derived to determine the fixed and variable components of a relationship between independent and dependent variables. Most computer installation libraries include programs that will calculate these estimates, together with a number of additional statistics about the estimates. Using one such program to analyze the data reported in Figure 2, the following estimates were obtained: fixed dietary department cost per week = $2,367, variable dietary department cost per patient day = $12.68. In Figure 8, this "best" line is drawn through the 13 data points from which it was estimated.

RELIABILITY OF LEAST-SQUARES ESTIMATE

As for the account analysis estimates and the high−low estimates, the least squares estimates of dietary department cost behavior may

be made for the past 13 weeks and compared to the actual data. This is done in Figure 9. The differences may be compared with the account analysis differences in Figure 3 and the high−low differences in Figure 7. The range in variation between actual values and estimated values for the regression estimates is −$1,334 to +$1,217—smaller than that obtained using either variable account analysis or high−low analysis.

SUMMARY

Four methods of determining cost behavior have been discussed: (1) account analysis, (2) graphic analysis, (3) high−low analysis, and (4) least-squares regression analysis. In using account analysis, it is assumed that a cost is either entirely fixed or entirely variable. Graphic analysis will confirm or contradict this assumption but does not lead to precise estimates of the pattern of cost behavior because each reader of the graph may see a slightly different pattern of variation. This problem

FIGURE 10   *Dietary department cost estimates obtained from various methods of cost estimation*

| Cost Estimates and Budget | Method of Cost Estimation | | | |
| | Account Analysis | | High-Low Analysis | Least-squares Regression Analysis |
	Fixed Classification	Variable Classification		
Fixed cost per week	$10,875	$ 0	$ 875	$ 2,367
Variable cost per patient day	$ 0	$ 16.26	$ 14.58	12.68
Budget for 850 patient day week	$10,875	$13,821	$13,268	$13,145

may be overcome by focusing attention on the highest and lowest points of activity, through which a straight line may be drawn. This approach, however, ignores useful data and may concentrate on abnormal rather than normal periods of activity. The last method makes use of all of the information available and yields precise estimates that may be used to draw a straight line that approximates the behavior pattern of the data points.

A hypothetical example has been used throughout this article: a dietary department for which 13 weeks of cost information was available and for which estimates for future planning were desired. Estimates obtained by applying each method of cost behavior estimation were reported throughout the article. They are reported again, for comparative purposes, in Figure 10, which also shows the dietary department expense budget for an 850 patient day week that would result from using the various cost estimates.

One way to test the reliability of these various estimates for budgeting purposes is to use them to make estimates for each of the past 13 weeks and, for each week, compare the budgeted figure with the actual value. The smaller the variation between the budgeted and actual values, the more reliable the estimate for budgeting purposes. The differences that resulted from this test of reliability for each of the estimation methods were also reported throughout the article. They too are reported again, for comparative purposes, in Figure 11. The total range of variation runs from a high of $7,000 for the account analysis method where the account is classified as fixed, to a low of $2,551 where the estimates are obtained from least-squares regression analysis.

Many hospitals, and other business enterprises, have used account analysis or high−low analysis to determine the pattern of cost variation in their cost accounts. The objective

FIGURE 11   *Range in variation between actual values and estimated values for various methods of cost estimation*

| Actual−Estimate Difference | Method of Cost Estimation | | | |
| | Account Analysis | | High-Low Analysis | Least-squares Regression Analysis |
	Fixed Classification	Variable Classification		
Largest positive difference	$3,215	$1,510	$1,488	$1,217
Largest negative difference	3,785	1,910	1,406	1,334
Total range	$7,000	$3,420	$2,894	$2,551

of this article has been to demonstrate that statistical estimation methods—in particular least-squares regression analysis—will provide cost estimates that will usually prove more reliable for planning purposes. Moreover, because most hospitals and other health care institutions today make some use of a computer, and because most computers have a programmed capability to perform least-squares regression analysis, this method of cost behavior estimation can probably be used as easily as the account analysis or high—low methods.

BREAK-EVEN ANALYSIS FOR HIGHER EDUCATION

L. Keith Larimore

In the field of educational administration, most methods of analysis employed for internal managerial control, or for justification purposes, emphasize either costs or revenues. Analytical methods which do tie costs and revenues together are generally too sophisticated and the resulting data are therefore difficult to explain. This is a situation which is becoming more and more serious since the demand for the services of colleges and universities has been negatively affected by tight money, reluctant taxpayers, population trends, and a number of other demand-depressing factors.

With regard to the relationship between the institution as the seller and the potential student as the buyer, a "buyer's market" is rapidly developing. This buyer's market has manifested itself in stable or declining enrollments following a decade of rapid expansion in physical facilities, curricula, and faculty size. In short, many colleges and universities have geared up for an unending growth in demand for their services only to find that the demand is shrinking. Thus, large numbers of institutions are left with excess capacity accompanied by declining enrollments—a situation which plays havoc with productivity and costs. Instead of virtually receiving a blank check from legislators who are now interested in trimming the fat from appropriations for higher education, college administrators are asked to justify objectively and quantitatively not only proposed new programs but also the existing programs and curriculum.

Top level administrators are thus caught on the horns of a dilemma in that they have almost constant pressure from above and below. The pressure from above comes from legislators and boards of control demanding more economical operation of the institution with orders to hold the line on, or even cut costs. The pressure from below comes from faculty members who typically want to add courses and programs to the curriculum.[1] The

Source. Copyright © 1974 by the National Association of Accountants. Reprinted with permission from *Management Accounting* (September, 1974), pp. 25—28.

[1]Many of these proposals are based on "pet" interests and are, more often than not, in addition to existing programs and courses which in themselves may not be justifiable in terms of enrollments or the costs and revenues associated with them. Some of these existing "financial losers" are necessary for a sound and complete academic program and should be carried by the more profitable courses.

resulting cost—revenue squeeze simply means that college administrators must do a more effective job of applying or adapting the available tools of management to their financial operations.

The objective in this article is to provide an effective yet easily understood method of analyzing costs and revenues together, whether the purpose be for curriculum decisions, resource allocation, costs and productivity analysis, or management effectiveness. The proposed method is nothing more or less than an adaptation and application to college and university operations of a simple management tool known as "break-even analysis."[2] If properly employed, the method aids the administrator to determine precisely that level of activity (enrollments) which will generate sufficient revenues to just cover the costs of operations. In addition, the magnitude of the losses or excesses associated with other levels of activity is also indicated. However, the process of generating the needed input data should not

exclude the generation of other information which is not specifically needed for break-even analysis.

REVENUES

Revenues may come from any one of a great many sources. However, for the most part, the revenues generated will depend on levels of enrollment. For most public colleges and universities, tuition and governmental appropriations (based on full-time equivalent enrollments) are the major sources of revenue. Therefore, revenues will increase as enrollments increase and decrease as enrollments decrease. The relationship between enrollments and revenues is for all practical purposes assumed to be linear.

COSTS

As in industry, most costs will fall into two categories, fixed costs and variable costs. Fixed costs are generally overhead costs which do not change as the level of activity changes. Some examples of fixed costs would be top level administrators' salaries, maintenance costs, and building and grounds expenses. Such costs are very broad and general in that they are difficult to associate with any academic area but represent necessary services for every phase of the institution. Variable costs, on the other hand, are those costs which vary directly with the level of activity. Faculty salaries and testing supplies are among examples of variable costs. As enrollments increase, the expenditures on these items will increase or vary within limits. It is important for the reader to realize that many such variable costs appear to be fixed within a budget or contract period. However, these variable costs do and should change with the level of activity from period to period.

However, even if such financial losers are not crucial to the overall curriculum, it is very difficult to remove such programs or courses for at least two reasons. First, the quantitative data upon which the courses were determined to be losers are not adequate to support such a determination, or such data are not easily understood by the cross-section faculty usually involved in the decision to drop courses or programs from the curriculum. Second, the welfare of the personnel who would be negatively affected by the elimination of programs or courses becomes a major consideration.

[2]Break-even analysis can be presented in the form of tables, formulas, or charts and graphs. The graphic illustrations are generally accepted as the most informative and most readily understood. However, the reader is reminded that break-even analysis is only a tool of management and not a "cure-all." The method should be used in conjunction with other more traditional measures of productivity and performance in an effort to improve the quality of decision required of college and university administrators.

COLLECTING BUDGET COSTS INFORMATION

It is suggested that the break-even approach be applied to the smallest subdivisions of the institution's total academic program for which budgets and enrollment data are available. It is also suggested that the time frame for the analysis include past as well as current budget periods. The budget data for the entire institution should be broken down by colleges, divisions, and departments. The more budget information can be broken down, the more meaningful the results will be.

A useful format for collecting budget information is shown in Exhibit 1. The column heads are for the most part self-explanatory. However, a question may be asked with regard to what budget items to include in the Department budget column. The recommendation here is to include the total known budget of the individual Responsibility center even

though an amount for equipment and other capital expenditures will be counted. A one-time expenditure for a building, a computer, or a comparable item should obviously not be included. This then assumes that all the amounts included are recurrent from budget period to budget period and are not a disproportionate amount of the total budget.

The main point is that the analysis be consistent from one responsibility center to another. The argument is well taken that a microscope, for example, may have a useful life of more than a year and should therefore not be charged to a single year's expenses. However, a portion of the microscope's life will be consumed during the current period, and since depreciation accounts are generally not maintained in college and university accounting systems, it is suggested that the entire cost of such recurring equipment expenditures be charged to current operations. A

EXHIBIT 1

Budget Costs Information

Responsibility Center	Dept. Budget	Dept. Salaries	Total Dept. Variable Costs	Allocated Overhead (Fixed Costs)	Total Dept. Costs	Credit Hours Taught	Costs per Credit Hours Taught (Actual Dollars)		
							Var.	Fixed	Total
College of X									
Division A	$20	$120	$140	$40	$180	5,000	$28.00	$ 8.00	$36.00
Dept 1	$ 5	$ 45	$ 50	$10	$ 60	2,000	$25.00	$ 5.00	$30.00
Dept 2	$15	$ 75	$ 90	$30	$120	3,000	$30.00	$10.00	$40.00
Division B	$25	$130	$155	$50	$205	5,500	$28.18	$ 9.09	$37.27
Dept 1	$10	$ 50	$ 60	$15	$ 75	2,500	$24.00	$ 6.00	$30.00
Dept 2	$15	$ 80	$ 95	$35	$130	3,000	$31.67	$11.67	$43.34
College of Y									
Division A	$18	$115	$133	$35	$168	4,000	$33.25	$ 8.75	$42.00
Dept 1	$12	$ 80	$ 92	$20	$112	3,000	$30.67	$ 6.67	$37.34
Dept 2	$ 6	$ 35	$ 41	$15	$ 56	1,000	$41.00	$15.00	$56.00
Division B	$22	$124	$146	$45	$191	6,000	$24.33	$ 7.50	$31.83
Dept 1	$ 8	$ 54	$ 62	$15	$ 77	2,000	$31.00	$ 7.50	$38.50
Dept 2	$14	$ 70	$ 84	$30	$114	4,000	$21.00	$ 7.50	$28.50

further justification for handling such expenditures in this manner is that depreciation costs for investments in physical plant and facilities will not be charged to the various responsibility centers, thus resulting in an understatement of fixed costs to some extent. The important point again is that the analysis be consistent from one responsibility center to another.

If salaries are not included in the department budgets, the contracted amounts for faculty and other personnel are simply listed in the Department salaries column. Thus, departmental administrative salaries which are clearly related to a single department as well as various clerical salaries are also included. Other administrative costs, which are not associated with a specific department, should be allocated on a credit-hour basis. The allocation would depend on the relationship which total credit hours taught in the department bears to the total credit hours taught by the organizational unit to which such costs can be specifically tied. For example, the salary of the dean of the college of arts and sciences should be allocated to the various departments of that college and should be based on the relationship which the credit hours taught by the individual departments bear to the credit hours taught by the entire college of arts and sciences. This amount should be included in the column labeled Allocated overhead.

Allocated overhead includes other fixed-cost items such as salaries of the president and other top level or staff administrators in addition to expenditures which are vital to the institution but which cannot be clearly tied to a specific department or responsibility center. These costs should also be allocated among the various departments on the basis of the number of credit hours taught by the individual department relative to the number of credit hours taught by the entire institution.

The column Total department costs is simply a summation of the Department budget, Department salaries, and Allocated overhead.

Credit hours taught are, of course, available from historical schedules and enrollment information. Knowing the credit hours taught, cost per credit hour taught can be obtained by dividing total department costs by credit hours taught. Once the cost per credit hour taught for a particular department is determined, the cost of offering a class in that department can be closely approximated.

The cost of the class, for all practical purposes, remains fairly constant regardless of enrollment, once resources have been committed to a given course offering. Certainly more students require more supplies, but the cost difference in most cases is not material. Therefore, the cost side of the analysis represented by the variable cost, the fixed cost, and the total cost, in Exhibit 2, are constant for the contract period.

REVENUE DETERMINATION

The revenues which are important for this analysis are those which are closely correlated with enrollments. Major sources of such revenues are tuition and state or federal appropriations based on full-time-equivalent (FTE) students. The FTE is determined by dividing the number of student credit hours by the criteria for full-time designation. For example, assume the attendance criterion for one FTE student is 24 hours per year or 12 hours per semester. Thus, a three-hour course with eight students enrolled would result in 24 student credit hours divided by the 12 hours per semester criterion. The number of full-time-equivalent students sitting in that class in that semester is two. The revenue associated with the course would be the governmental appropriation per FTE student for the semester multiplied by two plus the tuition per credit hour multiplied by 24.

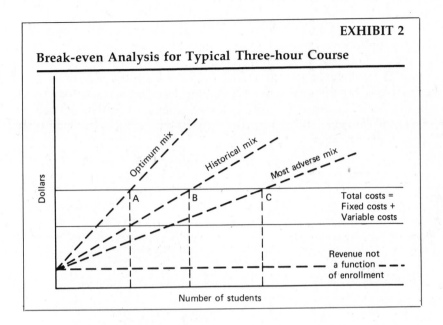

EXHIBIT 2

Break-even Analysis for Typical Three-hour Course

Dollars

Optimum mix

Historical mix

Most adverse mix

A   B   C

Total costs =
Fixed costs +
Variable costs

Revenue not
a function
of enrollment

Number of students

Another way of handling this situation is to divide the annual appropriation per FTE student by the annual criterion for FTE designation. The resulting amount is the appropriation per student credit hour. This value, when added to the tuition rate and then multiplied by the number of hours in the course in question, provides the revenue per student enrolled. The revenue per student enrolled is recommended here because this is the manner in which costs have been defined to this point. Enrollment then becomes a common denominator, allowing the costs and revenues to be analyzed simultaneously.

It should be emphasized that revenue per student enrolled will vary in most institutions depending on whether the students are resident, nonresident, graduate, upper division, lower division, and so on. The recommendation here is to calculate the revenue per student enrolled under the optimum revenue mix, the most adverse revenue mix, and the actual revenue mix through time. These values can then be illustrated as shown in Exhibit 2.

In some junior colleges, additional governmental aid is often received when certain vocational or technical programs are offered. If this aid can be expressed on (or converted to) a per course basis this amount would be added as a fixed revenue amount in Exhibit 2. The sloped revenue lines would then intersect the vertical axis rather than the origin.

BREAK-EVEN POINTS

With the revenue data superimposed over the cost information, the break-even points under a number of circumstances can be determined. The points A, B, and C represent break-even points under different revenue conditions and provide the basis for review and control of operations. The level of enrollment which is associated with the most realistic revenue situation is the key at this point. Classes with consistent historical enrollments below the break-even level can easily be "red flagged" for appropriate action, whether it be reductions in sections offered or elimination from the curriculum. However, it is advisable to allow courses or programs to continue for a short time (possibly more than one contract period) even though enrollments are not sufficient to reach the break-even point, provided variables costs are being covered by current enrollment levels. If variable costs are not being covered, immediate corrective action will be required.

Classes with consistent historical enrollments above the break-even point can be readily identified also. The net revenues generated by such classes are measured by the vertical difference between the appropriate revenue curve and the cost level. A trend of growing enrollments beyond the break-even point

would probably justify plans for the allocation of additional resources. The reallocation of resources need not result in increases in total expenditures but may necessitate intra- and/or interdisciplinary transfers of resources from low demand nonessential courses or programs to growth areas of the institution.

CONCLUSION

The adaptation of break-even analysis for use by college and university administrators, while not a cure-all, can be a valuable management tool in coping with the buyer's market which now exists in higher education.

THE HIGH COST OF DELIVERING SERVICES

Alan R. Gruber

Social welfare financing has traditionally been based on the concept of providing enough money for an agency to employ enough staff to carry out the functions set forth in its charter. The important element has been the provision of funds so that staff would be available to carry the necessary responsibilities. Whether or not they efficiently did so has almost never been directly related to the the funding picture.

United Way organizations, for instance, have not provided grants to agencies based on actual time that staff spent delivering services directly to recipients. Rather, they have based allocations on aggregate data, that is, the

Source. Copyright © 1973 by the National Association of Social Workers, Inc. Reproduced with permission from *Social Work,* Vol. 18, No. 4 (July, 1973), pp. 33–40.

number of cases (even though some cases may not have been seen for months), budget, number of staff, and so on. Worse, of course, has been funding based on who on the requesting agency's board knew whom on the funding agency's budget review committee. The accepted and typical procedure has been for the agency executive and a selected board member to go into the budget hearing with colorful charts, the agency's annual budget summary, and most important, a few good case examples designed to tear at the purse strings of budget review committees.

Collecting and transforming data into usable information has been at best a haphazard activity in most health and social welfare organizations. Gathering information has been largely construed to mean compiling case records, often without even a standard outline, or completing forms such as fact sheets and sometimes employee time forms. Traditionally, the social worker's sophistication in this area has not gone beyond counting or categorizing client contacts, counting cases, and tracking cases that are new, opened, reopened, or closed.

It has, then, been on the basis of such information that important administrative and program decisions have been made—or just as often not made. Terms such as cost analysis, cost benefit, service and overhead ratios, service accounting, and others denoting concepts common in business and industry have seldom been relevant to social welfare administration.

ACCOUNTABILITY

Thomas has made the point that a system of collecting statistics about an organization must serve as an administrative tool to expedite accountability. He has further pointed out that it also can serve to monitor program development, maintain program control, check and guide staff development and evaluation, and provide a basis for research.[1]

It is primarily the first issue—accountability—that supports the need for more knowledgeable, accurate collection of information than the vast majority of public and private nonprofit organizations currently do. Accountability has always been espoused as an extremely important component of the social work profession, and yet most social agencies have not implemented it enough so that it has become an ongoing element in their pattern of work. Sanction has often replaced accountability in that as long as funding and other mechanisms permitted an organization to function, it was assumed to be fulfilling its stated purposes.

Accountability becomes all the more imperative for the private, nonprofit service organization when it depends on the public dollar—and to many persons in the business of delivering health and welfare services from the voluntary sector it is agonizingly clear that such dependence will grow in the next few years.

Over the last decade, for instance, private philanthropic giving to support social welfare services has substantially decreased while giving to other endeavors of nonprofit organizations—except religious work—has substantially increased.[2] Large donors particularly have created this situation by generally providing more support to cultural, educational, and health facilities and assuming that the federal and state governments would support the social services.

Added to this—assuming that Boston is typical of large metropolitan areas—support of social agencies by United Way has decreased appreciably in the last decade: a reduction in Boston from 28 percent of the annual operating budgets in 1962 to 18 percent in 1972.[3] This loss has largely been made up through public funds, that is, purchase-of-service contracts. In agencies of the Child Welfare League of America, for example, government payments for services increased by 33 percent between 1968 and 1971.[4] Social agency executives are no longer shocked to hear at their gatherings someone from funding agencies state that in five years approximately 25 percent of the voluntary agencies will no longer exist. Even today, news is often heard of the closing or radical restructuring of a private agency because of its lack of funds.

To counter this trend and attempt to strengthen public faith in private agencies, farseeing agency administrators have recently been turning to service accounting and cost accounting. By using these systems, they are hoping to find the answers to questions that taxpayers are asking about services, costs, benefits, and the wise use of funds.

SERVICE ACCOUNTING AND COST ACCOUNTING

The primary objective of a system of service accounting (sometimes called management information) is the collection of systematic data that will enable an organization to improve its decision-making processes and thereby allocate its resources more efficiently—that is, its funds, personnel, space, and so on. Thus in a social welfare organization, with greatly improved management, the delivery of social and health services should become considerably more efficacious. Specifically, with regard to service delivery, an effective system of service accounting allows for collecting and measuring data related to recipients and provides information from which programs and techniques can be developed and refined.

No system of service accounting has yet been devised that will, in itself, make the decisions required. The function of such a system is to define and illuminate the issues so that appropriate personnel may take rational and informed action. Given our increased technological abilities, service accounting in a social welfare organization aims not only to improve the administrative operation but to reinforce existing information sources and strengthen current practices so that they effectively promote the attainment of social welfare goals.

Cost accounting is a long-accepted practice in commerce and industry. Its objective is simply to determine how much it costs an organization to produce, market, and deliver a product. Knowing that, management is able to make decisions regarding the utilization of manpower, space, and other resources. Management then knows how much it is making—or losing—on its various endeavors and is able to decide whether or not the organization will continue certain practices and products, according to the resulting benefit.

One must remember that benefit need not always be financial reward. Many organizations continue to produce and deliver products on a break-even basis—perhaps even at a loss—because of other benefits derived, such as favorable public relations, worthwhile service to the community, or professional acclaim.

Cost accounting has not been utilized extensively in social welfare. By and large, administrators have taken the position that it is irrelevant since there is no product, that it is impossible to implement, or simply that no one in the organization knows how to do it. However, the thesis of this article is that a specific unit of service rendered by an organization can be considered to be synonymous with a product; therefore, cost accounting and service accounting can be quite readily implemented.

A service unit may be arbitrarily defined in whatever way the administration chooses. For instance, a service unit for an entire day of day care may be defined as (1) a full day of day care for a child, (2) two half-days of day care for a child, (3) nine hours of day care for a child, or (4) any suitable period.

The number of administrators who have recognized the feasibility of using service accounting and cost accounting in social welfare has been growing in recent years. Increasingly, social agencies are combining cost accounting functions with service accounting systems and beginning to implement them.

As a result of such implementation, administrators and board members are being forced to deal with some embarrassing and revealing facts. Why, for instance, does it cost some social agencies or clinics so much more than one dollar to support the delivery of one dollar's worth of service? Why do some administrators estimate that it costs forty to sixty dollars or more per hour to deliver casework/psychotherapy services to individuals or families, although these services are often delivered by students or paraprofessionals? Why do professional personnel, on an average, deliver only about twenty hours a week of direct service, including travel and collateral contacts?

It is important to note that the most progressive and competent administrators are the ones likely to be caught in the squeeze of these issues. Quite obviously, the board members and other decision-makers who are able to ask such questions in the first place are those in organizations that have instituted and implemented service and cost accounting systems. These systems have provided the controversial data. Administrators who continue to use traditional accounting procedures tend to remain blissfully ignorant of such issues.

PURCHASE-OF-SERVICE CONTRACTS

The beginning of a system of service and cost accounting has recently been introduced in Massachusetts for purchase-of-service contracts. Since both federal and state funds are involved, this is a situation in which the significance of accountability cannot be overemphasized.

The author chaired a task force responsible for developing procedures of cost determination, monitoring, and evaluation to utilize Title IV-A funds for purchase-of-service contracts with the Massachusetts Department of Public Welfare. Title IV-A is a part of the social security law, which provides that the federal government under certain conditions will match each dollar supplied by the state with three dollars when the funds are expended for certain social services.

Through this mechanism, the Commonwealth of Massachusetts expects to spend approximately $12 million each year on day care, homemaker services, protective services, services to unmarried mothers, and counseling and emergency services. A large portion of these funds will be spent through purchase-of-service contracts with private agencies.

Purchase-of-service contracting is of course not a new concept in social welfare. In the past, however, such contracts have almost always been based on arbitrary cost figures— for example, twenty-five dollars per week per case, even though generally neither the contracting organization nor the contractor knew how much it would actually cost to deliver the services requested. In most such contracts, grants are given to the contractor, who agrees to provide certain defined services. Then the funds are used, for instance, to hire social workers who theoretically will provide the services. Generally, there is no provision requiring a contractor to account for what has actually been done on the case, how much of the service specified has been rendered, and what benefit has accrued from delivering the service.

In a situation like this, the less a contractor does while still meeting the basic although loose provisions of the contract, the more money he makes. In essence, this type of loose contracting rewards organizations that do the least, beyond an established minimum. From a practical viewpoint, there is a financial disincentive that prevents an organization from doing too much.

On the other hand, organizations working on some contracts found, after they had instituted systems of cost and service accounting, that they were losing literally tens of thousands of dollars. With that in mind, the cost determination system for use of Title IV-A funds in Massachusetts was established with two primary principles: (1) the contractor must be assured of being reimbursed one dollar for each dollar he spends on a contract, including administration and overhead expenses, and (2) the contractor must be assured of maintaining his autonomy and his freedom to design the service delivery system in the way he feels is most efficient and effective.

In line with the latter principle, the system was planned in a way to assure that contracts were not let simply on the basis of price. If they had been, then there would have been a simple, competitive bid system, which again would have rewarded those who delivered the least possible service beyond the established minimum. It was even more important, however, to make sure that contractors were paid dollar for dollar for what they actually delivered, not for the staff they hired, who might or might not deliver the requested services.

To assure attaining these results, a rather tight system of cost determination evolved. It benefits both parties to the contract by assuring that the agreed-upon services are in fact delivered and that the contractor is totally reimbursed. The client obviously is the ultimate beneficiary, and at the same time, the taxpayer is happy because of the maximized accountability and cost benefit.

This system was presented by the Massachusetts Department of Public Welfare at seventeen meetings across the state, which were attended by executive directors of private agencies. At one meeting, the director of a relatively large family counseling agency, clearly recognizing the implications of establishing direct service costs versus general costs, brought up an important issue.

"I'm in private practice," he said, "with a group of social workers and other well-trained and experienced professionals. We could deliver services, say, to unmarried mothers at a price of about twenty-five dollars an hour and make quite a bit of money for ourselves. I could never do it at that price in my agency, however, because of the cost of meetings, training, fringe benefits for my staff, and all the other elements that go into my overhead." Therein lies the issue: he was probably right. In private practice such as he described, he could offer services, delivered by exceptionally well-trained and experienced personnel with full credentials, at a lower rate than his own agency could offer these services with delivery by much less qualified persons. Why?

USE OF TIME

To answer that question, it will be helpful to look at social workers' use of their time. When an agency with a thirty-five-hour working week employs a social worker to deliver services, theoretically that worker is being paid to deliver thirty-five hours of services each week. But it is obvious that he will not do so—and no one expects him to.

Table 1 shows how an average social worker in a large multifunctional agency, Boston Children's Service Association (BSCA), spent his time in 1971. The data for this table were collected for more than a year by the BCSA service and cost accounting systems. Continued use of the systems led to the development of improved administrative procedures that made it possible to redistribute the proportions of time and subsequently reduce the costs of service delivery. The BCSA service and cost accounting systems have also been used to test costs in other agencies, and the figures from those tests are consistent with the data shown in the table.

Costs are figured on the basis of a thirty-five-hour week, an annual salary of $10,000, and thus an hourly rate of $5.49. Time is distributed according to the way the agency's total professional staff—excluding top administrators—spent their working hours.

As Table 1 indicates, an average social worker spends only 19.5 percent of his time delivering services directly to clients. Adding collateral services to the direct services accounts for only 29.5 percent of his time. When all the activities are combined that can be charged directly to specific cases—that is, direct and collateral services, plus the reporting, administrative, and supervisory responsibilities, and travel related to cases—they still take up only 49.5 percent of his time. Thus slightly more than half that social worker's salary should in reality be charged to overhead.

TABLE 1
Distribution of Time for a Typical Social Worker

Activity	Hours[a]	Percent of Time	Cost[b]
Charged directly to specific cases			
Face-to-face services to clients[c]	354.9	19.5	1,950
Collateral services on behalf of clients[c]	182.0	10.0	1,000
Dictation, administration, and supervision	236.6	13.0	1,300
Travel	127.4	7.0	700
Charged to overhead			
Fringe benefits (vacations, holidays, etc.)	182.0	10.0	1,000
Community activity	72.8	4.0	400
Agency activity (staff meetings, staff development, etc.)	309.4	17.0	1,700
Unspecified and unaccounted-for time[d]	354.9	19.5	1,950
Total	1,820.0	100.0	10,000

[a] Hours per year based on a 35-hour week.
[b] Dollars per year based on an annual salary of $10,000.
[c] These figures include time on the telephone.
[d] It is estimated that, at best, approximately 20 percent of the unspecified and unaccounted-for time (71 hours, for a cost of $390) is used for general administrative purposes such as completing statistical forms, program reports, etc. At least $1,560, therefore, is spent to support activity irrelevant to the agency but important to the worker, e.g., coffee breaks, short shopping trips, etc. Note that all social action, education, and other important noncase costs would be accounted for under the categories of community activity and agency activity.

Source. The figures in this table were obtained at Boston Children's Service Association (BCSA), Boston, Massachusetts, through the use of the BCSA service and cost accounting system.

These ratios have significant operational implications for agency administrators. Seemingly, however, most administrators have not been concerned about the problem—at least, if they have, not many have allowed their concern to become public knowledge.

EXEMPLAR AGENCY

The data in Table 1 showing how the average social worker in a large agency spends his time—along with other data based on analyses of actual agency budgets—are used in demonstrating how an exemplar agency establishes costs. For purposes of illustration, it is assumed that the agency renders casework services only; therefore, the service unit (product) is one hour of casework services delivered.

The exemplar then is a large casework agency that carries responsibilities for approximately 2,000 active cases and has an annual budget of $2 million. A traditional system of case costing—simply dividing the budget total by the number of cases—yields a figure of $1,000 per case. That figure, however, provides little if any usable information.

Most social welfare organizations are more sophisticated about case costing and, therefore, figures are not constructed in this traditional way as often now as in the past. Instead, increasing attention is being paid to the overhead rate, which can be defined simply as the portion of the agency budget that is used to enable the agency to deliver its services, as opposed to the portion used for actually delivering them. Services obviously differ from organization to organization. A community organization agency delivers services that a family service agency might carry as overhead—for example, organizing tenants.

It is usually assumed, in considering personnel needs and estimating costs, that staff who deliver services are using their time efficiently to do so. Granted that this assumption is correct, how does an administrator proceed to figure costs of services, costs of overhead, and overhead rate?

First, he recognizes that, out of the agency's $2 million budget, a considerable sum must be set aside for reimbursables. Reimbursables make up the portion of the budget that is essentially cash flow; they include, for example, expenditures for foster care or for a child's residential treatment.

After allocating $600,000 for reimbursables, he subtracts from the balance of $1.4 million the amount required for salaries of workers who are theoretically devoting all their time to the delivery of services to clients—that is, the social workers who are not administrators. He decides on $600,000 for these salaries. The remainder, $800,000, is the overhead.

Next, the overhead rate is calculated by establishing the percentage by which $600,000 must be increased to get $1.4 million. The rate is found to be almost 234 percent.[5]

There may be legitimate reasons that justify an overhead rate of this size. The agency, for instance, may be performing many functions in the community that cannot be charged to specific cases. Action geared to solving problems of racism, housing, poverty, and so on are not always or even usually based on circumstances or events that can be dealt with on a case-to-case basis. Thus the overhead rate for these agencies is generally higher.

As a rule, however, agencies that attempt to deal with social conditions affecting the lives of their clients make more significant contributions to their communities than those that do

not. The costs of such efforts, as well as those for education and consultation, are usually justifiable and warrant support from funding sources. Because of these factors, the simple comparison of costs per unit of service in a large multifunctional agency and in private practice may be inappropriate and unfair.

SERVICE COSTS PER HOUR

Looking at Table 1 from another viewpoint, it can be seen that the typical social worker spent 354.9 hours during the year delivering face-to-face services to clients. Dividing his salary of $10,000 by those hours yields a cost of $28.18 per hour. However, considering only direct services as relevant is a rather regressive concept in social work practice. Including also the hours spent on collateral services, the total comes to 536.9 hours and the resulting cost is $18.63 per hour of service.

Since this worker was theoretically hired to work full time (1,820 hours) delivering services, those services are being delivered at a salary rate of approximately $34,000 per year. Even so, the major problem is yet to be addressed. These costs reflect only salary; how does one allocate the overhead?

It must be remembered that the issue here is cost per service unit. If that service unit is defined as one hour of service delivered directly to a client, then as Table 1 indicates, only 19.5 percent of the worker's time was actually devoted to such functions. Consequently, only 19.5 percent of the $600,000 that the agency spent for salaries of direct service workers (or $117,000) actually represented services delivered directly to clients. Therefore, 80.5 percent of $600,000, or $483,000, should be transferred to overhead costs. Adding this to $800,000 already allocated to overhead means that it has taken $1,283,000 to deliver $117,000 worth of direct worker-to-client services. That represents an effective overhead rate of almost 1,200 percent. Put yet another way, it has taken almost twelve dollars to deliver one dollar's worth of service!

Using the more progressive model—including collateral services as a legitimate part of a service unit—means that 70.5 percent of $600,000 should be transferred to overhead. Then it would take $1,223,000 to deliver $177,000 worth of services with an overhead rate of almost 800 percent—that is, a ratio of almost eight dollars for one dollar's worth of service! Even including dictation, administration, supervision, and travel, the overhead rate would still be approximately 472 percent.

Using the latter ratio, for each dollar that the agency is spending for service directly chargeable to a case, it is spending four to five dollars for overhead. This covers costs of staff meetings, vacations, staff development, conferences, secretarial and clerical assistance, fringe benefits, administration, record-keeping, accounting, and a whole host of other elements—including a significant amount of unaccounted-for time.

SOURCES OF PROBLEMS

It should be pointed out that the data in Table 1, showing the number of hours and the percentage of time devoted to various activities, are based on the records of how working hours were spent in a large agency by the entire professional staff, excluding top administrators. The costs of direct services, costs of overhead, and overhead rates are of course calculated on the same time distribution.

When the time distribution for social workers in *direct service positions* was analyzed, the findings indicated that they spent about 70 percent of their time on activity that could be charged directly to specific cases. Thus the picture regarding overhead costs and overhead rate would be much brighter in an agency having a high proportion of its professional staff in direct service positions.

The data revealed, however, that some

workers averaged only twenty or twenty-five client contacts per month. And in the average bureaucratic agency there are whole groups of workers who deliver virtually no case services, but rather spend the greater part of their time on such functions as liaison with other organizations, supervision, and the processing of information.

The proportion of time that must be charged to overhead is of vital significance to the private practitioner. Suppose that a social worker in private practice, full time, is spending only 29.5 percent of his time actually seeing clients or providing collateral services to them. Then less than one-third of his time is generating income, and he is in serious financial difficulty. To stay in business, he must devote a larger proportion of his time to direct and collateral services. Does this perhaps help to explain why the director of the family counseling agency previously referred to could offer services through his private practice at a lower rate than his nonprofit agency could offer them?

It should also be noted that the overhead rate is of paramount importance when a purchase-of-service contract is involved. It is from that segment of the payment that an agency will obtain its general fiscal support.

CONCLUSIONS

Data collected for more than a year in a number of private social agencies indicate that, in general, the ratio of service costs to overhead costs is quite unreasonable. The author believes that the main reason for uncontrolled costs and minimal benefits lies in the system itself, in that organizations are too heavily staffed by bureaucratic personnel who spend little if any time in actual service delivery—and the larger the organization, the more frequently this occurs.

Although line workers seem to be spending most of their time on services, some deliver little, and this is undetected because of the loose or nonexisting procedures of service accounting. Thus it is probably true that the unproductive line workers account for a small proportion of the uncontrolled costs.

The inevitable and disturbing conclusion, however, is that the costs could be much less and the benefit could be much greater. The real issue is probably more visible when seen in terms of Parkinson's Law, i.e., people fill time with work, whether the work is necessary or not.

Evaluation is certainly not a new concept in social welfare organizations. Combining general program evaluation with cost and service accounting leads to the analysis of cost benefit. Only when more agency administrators and board members recognize that they must know what is actually occurring in their organizations—that is, how time is being spent and what service delivery costs—will more efficient and efficacious services begin to appear.

NOTES AND REFERENCES

1. Thomas, Marvin, "Service Accounting for the Large Multi-Purpose Family Agency" (Seattle, Washington: Family Counseling Service of Seattle, 1968). (Mimeographed.)

2. See *Giving U.S.A.*, annual reports (New York: American Association of Fund-Raising Counsel).

3. Personal communication with Dr. Howard Demone, Director, United Community Services, Boston, Mass.

4. *See* Michael J. Smith, *Child Welfare Agency Income: Amount and Source, 1970–1971* (New York: Child Welfare League of America, 1971), p. 5.

5. Keeping in mind that the reimbursables are simply cash flow for the agency, the following formulas show how to calculate an effective overhead rate. Given:

S = salaries for providing direct services to clients.

R = reimbursables, that is, funds returned to the agency by third parties for costs of foster care, residential treatment, hospitalization, and so on.

O = overhead, that is, cost of space, telephone service, heat, light, and the like; also, salaries of administrators, secretaries, maintenance personnel, and so on.

T = total operating budget of agency.

C = cost of delivering service.

We know that $S + R + O = T$.

We also know $C = S + O$ or $C = T - R$.

The formula used to calculate the overhead rate (OR) is, therefore:

$$OR = \frac{S + O}{S} \times 100.$$

THE VOLUNTARY AGENCY AS A VENDOR OF SOCIAL SERVICES

Darrel J. Vorwaller

Recent government activity in the development and extension of social services to low-income, disadvantaged populations provides an interesting development in the long-standing question of the roles of voluntary and government agencies in meeting social service needs. In several recent projects, state departments of public welfare have arranged to purchase social services from voluntary agencies. The use of the purchase strategy is indeed on the increase. The road to this approach was paved by permissive guidelines prepared by the federal government for the administration of Title IV-A and Title XVI programs of the Social Security Act.

The Model Cities program provides another example of government purchase of social services from voluntary and government agencies. Most often the purchase arrangement follows traditional fiscal allocation procedures, in which the expansion of specific agency programs is financed by subsidy. Less often the purchase transaction specifies the unit of service and the amount to be paid per unit. The latter approach has been applied to institutional child care and more recently to child care in day care centers, where definition of the unit of care is amenable to quantification. Where conventions for service units are not yet in vogue, the subsidy approach is used. The discussion in this paper pertains to the purchase transaction based on service units, which appears to be gaining in popularity.

Source. Darrell J. Vorwaller, "Voluntary Agency as Vendor of Social Services," *Child Welfare* (Vol. LI, No. 7), pp. 436–42. Reproduced with permission from Child Welfare League of America.

The service-unit purchase strategy is similar in intent and format to that employed in Medicare, Medicaid, and vocational rehabilitation programs, in which government makes services available through purchase transaction with existing community resources. In such programs the government serves as a third-party purchaser in behalf of clients depending on government assistance. The third-party purchase arrangement protects the integrity of the government role where there are effective constraints against government involvement in the direct operation of a service enterprise.

The Medicare system is particularly instructive here. In it an even wider protective span was created between the government and physicians by the use of an independent medical insurance firm as the administrator of the program. Whether the increasing purchase of services from voluntary agencies is intended to assure a balance between government and voluntary agency participation cannot be argued here because of the scanty evidence available. The apparent reason for the action is the scarcity of government agency services required to meet the full range of services called for in federal legislation. At any rate, we can anticipate that the experience of the government in the medical care and vocational rehabilitation programs will provide guidelines for developing policies and procedures affecting the purchase of social services.

Government purchase of social services provides a monetary assurance of a relevant and expanded role for voluntary agencies. It also creates a role unfamiliar to most voluntary agencies, namely, that of vendor. To participate successfully in such a venture, voluntary agencies must be aware of the dimensions of this new role, particularly of changes in the management of the agency from a sales-transaction point of view, in contrast to the traditional subsidized-service approach. In this article, pertinent management requirements are considered for voluntary agencies as vendors of social services.

The sale of social services in a noncompetitive buyer's market such as that created when government is the sole purchaser of services permits the purchaser to exert considerable control over the sales transaction. The government as purchaser may set the conditions for defining the scope of services to be purchased, the unit of service to be reimbursed, and reimbursable costs to be included in the calculation of rates. Government may seek to assure uniformity of purchase procedures and equity to all agencies participating in the service market. It can be expected that government will want to assure clients and taxpayers through systematic evaluation and standard setting that quality services are provided.

THE KEY QUESTIONS

The voluntary agency seeking to participate in the market as a vendor of social services must eventually expect to provide suitable answers to the following questions:

1 Is the service provided clearly defined, specifying the activities that constitute the service?

2 Is the unit of service so defined that it is compatible with a sales orientation? Does the service definition facilitate delivery to clients? Does the defined service lend itself to service accounting?

3 Is the fee charged for a unit of service related to actual costs? How sound is the cost-determination procedure?

4 What documentable evidence can the agency give that the service is effective in accomplishing the changes ascribed to its capability by professional practitioners?

The agency that is able to respond affirmatively to these questions is well on its way to participating in the social services market on a sound and defensible basis.

Service Definition

The service definition provides the basis for letting the purchaser know precisely what he is getting in the social service transaction. The service definition is also an integral part of the agency management system, providing a basis for service and cost accounting, which is essential in a sales system based on units of service provided. A service is defined as an entity that constitutes a major objective of the agency. All activities devoted to the accomplishment of that objective serve to identify the service entity. Where certain activities not clearly related to a direct service are ascribed to more than one objective, a procedure is developed to prorate them among services. Activities defining a service should be event-oriented, each recognizable by a clear beginning and ending. Examples of service definitions are shown in Figure 1.

FIGURE 1 *Children and family social service agency elements of an objectives format for defining social services January to December, 1970*

Service Category	Type of Activity	Examples of Activities
Family Relationships	Activities for assisting family members to improve and strengthen relationships.	(1) Classroom instruction for parents. (2) Group counseling with parents.

FIGURE 1   *(Continued)*

Service Category	*Type of Activity*	*Examples of Activities*
		(3) Counseling parents in family relationships.
		(4) Classroom training in family life.
		(5) Family field trips.
Family Planning	Activities for assisting parents or potential parents in planning the number and spacing of children in the family and for preventing unwanted or out-of-wedlock pregnancies.	(1) Classroom or group instruction (2) Individual counseling.
Foster Home Care	Activities for providing foster homes and training foster parents; activities for assisting adjustment of the child to the temporary foster home placement; activities for preparing the child for return to his own home.	(1) Finding foster homes. (2) Classroom or group instruction of foster parents. (3) Counseling foster parents. (4) Counseling with children in foster placements. (5) Counseling natural parents. (6) Group counseling for parents whose children are in foster placement.

Service Unit

The service unit is a measure of production that is observable and that can be counted. The service unit is one of the bases for the billing and reimbursement of social services that have been purchased. It is also a factor in the determination of cost. To serve this purpose, the service unit should (1) be consistent from year to year, (2) measure a meaningful unit of the service that represents a transaction that is valued by the purchaser, (3) contribute to the alleviation of the problem of the client, and (4) serve as a basis of management control. Examples of service units include foster care day, child care day, institutional care day, client interview, group meeting, client tutorial session, and home visit.

Cost-Based Fees

Conventionally, voluntary agencies have depended on community subsidy of service operations administered on a deficit financing basis. The deficit financial procedure is consistent with the service subsidy approach and does not inherently require rigorous definitions of service, service unit, and service cost. As a result, most social service agencies have limited experience in the determination and use of costs in agency administration. Those United Way agencies that have been introduced to functional budgeting have the advantage of a working acquaintance with cost procedures, although the cost figures are used for budgeting and control purposes, and not sale of services.

In a social service market, albeit a noncompetitive buyers' market, it is necessary to establish the price to be paid for service, expressed as a service fee or reimbursement rate. Unless the fee is based on actual cost, the agency is likely to run into difficulties. Charging what the market will bear is precarious because it may not reflect the actual cost of providing the service. An understatement of cost adds to the fiscal strain already burdening voluntary agencies and community funds. It also leads to unrealistic service policy and purchase practices, which in the long run are detrimental to the survival of the voluntary agency. An overstatement of cost implies a profit motive and jeopardizes the not-for-profit status of the agency.

Conventional cost-accounting procedures developed in the child welfare services can be adapted to other types of voluntary agencies to determine costs. All costs of operating the agency are allocated to the defined services of the agency. Costs not directly identifiable with a specific service can be prorated on the basis of several alternative procedures, including the time-use study. Special problems presented by depreciation, facility-use rates, and costs imputed from volunteer or nonsecular staff can be resolved by a cost accountant acquainted with standards of financial accounting and reporting in the social service field. Unit cost is derived by dividing the total cost of a service encumbered in the fiscal year by the total units of service provided during the same period. Unit cost may be overstated where service utilization has fallen below normal levels. This is something the government purchaser will seek to prevent through the use of minimum-utilization floors for calculating unit cost, in order to control the reimbursement rate of services purchased. The voluntary agency vendor can anticipate such a policy requirement through management procedures that minimize the underutilization of services.

Agency Accountability

Increasingly, agencies are being expected to document the effectiveness of services they

FIGURE 2 *Social service objectives and quantitative measures*

Service	Objective	Quantitative Measure
Foster Home Care	To reduce the rate of children returned to foster home placements after reunion with their own parents or guardians.	The ratio of children returned to foster home placement *to* all children who have been reunited with their families or guardians.
	To reduce the rate of children being moved from one foster home to another because of failure in the adjustment between the children and the foster parents.	The ratio of children moved from one foster home to another because of failure of adjustment between the children and the foster parents *to* all children in foster home placements.
Protective Services	To reduce the rate of cases being served requiring the separation of children from their parents.	The ratio of cases requiring the separation of children from their parents *to* all cases being serviced.
	To reduce the rate of child desertion in cases being served.	The ratio of child desertion in cases served *to* all cases being served.
Family Planning Services	To reduce the rate of pregnancies occurring in families that have registered for family planning services.	The ratio of families in which pregnancies occurs after registration for services *to* all families registered for services.

provide. Do services bring about intended changes in the condition or circumstances of the client? Are the objectives related to social services being accomplished? The government, as a purchaser of services, wants to know if it is getting its money's worth. To provide such documentation, agencies must look to a quantified system for periodically evaluating the effectiveness of services. Such a system requires the definition of quantitative measures that indicate whether objectives of services are being achieved. Such quantitative measures are based on observable events and conditions indicating whether intended changes are being brought about.

The second requisite of an effectiveness evaluation system is a uniform system for collecting data to be applied to the quantitative measures. For most voluntary agencies, the mounting of a quantified evaluation system will require considerable change in orientation to the collection of statistical information. Traditionally agencies have collected data regarding practice activities or the process of providing the service, and the outputs of the agency, such as closed cases or completed adoptions. Effectiveness evaluation requires a focus on events indicating intended change in the condition of the client. Examples of changes expressed as objectives and their related measures are shown in Figure 2, for foster home care, protective services, and family planning services. The measures are expressed as a ratio that is a conventional quantitative indicator. Properly applied, means and medians may also be considered for use in quantitative evaluation of effectiveness. Analysis of effectiveness may relate the achievement of the current to the preceding year, or to quantitative standards used for setting objectives at the beginning of the program year. This type of

quantitative evaluation of effectiveness provides the agency with the documentation required for establishing its accountability to the contributing public or to the government purchaser.

SUMMARY

It is unknown what effect the advent and expansion of government purchase of social services will have on voluntary agencies. Some herald this development as the possible salvation of the voluntary agency from an ultimate disappearance from the American scene. Some fear for the continued autonomy of voluntary agencies that enter contractual agreements with the government and become subject to required service and management standards and the accompanying monitoring of performance. Government utilization of social services will focus its efforts on low-income, disadvantaged populations, and some agencies may regret this. It may selectively weed out services or practice approaches found to be ineffective in bringing about desired change in the target population involved. It could create opportunities to seek improved intervention procedures and upgrade service programs.

Whatever the outcome, it is evident that at least for the present, government is increasing its activity as a purchaser of social service. It is also likely that government will insist on sound management procedures, requiring the definition of services, service units, cost of service, and evaluation of service effectiveness. Although government may provide guidelines and technical assistance to accomplish such requirements, it is obviously to the advantage of the voluntary agency to initiate actions directed at mounting required procedures.

CHAPTER 4

A General Approach to Designing Management Control

The word *control* often produces connotations of coercion, manipulation, and restriction. A system of control, however, is a requisite part of organizational success, just as it is necessary to the survival of biological phenomena. All living forms, from the complex human body to the simplest amoeba, require a control system to insure that the various processes of the organism are in harmony with one another. When these "control" systems go awry, the quality of life for the organism suffers. Such is also the case with human organizations.

In the latter, however, the process which insures that the various parts of the organization are in harmony with one another is a manmade system of policies, goals, objectives, performance evaluations, and human motivations. The success of the organization in achieving its goals depends to no small degree on the success that management has in designing a control system.

Management control is a complex process in which top management seeks to motivate individuals to make decisions that are in the best interests of the organization. "The best interests of the organization" are defined in terms of what enables the organization to make progress toward the goals established by the management coalition. If the control system is to achieve congruence between the goals of the organization and its employees, it must insure that what is in the best interests of the organization is also in the best interests of the individual.

An understanding of the management control process requires that one be able to see the linkages between the organization's goals and objectives versus the individual motivational process. This implies that one has both a clear understanding of the social organization and the behavior of individuals in small and large groups. The readings in this chapter provide an overview of this complex process known as management control.

Measurement of performance and the communication of that information are at the center of any management control system. Since people are the recipients of such data and it is they who are motivated by the information, it is imperative to know what impact measurement and communication of accounting information has on the behavior of the individuals in organizations. The literature covering this subject crosses many academic disciplines, as is reflected in San Miguel's synthesis of the behavioral and accounting literature in "The Behavioral Sciences and

Concepts and Standards for Management Planning and Control." San Miguel provides a quick introduction to the many facets of the subject and examines the extent to which existing research findings can be applied to the nonprofit sector.

The starting point of any management control system is a clear identification of the goals of the organization. In their article entitled "Evaluating the Effectiveness of Social Services," Elkin and Vorwaller not only present a good case for the importance of goal statements but also provide a step-by-step approach for constructing them. In turn these are translated into objective statements that constitute the basis for determining the organization's efficiency and effectiveness. An important advantage of the use of sound statements of organization goals and objectives is that it forces the decision maker's attention onto the outputs of the program rather than the inputs. In many nonprofit organizations this represents a sharp break with past tradition and is an important first step in gaining effective control over the organization.

While the two preceding articles emphasize the fact that communication of performance measurement is at the heart of any management control system, Finz in his article "Productivity Analysis: Its Use in a Local Government" stresses the need for measures of performance. Finz argues that one cannot measure performance without first identifying the goals and objectives of each agency. The first step, therefore, in what Finz calls a management-indicator system is identification of the goals of each agency. The second step is to develop specific targets for each achievement. It is important that these targets or objectives be capable of being measured so that it is possible to tell, that is, measure, whether a target has been achieved. If it has, then the agency is on its way toward meeting its ultimate goals. The objective statements, therefore, help to identify the measures of effectiveness.

THE BEHAVIORAL SCIENCES AND CONCEPTS AND STANDARDS FOR MANAGEMENT PLANNING AND CONTROL*

Joseph G. San Miguel

Technological developments in recent years have greatly increased our capacity to design planning and control devices in modern organizations. The emergence of applications of logical and mathematical tools and the advent of the computer are two primary sources of these technological developments (Churchman, 1961; Simon, 1959). The important question is how do these techniques and tools benefit organizational planning and control in a real sense? One test of these developments must rest in how they improve management control systems (Arrow, 1964). The techniques are only a means to an end. The end is a system that enables managers to make sound decisions as to the efficient and effective allocation of human, physical, and financial resources to attain the objectives of the organization. This is the essence of modern planning and control (Anthony, 1965; Barnard, 1938).

Since human resources are an integral part of planning and control systems, a com-

prehensive understanding of the behavior of managers and those they seek to manage, or more properly motivate (Roethlisberger & Dickson, 1939), is necessary to the development of standards for planning and control. However, we are discovering that behavioral implications of management control systems are extremely complex (Argyris, 1952; Bruns, 1968; Burns, 1969). And as if the behavior of human resources were not complex enough we must also contend with the effects of uncertainty on behavior (Edwards, 1954; Simon, 1959).

Quantitative and economic decision tools attempt to deal with uncertainty and its concomitant effects on human decision makers in an impersonal, objective way (Marschak & Radnor, 1972; Simon, 1957; von Neumann & Morgenstern, 1953). However, the assumptions underlying the specified decision models are simplistic. The richness of decision situations actually encountered in large-scale organizations defy these simple notions of behavior (Bonini, 1963; Churchman, 1961). The interaction of human behavior and uncertainty in even simple decision situations reminds us of the little knowledge we have about human information processing and decision making.

Because of this lack of knowledge of human behavior in organizations, intensive research is needed to establish the constraints or requirements for designing planning, reporting, and control systems. To provide an overview and possibly encourage fresh approaches to research as it concerns managerial

Source. Copyright © 1977 by *Accounting, Organizations,* and *Society*. All rights reserved. Reprinted with permission from *Accounting, Organizations, and Society* (Vol. 2, No. 2), pp. 177–186.

*The idea for this paper was conceived while the author was a member of the American Accounting Association's Committee on Concepts and Standards for Management Planning and Control. The comments of William J. Bruns, John K. Shank, Andrew C. Stedry, an anonymous referee, and especially Anthony G. Hopwood are gratefully acknowledged. Also, the financial support of The Associates of the Harvard Graduate School of Business Administration is acknowledged.

accounting, several areas of relevant behavioral science literature will be examined. The contributions come from various disciplines and the literature review is by no means exhaustive. One of the difficulties in gaining an understanding (for student and instructor alike) of this subject area is the dispersion of publications across the various disciplines.

Behavioral research on information processing and decision making can be examined at three levels: research on the individual, on small groups, and on large, complex organizations. This does not imply that the levels of research are distinct or independent. Rather they are very interrelated and hierarchical. This follows the chronological development of behavioral research from individual transactions to transactions within and between large organizations. Research on individual behavior has helped to formulate theories and conduct research on small groups. The research on individuals and small groups in turn has had an influence on our understanding of behavior in larger organizations.

RESEARCH ON THE INDIVIDUAL

Individual information processing and decision making are strongly rooted in theories of personality, learning, perception, and cognition. The success of individuals in managerial positions and risk taking has been explained by personality theorists such as McClelland, Atkinson, Clark, and Lowell (1953) in terms of their motive to achieve. Also, Maslow (1954) has broken down motivation into five hierarchical levels. These theories bear directly on how management control systems affect behavior. For example, Lawler (1973) and Lawler and Rhode (1976) have related these and other motivation theories to information and control systems in organizations. They emphasize that information and control systems have a significant impact on individual behavior. The un-

derstanding of this impact on behavior is important to anyone concerned with organizational effectiveness, those concerned with designing and implementing information and control systems, and managers who must understand the effects on subordinates' motivation and performance.

Whether the individual participates in goal setting and decision making is often cited as a critical factor in motivating performance. There have been numerous, and often controversial, research efforts on the effects of participation. Stedry (1960) and Becker and Green (1962) have provided a forum for the discussion of the motivational effects of cost standards and budgets, and more recently research has started to investigate the relationship between managers' attitudes and participation (Tosi, 1975). In one study, Onsi (1973) investigated managers' attitudes toward budgets, budget pressure, and budget slack and concluded that "positive participation" could lessen managers' perceived need for budgetary slack. In addition, Swieringa and Moncur (1975) used organizational, personality, and interpersonal variables to explore the effects of participation on managerial attitudes. They found that personality and attitudinal data were relatively less important than organizational data in explaining managerial attitudes. However, they reported that participation in budgeting was related to the individual's self-actualization.

Vroom (1960) first attempted to relate personality traits to the effects of participation in budgeting. Recently, Heller (1971) and Vroom and Yetton (1973) have extended this research into motivation by taking a contingency view of participation. This not only incorporates managers' personal characteristics but also includes situational factors such as organizational structure and context. Heller (1971) studied the effects of influence and power sharing on managers' attitudes and found that perception of skill, experience, span of control, job function, importance of the decision, and proximity of decision are important factors that determine the location of influence and power. Vroom and Yetton (1973) examined the effects of styles of leadership on participative decision making and found that situational variables were relatively more useful than personal variables in explaining managers' participative decision making. This is consistent with the findings of Swieringa and Moncur (1975).

One hypothesis that has emerged from this research on motivation is that extrinsic rewards, such as money, do not continue to motivate performance. Furthermore, intrinsic factors, such as participation, that lead to self-actualization are important variables to consider (Lawler & Rhode, 1976). Extrinsic motivation of individuals is influenced by the organization's reward and punishment system. Intrinsic motivation is not visible nor so readily controllable by the organization. Thus, the organization through its information and control system must provide an environment in which the individual can relate intrinsic rewards to performance (Lawler & Rhode, 1976; Porter & Lawler, 1968).

Learning theorists have contributed to our understanding of concept formulation and mental development (Bruner, Goodnow, & Austin, 1956; Piaget, 1950; Skinner, 1953). There then followed an interest in perceptual research (Brunswick, 1956; Harvey, Hunt, & Schroder, 1961) and cognitive research (Neisser, 1967; Zazonc, 1969) which appears to be influencing the direction and scope of behavioral research on accounting information and control systems (Burns, 1969, 1972; Fertakis, 1970).

For example, an individual's perception of information is receiving more attention from behavioral researchers than the amount of information transmitted in an information theoretic sense (Rapoport, 1956). This research

recognizes that simply providing more and more data to individual decision makers does not necessarily lead to better performance if the decision maker does not attach importance to the information. In this regard, perception plays an important role in communication (the flow of information) because if information is not perceived in the manner intended, then communication does not occur (Cherry, 1966). Research in information processing has recognized that factors such as intelligence, motivation, and experience influence perception in different ways (Harvey, Hunt, & Schroder, 1961). Dearborn and Simon (1958), for instance, have shown that we perceive only those things that are congruent with our predispositions and beliefs (selective perception). These personal characteristics of the user of information are thus important considerations in the design of information systems.

Psychological research on individual differences in information processing (Irwin & Smith, 1957; Schroder, Driver, & Struefert, 1967), risk taking (Kogan & Wallach, 1964), and decision making (Simon, 1959) has particular promise in our need to understand the behavior of participants in organizations. For example, Revsine (1970) has emphasized the importance of research into questions of information overload and data disaggregation. Although he addressed human information processing and decision making in the external reporting environment, his recommendations are equally applicable to internal reporting and control systems. Cravens (1970) studied individual information processors in an industrial research organization and discovered that risk-taking propensity and information-processing efficiency were related. This exploratory study serves to emphasize the importance of relationships between the decision maker, the task, and information-processing behavior.

Cognitive theorists have advanced our

knowledge concerning decision-making behavior (Zazonc, 1969). Festinger (1957) provided an impetus to this area with his theory of cognitive dissonance. Zimbardo (1969), Simon (1957), and Driver and Streufert (1969) have hypothesized the usefulness of these theories in explaining management behavior. In a management accounting setting, Dermer (1973) investigated how users' cognitive characteristics affect the perceived importance of information. He found that individuals who are intolerant of ambiguity (conceptually concrete processors) seek out more information than those who are more tolerant of ambiguity (conceptually abstract processors) and that the utility of information cannot be determined separately from the user of that information. In a laboratory experiment, Huysmans (1970) tested the effects of two cognitive styles (analytical vs. heuristic) on the implementation of operations research recommendations and discovered that matching the method of recommendation with the subject's cognitive style is an important factor in achieving managers' implementation of the recommendations.

Other perceptual and cognitive research in accounting has focused on the human information processing and decision-making interface. Ashton (1974a, 1974b), for example, examined internal control judgments of independent auditors and generally found high levels of group consistency. He also pointed out the need for additional research into individual inconsistencies. Driver and Mock (1975) used decision styles in a laboratory experiment to study the effects on information-purchasing behavior. They found that "complex" decision makers purchase more information and that "decisive" decision makers become quickly overloaded and cannot function effectively in complex decision tasks. Libby (1975a, 1975b) found a strong relationship between perceived usefulness of financial accounting ratios to bank loan officers and their predictive accuracy and

individual behavior. In a laboratory setting, San Miguel (1976) found strong relationships between levels of information purchasing behavior and psychological characteristics but only a moderate relationship between information purchasing behavior and levels of integrative complexity. Not surprisingly, all of the above research studies point to the need to explicitly consider individual behavior in accounting research on information processing and decision making.

Communication of accounting measurements is at the heart of management control systems (Ackoff, 1958; Anton, 1964; Fertakis, 1970). Consider the discussions in the management accounting literature of "perceived fairness," "responsibility centers," and "goal congruence." Since performance is linked to these concepts, individual behavior plays an important role in successful management control systems. Argyris (1952) first pointed out the importance of interpersonal relationships and the humanistic approach to communicating profit budgets to managers. On the other hand, Schiff and Lewin (1970) have shown how misunderstanding and improper communication can lead managers to manipulate budgetary data to their advantage. Also, Hofstede (1967) has found that the motivational impact of goals and standards can be influenced by managers' perceived goal difficulty. Neither too high nor too low goal difficulty motivates good performance. Thus, communication between the manager, top management, and the managerial accountant are vital to the successful use of budgets and cost controls. Effects of budgets on personal characteristics are also important. For example, DeCoster and Fertakis (1968) have found evidence of a relationship between budget-induced pressure and managers' leadership styles.

What can we learn from the above and what are the implications for managerial accounting research and methods? First, behavioral science theories concerning individual behavior have evolved from painstaking research on individuals in different settings. Second, rarely, if ever, have behavioral scientists studied individuals in settings where accounting information comprised the stimuli (Burns, 1972; Fertakis, 1970). As a result we lack firsthand knowledge of the implications of behavioral science theories for explaining the behavior of individuals in cost accounting and management control systems (Miles & Vergin, 1966; Ridgway, 1956). However, we can distill this knowledge from laboratory research in which existing and new theories can be tested and from field research in which laboratory findings or research hypotheses are submitted to tests. Since the purpose of managerial planning and control systems is to motivate performance, we need fundamental research on individual behavior. Research areas include how decision makers handle uncertainty (Irwin & Smith, 1957), the needs and preferences for information (Lanzetta & Kanareff, 1962), the effects of information overload (G. Miller, 1956; J. Miller, 1962), and the motivational impact of management planning and control systems on users and their decisions (Lawler & Rhode, 1976).

RESEARCH ON BEHAVIOR IN SMALL GROUPS

The study of small-group behavior has helped behavioral scientists bridge the gap between understanding individual behavior and the behavior of complex organizations. It is understood that to speak of the "behavior" of organizations really means the collective behavior of individuals and groups of individuals in a social institution that has a defined mission (Homans, 1950; Zaleznik & Moment, 1964). Since large, complex organizations evolve from small groups, research on the latter provides valuable insight in understand-

ing the former (Cartwright & Zander, 1953; Guetzkow, 1951; Schein, 1965). For example, much of the current thinking concerning bargaining and labor negotiation processes stems from the experimental research on small groups by Siegel and Fouraker (1960).

Each individual in a group brings to it his own personal experience, attributes, and values. The major distinction is that the individual is now studied in a social setting in which he must interact with others to accomplish some task. This was emphasized in Roethlisberger and Dickson's (1939) early research on informal organizations. Subsequent research has focused on how leadership is established in group behavior (Fielder, 1967), how role differentiation and expectations affect the group (Etzioni, 1961), how authority is distributed and accepted (Homans, 1950), and how communication takes place (Bavelas, 1950). The development of group norms and rules are of particular interest to some researchers in this area. March and Simon (1958) in particular have extended Barnard's (1938) pioneering work on group participation and rewards to larger organizations.

As with research on individual behavior, research on small-group behavior considers personal characteristics of the members of the group, environmental variables, and task variables. However, accounting researchers have not explicitly studied these factors as they relate to the effectiveness of group risk taking, resource utilization, and decision making. This is unfortunate, because group processes exist in organizations and influence, or are influenced by, information and control systems. For example, production-line groups frequently set up norms against which performance is judged. This obviously impacts the setting of productivity standards. Budgeting decisions also frequently result from group processes between marketing, production, and finance functions, but performance evaluation systems are usually designed around individual behavior. There are no existing management control systems for considering group performance. The negotiation of transfer prices between managers is also a group process that impacts the effectiveness of management control systems.

Another example which is illustrative of the information-processing and decision-making behavior of groups is the research and development project team. Here individuals are assigned responsibility for certain tasks in the overall project. To succeed as a group these tasks require cooperation and communication between group members. The research committee responsible for the research efforts is also a group worthy of investigation. The effectiveness of this group's information processing and decision making is vital to the success of the company's products and processes. Group cohesiveness, group size, group structure, and communication networks are important factors to consider in group motivation and performance. These factors should be receiving more attention from accounting researchers examining management planning and control system.

BEHAVIORAL RESEARCH OF ORGANIZATIONAL BEHAVIOR

Modern organizations range from very large, multinational, and conglomerate corporations to extremely large multi-service institutions such as hospitals and universities. These organizations have emerged from relatively small organizations during the past half century. In a world of scarce resources, the way we plan and control these organizations can have a serious socioeconomic impact (Churchman, 1961; Drucker, 1954; Etzioni, 1961).

The primary purpose of behavioral research at the organization level is to improve internal decision-making processes such as re-

source allocation, innovation, and change (Likert, 1961, 1967). These are human decisions. Information is received, processed, and acted upon by internal decision makers. The information may be internally generated in the organization or gathered from external sources.

As a result of behavioral research on the individual and groups of individuals, the economic theory of the firm and the assumptions of the behavior of participants in the firm have been questioned. Cyert and March (1963) and March and Simon (1958) have given us new concepts of decision making and information processing in the firm such as satisfying behavior, bounded rationality, and the effects of organizational structure on goals. Extensions by Charnes and Stedry (1964) to multiple objectives and Williamson (1964) to discretionary managerial control and utility functions combine theories of individual behavior discussed earlier (i.e., Maslow and McClelland) with these theories of organizational behavior.

During the period that these new theories of managerial behavior in organizations have been developed, there has been no discernible impact on the design of cost accounting and reporting systems (Rosen & Schenck, 1967). Too often, cost standards and budgets are based on idealized models of economic behavior that conflict with the complex realities of behavior in large organizations. For example, cost standards and budgets require efficient, machine-like compliance of workers and managers. This assumes that workers and managers as physiological machines can be controlled through basic drives and emotions. Performance evaluation based on profit targets and return on investment also reflects this technical view of managerial accounting. A broader framework is needed for examining the impact of organizations and organizational design on management planning and control systems (Hopwood, 1974).

Recognizing the rather limited and out-moded assumptions of traditional internal accounting, Caplan (1966) developed a list of behavioral assumptions that reflect modern organization theory. His work was based primarily on the recommendations of Drucker (1954) and McGregor (1960) concerning management by objectives and self-control. By studying the effects of various styles of performance evaluation on job-related tension, interpersonal relations, and manipulation of accounting information, Hopwood (1973) sought explanations of the actual behavior of individuals. Although not a broad enough field study for drawing conclusions, his findings are suggestive of the significant impact that actual, rather than presumed, managerial attitudes can have on management control systems.

Recent research on formal organizations has been extremely useful to the formulation of new organizational theories, and understanding the behavior of individuals and groups has been important to this research (Katz & Kahn, 1966). Research on organizations, like research on individuals, has incorporated situational factors such as the organizational setting—its structure, technology, and environment (Sathe, 1975). Among others, Woodward (1965) identified technology (routine vs. non-routine production) as a determinant of organizational structure and the distribution of authority for maintaining internal control and coordination. Thompson (1967) proposed a theoretical framework for organizational structures which treats both technology and environment. In turbulent environments characterized by uncertainty, he argued, organizations structure themselves around their primary technologies to reduce uncertainty and best maintain control and coordination among the organization's subunits.

The field work of Lawrence and Lorsch (1967) on organizations and their environment is probably the most influential organizational research in recent years. Their contingency theory views the organization as an information-processing system that must adapt to its external environment by internally manipulating states of differentiation and integration between the various subunits. They found that financially successful firms had organization structures that were consistent with the demands of the environment confronting the firm. These organizations used differentiated structures to cope with different environments faced by different subunits. In addition, successful organizations required a high level of integration among the subunits. Among other things, the findings suggest that there is no one optimal structure for all organizations.

Reflecting the influence of the works of Cyert, March, and Simon, Galbraith (1973) has taken a similar approach to organizational information processing as Lawrence and Lorsch (1967) except that he uses task uncertainty to specify the need for processing information for decision making. The higher the task uncertainty the greater the amount of information that must be processed among decision makers in order for the organization to succeed. Thus, the information requirements of the task must be matched by the information-processing capacity of the organization.

The implication of the above research on contingency theories of organization structure is that the internal reporting and control system should match the organization structure. This is particularly stressed in Galbraith's (1973) research. The accounting information system is the major means by which production, marketing, and finance subunits effectively communicate their plans, budgets, and decisions to achieve overall coordination and control. The information flows and decision making are largely determined by the structuring of responsibility and authority across and within each of the organization's subunits. Devices used within organizations to fix financial responsibility are cost centers, revenue centers, profit centers, and investment centers. Therefore, questions of divisionalization, decentralization, and related issues such as transfer prices are usually resolved in the design of the organization's structure and management control system. And these designs are a function of the environment and key social and economic characteristics faced by the individual firm.

There is evidence that accounting researchers are beginning to use contingency theory in their research. In the section on individual behavior we discussed recent works that have concluded that situational factors, in addition to personal characteristics, are important variables to consider when examining managers' attitudes toward budgets and participation (Heller, 1971; Swieringa & Moncur, 1975; Vroom & Yetton, 1973). In addition, recent work by Sathe (1975) and Watson (1975) has stressed the importance of contingency theory to management planning and control. In a related study, Bruns and Waterhouse (1975) have investigated the relationship between formal properties of organization structure and budgetary control in twenty-five firms. Several findings have emerged from their research that bear upon the importance of contingency theory to management control systems. First, high participation and perceived budgetary control were related to organization structure. Second, organization variables such as size and technology were related to structure, which is consistent with organizational research findings (Lawrence & Lorsch, 1967; Woodward, 1965). Thus, organization structure variables should be a requisite part of future studies of budget-related behavior and managerial performance. Similar to the recommendation that no one structure is optimal for all organizations, Bruns and Waterhouse

advise against a universal policy about budget preparation.

Although still relatively young, the research on contingency theories of organization structure suggests the need to examine organizational, environmental, and personal variables as multidimensional systems with complex interrelationships among the variables. This requires the study of large numbers of organizations and an increase in sample size as more variables are studied (Sathe, 1975).

We have seen in this section that behavioral research has come full circle—from an emphasis on individual behavior to an emphasis on complex organizations and then back to an emphasis on the individual as an active participant in large, complex ortanizations. Before the rise of large organizations, behavioral scientists were concerned with individuals' motives, personality, and cognitive processes. This research dealt with relatively simple problems such as entrepreneurial behavior and relationships between the worker and manager where the owner was usually the manager. The problems became more complex as ownership and stewardship separated and owners sought control over managers who in turn sought control over subordinates. Thus, as organizations grew, interpersonal relations and communication between individuals and groups of individuals became more and more important. At the same time the complexity of the technology and environment increased. The emergence of large, complex organizations initially inspired research that viewed organizations as information-processing entities that structured themselves according to technological and environmental demands. There is evidence that recent research in behavioral science and management accounting has begun to include the study of individual behavior along with organizational structure and environmental variables.

One of the primary reasons for this re-emphasis on individual behavior stems from the way organizations have structured their activities. Organizations have coped with dynamic environments and technologies by assigning responsibility for information processing and decisions to fairly autonomous subunits. This movement to decentralization and divisionalization of lines of business and functions has placed a great deal of pressure on management control systems to provide accurate and timely information to individuals or groups of individuals who are responsible for efficient and effective performance of the organization. Thus it is not the information-processing capacity of the organization per se that determines the success of the organization, but the collective information-processing capacity of the organization's individual decision makers. Different individuals have different needs, preferences, and attitudes which influence their information-processing and decision-making behavior. Environmental factors also influence this behavior. In this regard there is a striking similarity between human information processing theories and contingency theories of organization. Human information processing relates the structuring of information processing activities in terms of differentiation and integration to efficient performance in the same way that contingency theory explains organization structure and performance. Therefore, it is extremely difficult to avoid including personal characteristics of the individual in research studies of effective organizations and vice versa.

CONCLUSION

The purpose of this view of behavioral science and management accounting was to provide a concise introduction into the literature for those interested in this area. To accomplish this we organized the literature into three interrelated categories: research on individual behavior, research on small-group processes,

and research on complex organizations. We have traced behavioral research from its early focus on individual behavior to its emphasis on individual behavior in small groups and large organizations. We have also traced behavioral research in management accounting along the same three levels of behavioral systems. Except in the area of small-group processes, accountants have indicated an interest in transferring behavioral science theories and concepts to research designs on the effectiveness of management planning and control systems. Although the research is relatively young and fragmented, we have at least gained vital, foothold knowledge. But a great deal of fundamental research remains.

Measurement and communication are at the heart of internal planning, reporting, and control systems. There is general agreement that how measurement and communication systems affect the behavior of individuals in organizations and how individual behavior affects measurement and communication systems are legitimate concerns for those responsible for their design and implementation. Because very few behavioral scientists have taken an active role in this area, it is incumbent on accountants to take responsibility for transferring behavioral science knowledge to the design and implementation of effective management control systems.

BIBLIOGRAPHY

Ackoff, R. L., Towards a Behavioral Theory of Communication, *Management Science* (April, 1958), pp. 218–234.

Anthony, R. N., *Planning and Control Systems: A Framework for Analysis* (Division of Research, Harvard Graduate School of Business Administration, 1965).

Anton, H. R., Some Aspects of Measurement and Accounting, *Journal of Accounting Research* (Spring, 1964), pp. 1–9.

Argyris, C., *The Impact of Budgets on People* (The Controllership Foundation, 1952).

Arrow, K. J., Control in Large Organizations, *Management Science* (April, 1964), pp. 397–406.

Arrow, K. J., *The Limits of Organization* (New York: W. W. Norton, 1974).

Ashton, R. H., An Experimental Study of Internal Control Judgments, *Journal of Accounting Research* (Spring, 1974), pp. 144–157.(a)

Ashton, R. H., Cue Utilization and Expert Judgment: A Comparison of Independent Auditors with Other Judges, *Journal of Applied Psychology* (August, 1974), pp. 437–444.(b)

Barnard, C. I., *The Functions of the Executive* (Cambridge: Harvard University Press, 1938).

Bavelas, A., Communication Patterns in Task-Oriented Groups, *Journal of the Acoustical Society of America* (1950), pp. 725–730.

Becker, S. & Green, D., Jr., Budgeting and Employee Behavior, *Journal of Business* (October, 1962), pp. 392–402.

Bonini, C. P., *Simulation of Information and Decision Systems in the Firm* (Englewood Cliffs, N.J.: Prentice-Hall, 1963).

Bruner, J. S., Goodnow, J. & Austin, G., *A Study of Thinking* (New York: Wiley, 1956).

Bruns, W. J., Accounting Information and Decision Making: Some Behavioral Hypotheses, *The Accounting Review* (July, 1968), pp. 469–480.

Bruns, W. J. & Waterhouse, J.H., Budgetary Control and Organization Structure, *Journal of Accounting Research* (Autumn, 1975), pp. 177–203.

Brunswik, E., *Perception and the Representative Design of Experiments* (Berkeley: University of California Press, 1956).

Burns, T. J., ed., *The Behavioral Aspects of Accounting Data for Performance Evaluation* (Columbus: College of Administrative Science, The Ohio State University, 1969).

Burns, T. J., ed., *Behavioral Experiments in Accounting* (Columbus: College of Administrative Science, The Ohio State University, 1972).

Caplan, E. H., Behavioral Assumptions of Management Accounting, *The Accounting Review* (July, 1966), pp. 496–509.

Cartwright, D. & Zander, A., eds., *Group Dynamics* (Evanston, Illinois: Row Peterson, 1953).

Charnes, A. & Stedry, A.C. Investigations in the Theory of Multiple Budgeted Goals, in *Management Controls*, ed. C. P. Bonini et al. (New York: McGraw-Hill, 1964), pp. 186–202.

Cherry, C., *On Human Communication* (Cambridge, Massachusetts: MIT Press, 1966).

Churchman, C. W., *Prediction and Optimal Decision* (Englewood Cliffs, N.J.: Prentice-Hall, 1961).

Cook, D. M., The Effect of Frequency of Feedback on Attitudes and Performance, Supplement to Vol. 5 of *Journal of Accounting Research* (1968), pp. 213–224.

Cravens, D. W., An Exploratory Analysis of Individual Information Processing, *Management Science* (June, 1970), pp. B656–670.

Cyert, R. M. & March J. G., *A Behavioral Theory of the Firm* (Englewood Cliffs, N.J.: Prentice-Hall, 1963).

Dearborn, D. C. & Simon, H. A., Selective Perception: A Note on the Departmental Identifications of Executives, *Sociometry* (June, 1958).

DeCoster, D. T. & Fertakis, J. P., Budget-Induced Pressure and Its Relationship to Supervisory Behavior, *Journal of Accounting Research* (Autumn, 1968), pp. 237–246.

Dermer, J. D., Cognitive Characteristics and the Perceived Importance of Information, *The Accounting Review* (July, 1973), pp. 511–519.

Driver, M. J. & Mock, T. J., Human Information Processing, Decision Style Theory, and Accounting Information Systems, *The Accounting Review* (July, 1975), pp. 490–508.

Drivet, M. J. & Streufert, S., Integrative Complexity: An Approach to Individuals and Groups as Information Processing Systems, *Administrative Science Quarterly* (June, 1969).

Drucker, P. F., *The Practice of Management* (New York: Harper, 1954).

Edwards, W., The Theory of Decision Making, *Psychological Bulletin* (April, 1954), pp. 380–417.

Etzioni, A., *Complex Organizations* (New York: Holt, Rinehart & Winston, 1961).

Fertakis, J. P., On Communication, Understanding, and Relevance in Accounting Reports, *The Accounting Review* (October, 1970), pp. 623–640.

Festinger, L., *A Theory of Cognitive Dissonance* (Palo Alto: Stanford University Press, 1957).

Fielder, F. E., *A Theory of Leadership Effectiveness* (New York: McGraw-Hill, 1967).

Galbraith, J., *Designing Complex Organizations* (Reading, Massachusetts: Addison-Wesley, 1973).

Guetzkow, H., ed., *Groups Leadership, and Men: Research in Human Relations* (Pittsburgh: Carnegie Institute of Technology Press, 1951).

Harvey, O. J., Hunt, D. E. & Schroder, H. M., *Conceptual Systems and Personality Organization* (New York: Wiley, 1961).

Heller, F. A., *Managerial Decision-Making: A Study of Leadership Styles and Power Sharing Among Senior Managers* (Assen: Van Gorcum, 1971).

Hofstede, G. H., *The Game of Budget Control* (New York: Van Nostrand, 1967).

Homans, G. C., *The Human Group* (New York: Harcourt, Brace & World, 1950).

Hopwood, A. G., *An Accounting System and Managerial Behavior* (Lexington, Massachusetts: Lexington Books, 1973).

Hopwood, A. G., *Accounting and Human Behavior* (London: Haymarket Publ., 1974).

Huysmans, J. H. B. M., The Effectiveness of the Cognitive-style Constraint in Implementing Operations Research Proposals, *Management Science* (September, 1970), pp. 92–104.

Irwin, F. W., & Smith, W. A., Value, Cost and Information as Determiners of Decision, *Journal of Experimental Psychology* (September, 1957), pp. 229–232.

Katz, D. & Kahn, R. L., *The Social Psychology of Organizations* (New York: Wiley, 1966).

Kogan, N. & Wallach, M. A., *Risk Taking: A Study in Cognition and Personality* (New York: Holt, Rinehart & Winston, 1964).

Lanzetta, J. T., & Kanareff, V. T., Information Cost, Amount of Payoff, and Level of Aspiration as Determinants of Information Seeking in Decision Making, *Behavioral Science* (October, 1962), pp. 459–473.

Lawler, E. E., *Motivation in Work Organizations* (Monterey, California: Brooks/Cole, 1973).

Lawler, E. E. & Rhode, J. G., *Information and Control in Organizations* (Pacific Palisades, California: Goodyear, 1976).

Lawrence, P. R. & Lorsch, J. W., *Organization and Environment* (Boston: Division of Research, Harvard Graduate School of Business, 1967).

Libby, R., The Use of Simulated Decision Makers in Information Evaluation, *The Accounting Review* (July, 1975), pp. 475–489.

Libby, R., Accounting Ratios and the Prediction of Failure: Some Behavioral Evidence, *Journal of Accounting Research* (Spring, 1975), pp. 150–161.

Likert, R., *The Human Organization* (New York: McGraw-Hill, 1967).

Likert, R., *New Patterns of Management* (New York: McGraw-Hill, 1961).

March, J. G. & Simon, H. A., *Organizations* (New York: Wiley, 1958).

Marschak, J. & Radnor, R., *Economic Theory of Teams* (Yale University Press, 1972).

Maslow, A. H., *Motivation and Personality* (New York: Harper & Row, 1954).

McClelland, D., Atkinson, J. W., Clark, R. A. & Lowell, E. L., *The Achievement Motive* (New York: Appleton-Century-Crofts, 1953).

McGregor, D., *The Human Side of Enterprise* (New York: McGraw-Hill, 1960).

Miles, R. E. & Vergin, R. C., Behavioral Properties of Variance Control, *California Management Review* (Spring, 1966), pp. 57–65.

Miller, G. A., The Magical Number Seven, Plus or Minus Two, *Psychological Review* (March, 1956), pp. 81–97.

Miller, J. G., Information Input Overload, in *Self-Organizing Systems*, ed. Marschall C. Yovits et al. (Washington: Spartan Books, 1962), pp. 61–78.

Neisser, U., *Cognitive Psychology* (New York: Appleton-Century-Crofts, 1967).

Onsi, M., Factor Analysis of Behavioral Variables Affecting Budgetary Slack, *The Accounting Review* (July, 1973), pp. 535–548.

Piaget, J., *The Psychology of Intelligence* (London: Routledge & Kegan Paul, 1950).

Porter, L. W. & Lawler, E. E., *Managerial Attitudes and Performance* (Homewood, Illinois: Irwin, 1968).

Rapoport, A., The Promise of Pitfalls of Information Theory, *Behavioral Science* (October, 1956), pp. 303–309.

Revsine, L., Data Expansion and Conceptual Structure, *The Accounting Review* (October, 1970), pp. 704–711.

Ridgway, V. F., Dysfunctional Consequences of Performance Measurements, *Administrative Science Quarterly* (September, 1956), pp. 240–247.

Roethlisberger, F. J. & Dickson, W. J., *Management and the Worker* (Cambridge: Harvard University Press, 1939).

Rosen, L. S. & Schenck, R. E., Some Behavioral Consequences of Accounting Measurement Systems, *Cost and Management* (October, 1967), pp. 6–16.

San Miguel, J. G., Human Information Processing and Its Relevance to Accounting: A Laboratory Study, *Accounting, Organizations and Society* (1976).

Sathe, V., Contingency Theory of Organizational Structure, J. L. Livingstone, ed., *Managerial Accounting: The Behavioral Foundations* (Columbus, Ohio: Grid, 1975), pp. 51–63.

Schein, E. H., *Organizational Psychology* (Englewood Cliffs, N.J.: Prentice-Hall, 1965).

Schiff, M. & Lewin, A. Y., The Impact of People on Budgets, *The Accounting Review* (April, 1970), pp. 259–268.

Schroder, H. M., Driver M. J. & Streufert, S., *Human Information Processing* (New York: Holt, Rinehart & Winston, 1967).

Siegel, S. & Fouraker, L. E., *Bargaining and Group Decision Making* (New York: McGraw-Hill, 1960).

Simon, H. A., *Models of Man: Social and Rational* (New York: Wiley, 1957).

Simon, H. A., Theories of Decision-Making in Economics and Behavioral Science, *The American Economic Review* (June, 1959), pp. 253–283.

Skinner, B. F., *Science and Human Behavior* (New York: Macmillan, 1953).

Stedry, A. C., *Budget Control and Cost Behavior* (Englewood Cliffs, N.J.: Prentice-Hall, 1960).

Swieringa, R. J. & Moncur, R. H., *Some Effects of Participative Budgeting on Managerial Behavior* (New York: National Association of Accountants, 1975).

Thompson, J. D., *Organizations in Action* (New York: McGraw-Hill, 1967).

Tosi, H., The Human Effects of Managerial Budgeting Systems, J. L. Livingstone, ed., *Managerial Accounting: The Behavioral Foundations* (Columbus, Ohio: Grid, 1975), pp. 139–156.

Von Neumann, J. & Morgenstern, O., *Theory of Games and Economic Behavior* (Princeton University Press, 1953).

Vroom, V. H., *Some Personality Determinants of the Effects of Participation* (Englewood Cliffs, N.J.: Prentice-Hall, 1960).

Vroom, V. H. & Yetton, P. W., *Leadership and Decision-Making* (University of Pittsburgh Press, 1973).

Watson, D. J. H., Contingency Formulations of Organizational Structure: Implications for Managerial Accounting, J. L. Livingstone, ed., *Managerial Accounting: The Behavioral Foundations* (Columbus, Ohio: Grid, 1975), pp. 65–80.

Williamson, O. E., *Economics of Discretionary Behavior* (Englewood Cliffs, N.J.: Prentice-Hall, 1964).

Woodward, J., *Industrial Organization: Theory and Practice* (New York: Oxford University Press, 1965).

Zaleznik, A. & Moment, D., *The Dynamics of Interpersonal Behavior* (New York: Wiley, 1964).

Zazonc, R. B., Cognitive Theories in Social Psychology, in *The Handbook of Social Psychology*, ed., G. Lindzey and E. Aronson (New York: Addison-Wesley, 1969), Vol. I, pp. 320–411.

Zimbardo, P. G., *The Cognitive Control of Motivation* (New York: Scott-Foresman, 1969).

EVALUATING THE EFFECTIVENESS OF SOCIAL SERVICES

Robert Elkin and Darrel J. Vorwaller

Current developments, including changes in Federal laws, regulations, and guidelines, have imposed on public welfare departments new requirements for managing and reporting social services. At the same time, too, that their departments are attempting to meet demands for more and better services, public welfare administrators are on yet another firing line as they are called to account more and more frequently by taxpayers, lawmakers, clients, and their professional peers. What populations are being served? What amount of what service is being provided? What changes in clients are brought about by social services? What programs are most powerful in bringing about desired changes? What programs are failing to achieve intended changes and must be weeded out? Such questions imply that a sound method should exist for evaluating the effectiveness of social services.

Many welfare programs are currently evaluated according to standards set by national or supervisory agencies, but these standards may not be suitable for evaluation purposes. Thus, the assumption is often made that a program is successful if its professional staff has attained a stated level of expertise, or if the staff-to-client ratio is at a recommended ratio. What is happening, however, is that the emphasis is on input into a program, while output is overlooked. Further, a case-by-case review of a sample of agency records may

represent an attempt at program evaluation. But such a review usually reveals only limited program data—whether a staff has worked within defined limits, or if eligible clients have received program services. While case reviews do eventually contribute some information on welfare programs, they cannot provide the timely data a welfare administrator needs for ongoing planning, budgeting, or crisis-resolving. Hence, many welfare agencies resort to operational statistics to evaluate programs. Here, sheer numbers are presumed to imply success. If a great number of clients are interviewed, home visits made, days of care provided, etc., it is assumed that the program is successful.

The approach to evaluation of social services described in this article is based on systems concepts. Essentially, this approach requires clear definitions of the goals and objectives against which to assess the outcome of programs. The following basic steps are involved in establishing a systems-based evaluation of social services:

- Identification and description of the social problems that are within the scope of the organization's interest.

- Development of goals for resolving these problems.

- Statement of the objectives of each service in quantifiable terms.

- Establishment of measures of effectiveness for all objectives.

- Formulation of evaluation standards for each service.

Source. Copyright © 1972 by Peat, Marwick, Mitchell, & Company. All rights reserved. Reprinted with permission from *Management Controls* (May, 1972), pp. 104–111.

Implementation of the system begins with the development of profiles for each of the services.

SERVICE PROFILES

A service profile is a convenient format for organizing and displaying the elements required in an effectiveness evaluation system. The profile, illustrated in Exhibit 1, includes the service category, program description, problem description, goal statement, objectives statement, and measures of effectiveness.

EXHIBIT 1

Profile of a Service Program

Service category

Family planning

Program

Training and counseling to enable families to plan the births of children and to enable unmarried persons to avoid pregnancies out-of-wedlock.

Problem description

Lack of knowledge and skills in family planning impairs family life and impedes the growth and development of children. This problem is reflected in unplanned births of children.

Goal

Assurance that the addition of children to families is by parental choice; and prevention of births out-of-wedkock.

Objectives

(1) To reduce the rate of unmarried females 14 to 44 years of age who become pregnant.

(2) To reduce the rate of pregnancies occurring in families who have requested family planning services.

Measures

(1) The ratio of unmarried females 14 to 44 years of age who become pregnant, to all unmarried females 14 to 44 years of age registered with the Project.

(2) The ratio of pregnancies occurring in families who have requested family planning services, to all families registered with the Project who have requested family planning services.

A service definition represents the boundaries of a specific area to be evaluated. In an ongoing social service program, the development of an evaluation system starts with the service to be evaluated. The service should be precisely defined, and once the service boundaries are clearly stated in the definition, the specification of problem goals and objectives can be controlled by relating them to the limits of the service boundaries. Thus, in Exhibit 1, the service is described as all activities provided to enable families to plan the timing of births of children and to enable unmarried persons to avoid pregnancies out-of-wedlock. Several programs of activities may be related to the service, such as individual training and counseling, group counseling, group courses in sex education, and medical examination and prescription. All of these programs relate to achieving the stated goal.

After the services or programs have been clearly and concisely described in profiles, they are grouped into related categories. Services may be classified as either operational or program goal-oriented. The organization of services on an operational basis is generally well established and documented in written directives. Basically, individual organizational units are normally assigned responsibility for the delivery of services in certain functional areas, such as protective services to children. A study of the organizational structure of a welfare department should provide knowledge of how services are delivered under the current operational structure. The operational classification of services does not always parallel the goal-oriented structure. To meet social needs as they develop, responsibility for providing service is frequently assigned solely on the basis of available resources. The most appropriate organizational unit is often not used for new assignments due to a lack of resources or of operational flexibility, so that services classified along operational lines are frequently not classified into a consistent goal structure.

In classifying services along goal-oriented lines, it is necessary to determine relationships in results being achieved. If progress toward the goal of one service is a component of goal accomplishment for another service, the two services should be related under a goal structure orientation. Some restructuring and classification changes of ongoing services and programs may prove necessary as the development of an evaluation system progresses.

Let us now turn to the basic steps entering into the development of an evaluation system, starting with the first—identification and description of the social problem.

PROBLEM DESCRIPTION

A problem is a situation or condition that adversely affects identified client populations. Examples of problems in the social welfare field are: children living in hazardous and substandard housing; lack of knowledge and skill in money management.

The basis of future measurement will be a determination of the amount of change that has occurred in the problem. Hence, a problem definition should be precisely drawn. In an ongoing service, the process of definition starts with an analysis of current programs, but in the case of new services, the process is inductive and more complex inasmuch as the service components have not yet been spelled out.

In some cases, the service title (for example, "Services to Unwed Parents") suggests the nature of a particular problem or target group. When the problem is not immediately suggested by the service title (for example, "Housing and Homemaking"), a careful analysis must be made to determine the scope of the problem toward which the service is directed.

A review of Federal and state regulations and guidelines will provide clues concerning the particular problem toward which a service is being directed. Guidelines often include statements of conditions which can be used as a basis for problem descriptions. A review of these guidelines increases the validity of the evaluation system and insures that appropriate problems are addressed by the services mandated under regulations.

Where the evaluations relate to new social problems not yet augmented by specific social services, an analysis of social indicators, specific client situations, and validated research data is necessary for developing problem statements. A careful analysis of social indicators and other data will yield the problem statement needed both for the development of appropriate services and the specification of the elements of the evaluation.

A close examination of welfare problem situations will reveal at least two identifiable types of factors—symptomatic and causal. Symptomatic factors are the unfavorable social conditions that are observable in the problem situation. As a general rule they are readily discernible because they rise to the surface. For example, in the welfare field there are ample cases to illustrate the existence of children living in hazardous and substandard housing, and families requesting emergency financial grants to pay rent. Both conditions are symptoms of problems facing clients. Causal factors are more difficult to identify in problem situations than are the symptomatic factors. Causal factors are those elements that generate observable unfavorable social conditions. In the case of children living in hazardous and substandard housing, inadequate family income might be a cause. In the case of requests for emergency financial assistance where adequate resources appear to exist, a causative factor might be the lack of knowledge or skill in money management.

One aspect of the causal–symptomatic relationship in social problem situations which is essential in developing problem descriptions is that of cause–symptom linkage. Cause-symptom linkage describes the relationship that exists between a symptom at one level of a problem situation and a causal factor at the next level. This linkage can be explained through a simplified illustration in Exhibit 2 of the relationship drawn from a particular social problem context.

This illustration does not attempt to define fully the multiple characteristics of the relationships involved in the problem situation. Comprehensive identification of the interrelationship between causes and symptoms requires extensive in-depth research. To determine the course of action to be taken, the linkage effect should be traced to a point where the agency is capable of addressing its resources to the problem in an effective manner. For example, it is possible that a decision could be made to treat the problem at level A of the situation. Treatment of the problem at this level could involve making arrangements to move the family to more adequate quarters. Indeed, such action could provide a short-range remedy for the immediate physical needs of the family indicated as the "symptom" at level A. However, the family would still lack the capacity and resources to be economically self-sufficient and to maintain the higher standard of housing. The move to better housing would not necessarily increase the family's opportunities for becoming economically self-sufficient, and might actually impair the family's chances for financial improvement by increasing the family's financial burden to an intolerable level. In this illustration, dealing with problem needs at "causal" level C would indicate the need for a program designed to train the head of the household in a skill that would lead to future employment, an adequate income, and eventual economic self-support. By attacking the problem at the proper level, the probability of achieving long-term success through service intervention is greatly enhanced.

Following analysis, a detailed description of the problem can be written. (See Exhibit 3 for examples of key words and phrases used in problem descriptions.) A problem description should include both symptomatic and causal factors appropriate to the level of the services being provided.

GOAL STATEMENTS

Goal statements should relate directly to specific problem situations or barriers requiring remedial social services. A service goal is a frame of reference for management decision-making and for program planning and evaluation. For example, the goal in providing assistance to past, potential, and expectant parents out-of-wedlock could be the prevention of births out-of-wedlock and elimination of the social, emotional, and legal problems associated with them. Such a goal is admittedly idealistic since the problem of unwed parenthood is a continuing one. However, the goal is still valid when viewed as an ideal outcome and a desirable state or condition toward which to direct service activities. Exhibit 4 provides some examples of key words and phrases used in goal statements.

A service effectiveness goal reflects the desired end state, and not the quantity or quality of activities and services to be applied to achieve the end state. For example, the goal for a family which is financially dependent could be the achievement of economic self-

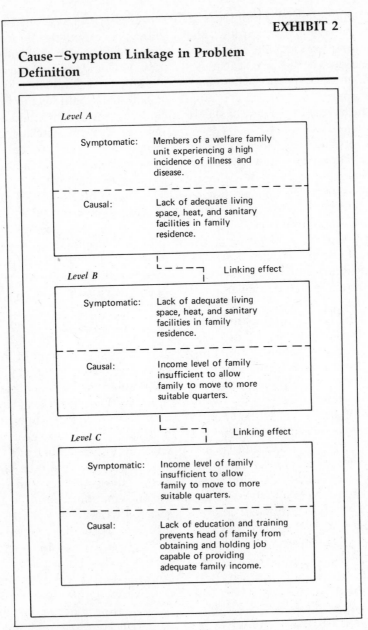

EXHIBIT 2

Cause—Symptom Linkage in Problem Definition

Level A

Symptomatic: Members of a welfare family unit experiencing a high incidence of illness and disease.

Causal: Lack of adequate living space, heat, and sanitary facilities in family residence.

Linking effect

Level B

Symptomatic: Lack of adequate living space, heat, and sanitary facilities in family residence.

Causal: Income level of family insufficient to allow family to move to more suitable quarters.

Linking effect

Level C

Symptomatic: Income level of family insufficient to allow family to move to more suitable quarters.

Causal: Lack of education and training prevents head of family from obtaining and holding job capable of providing adequate family income.

sufficiency. The statement of the goal does not specify the activities that will be employed to develop the economic self-sufficiency.

The very existence of goals can help to redirect program emphasis from its tendency toward process orientation (what was applied), to a stress on progress (what was the effect). An orientation directed toward achievement provides the foundation on which a system of social services evaluation of effectiveness can be established. In addition, goals for services indicate a commitment of the organization to purposeful action to bring about meaningful and significant improve-

EXHIBIT 3

Key Words and Phrases Used in Problem Descriptions

A problem description consists of an antecedent (causal) event or state; a subsequent action; the recipient (target) of the action; and the consequent (symptomatic) conditions.

Example

Antecedent state:	living in substandard housing; practicing unhealthy housekeeping
Action:	endanger and impede
Recipients of action:	family and children
Consequent condition:	unrealized potential for growth and development

Words describing antecedent states

absence	inadequate
default	incompetency
deficiency	interruption
deterioration	lack
disturbed	loss
disfunctional	maladjustment
failure	omission
inability	unmet

Action words transmitting the cause to the object

abuse	impair
damage	impede
endanger	injure
exploit	neglect
hamper	obstruct
hinder	prevent

EXHIBIT 4

Key Words Used in Goal Statements

Used to describe end states:

assured	maintained
attained	preserved
eliminated	rehabilitated
improved	restored
insured	retained

Goal statements should reflect the realistic constraints upon the organization offering the service, including availability of resources, authorization to provide a service, and geographic limitations. For example, it is not realistic for a social service agency to set as its goal the prevention of all unwed pregnancies when it has a legal mandate and finances for serving only a specified portion of a community.

Broad participation of staff personnel in goal development assists in insuring the accuracy and completeness of goal content. In addition, broad participation aids in developing a more willing acceptance and a deeper commitment by those who will ultimately play a significant role in goal attainment. The participation process of goal setting many times brings to the surface different orientations of different levels of staff. Thus, administrators tend to emphasize legal and financial constraints of the organization. Caseworkers tend to emphasize professional autonomy in decision-making in determining specific programs for their clients. Supervisors and program directors tend to emphasize unmet needs and additional staff required to meet these needs. Concern is expressed in the field for the appropriate way to involve clients in the goal-setting and evaluation process; but while consensus has emerged on the inadequacy of token client membership on advisory committees, other more effective measures have not as yet been identified.

ments in conditions or problem situations that are adversely affecting the lives of client populations. The development of goals thus becomes an important step toward the initiation of effective services by social welfare organizations.

OBJECTIVES

Objectives are specific targets for achievement which represent interim steps or progress toward a goal within a specified time span. Objectives should be comprehnsive in nature and cover all activities leading to the achievement of a particular goal. Objectives describe the desired impact on a problem situation which should be produced by the services provided.

While goals provide the basic guidance for all activities in a service, they are, by definition, general and timeless and do not provide the explicitness required for measuring results. Objectives provide the detail necessary to enable decisions to be made, actions to be taken, plans to be implemented, and results to be evaluated. Objectives of a service should be determined after problems and goals have been identified and described.

Objectives should be stated in terms that permit quantitative measurement of achievement, wherever possible. When problems have not been clearly analyzed and defined, objectives are frequently described in terms that do not lend themselves to such measurement.

Both quantifiable and nonquantifiable objectives should indicate the direct relationship between the objectives and the goals of the service being provided. Thus, the aggregate of objectives established for a service indicates the results expected from the application of the service to a specific social problem. The function of quantifiable and nonquantifiable objectives may be illustrated using the example of a social service program that has as its goal, "To increase the number of AFDC families who are economically self-sufficient." Since economic self-sufficiency depends on a steady and adequate family income, and job training normally aids in achieving an adequate income, a quantifiable objective which would serve as an indicator of measurable progress toward achieving the service goal could be, "To increase the rate of AFDC family members completing a work training program." The percentage of AFDC family members completing such programs can be determined quantitatively, and thus the objective is measurable in numeric terms.

A nonquantifiable objective for the same goal could be, "To develop in AFDC family members the sense of self-esteem necessary to be functioning members of the community." Though it is difficult with present measurement devices to know precisely when a desired level of self-esteem is acquired or the precise level of self-esteem attained, it is possible to determine whether or not there has been a change in the self-esteem level. An increase in the self-esteem level would indicate progress toward the goal. Such nonquantifiable objectives should be used sparingly and avoided, if at all possible, in developing an objectively based evaluation system.

The detailed development of objectives requires an analysis of the service description, a study of legislation, and an understanding of the problem. A review of existing service descriptions is the first step in attempting to determine objectives for an ongoing service. Frequently, objectives are suggested in the service descriptions in the organization's social service handbook or manual. However, objectives shown in manuals are not always developed in a parallel or consistent manner; objectives, goals, and benefits are often used interchangeably. As a consequence, objectives as described in such manuals may require refinement before being acceptable in an evaluation system. Federal and State legislatures have enacted statutes stating objectives for certain social services, and all such mandated objectives should be considered in service profiles.

By definition, achievement of an objective

EXHIBIT 5

Key Words Used in Objectives

Words indicating direction of impact

Negative direction	*Positive direction*
decrease	increase
reduce	expand
diminish	enlarge
minimize	maximize
lower	raise

---

advances the service toward its identified goal. Accordingly, care must be taken in the development of objectives to insure that objectives reflect and support achievement of all established goals. The objectives must be precisely defined, however, and not become a new description of the goal. The requirement for developing quantitative measures is an effective restraint which assists in preventing the use of qualitative words such as "better," "acceptable," "appropriate," etc. in objective statements. Objectives must be measurable in a given time period and qualitative words such as the preceding are normally difficult to measure. Illustrations of key words and phrases used in objecties statements are shown in Exhibit 5.

MEASURES OF EFFECTIVENESS

One requirement of a system of evaluation is a method for determining whether or not objectives, and consequently goals, are being achieved. Measures of effectiveness provide this essential function in a social services evaluation system designed to appraise service impact. By clear and accurate identification of the extent to which objectives are being met, the effectiveness measure indicates the level of tangible impact of the service on the problem.

Typically, effectiveness is measured by determining the amount of change that has occurred in specified conditions of the client group.

Measures of effectiveness for social service objectives should be capable of providing data that can be used in the following activities:

- Measuring the extent to which objectives are met.
- Recording the tangible impact of program services in the stated problem situation.
- Evaluating the adequacy of service efforts to accomplish an objective or produce an intended or expected result.

In complying with these conditions and establishing criteria for determining the degree of success or impact of social services, recognition and awareness of current community opinion should be included as a basis for measuring change.

Measurement of change in social situations is usually expressed in such terms as trends, ratios, and comparisons. To be viable, the measurement should possess the following characteristics: be observable; be quantifiable; and have social consequences. Measures having these characteristics will permit the evaluation of social programs in quantifiable terms.

In determining the impact of social services on client groups, it is often necessary to measure changes in social behavioral patterns. Such measurable social behavior may be evidenced by an event (an occurrence involving one or more persons) or a state (a mode or condition of being). Social behavior is also evidenced in the material things which man creates and uses or the factors which reflect the substance and quality of human social existence.

Technically speaking, all events and states are ultimately observable and therefore measurable. However, phenomena that are observable on only a limited basis require elaborate and costly observation devices suited for use only by the sophisticated investigator, and thus are not applicable to the routine, ongoing evaluation system. Such measurement techniques are required for in-depth special evaluations and are elements of evaluative research techniques. Accordingly, for purposes of the ongoing evaluation of social services, events and states which are highly susceptible to observation and measurement are used. Generally speaking, events are more easily observed than states and therefore are more often used for measurement. Examples of observable behavior, human conditions, and material factors are listed in Exhibit 6.

The following considerations should be incorporated in the development of effectiveness measures to insure that the evaluation system is useful:

EXHIBIT 6

Examples of Observable Phenomena

Social Behavior

Event (occurrence)	*Observation of Act*
Child abuse	Parent beating child
Job application	Potential employee makes application
Physician appointment	Individual keeps appointment
Change of residence	Family moves to different quarters
Enrollment of child in day care	Parent enrolls child in day care
Adoption of child	Child moved to adoptive family
Runaway child	Child leaves home

Human Conditions

State of Being	*Observation of State*
Injured child	Bodily injuries
Unemployed	Person without job
Illness	Symptoms of illness
Unsupervised child	Child left alone
Homeless child	Child without parents

Material Factors

Factors	*Observation*	*State or Condition Based on Criteria*
Housing	Presence	Standard–Substandard
Income	or	Adequate–Inadequate
Food	Absence	Nutritious–Non-nutritious
Toilet	of a	Usable–Nonusable
Clothing	Specific	Sufficient–Insufficient
Transportation	Factor	Satisfactory–Nonsatisfactory

- Measures should relate directly to a specific objective.
- Measures should be clearly stated.
- Measures should provide the basis for defining statistical data to be collected.
- Measures should not create a data-collection burden out of proportion to the utility of the data.

Appropriate program directors and supervisory personnel should be consulted in the process of developing measures of effectiveness. Their participation is beneficial for the following reasons:

- The measures of effectiveness should relate directly to the actual objectives of those individuals delivering the service.
- In most instances, the data needed for measurement must be collected by field operations personnel, who are probably most aware of potential problems involved in interpreting and collecting specific types of information.
- Field operations staff will be more willing to make the additional effort required for the data collection if they participate in determining the data to be collected.
- Participation contributes to the development of more knowledgeable and more effective staff members at the field operations level.

The process of developing measures is iterative in nature. It can be expected that progressively higher staff competence and skill levels in the technique of measures development will be attained as the process is repeated. Examples of effectiveness measures are given in Exhibit 7. Several important characteristics consistently presented in these examples should be noted:

- All measures relate directly to objectives, which in turn are related to the service goals.
- In each measure, the scope is carefully defined.
- Each objective and corresponding measure related to a specific goal appraises different aspects of service impact that would indicate progress toward goal achievement.

In certain service programs, it may be difficult to establish quantitative measures of effectiveness. In such cases, efficiency measures are sometimes used as an alternative. Efficiency refers to the manner in which agency resources are applied for the purpose of providing services. An efficiency objective is process-oriented. Objectives relating to efficiency may stipulate minimum levels below which service activities should not fall, such as to provide a minimum number of interviews per client. Efficiency objectives may also set as a target the reduction of manpower required to complete a service activity. Or an efficiency objective may call for an increase in the frequency or intensity of a service activity, reflected in the number of contacts per week. Essentially, efficiency measures are directed to *output* (numbers of interviews or days of care) while effectiveness measures are directed to *outcome* (impact on client). Certain service programs have traditionally been regarded as acceptable professional practice, but there has been no quantifiable measurement of the effectiveness of these programs. Attempts to define such service programs in the context of this evaluation system have often been unsuccessful because the objectives are frequently ill-defined.

It is important, wherever possible, to avoid the traditional practice of activity counting (process orientation) as a substitute for measuring social service impact (results orien-

---

EXHIBIT 7

Key Words Used in Measures

Describing Numerator and Denominator Components of Ratios

Key Word	Use	Definition	Example
Total population	Denominator	All individuals falling within the scope of the social service agency's accountability.	All families residing in a geographically bounded area; all persons registered with an agency.
Risk group	Denominator	A subunit of a population in jeopardy of being affected by a specific problem.	All unmarried female youths age 13 to 18; all married females age 19 to 45; all children age 1 to 17.
Target group	Denominator	A subunit of a population affected by a problem to which social services are directed.	All married females age 19 to 45 registered for family planning counseling; all children age 1 to 17 placed in foster care.
Impact group	Numerator	All members of a risk or target group affected in a specified way, either positively or negatively.	All unmarried females age 13 to 18 in risk group who become pregnant out-of-wedlock; all children age 1 to 17 in foster care who are reunited with their parents.

---

tation). If program administrators overwork the use of efficiency measures, rather than devote the effort required to develop effectiveness measures, an evaluation system will be seriously impaired and have limited utility.

QUANTITATIVE STANDARDS FOR EVALUATION

Quantitative standards for evaluating effectiveness may be defined as specified levels of attainment expressed in discrete units of measurement. Evaluation standards specify quantitative results to be expected from a particular service within a predetermined period of time. Examples of quantitative standards are presented in Exhibit 8.

Although evaluation standards perform a valuable function in establishing expected levels of attainment for welfare services, two significant problems occur. The first involves a misinterpretation of quantitative standards by operational personnel. Effectiveness standards may mistakenly be viewed as maximum objectives for attainment rather than as benchmarks. Operational personnel may thus tend to strive for achievement of only the level of attainment indicated by the standard rather than for maximum achievement. Administrators may avoid the problem by communication of the purpose of standards to all personnel involved.

A second problem is the tendency for a

EXHIBIT 8

Some Standards Used in Measures

Mathematical Term Used in Measure	Range of Scale	Hypothetical Documented Performance at Time 1	Hypothetical Objective for Performance at Time 2	Example of Objective Based on Standard
Ratio	1/100 to 100 or .01 to 1.00	25/100 .25	20/100 .20	Reduce pregnancies out-of-wedlock in target group from 25/100 to 20/100.
Percent	1% to 100%	25%	20%	Reduce pregnancies out-of-wedlock in target group from 25% to 20%.
Average	1 to 9 (theoretically from 1 to ∞)	7	6	Lower from the 7th to the 6th the average month of pregnancy at which time the first contact with the maternal child care clinic is made.

---

standard to be accepted as permanent, never requiring revision. As a standard is approached or reached, it becomes increasingly difficult to change the standard, especially if the change would represent a higher level of desired accomplishment than is currently expected. When such a condition develops, effectiveness standards become retardants rather than motivators to achievement, thereby weakening the evaluation process. Administrators similarly should be aware of and remain alert to these and other potential problems which may develop in using standards of evaluation. All standards should be periodically reviewed to insure that they are recognized as benchmarks for measurement and not as ceilings for accomplishment.

CONCLUSION

Effectiveness measures concentrate on the results of a program, rather than on the operation of a program, and can alter the traditional focus of welfare managers from emphasis on process and input into services, to concern with the product turned out by these investments. This new welfare orientation can establish a new framework in which goals and objectives buttress a program's intent. On a day-to-day basis, therefore, welfare administrators may well begin to manage by objective. Management by objective is a powerful tool with considerable potential in welfare work. As it is increasingly accepted in the welfare field, it can help welfare administrators in three primary management functions—program planning, personnel administration, and internal and external communication. Effectiveness measures can pinpoint program areas where objectives are not achieved and can cast a spotlight on those where additional study is needed. The end product will provide an improved basis for decisions as to which welfare programs should be maintained, which should be modified, and which eliminated so that a greater impact may be made on defined problems.

The concept of effectiveness measures for welfare programs has already been demonstrated as feasible and promising for improving welfare management. Of course, no management method, however enlightened, offers a ready resolution on how this nation's manpower and money can best be deployed to help millions of Americans improve the quality of their lives. Measures of effectiveness do, however, provide welfare administrators with a promising new tool for charting a new course among uncertain currents of social problems.

PRODUCTIVITY ANALYSIS: ITS USE IN A LOCAL GOVERNMENT

Samuel A. Finz

In a letter dated September 21, 1970, to Elmer Staats, Controller General of the United States, William Proxmire, Senator from Wisconsin, urged that the Federal sector of the economy undertake a comprehensive evaluation of the possibilities for measuring productivity. In that letter, he recognized the major conceptual and practical difficulties involved in measurement of government services, particularly from the standpoint that performance of many of the service activities of government is difficult, if not impossible, to describe in quantitative terms.

Measurement of local government services faces the same basic conceptual problems. Nevertheless, as in the case of the Federal sector, to insure the most efficient and effective levels of local government service, the tools necessary to evaluate performance must be developed and utilized. The emphasis on productivity and its measurement in this paper

Source. Copyright © 1973 by the Municipal Finance Officers Association of the United States and Canada. Reprinted with permission from *Governmental Finance* (November, 1973), pp. 29–33.

is related to local government, in particular, Fairfax County, Virginia. It is, however, by no means unique to this local government.

Peter Drucker points out[1] that in the past it has been management's task to make the manual worker productive. It was Frederick Taylor's insistence on studying and measuring work habits to which the affluence of today's industrial states can be attributed. On the other hand, Harry Hatry of the Urban Institute points out[2] that productivity measurement reveals how successful local government has been after action is taken, and helps to identify new procedures or approaches that are worth pursuing and those that are not. As Edward Hamilton, Deputy Mayor of New York City puts it,[3] New Yorkers and urban dwellers everywhere have a right to a more solid measure of productivity. They have a right to know where the government is succeeding, where it is falling short of its potential, and why.

Some, on the other hand, like Frederick Thayer, Associate Professor of Public Administration, University of Pittsburgh, would argue that suitable productivity standards of output should not be devised.[4] The thrust of his argument is that under present economic conditions, the trend will be not to increase productivity, but instead to restrain it. He points out that as an issue, growth is on the verge of producing the greatest national debate in at least a century, and that increased productivity is tied to infinitely increasing growth. He suggests that there will be more emphasis on a shift in service rather than the level of service as growth is restrained.

One cannot, however, overlook the growing demand for public services directly proportionate to growth, especially in cities that are in the process of rapid growth. In some cases, particularly in those jurisdictions where the average income and level of education is high above the national norm, the quality of service, not necessarily the quantity of service, is of primary importance. An educated populace no longer will accept just a median level of service. They are interested instead in quality of service and cite relatively high tax rates as their right to this type of service.

Regardless of what the national policy will be toward growth, expansion at the local levels will continue to occur and bring about a much greater, and in some cases, a shift in demand for performance on the part of local government. In Fairfax County, for example, the estimated household population in January, 1972, was 494,600, an increase of 252,000 persons or 104 percent of the household population of January, 1961. This is growth which cannot be denied and by no means overlooked, because along with these increases have come expanded school, police, fire, library, social services, etc. If one views statistics, increases can be found in many areas, such as the number of schools, the number of police officers, the number of pieces of fire fighting equipment, the number of library books in circulation, and the number of welfare recipients. While these statistics provide the basis upon which to evaluate trends over a

given period of time, the approach falls short in providing the means to evaluate the quality of services, as it applies to productivity in the sense of effectiveness or efficiency of programs of improvements.

This concept of quality services is related to what Drucker points out as his number three assumption in keeping with the "new realities."[5] He argues that it is management's task to make knowledge more productive. When one draws similarities between the quality of services being demanded in today's "affluent" society by a knowledgeable public and Drucker's "knowledge worker" and the types of tasks he is called upon to perform, then we have to accept Drucker's emphasis on management sciences and the need to monitor changes in job structure, careers, and organizations. In the same vein, we must monitor changes in the structures, careers, and organizations at the local level of government to be able to expect an equally high level of service which is not merely quantitative and responsive to growth, but qualitative or reflective of "knowledge workers" and a knowledgeable citizenry.

The "intent" of a planning, programming, and budget system (PPBS) originally introduced to the civilian agencies of the Federal Government in the Department of Defense was to improve the Budgetary process by a more rational allocation of finite resources to accomplish infinite goals and objectives. This process requires:

1 Careful specification and systematic analysis of objectives.
2 Identification of the relevant alternatives, the different ways of achieving the objectives.
3 Estimation of the total costs associated with each alternative, including direct and indirect costs, initial costs as well as those to which an alternative commits an admin-

istration for future years, and pecuniary and nonpecuniary costs.

4 Estimation of the effectiveness of each alternative, of how close it comes to achieving the objective.

5 Comparison and analysis of the alternatives that promise the greatest effectiveness, for given resourcces, in achieving the objectives.

A system such as the one described provides the means for a more systematic approach to providing quality services. In the absence of such an approach, the quantity of services becomes directly proportionate to the growth of the community without regard to the quality of the services provided, nor the identification of a set of clearly defined goals, objectives or policies. On the one hand, quantity of service is the immediate solution to the growth of demand for public services or benefits. However, without systematic evaluation of these services, government ultimately may be expending scarce resources in the entirely wrong programs.

Thus, in the conventional sense, the issue is not truly of productivity, where the attempt is to maximize output per man hour expended, but instead one of the "productivity of knowledge" as Drucker defines it, where a systematic approach is employed to define the quality, not the quantity of demand and services provided. Such an approach entails identification of the needs of the citizenry and the goals and objectives of each program geared toward satisfying these needs.

For example, it is not enough merely to appropriate funds for an additional social worker without consideration for the goals and objectives of the social services agency and specific programs which they are responsible for. If, for example, one of the goals of social services were the prevention of out-of-wedlock births and the elimination of the ac-

companying social, emotional, and legal problems, and the objective was to reduce the rate of births out of wedlock among individuals in risk groups receiving social services, then appropriations must be earmarked for individuals to work toward achieving this specific objective. Productivity is not measured, then, in terms of total number of social services provided, but in this instance in terms of the reduction in out-of-wedlock births attributable to the efforts of an additional social worker engaged in that particular program. This is a different kind of productivity and the quantitative measures to evaluate achievement can and have been developed on some local jurisdictions in the country, Fairfax County being one of those.

The question arises as to what is the purpose of productivity analysis (the use of measures of effectiveness) in local government. How can it be used and why? In general, given a set of clearly defined statements of goals and objectives relative to the mission of each county agency, certain statistics could be identified which would serve as measures of effectiveness. Policies and programs would be determined only after consideration were given to the basic importance of individual agency objectives and the current level of achievement of these objectives as indicated by the associated measures of effectiveness.

The inherent advantages to having such information:

Provides the means for middle management to evaluate the performance of its agency and personnel in carrying out routine functions geared toward achievement of a set of well defined goals and objectives.

Provides the means for upper management to evaluate the performance of all agencies in achieving their purpose effectively.

Provides the means for the citizenry to evaluate the performance of the county as a whole in accomplishing its goals and objectives as described in a series of adopted countrywide policies.

In general, the major utility of measures of effectiveness lies in either a reduction in operating expenditures or the equivalent in terms of improved effectiveness of the delivery of public services to county citizens.

Briefly, measures of effectiveness are statistics which are geared specifically to goals and objectives, but afford one the opportunity to compare performance over time, as a function of population growth, as a percentage of a total program, or as a ratio to some significant variable which provides the basis for evaluation. Measures of effectiveness can be chosen simply by evaluation of an agency's purpose, analytically through empirical testing of a series of potential variables, or through surveys undertaken to measure user responsiveness and satisfaction.

In June, 1972, the county executive of Fairfax County, Virginia, established the Management Statistics Committee. The purpose of this committee was the development of a management indicator system consisting of those elements or groups of data elements which would be useful in determining the effectiveness and progress of various county agencies and programs toward achievement of specific goals and objectives. A system of indicators provides the means to monitor countywide efforts, assess progress, determine levels of time and cost effectiveness of programs, and determine the future requirements for information useful in the decision-making process of the county.

In general, the work program was subdivided into three major tasks.

1 Development of a series of goals and objectives for each county agency.
2 Development of a series of management indicators or measures of effectiveness which reflect progress toward achievement of goals and objectives.
3 Determination and evaluation of the needs and availability of information in the county which would allow the reporting of the information identified as indicative of performance.

The responsibility for implementation of the productivity program suggested by the Management Statistics Committee has since been given to a separate county agency, the office of research and statistics. This office has a staff of research analysts, each assigned to different county agencies, who are responsible for collecting information and providing analysis and evaluation of significant deviations from targeted levels of performance.

The ultimate utility of this information is in the form of a report which, when submitted by each agency to the office of the county executive, provides the means to evaluate the performance of agencies and programs and the progress toward providing government services to satisfy the demands of the community as a whole. As a general rule, the cost of collecting data elements as measures of effectiveness should not outweigh the utility to be derived from possessing such information.

Measures of effectiveness or management indicators focus on meausres that most truly reflect the impact various programs have on other agencies and citizens of the county. For example, the total number of playgrounds and attendees give no indication of the percentage utilization of a given recreational facility. Much more useful would be the overall perceived recreational satisfaction of attendees and, hence, would provide a practical indication of program effectiveness.

Measures of effectiveness are derived from overall objectives developed by each agency. Policies and programs can be determined only after consideration is given to the basic importance of individual agency objectives and the current level of achievement of these objectives as indicated by the associated measures. Each objective and each measure of effectiveness is intended to reflect some important service characteristic of an agency that no other objective and measure combined reflects.

The first step in the development of a management indicator system is the identification and definition of the goal(s) of each agency. This is not an enumeration of what the agency does, but a statement of *why it does what it does*. A goal statement is not a description of action but the result, state, or condition to be achieved by the action.

The second step in the process is to develop specific targets for achievement. These specific targets or objectives describe the desired results flowing from an operation or action. Every effort should be made to state the objectives in terms that permit quantitative measurement of their achievement. However, many agencies, because of the type of service they provide, will find it difficult, if not impossible, to quantify some of their objectives. The following represents the classification of types of objectives.

1 Objectives which provide quantitative levels to be achieved, e.g., rate of return on investment of at least $3\frac{1}{2}$ percent per annum, reduce the average response time on emergency calls to a maximum of 5 minutes, etc.
2 Objectives which do not provide quantitative levels to be achieved, but which do provide a measure in terms of time and budget constraints, e.g., to process all requests within 24 hours, to reduce the cost of processing to a maximum of $10 per request, etc.
3 Objectives which cannot be expressed in terms of specific levels of quantification,

but which can be expressed in terms of full, reduction, maximum, all, etc. Examples are to: achieve full employment, keep records on all county residents, lower fire insurance rates, etc.
4 Objectives which can be expressed in terms of satisfaction or public acceptance of those affected by the services provided, e.g., the performance of a given recreation facility can be measured in terms of the percentage of people who use the facility who are satisfied, dissatisfied, would like improvements, etc. This objective can be measured through survey and personal interview with recipients of recreation services.
5 Objectives which cannot be expressed in the form of positive quantification and yet are more specific than goals. For example, to maintain machinery, insure continuous operation and efficient performance, etc.

The next step after setting the goals and objectives for each agency is to establish management indicators or measures of effectiveness. A measure helps to evaluate the extent to which an objective is being met. Each measure, ideally, should be capable of meaningful quantification. A measure could be in one of the following forms: change in a number or rate; percentage change a percentage, rate, or ratio; elapsed or average time; number or number per "xx" population. Management indicators can be of various forms and levels of sophistication. In the simplest case, they consist of individual data elements each of which measures effectiveness. In a more complex case, they consist of a series of data elements, the total of which provides useful information.

Examples of goals, objectives, and measures of effectiveness actually developed for Fairfax County are shown in Table 1 from excerpts from the Fairfax County department of fire and rescue services.

TABLE 1

A Sample Set of Goals, Objectives, and Measures of Effectiveness: Fire and Rescue Services

Goal 1

Control and extinguish fires should they start.

Objective 1-a

To reduce the response time on fire calls to a maximum of five minutes.

Measures of Effectiveness

- Average time between fire call received and equipment dispatched.
- Average time between fire equipment dispatched and time of arrival on scene (10-97).
- Average time between fire equipment on scene and time equipment returned to service (10-8).

Objective 1-b

To insure and coordinate the use of adequate equipment for fire and emergency situations.

Measures of Effectiveness

- Average estimated property loss.
- Percentage of estimated total value.
- Percentage of fire alarms requiring fire fighting attention, i.e., not false alarm, smoke scare, etc.

A final step is the establishment of standards for evaluation. Standards for evaluating effectiveness may be defined as specified levels of attainment expressed in discrete units of measurement. They specify quantitative results to be expected from a particular program within a predetermined period of time. For example, the standard set by the police department could be a 20 percent reduction in the crime rate in 1973, while the health department could set as a standard a 10 percent reduction in the annual mortality rate by major cause for the entire county population. Through the establishment of these standards, specific anticipated levels of effectiveness for agencies can be established and their attainment measured.

However, care must be taken that standards are not misinterpreted by operational personnel as maximum objectives for attainment instead of a merely benchmarks. Furthermore, program administrators and operational personnel would have to avoid the tendency to accept the standards as something permanent and never requiring revision. Standards should be periodically reviewed to insure that they are used only as benchmarks for measurement and not as permanent goals.

Each county agency has a mission to perform and therefore has a set of goals and objectives which it seeks to achieve, and therefore measures of effectiveness established for each agency vary accordingly. However, in a very general sense, certain indicators are not only indicative of the performance of an agency but are indicative of the performance of the county as a whole, toward meeting specific countywide policy goals. For example, the planning office has the goal of developing countywide plans which reflect the established policies of the county. Population, employment, income levels, and housing are those categories of data which provide the basis for measurement as to the effectiveness of these plans in achieving these policy-oriented goals. However, in addition to the planning office, this information is extremely important as a source of data useful to other county agencies, builders, citizenry, etc., to accomplish their goals and objectives.

The successful implementation of a productivity program will help fill a gap which a PPB system might have filled—the constant review and analysis of programs and the choice of the best alternative(s) to accomplish a given objective. While a PPB system assists in making rational decisions concerning the allocation of scarce resources to meet various objectives, a management-indicator system helps in assessing whether the programs designed to achieve a given objective(s) are effective. Thus, in a fully developed PPB system, a management-indicator system should be one of its basic elements. But where no PPB system exists, the development of a management-indicator system or productivity program would help provide the experience and the skills required for the development of a PPB system.

The utility of management indicators, therefore, is as a basic set of criteria for making decisions which affect manpower and budgetary commitments by the jurisdiction. Such a system conceivably provides the justification for such endeavors as program funding, changes in staff reorganization, allocation of funds, and shifts in emphasis or priorities regarding existing programs.

NOTES

[1]Drucker, Peter, F., "Management's New Role," *Harvard Business Review,* November–December 1969, pp. 49–54.

[2]Hatry, Harry P., "Issues in Productivity Measurement for Local Governments," *Public Administration Review,* No. 6, November–December 1972, pp. 776–784.

[3]*City of New York Productivity Program for FY 1972–1973,* City of New York, Office of the Mayor.

[4]Thayer, Frederick C., "Productivity: Taylorism Revisited (Round Three)," *Public Administration Review,* No. 6, November–December 1972, pp. 833–840.

[5]*Op. cit.,* Peter F. Drucker.

CHAPTER 5

Unique Characteristics of Nonprofit Organizations

Without a complete understanding of the theoretical traditions and economic forces that interact within each sector, the question of the applicability of private-sector management techniques to the nonprofit sector cannot be answered. The readings in this chapter explore these traditions and forces.

Classifcal economic theory of the firm is highly developed, and over the years a sophisticated theory has evolved. Economists are well versed in its predictive power, its assumptions, and its limitations. Such a rich background has provided management scholars a basis for developing their own management control theory. The keystone of that theory is that the firm attempts to maximize profits, seeking to allocate resources within the firm in such a way as to realize this objective. The goal is straightforward, simple, measurable, and easily decomposed and assigned to the various subparts of the firm.

Such a general theory does not exist in the nonprofit sector. There is no cohesive "theory of the nonprofit agency" that is analogous to the "theory of the firm" in the private sector, nor can the theory of the firm be applied to the public sector. The purposes of the two sectors are fundamentally different. While the firm attempts to maximize profit by efficiently allocating resources *given* a Pareto optimal point, the role of the public sector is to move society to a more socially desirable Pareto optimal equilibrium point.

The term *Pareto optimal point* refers to an economic equilibrium point where it is impossible to make any one person better off without anyone else being worse off. Given the assumptions of perfect markets, utility-maximizing consumers, and profit-maximizing producers, economists can prove that the market will achieve a Pareto optimal equilibrium point. Economists can also demonstrate that there are many alternative Pareto optimal equilibrium points available, depending upon the initial wealth distribution within the society.

Traditional economic theory is neutral toward alternative Pareto optimal equilibrium points because economists have considered it impossible to construct a ranking of such points without making individual value judgments. This conclusion implies the impossibility of evaluating alternative wealth distributions within society. The nonprofit sector, however, must make such value judgments, for an essential reason for its very existence is to move society toward a more socially preferred Pareto optimal equilibrium point.

An additional major difference between the two sectors is the relative complexity of the production function, that is, the relationship between inputs and outputs. In the private sector it is usually easy to identify a clear relationship, in many cases a mathematical function, between the inputs and outputs of the system. Given changes in the input side, one can predict the effects on the outputs.

In contrast, the production function in the public sector is complex and uncertain. The input side is dominated by skills, attitudes, and treatments. The output frequently is behavioral change in the client that may or may not be capable of measurement. The relationship between the input and output is not clear, and it is usually not possible to predict changes in the output given changes in the input.

In "Economic Behavior of Social Institutions," Wittrup presents basic differences between profit-seeking organizations and what he refers to as social organizations. Profit-seeking organizations are a consequence of the market forces of supply and demand. A product or service will be exchanged in the market place if there exists adequate demand and supply. On the other hand, a nonprofit organization exists because society is not satisfied with the rate of consumption and investment provided by the market. Thus, nonprofit organizations represent a deliberate interference in the market. As a consequence, attempts to judge organizational performance using market based criteria are inadequate. Instead, as Wittrup notes, nonprofit organizational success is measured by the extent of its public approbation. The fact that "the public" is not a homogeneous group but rather comprises many groups and individuals makes the process all the more difficult. Additional differences that Wittrup discusses between the two types of organizations can be derived from this one basic dissimilarity.

Klein, in "Plan Accounting Systems for Special Needs," uses the college and university setting to further explore the issue, already raised in the Wittrup article, of the difficulty of satisfying the multiplicity of groups that make up the nonprofit organization's "public." Klein addresses the complexities inherent in reporting financial information to the organization's constituencies. In Klein's view, management's concern for satisfying the legal reporting requirements for external reports has meant that the unique information needs of management are infrequently met. Control over the financial resources of the organization require that management be able to compare actual expenditures with planned (budgeted) ones. Such comparisons require that expenditures be classified in numerous ways beyond the needs of the external reports. This is the subject of Klein's paper.

In contrast to the narrow fiscal concept given to control by Klein, the article by Newman and Turem employs a much broader concept. In "The Crisis of Accountability" the authors argue that accountability cannot be fully shown unless one is able to demonstrate efficiency, effectiveness, and fiscal stewardship. Viewed from an economic perspective, accountability requires that scarce resources be allocated in an efficient and effective manner. In the profit-oriented sector of the economy this is insured by the marketplace. The fact that the market is not used to allocate social services nor to value its output places the problem in the hands of the decision maker, who must determine how to allocate resources in the most efficient manner. While the authors offer no ready solutions, they point to the need for social workers to recognize the problem and to begin investigating ways of demonstrating accountability.

ECONOMIC BEHAVIOR OF SOCIAL INSTITUTIONS

Richard D. Wittrup

John Maynard Keynes, the famous British economist, once wrote that most practical men of affairs, who believe themselves devoid of any intellectual influence, are, in fact, the slaves of some defunct economist.

That observation still holds. Most of what we take for granted in the field of economics is, in truth, a reflection of doctrines being taught by professors decades ago. Even former President Nixon confessed to having become a "Keynesian." Keynes published his General Theory in 1936.

For reasons about which all are free to speculate, economics as an intellectual discipline has been mainly oriented to business, i.e., the profit-motivated sector of the economy, and there exist no very clearly articulated concepts which serve to explain the economic behavior of social institutions.[1]

It is, of course, recognized that governmental fiscal and monetary practices have important effects on the economy as a whole, and in that way social institutions enter into economic thought.

But most prevailing concepts about the economic behavior of the institutions themselves derive from theories developed to understand businesses. Adapting Mr. Keynes' observation to social institutions, most practical men of affairs are the slaves of defunct

Source. Reprinted with permission from the quarterly journal of the American College of Hospital Administrators' *Hospital Administration* (Winter, 1975), pp. 8–16. (Retitled *Hospital & Health Services Administration* in 1976).
[1]The term *social institutions* is used here to describe nonprofit corporations and governmental agencies which provide services to the public. Examples would include hospitals, schools, libraries, and museums.

economists who were talking about something else.

One of the distinguishing economic characteristics of a social institution is that its equity capital has been donated. That is to say, the sources of equity capital retain no proprietary interest in it.

In contrast, the equity capital of a business has been invested, i.e., the providers of capital retain a proprietary interest through the holding of shares or other means. In such cases, the investors expect to realize an economic return, either in the form of dividends or through an appreciation in the value of the interest they hold.

Speaking generally, what we call free or private enterprise is a decentralized system of economic decision-making. Within the limitations of his economic capabilities, each purchaser makes his own selections from the goods and services available. Entrepreneurs compete for the purchaser's favor and prosper in accordance with their success.

THE "INVISIBLE HAND"

Under this arrangement, it is assumed that everyone acts according to his perception of economic self-interest. The distribution of available goods and services is determined by what Adam Smith called the "invisible hand," a term used to describe the sum of forces operating in the market place.

There are times, however, when society decides to override the "invisible hand" and impose a collective judgment influencing how goods and services should be distributed. In some cases, the decision is to restrict consumer preferences. For example, laws are passed limiting the practice of medicine to licensed physicians. Gambling, prostitution, and the open sale of addicting drugs are prohibited, even though there is consumer demand for these services and products.

Conversely, society sometimes determines that the consumption of certain items, usually services, should be at a level beyond that which ordinary market forces would generate. Our educational system, for example, is larger than it would be if each family had to purchase educational services privately in the open market. Few, if any, public libraries or museums could finance their collections from fees charged to users. Orphans' homes and certain other charitable institutions have no opportunity at all to be supported by the consumers of their services.

These decisions to expand consumption are commonly implemented through social institutions. Financed by donated capital, social institutions have no concern with the generation of any economic return for investors. Instead, they are expected to provide as much service, quantitatively and qualitatively, as they can within the limits of their resources. In other words, whereas businesses seek to maximize economic return, social institutions seek to maximize service.

To understand the matrix of forces which shape this pattern of behavior, it is necessary to shift from the framework of traditional economic thought to the framework of political thought, using that broad term to encompass the many and varied factors that influence social organization and social decisions. As we will attempt to show, service is maximized only when those concerned reach a consensus of judgment to that effect. It is through political processes that such a consensus is reached.

POLITICAL MOTIVATION

Typically, social institutions operate under the control of elected officials or voluntary trustees. People generally do not seek or accept these positions because of the economic rewards involved, cynical opinions to the contrary notwithstanding. Neither is pure altruism the primary motivation.

What these positions offer is personal gratification arising from power, prestige, and achievement. To obtain that gratification can require complex choices, such as making unpopular decisions in the expectation of future vindication or taking action in the face of public controversy. Sometimes unsavory behavior results, including deceit and abuse of power. But withal, performance strives to elicit the public support necessary to maintain or improve one's position in the social structure.

To do so, it is necessary to create a record of accomplishment. It is no accident that social institutions have public relations programs, through which they attempt to bring their good deeds, accomplished and projected, to the public's attention. The pronouncements regularly make use of such terms as "long tradition of public service," "meeting social need," "imaginative approach," "expanded program," "improved quality," "responding to public demands," and so on.

It is these motivations that create the drive for expansion and growth which, in turn, generate more service than would result from the ordinary interplay of market forces. For example, operating a revenue-producing activity at a loss solely to avoid reducing the scope of operations is not considered acceptable business behavior. But social institutions do so with enthusiasm and pride, particularly if it can be claimed that the public benefits thereby.

MARKETING QUALITY

For another example, businesses view quality as a marketing consideration, to be evaluated according to the expected influence on profits or sales. Reduced quality, though not a likely subject for an advertising campaign, can be an acceptable business decision if it improves economic return. Social institutions, on the other hand, have to justify any voluntary reduction in quality as being in the public interest. Such justifications are politically treacherous. No elected official or voluntary trustee likes to be found on the side of reduced quality. The safer and more common course is to strive for improved quality and to seek the resources necessary to support it.

The internal leadership of social institutions tends, if anything, to be even more attuned to expanding and improving service. For that group, the rewards are material as well as psychological. It is by creating a record of achievement that one becomes eligible for better jobs, paying higher salaries.

In professional institutions, such as hospitals and universities, internal leadership has great influence on the criteria of accomplishment. If, for example, a hospital medical staff or a university faculty classifies a proposed course of action as leading to more or better service, then the voluntary or elected leadership has great difficulty maintaining a contrary position. This creates an almost constant state of tension, with the professional leadership pressing for more achievement than the voluntary or elected leadership can find resources to finance.

As indicated above, service is maximized by social institutions within the constraint of limited resources. The most obvious way, in any situation, to deal with this constraint is to enlarge the quantity of resources available. This creates pressures for increased taxes and higher charges for service and, in the case of private institutions, solicitation of charitable donations.

In any event, the funds must be acquired from the public. The willingness of the public to accept taxes or to donate funds depends upon its being convinced that the benefits are commensurate with the costs. Public opinion also influences charges for service. Charges seen to be too high result in public disapproval. A common alternative in such cases is

to opt for lower charges and seek sources from which the costs involved can be subsized.

CREATING A FAVORABLE PUBLIC IMAGE

Consequently, institutions emphasize the importance of the service they provide and strive to create a public image conducive to acquiring the desired funds. By this tack, they compete for favorable positions in the list of public priorities.

Within available resources, maximizing service involves the exercise of sound judgment. Any institution has the possibility of shaping its programs in alternative ways. A university might choose between a small, well-paid faculty or a larger faculty at lower salaries. A library might elect to buy more books but be open fewer hours. In each case, the effort is to find that combination which will be viewed as the most "efficient" or "productive" utilization of resources; that is, the combination which maximizes service. Quantitative measures have limited value in this connection. In the library example cited above, it is useful to know how many books could be bought in return for a certain number of reduced hours of staff coverage, but choosing among the alternatives is wholly a judgmental matter.

In making these judgments, institutional decision-makers obviously are guided by their own personal values. But, in the end, it is public approbation they seek, and their judgments are influenced accordingly. The ability to anticipate public reaction, or to persuade the public, is an important determinant of success in institutional leadership. At this point, it is appropriate to mention again the important role of professionals in this decision-making process. In its evaluation of these judgments, the public gives considerable credence to the opinions of those whom it sees to be competent in the particular area involved, i.e., the professionals. It is, therefore, inevitable that in institutions providing professional services, the professionals themselves will exercise strong influence on economic behavior. Only in unusual circumstances can voluntary or elected leadership risk the disapproval of the professionals, and, even then, political skill is required to obtain public understanding and acceptance of the course of action chosen.

THE AMORPHOUS "PUBLIC"

It might be noted, in passing, that the "public" whose approval is sought varies from time to time, from place to place, and from group to group. Professionals, for example, tend toward strong peer group identification, which can be important for career success. Thus, a professional person may be pursuing the approval of people who are disassociated and distant from the institution. Voluntary trustees have constituencies usually vaguely defined to which they owe their position and to which they tend to be responsive. The constituencies of elected officials can, in one sense, be readily definable as the voters in the electing jurisdiction. On the other hand, elected officials are involved in all aspects of public liffe, and, thus, their actions, with respect to any social institution, can be influenced by forces associated remotely, if at all, with the institution's particular purposes. For example, a construction program for an institution may be stopped to avoid higher taxes in an election year or, conversely, approved to avoid antagonizing construction unions.

The recent consumerism movement has suggested that those being directly served by social institutions should have a larger, perhaps even the dominant, "public" role. The problem has been to develop and maintain the degree of consumer organization and group identity required to exercise influence.

However amorphous any institution's "public," and however irrelevant to institutional objectives certain influential groups may seem to be, it is primarily in their attitudes and

interests that the determinants of institutional behavior, economic and other, are to be found.

At the beginning of this essay, it was suggested that social institutions represent a deliberate interference into market forces so as to increase consumption of the services involved. Put another way, the intention is to stimulate a higher level of expenditures for the provision of these services than would otherwise occur.

For businesses, economic incentives can also be viewed as stimulants to expenditure, but these incentives are restrained by market forces which affect the ability to generate an economic return on invested capital. Only if goods and services can be sold at a profit are the expenditures required to produce them likely to be made.

SOCIAL INSTITUTIONS AND RESOURCE ALLOCATION

Consequently, social institutions tend to be more expenditure oriented than are businesses. Businesses are inclined to look with caution on expenditure proposals, since it is much easier to operate at a loss (dissipate invested capital) than at a profit (earn an economic return). Social institutions, on the other hand, attempt to maximize service and, thus, ara apt to expend all the resources they can acquire.

Occasionally, an institution finds that all of its available opportunities for improving or expanding service involve unreasonable costs with the result that it does not expend all of its available resources. These situations arise when, for example, the needs for the institution's services have been substantially satisfied. It might be pointed out in passing, however, that the ability in such cases to redirect institutional purposes into some related area of need is generally looked upon favorably as an indication of vigorous and imaginative leadership.

It also happens that an institution comes to be controlled by people who sequester funds in the interests of what they see to be fiscal prudence. Circumstances can justify this approach, but the more common result is a decline in institutional vitality, sometimes to the point of extinction.

But these are exceptional situations. As a general rule, behavior is toward the maximizing of service and, therefore, of expenditures.

This pattern of behavior has important implications for public policy. On the positive and most important side, it has provided our society with a reliable vehicle for meeting social needs. However much social institutions may be criticized for their proclivities to expand, public decisions to devote resources into some area of perceived need have, in most cases, found social institutions eager to implement those decisions. Consider how serious a problem would arise in the absence of such a response. The urge to maximize service can be restrained, but programs such as Medicaid, Medicare, and federal aid to education would come to naught if social institutions were not energized to provide the desired services.

But social services are now so highly developed, particularly in fields such as health and education, that there is public concern that expenditures, in some cases, may be too high and rising too rapidly. In the search for remedial measures, the tendency is to apply economic concepts derived from businesses, often with counterproductive results.

For example, there is a common belief that the consolidation of small, social institutions into larger units produces economies of scale and, therefore, lower costs. But consolidation also creates a more powerful base from which to to maximize service. That could explain why large universities tend to have a higher cost per student than small universities, and large hospitals, a higher cost per patient than their smaller counterparts. To say that this different-

ial reflects a higher quality and broader scope of services is most likely true, but confirms the proposition that large institutions are more successful in improving and expanding services.

Another concept lifted from business is that costs can be contained by improving the quality of management. But it should also be recognized that able executives will see opportunities not apparent to the less imaginative for acquiring resources and developing programs, and will be more likely to exploit those opportunities successfully.

It seems appropriate to mention at this point that in any economic analysis relative to social institutions, it is necessary to draw clear distinctions between expenditures, costs, and prices.

Expenditures describe the actual movement of funds out of an institution in payment for goods and services.

Costs, while ultimately derived from expenditures, represent a judgment as to the portion of total expenditures which should be attributed to some particular service or category of service. The term *cost* tends to be used very loosely. For example, the amount paid for a barrel of heating oil can be quoted as "cost." But the institutional cost per student per hour of credit in a college is a highly abstract figure which can br influenced over a wide range by the criteria applied in the many allocations required.

Prices, on the other hand, are the particular amounts which an institution charges for various services. Prices may bear only the most remote sort of relationship to either expenditures or costs. College tuition, for instance, is a price but, as is commonly known, seldom reflects cost in any direct sense. However, price becomes "cost" to the consumer, thus illustrating the opportunities for confusion arising from loose usage of terms.

Planning is often advocated as another approach to restraining expenditures, but here again, there are countervailing influences. Planning for services usually begins with an identification of need, in the process of which new public demands for services can be generated and expectations heightened. Alert social institutions will capitalize on that possibility wherever it arises.

Some advocate competition as a means to regulate expenditure growth. For social institutions, however, competition relates to the maximizing of service. If one institution expands or improves service in some way, other institutions feel challenged to match or surpass that performance. If, as mentioned earlier, this results in costs which seem excessive, efforts will be directed toward finding ways to relieve that effect through grants in aid, subsidies, prepayment, endowment, etc.

Abraham Lincoln said, "As our case is new, so much we think anew and act anew." If it is true that the tendency of social institutions to maximize service is creating problems which are without substantial precedent, then there is need for new and effective solutions. To that end, it will be useful to develop an adequate understanding of the economic behavior of social institutions.

PLAN ACCOUNTING SYSTEMS FOR SPECIAL NEEDS

David C. Klein

In a recent *Wall Street Journal* article, Peter Drucker noted that not-for-profit institutions are "more complex than either businesses or government agencies." This inherent complexity is especially evident in accounting and reporting requirements.

Even a small college must provide financial information to external parties, such as actual and potential donors and state and federal agencies responsible for monitoring educational organizations. It must report on expenditures to individual funding sources, including government agencies and its own board of trustees. And it must accumulate and clearly present financial data so that its own administration can effectively control its operations.

This diversity of objectives and uses for financial information has led to the design of accounting systems that in trying to satisfy the needs of all concerned people actually prove inadequate for most. Confusion and misunderstanding all too often arise from the failure to distinguish between the information needs of outsiders and those of management. This article will, therefore, concentrate on some concepts that must be incorporated into the accounting and reporting systems of educational institutions in order to help their managements maintain control.

STANDARDS ALREADY EXIST FOR EXTERNAL REPORTING

For financial reporting to external parties, a body of standard practices developed for some segments of the not-for-profit sector defines how financial information should be presented. These practices are promulgated in various audit guides of the American Institute

Source. Copyright © 1979 by Peat, Marwick, Mitchell, & Company. All rights reserved. Reprinted with permission from *Management Focus* (March/April, 1979), pp. 22–25.

of Certified Public Accountants (AICPA). They identify formats for financial statements and specify the necessity for reporting activities according to standard fund groups and expenditures by function or program.

The audit guide for colleges and universities, for example, defines reporting of expenditures of the current funds by function. The audit guide for voluntary health and welfare organizations specifies that expenditures be classified as to object of expense (e.g., salaries, supplies, etc.) and program service or supporting service.

Recently, AICPA has published a Statement of Position entitled *Accounting Principle and Reporting Practices for Certain Nonprofit Organizations*, covering financial reporting for nonprofit organizations not covered by existing AICPA audit guides. Furthermore, the Financial Accounting Standards Board (FASB) is currently studying the objectives of financial reporting by "non-business" organizations. This work is likely to lead to standard accounting principles that will be applicable to all nonprofit and not-for-profit organizations, including colleges and universities.

In addition to these reporting standards, individual funding sources may each have their own requirements for reporting expenditures. Clearly there are many external requirements that must be considered by not-for-profit organizations in developing an accounting and reporting system. The requirements are more complex when internal needs are considered. For internal reporting, each organization must define its own management information needs and develop accounting systems (manual or computer-based) that satisfy them.

MANAGEMENT HAS BEEN NEGLECTED

Given these sometimes competing demands for financial information, the priroity has often been allocated to the development of account-ing and reporting systems that satisfy external requirements, because they have the weight of official public pronouncement. Internal reporting requirements do not have any such official sanction; so the accounting systems are not always designed to meet management control needs.

This emphasis has led to the development of accounting systems that organize, classify, and report financial transactions to meet reporting requirements for stewardship fashioned by external requirements but not for management action. The priority can be attributed, in part, to the orientation of the public accounting profession toward external reporting and presenting expenditures by function. But organizations *do not* manage their day-to-day operations on the basis of expenditures classified by function. They manage by controllable budgets assigned to individuals with authority to make decisions on spending the funds.

ACCOUNT CLASSIFICATIONS ARE COMPLEX

External as well as internal information needs can require complicated accounting systems and classification structures. The latter must allow for classifications by funding source, responsible organizational unit, object of expense, revenue type, balance sheet category, and expenditure functions. Exhibit 1 illustrates the interrelationship of current fund expenditure classifications for colleges and universities. Consider the complexity of accounting—at the same time—by funding source, by responsible organizational unit, by function, and by object of expenditure when:

- different functions are performed by one organizational unit
- different types of expenditures are incurred for different functions
- different organizational units perform common functions

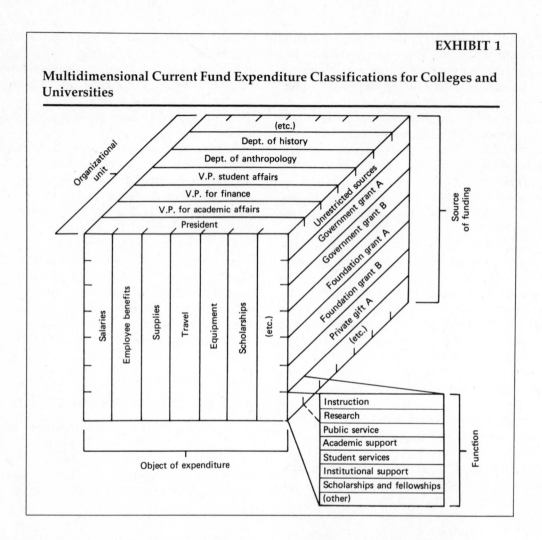

EXHIBIT 1

Multidimensional Current Fund Expenditure Classifications for Colleges and Universities

- different funding sources fund one function
- one funding source supports more than one function

The need to account for costs to meet each of the reporting requirements on a regular basis can require a complex accounting system. Each organization must analyze multifold information needs to determine the accounting system that is best. The management information requirements of a not-for-profit institution is one of the most important considerations.

ADMINISTRATORS NEED DIFFERENT INFORMATION

What kinds of reporting systems are needed for the managerial function in the not-for-profit environment? Primarily, they should be those that help administrators of the institution to manage and control their day-to-day operations and their resources. It is essential to report in a timely way actual financial activity with comparisons to planned activity and other bases, such as prior year activity, by each responsible organizational unit.

What are some of the most important concepts, then, that accounting and reporting systems must incorporate to meet not-for-profit management reporting needs? They include:

Hierarchical Reporting

Different organizational levels need different levels of aggregation of financial information. The lower the organization level, the greater is the need for detailed information on financial activity. If a unit is to be held accountable for its budget, it must receive reports that show budget status for the budgeted line item. The higher the organizational level, the lesser the need for detail and the greater the need for information concerning the aggregated financial activity of the lower units. Thus, the principal investigator responsible for administering a federal research grant or an academic department head responsible for a departmental budget should receive reports covering expenditures compared to those budgets. A dean, who has many department heads and principal investigators reporting to him, may need reports on only the summary status of each of these activities. Clearly, the need to report by responsible budget unit in hierarchical fashion must be recognized as a key ingredient in an effective accounting system.

Reporting Controllable Costs

Financial activity for which a department head or administrator is responsible and exercises some measure of control should be reported to that person. Those activities that can be attributed to a unit but are not controlled by that unit should be reported separately in detail and aggregate.

An illustrative example, chosen for simplicity's sake, is telephone charges, if they are treated as a material expense requiring control. Telephone costs often include a basic charge plus charges for long distance toll calls. A departmental charge for telephone costs in one line item that includes both of these elements does not distinguish between the controllable portion and the uncontrollable portion. For purposes of identifying the full cost of a department's operation, it may be appropriate to charge the department with a share of the base telephone costs. But the controllable portion, the toll calls initiated by the unit, should be separately identified and compared to a budgeted line item for toll calls.

Reporting by Levels of Budgeting Control

Levels of budgeting control refer to the aggregation of expenditure accounts, each having a budget, over which a responsible official has spending authority. This authority can be exercised so that an individual account may exceed the budget without formal budget modifications as long as the aggregate does not exceed the budget. Such levels depend on policy established at each institution.

A set of budgeting control levels commonly found in not-for-profit institutions is personnel compensation, supplies and expenses, travel, and equipment. Within each category, an institution may have many detailed expenditure accounts, for which budgets have been established. For example, in the supplies and expenses category there may be an office supplies account, a reproduction services account, and an office equipment repairs account. These accounts are established to permit analysis of expenditures in some detail, but the budgets for each of these accounts do not serve to control the expenditures except in the aggregate. A responsible official can spend more or less of the budget in any one detailed account as long as the aggregate does not exceed the budget. Accordingly, a well-designed accounting system must permit reporting at detailed levels, but allow aggregation of balances at levels of budgeting control that may vary depending on the type of account.

Budget Comparison Reporting

Reporting activity against budget or plan is a primary objective of management reporting for not-for-profit institutions. A format for such reporting has many variations depending on budgeting philosophy and the management information needed. At a minimum, activity to date in the fiscal year must be comparable with the annual budget. Refined variations include:

- monthly activity comparable with monthly budget
- year-to-date activity comparable with year-to-date budget
- reporting both original budget and revised budget (This allows for modifying the budget based on authorized revisions but still indicating deviations from the original budget.)

Other Period Reporting

Not-for-profit institutions receiving grants from governmental agencies for research and other activities often must control the use of and account for funds on a period different from that of the fiscal year of the institution. The accounting system must be able to capture financial transactions for results on project inception-to-date as well as on the institution's own fiscal year. Reporting for management control is required on the project's fiscal period.

Encumbrance Reporting

Emcumbrances represent formal legal commitments of the institution for goods and services that can result from the issuance of purchase orders or contracts. These commitments properly should be reported as reductions in the available budget balances. In this way, the institution can control the budget better. Encumbrance reporting showing reductions of applicable budgets available is an early warning device for management. It permits budgeting control by including in management reports future expenditures that are in the "pipeline."

Reporting on Cash Balances

Fund accounting calls for maintaining a self-balancing set of accounts, including a cash account, if appropriate, for each fund. For example, a restricted research fund would have a cash account to identify the excess of cash received over the money spent. For cash management purposes, however, it should not be necessary to maintain a separate bank account for each fund. The system, therefore, should be able to account for and report separately cash by bank and cash by fund.

TOP PRIORITY FOR MANAGEMENT

An accounting and reporting system for a not-for-profit institution must be designed to satisfy management control needs. Although reporting financial results to external parties is an important consideration in the design of such a system, the concern for timely control over the budget should be the primary concern. The design of the account classification structure and the reporting formats must consider above all the information needed for effective management.

THE CRISIS OF ACCOUNTABILITY

Edward Newman and Jerry Turem

Accountability is an elusive concept. As addressed in this article, its terms of reference are personal social services in the broad spectrum of human services, concentrating in the main on social services available in either the public or private sector under the Social Security Act. The problems of social services that are publicly delivered or publicly supported are not necessarily different from those of services funded through other sources. However, in the case of services having governmental assistance, the problems of accountability— problems that are related to political action, ideology, policy-making, program effectiveness, and professional responsibility—are today more striking and visible. They are therefore more symptomatic of the current crisis of accountability.

This article will focus on issues that go beneath the surface of political polemics, administrative style, or intergovernmental issues to the raison d'etre of the social service profession—the problems, the goals, the means of achieving these goals, and the value of the profession's efforts according to the extent to which tasks are accomplished. Implications of accountability in social services will then be considered from the vantage point of public responsibility.

Finally, a perspective on accountability will be presented that explores why, in publicly supported programs, accountability does not simply involve accounting for the "quality

of service delivery," as stated by Austin and Caulk in a paper prepared for the 1973 Delegate Assembly of the National Association of Social Workers (NASW).[1]

Indeed, that view largely misses the point that accountability comprises a series of elements ranging from problem identification to goal formulation, and it raises the central questions of efficiency and effectiveness in reducing social problems. To be accountable, in this sense, means addressing a real problem that can be remedied. It means that professional and technical work can be provided if society makes the resources available, that this work will be provided in the manner promised, and that the problem may then be effectively minimized at the least possible social cost.

Accountability is an emotionally laden issue for social workers. The profession naturally reacted vigorously when news reports of the president's former chief domestic adviser stated:

There seems to be a folk tradition around this town that it's somehow indecent to cut any social program. I don't think the second administration will be a believer in that folk tale. I think a President with a substantial mandate, who feels that the majority of the people are behind him, will feel very comfortable in saying to a vested interest group, such as the social workers, "Look, your social program of the 1960s isn't working, and we're going to dismantle it so you'll just have to go out and find honest labor somewhere else."[2]

In March 1973, Mitchell I. Ginsberg, then president of NASW, pointed out to members

Source. Copyright © 1974 by the National Association of Social Workers, Inc. Reproduced with permission from *Social Work* (January, 1974), pp. 5–16.

the unprecedented challenge presented by "program and fiscal cutbacks at all levels of government, [which] presage fewer services for those in need." Ginsberg called on NASW "to see to it that social services are not decimated, that government does not abdicate its responsibility" and to focus its efforts "on a program of professional action which will counter the erosion of services to people and the assaults on social work."[3]

Austin and Caulk recommended to the NASW Delegate Assembly program objectives and actions concentrating on political, governmental, administrative, and fiscal strategies.[4] They outlined the following roles for the federal government and the states:

- The states rather than the federal government should set priorities for social services.

- The federal government should not set forth detailed regulations and rules and keep changing them.

- The states should develop machinery to maximize rationale, technically sound programs that include full participation by consumers, providers, and other individuals and groups.

- The federal government should finance the system and distribute funds to states through relatively unencumbered procedures.

These proposals reflect a concept closely allied to issues of public responsibility. Austin and Caulk seem to suggest that politically the federal government is either untrustworthy or unresponsive. Ideologically, they find a federally directed public social service strategy repugnant. Administratively, they consider federal priority-setting more aloof from the public interest than state and local priority-setting would be. Their view slides over some critical factors as to why the crisis of accountability exists.

POLITICAL AND ADMINISTRATIVE ACCOUNTABILITY

One often hears complaints that political influence is diverting the good intentions of planners and practitioners. This sounds as if planners and practitioners have a rational and comprehensive approach to developing goals—and the means to achieve them—which politicians distort or pervert. Planners tend to ignore or underrate political considerations, that is to say, the roles of power and influence. They do not realize the extent to which the political process is a means for identifying and allocating social values and for legitimating the means and resources to achieve the ends that those values define. It is in this sense that politics inevitably influences the outcome of any planning process. More strongly stated, effective planning in the public sector is always politicized.

The pluralistic American approach to services will, for the foreseeable future, be based on choices made by providers representing disparate interests who may choose to be "in" or "out" of any national scheme. So far, no interest group or coalition of like-minded interests (including the organized social work profession) has brought together sufficient influence to interest the Administration, the Congress, or other important elements of the American public in a plan to organize social services. It is particularly disconcerting that neither NASW nor professional social workers acting independently or under other auspices have successfully influenced recent decisions in more appealing directions.

A strategy that points the states as priority-setters and orchestrators for the services within their domain moves away from a national, unified, comprehensive approach. The federal executive branch does have a point of view about services (even though social workers may not like many of its components) and has the potential power to impose decisions and make binding proposals (about which many social workers may raise questions). But the federal government is the only source from which both significant funding and comprehensive programs can develop.

The question of accountability is raised at this time because of recent events in Washington. Congress approved a ceiling of $2.5 billion on formerly open-ended public social services and narrowed the range of clients who could be served. The Administration proposed regulations that narrowed the range even further. Why has this happened and why now? What does it portend? A few years ago most social workers would have thought $2.5 billion for social services was unattainable. Now it is considered inhibiting. Why? What impelled the growth? Is there a real "crisis" in services, or are social workers reacting without even a moment's reflection? Could it be a return to normal growth after an aberrant spurt?

THE BUDGET CRISIS

When the president delivers his annual budget message some time in January, the major newspapers of the country usually greet it with a "canned" description of his recommendations of the ensuing fiscal year. Their descriptions contain summaries of the budget's major sectors—national defense, human resources, natural resources, the national interest, and "other." Their source material is provided annually in a prereleased pamphlet. The real news related to the budget announcement usually revolves around its total magnitude and legislative initiatives. Within a day or so after the president presents the message, the budget no longer is news.

In 1973, however, the budget, especially its recommendations in the human resources sector, was big news for those interested in the progress of social services.[5] Reaction to this budget generated the crisis in human services.

Various groups interested in human resources agitated and formed coalitions spanning previously autonomous fields.

In most years the presentation of the budget and its appropriations processes have resulted in incremental changes in the existing budget authority and have given a slight leeway for substantial starts in any new program. As Newman and March haved noted:

The complexities of institutional arrangements guard against radical departures. These complexities also make it very difficult to adjust priorities on a major scale to adjust to changing social needs.[6]

In 1973 actions on the president's budget in the human services sector involved more than incrementalism. A number of economic and administrative premises incorporated in the executive budget are difficult to attack; others go beyond substantive differences and relate to more basic political and constitutional questions of the separation of powers. The serious questions are the choices that must be made about the human services, given a relatively limited level of federal funds.

One may agree or disagree with an overall $268.7 billion maximum for fiscal year 1974. Most people would agree, though, that a budget of this magnitude will have a significant impact on prices, wages, and employment. Social workers and others may disagree with the distribution among national defense, human resources, and natural resources. Many would agree, however, that some level for defense expenditures should be preserved. They may disagree with the rise in expenditures for natural resources, although most are sympathetic to efforts to reduce air and water pollution, preserve the physical environment, and deal with the energy crisis.

The rhetoric supporting the federal government's role in promoting national priorities, while decentralizing authority and decision-making to states and local governments and moving away from central control in Washington, Appeals to some social workers but not to others. Traditionally, social work support was often directed to the centralist programs of the· New Deal and the Great Society. It is indeed difficult now to counteract a rationale that professes to maximize economic well-being, stresses concentration on national priorities "which really work," and justifies its humaneness on grounds that the comparative levels of defense expenditures will have decreased from 41 percent in fiscal year 1969 to a projected 30.2 percent in fiscal year 1974, while human resources will have risen from 39 percent to 46.7 percent during the same period.

In examining the human resources sector we find that of an estimated $93.9 billion proposed for fiscal year 1974, over $80 billion are tabbed for income security (mostly social security and income maintenance). These resources are allocated without regard to congressional authority to make annual appropriations and are expended from trust funds and from ostensibly uncontrollable matching funds disbursed through state and local authorities.

Responsible groups cannot ignore the implications of extending all programs under the Department of Health, Education and Welfare (HEW) to all potential recipients. In December 1972 the secretary of HEW estimated that the department's service delivery programs, which then cost $9 billion, would cost $250 billion (about the total of the federal budget) if they were actually extended to all who could be covered.[7] Also, a recent study estimated that meeting the objectives of two major programs in compensatory education and four in social service would require the recruitment and training of an additional 6 million professionals, paraprofessionals, and volunteers.[8]

This recounting is presented neither to defend nor to scare those who may be in-

censed by current efforts to roll back commitments to social programs. It is meant, rather, to remind social workers that fiscal and human resources are not unlimited even in this affluent nation and that choices must be made among goals for programs.

SERVICES UNDER SOCIAL SECURITY

The treatment of the social services under the Social Security Act presents a special case of gross inconsistency between the rhetoric of decentralization and the reality of Administration proposals. Detailed federal regulations set priorities and limit eligibility and allowable services. Financial penalties for noncompliance place the states in an advocacy relationship to the federal bureaucracy. Yet Nixon's New Federalism affirms that state and local governments should have discretion in setting priorities for social programs and that the federal bureaucracy should disengage itself from handling problems that are state or local.

How closely do specific public benefits or services approximate generally accepted "rights"? For example, in the field of education, the idea that elementary and secondary education should be available to all has wide acceptability. But no such broad consensus has developed for social services, either on their parameters or on their separate components.

Services available under the Social Security Act are still generally associated with actual provision of or at least control by public welfare agencies, even though advocates of a comprehensive social service system would like it otherwise. The great growth in expenditures for social services, which some thought would reduce welfare, parallels growth in case loads and payments. Finally, and perhaps most significantly, a basic income floor under all Americans has given way as a major public issue to questions of how much income, for what categories of people, under what condi-

tions. Some programs still include maintenance benefits as an ingredient in a plan for
training or treatment. In these instances,
maintenance payments may be used as incentives to continue participation in such programs.

Given lack of consensus on the scope and
effectiveness of social services, along with the
growth of expenditures in public assistance,
changes at the federal level over the past few
months are best explained as attempts to control the anticipated overall expenditures av-
vailable for welfare-related services, to reduce
the numbers eligible to receive such services,
and to circumscribe the categories in which
available resources may be expended.

Observers both within and outside the
field warned, even during the early 1960s, that
tying services to the goal of reducing dependence on public assistance would weaken their
public credibility. At least three developments
can be cited for the unhappy consequences of
not heeding these warnings—all dealing with
the central theme of accountability.

First, studies of service effectiveness do
not convincingly show that direct service intervention, especially casework, leads to client
improvement.[9] Second, federal, state, and
local welfare agencies have failed to find adequate monitoring or reporting devices for
separating administrative from service costs or
to account adequately for the use of purchased
services under the 1967 amendments to the
Social Security Act. Third, state and local governments were caught short fiscally in the last
few years and abused the purposes of the
services amendments by replacing at least
some state and local funds with federal
moneys probably illegally in some instances,
such as charging for social services activities
properly reimbursed at the lower administrative rate authorized by the Social Security Act.
Accountability was therefore increasingly challenged on grounds of effectiveness as well as

evidence of inadequate responsibility to the
taxpayer and intended recipients.

No one is convinced that the building
blocks for social services that are clearly accountable to the public are yet available. Existing programs become exceedingly vulnerable
to a cost-conscious leadership unsympathetic
to unsupported claims.

What are the first steps that go beyond the
political awareness necessary to make any profession responsive to societal needs? Can social
workers meet the following challenge Eulau
recently threw to all the humanistic professions?

. . . the professionals must bring to the treatment of
public issues professionally pertinent criteria of substance and conduct that warrant their being re-
spected for their knowledge and skills rather than
for the particular ideological predilections that may
be the fashion of the moment. The winds of politics
are moody and have a way of changing faster than
professional responses to these winds.[10]

As indicated, budget restrictions are
symptomatic of a more deep-seated problem:
lack of recognition of the effectiveness of social
service programs. In large measure, this is
because social work has not sustained the
burden of proof of cost effectiveness and because service programs often operate without
regard for basic accounting and the requirements of program data collection. Also, the
squeeze on social service programs is part of an
overall program of resource allocation within a
given budget.

THE VALUE OF SERVICES

Are social work services valued? This is a
question central to the concern of social workers. If services are valued, the problem of
demonstrating effectiveness is easier. This is
not the same as asking if they *are* effective. The
term *valued* is used in the sense that someone

believes services are worth spending money on. Worth could be established by a given individual who elects to spend some of his income to purchase a service. Or it could be established by society wishing to buy a set of activities from which it gains satisfaction. This latter is a bit tricky since society may gain satisfaction from results other than what practitioners actually attain. Thus, society may indicate that it values social services by making donations to support philanthropic institutions or by providing direct tax subsidies. However, such actions may be taken primarily because they reduce social guilt rather than because they bring about change in individuals or conditions.

Consider the legal profession by analogy. The fact that people are willing to purchase unsubsidized legal services from lawyers is evidence that these services are valued in the private sector. To the extent that an attorney is effective he will usually prosper. If he is ineffective, then his income will likely be less than that of his successful colleagues.

When publicly subsidized programs of legal services for the poor were established, lawyers held that the subsidies were required only for those incapable of paying. Some lawyers claimed that no such programs were necessary since there are existing societies that provide services and since many lawyers reduced their fees to the poor. The recent attack on programs of legal services for the poor did not occur because of lack of demonstrated effectiveness but because of the alleged practice of too little "personal service" law and too much "social action" law. But these are questions of emphasis and arguments as to whether government should sponsor litigation against itself, not whether people value the legal profession.

In the social services there are some, but few, comparable programs so valued. Child care, for example, can be shown to be valued; that is, one can point to programs of child care operated solely by parent subscription. Child care becomes controversial when, with government subsidy, program operators and planners develop standards that tend to price the services higher than people are willing or able to pay. The wish to subsidize, then, all "extras" for all users becomes subject to the question: What differences, if any, do these extras make?

If social work was an essentially private profession supported in the marketplace by persons willing to purchase whatever they thought gave them satisfaction, then the question of public accountability and the question of effectiveness would be less compelling. Since professional social work activities largely depend on public sources of funding, society requires some accounting. And alternative uses of limited resources will always be a major issue.

It is a simple fact, although often unappreciated by professionals, that resources expended on one person are unavailable for another—and this is true of money, time, or talent. Thus resources used for a person with a long-term, intractable problem are not available for one or two or three other persons with serious, tractable problems.

If left up to the marketplace, the problem works itself out to some extent, although one might quarrel with the distribution that results. To the extent that people perceive that they need something badly enough to spend their scarce resources to demand it, and to the extent that other people will agree to supply that amount of resources, then the allocation of resources becomes efficient. If a provider does not meet the individual's needs, a new provider is sought. To the extent that the individual is unwilling, rather than unable, to meet the provider's price, then his need cannot be said to be great in relation to other things he wants to spend his resources on. If this was the way social work operated, and if the main problem was to extend services to persons unable, rather than unwilling, to pay a price, then it would be easier to defend programs and budgets.

In the absence of a market mechanism by which individual tastes can be expressed and individual offerings may be accepted or rejected, some other way of expressing value must be developed. When the government subsidizes a program, the effect is to reduce the price to the user, thus encouraging use even by those who would not value the service enough to pay full price. When services are provided without charge, the maximum number of potential users would be expected. Without a pricing mechanism, inefficiency and ineffectiveness can be masked. Without competition among providers, there is little incentive for innovation and efficiency.

Thus, in a market context, the allocation of resources occurs through the expression of individual tastes with demanders offering a certain amount of money and suppliers offering services if an acceptable amount of money is offered. Once an equilibrium price is reached, then the exchange occurs. Without this mechanism, conscious decisions regarding allocation must be made since too few resources are available to serve everyone, especially at zero price.

One way to handle the problem of persons with low income is to have a price that varies with income. This is usually called a sliding fee. It tends to reduce the price for users, but not to zero. It requires that persons pay for some portion of their services, thereby giving an indication of how much they value them. However, with sliding fees there must either be a third-party subsidy to the provider, or else persons with higher incomes must pay enough

to offset the deficit created by persons paying less than full cost. Any private practitioner realizes that, to maintain a solvent practice, full costs must be paid by someone for all clients. Charging a few affects a program by (1) showing how those most willing to pay—presumably those in greatest need—line up for the service and (2) making additional funds available, which may permit extending the program.

The concept of pricing social services in the open market without subsidy is abhorrent to some social workers. Often, they point out, persons need services but cannot afford them. In addition, they say, "Anything that helps a person is worth the price." However, definitions of need are elusive. People have many needs they would not be willing to transform into effective demands. And not everything is "worth the price."

SCREENING AND ELIGIBILITY

It is virtually in the nature of the social work profession to try to assist an individual who lays claim to assistance, regardless of whether anything can actually be done to help. Of course a specific agency may turn away some persons seeking help because it does not provide that range of services usually identified as meeting their needs. For example, some agencies specializing in counseling may turn away persons presenting problems that require tangible resources. Some studies have indicated that the poor and minority groups are often turned away or dropped without assistance.[11] However, once a person is labeled *client*, there seem to be few bounds of the investment to which he can lay claim. Thus a clear conflict is evident between a professional ideology of full services to all persons in need and the practical necessity to ration scarce resources.

Suppose one thought that services should

be targeted to certain individuals, or that society would be better off if certain persons were required to have services. Price screening would not be an appropriate first step, although it could be used at some point. The problem would be that all people cannot be served, either because resources are limited or because limited technology prevents help being given to some.

The usual step is to provide screening according to eligibility criteria. These may be based on income or capital resources, demographic or geographic characteristics, type of problem, or other such variables. Basically, eligibility requirements tend merely to reduce the universe of potential users rather than select among potential clients those whose utilization does most to accomplish the program's ends. Once the eligibility hurdle has been cleared, the individual is usually put on a waiting list or accepted for service and carried until closed. The first-come, first-served technique tends to be inefficient in that it does not identify the range of clients from whom those who would use the service resource most efficiently might be selected.

One can view eligibility screening as a form of tax or a price people pay to get services. For example, when government-sponsored services are free to those in the population who meet certain criteria, then persons who do not meet the criteria must pay for the services, assuming they are available in the market. Thus some people pay the total costs of such services while others pay nothing. This example is not intended to support the position that all services should be free to all people but to point out that eligibility requirements provide a way to ration scarce resources. The case has already been made against providing all things to all people. There just is not enough to go around.

If the profession operated in the mar-

ketplace, individuals could translate their preferences into demands by bidding dollars for services. Many services, such as homemaking, child care, and marital counseling, are provided in this way. When there is no market mechanism, society defines its preferences by processes that are essentially political. The rules then change drastically.

When individuals make their own way in the private sector of our society, they are accountable only to their customers, their professions, and themselves—except for certain requirements to keep fraud and dishonesty to a minimum and licensing requirements to assure some minimal level of standards. When one turns to philanthropy or taxes, then stricter requirements for accountability are imposed. Since this involves society's money, administered through its public agents (whatever one may think of them at the time), supplicants are bound to accept certain limitations as well as responsibility for their own actions. Their alternative is to abandon this source of funds or seek to change the rules by the political clout.

Accountability, at a minimum, is utilized to assure the criterion of honesty. Honesty is a necessary but not sufficient condition for a fully accountable system. When funds are misappropriated for personal use, that is clearly dishonest. When those operating programs act in capricious and discriminatory ways—that is, when they are lawless in the literal sense of having no authority to behave as they do—they are socially irresponsible. When evidence of ineffectiveness and waste is neglected or covered up, then too there is a lack of accountability. The requirements for full accountability protect everyone, in the social services, defense contracting, or whatever area. Such a system of accountability presumes having ethical persons at the top who recognize that society's resources are never adequate to meet all needs and who insist therefore that these resources should at least be expended honestly and legally.

THE CRITERION OF RESULTS

A sound system of accountability goes beyond honesty and is based on results. The techniques oriented to relationships and processes, which are the heart of the social work profession, are the most "soft" and most in need of being put in proper perspective. If credible professional accountability is to occur, casework and group work must be viewed as inputs that may or may not reduce the incidence of definable social problems, and the profession must develop a new orientation based on outputs that can be measured objectively.

Accountability, in a political system, requires a reasonable expectation that the purposes for which dollars were raised have been or could be achieved with maximum efficiency and effectiveness.

Social workers worry about accountability to clients, but there are no fiscal incentives to assure it, since clients have no market mechanism for expressing their preferences. Other mechanisms, such as having users participate on boards, are required. But to the extent that clients do not pay the bill, the focus is on the social institutions that do.

The authors are concerned with the type of accountability that argues it is wrong to continue to demand pay from society for an elegent surgical operation that impresses the interns but never saves a patient's life. The resources required might well have been used for many other untreated patients who could benefit from known procedures.

Not all outputs have to be successful nor must all interventions be measured and be statistically and methodologically precise. The concern is with accountability in a political environment in which reasonable men do not require anything resembling perfection. In vocational rehabilitation, for example, many cases are closed without attaining success. Yet a preponderance of cases are closed with a claim that clients were rehabilitated since many can be accounted for in addition to those able to meet program objectives. But these are questions of efficiency, which is but one component of accountability. In government policy-making it is recognized that reasonable levels of success and a reporting system that retrieves most of what actually occurs are "good enough."

GOALS AS OUTPUTS

Mogulof has noted the following with respect to goals of social work:

Our goals are couched in the kind of generalities which are unable to inform action. The actions we take are not subject to measurement, and are not conceived of as leading to goals larger than the actions themselves. In effect the instrument (Family Planning, Day Care, Counseling, etc.) becomes the ends, and our administrative energies go toward the preservation of instruments. In a sense, it is a remarkable performance by a society whose great technical achievements have come through the employment of the scientific method, where all action is potentially subject to test. We seem uninterested in viewing our social services as action probes which may or may not achieve desired states. Is it because we really don't know what these desired states are? Or is it evidence of a misguided professionalism, which develops a stake in a particular probe (e.g., Headstart) and pushes all of us (the Congress included) to see the probe as an end in itself?[12]

Characteristically, the social work profession does not define goals in terms of output, but rather input (for example, casework hours, number of persons served). One reason for emphasizing new output conventions is that better program analysts are advising decision-makers who are more sophisticated. Future decision-makers will increasingly include state and local elected officials and superagency manager-budget types. The categorical program managers at both federal and state levels will no longer define the scope of the problem and the resources needed through the traditional device of continuing to expand the programs. Tougher questions will be asked. To a greater extent, demonstrated results will be demanded because of greater exposure to a more open political process.

Social work needs an improved technology for defining goals in terms that entail not only measures of effectiveness but also measures of efficiency. There may have been a time when it was sufficient to state objectives in obscure terms, but this is no longer the case.

Seemingly, the profession is in a poor position to claim it knows best. In principle, it might be said that those providing the funds to pay the piper should call the tune, but social workers should try to be included in that essentially political process. It might also be argued that the means of achievement should be in the hands of professionals—but only as long as they are effective and do not displace or obscure the achievement of goals.

Defining goals more rigorously is so large a first step for social work practitioners and supporting scholars to develop that a concerted effort to do so would probably satisfy critics for a while. Merely redefining our set of abstractions with another may give the illusion of movement, but in fact goes nowhere. The day of reckoning comes closer with each attempt. Devising new catchwords or slogans or grasping for the latest fad in rhetoric can no longer suffice. Nor are fancy new delivery systems required. Social workers must simply define what they already do best.

Those active in the social work profession must learn to focus on the few, perhaps narrow, areas in which they can demonstrate that what they do makes a difference, a difference not possible by other means for fewer resources. They cannot afford to make promises that, given the resources, they will reduce welfare rolls, eliminate delinquency, cure the mentally ill, or educate the poor. They must learn to talk about which of how many, at what price, with what expected success, and why this is the way society should do it.

Knowledge bases and the role of schools of social work in relation to accountability have been covered by Briar.[13] To echo his views, truth, beauty, justice, and mental health are goals, but they are not useful for stimulating specific actions, and it is difficult to know when one has such a goal in hand. Systematic evaluation requires ability to state goals in objective, measurable terms. Evading such a statement leaves one open to the accusation of masking ineffectiveness or of committing a form of fraud and leads to a discounting of claims of credibility that may be sound.

If, for example, social workers claim that working with juvenile delinquents can reduce recidivism, and then recidivism is not reduced, they have demonstrated that what they were doing could not achieve the end promised. They have not made the case for the total ineffectiveness of what they were doing or denied that it accomplished some things for some people. (For example, it may have reduced the severity if not the incidence of offenses.) Nevertheless, they may have shown that it is not the best tool for reducing juvenile recidivism in general. The argument that some good was done anyway, even if it was not what was primarily intended, saves little face in the budget shop.

Delinquency has many roots: economic conditions, community and neighborhood influences, social class, the educational system, the local police and court systems, and the like. Social work cannot influence many of these factors. Therefore, the objectives should be expressed in terms of whether, for some subset of juveniles who have certain characteristics and whose offenses stem from, say inadequate parental supervision, social work can help reduce recidivism by a specified percent through working with the parents. Casting objectives in such a fashion makes headway in defining credible goals.

This approach, however, would only help determine whether the intervention worked at all. The vital questions: Does it offer the best way? Are there alternatives that, with the same resources, would have further reduced recidivism? Or are there alternatives that would have reduced it to the same extent at less expense? Together these questions define the effectiveness and efficiency of the system of accountability.

What should be measured and how it should be measured involve a mixture of technical and political concerns. How precise the measurement should be depends on its purpose and on the person prompting it, who may be a cost-benefit expert concerned with the discount rate on future income, a politician who wants to make sure someone is really being "helped," or a program operator who wants to stay in business. The system should produce sufficient information to provide a record for audit showing that the funds were spent honestly. After that the question of how much one wishes to know to evaluate the program can vary widely. The minimum, then, is an acceptable fiscal reporting system and a management-information system covering program data.

EFFECTIVENESS AND EFFICIENCY

Briar has discussed many factors involved in the inability of social work to show effectiveness—its sliding from theory to theory, from technique to technique, but seldom grappling with the question of whether what was accomplished did the clients any good.[14] Effectiveness may be the heart of the truly legitimate question of what benefit professionals, or the profession as a whole, may be bringing clients.

If social services help people, and social workers think many of them do, then it behooves the profession to demonstrate how. Again, the authors take the hard line that case studies and case histories do not constitute evidence since they do not show controlled conditions, the influence of the intervention, the relative overall numbers of successes and failures, and the long-term effects and costs. Nor do they control for enough variables. Who asks what percentage of his clients improved? Further, how would one show it, and at what cost was the client improved? Could more have been done for others at the same cost?

As for efficiency, it would be monumental to show that any intervention worked. Before the cheers died down, one should look at the problems facing those who want to find out whether this intervention works better than another, or if the same result could be attained for less money. Efficiency in this instance does not mean that what is done is done for the lowest cost but that the ends achieved cannot be brought about in another way or at an even lower cost.

Efficiency involves weighing alternatives against costs. To a large degree, many trade-offs are not precisely comparable. For example, looking at trade-offs—say, between two techniques for reducing recidivism among inner-city delinquents—is only one way of judging efficiency. The comparisons could be between casework and group work or between counseling and manpower programs and compensatory education. Each has a different approach and different techniques, but the comparison should be with regard to degree of impact on the same meausre of outcome.

Another set of issues related to efficiency deals with normative judgments as to the choice of what to do at given levels of expenditures to make society better off. Should the money go, for example, to nursing homes for the aged, foster homes for neglected children, rehabilitation of the handicapped, or services to reduce delinquency? If all are worthy, what should the mix be? When a program is fully accountable, those responsible for it can show not only that what it accomplishes is done with fiscal economy and that it is effective, but also that it does what it does better and less expensively—given quality and quantity levels—than any other program could.

SUMMARY AND CONCLUSION

The current crisis in social services is a crisis of credibility based on an inadequate system of accountability. Social programs are in trouble because they focus on processes and not results. A society with limited resources can agree on an endless catelog of needs, but it needs must be ranked to concentrate enough resources to do some good. An analogy to the marketplace indicates that when individuals translate their needs into demands by showing how much they are willing to pay, then many of the issues surrounding accountability recede. When the market mechanism is weak or missing and the support of social institutions is necessary, then political interplay influences preferences and those providing services are required to show that available resources are spent on the most pressing problems with maximum effectiveness and efficiency.

With respect to the "soft" services—those that primarily involve relationships, counseling, and process technologies—it is difficult to attribute changes in the individual's status to the service activity. Testimonials are suspect, and few instruments are available that validly measure before-and-after impact. When the bulk of activity is based on individual or group

processes, changes take a long time. Experimenters and practitioners experience difficulties when they try to isolate the intervention as the key to change over time. In most cases, however, claims that the successful outcome was based on the intervention would be given benefit of doubt if the intended outcomes had been clearly specified and believable.

Occasionally one hears that programs of social work produce outcomes so subtle they cannot be measured but that somehow without them society would be worse off. When the outcome is not measurable, social workers are probably engaging in self-delusion.

At the end, these are the paramount questions: Are social workers useful? Do the programs in which they work leave society better off than it would be if the programs were abolished? In general, the authors think many aspects of society would be worse off were there no social workers and no social programs, but they hold no brief for the sacredness of any one program or any one intervention technique. It is cause for despair, however, that social workers, while indulging in rhetoric about their social responsibilities, often do not have even the most elementary regard for the mechanics of social accountability.

Many programs or specific aspects of services are in a favorable position for sophisticated defense on a limited scale, with modest claims for accomplishment. Family planning, rehabilitation, day care, homemaking, protective services, and the like, should be able to prove their worth if the necessary rigor were applied. It could be shown that other services can accomplish desired ends less expensively than alternative techniques—for example, in-home care for the retarded, the elderly, and the severely handicapped.

This article has tried to show what accountability is about, where the profession falls short, and what might be done. The rest is

up to all of us in the social work profession—
and time may be short.

NOTES AND REFERENCES

1. David M. Austin and Robert S. Caulk, "Issues in
Social Services: A Program for NASW," *New Directions for the Seventies* (Washington, D.C.: National
Association of Social Workers, 1973), p. 16.

2. John D. Erlichman, cited in James P. Gannon, "If
President Wins Again, the Nation May Have a Do
Less Government," *Wall Street Journal,* October 18,
1972, pp. 1, 20.

3. Mitchell I. Ginsberg, "A Letter from Our President," *New Directions for the Seventies,* p. 1.

4. Austin and Caulk, op. cit., pp. 7–18.

5. "The United States Budget in Brief, Fiscal Year
1974" (Washington, D.C.: U.S. Government Printing Office, 1973).

6. Edward Newman and Michael S. March, "Financing Social Welfare: Governmental Allocation Procedures," *Encyclopedia of Social Work, 1971* (New York:
National Association of Social Workers, 1971), p.
433.

7. Internal HEW memo.

8. Elliot L. Richardson, "Responsibility and Reponsiveness," Monograph on the HEW Potential for the
Seventies (Washington, D.C.: U.S. Department of
Health, Education & Welfare, 1972), p. 3. (Mimeographed.)

9. See, for example, Joel Fischer, "Is Casework
Effective?" *Social Work,* 18 (January 1973), pp. 5–20.

10. Heinz Eulau, "Skill Revolution and Consultive
Commonwealth," *American Political Science Review,*
67 (March 1973), p. 188.

11. For a review of studies, see Richard A. Cloward
and Irwin Epstein, "Private Social Welfare's Disengagement from the Poor: The Case of Family Adjustment Agencies," in Mayer Zald, ed., *Social Welfare Institutions,* (New York: John Wiley & Sons,
1965), pp. 623–643; and Cloward and Frances Fox
Piven, *Regulating the Poor: The Functions of Public
Welfare* (New York: Pantheon Books, 1971).

12. Melvin Mogulof, "Special Revenue Sharing in
Support of the Public Scoail Services" (Washington,
D.C.: Urban Institute, March 1973). (Mimeographed.)

13. Scott Briar, "Effective Social Work Intervention
in Direct Practice: Implications for Education."
Paper presented at the annual meeting of the Council on Social Work Education, San Francisco,
California, February 1973.

CHAPTER 6

Control Design for Expenditure and Cost Effectiveness

The most common method for controlling expenditures in nonprofit organizations is through the use of budgets and expenditure centers, which are subunits of the organization. When this method of control is employed, the amount of expenditure authorization, that is, the budget appropriation, is determined at the highest level of the organization. Subordinate managers are expected to maintain expenditures at the budgeted level.

An important assumption with expenditure control at the operating-manager level is that the amounts of expenditures specified in the budget are implicitly correct; nothing could be gained by spending either more or less than the monies allocated. Hence, the objective is absolute compliance with the budgeted spending patterns. Since the budget, therefore, performs such a vital role in this type of control process, it is made a formal part of the accounting records. This feature of governmental accounting clearly distinguishes it from accounting for business entities.

An additional characteristic that distinguishes nonprofit accounting from that used in the private sector is the use of "funds." Funds, which are separate fiscal and accounting entities, represent a very effective device for achieving dollar accountability. Stewardship over revenues and their ultimate expenditure is achieved by earmarking certain revenues for specific purposes. If, for example, the city council identifies city auto license revenue for the support of the city motor pool, then a special revenue fund would be established. The revenue from the sale of such licenses would be recognized in the fund, and the only expenditures made from these resources would be for motor pool operations. This process of earmarking revenues for specific purposes has resulted in many accountants likening it to "cookie jar accounting."

Frequently, a line item budget is used within each fund to gain additional control over spending by subordinate managers. Rather than establishing only a lump sum authorization for the motor pool of the above example, the city council would specify spending limits for such line items as salaries, vehicle purchase, and maintenance.

Should it be possible, however, for the organizational spending unit to influence the results achieved through the expenditure, then management control design can be strengthened by *linking* expenditures to their outputs. The assumptions here are that the spending unit can best determine the optimum amount of expenditures and that expenditures can be increased so long as the benefits achieved are greater than the costs incurred. Evaluation of the spending unit is based on improvements in the ratio of benefits to expenditures rather than on simple compliance with a line item budget.

In "A Study of a Program Budget for a Small City," Lawrence demonstrates the weaknesses in the traditional expenditure approach for reporting financial results through the example of a small municipality. In contrast to the traditional method of reporting, which identifies dollar expenditures with municipal departments, the financial report that the author advocates relates dollars to programs. Such a report identifies expenditures with specific programs within, for example, the police department. A report so designed simplifies the identification of costs with the specific programs of that particular department.

In his brief letter, labeled "Accounting in the Small City," Cunitz charges Lawrence with failing to confront the allocation of line item costs to various programs. Cunitz concedes that in many cases municipal accounting does not provide sufficient detail to accomplish this, but he faults Lawrence for avoiding the issue since it is the essence of program budgeting. In short, Cunitz views the Lawrence example as oversimplified.

Still, the Lawrence proposal represents a substantial improvement in communicating to both the citizenry and the city council the results achieved with the dollars spent. It does not, however, link expenditures with the results in such a way that benefits can be identified with costs. This makes it difficult to determine whether additional dollars spent are in fact achieving additional benefits.

At this juncture it should be pointed out that "costs" are not identical with "expenditures." Costs represent the consumption of resources used in the production of products and/or services. Expenditures, on the other hand, simply represent the outflow of resources incurred if the city council purchases a snowplow for $20,000 in 1980, the $20,000 payment represents a $20,000 expenditure. However, since the estimated life of the snowplow is ten years, its "cost" is $2,000 per year over its estimated economic life. One way to measure the benefit–cost ratio of the snowplow is to match the yearly benefits produced by the vehicle with the yearly $2,000 cost.

The distinction between expenditures and costs should be borne in mind when reading the article by Ross, "Efficiency, Equity, and Higher Education." He contends that greater cost control emphasis could be achieved in universities if they identified the costs incurred in their various programs and based tuition fees on these actual costs. Two important consequences emanate from such a proposal. First, such a pricing structure would encourage program innovation and cost consciousness on the part of management, as high-cost programs would not be subsidized by low-cost ones.[1] Second, the consumption of services by students

---

[1]Editors' note: It is quite likely that cost consciousness would result in the simple reporting of such information without changing the pricing philosophy.

could be expected to change as they sought to maximize the utility obtained from each tuition dollar spent.

Ideally, the existence of a marketplace where goods and services are sold imposes cost control upon organizations competing within the market. A pricing policy like the one Ross presents may have application in other parts of the nonprofit sector where it is possible to sell the services to the consumer. A characteristic common to many nonprofit organizations, however, is the lack of a marketplace. For example, the class of services that economists define as public goods cannot be sold in a connventional marketplace because they cannot be withheld from nonbuyers.

An alternative to the market test for such commodities is a comparison of costs and benefits. In "Payment for Foster Parents: Cost–Benefit Approach," Peterson discusses Oregon's attempt to establish a linkage between input costs and outcomes in a foster-parent program. Described in the article are only direct costs such as payments to the foster parent plus out-of-pocket costs incurred by the foster parent. Outcomes of the program are measured at the end of each year when the foster parent and social worker jointly compare actual progress made by a child with the objectives set out at the beginning of the year. Although more work needs to be done in identifying the total costs of the program and in quantifying the benefits, the case described by the author represents a significant contribution in the area of cost–benefit analysis.

A STUDY OF A PROGRAM BUDGET FOR A SMALL CITY

Charles Lawrence

The accounting results of private businesses remain mysterious to millions of persons uninitiated into accounting lore. However, these people have several consolations. (1) Generally, contribution to a private organization is a strictly voluntary act. It is of small concern to a person if he chooses not to be interested in a given private enterprise, for the organization will probably have little direct influence on him. (2) An investor having but little financial knowledge can use the reported profits test to measure the organization's results of pitting efforts (and costs) against accomplishments (and revenues). The rule of thumb that a business reporting profits is one worth investing in has served otherwise uninformed investors reasonably well.

Unfortunately, the same consolations are not available to the citizenry of governmental (nonprofit) organizations such as the state, the school district, or the city. In the first place these organizations extend to their individual constituents an undeniable mandate to contribute funds (i.e., taxes). The citizen's funds are le-

Source. Copyright © 1972 by the American Institute of Certified Public Accountants, Inc. Reprinted with permission from *The Journal of Accountancy* (November, 1972), pp. 52–57.

gally removed from him and as legally spent by the concerned governmental organization. In the second place, the profit motive does not operate as a measure of the quality of the government's operations. Under present practices the "best" governmental unit is likely to be one that ends the period with the least amount of unspent citizen's funds. Thus the financially uninformed citizen must contribute to an organization which generally regards the spending of the full amount of citizen dollars available as its prime measure of success.

One might think that under these circumstances the government's reporting system might accommodate the citizen's viewpoint. Such is not the case. The purpose of this article is to develop some insights into how that accommodation could be made in reporting municipal financial operations.

Of the two considerations outlined above, little can be done about the government's inalienable right to demand financial support for its operations from the citizens. However, a great deal remains to be done at the municipal level regarding the way the city can report to the citizen on the use of those funds.

The traditional municipal accounting system—including reporting—centers on the spending of funds. The system encompassed here consists of the budget, the recording of expenditures, and the comparative reporting of these two items to the deadly penny. This system primarily serves as a mechanism for validating the expenditure records by referencing each expenditure to an appropriate authorization in the budget document.

Necessary as this system is, legally it encourages a unique variety of spendthrift stewardship. The resultant public reports are generally dull and lifeless; they do not, in the popular parlance, "relate to the people"; they merely absolve the municipal management from legal liability to them.

The heart of the problem lies in the formulation of the usual budget solely in terms of functions and functionaries. The most common budget request appeals for dollars for the police department, the engineering department, the dog catcher, and the sanitarian. The Indian City budget (Exhibit 1) is a typical presentation. The municipal management envisions the needs of the city and presents this functionally organized budget to the city council (or other governing group) for adoption or general information. (The most enlightened of these budgets divide the gross amounts into personnel, supplies, and capital expenditures.)

Each expenditure is generally tied to an office; justification to the citizen, if any, is by way of that now familiar cameo—"5 percent for inflation and (say) $10,000 for a specific capital

---

EXHIBIT 1

Indian City Budget for the Year Ending June 30, 19__[a]
General Fund

Mayor's office	$ 21,540
Controller	22,575
City clerk	18,821
City court	13,800
City council	38,780
City attorney	8,470
City engineer	22,675
Public works and safety	308,037
Electric department	18,570
Fire department	915,980
Human relations	320
Police department	739,800
Health department	40,792
Sanitation	188,000
	$2,358,160

[a]Services in each department's expenditures typically broken down by salaries, supplies, and capital items.

EXHIBIT 2

Indian City Budget in Program Form For the Year Ending June 30 19___

	Public Protection and Adjudication	Health	Community Environment	Social and Economic Improvement	Administration and Support	Total
Mayor's office					21,540	21,540
Controller					22,575	22,575
City clerk					18,821	18,821
City court					13,800	13,800
City council					38,780	38,780
City attorney					8,470	8,470
City engineer			22,675			22,675
Public works and safety			308,037			308,037
Electric department			18,570			18,570
Fire department	915,980					915,980
Human relations				320		320
Police department	739,800					739,800
Health department		40,792				40,792
Sanitation			188,000			188,000
TOTAL GENERAL FUND	1,655,780	40,792	537,282	320	123,986	2,358,160

item." The inevitable result is that each functionary is seized by the "legal spender concept" and attempts forthwith to spend his entire appropriation.[1]

The real difficulty in communicating with citizens by this kind of report is its emphasis upon the citizen as the dollar payer and upon the functionary as the dollar spender.

Suppose this function-oriented budget were supplemented by a budget that emphasized the citizen-benefits of the funds spent (Exhibit 2). It is possible to divide the dollars spent by the city into meaningful spent-for-citizen categories. Though exact categories

would vary by local choice, categorized lists of workable divisions exist in readily available literature.[2] This view emphasizes the kinds of benefits and services received by citizens rather than the dollars collected for functionaries. The focus on benefits in itself (almost regardless of the grossness of the allocations) gives a different perspective to government spending.

A citizen can more easily grasp the priorities of the city management's goals if the budget relates the dollars a municipality asks

[1]The "legal spender concept" holds that any funds should be unwisely spent rather than show a balance that may be subtracted from the following year's budget.

[2]See "Innovations in Planning Programing and Budgeting in State and Local Governments," *A Compendium of Papers Submitted to the Subcommittee on Economy in Government of the Joint Economic Committee—Congress of the United States*, U.S. Government Printing Office, 1965, for alternative workable divisions.

for to the activities it performs for citizens. The central theme of such a report is apparent—dollars should be spent for the benefit of the citizens and not primarily for the benefit of the city clerk, police chief, or other functionary.

The case for the program budget is only partly made with the inclusion of an alternative program budget to supplement the usual line-item city budget. That program budget of course should identify separate divisions of the city budget, such as health, public protection, adjudication, etc.[3] However, several additional steps need to be taken to make this budget an effective report of fund uses to interested readers. The first step is to identify objectives useful to or desired by the citizens within each program budget category; the second step is to seek a measure of the effectiveness of the use of funds under each program.

These steps can be illustrated by examining further a segment of a typical area of the Indian City budget in program form—public protection and adjudication. This area includes both the police and fire departments. For each department, the processes of goal-setting and measurement would have to be accomplished. The processes for the police department are tentatively described in the following pages.

DEPARTMENTAL BUDGETING OF OBJECTIVES

If uses of citizen funds are to be understood, reporting should center on citizen uses. The typical Indian City police department report does little to explain uses. The annual report details (1) the organization and personnel of the department, (2) the major offenses reported and cleared, (3) the property stolen and recovered, (4) the adult convictions by crime, and (5) statistics on traffic accidents. The only financial

[3]George Mead, "A Managerial Approach to Governmental Accounting," JofA, Mar. 70, pp. 50–55, illustrates a program budget formulated for governmental use.

report lists categories of expenditures (salaries, school guards, etc.) according to appropriation, expenditure, encumbrances outstanding, and unexpected balances. The "legal spender concept" is validated by the implication that an unexpended balance is a gross mistake (Exhibit 3). The facts about the operations of the police department are undoubtedly useful and necessary to the internal operations of the department. However, an alternative report which answers questions like those below can probably elicit a great deal more citizen support:

1 What are the several objectives of the department?
2 How are the resources allocated among these objectives?
3 How do the requested changes in budget funds relate to the carrying out of its objectives?

The objectives of the Indian City police department might well be divided into the following: adult crime, juvenile crime, traffic control, and general administration. Other objectives might be added, or these might be subdivided, but in any event, some general objectives for the use of citizen funds should be set forth. Given the several objectives stated, it seems most appropriate that the report contain some indication of how the objectives are to be attained. Perhaps the most important way would be by the allocation of personnel. One such disposition might be shown in the police department's report of resource allocation to programs (Exhibit 4). A second way of attaining objectives is by the allocation of funds between programs. Financial allocations are difficult. Perhaps in the salaries and capital areas they are more useful than in the "supplies and all other" category, which is a more tentative allocation. Reports such as these show how the departmental resources are being allocated annually to meet departmental goals. The reader can

EXHIBIT 3

Indian City Police Department Financial Report for Year June 30, 19___

	Appropriation	Expenditures	June 30 Outstanding Encumbrance	Unexpended Balance
Salaries	$604,096.49	$598,753.15	$	$ 5,343.34
School guards	32,448.00	27,705.30		4,742.70
Travel	500.00	258.93		241.07
Investigative	300.00	300.00		
Instruction	3,987.69	3,884.77	76.75	26.17
Printing	1,400.00	1,310.25	52.50	37.25
Repair of equipment	8,389.18	7,619.38	750.00	19.80
Maintenance of contracts	2,860.65	948.15	160.65	1,751.85
Care of prisoners	25.00			25.00
Civil defense	1,000.00	840.40	156.00	3.60
Contractual comm.	5,160.00	4,789.95		370.05
Gasoline & oil	18,000.00	17,051.35	930.00	18.65
Tires—tubes	2,425.80	1,892.98	532.82	
Laundry & cleaning	50.80		.80	50.00
Medical services	1,029.00	585.05	443.95	
Lab & photo supply	549.45	492.82	56.00	.63
Office supplies	680.00	570.76	108.00	1.24
General supplies	564.80	394.56	66.00	104.24
Ordnance	4,830.49	4,830.49		
Radio supplies	549.00	416.65	110.00	22.35
Clothing allowance	18,759.50	17,159.89	1,592.44	7.17
Insurance	6,500.00	5.706.20		793.80
Subscription & dues	157.00	127.50		29.50
Motor equipment	15,683.00	14,661.00		1,022.00
Lab equipment	5,542.15	5,492.02	35.00	15.13
Radio equipment	3,612.00	3,612.00		
Office equipment	700.00	634.61	65.00	.39
TOTAL	$739,800.00	$720,038.16	$5,135.91	$14,625.93

readily rate the congruence or divergence of stated goals and resource allocations.

DEPARTMENTAL REPORTING OF ACHIEVEMENT

The specification of goals and the allocation of resources are fitting preludes to the important question: What kind of results are being achieved with this pattern of allocation? Innovative reporting should be the key here: several reports might be more useful to the citizen reader than the bald recitation of the functional categories of money spent (recheck Exhibit 2). Effective reports to citizens might analyze the "success" in dealing with the stated goals. Regarding control of adult and juvenile

EXHIBIT 4

Indian City Police Department Report of Resource Allocation to Programs

	Adult Crime	Juvenile Crime	Traffic Operation	Adminis- tration	Total
			Major Programs		
Resource Allocation:					
A. Personnel					
Radio cars	28	10			
Other					
Detective	8				
Juvenile		4			
Traffic			13		
Administration					
Identification				17	
Total personnel	36	14	13	17	80
B. Funds					
Salaries	$275,000	$107,000	$102,000	$122,000	$606,000
Capital (equipment)	10,000	6,000	3,600	6,200	25,800
Supplies and other (allocated)	16,800	8,800	44,350	38,050	108,000
Total funds	$301,800	$121,800	$149,950	$166,250	$739,800

crime, the several stages of crime investigations—(1) crimes investigated, (2) crimes cleared by arrest, (3) persons arrested who were held by the department, and (4) persons convicted (or cleared) of crimes charged—could be detailed and compared. Other measures might be suggested. The exact measures are not as important as the necessity of developing some measure of the effectiveness of spending citizen funds. A report of program results (such as Exhibit 5, Part A) gives a clue to the crime protection program's effectiveness. The report of traffic control success might well include a supplementary analysis of the rate of accident or death compared to the density of the local traffic determined to be in the jurisdiction of the police. Probably the citizenry would be most interested in having that report described by geographical area.

Another, perhaps more useful, view of noting how well the citizen's police funds are spent could be illustrated by a report which compared the patrol areas, the estimated population, the property value, and the types of crimes investigated (classified by adult and juvenile or perhaps property and persons crime) to the arrests made and man-days used[4] (Exhibit 5 Part B). This report gets down to the citizen, to his councilman, and to those most

[4]See comment in "Program Budgeting for Police Department," *The Yale Law Journal* (March 1967), pp. 822–838.

EXHIBIT 5

Indian City Police Department Report Program Results

Results (A)	Adult	Juvenile	Traffic	Total
Crimes investigated	4,840	860	3,000	8,700
Cleared by arrest	1,573	704	2,349	4,626
	33%	82%	78%	53%
Held by department	1,060	262	2,068	3,390
	68%	37%	88%	73%
Convicted (or cleared)	750	262	1,673	2,685
	70%	100%	80%	79%

Results (B)

Patrol Area	Estimated Population (000 omitted)	Property Value (000 omitted)	Number of Nontraffic Crimes Investigated		Arrests	Man-days Spent
			Against			
			Persons	Property		
1	10,000	$ 1,000	200	300	200	3,000
2	2,000	2,000	400	200	177	3,000
3	16,000	14,000	1,000	350	600	3,000
4	9,000	60,000	2,000	320	1,000	3,000
5	5,000	3,000	400	200	100	3,000
6	3,000	4,000	200	130	200	3,000
	45,000	$84,000	4,200	1,500	2,277	18,000

involved in supporting local police activities. It should be useful in soliciting citizen support for increases in budgets, because its focus is on output—results—rather than on dollar inputs.

The reporting approaches should lead to the examination of alternative ways in which stated goals could be reached. The problems of cost allocation and of measurement of effectiveness in program budgeting are complicated. However, only if program goals have been incorporated into the budget can measurement of the use of resources for citizen-oriented uses be effectively reported. There is little if any hope that they can be effectively reported if solely the "legal spender" reporting of municipal accounting is continued into perpetuity.

PROBLEMS AND PROSPECTS

There are, of course, substantial barriers to the immediate implementation of program budgets at the municipal level. One of the greatest is the lack of persons available to guide or give advice in the reformulation of the city's expenditures from a functional into a program pattern. As great a deficiency is the lack of persons in local government aware of, trained in, or even interested in an alternative supplement to the line-item budget formulation. Traditional state laws specify only the "legal spender" reporting of government expenditures.[5] Finally, most municipal accounting texts emphasize this system exclusively without mention of the possibility of soliciting citizen support by supplementary reporting.

However, the change from inputs to outputs reporting is an educational process. Con-

[5]Indian City's state legislature recently passed a law requiring school districts to submit their budgets to the state in program form, a break with tradition certain to be applied to other governmental units.

tinued publicizing of the possibility, practicality, and constituent benefits of supplementary program budgeting offers a good deal of hope for more understandable reports of uses of public funds. The important first step is to examine the possibility that total governmental expenditures reported in a supplementary way can evoke greater understanding and support from the citizenry who foot the largest part of the local governmental cost. Accountants are dedicated to the proposition that contributors to a fund should be informed about the uses of their funds in the clearest possible manner. Program budget formulation and reporting of governmental expenditures would be a big step in that direction.

ACCOUNTING IN THE SMALL CITY

Jonathan A. Cunitz

Professor Charles Lawrence, in his article, "A Study of a Program Budget for a Small City," presented the application of traditional program budget concepts to a small municipality. In my opinion, his approach completely ignores the political and behavioral realities inherent in such situations. This same failing has already led to the misuse and demise of program budgeting (and PPBS) in many governmental organizations.

As a practitioner of management accounting in various government organizations for a number of years, I have seen considerable evidence that Professor Lawrence's approach

Source. Copyright © 1973 by the American Institute of Certified Public Accountants, Inc. Reprinted with permission from *The Journal of Accountancy* (May, 1973), pp. 35–36.

just won't work that way. In his Exhibit 2 for Indian City, the 14 traditional line items are classified under one of five programs in order to illustrate a program budget format. Yet, since none of the line items have to be allocated to two or more programs, his program budget has not changed anything and has merely categorized the traditional budget as shown in Table 1.

Here is the first constraint that has been ignored—allocations of the line budget almost always must be made among various competing programs. Such allocations are often quite arbitrary because traditional municipality accounting cannot provide the cost detail necessary to accomplish them properly.

For effective application of the program budget, objectives must be established for each

TABLE 1
Indian City Budget for the Year Ending June 30, 19___
General Fund

Administration and support		
Mayor's office	$ 21,540	
Controller	22,575	
City clerk	18,821	
City court	13,800	
City council	38,780	
City attorney	8,470	$ 123,986
Community environment		
City engineer	22,675	
Public works and safety	308,037	
Electric department	18,570	
Sanitation	188,000	537,282
Public protection and adjudication		
Fire department	915,980	
Police department	739,800	1,655,780
Health		
Health department	40,792	40,792
Social and economic improvement		
Human relations	320	320
Total general fund		$2,358,160

program category. In reality, this proves to be difficult since objectives are strongly influenced by political motivations, which change all too rapidly. Even if agreement can be attained on objectives, translating them into budget dollars becomes frustrating when municipalities have not yet found clear-cut alternatives for achieving specific goals.

The subsequent effort to measure the effective use of funds under each program is likewise exhausting. Output and productivity measures are only in their early stages of development for municipalities and it is rarely proved that a given measure relates directly to the accomplishment of an objective. Even if it did, municipalities find it difficult to collect data on operations which are valid and not subject to political or managerial distortions.

Finally, the problem of program responsibility has not been contended with at all. Who is responsible for the program budget which cuts across organizational and budget lines? How can he control program implementation and data collection over areas in which he has no direct authority? And where will the money come from to pay for a new layer of financial reporting superimposed over the existing, ingrained system?

Granted that municipal accounting is a weak link in the operation of local government; but I don't believe program budgeting is the means to improve it. Rather than introducing a new concept which creates greater conflict than it cures, it would seem far better to simply apply the vast array of proven managerial accounting techniques within the regular municipal accounting structure.

EFFICIENCY, EQUITY, AND HIGHER EDUCATION

Myron H. Ross

Higher education is a powerful and beneficent force in society, but it is not a free good. Since it is not a free good it requires that we allocate our educational resources wisely so that we receive maximum benefits.

THE FISCAL CRISIS OF HIGHER EDUCATION

The Carnegie Commission on Higher Education has zealously documented the fiscal crisis of higher education. This crisis is a compound of two interrelated elements. Foremost is the fact that productivity of college faculties has been virtually unchanged since 1929. The second element is the fact that there is little motivation or incentive for college administrators or faculties to be more efficient. If a department becomes more efficient, frequently it will receive a smaller budget.

Placing these two facts next to the fact that enrollments are relatively inelastic with regard to tuition leads to the conclusion that university budgets will grow faster than GNP. To see the logic of this we must compare universities with the situation for competitive firms in the rest of the economy. In the United States productivity and real wage rates increase by about 3 percent annually on the average.

Thus for the typical firm average real costs of production are constant. In sharp contrast, higher education is characterized by the condition that wage rates rise by about 3 percent (since the university is in competition with the

Source. Reprinted with permission from *Western Michigan University Magazine* (Fall, 1973), pp. 11–18. (Originally published under the title "The Economics of Higher Education.")

rest of the economy for labor), but because productivity is unchanged, real costs of production rise by 3 percent. In order to cover these additional costs, revenues—some combination of state appropriations, private endowment, or tuition—must be increased by 3 percent annually.

If tuition were increased by 3 percent along with state appropriations and endowments, it is probable that enrollments would not diminish by 3 percent, but by some smaller percentage. It follows that we can expect university budgets to expand faster than GNP. This is probably illustrated by Western Michigan University's experience between 1962 and 1972. For this period, state appropriations in real terms increased by 250 percent, while credit hour production increased by 140 percent. Some of the increase was no doubt caused by the fact that graduate programs grew at a faster rate than undergraduate programs.

The implications of a constant productivity-weak incentive syndrome are clear. With the "taxpayers' revolt" much in evidence, one would expect that taxpayers will become more and more reluctant to cover the increased costs of university education. It would therefore be expected that tuition will rise faster than the 3 percent increase in costs of university education. This means that public universities will be financed increasingly from private sources and will, as a result, assume characteristics of a private institution.

The grim prospect of elephantine budgets can be avoided if the productivity of university inputs is annually increased by at least 3 percent. Too often faculty behave like frightened

Luddites when faced with any potential technological advance in teaching methods. For some professors the definition of optimal class size is "much smaller than last year's." Political and bargaining power are foremost in determining "proper class size" at the university, with little attention paid to the few valid objective studies that exist.

To implement potential economies, stronger incentives are required. Under present conditions incentive to economize is weak and the situation becomes increasingly exacerbated. This is what economists call "market failure." To put the quietus on such market failure it is essential that we restructure the university price system so that incentives for a better allocation of resources exist.

FULL-COST PRICING

Many economists have urged that the university employ full-cost pricing. This would mean that the student would pay the costs associated with his education. This is synonymous with "marginal-cost" pricing in that such a policy would equate price to the marginal cost of education. Along with a full-cost pricing policy, it is required that there be government loans for students who do not have access to the private loan market.

Full-cost pricing does not propose to charge all students the same tuition, as is currently practiced. Quite the contrary. To charge all students the same fees ignores the fact that supply and demand conditions differ for different courses and curriculums. One does not expect General Motors to charge the same for a Cadillac and a Chevrolet. Yet this is precisely what most universities are currently doing. A course in physics with expensive equipment or a seminar with five students costs the student the same as a class with 500 students and no expensive equipment.

While there is currently some differentia-

tion by use of laboratory fees, this is quite negligible relative to the cost differences involved. Under the present system, the student in the humanities subsidizes the student in physics. This is inefficient and inequitable. It is inefficient because we produce too many credit hours in physics and not enough in the humanities. It is inequitable because it shifts income from the student in the humanities to the student in physics on a random basis—and more often than not subsidizes the not-so-poor student to a greater extent than the poor student.

An examination of Table 1 should dispell the belief that cost differences are small. At the University of Minnesota the average and marginal cost of education between colleges is

TABLE 1
University of Minnesota Costs
of Undergraduate Degree (1969 Prices)[a]

College	Average Cost[b]	Estimated Marginal Cost[c]	Marginal Cost Confidence Interval[d]
Agriculture	$7,619	$4,398	$3,516 $5,280
Liberal Arts	3,318	1,915	1,531 2,299
Business Admin.	3,121	1,801	1,440 2,162
Education	4,861	2,806	2,243 3,369
Technology	4,686	2,705	2,162 3,248
Biological Sci.	5,706	3,294	2,633 3,955

[a]Costs are adjusted for fact that teaching assistants bear part of costs because they receive educational benefits, and for research by senior faculty.
[b]Based on cost per student credit hour of spring 1969.
[c]Based on equation: $E = aCH^e$ where E is total expenditure and CH is number of student credit hours. e was equal to .5722, indicating that a 10 percent increase in credit hour would increase total expenditures by 5.72 percent. (All costs are expressed in 1969 prices.)
[d]For 95 percent level of confidence, or alternatively, only 5 percent of observations will be outside range.
Source. Assaf Razin and James D. Campbell, "Internal Allocations of University Resources," Western Economic Journal, September 1972, p. 314.

surprisingly large. A student in business administration can be educated for less than one-half the cost of educating a student in agriculture. The subsidies to students in 1969 at the University of Minnesota ranged from $2,841 in agriculture to $153 in business administration.[1] The "Cadillac" (majors in agriculture) buyers get a bargain. In addition, differences within colleges are also quite large. Within the 95 percent confidence interval the range is in the neighborhood of $1,000 or about 50 percent of marginal cost. Some "Chevrolet" buyers (those getting small classes) get more of a bargain than other "Chevrolet" buyers (those getting large classes).

Assuming for the moment that a graduate in business administration has as much social value as a graduate in agriculture, full-cost pricing implies that the University of Minnesota, if it wants to be efficient, should charge the student in agriculture twice as much tuition as the business administration student. Even if costs were identical under present tuition policy the University of Minnesota would be misallocating resources because the benefits from agricultural education are probably below that of business education (see Table 2). While data for lifetime income for business education are not shown in Table 2, it is probably above $300,000 in line with the lifetime income of such competitive fields as economics, statistics, and computer science.

If tuition were based on full costs, one would expect profound changes to occur in teaching methods. The lecture method, which currently predominates, originated in the medieval period when the cost of books and other written matter were quite high relative to faculty costs. Lectures made good economic sense in the 12th and 13th centuries. However,

[1]Assaf Razin and James D. Campbell, "Internal Allocation of University Resources," *Western Economic Journal,* September 1972, p. 317.

TABLE 2
Present Value of Lifetime Earnings for College
Graduates With Bachelor Degree (1969 Dollars)[a]

	Mean	Standard Deviation	Sample Size
Economics	$339,482	$20,236	1,027
Sociology	213,590	13,063	698
Political Science	300,000	21,194	157
Psychology	262,127	11,300	248
Mathematics	342,068	17,713	5,147
Physics	282,758	13,998	7,239
Statistics	318,421	13,998	7,239
Computer Science	306,733	10,751	3,513
Biological Sciences	215,691	10,802	6,363
Agricultural Sciences	225,118	9,325	6,880

[a]Based on data in National Science Foundation, American Scientific Manpower, 1968 report and supplementary data. A 40-year earning period with a 3 percent rate of discount is used.
Source. Assaf Razin and James D. Campbell, "Internal Allocations of University Resources," *Western Economic Journal,* September 1972, p. 315.

the economic virtue of the lecture method is doubtful with the advent of the printing press and the fact that a reading ability of English is a requirement to matriculate at most universities.

Why then has the lecture method persisted? It has probably persisted because there is no penalty associated with its use. Under the current tuition system there is little or no distinction between efficient and inefficient teaching methods. Reform requires that the compensation of faculty depend on more extensive use of merit from the viewpoint of the student. Perhaps part of faculty compensation should be based on the number of students the faculty member has, making appropriate distinction between graduate and undergraduate classes and so forth. With all the intellectual powers at the university it should not be difficult to devise a merit system that will encourage better teaching.

There is little doubt that consumer or student sovereignty should be maximized. However, there is a potentially serious disadvantage when the teaching and evaluation functions of education are combined. Regular publication of student evaluations may cause a serious decline in the grading of students because professors attempt to curry favor with the student. One can see this effect at Western Michigan University. Between 1969 and 1972, when student evaluation became increasingly important, the mean university grade point average (using departmental averages) increased from 2.75 to 2.91, an increase of about 7 percent.

Perhaps grading should be done independently of the teaching function as in Great Britain and Yugoslavia. This means that the student has limited sovereignty, which she shares with the faculty. The university is more like a republic than a democracy. Perhaps we can and should expect no more. For those devotees of full student sovereignty, would one argue for full patient sovereignty so that the doctor is paid only if he cures the patient? If such a system were employed, it is probable that the "cure" rate would increase significantly, just as the "quality" of student performance has increased with the inception of student evaluation.

ARGUMENTS AGAINST FULL-COST PRICING

1. *Administrative feasibility.* If we applied full-cost pricing to all activities at the university from football tickets to parking facilities, to the coffee pot in the economics department, full-cost pricing no doubt would be too costly to administer. However, we are not arguing here for (in the words of J. M. Clark) an "irrational passion for dispassionate rationality." Rather we are recommending that the university move in a direction of a more extensive but not complete application of full-cost pricing, ob-

serving that the administrative marginal costs be no greater than the expected marginal benefits.

Administrative costs are probably exaggerated. The computer has eliminated many of the problems of handling enrollments as well as handling detailed accounting problems. The computer is a wonderful machine that can inexpensively implement a full-cost tuition policy. Current practice of charging one price for all courses is misguided. It minimizes administrative costs but involves a large-scale misallocation of the university's resources.

2. *There are significant externalities, so universities must be subsidized.* If benefits accrue to third parties, then it makes sense for the third party to make some contribution toward the support of the university. However, the "externality" argument appears to be greatly overworked. It is doubtful, for example, that college attendance reduces the crime rate significantly. Further, any subsidy that is justified should be given to the student and not to the university. This gives the student the opportunity to exercise some consumer sovereignty.

Substantial subsidy may be justified with regard to research activities at the university. Research activities are a public good, with consumption of research results by one individual not interfering with the consumption of research results by another individual. In this case full-cost pricing is inappropriate and would result in the underproduction of research activities. In sharp contrast, a seat at a university is a private good because if the seat is occupied by one individual it excludes others from using the seat. In this case full-cost pricing is appropriate.

3. *The university will not get enough revenue to cover its costs.* This would be true if universities are subject to economies of scale so that marginal cost is below average cost. However, there is little evidence of economies of scale once a university achieves an enrollment of perhaps

6,000. Below this enrollment level there appears to be substantial economies of scale because there are indivisibilities with regard to computer facilities, laboratories, internationally known faculty, and so forth. There is apparently no effective way of employing one-fiftieth of Paul Samuelson. This suggests that schools of less than 6,000 students are probably uneconomic and in a free market will disappear just as the large supermarket has supplanted the "mom and pop" store. For schools in excess of 6,000 enrollment there is no problem in obtaining sufficient revenues with full-cost pricing.

Note that in Table 1, University of Minnesota marginal costs are below average costs. However, this is not because of economies of scale which refer to average costs declining because all inputs are increased. Rather, the University of Minnesota data refer to a situation where plant is fixed and illustrate the significant uneconomic use of that plant because of the existence of large-scale excess capacity. To put this another way, if the University of Minnesota doubled all inputs, it is unlikely that average costs would fall, but if enrollments increased and there was no expansion in physical capacity, average costs will fall.

4. *Lower-income students will not be able to attend college and we will end up with a situation where only the rich attend college.* For those concerned with whether lower-income students can attend college, it is necessary to emphasize that the present university system subsidizes the upper-income brackets to a greater extent than the lower-income brackets. This is so because the not-so-poor students take advantage of subsidized higher education to a greater extent than poor students. And when we speak of "poor students," do we mean poor before or after receiving their education? Since many of these students are poor before they are educated, but not so poor after they are educated, the essential problem is one of finding means of financing education. This suggests that a system of governmental loans for poor students is needed to supplement private sources, because poor students have imperfect access to the loan market.

5. *The fear of failure may prevent a policy of full-cost pricing from being implemented.* University administrations are in the position of the subsistence farmer in the less-developed country. The farmer has knowledge that there are probably better methods of farming than those currently practiced, but the fear of failure prevents such methods from being adopted. In order to overcome this during the transition period the farmer be ensured that if failure results, much of the burden will be borne by the government rather than by the farmer. Similarly, if full-cost pricing is to be implemented it seems that some foundation (why not the Carnegie Foundation?) or governmental agency will have to enter the picture with subsidies during the transition period from the present policy to one of full-cost pricing. Otherwise, each university, for fear of failure, will wait for others to take the initiative, with the result being that none will take the initiative.

BENEFIT–COST ANALYSIS AND HIGHER EDUCATION

Even if the marginal cost for all programs were identical, this is not a sufficient condition for their existence of one price. On the basis of the present value of lifetime earnings in Table 2, one must conclude that the mathematics and economics curriculums should be expanded relative to the biological sciences and sociology.

One would expect student demand for education to move from the low to the high payoff areas. And, as this occurs, the university must be in a position to shift resources in complementary fashion.

This last point is of some significance. If the university is to be responsive to changing demands, it is necessary to keep faculty in a flexible position, so that contraction and expansion of different programs is possible. If there are too many tenured faculty, it is more difficult to contract faculty in some areas than to expand faculty in other areas. Compared with most economic units, universities are unique with regard to their labor force. For most firms labor cost is generally a variable cost; for universities labor cost is a fixed cost.

Students are sensitive to changing benefits. T. W. Schultz contends that there ". . . is strong evidence of the economic calculus at work once opportunities are at hand. I would venture to the view that college students are in general as efficient in this context as firms for profit in their domain."[2]

James V. Koch in a study of student behavior at Illinois State University lends support to Schultz's contention. He shows that marginal changes in the rate of return on an education are associated with student choice of major fields of undergraduate study.[3] An attempt to see if these results would be repeated at Western Michigan University showed no significant correlation between rates of return and enrollment changes, casting doubt on Koch's findings. One can only lament that further research along this line is needed.

The application of benefit—cost analysis to human capital is deceptively simple. If the student can earn a return higher than the cost of funds to finance his education, then we may say that the student should make the investment. For example if the additional income resulting

from four years of college will equal about $5,000 for 40 years and the cost of the education (tuition, books, forgone earnings) equals $20,000 then the rate of return is roughly 25 percent. If the student can borrow funds for less than 25 percent, then he should invest in an education.

While economists are wont to make such calculations, they are also aware of the many qualifications and pitfalls involved. Let us briefly indicate some of these:

- Education is subsidized, so that the return from the student's point of view is higher than the return from society's point of view. In the above example, while the cost to the student may be $20,000, the total cost of the student's education may be in the neighborhood of $30,000, thereby reducing the rate of return. Unless there are significant externalities, subsidization will result in overproduction of college-trained people.

- The product of education becomes embodied in the student. This means that private financing of education will be more difficult than financing nonhuman capital because one cannot separate these skills from the individual, as a bank can separate property from the individual when they foreclose a mortgage. This imperfection in the marketplace signifies that federal or state aid for financing is required in the field of higher education.

- Education may be valuable per se as a consumption good. Taking a course in music appreciation probably produces little increment in earnings, but for many has significant utility. One is, however, left with the suspicion that the consumption element in higher education is exaggerated. If there was no increment in earning power associated with a college education, enrollments in universities would probably contract like a punctured balloon.

[2]T. W. Schultz, "Investment in Ourselves: Opportunities and Implications," in Myron H. Ross (ed.), *The Economics of Education*, Graduate School of Business Administration, University of Michigan (forthcoming). Also see Richard Freeman, *The Amerket for College-Trained Manpower: A Study in the Economics of Career Choice*, Harvard University Press, 1971.

[3]James V. Koch, "Student Choice of Undergraduate Major Field of Study and Private Internal Rates of Return," *Industrial and Labor Relations Review*, October 1972, p. 685.

- Higher earnings are associated with family background, IQs of students, mere college attendance (the screening function), as well as skills. Separating these elements out statistically is extremely difficult.

- Current earnings are not necessarily related to the return on an education. Some occupations will have a higher than average income to compensate for risk. The return on a medical education may be smaller than most people would guess, not only because the cost of a medical education is high, but because doctors enter the labor force later than most professional people. The shorter earning period requires that current earnings be higher to compensate those entering the medical profession.

- There are many nonmonetary factors that must be considered. Some occupations are more enjoyable, have more status, or offer more opportunities than others. It follows that over the long run monetary rates of return will not be equalized because of the presence of nonmonetary benefits and costs.

Economists are in the habit of reminding people that "there is no such thing as a free lunch." This is true as long as resources are allocated in a situation in the neighborhood of equilibrium. However, current operation of universities is in a state of disequilibrium. By moving toward equilibrium, there is available a "free lunch." Considering the great benefits, it is a puzzle why more administrators and faculty are not interested in such policies.

PAYMENT FOR FOSTER PARENTS: COST—BENEFIT APPROACH

Virginia Peterson

More study and research, formulation and testing of hypotheses, and innovative approaches need to be included in the literature about whether, how much, and on what basis agencies should make payments for specialized foster care.[1] With respect to these needs, the author of this article will provide an account of the procedure used by one public child care agency to deal with specialized foster care.

The Children's Services Division in Salem, Oregon, which is a state-administered agency, has approximately 4,500 children in paid foster care on any given day. Eighty-five to 90 percent of these children are in homes in which the person caring for them receives a basic rate of payment according to the child's age group. See Table 1. The other 10 to 15 percent of the children are in homes in which the person caring for them receives a special rate ranging from $35 to as high as $350 over the basic rate per month because these children have special needs or problems that the person caring for them must work with. Historically, these special rates have been determined, authorized, and administered locally.

However, since there was no way to document what was being achieved by paying higher rates, the Children's Services Division decided that it needed to develop a new procedure to govern how special rates would be

Source. Copyright © 1974 by the National Association of Social Workers, Inc. Reproduced with permission from *Social Work* (July, 1974), pp. 426–431.

TABLE 1
Basic Rate Schedule for
Foster Children of Various Ages, 1971−73[a]

Item Provided	Amount Paid for Given Age Groups Per Month		
	0−5 Years	6−13 Years	14−18 Years
Food	$23.80	$34.73	$45.17
Shelter	31.45	29.27	30.33
Clothing	10.00	12.00	15.00
Allowance	.75	2.50	5.50
Personal incidentals	4.00	6.50	9.00
Total	$70.00	$85.00	$105.00

[a]These rates were increased by legislative action for 1973−75.

determined and paid. This new procedure would include a central system in which means existed for measuring both the cost and effectiveness of specialized foster care programs.[2] It would also provide information to aid the further design and improvement of specialized foster care programs. Later, the agency also decided to accumulate empirical data that in time would benefit research in specialized foster care.

The agency found that, although a great deal of information was needed, its resources for obtaining this information were limited by several factors: (1) The findings that were available on the growing size and changing profiles of the national foster care population failed to provide the agency with a reliable basis for predicting the needs of its children in specialized foster care.[3] (2) Little was known in general about the characteristics of persons who elected or were selected to work with the special needs of some children in foster care, and the literature only confirmed that it was the responsibility of the practitioner and the researcher to determine whether any characteriz-

ing patterns existed.[4] (3) There was a lack of information about how workers actually arrived at a given special rate determination.

Further, the absence of unanimity regarding the goals of foster care in general and those of specialized foster care in particular also presented a problem. The agency found it impossible to make an accurate account of the broad social goals advanced customarily to justify public subsidy of foster care. And because the goals that could be measured were so specialized, they failed to serve as principles that would help the agency design a procedure with wide uniform application for similar child care agencies.

DUAL STRATEGY

The agency decided it needed a dual strategy to develop the new procedure. The first strategy was to centralize the function of authorizing special rates of payment. All requests for special rates were to go directly to the central office of the division for authorization by the state foster care program supervisor, and the requests were to include an explanation of why the worker recommended the extra payment. Such explanations would include information about the child's exceptional needs, what extra services were required of the person caring for him, and how long the additional amount would be needed. Workers were asked to identify direct costs of reimbursement other than those included in the standard costs of room and board, such as special food or clothing needed because of a medical condition. Initially, the worker was also asked to assess the special qualifications of the foster parent. But this requirement was eliminated when it became apparent that no common elements were being uncovered. In his report, Fanshel suggests why it is difficult to compile index characteristics of foster parents who can deal with special problems.[5]

The agency's second strategy involved devising a system for paying those persons who provided specialized services for foster care. The literature was reexamined for clues to characteristics of a system of payment that would permit cost–benefit evaluation. Although only a small number of systems were available for review, the agency did attempt to classify them.[06]

All systems studied used one of two means to pay specialized foster parents: salary or fee-for-service. The systems that paid by salary tended not to factor out service from the cost of maintenance in arriving at a payable rate, while those that made payments on a fee-for-service basis usually separated the costs of service from those for room and board. Paying a salary carries implications relating to the status of the employee. Since the agency was unable to indicate employee status, it decided to pay foster parents on a fee-for-service basis.

One or more of three categories—child, need or problem, and service—determines how payments on a fee-for-service basis are to be made. The child category includes children returning from institutional care, diabetics, the mentally ill or retarded, and so on. Payment based on this category is common since the children who fall into it are easy to identify and are likely to require specialized services.

The need or problem category is similar to the child category, but it permits greater precision in determining a rate of payment. Many problems that must be handled in foster care—chronic bedwetting, drug use, truancy, sexual acting out, and so on—are unaccompanied by medical diagnosis or other easily classifiable conditions. For this reason payment is based on the nature of the problem rather than on the category in which the child is placed.

The category of service places the emphasis on the foster parent. Payment in this category is based on what the foster parent actually does in caring for the child, such as feeding, dressing, lifting, transporting, teaching, or tutoring him;

managing some of his medical needs; and so on.

Generally, a schedule of maximums in each category of payment established the highest amount that parents could be paid, with discretion in payment permitted below the maximum. Two or three categories might be combined or a weighting formula assigned to items of importance within a category to correct for unusual severity of a problem or to allow for the extra time, physical labor, cost, or stress involved in meeting the child's needs.

PATTERNS PERCEIVED

While this analysis of how payments were being made was in progress, the first strategy was bringing in results. Empirical data were being accumulated from the requests for special rates. Patterns were sought and found, especially those regarding the need characteristics of the foster children for whom the special rate was recommended. Needs were grouped, without excessive overlap, in such areas as need for supervision of behavior, need for medical attention, need for school adjustment, and need for social or cultural rehabilitation.

However, it was more difficult to find patterns in the services provided by foster parents. Ideally, and for the most part, services provided by foster parents related directly to the need of the child, but the same service might meet a need in any area. However, all services presented common elements of cost to the foster parent, including out-of-pcoket expense, extra time required to work with a child, developing a child's unusual skill or aptitude, special self-training to accommodate a child's needs, additional physical labor, or extraordinary tolerance of stress.

The assumption was made, based on the premise that workers are consistent and objective in identifying special needs and required services and in estimating costs of providing those services, that variation in rates was a function of variation in and among identified cost factors only. For easier management and for keeping intangibles to a minimum, the agency limited cost factors to three specific variables—direct cost, time, and skill. Thus the assumption, stated simply, is that after direct costs are deducted and when time is held constant, payment will vary with the skill the foster parent must have to provide the service. Conversely, when similar skill levels are involved, payment will vary with the number of units of time required to provide the service.

This assumption operates on the basis of the equation: $x = a + (bc)$, in which x = rate of a special payment above the standard rate for the age group, a = direct cost factor, b = value of time, and c = skill level.

Further examination and analysis of individual requests for paymen.₃ tended to support the assumption and to suggest an optimum skill level scale of "3," with "1" and "3" representing the lowest and highest skill levels respectively. The scale arbitrarily assigned a relative value to the aptitude, training, level of tolerance, and so on the parent must have to provide a specific service. The skill levels reflected no monetary value but operated on the time factor to produce variations in the rate, for example, a skill level of "1" would not by itself increase the value of a service beyond the value of the extra time required to provide the service. But assigning a skill level of "3" to a given service would triple the value of the time factor. Guidelines were given for using this scale, but the assignment of a skill level and the estimation of units of time required to provide a given service were left to the judgment of the practitioner. This permitted the agency to retain a considerable measure of individual discretion in determining the rate of payment, while standardizing the reporting.

Two case examples may clarify how the scale worked. In one, a foster mother who had

teaching credentials agreed to spend an hour a day tutoring her tenth-grade foster daughter who read at the second-grade level. The goal was to raise the child's reading level by four years in one school year. The agency requested a $35 increase in rate, which was determined by three variables of cost: direct costs for books and other supplies, $10–$15; units of time, five to seven hours per week; and skill level, "3." By applying the equation, the range of payment was determined to be $25–$36 per month.

In the other example, the agency requested a similar rate for foster parents who were willing to spend extra time training their mentally retarded foster child to perform self-help skills that were within his capability. In this instance, no direct costs were involved. Together, the foster parents and caseworker estimated the extra time required would be twenty-five to thirty hours per week. Since achieving the goal appeared to depend more on the patience and persistence of the parents than on skill and technique, the skill level was set at "1." The range of payment was determined to be $25–$30, a little less than the $35 that was requested and authorized. When individual circumstances justified a rate of payment that could not be supported by manipulating the cost variables, the service need was classified separately and no cost distribution was attempted.

RESULTS

The agency standardized the means for figuring and reporting special rates in foster family care by adapting the equation to a cost-computation schedule for use throughout the state. In theory, this schedule could be used by workers to compute a rate by multiplying estimated units of time by assigned skill levels and adding direct costs, expressing the result in dollars per month. In practice, it has probably been used more often to distribute cost components of an already agreed-on rate by deducting direct costs and dividing the remainder first by the assigned skill level and then by the estimated units of time. Either way, the objective of analyzing cost is achieved.

However, cost analysis tells the agency only what is being invested in a given area. If return on the investment is to be gauged, then benefits must be measured. To measure benefits, the agency must project the goals it expects to achieve by paying special foster care rates.

The three categories—child, problem, and service—that are commonly used as a basis for paying specialized foster parents do not lend themselves to cost–benefit analysis. This is so primarily because the categories make no reference to goals, although goals can frequently be inferred. Such categories, used alone or combined with a weighting formula, can tell an agency with varying degrees of precision what it is paying for. But they fail to help the agency determine if it is getting a fair return on its investment. Therefore, to obtain cost–benefit information, the agency incorporated the service-objective category with a provision for periodic feedback into its cost-computation schedule.

Essentially, the service-objective category required the worker to state the objectives he expected to be achieved by provision of the services for which the foster parents received a special rate.[7] Broadly speaking, these objectives would describe a desired change to be brought about, an undesired change to be prevented, or an optimum state to be maintained. The worker also had to predict the earliest date his reevaluation could be expected to show progress toward achievement of the stated objective. The reevaluation would then serve as a basis for redefining the objective.

The earlier case examples can be used here to show how the service-objective category works. In the first case example of the tenth-grade child who read poorly, the initial objective was to promote a desired change in her level of reading. Improvement in this child's ability to read probably would not be evaluated until the end of the school year. At that time, the caseworker, foster parent, and the child would decide together whether improvements that still needed to be made justified continuing the program and the special rate or whether the major improvements had been achieved and the child could now continue on her own.

In the other case example of the retarded child, progress toward the objective to get the child to acquire and use self-help skills would be evaluated at a time designated by the foster parents and worker together. The foster child might or might not participate, depending on his understanding of what was happening and on his prior involvement. At the time of the evaluation, the parents and worker might decide that another skill could be included or that a skill should be put aside. Or if a plateau seemed to have been reached, they might redefine the objective to maintain and consolidate gains already made or to prevent threatened deterioration. A change in rate would not be necessary, assuming no significant change occurred in any of the cost components. On the other hand, the foster parents might have found patience and persistence alone insufficient to bring about the desired changes and might have consulted with the worker or some other source to develop and subsequently apply skills that would warrant assigning a higher skill level and would also warrant a corresponding increase in rate.

STAFF REACTIONS

Although the procedure devised by this agency was introduced as a "new" way to determine special foster care rates, its principal innovation was the provision for returning information on a large-scale systematized basis. Many workers displayed understandable resistance to additional paperwork, but many others reported that they found the schedule an aid in focusing their efforts. And most of them showed steady improvement in defining operational goals.

Other secondary gains could also be claimed as a result of the schedule: (1) The focus of payment for specialized services was redirected from pathology to potential. The strengths of the child rather than his disabilities were illuminated. Thus the agency could estimate the progress that could realistically be expected, given the provision of specialized services in foster family care. (2) Systematized communication between practitioners and foster parents was promoted; that is, the schedule provided practitioners and parents with a tool for working with each other on the special problems the child presented in foster care. Foster parents are frequently in a strategic position to assess the feasibility of objectives and to suggest alternatives. The resource their unique relationship with the child presents is one no agency can afford to underuse. (3) Finally, another accomplishment was the encouragement of more realistic levels of payment. Even at the highest skill level, the rate of payment for service according to the schedule rarely exceeded seventy-five cents per hour.

However, this system was not without certain problems, the major one being the difficulty in quantifying intangibles and translating them into operational measures. Others included these: (1) The system was based on untested or even unformulated assumptions. (2) No studies of reliability were conducted to determine whether practitioners of similar competence would arrive at similar objectives and rates payable for the same foster parent–child combination. (3) The system had imposed a questionable requirement on practitioners to demonstrate proficiency in a skill not yet generally accepted as essential to practice—that of writing operational objectives.

CONCLUSIONS AND IMPLICATIONS

The Children's Services Division in Oregon essentially pays specialized foster parents on a fee-for-service basis. Payment for service is based on agreement between the caseworker and the foster parent on identified objectives that are to be achieved through services provided by the foster parent. The rate of payment the parent receives is based on three variables of cost: direct cost, time, and skill. Periodic evaluation of the degree that objectives are realized is a condition for continued payment for service.

This approach was prompted by the agency's administrative need to introduce measurement and accountability into an area that had been largely without both. The large-scale systematic accumulation of empirical data resulting from this approach promises to serve research purposes as well by providing the opportunity for constructing research experiments designed to test and evaluate some of the assumptions on which foster care payments are based.

NOTES AND REFERENCES

1. See John Dula, "Future Directions in Foster Care for Children," in *The Social Welfare Forum, Official Proceedings of the National Conference of Social Work* (New York: Columbia University Press, 1952), p. 137; Elizabeth Glover and Joseph H. Reid, "Unmet and Future Needs," *Annals of the American Academy of Political and Social Science*, 355 (September 1964), pp. 9–19; Mary Lewis, "Foster Family Care: Has It Fulfilled Its Promise?" *Annals of the American Academy of Political and Social Science*, 355 (September 1964), pp. 31–41; Delores A. Taylor and Philip Starr, "Foster Parenting: An Integrative Review of the Literature," *Child Welfare*, 16 (July 1967), pp. 371–385; Joseph Meisels and Martin B. Loeb, "Unanswered Questions About Foster Care," *Social Service Review*, 30 (September 1956), pp. 239–246; Elizabeth Glover, "Improving and Expanding Foster Care Resources," Editorial, *Child Welfare*, 44 (May

1965), pp. 244, 286; Richard Haitch, "The Foster Home Problem—Children in Limbo," *The Nation*, 196 (April 1963), pp. 279–281; and Ann F. Neel, "Trends and Dilemmas in Child Welfare Research," *Child Welfare*, 50 (January 1971), pp. 25–32.

2. See Abraham S. Levine, "Cost-Benefit Analysis and Social Welfare Program Evanuation," *Social Service Review*, 42 (June 1968), pp. 173–183; and Darrel J. Vorwaller, "The Voluntary Agency as a Vendor of Social Services," *Child Welfare*, 51 (July 1972), pp. 436–442.

3. See, for example, *The Need for Foster Care: An Incidence Study of Requests for Foster Care and Agency Response in Seven Metropolitan Areas* (New York: Child Welfare League of America, 1969), pp. vi, 73; Glover and Reid, op. cit.; and Taylor and Starr, op. cit.

4. See David Fanshel, "Specializations Within the Foster Parent Role: A Research Report, Part I," *Child Welfare*, 40 (March 1961), p. 21; and Part II of the Fanshel report, *Child Welfare*, 40 (April 1961), pp. 19–23.

5. See ibid., Part II.

6. See, for example, Benson Jaffee and Draza Kline, *New Payment Patterns and the Foster Parent Role* (New York: Child Welfare League of America, 1970), pp. vii, 96: and *Foster Family Care for Emotionally Disturbed Children*, a compilation of ten published papers (rev. ed.; New York: Child Welfare League of America, 1962), p. 72; and Chandrakant Shah, "Assessing Needs and Board Rates for Handicapped Children in Foster Family Care," *Child Welfare*, 50 (December 1971), pp. 588–592.

7. See Levine, op. cit., p. 175.

CHAPTER 7

Control Design for Benefit—Cost Effectiveness

Readings in the preceding chapter alluded to the variety of problems that nonprofit organizations encounter in budget management. Two methods were reviewed in general: expenditure control and input cost control. The readings in this chapter examine in greather depth the use of input/output effectiveness ratios for resource allocation decisions.

A ratio commonly employed by social organizations to evaluate the effectiveness of programs is an outcome/output measure. For example, an alcohol rehabilitation program might report that 87 (outcome) of 115 (output) participants have successfully completed its treatment. A measure of this type can be an effective control device for monitoring efficiency of a program over a period of time, assuming that technology remains constant and that the program is limited to one output. If one is evaluating two different treatments for alcohol rehabilitation or if a program treats both drug and alcohol abusers, then a simple outcome/output ratio cannot be used due to the lack of a common valuation base. Different treatments mean different inputs with different costs, while different outputs imply that we cannot equate one output with another. For example, the benefits accruing to society are likely to differ if one is measuring positive aspects associated with rehabilitating one alcoholic or curing one drug addict.

The search for a common denominator to measure outcomes and outputs most frequently results in the quantification of such activities with the dollar. Theoretically, if one compares the dollar value of the benefits obtained through an alcohol rehabilitation program with its total dollar costs, that is, a benefit/cost ratio, that ratio can be compared with the ratio for a drug-abuse treatment program. A manager would assign additional resources to the program having the highest ratio.

In practice there are numerous conceptual problems related to benefit/cost ratios. These include the difficulty in identifying total benefits and total costs, the problem of assigning dollar valuation to inputs and outputs, and the determination of the appropriate discount rate. These issues as well as others are considered in the readings in the present chapter.

In "Problems Associated with the Cost—Benefit Analysis Technique in Voluntary Hospitals," Knobel and Longest provide a sound theoretitic discussion of a number of problem areas that must be dealt with before one can apply cost—benefit analysis. The authors do not pretend to offer solutions to the problems of proper discount rates, externalities, lack of external markets, and multiple objectives.

Instead, they present a lucid discussion of the important theoretical issues confronting the decision maker, emphasizing that cost—benefit techniques should not be applied without adequate conceptual analysis.

Many techniques are available today for aiding the decision maker involved with allocating scarce resources in an environment with objectives that are difficult to quantify. King, in "Cost-Effectiveness Analysis: Implications for Accountants," discusses one of these methods in a general and nontechnical manner. The basic concepts of cost-effectiveness design are so presented in the article as to permit the reader to apply the ideas to such closely related decision tools as cost—benefit analysis, planning, programming and budgeting, and cost—utility design.

Of particular interest is King's discussion on choosing measures of effectiveness and the selection of a decision criterion. Effectiveness measures gauge the efficacy of each alternative being selected. Care, however, must be taken that such measures are good surrogates for the outcome. The decision criterion is used for making cost-effectiveness trade-off decisions of various alternatives. The synthesizing model that King employs demonstrates well the issues involved in establishing an appropriate decision criterion.

Because the two preceding articles have considered some of the theoretical and empirical problems of applying cost—benefit analysis, the reader may have the impression that with so many potential hazards it would be fruitless to try this technique. Hannan, in "The Benefits and Costs of Methadone Maintenance," makes a rigorous attempt to overcome these problems in a case study of a methadone-maintenance treatment center in New York City. The problems of valuation of benefits and costs, external benefits versus direct benefits, and subjective estimates are dealt with in a well-documented application of the cost—benefit technique. Of considerable importance is the method by which Hannan is able to demonstrate the degree of sensitivity of the various analytical assumptions employed.

As was discussed in Chapter 5, a dilemma of classical economics has been its inability to use mathematical logic to rank alternative Pareto optimal equilibrium points without resorting to individual value judgments. In "How to Determine Who Should Get What," Goodin proposes an approach that would allow economists to make interpersonal utility comparisons and in turn to rank alternative Pareto optimal points. The article does not solve the problems of making simultaneous considerations of heterogeneous utility functions, but it does identify the ethical judgments that must be made in the course of solving distributive questions. A solution to one question is postulated, while others remain unresolved.

PROBLEMS ASSOCIATED WITH THE COST—BENEFIT ANALYSIS TECHNIQUE IN VOLUNTARY HOSPITALS

Roland J. Knobel and Beaufort B. Longest, Jr.

The desire to provide adequate community health facilities is not a new phenomenon. It draws upon both the egalitarian principles which espouse "health care as a right, not a privilege," and economic pragmatism which calculates the social costs of ill health and the values of improving or maintaining the stock of human capital.

Health care institutions that have as an objective the provision of adequate community health facilities must choose from among alternative uses of resources in their efforts to meet this goal. Therefore, let us look at the voluntary hospital as an institution which must choose from among alternative uses of its resources and examine some of the basic problems associated with the process of cost—benefit analysis as a technique to decide among alternative uses of capital resources by individual hospitals.

Muller and Worthington have described the present and past treatment of capital by hospitals:

Capital has not been placed by hospital management under the same accounting rules as other inputs. Administrators have not sought to collect the full cost of capital services through pricing policy, i.e., depreciation expense and imputed interest on internal funds have been omitted. Before Medicare, inventories of capital assets were rare. There have been no systematic and accepted means of funding capital accumulation within institutions and within a group of institutions in a region. There has been little expectation that charges would cover capital costs—indeed, even meeting non-capital operating costs was not assured. The organizations made a virtue of their lack of business orientation with respect to capital, and to a considerable extent this is still the case.[1]

The future is, of course, brighter as more and more attention is being paid to the way hospitals utilize their capital resources and to the manner in which they select from among alternative uses of their resources. One of the most promising tools in improving the process is cost—benefit analysis. Richard F. Wacht has suggested its incorporation into a "hospital capital budgeting" approach where the object is "to determine the numeridal value of the ratio of the present value of benefits expressed in dollars to the present value of money costs."[2]

Since we are looking at the problems associated with the voluntary hospital's use of cost—benefit analysis for determining the amounts of capital to be used in various alternatives, we should, perhaps, examine a brief summary of cost—benefit analysis since it is the predominant tool suggested in the literature with which hospitals are to make this choice.

Source. Reprinted with permission from the quarterly journal of the American College of Hospital Administrators' Hospital Administration (Winter, 1974), pp. 42—52. (Retitled Hospital & Health Services Administration in 1976.)

[1]Charlotte F. Muller, and Paul Worthington, "Factors Entering Capital Decisions of Hospitals," Empirical Studies in Health Economics, Ed. Herbert E. Klarman (Baltimore: The Johns Hopkins Press, 1970), p. 399.

[2]Richard F. Wacht, "Capital Budgeting Decision-Making for Hospitals," Hospital Administration, Fall 1970, pp. 16—17.

COST—BENEFIT ANALYSIS

A cost—benefit ratio (Z) is defined as the ratio of the value of the benefits of an alternative to the value of the alternatives' costs:

$$Z = \frac{\text{present value of economic benefits}}{\text{Present value of economic costs}}$$

Clearly, if the ratio is greater than one, expenditures for the alternative may be judged to be economically worthwhile. This analysis serves three purposes for the decision maker: (1) It assists him in developing the optimum size program or project. (2) It assists him in designing the program to be of maximum efficiency. (3) It assists him in choosing from among the alternatives open to him the set of options that is the most productive.[3]

PROBLEMS ASSOCIATED WITH COST—BENEFIT ANALYSIS

Before hospitals utilize cost—benefit analysis as the method by which they will make the choice for alternative uses of capital they must consider certain inherent problems in this process: (1) treatment of time, (2) valuing with imperfect markets—shadow pricing, (3) valuing with multiple objectives, (4) doctor—hospital relationships, (5) spillover effects, and (6) multiple sources of funding.

Any consideration of the problems associated with the allocation of capital assumes that capital is available. At this point it is appropriate to describe briefly the trends in sources of capital for hospitals.

Nonprofit financing has run a cycle from almost complete dependence on individual philanthropy to dependence on contributions from the entire community, grants from the federal government, and funds generated internally.

SOURCES OF HOSPITAL CAPITAL

These sources now are undergoing significant and far-reaching changes. There is a downward trend in the annual flow of contributions relative to the need for capital.[4] The federal preference is to shift from direct to indirect support in the form of interest subsidies and government guaranty of borrowing in the private capital markets.[5] Reliance upon internally generated funds, particularly from third-party payers, may worsen before it improves because of "pressure to reduce Medicare expenditures and the desires of other third-parties to reduce their reimbursement to Medicare levels."[6]

Hopefully, replacement of retrospective, cost-based reimbursement being replaced by some form of prospectively set prices will be widely accepted. Health Legislation, now pending in Congress, includes this feature.[7]

For the present, hospitals are forced to rely on long-term debt repaid with cash generated from operations to an increasing extent.

TREATMENT OF TIME

An object's value depends on when it will be used. In other words, the value of a dollar is specific only on a specific date and to a specific person under specific circumstances. This presents a problem in evaluating investments when they are long-lived undertakings because of the different time periods in which benefits and costs are experienced. To circumvent this

---

[3]Robert H. Haveman, *The Economics of the Public Sector* (New York: John Wiley and Sons, 1970), pp. 151—152.

[4]C. R. Rorem, *Capital Financing for Hospitals* (New York: Health and Hospital Planning Council for Southern New York, Inc., 1968).
[5]Kenneth W. Williamson, "Trends in Federal Spending—and Some Predictions," *Hospitals*, 16 October 1968, p. 68.
[6]Edward L. Walls, "Hospital Dependency on Long-Term Debt," *Financial Management*, Spring 1962, p. 45.
[7]*Ibid.*

problem, it is necessary to state both present and future flow of benefits and costs in terms of their present value.

In symbolic terms, the numerator of the cost—benefit ratio can be restated to reflect time preference:

$$\Sigma \frac{B_t}{(1 + r)^t}$$

The symbol Σ is summation over all the years, B_t is the benefits expected in the t-th year and $(1 + r)$ is the discounting factor by which values expected in the future are converted to today's values. The denominator of the cost—benefit ratio is shown here:

$$K + \Sigma \frac{O_t}{(1 + r)^t}$$

K is the capital or construction costs (assumed to occur in the current year) and O_t are the operation, maintenance, and repair costs expected in the tth year. The cost—benefit ratio then becomes the following:

$$Z = \frac{\Sigma \dfrac{B_t}{(1 + r)^t}}{K + \Sigma \dfrac{O_t}{(1 + r)^t}}$$

It is the ratio of the present value of the benefits over the present value of the capital plus future operation costs.[8]

Most of the revealed cost—benefit analysis in hospitals today makes a basic assumption that the amount of capital to be distributed among the various costs and benefits in the hospital is a given. This assumption ignores the

[8]Haveman, *op. cit.* pp. 158–160.

need to assess the benefits accruing from the investment against the opportunity benefits that might accrue from social investments extramural to the hospital.

At this point the determination of the value of "r" should be faced. This can present considerable difficulty to the administrative decision maker. As a first approximation he could set "r" arbitrarily at the market rate of the cost of borrowing funds in the present money market. If he does so, he will be making mistakes a good percentage of the time.

Rational consumers are reluctant to reveal the true utility they assign to public goods. The hospital combines, in its output, both private and public goods. The private goods are the treatment and medical services provided to individuals, that can be internalized by them. The public goods include community services, disease control which has "neighborhood" qualities, medical education, and research. It is very probable that the facilities and equipment, provided by hospital capital expenditures, are jointly used to produce these private and public good outputs.

Since market interest rates do not properly reflect social externalities (the economic man would prefer that the rest of society make the intertemporal concessions which lead to the production of public goods), a number of hospital capital investments, which have a high public good or social content, would not be made based on a market rate of return. This may call for the establishment of a social rate of return (r) and its substitution for the market rate of return, which is based on the interest rate set in the market place.

The investment in the health of future generations also must be considered in allocating available capital expenditures. McKean says of this:

The way to provide more wealth (or fewer hardships) for future generations is surely to choose investments with the highest rates of return and to increase the size of current and future investment budgets. To use a discount rate lower than the marginal rate of return in *comparing* projects does nothing to increase the volume of investment; it merely discriminates in favor of proposals whose benefits occur in the distant future and against projects (education? training?) whose benefits occur in the near future.[9]

Another authority on public investment criteria considers the interdependence of public and private investments. He points out the distortions in public versus private utility maximization which derive when a government makes hospital capital expenditures based on social rates of discount which compete with private investments. Under such circumstances he suggests that the cost—benefit equation be modified to reflect the value to individual consumers of the money withdrawn from the market.[10] These withdrawals reduce the private consumption and are not a available to underwrite private investments based on private time preferences.

An additional problem which has been dealt with by Muller and Worthington concerns the translation of funds into capital formation in order to help solve problems in the delivery of medical care. They suggest the following:

Where continuing programs of modernization and expansion are the objectives of an individual hospital or group of hospitals, capital funding and capital formation may fail to correspond. This cannot be dismissed as a short-run problem which is self-correcting in the long-run. The translation of funds into plant and equipment may be permanently impaired.[11]

Their study concerned the time required to translate funds into facilities within the municipal hospital system of New York City. The study dealt with the structure of time requirements for adding value to capital projects. The design activity in construction was singled out for special attention. The study concluded that (1) it will take as long to design a project as it will to built it, and (2) larger projects will economize on time per dollar of project value. However, the primary source of this economy will be in construction, not in design.[12]

Another problem that must be considered over a given period of time is that of population shifts and changes. For most hospitals this cannot be considered a static situation and the analysis, therefore, cannot be considered static.

VALUING WITH IMPERFECT MARKETS—SHADOW PRICING

If one could actually describe all markets as competitive, effective, and comprehensive, prices for all outputs would be available and reliable. The practical implementation of cost—benefit analysis would be greatly eased. Unfortunately, markets are imperfect and, therefore, observed prices fail to reflect social values accurately. These imperfections run the gamut from monopoly power to immobilities to externalities or spillovers to lack of market information. Because of these market imperfections, many prices observed in the real world are not reliable and must be "corrected" in doing a cost—benefit analysis. The process of adjusting faulty market observations is called shadow pricing. A shadow price can, therefore, be defined most simply as "a synthetic value attached to a unit of input or output which represents the social value of the item used up or produced."[13] This social value incorporates externalities, among other things, and can be an

[9]R. N. McKean, *Efficiency in Government Through Systems Analysis* (New York, John Wiley and Sons, 1958), p. 118.
[10]S. A. Marglin, *Public Investment Criteria* (Cambridge, Mass.: The M.I.T. Press, 1967), pp. 52—57.
[11]Charlotte F. Muller and Paul Worthington, "The Time Structure of Capital Formation: Design and Construction of Municipal Hospital Projects," *Inquiry* VI, no. 2 (June 1969); 42.

[12]*Ibid.*, p. 51.
[13]Haveman, *op. cit.*, p. 163.

approximation at best, as McKean has pointed out.[14]

VALUING WITH MULTIPLE OBJECTIVES

Even if the decision-making administrator has made specific the objectives for the hospital in terms of quality, prestige, and quantity,[15] he is faced with the knotty problem of rationalizing the various factors of output objectives as they relate to the capital expenditures. Teaching and research programs affect the prestige and quality of care provided by the hospital and have effects on the quantity of inpatient, outpatient, and community services it puts out. Each of these programs requires different mixes of capital and human resource inputs and has different spillover effects and probably different social rates of return. The latter are embodied in the different time horizons that programs entail and the different populations they provide utility to.

The complexity of valuing with multiple objectives begins to come into focus when you see that society, the individual, and the hospital can have different utility functions (both total and marginal). Perhaps one more complicating factor should be noted here: patient-care, research, or training all have different social values or, technically, all have variable rates of return to society.

Some attempts have been made to disaggregate the costs assignable to private and public good output producing operations in a hospital. An example is the attempt to break down the inputs that lead to patient care and teaching outputs in teaching hospitals. It is easier to do this for the variable costs than for the capital and overhead costs involved in these operations. A pioneering effort to identify these different program bases was made by Augustus Carroll at Yale New Haven Hospital. In commenting on this effort, M. F. McNulty, Jr. said:

> Program cost finding for teaching hospitals does not solve the greatest problem facing the hospital administrator, the compartive evaluation and leadership in decision making among projects, functions or activities and the allocation of resources, always limited in proportion to the opportunities for individual and institutional contribution to society. Although program cost finding does aid such determinations by bringing functions or activities into sharper focus, more frequently than not the functions or activities are not comparable.[16]

THE DOCTOR—HOSPITAL RELATIONSHIP

One of the significant factors which is felt to influence the evaluation of alternative use of capital resources by hospitals is the hospital—doctor relationship.[17]

Doctors, when they have a choice, tend to practice in hospitals that provide the best array of services and facilities in support of their private practices. Hospitals, therefore, are motivated to take "into account the capital it will require both for the patient load it anticipates and for satisfaction of the requirements of the physicians admitting the patients."[18] If one assumes that those doctors with the levels of skill and range of specialization which the hospital would like to retain or attract are relatively scarce, then the hospital must respond to doctor's requirements or the doctor can withdraw his affiliation if he becomes dissatisfied with the hospital's services.[19]

---

[14]R. McKean, "The Use of Shadow Prices," *Problems in Public Expenditure Analysis*, Ed. S. B. Chase (Washington: The Brookings Institute, 1968), p. 34.

[15]J. P. Newhouse, "Toward a Theory of Nonprofit Institutions: An Economic Model of a Hospital," *American Economic Review*, March 1970, pp. 64—74.

[16]A. J. Carrol, *Program Cost Estimating in a Teaching Hospital, A Pilot Study* (Chicago: Association of American Medical Colleges, 1969), p. 108.

[17]Melvin W. Rider, "Some Problems in the Economics of Hospitals," *American Economic Review Papers and Proceedings* 55 no. 2 (May 1965):472—480.

[18]"Factors Entering into Capital Decisions of Hospitals," *op. cit.*, p. 402.

[19]*Ibid.*

SOCIAL CAPITAL INVESTMENT

A physician's demands for social capital investment exceed the expenditures he would be willing to make if he were developing his own technical production function as an entrepreneur. Fuchs suggests that the "technological imperative" of the physician overpowers all economic and resource allocation considerations that might apply in the treatment of patients even in cases where he has knowledge of the opportunity costs of his efforts.[20] This "technological imperative" would have added force in the hospital setting where the reproducible capital is provided by society.

Muller and Worthington have summarized this problem:

> The tendency of hospitals to duplicate facilities flows from their competition for doctors. The result is that unmet needs coexist with excess capacity, and the community loses services. The present relationship, in which doctors, although neither owners nor employees, have a voice in management decisions, may pass into history as a transitional form of hospital organization as more doctors assume full-time posts at hospitals. However, given the relative scarcity of doctors, the incentive for hospitals to try to provide doctors with technically optimal facilities will remain.[21]

The capital expenditure in these facilities exceeds those that the physician as an entrepreneur would be willing to make. As Penchansky and Rosenthal have suggested, the physician is capturing socially provided capital in his income.[22]

SPILLOVER EFFECTS

If a market is to function ideally, the goods, services, and factors of production must possess the characteristic called the exclusion property. Put simply, this means that for a good, service, or factor of production to be "exclusive," everyone but the buyer of the good must be excluded from the satisfactions it provides. For example, a pair of shoes is a good which is consistent with the exclusion principle. When one buys the shoes, he alone gets the satisfaction of wearing them. Conversely, medical education and research in a hospital are clearly not subject to the exclusion principle. In this regard, Robert Haveman has suggested the following:

> Commodities which are not subject to the exclusion principle are said to possess *spillover* effects. Their benefits and costs spill over onto third parties. When their effects are present, demand curves fail to capture the full costs. The demand curves, for example, would capture the willingness-to-pay of buyers of the good, but not the willingness-to-pay of those who are indirectly benefited through no action of their own.[23]

The relationship of this phenomenon to the services provided by the hospital cannot be overlooked.

MULTIPLE SOURCES OF FUNDING

Sources of funding for capital expenditures by hospitals are multiple. Generally, the funds are developed either internally through operating funds or externally through a number of sources. If the capital expenditure is a large one, sources of funding must normally be developed outside of the operating revenue. It is these external funds that are of concern here because internally generated funds are available for whatever use the hospital decides to put them;

[20]Victor R. Fuchs, "The Growing Demand for Medical Care," *New England Journal of Medicine*, 25 July 1968, pp. 190–195.

[21]"Factors Entering into Capital Decisions of Hospitals," *op. cit.*, p. 402.

[22]R. Penchansky and G. Rosenthal, "Productivity, Price, and Income in Physician's Services Market: A Tentative Hypothesis," *Medical Care*, December 1965, pp. 240–244.

[23]Haveman, *op. cit.*, p. 25.

the major consideration in deciding among uses for them being opportunity costs.

However, those funds from outside sources usually have certain restrictions on their use by the hospital. These restrictions ultimately will have to be taken into account in the decision-making process and may even make a cost—benefit analysis meaningless in extreme cases. Furthermore, these external funds will generally be obtained at different rates.

The basic criterion for the use of cost—benefit analysis is maximum net benefits. The presumption is that the goal of gaining the greatest value of output for resources (input) is desirable. It would be an exceptionally good approach to the decision among alternative uses of resources by hospitals if it were not restricted to comparing the dollar value of outputs and inputs. However, its usefulness is limited by the fact that the six problem areas as outlined above must be defined as explicitly as possible and included in the decision process.

FURTHER READINGS

"A Symposium on Hospital Financing." *Financial Management,* Spring 1972, pp. 41–47.

Comptroller General of the United States, *Study of Health Facilities Constructions Costs* made pursuant to Section 204 of the Comprehensive Health Manpower Training Act of 1971, (U.S. Government Printing Office, December 1972).

Feldstein, M. *Hospital Cost Inflation: A Study of Non-Profit Price Dynamics.* Harvard Institute of Economic Research, Discussion Paper, no. 139, October 1970.

Forsyth, G. and Thomas, D. "Models for Financially Healthy Hospitals." *Harvard Business Review,* May 1971, pp. 106–117.

Ginsburg, P. *Capital in Non-Profit Hospitals.* Ph.D. dissertation, Harvard University, 1971.

Haveman, R. H. "Benefit Cost Analysis: Its Relevance to Public Investment Decisions: Comment." *Quarterly Journal of Economics,* 1967, pp. 695–702.

Mass. "Benefit—Cost Analysis: Its Relevance to Public Investment Decisions." *Quarterly Journal of Economics,* 1966, pp. 208–226.

COST-EFFECTIVENESS ANALYSIS: IMPLICATIONS FOR ACCOUNTANTS

Barry G. King

Selection from among alternative uses of sizable, but limited, financial resources in order to meet stipulated, but often vague, objectives is a challenge to modern management of both private and public enterprise. Particularly challenging are those situations in which the immediate objectives of management cannot be conveniently reduced to the profit motive, so

Source. Copyright © 1970 by the American Institute of Certified Public Accountants, Inc. Reprinted with permission from *The Journal of Accountancy* (March, 1970), pp. 43–49.

that alternative means of meeting these objectives cannot be compared on the basis of relative profitability. Recent years have seen the development and refinement of a number of analytical approaches for meeting this challenge. A family of these approaches has become known under such names as (1) systems analysis, (2) cost-effectiveness analysis, (3) operations analysis, (4) cost—benefit analysis, (5) cost—utility analysis and (6) planning, programming, and budgeting system (PPBS). No attempt is made in this article to distinguish the shades of meaning in these terms as they are used in the field and in the literature. All refer to the attempt to apply a systematic, analytical approach to problems of choice. *Cost-effectiveness* analysis has been selected for this discussion, but much of what follows could be said about others of the group.

Cost-effectiveness is a term which has been used in a formal sense only in recent years. Wide publicity was given to the use of the technique in managing the activities of the Department of Defense under Robert McNamara. Many of the top people brought into the Defense Department by McNamara came from the Rand Corporation, where they had been working on problems concerning "the economics of defense,"[1] and where the formal approach had been developed.

In its narrowest sense, cost-effectiveness analysis may be defined as a technique for choosing among *given* alternative courses of action in terms of their cost and their effectiveness in the attainment of *specified* objectives. Treated as given by the analyst are: (1) A specific statement of objectives, (2) a complete listing of the alternative solutions to be considered, and (3) acceptable measures of effectiveness in meeting objectives. The decision-maker is viewed as a "higher-order" system who sets these constrains and for whom the analysis will provide informational inputs for making his choice.

In a broader sense, cost-effectiveness has been defined as simply a "technique for evaluating broad management and economic implications of alternative choices of action with the objective of assisting in the identification of the preferred choice."[2] Here the analyst takes a somewhat more general view of the decision-maker's problem and is concerned with (1) less explicitly stated objectives, (2)

undefined alternative solutions, and (3) more subjective measures of effectiveness.

For example, cost-effectiveness analysis may be applied in its narrower sense to the problem of deciding among three proposed aircraft systems. The objective may be one of providing capability of transporting personnel, with effectiveness to be measured in terms of the aircrafts' technical characteristics, such as payload, speed, and reliability.

On the other hand, the approach may be utilized in its broader sense, in the case where the objective above becomes one of providing personnel at key locations when needed. The alternatives for meeting this objective go far beyond three competing airplanes and involve strategies of personnel assignment as well as logistical considerations. Most of the more interesting problems arise in this latter, broader context, and it is this view of cost-effectiveness which is pursued in this article.

Two characteristics of the analysis deserve special emphasis. First, cost-effectiveness analysis is output-oriented. As such, decision situations are analyzed from a program, or mission, viewpoint rather than from a functional one. Problems are treated not as production, marketing, or financing problems but as problems in carrying out a specified program. The impact of this thinking is seen in the increasing tendency on the part of industrial firms to organize their activities, especially those of a planning nature, along project lines as opposed to the more traditional functional organization.

Second, the approach emphasizes effectiveness as opposed to technical economic efficiency in the allocation of resources. In a technical sense, resources are allocated efficiently when an increase in one output can be obtained only at a sacrifice of another output or with an increase in input, whereas effectiveness measures, in terms of an objective, the comparative desirability of alternative efficient allocations. For example, a company's computer and data processing system may operate effi-

[1]See Hitch, Charles J., and McKean, Roland N., *Economics of Defense in the Nuclear Age* (Cambridge: Harvard Press, 1960).
[2]Heuston, M. C., and Ogawa, G., "Observations on the Theoretical Basis of Cost Effectiveness," *Operations Research*, March—April 1966, pp. 242—266.

ciently, in that it operates 24 hours a day. Furthermore, it may be programmed to perform the tasks assigned to it efficiently. Any additional work required of the system will be at the sacrifice of some task it is currently performing. Still this efficient system may well be made more effective in meeting the objectives of the firm for the system by making changes in the makeup of its workload.

Most of the applications of cost-effectiveness analysis reported in the literature have dealt with governmental programs. This was to be expected because these programs require decisions for carrying out policies, the effectiveness of which cannot be measured in terms of profit. Cost-effectiveness analysis has provided a framework for aiding in these decisions. Now we are finding that more and more such decisions are being required of those in profit-oriented organizations. For example, business is being called upon to embark on programs of antipollution and training of the unemployed. Programs such as these cannot be evaluated on the basis of profitability to the individual firm but must be measured in terms of meeting social objectives. Thus cost-effectiveness will, I feel, be found to be increasingly valuable to the profit-seeking enterprise.

It is the purpose of this article to describe and illustrate the methodology of cost-effectiveness analysis in a nontechnical manner and to specify some implications that the approach seems to have for accountants.

METHODOLOGY

Although it may include the use of models developed as operations research techniques, cost-effectiveness analysis should not be considered as simply another OR tool or technique. Unlike such tools as mathematical programming and queuing theory, which are useful only in solving particular classes of problems which can be structured according to prescribed formats, cost-effectiveness analysis is designed to

yield solutions that are uniquely responsive to particular problems. It deals with problems which are ill-structured and which have objectives that are less precisely defined. Thus, the methodology of cost-effectiveness analysis cannot be set forth as a set of standard procedures, but must be outlined as a sequence of general steps which constitute an approach. These include:

1 Definition of objectives
2 Identification of alternatives
3 Selection of effectiveness measures
4 Development of cost estimates
5 Selection of a decision criterion
6 Creation of models relating cost and effectiveness.

Objectives

The beginning point for any analysis must be a consideration of objectives. Objectives, the desired goal (or goals) to be attained by the use of resources, must be defined as explicitly as possible. Careless selection and specification of objectives can lead to solution of the wrong problem. Much of the misunderstanding of U.S. defense policy, for example, seems to be related to misunderstanding of objectives. For instance, providing capability to *deter* attack reflects a different objective from providing capability to *repel* attack. In one case the attack is assumed to occur, while in the other the objective is precisely to prevent its occurrence. Thus given strategies may be effective in one case and not in the other.

For another example, reduction of traffic *fatalities* represents a different objective from a reduction of traffic accidents. Wearing seat belts has some effectiveness toward meeting the first objective, but none toward meeting the latter. Also, in industrial employee relations the objective of maintaining a stable size for the labor force is quite different from an objective of reducing employee turnover. In many cases the analyst can make a significant contribution by pointing out confusing or conflicting objectives.

Alternatives

The alternatives represent the competing "systems" for accomplishing objectives. They represent opposing strategies, policies, or specific actions as well as the necessary elements, such as materials, men, machines, etc. Even though certain elements or tactics may overlap, each alternative is viewed as a complete system. These alternatives need not be obvious substitutes for each other or perform the same specific function. Thus education, antipoverty measures, police protection, slum clearance, and various combinations of these, may all be alternatives in combating juvenile delinquency.[3] Creativity is needed to insure that as many legitimate alternatives as possible are considered. Often new ones are conceived as the analysis of the original alternatives is being performed.

Effectiveness Measures

Overall performance must be combined into appropriate measures that gauge the effectiveness of each alternative. Choosing appropriate measures of effectiveness is probably the most difficult, unique problem in cost-effectiveness analysis. The challenge is to provide measures that are relevant to the objective sought and measurable in terms that allow comparisons of effectiveness among alternatives.

The well-known story of the Soviet nail factory exemplifies the faulty results of optimizing irrelevant measures of effectiveness.[4] An objective of providing nails for a segment of Soviet industry was to be measured on the basis of weight of the output. Soon the factory optimized by producing only huge railroad spikes very efficiently. When the surplus of railroad spikes became quite large, the effectiveness measure was changed to quantity of items produced. The manager was able to quickly switch over to production of huge quantities of tiny tacks, brads, and staples, also very efficiently.

In order to compare alternatives, a single quantitative indicator of effectiveness would be the ideal. For example, to measure the effectiveness of a program having the objective of improving employee morale, one would like to have a means of quantitatively measuring "morale score." As is the case in most situations, such a single measure is not available. However, there are several factors which relate to employee morale which can be quantified to some degree—e.g., absenteeism, turnover, and grievances. These measures tempered with judgment concerning nonquantifiable aspects should lead to satisfactory comparisons of effectiveness of given alternatives.

Cost Estimates

To implement a given alternative, it is anticipated that certain resources must be used. Forgoing the use of these resources elsewhere represents a cost in the economic sense. Estimation of the cost of the alternatives constitutes a very important and difficult step in cost-effectiveness analysis.

Basically, two issues are involved: (1) what costs to include and (2) how to measure them. What is desired, of course, is an estimate of all *relevant* costs of each alternative. The concepts of sunk costs, incremental costs, and joint costs, all familiar to accountants, are applicable in the same manner as in traditional accounting analyses.

Many costs are general and can be ade-

[3]Quade, E. S., "Systems Analysis Techniques for Planning-Programming-Budgeting" in *Systems, Organizations, Analysis, Management: A Book of Readings*, edited by David I. Cleland and William R. King (New York: McGraw-Hill, 1969), p. 195.
[4]Niskanen, William A., "Measures of Effectiveness," *Cost-Effectiveness Analysis*, edited by Thomas A. Goldman (New York: Frederick A. Praeger, 1967), p. 20.

quately measured in terms of money. Long-range planning problems anticipate largely this type of cost. Often the only constrained resources being forgone are in the future, and, since money can be used to purchase these resources, it provides an adequate measuring tool. However, consideration should also be given to those costs for which money is not an entirely adequate measure. For instance, the cost in terms of human lives of specific defense alternatives can never be adequately measured in terms of money.

Sometimes a nonmonetary cost may be more rationally expressed as a negative factor in effectiveness, thus leaving the cost portion of the analysis in a "pure" money form. Thus instead of considering the loss of life by friendly forces as a cost, it may be more reasonable to consider it as a negative factor in measuring the effectiveness of a given defense alternative.

Selection of a Decision Criterion

The decision criterion is the standard by which all alternatives are evaluated in terms of cost and effectiveness. Three types of valid criterion from which the analyst must choose are: (1) maximize effectiveness at given cost; (2) minimize cost while attaining a given effectiveness; or (3) some combination of these two which recognizes a trade-off cost for effectiveness to maximize a selected utility function of the two factors (e.g., maximize effectiveness minus cost, where the two can be expressed in common terms). Many governmental objectives which are limited to fixed budgets are guided by the first criterion. Industrial firms may be guided by the second.

Adoption of an invalid criterion can be deceptively easy. For example, the statement "maximize effectiveness at a minimum cost" reflects a criterion that can seldom be met. It is not reasonable to believe that the best alternative from a number of feasible ones in terms of effectiveness will also be the one that costs the least. Also, the criterion—maximize the *ratio* of effectiveness to cost, or "effectiveness per dollar"—can also be seen to be invalid unless the ratio remains constant for all levels of activity. For example, an alternative which provides up to 10,000 square feet of warehouse space at a cost of $10 per square foot is not preferable over another alternative which provides up to 20,000 square feet at a cost of $15 per square foot if the objective is to produce a warehouse with 15,000 square feet of space. Obviously if the ratio, $ per square foot, remains constant at all levels of activity the ratio criterion is adequate. However, it provides no better criterion than the valid criterion mentioned above—minimize cost of providing 15,000 square feet of warehouse space.

Creation of Models

Having determined adequate measures of cost and effectiveness, and a criterion by which to compare alternatives, there remains the problem of formulating analytical relationships among costs, effectiveness, and environmental factors. Needed are cost models, effectiveness models, and a synthesizing model based on outputs from them.

Cost models attempt to describe relationships between the characteristics of a given alternative (system) and its costs. Thus the result of operating a cost model should be an estimate of the cost of each alternative. Effectiveness models attempt to describe relationships between an alternative's characteristics and its effectiveness. The result of operating an effectiveness model should be an estimate of the effectiveness of each alternative. Additionally, and very significantly, these models should provide trade-off relationships between system costs and characteristics as well as trade-offs between system effectiveness and characteristics. For example, besides outputt-

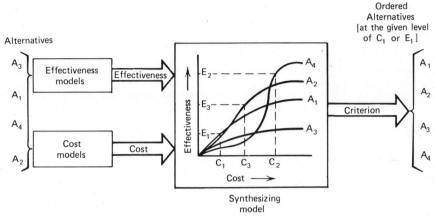

FIGURE 1 *Structure of cost-effectiveness analysis*

ing the fact that alternative A has characteristics X, Y, and Z with a cost of C, the cost model should provide relationships such as estimated marginal cost of changes in system characteristics. The synthesizing model should provide relationships between cost and effectiveness among alternatives. It should provide aid in answering such questions as: (1) How much effectiveness can be bought with an additional $X spent on alternative A? (2) What is the cost of a given increasee in the effectiveness of alternative B?

Model structure depends on how well the analyst knows the relationships which are to be expressed in the model, along with the complexity of the alternatives involved. If relationships are fairly well known, they may be expressed in algebraic terms and solved by use of the calculus. Other well-developed and understood techniques of operations research, such as mathematical programming and simulation, are available when applicable. Operational gaming may be used to determine less well-known relationships when the human element is crucial. Finally some relationships may be so uncertain that the only acceptable model is verbal.

Figure 1 is an attempt to depict in pictorial form the structure of the analysis.[5] In this figure, the curves relating cost and effectiveness permit illustration of both the criterion of maximizing effectiveness with given cost and minimizing cost of given effectiveness. For example, effectiveness is maximized with a given cost of C_1 by using alternative A_1 or with a given cost of C_2 by alternative A_4. Cost is minimized with a given effectiveness of E_3 by choosing alternative A_2. The ordered alternatives shown in the figure are the result of applying either criterion at the level of C_1 or E_1.

LIMITATIONS

Several limitations of cost-effectiveness analysis should be considered. First, it must be realized that all results are merely inputs to be judged along with other less systematic factors by a higher-level decision-maker. While the approach should emphasize consideration of as many factors as possible, there will always remain the necessity for the decision-maker to

[5]This illustration is adapted from one used by Quade, E. S., "Introduction and Overview," in Goldman, *Cost-Effectiveness Analysis, op. cit.,* p. 6.

exercise judgment of his own. The breadth of scope of the analysis allows a wide range of problems to be attacked; however, this leaves a good deal of the specifics to the analyst. Judgment is necessary to design the analysis, to determine alternatives, to delineate relevant factors and interrelationships, and to interpret the results. Quade summarizes this limitation by saying,

> No matter how we strive to maintain standards of scientific inquiry or how closely we attempt to follow scientific methods, we cannot turn cost-effectiveness analysis into science. Its objective, in contrast to that of science, is primarily to recommend—or at least to suggest—policy, rather than merely to understand and predict.[6]

A second limitation of the analysis is the difficulty in selecting measures of effectiveness. The best that can be done is to reasonably approximate objectives with measures which can aid in guiding decision-making. For example, employee welfare is an objective which everyone understands but which is extremely difficult to measure.

A third limitation results from imperfect information. Insufficient input information in terms of costs and benefits of various alternatives may result in an analysis that is misleading or downright erroneous. Neglect of benefits which are difficult to quantify or which occur in an indirect manner may lead to dismissal of some very advantageous alternatives. On the other hand, exclusion of costs which are difficult to quantify or which result indirectly may make undesirable alternatives seem desirable.

A final limitation which should be mentioned is the lack of a probability orientation in most cost-effectiveness analysis. Whereas several techniques for including probability factors in quantitative models have been developed in

an attempt to measure uncertainty, almost no use has been made of these in cost-effectiveness analysis.

IMPLICATIONS FOR ACCOUNTING

The foregoing has been very general and non-technical in an attempt simply to introduce some basic concepts of cost-effectiveness analysis. Avoided were the very relevant, but somewhat technical, aspects of the mathematics of maximization,[7] which is the basis for most of the quantitative models in the analysis. There appear to be some germane implications for accounting. These fall conveniently into four categories:

1. Implications for an expanded concept of organizational objectives.
2. Implications for an increased knowledge of quantitative management science.
3. Implications for design and operation of management information (data) systems.
4. Implications for more sophistication in cost estimation and forecasting.

Expanded Concept of Organization Objectives

Accountants have been performing a form of cost-effectiveness analysis for some time. Capital budgeting analysis, incremental cost analysis, and financial source selection are all decisions in which the basic cost-effectiveness aprpoach is used. All involve evaluation of alternatives for which return is compared with cost as a criterion for selection. The common factor which they exhibit is that effectiveness is measured in terms of return (profitability). Thus cost and effectiveness are stated in terms of a common denominator—dollars.

Modern management must initiate, plan,

---

[6]Quade, E. S., "Systems Analysis Techniques for Planning-Programming-Budgeting," *op. cit.*, p. 201.

[7]For a discussion of the "Mathematics of Maximization," see Hitch, Charles J., and McKean, Roland N., *op. cit.*, Appendix A.

and control activities which are designed to meet objectives which are not primarily profit-oriented and whose effectiveness cannot be adequately measured in dollars. Accountants must be willing and prepared to provide information about the perform analysis of such activities. This includes understanding and helping to define objectives explicitly as well as searching for adequate measures of effectiveness.

Perhaps even more significant for accountants than this responsibility to management for aid in their decision-making is an implied responsibility for external reporting of the results of such activities. Viewed as an institution in our society with goals other than financial ones, business enterprise is being asked to assume a more active part in programs of social action such as manpower training and development of urban areas. We see a trend toward increased protection for the consumer in demands for assurance of quality. Business has a responsibility to the general public in such areas as antipollution and conservation. Along with the responsibility for initiating and carrying out such programs is that of evaluating and reporting the results. Perhaps accountants will adopt a broader view and go beyond reporting on merely the financial objectives of the firm.

Quantitative Management Science

Several concepts of management science are exemplified in cost-effectiveness analysis. These serve to point out areas in which accountants should become knowledgeable. First, the accountant must understand the concept of a model and the modeling process, its uses and limitations. He needs to view models as descriptions or representations of the real world, quantitative or nonquantitative, which are valuable only to the extent that they accurately depict the situation. Also there needs to be the ability to conceptualize problems in an "input—output" format. That is, the accountant must take the approach which takes controllable variables as inputs and manipulates them to learn more about the uncontrollable variables, eventually resulting in an output which optimizes, or at least satisfies, the objectives.

Another valuable aspect of the mathematics in management science is the capacity to express and manipulate relationships in functional form. Cost-estimating relationships (CERs) are nothing more than functions which treat cost as a dependent variable and other factors as independent variables.

Information and Data Systems

Perhaps the weakest link in cost-effectiveness analysis is the "data gap." Models of cost and effectiveness are no better than the data used in developing them and as input to them. Too often, accurate timely data of the type needed are not available. Brussell has the following comment:

Today the modeling aspects of cost-effectiveness analysis are firmly entrenched. However, there has been a misallocation of research resources as between model building and data inputting or estimating. The conceptual problem of formulating models is relatively easy but probably more interesting and prestigious than the actual bird-dogging, collection, understanding, and estimation of grubby old numbers. There are undoubtedly increasing returns to analysis by improving the input numbers, both cost and performance data, whereas there are diminishing returns when the aim is at better models, cost models included.[8]

The same data gap exists in the use of most management science models and techniques. Information gathering, retrieval, processing,

[8]Brussell, Eugene R., "Defense Contractor Use of Cost-Effectiveness Analysis," in Goldman, *Cost-Effectiveness Analysis, op. cit.,* p. 114.

and dissemination are only now getting some of the attention which they deserve. Accountants, because of their interest in information and data processing, should be vitally concerned with development of systems which improve the quality of input data for decision models.

Cost Estimation

Cost-effectiveness analysis offers the challenge of estimating costs of activities which are unique and for which past cost data are unavailable. Here unavailability is not caused by the cost system, but the fact that the activity has not been tried before. More sophisticated estimating and forecasting techniques must be used. Effects on cost of many factors must be predicted. Accountants have for a long time realized the value of analytical techniques which employ the concept of variable costs. Thus the effect of volume on cost is well recognized. What has not been developed on the part of many accountants is the capability of analyzing costs in terms of other potential independent variables. Techniques of regression and correlation analysis should be mastered.

A related point involves the approach taken with regard to cost estimation. Accountants have traditionally taken a "micro" or "building block" view of cost estimating, based on the breakdown of cost present in the accounting system. Costs of the smallest elements into which costs can be divided are estimated and total cost is derived by aggregating these elementary costs. Such detailed procedures are rather expensive to employ and may not be very responsive to changes in parameters. Trade-off relationships between cost and effectiveness and between costs of two or more competing alternatives are difficult and time-consuming to determine. The alternative is to take a "macro" or "broad-brush" approach to estimating costs. This approach involves costing the total system in terms of its parameters, i.e., system characteristics and capabilities. For example, estimating costs of a new airplane may be done in terms of its speed, range, reliability, payload, etc., based on historical data for similar planes, as opposed to a detailed costing of all elements of labor, materials, indirect costs, etc., involved in designing and producing it. It should not be inferred that detailed costing procedures are of no value in cost-effectiveness. They still provide some valuable inputs to the cost model. The point is that accountants should be capable of taking the overall total systems view and become familiar with estimating techniques based thereon.

In summary, the framework for cost-effectiveness analysis has been outlined in a nontechnical manner. This form of analysis is being used extensively, although sometimes under other names, in government and will be used more extensively in the future in private enterprise. Therefore, accountants should be aware of it, its uses and limitations. These implications are certainly not brought about solely by cost-effectiveness analysis, but reflect some very significant directions for accounting to take as a result of current developments in management science.

THE BENEFITS AND COSTS OF METHADONE MAINTENANCE

Timothy H. Hannan

In recent years the number of heroin addicts receiving the treatment known as methadone maintenance has risen dramatically. Proponents of methadone programs have argued that by providing the heroin addict with methadone, a low-cost substitute for illegal heroin, methadone maintenance reduces the addict's need to engage in criminal activity, frees him to seek legal employment, and reduces his susceptibility to narcotic-related illnesses.

Despite this rapid expansion, however, the controversy surrounding methadone maintenance has not subsided. Although proponents speak glowingly of its successes, opponents point with alarm to its drawbacks. Indeed, in a recent issue of *The Public Interest*, Edward Epstein [11] pronounced treatment of heroin addicts by methadone maintenance a "forlorn hope." Unfortunately a simple description such as Epstein's, documenting how the performance of methadone programs falls short of exaggerated expectations, is of little use in determining public policy. Decisions to invest or not to invest in methadone programs require a comparison of the gains to be derived from methadone treatment and the costs of achiev-

ing those gains, not a simple enumeration of shortcomings. It is for this reason that the application of benefit−cost techniques to methadone maintenance treatment can prove useful to those interested in policy.

Few benefit−cost analyses of methadone-maintenance treatment have been attempted by economists, and of those attempted, excessive reliance has been placed on either subjective guesses or varying assumptions about program effectiveness.[1] This paper attempts to correct for these deficiencies by developing a benefit−cost analysis based on actual data generated by the nation's largest methadone-maintenance program. Policy considerations are then addressed in the light of the results obtained.

THE BENEFITS OF METHADONE TREATMENT

It is important to note at the outset that the impact of methadone treatment may go beyond merely altering the economic behavior of those individuals who actually enter the program. If, for example, the provision of methadone treatment results in a change in the price of heroin or induces a change in the number of new addicts created over time, the behavior of individuals not in the program may be of considerable importance in determining the total benefits and costs of methadone treatment.

In the empirical work to follow, it will be possible to capture only what will be termed the *direct benefits* of methadone treatment, i.e.,

Source. Copyright © 1976. Reprinted by permission of John Wiley & Sons, Inc., from *Public Policy* (Spring, 1976), pp. 197−226.

This article is drawn from the author's larger study of methadone maintenance treatment, *The Economics of Methadone Maintenance* (Lexington, Mass.: D. C. Heath and Company, 1975). For their helpful comments on substantive issues treated in this paper, the author would like to thank Eugene Smolensky, Robert Haveman, and Morgan Reynolds. The referees for the paper also made many valuable comments.

[1] For examples of the use of hypothesized outcomes in benefit−cost analyses of methadone-maintenance treatment, see Fernandez [12], Holahan [18], Jeffers and Johnson [20], and McGlothlin [22].

those benefits that result directly from the changed behavior of individuals who participate in the program. Once the benefit–cost calculations have been made, we will reconsider the indirect effects of methadone treatment and assess their importance in light of the results obtained.

Benefits will be presented from the standpoint of the maximum amount of money that members of society should be willing to pay for the provision of methadone treatment. This will be done by dividing society into several nonmutually exclusive groups and determining the value of methadone treatment to each group.

First, let us consider a group in society that can be called "potential victims of addict crimes" and ask what the value of methadone treatment is to these individuals. The total loss to potential victims of crime can be broken down into four basic areas: (1) the expenditures on private protection that potential victims find it necessary to make, (2) the value of forced transfers successfully extracted from them by criminal offenders, (3) the value of whatever property damage or physical injury results from criminal victimization, (4) the negative value placed on the fear and mental anguish brought on by crime. If methadone treatment is responsible for reduced crime, then potential victims are better off by whatever reduction in the sum of these four areas of loss occurs, and this reduced total loss should approximate the maximum amount they would be willing to pay for the existence of methadone treatment.[2] Note that the *exact* amount that potential victims should be willing to pay will depend, among other things, on their risk preference. Only if they are risk neutral will the reduction in

the sum of the above four areas of loss exactly measure improved welfare.

Taxpayers, as distinguished from potential victims, may also benefit from the provision of methadone treatment. First, taxpayers are better off by whatever reduction in criminal justice expenditures results from a methadone-induced reduction in crime. In addition, because taxpayers usually bear the medical costs of various narcotic-related illnesses and injuries sustained by heroin addicts, we can also regard the taxpayer as better off by whatever reduction in such expenditures results from methadone treatment.[3]

Because all individuals will be regarded as members of society, it is important that we also determine the value of methadone treatment to methadone patients themselves. Unfortunately, many of the elements of such a determination are unmeasurable.

The new methadone patient, for example, loses consumer satisfaction from reduced heroin consumption but gains consumer satisfaction from methadone consumption. As a heroin addict he suffers from frequent arrests and prison terms, periodic withdrawals, and constant health problems. As a methadone patient, however, he may face an undesirable amount of regulation, and it is not possible to determine how such considerations "balance out" in the addict's evaluation of his alternatives.

There are, however, some elements in the decision to enter treatment that are potentially quantifiable. Because methadone patients or-

---

[2]Note that because of high contracting costs, it is not reasonable to expect potential victims to make such a payment for the service of methadone treatment. Note also that there does exist some interdependence in these four areas of reduced loss. The degree to which private

protection expenditures are reduced in response to a methadone-induced reduction in crime, for example, will clearly affect the reduction in other losses from criminal victimization. This, however, does not alter the fact that the benefit to potential victims is the sum of whatever reduction in losses occurs.

[3]No distinction is made here between original taxpayers and new taxpayers created by the program. If by virtue of their increased earnings, program participants bear more of the tax burden, an additional improvement in the welfare of original taxpayers will result.

dinarily pay nothing for methadone, an addict entering treatment is, ceteris paribus, better off by the reduction in the cost of his heroin consumption. In addition, if as a result of methadone treatment he shifts his labor services from criminal activity to legal employment (and abstracting from changes in leisure), he is better off by his increased legal earnings and worse off by the resulting decrease in illegal "earnings." Assuming that the unmeasurable considerations mentioned above roughly balance out, we will use these measures to approximate the improved welfare of methadone patients. To the extent that the unmeasurable considerations do not balance out, then these measures represent simply a rough proxy for the actual value that methadone patients place on methadone treatment.

These derived measures of increased welfare on the part of potential victims, taxpayers, and methadone patients are presented in the following list.[4]

THE DIRECT BENEFITS OF METHADONE TREATMENT

1 Benefits to Potential Victims
   a. Decrease in private protection expenditures
   b. Decrease in the value of damage to victim resources
   c. Decrease in the value of forced transfers
   d. Decrease in the negative value placed on fear and mental anguish
2. Benefits to Taxpayers
   a. Decrease in criminal justice expenditures
   b. Decrease in medical expenditures for narcotic-related illnesses

3. Benefits to Methadone Patients
   a. Decrease in expenditures on heroin
   b. Increase in legal earnings, minus the decrease in illegal earnings

In jumping from a theoretical discussion of program benefits to the actual implementation of a benefit–cost analysis, the form and availability of data will require several compromises with reality. It will not be possible, for example, to measure the decrease in private protection expenditures of potential victims, the decrease in damages to victim resources, or the value of reduced fear and mental anguish resulting from a reduction in crime. In addition, because addict illegal activity is aimed primarily at obtaining a forced transfer from victims, we will assume that the decrease in illegal "earnings" of methadone patients exactly equals the decrease in forced transfers extracted from victims.[5] These two categories appear in the above list with opposite values, and thus drop out of the calculation, leaving the following empirically measurable direct benefits of methadone treatment.

THE EMPIRICALLY MEASURABLE DIRECT BENEFITS OF METHADONE TREATMENT

1. Decrease in criminal justice expenditures
2. Decrease in medical expenditures for narcotic-related illnesses
3. Decrease in expenditures on heroin
4. Increase in legal earnings

---

[4]In addition to the benefits attributed to potential victims, taxpayers, and methadone patients, it is also likely that society as a whole places a positive value on reduced crime beyond any of the considerations mentioned thus far.

[5]This is clearly not true if the role of the fence is introduced into the analysis, but the end result can be the same. With the complication of the fence introduced, the equivalent assumption is that the decrease in illegal earnings of methadone patients and fences exactly equals the decrease in forced transfers extracted from victims. It is possible, however, that stolen goods are valued less because they are "hot." If this is true, then the decrease in forced transfers extracted from victims will exceed the decrease in illegal earnings of methadone patients plus fences, and the measurement procedure may understate program benefits as a result.

Note that the decreased cost of heroin consumption is presented as a benefit of methadone treatment.[6] This value will overstate the true social benefit of reduced heroin consumption if (1) monopoly rents exist in the heroin trade (in which case the reduction in consumption will leave the seller of heroin worse off) or (2) resources released from the heroin trade flow into other illegal pursuits (in which case victims of these crimes will be left worse off). Because of these possibilities, the benefit of reduced heroin consumption must be taken as something less than the reduction in heroin expenditures, and we must treat it accordingly in the calculation.

Interpreting the benefit associated with reduced criminal justice expenditures must also be approached with great care, because a reduction in criminal justice expenditures brought on by a decrease in crimes committed by methadone patients may change the level of enforcement faced by other criminal offenders and hence the involvement of these others in criminal activity. If we could constrain enforcement authorities to keep constant the amount of resources devoted to each criminal offense in the face of such a reduction in crime, then the total decrease in crime would be no more or less than the decreased number of crimes committed by methadone patients (because other criminal offenders would presumably face the same level of deterrence). Under such an artifical constraint, the *criminal justice benefit* could then be measured by the value of criminal justice resources formerly devoted to crimes eliminated by methadone treatment.

In reality, of course, enforcement authorities are free to maintain such resources in the criminal justice system and use them to deter or prevent other crimes. In this case, part or all of the criminal justice benefit would be in the form of reduced crimes committed by other members of society. Following a standard assumption treated by Gary Becker and others, it will be assumed that society acts to minimize the sum of damages inflicted by crime plus the cost of enforcement designed to reduce such damages.[7] This assumption means that even if enforcement authorities do not release all criminal justice resources devoted to crimes eliminated by methadone treatment, we can calculate the benefit as if they did and know that the resulting measure is if anything an underestimate of the true criminal justice benefit.

THE COSTS OF METHADONE TREATMENT

As do all types of economic activities, methadone programs must employ scarce resources to generate the potential benefits associated with their operation. To the extent that such resources could have been employed productively in other pursuits, their diversion to methadone treatment represents a true social cost.

In general, methadone programs employ a wide range of personnel, including, physicians, supervisors, counselors, nurses, and clerk typists. In addition to paying the salaries of these individuals, funds are expended on rent, supplies, methadone, and pharmacy services. Besides expenses related specifically to the distribution of methadone, expenditures are made on central administrative functions and, in the case of some of the larger programs, on legal and data-collection services. Assuming that these program expenditures measure the true opportunity costs of the factors employed, program accounting data will be used to measure true program costs.[8]

---

[6]Because we will count the costs of providing patients with methadone, the decreased cost of providing them with heroin should clearly be treated as a benefit.

[7]See Becker [2] for a discussion of observable phenomena consistent with this assumption.

[8]Note that other potential costs of methadone maintenance, such as those associated with its impact on the addict death rate and its effect on the number of new addicts created, will be discussed in a later section.

METHODOLOGY

It has been noted that for many reasons, both theoretical and empirical, it is not possible to measure all of the benefits of methadone treatment. Because of lack of data, some potential benefits, such as the value of reduced fear and mental anguish on the part of potential victims of crime, must be totally excluded from the calculation. Others, such as the criminal justice benefit, can be measured only partially. Because of this and because of other sources of benefit underestimates to be encountered below, it will be necessary to follow a research strategy in which the aim is to compare only a minimum measure of program benefits with a full measure of program costs. Thus, whenever uncertainty presents itself, a deliberate attempt will be made to err on the side of conservatism in measuring program benefits.

THE PROGRAM AND ITS PARTICIPANTS

For our benefit–cost calculation, we will focus on New York City's Methadone Maintenance Treatment Program (MMTP). This program is particularly suited to our purposes, for it is the largest program in the nation and provides operational patient performance data for more years than does any other program. In addition, since 1965 data from the MMTP have been collected and reported by an independent evaluation unit at the Columbia University School of Public Health and Administrative Medicine. This should increase confidence in the reliability of the data.

It is important to note that patients receiving treatment in the numerous clinics of the MMTP are a selected group in several respects. First, an attempt is made to exclude from the program both overtly psychotic addicts and addicts with multiple drug dependence.[9] In addition, although admission to the program is totally voluntary, an addict must be at least 18 years old with a minimum of two years of known heroin addiction to qualify for admission. Perhaps as a result of such admission requirements, the age and ethnic distribution of program participants are somewhat different from those of the addict population in general. The average age of patients at time of admission to the program is 33.2 years, whereas that reported by the New York City Narcotics Register is only 28.6 years. Moreover, the ratio of whites to blacks in treatment is somewhat greater than that found in the general addict population. Thus, it is important to remember that in at least some respects, MMTP patients do not represent an unbiased sample of the addict population. This point must be kept in mind in generalizing the results of our bene-fit–cost analysis and in considering its policy implications.

THE CHOICE OF CONTROL GROUPS

Patient performance characteristics such as arrest rates and legal earnings can be directly or indirectly obtained from MMTP data. The question arises, however, as to how we should measure what patient performance would have been in the absence of the program. Two alternatives are available. (1) We can measure the performance over time of a group of heroin addicts who have not expressed interest in entering the program but whose personal characteristics correspond closely to those of the program participants, or (2) we can simply measure the performance of program participants before they entered the program.

Both procedures are subject to legitimate criticism. Using a group of similar addicts as a control group may result in an overestimate of program benefits if, as seems likely, those

---

[9]See [4], p. 149. Overtly psychotic addicts are not generally considered a significant portion of the addict population. The problem of multiple drug dependencies, however, is

much more prevalent and hence more significantly limits the generality of the results.

addicts who enter and remain in methadone treatment are more highly motivated than those who do not. Likewise, the simple comparison of patient performance before and after admission to the program may result in a biased estimate for at least three different reasons. (1) If individuals enter the program because of a temporarily low level of performance, the results of the before-and-after comparison will not only include the true impact of treatment, but will also register the improvement in patient performance as they recover from their temporarily low level of performance. (2) Changes in environmental variables over time—variables such as employment opportunity, the probability of arrest, and the price of heroin—may affect performance and thus bias the measurement of the program's true impact. (3) Finally, certain personal characteristics, such as age and the duration of addiction, vary over time and may thus cause changes in individual performance that should not be attributed to the program.

Because the before-and-after comparison is relatively attractive from the standpoint of data requirements, it is important that we examine more closely these three potential problem areas. First, the distinction between temporary and long-term behavior outlined above is not regarded as a significant source of bias in the case of MMTP methadone treatment, for there is little evidence that heroin addicts apply to the program because of a temporary reduction in performance—a lost job or a reduction in income, for example.[10] Changing environmental variables and changing personal characteristics over time, however, may indeed distort the results of the before-and-after comparison, and the bias introduced is likely to be in the direction of benefit underestimation.

In regard to the influence of environmental changes over time, it is important to note that because of the years for which MMTP data are available, any comparison will be limited primarily to the years 1967 through 1971—a period during which the New York City unemployment rate, the probability of being arrested for a property offense, and the price of heroin were generally increasing.[11] Because the before-and-after comparison will register the increase in unemployment and in reported arrests associated with such changes over time, it should for this reason understate related benefits of methadone treatment.

Changes in such personal characteristics as age and the duration of addiction may also cause the comparison to understate program benefits. In regard to criminal activity and heroin comsumption, it is important to note that the daily cost of an addict's habit and his participation in criminal activity generally rise with the number of years of addiction.[12] Because the "before" situation may thus underestimate criminal activity and heroin consumption that would have taken place in the absence of treatment, the effect of treatment in reducing criminal activity and heroin consumption may thus be understated. In regard to legal employment, data covering the employment of addicts entering the MMTP indicate that older heroin addicts do not exhibit higher rates of employment than do younger addicts.[13] Thus to the extent that changing personal characteris-

---

[10]This is supported by the employment histories of MMTP patients, which show no evidence of a temporary reduction in employment during the period immediately preceding admission. See [13], p. 534.

[11]The New York City unemployment rate increased from 3.7% in 1967 to 5.3% in 1971 [23]. The upward trend in the probability of arrest over time was calculated from data taken from the Annual Reports of the New York City Police Department for the years 1967, 1968, and 1969 [27]. That the price of heroin has been rising over time is a judgment on the part of the Bureau of Narcotics and Dangerous Drugs [6].

[12]These relationships have been demonstrated empirically from data gathered and reported by a number of drug treatment programs. See [17] for more detail.

[13]See [14], p. 14.

tics bias the results of the before-and-after comparison, the distortion is again likely to be in the direction of benefit underestimation.[14]

We have emphasized the need to err on the side of a conservative measurement of program benefits whenever uncertainty presents itself. We have also noted that using similar addicts as a control group may overestimate program benefits. Because the before-and-after comparison should if anything understate the benefits of methadone treatment, we will rely on this method of control in measuring program benefits.

THE BENEFIT—COST CALCULATION

The patient performance data to be used in the calculation will be taken primarily from periodic reports authored by Frances R. Gearing, chairman of the independent Methadone Maintenance Evaluation Unit charged with gathering and reporting such data. In the calculation we will follow the progress of a cohort of 1,230 patients admitted to the MMTP between 1964 and 1968, inclusive. Of this group 85% were male, 15% were female; 40% were white, 40% were black, and 20% were of Spanish extraction. As with most patients in the MMTP, members of this cohort can generally be termed "hard core" addicts, for they experienced an average of 8 years of addiction before admission to the program and exhibited extensive criminal records.

Although the concept of methadone maintenance requires the continued supply of methadone to heroin addicts under supervised conditions, many patients do eventually leave the program, and it will not be possible to ascribe benefits to these patients once they have dropped out. A number of follow-up studies

TABLE 1
The Estimated Number of Cohort Patients in
Treatment at the Beginning of Each Year of Treatment

At Admission	2nd Year	3rd Year	4th Year	5th Year	6th Year	7th Year
1,230	1,093	983	866	814[a]	782[a]	743[a]

[a]Derived by assuming a 6% dropout rate in the fourth year, a 4% rate in the fifth year, and a 5% rate in the sixth year.
Source: Frances R. Gearing, "Methadone Treatment Five Years Later—Where Are They Now?" (Paper presented at the One Hundreth Annual Meeting of the American Public Health Association, Atlantic City, N.J., November 13, 1972), Figure 2.

have found that patients discharged from methadone-maintenance treatment generally return to heroin consumption and the drug-centered way of life.[15] Because of this and because data from such studies are not sufficiently detailed for the present purpose, it will be assumed that all benefits, as well as costs, cease once an individual has left the program. Therefore it is crucial that we determine how many cohort patients remain in the program for each year of treatment. This information can be derived from MMTP data and is presented in Table 1. Because many patients had not entered the program early enough to have reached the fifth, sixth, and seventh years of treatment by March 31, 1972 (the last date of observation), figures for these years were derived by use of dropout rates registered by those in the program for these greater lengths of time.[16]

The Increase in Legal Earnings

Unfortunately, patient earnings data are not available from the MMTP and must be derived from the rather extensive employment data

[14]This argument does not account for the possibility that some heroin addicts become unhooked in later years. This is obviously an important issue and will be discussed more fully below.

[15]For a follow-up study of patients, discharged from the MMTP, see [15].
[16]The dropout rates for the fourth, fifth, and sixth years were 6%, 4%, and 5%, respectively. See [14], p. 9.

gathered from patient employment records and reported by Frances Gearing. Table 2 presents the percentage of cohort patients who were employed, in training, or considered homemakers on the date of admission and on the date of March 31, 1972.

The two distributions presented in Table 2 represents the earliest and latest dates on which such employment data are available for our cohort.[17] Although employment data for intermediate points in time are not available for the cohort of 1,230 patients, such data are presented for a cohort of 1,000 men and another of 325 women admitted to the program through December 31, 1969 (see Tables 3 and 4). Because these cohorts should include most of the members of our study cohort, they can be used to approximate the employment percentages that our 1,230 patients were registering for intermediate periods of treatment. Table 5 presents the results of extrapolating from these two cohorts to our study cohort of 1,230 patients.[18]

The only before-treatment employment data refer to the percentage of patients employed upon admission. Other types of employment data gathered from the MMTP have indicated a small rise in employment during the period immediately preceding admission[19]—a result often attributed to increased motivation as prospective patients wait for admission. If true, use of employment upon admission as a control will for this reason also tend to understate program benefits.

[17]Although all patients entered the program during the period 1964–1968, it should be noted that the vast majority of admissions were confined to the years 1967 and 1968.
[18]Because the study cohort is 85% male and 15% female, employment percentages for intermediate points in time in Tables 3 and 4 were combined in these proportions to approximate the employment percentages of our 1,230 patients for intermediate points in time. Note that because the two cohorts presented in Tables 3 and 4 provide so few observations of patients in the program for 4 years or more, these cohorts have not been chosen for separate study.
[19]See [16], p. 15.

TABLE 2

Percent of Patients Employed, Considered Homemakers, or in Training—on Admission and on March 31, 1972

	On Admission	March 31, 1972
Employed	33%	74%
Homemakers	1	4
In training	2	4
	$N = 1,230$	$N = 810$

Source. Gearing, "Methadone Treatment Five Years Later," Figure 3.

A common and quite legitimate criticism of the way the Methadone Maintenance Evaluation Unit reports this type of data involves the question of "creaming." As can be seen from Table 5, the percentage of patients employed upon admission was obtained from all 1,230 individuals, whereas because of the dropout problem, the percentage of patients employed at later dates were calculated for fewer individuals. If creaming is in evidence, then those individuals who remain in the program have a higher employment percentage on admission than do those who drop out. This means that the use of such admission data would underestimate the employment upon admission of patients in the program and therefore would overestimate their employment gains.

Fortunately, data exist by which we can adjust for the problem. Of those 810 individuals who remained in the program as of March 31, 1972, it can be determined from other MMTP data that approximately 41% were either employed, in training, or considered homemakers upon admission.[20] As can be seen from Table 5, the equivalent figure for all 1,230 members of the cohort is 36%, a difference of 5%. To ensure that no such bias toward benefit overestimation enters the calculation because of creaming, the percentage employed upon admission will be

[20]See [14].

TABLE 3
Employment Status and School Attendance for a
Cohort of 1,000 Men Admitted through December 31, 1969

	At Admission	6 mo.	12 mo.	18 mo.	24 mo.	30 mo.	36 mo.	42 mo.	48 mo.
Employed	26%	51%	61%	63%	67%	67%	70%	68%	82%
In training	?	3	4	4	5	6	6	5	4
N =	1,000		964		673		408		180

Source. Frances R. Gearing, "Methadone Maintenance Treatment Program, Progress Report Through March 31, 1971—A Five Year Overview," Report of the Methadone Maintenance Evaluation Unit, Columbia University School of Public Health and Administrative Medicine (New York, May 19, 1971), Figure 3.

TABLE 4
Employment Status and School Attendance for a
Cohort of 325 Women Admitted through December 31, 1969

	At Admission	6 mo.	12 mo.	18 mo.	24 mo.	30 mo.	36 mo.	42 mo.	48 mo.
Employed	18%	30%	35%	34%	42%	45%	46%	46%	
Homemaker	16	15	25	28	36	33	27	24	
In training	0	4	6	5	4	4	3	2	
N =	325			260	135	84	14		

Source. Gearing, "Progress Report Through March 31, 1971," Figure 4.

TABLE 5
Actual and Estimated Employment Status and School
Attendance for a Cohort of 1,230 Patients Admitted During the Period 1964–1968

	At Admission	6 mo.	12 mo.	18 mo.	24 mo.	30 mo.	36 mo.	42 mo. or more
Employed	33% (38%)	49%	57%	59%	63%	64%	67%	74%
Homemaking	1	2	4	4	5	5	4	4
In training	2	3	4	4	5	6	6	4
	N = 1,230	1,102[a]	1,093	1,038[a]	983	925[a]	866	

[a]Calculated as the average of the number of patients in the program at the beginning and end of each 12-month period.

adjusted upward by 5%. This change is noted in parentheses in Table 5.

Despite numerous shortcomings, the data presented in Table 5 can be used to obtain a minimum estimate of increased patient earnings attributable to methadone treatment. First, a minimum estimate of the average employment for each 6-month period of treatment can be approximated by the employment percentage observed at the beginning of each period. Next, the average number of cohort patients in the program for each 6-month period can be approximated by the average of the number of patients at the beginning and end of each period. With this information, we can calculate the employment-months registered by cohort patients for each 6-month period of treatment and (from before-treatment data) the employment months they would have registered in the absence of the program.

Earnings per employment-month, both with and without treatment, can be approximated by use of two different data sources. First, information is available on the occupational distribution of our cohort patients both upon admission and after admission to the program.[21] In addition, from the 1970 Population and Housing Census [5], we can obtain the median monthly earnings, by occupation, of workers who reside in New York City's low-income areas. Assuming that the occupational earnings of such individuals are roughly representative of the earnings of cohort patients who worked in the same occupations, we can use these data, along with the estimate of employment-months and the average number of patients in each 6-month period, to calculate increased earnings for each 6-month period of treatment. The results of this calculation are presented in Table 6.[22]

TABLE 6

Increased Legal Earnings, Criminal Justice Cost Savings, and the Value of Reduced Heroin Consumption by Period in Treatment for a Cohort of 1,230 Patients

Period in Treatment	Increased Earnings	Criminal Justice Cost Savings	Value of Reduced Heroin Consumption
0−5 + mo.	$0,000,000	$703,000	$3,456,000
6−11 + mo.	414,000	664,000	3,260,000
12−17 + mo.	707,000	708,000	3,078,000
18−23 + mo.	745,000	673,000	2,922,000
24−29 + mo.	852,000	667,000	2,757,000
30−35 + mo.	840,000	626,000	2,589,000
36−41 + mo.	874,000	608,000	2,465,000
42−47 + mo.	1,049,000	593,000	2,405,000
48−53 + mo.	1,016,000	574,000	2,329,000
54−59 + mo.	999,000	564,000	2,289,000
60−65 + mo.	973,000	550,000	2,231,000
66−72 + mo.	961,000	544,000	2,202,000

Note that because of the care taken to ensure a conservative estimate, no increased earnings are ascribed to the first 6 months of treatment. This is because the employment and earnings attributed to each period of treatment actually refer to the first day of each period. The first day of the first period is the day of admission; hence no benefit is assigned to the first 6 months of treatment. Because employment and the occupational distribution "improve" with time in the program, this procedure will underestimate the increased earnings attributable to other periods of treatment as well. Finally, it should be noted that after 48 months of treatment, the measure of increased legal earnings decreases with time in the program. This is due solely to the fact that fewer

---

[21]See [14].

[22]In the interest of ensuring a conservative estimate, only the typically lower occupational earnings of black residents of New York City's low-income areas were used to repre-

sent the earnings of employed cohort patients. The median earnings of female black private household workers were used to obtain what is regarded as a minimum estimate of the value of homemaking services. See [17] for a fuller discussion.

patients remain in the program for successive periods of treatment.[23]

The Criminal Justice Benefit

As argued above, the costs of criminal justice resources formerly devoted to crimes eliminated by methadone treatment can be regarded as a minimum measure of the criminal justice benefit. Such a measure can be obtained by first calculating the reduced number of arrests and incarcerations by type of offense attributable to the treatment of our 1,230 cohort patients over time. According to data reported by Frances Gearing, members of the cohort were arrested an average of 3.5 times in the 3-year period prior to admission.[24] It can also be determined from similar data that the arrest rate for the first year of treatment was approximately 81% lower than the before-treatment arrest rate, 92% lower for the second year, 96% lower for the third year, and 98% lower for the fourth and later years of treatment.[25] It should be warned that this rather dramatic decline in the arrest rate may be overstated if creaming is in evi-

dence, in which case at least some of the decline is due to the more criminally inclined individuals' dropping out of the program. However, most of the arrest reduction occurs during the first year of treatment, when (as can be seen from Table 5) few patients have dropped out of the program. Thus it is likely that such a bias, if it exists, is relatively small. Because of this and because a more detailed study of 119 MMTP patients by Cushman [7] shows similar results, these estimates will be regarded as a reasonable approximation. The arrest reduction *by type of offense* for each period can be calculated from arrest breakdowns obtained by Cushman [7] and Langrod and Lowinson [21] from police records of methadone patients before and after admission to the program.[26]

With this information and our knowledge of the number of cohort patients in treatment for each 6-month period, we can estimate the reduction in arrests by type of offense for each 6-month period of treatment. From MMTP data on the average sentence length and the proportion of arrest resulting in incarcerations both before and after admission, we can also derive the reduction in jail-days and court appearances for each period of treatment.[27]

Data on the average variable costs of police, courts, and correction that are attributable to various types of offenses are available from several sources. This information can be applied to our estimated reduction in arrests, court appearances, and jail-days to obtain a minimum measure of the criminal justice cost savings resulting from methadone treatment. To approximate New York City police costs, we will use estimates obtained by Blumstein and Larson [3] from a linear activity model of police

---

[23]A problem encountered in many applications of benefit–cost analysis involves the possibility that increased employment is achieved by displacing other workers in an underemployed economy. In the present case, however, the results of the benefit–cost calculation can be shown to be relatively unaffected even by very extreme assumptions concerning the magnitude of this displacement effect. See [17] for more detail. It should also be noted that a few patients work within the program itself, and it is arguable that counting their earnings as a program benefit is not appropriate. Because their earnings also show up as program costs and because in any case they represent a very small percentage of all patients, omitting this consideration is not regarded as serious.

[24]See [14], p. 3. These data were obtained both from patient interviews and from the New York City Department of Health's Narcotics Register, which collects arrest data for New York City narcotics addicts.

[25]Because arrests occurring during treatment are not reported for our cohort of 1,230 patients, these percentage reductions in the rate of arrest refer specifically to a cohort of 1,000 men and a cohort of 325 women, both of which significantly overlap with our study cohort. See [15.b, p. 6.

[26]See [17] for more detail.

[27]Unfortunately, the number of court appearances cannot be obtained directly from MMTP sources. We can, however, calculate directly the reduction in incarcerations. Because addicts incarcerated must have passed through the courts, this number is used as a minimum estimate of the reduced number of court appearances.

operations. Because of the lack of New York City court data, New York City court costs will be approximated by estimates obtained from Holahan's rather detailed study of 1969 Washington, D.C., court costs [19]. Correctional costs per jail-day can be obtained from estimates of the New York State Department of Corrections as reported by Cushman [8]. From these data we can calculate an approximate criminal justice cost savings of $1,265 associated with a reduction of one arrest.[28] The criminal justice cost savings obtained by applying this figure to the estimated reduction in arrests over time for the 1,230 members of our cohort are presented in Table 6. Because the costs of an addict's habit and hence his involvement in criminal activity generally increase over time, and because the criminal justice cost data do not reflect fixed costs, these estimates are expected if anything to understate the full long-run criminal justice cost savings attributable to methadone treatment.

The Medical Cost Savings

There also exists evidence to indicate that methadone patients experience a substantial reduction in the incidence of narcotic-related illnesses. A study of 81 patients in the MMTP's St. Luke's methadone clinic, for example, found that whereas 12 days were spent in the hospital during the year prior to treatment as a result of narcotic-related illnesses, no such hospital-days occurred during the year after admission to the program [8]. From data on the cost per hospital-day of such treatment, it is possible to estimate the resulting medical cost savings. Because, however, there is little information on how such medical problems vary

---

[28]Because of a number of conservative assumptions involved in calculating police and court cost savings, the estimate for correctional cost savings, which is regarded as the best of the three cost estimates, accounts for nearly 90% of this figure. See [17] for a fuller discussion.

over time, it will not be possible to calculate this benefit for our cohort of 1,230 patients, and its omission should be considered yet another source of benefit underestimation.

The Value of Decreased Heroin Consumption

To estimate the reduction in heroin consumption caused by methadone maintenance treatment, we will rely on a 1969 study of 174 MMTP methadone patients. In this study urine analyses were conducted three times weekly for the first full year in treatment. According to Dole, Nyswander, and Warner [10], the directors of the study, 55% of the patients did not show a single positive result for self-administered heroin. On the other hand, a minority of about 15% continued to use heroin intermittently (e.g., on weekends).

In order to make these results operational, it will be assumed that the 15% intermittent users consumed heroin half of the time and that the remaining 30% used heroin one-fourth of the time. In total, then, this group of 174 methadone patients appear to have consumed approximately 15% of a full year's consumption of heroin during the year of observation.

In determining heroin consumption in the absence of the program, it is important to realize that addicts do not consume heroin every day of the year. For example, from our knowledge of the incarceration rate and average sentence length, we can deduce that the typical methadone patient spent approximately 25% of his time in jail during the period preceding admission to the program. To obtain a conservative estimate of the amount of heroin consumed in the absence of the program, it will be assumed that no heroin is consumed during incarceration. In addition, a study of patients from the MMTP's St. Luke's clinic indicates that patients spent approximately 4% of the last premethadone year in voluntary abstinence [8]. We will thus assume that in the absence of the program, approximately 29% of the year would have been spent in abstinence, giving us an estimated reduction in heroin consumption caused by methadone treatment of approximately 56% of a full year's consumption.

An estimate of the mean daily cost of a heroin habit can be obtained from a sample of 5.804 addicts under the care of New York's Narcotics Addiction Control Commission as of March 31, 1969 [26]. Applying this figure ($28.32) to the estimated reduction in heroin consumption resulting from methadone treatment, we can approximate the market value of reduced heroin consumption for our cohort over time. The results of this calculation are also presented in Table 6.

Because the cost of an addict's habit typically increases over time in the absence of treatment, these estimates should if anything understate the reduced value of heroin consumption attributable to the program. We have noted, however, that the social benefit of reduced heroin consumption will be less than the market value of reduced consumption if (1) monopoly rents exist in the heroin trade or (2) resources released from the heroin trade flow into other criminal pursuits. Inasmuch as we do not know the extent to which these factors are operating, we will be able to present this benefit only in the form of a likely range. Thus, the benefit will be calculated under the varying assumptions that all, half, and none of the value of reduced heroin consumption results in a social benefit.

Program Costs

In determining the costs of treating 1,230 patients over time, we must introduce a complication not explicitly considered up to now. Until 1969, most patients were introduced into the program by a process known as inpatient induction. This means that new patients underwent 4 to 6 weeks of residential care in order

TABLE 7

Estimated Costs of Treating a Cohort of 1,230 Patients by Period in Treatment, Inpatient Induction

Period in Treatment	Treatment Costs
0–5 + mo.	$3,000,000
6–11 + mo.	856,000
12–17 + mo.	799,000
18–23 + mo.	758,000
24–29 + mo.	716,000
30–35 + mo.	672,000
36–41 + mo.	640,000
42–47 + mo.	624,000
48–53 + mo.	605,000
54–59 + mo.	594,000
60–65 + mo.	579,000
66–72 + mo.	572,000

to be gradually converted from heroin to a stable maintenance level of methadone. Since 1969, the vast majority of new methadone patients have undergone ambulatory induction, which requires no such residential treatment. Because this initial residential phase of treatment is quite expensive, it is important that it be treated explicitly. According to the New York State Executive Budget [24], this residential phase of treatment cost in 1969 about $1,850 per addict, whereas the regular outpatient treatment cost about $1,500 per patient year.[29]

Assuming that all patients were inpatient inductees, we can construct the costs of treating the cohort of 1,230 patients by period in treatment. The results of this calculation are presented in Table 7.

Available evidence from the MMTP indicates that the performance of patients inducted on an ambulatory basis is very similar to that of

[29]These costs include expenditures for rent, salaries, methadone, and pharmacy and other auxiliary services; and, as far as can be determined, include all relevant costs of the program. For more detail, see Program Audit 2.2.71 reported by New York State's Legislative Commission on Expenditure Review [25].

patients who have undergone the more expensive inpatient induction process.[30] Because most patients are now inducted on an ambulatory basis, it is important for policy purposes that we also perform a benefit—cost calculation under the assumption that all patients are ambulatory inductees.[31] Applying this assumption will mean that the costs of treating the 1,230 cohort patients for the first 6 months of treatment is $897,000 instead of the $3,000,000 registered in Table 7. The costs for later periods of treatment will remain the same.

The Results of the Benefit—Cost Calculations

It is possible to make many different benefit—cost calculations under varying assumptions about discount rates and about the relevant benefits and costs to be included in the calculation. To be conservative we will use throughout the calculations a 10% annual rate of time discount (or approximately 4.88% for each 6-month period). Calculations will be made under the two assumptions of total inpatient induction and total ambulatory induction and under three varying assumptions concerning the magnitude of the benefit of reduced heroin consumption.

Because we do not have observations of individuals who have been in the program more than 6 years, the stream of benefits and costs listed thus far refer only to the first 6 years of treatment. Many cohort patients will undoubtedly remain in the program for periods longer than 6 years, and we will for this reason consider two types of calculations—one for the 6-year period for which data are available and the other projected for a much longer period of time.

The results of projecting benefits and costs

well past the 6-year time horizon must be regarded as more tenuous, for among other things less is known about performance in the absence of the program for periods far into the future. We will in fact investigate the sensitivity of our results to qualifications which may be of particular importance in distant time periods.

Here, however, we will abstract from these qualifications and project benefits and costs into the future under the assumptions that (1) the same benefits and costs calculated for patients who have been in the program at least 4 years apply equally to those in the program for all later periods of treatment, and (2) the drop-out rate of approximately 5% registered during the fifth and sixth years of treatment applies equally to all later years. The time horizon used in this second calculation will be 33 years, at which point the average age of our cohort patients will be 67.[32] We will also assume that the benefit of increased market earnings terminates at an average age of 65. The ratios of benefits to costs calculated under these varying assumptions are presented in Table 8.

As can be seen, even in the absence of the benefit of reduced heroin consumption, calculated benefit—cost ratios are significantly greater than one, despite the fact that many benefits could be only partially measured and others could not be measured at all. Rather than review completely every possible source of benefit underestimation, let us simply note where the largest source of benefit underestimation is likely to occur. As is well known, only a small fraction of total addict offenses are ever "cleared" by an arrest. This means that we have not accounted for a rather substantial reduction in crime attributable to methadone treatment. Because benefits such as

---

[30]See, for example, [15], pp. 5—6, and [16], p. 4.
[31]This calculation is also directly relevant to the decision to continue patients in treatment once the cost of their induction has become a sunk cost.

[32]Death rates among MMTP patients have been shown to be similar to those of the general population, and therefore 67 years is regarded as an appropriate estimate of life expectancy. See [15], p. 4.

TABLE 8

The Ratios of Benefits to Costs Calculated Under Varying Assumptions for a 6-Year and a 33-Year Time Horizon

Benefits Included in the Calculation	100% Inpatient Induction		100% Ambulatory Induction	
	6-Year Time Horizon	33-Year Time Horizon	6-Year Time Horizon	33-Year Time Horizon
$B_y + B_{cj}$	1.47	1.86	1.94	2.21
$B_y + B_{cj} + B_{h1}$	2.94	3.48	3.87	4.14
$B_y + B_{cj} + B_{h2}$	4.40	5.09	5.80	6.06

B_y represents the benefit of increased legal earnings, B_{cj} the criminal justice benefit, and B_{h1} and B_{h2} the benefit of reduced heroin consumption if half or all of the street value of reduced heroin consumption results in a social benefit, respectively.

the value of reduced fear and mental anguish on the part of potential victims are closely associated with the reduction in total offenses, and yet these benefits have not been measured, the omission of these types of benefits should constitute a particularly notable underestimation of program benefits.

QUALIFICATIONS

Before reaching any conclusions, however, it is important that we consider the sensitivity of these results to a number of potentially significant qualifications. First, we must consider the possibility that in the absence of methadone treatment, at least some cohort patients would have "matured out" of addiction on their own accord. Although expert opinion is divided on the question, at least two long-term follow-up studies have concluded that after the age of 40 years, as many as one-third of all heroin addicts eventually discontinue heroin consumption and abandon the drug-centered way of life[33]—a result with potential significance for our benefit−cost calculation.

[33]See [1] and [28].

Because MMTP patients were addicted an average of 8 years before admission and generally showed in that period a history of repeated failure of withdrawal treatment, these results may very well exaggerate the degree of maturation that our cohort patients would have registered in the absence of treatment. Nonetheless, it will be instructive to check the sensitivity of these results to this potential problem by assuming that one-third of all cohort patients would have achieved abstinence at the average age of 40 in the absence of the program. For want of actual data, we will also assume that the performance of ex-addicts is the same as that of long-term methadone patients. These assumptions thus imply that one-third of all benefits disappear after the sixth year of treatment. Under these assumptions (and again using a 10% annual rate of time discount), calculated benefit−cost ratios are as shown in Table 9.

As can be seen, all benefit−cost ratios remain significantly greater than one, and in fact do not diverge too markedly from those calculated under the assumption of no maturation. This is not surprising, for the maturation hypothesis has significance only for later periods of treatment, periods that are more

TABLE 9
The Ratios of Benefits to Costs Calculated Under the
Assumption That in the Absence of the Program, One-third
of All Cohort Patients Would Have Discontinued Heroin
Consumption at Age 40 Years, 33-Year Time Horizon

Benefits Included in the Calculation	100% Inpatient Induction	100% Ambulatory Induction
$B_y + B_{cj}$	1.57	1.86
$B_y + B_{cj} + B_{h1}$	3.00	3.53
$B_y + B_{cj} + B_{h2}$	4.37	5.20

See Table 8 for term definitions.

heavily discounted and that refer to fewer
patients in the program. It therefore appears
quite unlikely that the prospect of maturation
will materially affect the results of our calculations.

Perhaps the most serious qualification to
the results presented thus far concerns the
possible impact of methadone treatment on the
behavior of individuals not in the program. If
the establishment of metahdone treatment (1)
causes a change in the price of heroin, (2) results
in a change in the rate of creation of new
addicts, or (3) causes increased deaths resulting
from the illicit use of methadone, then the
impact on addicts and potential addicts not in
the program is clearly relevant, and we must
consider the likely bias resulting from our
inability to account for these "indirect" effects.

First, methadone is a substitute for heroin;
therefore the establishment of methadone
treatment should under most circumstances
reduce the market price of illicit heroin. If, as
seems likely, addicts "on the street" reduce
their involvement in criminal activity in response to such a price change, then we have
clearly underestimated the reduction in criminal activity attributable to methadone treat-

ment.[34] Thus, although the inability to include
this price effect in our calculation is regrettable,
it is at least in line with a strategy of obtaining a
minimum measure of program benefits.

The effect of methadone treatment on the
rate of creation of new addicts, however, is
much less clear, and because the presence of an
additional heroin addict in society constitutes a
considerable additional cost (at least in the
context of current legal sanctions), it is an
important consideration not accounted for in
the calculations in Tables 8 and 9.

On theoretical grounds, the net effect of
methadone treatment on the creation of new
addicts is ambiguous. On the one hand, by
reducing the lifetime cost of addiction, the
availability of methadone treatment will unam-
biguously reduce the incentive of potential
heroin addicts to avoid heroin consumption.
This effect, however, may be significantly mod-
erated by the fact that potential addicts evidence high rates of time discount and by the fact
that methadone programs require a number of
years of proved addiction before allowing admission to the program. On the other hand,
methadone programs may retard the rate of
creation of new addicts by reducing the number
of contagious elements capable of introducing
others to heroin consumption and by reducing
the profitability of investing in the creation of
new heroin addicts on the part of those who sell
heroin. Although there is weak evidence to
indicate a negative effect on balance,[35] this

[34]Assuming that addicts can devote labor time only to
criminal activity, legal employment, and leisure, a reduction in time devoted to crime must also involve an increase
in labor time devoted to leisure plus legal employment.
Thus, increased market income and/or income imputed to
leisure are also understated.

[35]The only significant piece of empirical evidence relating to
this question is the overworked and somewhat unsatisfactory comparison between the results of the maintenance
system practiced in Great Britain and the nonmaintenance
approach traditional to the United States. Although caution

relationship must in the final analysis be regarded as a potential qualification to our benefit—cost results, and its magnitude and direction must in the end be left to the reader's interpretation. [36]

Another qualification concerns the number of addict deaths that have resulted from the illicit diversion of methadone from methadone programs. Although the decline in death rates among legal participants of the MMTP is well documented,[37] the highly publicized increase in deaths among users of methadone illegally obtained does indeed represent a significant drawback to the program in particular and to methadone treatment in general. But if we are interested in policy toward methadone treatment, as opposed simply to documenting how its performance falls short of exaggerated expectations, we must consider whether methadone treatment has resulted in more deaths than would have occurred from heroin consumption in the absence of methadone treatment. What is required then is not a mere statement that methadone deaths have increased, but rather a comparison of increased methadone deaths with the methadone-induced decrease in heroin deaths. Unfortunately, data of sufficient quality to make such a comparison is not currently available, and the

issue of the program's impact on addict deaths must therefore be left as a potential qualification to the results obtained.

CONCLUSION AND POLICY CONSIDERATIONS

Subject to these qualifications, it appears from the evidence now available that under present conditions, the benefits of methadone programs of the type studied here exceed their costs, and most likely by a very wide margin. In translating these results into policy, however, a number of warnings are in order. First, because methadone programs vary considerably in the provision of auxiliary services and in requirements for admission, and because methadone patients do not represent an unbiased sample of the addict population, these results apply directly only to a subset of all programs and to a subset of all addicts. Indeed, methadone treatment may be totally inappropriate for addicts with multiple drug addictions and for other classes of addicts not represented among those allowed to enter the program. That this does not excessively limit the generality of the findings is readily demonstrated by the fact that as of July 31, 1972, approximately 20,000 patients in the Greater New York area were in programs roughly similar to the program examined, with many more on waiting lists for admission.[38] Nonetheless, these restrictions on generality should be kept in mind.

Second, these findings are clearly dependent on the assumption that current legal sanctions against the sale and consumption of heroin will remain constant. Although the achievement of a "global optimum" may indeed involve radical changes in current legal sanctions, it is for political reasons unlikely that enforcement directed against the sale and consumption of heroin will be materially altered in

---

is clearly in order in making this comparison, it is interesting to note that despite the fact that the lifetime cost of addiction is extremely high in the United States and extremely low in Great Britain, the proportion of addicts in Great Britain is extremely small compared to that existing in the United States. Although the results of this comparison are consistent with the hypothesis that methadone treatment will if anything reduce the rate of creation of new addicts, the rather serious violation of the ceteris paribus assumption will not allow a definitive conclusion.

[36]The illicit diversion of methadone to the black market presents a similar problem. Although it should serve to reduce the price of heroin, its effect on the creation of new addicts is theoretically ambiguous.

[37]See [15], p. 10.

[38]See [15], p. 2.

the near future, and hence the assumption of no change in enforcement policy is regarded as a reasonable one for the present.[39]

Finally, it is important to note that in addition to methadone maintenance treatment there are other treatment regimes or modalities designed to treat heroin addiction, and we have not considered the possibility that other treatment modalities may do the job better. A few relevant points concerning this question should be noted. First, if the various treatment modalities are designed primarily to treat separate parts of the addict population and hence are relatively independent of each other, our findings are relevant to policy no matter how effective are other treatment modalities in their respective shares of the addict population. It is worth noting in this connection that methadone patients in the MMTP are not representative of the addict population as a whole and should in general represent those addicts who are less willing or less able to accept the philosophy of abstinence, the primary goal of almost all other treatment modalities.[40] If, however, the relevant treatment populations of the various treatment modalities significantly overlap, then for policy purposes it becomes all the more important to measure the relative performance of all types of treatment programs—a task well beyond the scope of this paper.

Clearly, methadone maintenance is not a panacea for all the ills associated with heroin addiction. As we have seen from the program

studied, it does not eliminate all the criminal activity or all the heroin consumption on the part of those who participate in it. Moreover, it may not be appropriate for a substantial portion of the addict population. But failure to meet such expectations is no reason to exclude it from policy considerations. Policy decisions require a comparison of the gains to be derived from methadone maintenance and the costs of achieving those gains. Subject to the inevitable uncertainties that arise in such a complex comparison, methadone maintenance of the type studied appears to have passed such a test.

REFERENCES

1. Ball, John C., and Richard W. Snarr. "A Test of the Maturation Hypothesis with Respect to Opiate Addiction." In *Committee on Problems of Drug Dependence*, pp. 6204–6212. Washington, D.C.: GPO, 1969.

2. Becker, Gary S. "Crime and Punishment: An Economic Approach." *Journal of Political Economy* 76 (March–April 1968): 169–217.

3. Blumstein, Alfred, and Richard Larson. "Models of a Total Criminal Justice System." *Operations Research* 13 (March–April 1969): 199–231.

4. Brecher, Edward M., and the Editors of *Consumer Reports. Licit and Illicit Drugs*. Boston: Little, Brown and Co., 1972.

5. Bureau of the Census, U.S. Department of Commerce. *Census of Population: 1970—Employment Profiles of Selected Low-Income Areas*. Final Report, PHC(3)–4, Manhattan Borough, New York City—Summary. Washington, D.C.: GPO, 1972.

6. Bureau of Narcotics and Dangerous Drugs, U.S. Department of Justice, Intelligence Staff. Personal Communications, March 1971. Cited by John Holahan, "Control of Illegal Supply of Heroin." *Public Finance Quarterly* 1 (October 1973): 467–477.

7. Cushman, Paul. "Methadone Maintenance Treatment of Narcotic Addiction." *New York State Journal of Medicine* 81 (July 1972): 1752–1755.

8. ———. "Methadone Maintenance in Hard-Core Criminal Addicts." *New York State Journal of Medicine* 71 (July 1971): 1768–1774.

[39]For a discussion of optimal policy toward methadone treatment when enforcement policies are allowed to vary, see [17].

[40]One obvious exception is heroin maintenance as opposed to methadone maintenance. Because heroin must be administered several times a day (compared to once a day for methadone), supervised heroin maintenance is expected to be considerably more costly than methadone maintenance if close supervision is maintained. However, more addicts may choose to enter heroin maintenance than methadone maintenance, and therefore its use as a policy instrument cannot be precluded.

9. ———. "Progress Report on Methadone." *Wall Street Journal*, July 2, 1974, p. 15.

10. Dole, Vincent P., Marie E. Nyswander, and Alan Warner. "Successful Treatment of 750 Criminal Addicts." *Journal of the American Medical Association* 206 (December 1968): 2708–2714.

11. Epstein, Edward Jay. "Methadone: The Forlorn Hope." *The Public Interest* 36 (Summer, 1974): 3–24.

12. Fernandez, Paul A. "Costs and Benefits of Rehabilitation of Heroin Addicts." Ph.D. dissertation, Claremont Graduate School, 1972.

13. Gearing, Frances R. "Evaluation of Methadone Maintenance Treatment Program." *The International Journal of the Addiction* 5 (September 1970): 517–543.

14. ———. "Methadone Maintenance Treatment, Five Years Later—Where Are They Now?" Paper delivered at the One Hundredth Annual Meeting of the American Public Health Association, Atlantic City, N.J., November 1972.

15. Gearing, Frances R. "Methadone Maintenance Treatment Program, Progress Report through March 31, 1971—A Five-Year Overview." Report of the Methadone Maintenance Evaluation Unit, Columbia University School of Public Health and Administrative Medicine, May 1971.

16. ———. "Success and Failures in Methadone Maintenance Treatment of Heroin Addiction in New York City." In *Third National Conference on Methadone Treatment, Proceedings*, pp. 2–16, New York: November 1970.

17. Hannan, Timothy H. *The Economics of Methadone Maintenance*. Lexington, Mass.: D. C. Heath and Company, Lexington Books, 1975.

18. Holahan, John. *The Economics of Drug Addiction and Control in Washington, D.C.: A Model for Estimation of Costs and Benefits of Rehabilitation*. A Special Report of the D.C. Department of Corrections. Washington, D.C.: District of Columbia Department of Corrections, 1970.

19. ———. "Measuring Benefits from Alternative Heroin Policies." In *Fifth National Conference on Methadone Treatment, Proceedings*, pp. 1219–1226, Washington, D.C.: March 1973.

20. Jeffers, James R., and James E. Johnson. *A Cost–Benefit Analysis of Heroin Abuse Control Programs*. Bureau of Business and Economic Research Working Paper Series No. 73–21. Iowa City: University of Iowa, 1973.

21. Langrod, John, and Joyce Lowinson. "The Scope and Nature of Criminality in a Group of Methadone Patients." In *Fourth National Conference on Methadone Treatment, Proceedings*, pp. 95–99, San Francisco: January 1972.

22. McGlothlin, William H., Victor C. Tabbush, Carl D. Chambers, and Kay Jamison. *Alternative Approaches of Opiate Addiction Control: Costs, Benefits and Potential*. Bureau of Narcotics and Dangerous Drugs Report SCID–TR–7. Washington D.C.: GPO, 1972.

23. Manpower Administration, U.S. Department of Labor. *Area Trends in Employment and Unemployment*. Washington, D.C.: GPO.

24. New York State Government. *State of New York Executive Budget, Fiscal Year April 1, 1971 to March 31, 1972*. New York, 1972.

25. New York State Government, Legislative Commission on Expenditure Review. *Narcotic Drug Control in New York State, Program Audit 2.2.71*. New York, 1971.

26. New York State Government, Narcotic Addiction Control Commission. *Fourth Annual Statistical Report*. New York, 1971.

27. Police Department of the City of New York. *Annual Reports of the Police Department of the City of New York, 1967–1969*. New York, 1968–1970.

28. Vaillant, G. E. "A Twelve-Year Follow-up of New York Narcotic Addicts." *American Journal of Psychiatry* 122 (1966): 727–737.

HOW TO DETERMINE WHO SHOULD GET WHAT

Robert E. Goodin

Apparently the "end of ideology" has at last met its own, not untimely, end. This happy state of affairs is no doubt attributable more to sheer exhaustion than to intellectual conversion, and one is naturally hesitant to risk reopening that sterile controversy. But some of the more pernicious side effects of the quest for a value-free social science remain entrenched in academic orthodoxy and, worse, continue to influence policymakers.

At the head of the list must be the proposition that interpersonal comparisons of utility are impossible and, therefore, that either economists and philosophers must refrain from passing judgment on the distribution of income and wealth altogether or else they must do so in terms of a "planner's preference," clearly anathema in a liberal democracy.[1] The alternative suggested here is that ethical judgments be provided to make interpersonal utility comparisons possible and hence to make discussion of distributive issues in comfortably utilitarian terms possible.

Underlying this essay is a particular view of the place of values in social sciences. It is identical in essential respects to the one suggested to Joan Robinson by Ibsen's *Peer Gynt:* "We cannot escape from making judgments and the judgments that we make arise from the ethical preconceptions that have soaked into our view of life and are somehow printed in our brains. We cannot escape from our habits of thought. The Boyg bars the way. But we can go round about. We can see what we value, and try to see why."[2] It is impossible to do social science without value judgments creeping into the analysis, and it is better to make them explicit than to try to sweep them under the theoretical carpet. Ideology, if ignored, does not go away.

This will no doubt strike the hard-nosed social scientist as stern stuff. So as not to put him off the project immediately, it must be emphasized that, strictly speaking, the present exercise requires no more than his grumbling acquiescence that there is a place in society (although not necessarily in his university department) for social philosophers whose business it is to make value judgments. Following Hume and Moore in steering clear of the "naturalistic fallacy," we must admit that the social philosopher cannot get any evaluative conclusions out of his philosophical system unless he puts some value judgments into it in the first place. The social scientist is therefore

Source. Copyright © 1975 by the University of Chicago Press. Reproduced with permission from *Ethics* (July, 1975), pp. 310–321.

[1]Early rumblings turned into a full frontal assault with publication of Lionel Robbins's *An Essay on the Nature and Significance of Economic Science* (London: Macmillan Co., 1932); see esp. pp. 122–25; and his follow-up comment, "Interpersonal Comparisons of Utility," *Economic Journal* 48 (1938): 635–41. Abram Bergson ("A Reformulation of Certain Aspects of Welfare Economics," *Quarterly Journal of Economics* 52 [1938]: 310–34) responds in terms of a social welfare function which is essentially a planner's preference notion.

[2]Joan Robinson, *Economic Philosophy* (Harmondsworth: Penguin Books, 1964), p. 19.

invited to look upon this essay as an attempt at providing reasonable value judgments to program into our evaluative machinery.

I

The case against interpersonal utility comparisons rests on the proposition that "every mind is inscrutable to every other mind and no common denominator of feeling is possible."[3] An individual can intelligibly say that the third-degree burn on his right thumb is more painful than the pinprick on his left thumb, but he cannot intelligibly say that his burn is more painful than another man's pinprick.

The argument is, to be sure, strikingly counterintuitive. Men make such comparisons all the time.[4] Then again, men are also constantly speaking of the sun's rising and setting. That such propositions are well entrenched in ordinary language might prove something about popular belief systems, or it might simply demonstrate the difficulty of reforming popular linguistic habits in the light of modern (post-Copernican?) scientific findings. Surely it proves nothing whatsoever about Truth.

Thus has been initiated a search for a scientific basis for interpersonal utility comparisons. To date the search has been peculiarly unproductive.

One attempt starts from the observation that individuals are usually incapable of detecting very slight changes in states of affairs. The blue of 4501 Å is, to the naked eye, indistinguishable from the blue of 4502 Å. Similarly, individuals will not notice slight changes in well-being. A meal providing 700 calories will probably not leave a man feeling any more hungry or listless than one providing 705 calories. Many hope to use this sort of fact to calculate the intensity of preferences.[5] Each time an individual can notice a change he is said to have passed through one "level of discretion." The intensity of his preference for a change from one state of affairs to another is figured as the number of levels of discretion through which that change would take him.

This procedure unreasonably presupposes that a level of discretion corresponds to the same increment of utility for every individual. If a man is for some reason less discerning and capable of fewer levels of discretion, he is simply said to get less out of life. This might be dubbed the aesthete's theory of human happiness. Unfortunately, it is patently absurd. An old man who is nearly blind quite definitely enjoys those few things he can see more than does his son with perfect sight, and this in spite of the fact that the old man cannot perceive all the subtleties that his son assures him are there. The farmer with rheumatism might be able to detect weather changes far better than his

[3]William Stanley Jevons, *The Theory of Political Economy*, 4th ed. (London: Macmillan Co., 1911), p. 14.

[4]For such arguments see Brian Barry, *Political Argument* (London: Routledge & Kegan Paul, 1965), pp. 44−47; and I. M. D. Little, *A Critique of Welfare Economics*, 2d ed. (Oxford: Clarendon Press, 1957), chap. 4. A. C. Pigou ("Some Aspects of Economic Welfare," *American Economic Review* 41 [1951]: 287−302) is even more impatient with what he regards as sophistry pure and simple: "Nobody can prove that anybody besides himself exists, but, nevertheless, everybody is quite sure of it. We do not, in short, and there is no reason why we should, start from a *tabula rasa*, binding ourselves to hold every opinion which the natural man entertains to be guilty until it is proved innocent. The burden is the other way. To deny this is to wreck, not merely Welfare Economics, but the whole apparatus of practical thought."

[5]E.g., Francis Y. Edgeworth, *Mathematical Physics* (London: Kegan Paul, 1881), pp. 59−61; W. E. Armstrong, "Utility and the Theory of Welfare," *Oxford Economic Papers* 3 (1951): 259−71; and Leo A. Goodman and Harry Markowitz, "Social Welfare Functions Based on Individual Rankings," *American Journal of Sociology* 58 (1952): 257−62.

neighbors without welcoming the rain either more or less.[6]

A second attempt turns on the proposition that the more intensely a man desires something, the more likely he is to undertake to obtain it, other things being equal. Some proceed from this to argue that, if there is an equal probability of two individuals engaging in goal-directed action, then that is evidence for saying that their desires for those goals are equally strong.[7]

Even within a single individual it is far from certain that the more he wants something, the more likely he is to act. Quite the contrary. Arrow's theory of increasing risk aversion simply formalizes everyday experience: the larger the stakes, the more favorable the odds which a man demands before agreeing to take the gamble.[8] As between different individuals the proposition is clearly false. Some men habitually overreact to practically everything; others stoically accept their lot. It is just a matter of temperament and glands.

What is really needed for interpersonal comparisons of utility is for a man to be able to imagine himself in another's place. It is hard enough to imagine oneself in very strange circumstances, but even this is not enough. As Bernard Shaw admonishes, "Do not do unto others as you would that they should do unto you. Their tastes may not be the same." In addition to imagining oneself in the circumstances of another, one must also imaging himself possessing the values and tastes of that other. This is all well and good for those who have actually led two lives; the thoroughly assimilated Pakistani in London can say where he is happier. But for most men this bold flight of imagination is too much to ask.[9]

It is often thought that the notion of a choice under uncertainty can be called into aid at this juncture. Impartial judgments are possible from an individual behind a Rawlsian "veil of ignorance" who is asked to choose a social structure not knowing which position he will come to occupy in it. But this does not get around the problem at all. One of the things the veil of ignorance is supposed to deny the chooser is knowledge of his own peculiar tastes. In Harsanyi's formulation the chooser is explicitly directed "to judge the utility of another individual's position not in terms of his own attitudes and tastes but rather in terms of the attitudes and tastes of the individual actually holding this position." Furthermore, this procedure makes the results suspiciously contingent on the chooser's attitude toward risk. Some might choose a society with great gaps between rich and poor, trusting to luck that

[6]Jerome Rothenberg similarly considers "the hypothetical case of a man with a capacity for 'great joy' and 'great suffering,' but whose perception of satisfaction changes between the extremes is poor, so that he has but few discretion levels. In the same tenor, one can conceive of a highly discriminating person, trained to make fine distinctions in his states of being, but who is not 'passionate' " (*The Measurement of Social Welfare* [Englewood Cliffs, N.J.: Prentice-Hall, Inc., 1961], p. 194).

[7]Ilmar Valdner, "The Empirical Meaningfulness of Interpersonal Utility Comparisons," *Journal of Philosophy* 69 (1972): 87–103.

[8]Kenneth J. Arrow, "The Theory of Risk Aversion," in *Essays in the Theory of Risk-Bearing* (Amsterdam: North-Holland Publishing Co., 1971), pp. 90–120.

[9]George Bernard Shaw, "Maxims for Revolutionists" (postscript to *Man and Superman*), in *Works*, vol. 10 (London: Constable, 1930). John C. Harsanyi ("Cardinal Welfare, Individualistic Ethics, and Interpersonal Comparisons of Utility," *Journal of Political Economy* 63 [1955]: 309–21) argues that individuals whose tastes have changed (who have "led two lives" in present terminology) can "make direct comparisons between the satisfactions open to one human type and those open to another." (Reflect on how much depends on the implicit assumption of homogeneity within "human types.") Amartya K. Sen (*Collective Choice and Social Welfare* [San Francisco: Holden-Day, Inc., 1970]) argues for making interpersonal comparisons by imagining oneself in the place of another, but privately he admits that a Hindu background makes this a good bit easier to envisage.

they will be among the well-off. A risk-neutral man will favor maximizing average utility across all the roles he might come to occupy. A man who is absolutely risk averse will join Rawls in choosing to maximize the well-being of the worst-off man.[10]

II

There seems to be no scientific way to compare interpersonal utilities, so modern welfare economics has come to rely on the notion of Pareto optimality as a means of avoiding them. A change is defined as a Paretian improvement if it makes at least one person better-off and no one worse-off. Pareto optimality is achieved when all possible Paretian improvements have been made.

This Paretian principle is doubly annoying, being at once too broad and too narrow. It is excessively broad in that it fails to pick out one specific state of affairs as optimal. Instead, it defines a set of several Pareto optima. Any outcome contained in the set is a Paretian

improvement on any outcome outside the set, but the Paretian principle provides no basis for choosing between the several optimal outcomes within the set. Suppose, for example, that three gentlemen are courting the same lady, who does not care which (if any) of them she marries. It is a Paretian improvement for her to favor one of the suitors with her hand, but the Paretian principle cannot say which.

Even without yielding determinate results, however, the Paretian principle goes far enough to be objectionably narrow. Suppose one of the suitors in the above example were a sheik with a dozen wives already in his harem and the other suitors were unmarried. Intuitively, the impartial spectator would not only go further than the Paretian principle to say that the lady at stake should go to one of the bachelors and not to the sheik; he would also actually violate the Paretian principle by suggesting that the sheik should give up his twelfth-favorite wife to the bachelor who does not win the woman in question. The transfer would make the sheik slightly worse-off but not by nearly so much as it would make the losing bachelor better-off, assuming he just wants a wife and does not care whom.

Such judgments need not be contaminated by interpersonal utility comparisons. All that is required is that gainers from the change be able to compensate losers.[11] If the bachelor could offer the sheik enough camels to compensate him for the loss of his twelfth-favorite wife and still come out ahead on the deal, then it is optimal for the transfer of the wife to occur. Indeed, if they do make the

[10]See John Rawls, *A Theory of Justice* (Cambridge, Mass.: Harvard University Press, 1971); James M. Buchanan and Gordon Tullock, *The Calculus of Consent* (Ann Arbor: University of Michigan Press, 1962), pp. 78 ff.; and John C. Harsanyi, "Cardinal Utility in Welfare Economics and in the Theory of Risk-Taking," *Journal of Political Economy* 61 (1953: 434–35, and "Cardinal Welfare, Individualistic Ethics, and Interpersonal Comparisons of Utility" (quotation from the latter). The argument in the text presupposes that choosers know (1) how well-off representative members of each class of citizens are and (2) how many citizens fall into each class. If the veil of ignorance prevents them from knowing (2), then they will be unable to calculate the probabilities of ending up in the various classes, so they will simply look at the well-being of the best-off and the worst-off classes (see Kenneth J. Arrow and Leonard Hurwicz, "An Optimality Criterion for Decision-Making under Ignorance," in *Uncertainty and Expectations in Economics*, ed. C. F. Carter and J. L. Ford [Oxford: Blackwell, 1972], pp. 1–11).

[11]The compensation principle was first proposed by Nicholas Kaldor ("Welfare Propositions in Economics and Interpersonal Comparisons of Utility," *Economic Journal* 49 [1939]: 549–52). It was endorsed with modifications by John R. Hicks ("The Foundations of Welfare Economics," *Economic Journal* 49 [1939]: 696–712) and Tibor Scitovsky ("A Note on Welfare Propositions in Economics," *Review of Economic Studies* 9 [1942]: 77–88).

swap of camels for the wife a Paretian improvement will have occurred. However, economists urging compensation principles as the test of efficiency stop short of insisting that compensation actually be paid, realizing that to do so would simply enshrine the distribution of well-being prevailing at the moment. This result is clearly unjustifiable unless, of course, the existing distribution is adjudged laudable on some other grounds entirely. While compensation principles avoid the need for interpersonal utility comparisons in evaluating the efficiency of resource allocations, then, they do so in a way that is of no assistance on distributive issues.

III

Both the Paretian and the compensation principles are serious attempts at banishing interpersonal utility comparisons and the value judgments on which they depend. If successful, the accomplishment would, of course, come at the price of precluding evaluation of alternative distributions of well-being among citizens. There is one other approach—the laissez faire line—which does attempt distributive judgments, but it does so on the basis of ill-concealed and obnoxious value judgments. The critique of the value premises of this approach leads directly into the more positive recommendations of this essay.

As handed down from Adam Smith, the traditional argument for laissez faire policies focuses on the celebration of the way in which economic markets make men respond to one another's desires. As that famous passage from *The Wealth of Nations* maintains, it is not from the benevolence of the butcher, the brewer, or the baker that we expect our dinner but from their regard to their own interest. At equilibrium, the market will have distributed goods in such a way that each fetches its highest possible

price. At a descriptive statement about how markets do (or, at any rate, about how perfect markets would) work, this analysis is unobjectionable.

Unfortunate evaluative judgments tend to creep into the positive economic analysis when it is couched in terms of supply and demand. Another way of saying the same thing as before is that interactions in a perfect market will result in scarce supplies of goods being used to satisfy the "most pressing" demands. Now, this seems like something which should certainly be done, until the language is unloaded and the notion of "most pressing demands" is examined. A demand is "most pressing" by virtue of having the highest bid attached, and spelled out in this way the phrase loses its air of innocent charm. Distributive systems should take into account the fact that different people have different tastes. But the way markets do this is to equate the weight of an individual's claim with the strength of his demand, defined as the amount he is willing to pay; and this, in turn, depends heavily on how much he can afford to pay. A millionaire might in a moment of frivolity spend a thousandth of his fortune on a purchase and thereby outbid a sharecropper willing to commit his all to the purchase of the same good. More dramatically, "while some are starving others are allowed to indulge in luxury."[12] Whenever some consumers are substantially wealthier than others this is bound to happen. Hence, there can be no moral case for allocating goods to individuals according to market demand without first establishing a case (or at least stating a presumption) that the present distribution of wealth is morally justifiable.[13]

[12]Oskar Lange, "On the Economic Theory of Socialism," *Review of Economic Studies* 4 (1936–37); 124; see also pp. 53–71, 123–42.

[13]Among those who overtly commit this sin are Richard A. Posner (*Economic Analysis of Law* [Boston: Little, Brown & Co., 1972], p. 14) and D. Goldstick ("Assessing Utilities,"

IV

Having found the ethical consequences of doing without interpersonal utility comparisons repugnant and at the same time having found no scientific basis for making them, one must now consider proposing an ethical basis for such comparisons. Actually this is precisely what Pareto, the father of the "new welfare economics," recommends:

We are to conclude . . . not that problems of simultaneously considering a number of heterogeneous utilities cannot be solved, but that in order to discuss them some hypothesis which will render them commensurate has to be assumed. And when, as is most often the case, that is not done, discussion of such problems is idle and inconclusive, being merely a play of derivations cloaking certain sentiments— and those sentiments we should consider alone, without worrying very much about the garb they wear.[14]

The proposal of this essay is that everyone is assumed to have an equal capacity for happiness. This postulate is described as "ethical" as opposed to "scientific" because its validity is not even in principle verifiable. A pair of definitions is required to operationalize this standard. A state p is said to be "good" for individual I if and only if he prefers p to its contradictory, not-p, that is, if I prefers its presence to its absence.[15] The "capacity for happiness" of individual I is the sum of the utilities derived by I from each good over the entire range of goods, that is, $\Sigma^n_{i=1} U^1(g_i 0$, where where I regards g_1 through g_n as goods.

Given the postulate of equal capacities for happiness, comparison of interpersonal utilities becomes a straightforward matter. Ask each man to determine through introspection how happy he would be at his "bliss point," that is, when his capacity for happiness is fully realized. Since everyone *ex hypothesi* has an equal capacity for happiness, interpersonal utility comparisons simply amount to asking men how far along toward their bliss points a change would take them and comparing their responses. Suppose, for instance, that there is some indivisible good to be distributed and that giving it to Ivan would take him one-fourth of the way nearer to his bliss point (from, say, one-half to three-fourths of the way there)

Mind 80 [1971]: 531–41, esp. p. 535). More frequently, the problem is simply ignored while economists preoccupy themselves with the quest for efficiency. Economic theorists are quick to emphasize that, given an equilibrium, if incomes change a new equilibrium will have to be established (see, e.g., John R. Hicks on income effects in *Value and Capital*, 2d ed. [Oxford: Clarendon Press, 1946], pp. 26–33). It is a short and frequently taken step to the argument that, since different equilibria correspond to each different configuration of income distributions, analysis of equilibria can be of no guidance on distributive questions (see Robbins, *Nature and Significance of Economic Science*, pp. 127 ff; Paul A. Samuelson, *Economics*, 4th ed. [New York: McGraw-Hill Book Co., 1958], p. 617; John Kenneth Galbraith, *Economics and the Public Purpose* [London: Andre Deutsch, 1974], p. 14; and Aaron Wildavsky, "The Political Economy of Efficiency Cost–Benefit Analysis, Systems Analysis, and Program Budgeting," *Public Administration Review* 26[1966]: 292–310, esp. pp. 294–95).

[14]Vilfredo Pareto, *Trattato di sociologia generale*, trans. and ed. Arthur Livingston and Andrew Bongiorno (London: Jonathan Cape, 1935), sec. 2137.

[15]This definition is borrowed from G. H. von Wright (*The Logic of Preference* [Edinburgh: University Press, 1963], sec. 14. In utilitarian theory there is a perfect symmetry between pleasure and pain. The present analysis concerns only the distribution of well-being, but a parallel utilitarian analysis of the distribution of ill-being could be constructed. It would start with von Wright's definition of a "bad," import the ethical assumption that everyone has an equal capacity for misery, and make interpersonal disutility comparisons by observing how far a change would take men toward their "despair points." Along these negative utilitarian lines, see Karl Popper, *The Open Society and Its Enemies* (London: Routledge & Kegan Paul, 1945), 1:284–85; R. N. Smart, "Negative Utilitarianism," *Mind* 67 (1958): 542–43; the symposium with H. B. Acton and J. W. N. Watkins on "Negative Utilitarianism," *Proceedings of the Aristotelian Society* (Supplement) 37 (1963): 83–114; and Barrington Moore, Jr., *Reflections on the Causes of Human Misery* (Boston: Beacon Press, 1970).

while giving it to Johan would take him one-eighth nearer to his bliss point (from, say, one-half to five-eighths). Then it can be said that the good "means more" to Ivan than to Johan. Redistribution of goods can be treated analogously. Suppose that depriving a tycoon of bread with his four-course lunch takes him one-eighth of the way further from his bliss point but giving it to a pauper takes him one-fourth of the way nearer to his. Again, it can be said that the bread means more to the pauper than to the tycoon.[16]

Significantly, this does not settle the distributive question. From the fact that a commodity means more to I than to J it cannot be inferred that it should be given to I rather than to J. There is another ethical judgment to be made here between efficiency and equality. Opting for efficiency would imply that resources should be allocated to the individual to whom they mean most. A choice in favor of equality would mean that resources should be allocated in such a way as to take everyone

equally far along toward his bliss point. Usually some compromise between these incompatible standards will be chosen.[17]

In no case will this necessarily result in an equal distribution of all goods. This procedure for comparing interpersonal utilities explicitly recognizes that men have different tastes by asking each to specify his own bliss point and to state how far any given change will take him toward it. (There is room in this for paternalistic interference insofar as such judgments depend on factual information which the individual involved lacks.) An equal distribution of goods is justifiable if and only if everyone has an identical taste for all things, which is clearly not the case in the real world.

Philosophers from Hume onward have emphasized the conventional nature of moral judgments, and the one under discussion is no exception. There is nothing special about the

---

[16]Nineteenth-century economists frequently assumed that individuals have an equal capacity for happiness. This, combined with the assumption that everyone has an identical welfare function (i.e., identical tastes), produced the recommendation that income and wealth be distributed equally. Robbins ("Interpersonal Comparisons of Utility," n. 1 above), sees quite clearly that an ethical postulate about relative capacities for happiness is the key to interpersonal utility comparisons, but he refrains from using it in defence to the canons of good value-free social science. My particular procedure is, so far as I know, original, although something vaguely similar is suggested by Sen (*Collective Choice and Social Welfare,* chap. 7). At least one of Sen's proposals resembles a procedure suggested by Jevons (*Essays on Economics* [London: Macmillan Co., 1905], pp. 128–30): make interpersonal utility comparisons by comparing the proportion of the total happiness an individual is presently experiencing which is attributable to each good. If an automobile contributes 35 percent of one man's well-being and only 10 percent of another's, then it can said that the automobile means more to the former than to the latter. This procedure neglects the fact that under the status quo some men are better-off (i.e., nearer their bliss points) than others.

[17]Brian Barry (*Political Argument,* chap 1) suggests that such trade-offs be represented on ordinary indifference maps, as follows:

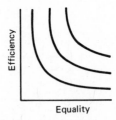

These indifference curves are drawn convex to the origin, suggesting that each good has decreasing marginal utility. Under these conditions, individuals would ordinarily choose a little of each instead of all of one or the other. Rawls correctly perceives that the efficiency criterion "implies that other things equal greater social utility results from educating people to have simple desires and to be easily satisfied" (*A Theory of Justice,* p. 323). This offends Rawls's considered moral judgments, but surely most would find the implications of the equality criterion even more offensive. It would result in a large share of commodities being allocated to those with bliss points which are difficult and expensive to attain; those who demand more would get more. This hardly seems reasonable.

presumption that individuals have an equal capacity for happiness. As Sir Henry Maine writes, "I have myself heard an Indian Brahmin dispute it on the ground that, according to the clear teaching of his religion, a Brahmin was entitled to twenty times as much happiness as anyone else."[18] What is attractive about this procedure for comparing interpersonal utilities is that it can be applied in any social context, provided only that there is some ethical judgment as to how much the happiness of each individual is to be weighted. If an additional elephant would take a Brahmin one-hundredth of the way nearer his bliss point but an untouchable one-tenth of the way nearer his, then within the Hindu value system it is quite clear that the elephant "means more" to the Brahmin and that, if resources are to be allocated efficiently, it must go to him.

One of the moral conventions in the Anglo-American community does seem to be that everyone should count for one and no one is to count for more than one. This principle is morally appealing in itself, and, more significantly, its results can be made to coincide nicely with our considered moral judgments. The most devastating objection to the traditional utilitarian theory of distribution centers around the "super-efficient pleasure machine," an individual who is very good indeed at converting material commodities into subjective utility. To look at the same problem from a slightly different angle, some people with special needs require more material goods than the average man to achieve the same measure of happiness.[19] It is frequently objected that utilitarians

would have to give virtually all material goods to super-efficient pleasure machines and deny handicapped persons virtually everything in order to maximize the sum total of subjective utility derived from a given lump of physical commodities. The present procedure for assessing interpersonal utilities does not automatically imply any such result. Everything depends on the second ethical judgment, the choice between equality and efficiency, and so long as equality carries any reasonably strong weight those with special needs will be accorded special treatment.

In principle, there is no reason that a society could not operate according to the dictates of a social welfare function based on interpersonal utility comparisons made according to the procedure described above. The same consideration that prevents individuals from misrepresenting their preferences in the marketplace also prevents them from doing so with this procedure: to some extent, individuals get what they ask for, so if they overstate or understate their liking for a good they will have to suffer the consequences. In practice, of course, it would certainly be time-consuming, and ultimately it might prove impossible for everyone to produce a complete schedule saying how far any conceivable change would take him toward or away from his bliss point. Most actual societies would therefore use this procedure only as a rough-and-ready guide.

---

[18]*Lectures on the Early History of Institutions* (London: John Murray, 1875), p. 399.

[19]On super-efficient pleasure machines, see Milton Friedman, "Lerner on the Economics of Control," *Journal of Political Economy* 55 (1947): 310–11; and Alan Ryan, *The Philosophy of John Stuart Mill* (London: Macmillan Co., 1970), p. 229. On special needs, see Amartya K. Sen, *On Economic Inequality* (Oxford: Clarendon Press, 1973), pp. 13

ff., and *Collective Choice and Social Welfare*, pp. 98 ff.; and Brian Barry, *The Liberal Theory of Justice* (Oxford: Clarendon Press, 1973), chap. 15. Francis Y. Edgeworth (*Mathematical Psychics*, pp. 56 ff.) derives the same implications from the utilitarian calculus, but his moral sensitivities are not particularly offended. As he writes in *New and Old Methods of Ethics* (Oxford: James Parker, 1877), p. 55. "This deduction agrees with common sense, as exhibited in the approved dealings of men with animals, of civilized with savage races, in the privileges of aristocracy approved in ages when aristocrats really represent a higher order of evolution."

One thing to bear in mind when using this procedure even in a rule-of-thumb sort of way is that individuals do change their minds from time to time, and they do so rather more frequently when their material circumstances are undergoing change. When living in the ghetto, Malcolm might think that a house in the suburbs would take him one-fourth of the way closer to his bliss point, but after he has moved into it he might find that he is not so keen on it after all and in fact it has taken him only one-eighth of the way nearer his bliss point. Since he was allocated the house on the assumption that it would be a one-fourth improvement for him, a wiser Malcolm is likely to be returned to his ghetto home when his new preference is registered. Someone who values the suburban house more will be given it, and Malcolm will be given something that makes more than a one-eighth improvement for him. The fact that men learn from their mistakes prevents the process from being hopelessly circular.

It is important to notice that there are no satisfactory procedural shortcuts for accomplishing the same results as the procedure suggested here. As has already been suggested, individuals must not be given equal portions of all goods because they have different tastes. This problem is partially overcome by allowing them to trade with one another after the initial allocation has been made, but, since bargaining is a costly business, it is certain that not all bargains that could be struck would be struck. Section III has exposed the folly of using market interactions as a substitute. The obvious response to the problems discussed there is to give everyone equal capacities for acquiring what they want, either by equalizing income and wealth or else by equalizing political power. Equalizing potential for want satisfaction, however, will not suffice because some individuals might have more expensive needs (or simply more expensive tastes) than others.

If everyone is given equal income and wealth, for instance, those requiring regular treatment with a kidney dialysis unit will not be able to get nearly so close to their bliss points as those with less costly necessities of life. A similar problem arises with equalizing political power. Some people (usually the poor) require relatively more services from the state than do those who can afford to purchase privately supplied substitutes. A further problem with equalizing political power without equalizing economic power at the same time is that rich men will buy votes either directly (e.g., in exchange for a bottle of whiskey) or indirectly (through campaign contributions for advertising). More fundamentally, the logic of coalition building is such that winning political coalitions will exclude unnecessary members so as to maximize the share of each of the remaining members. At the least this means that on each occasion some will gain more and others less than justifiable in terms of a comparison of their relative utility gains. Over the long run these effects will balance out, provided that everyone stands an equal chance of being in each winning coalition, but where there are persistent minorities who are always in the losing coalition time will only compound the problem.[20]

V

The major difficulty in discussing distributive principles solely in the foregoing terms is the possibility of incentive effects. Men must be

[20]The U.S. Supreme Court tried to equalize political power with its "one man, one vote" ruling in *Baker* v. *Carr*, 369 U.S. 186 (1962), and subsequent cases. For analysis of its shortcomings, see Nelson W. Polsby, ed., *Reappportionment in the 1970s* (Berkeley: University of California Press, 1971). Political theorists have long been familiar with problems of persistent minorities (see John C. Calhoun, *A Disquisition on Government* [Charleston, S.C.: Walker & James, 1851], and Robert A. Dahl, *A Preface to Democratic Theory* [Chicago: University of Chicago Press, 1956]).

rewarded according to their works if they are to be stimulated to actualize fully their potential. Where all members of society are guaranteed their share no matter what they do there is no inducement for them to contribute as much as they can.[21] Quotas only partially solve these problems because they must necessarily be aimed at those with the lowest abilities.

Presumably the equality-efficiency compromise and maximizing the sum total of goods available in a society both represent desirable goals. Since they are incompatible, there is need for a third ethical judgment as to how one is to be traded off for the other. Unlike the principle that each man is to count for one and none for more than one, there is no community consensus on this issue. Egalitarians insist that differential well-being not be allowed unless it results in some substantial gain for the disadvantaged; meritocrats insist that individuals should enjoy the full fruits of their own labors so long as they have not actually made anyone else worse-off. Heated though this controversy might be, however, each of the contesting parties would surely agree that it is better to pursue some mixture of both goals than to pursue one to the exclusion of the other.[22]

This ethical judgment is very different from the other two in several respects. Whereas the others concern matters of high principle, the third concerns a matter of low expediency. It is hardly an "ethical" judgment at all but, instead, a sop to practical necessity. As Rawls so ably argues, there is no moral sense in which talented people *deserve* extra rewards.[23] They can hold society to ransom unless they get them, of course, but that is something different. The extent of incentives, then, is an ethical question only insofar as it concerns how far to go in sacrificing moral principles to expediency. The third judgment differs from the others also in that it turns heavily on questions of empirical fact. The extent to which incentives need to be offered depends on the distribution of talents among the citizenry, how much of a bribe it takes to get individuals to work at full stretch, etc.

It should be mentioned that the decision to offer incentives need not work against the poor. If salary differentials are justified exclusively in terms of the need to attract people to the job, then the more tedious and less prestigious positions should carry the higher wages. There is no need to pay U.S. presidents hundreds of thousands of dollars when qualified men such as Herbert Hoover and John Kennedy will do it for nothing. The hourly wage of the plumber is and should be higher than that of the doctor because there is inherently less job satisfaction in mending pipes than in mending human bodies.[24]

VI

In a way this essay delivers something less than its title promises. It argues that three ethical judgments must be made in the course of resolving distributive questions, but it suggests a solution to only the first problem. The other two are left as very open questions, hence leaving the essay devoid of substantive recommendations as to who is to get what. While such failure to deliver on the title's promise ordinar-

[21]See Herbert Spencer, *The Principles of Ethics* (London: Williams & Norgate, 1897), pt. 1, chap. 8; Henry Sidgwick, *The Principles of Political Economy* (London: Macmillan Co., 1883), bk. 3, chap. 7; Francis Y. Edgeworth, "The Pure Theory of Progressive Taxation," in *Papers Relating to Political Economy* (London: Macmillan Co., 1925), 2:100–116; A. C. Pigou, *The Economics of Welfare*, 4th ed. (London: Macmillan Co., 1932), pt. 4, chap. 9; and J. A. Mirrlees, "An Exploration in the Theory of Optimum Income Taxation," *Review of Economic Studies* 38 (1971): 175–208.

[22]See the figure in n. 17 above, relabeling the axes "productivity" and "equality-efficiency compromise."

[23]Rawls, *A Theory of Justice*, sec. 48.

[24]Lange, "On the Economic Theory of Socialism," p. 124.

ily warrants a charge of scholastic sensationalism, a plea in mitigation must be entered in the present case. The failure does at least serve to highlight two important sub-themes of the essay: first, until some solution is offered to the first problem (interpersonal utility comparisons) there will be no critical discussion or crystallization of scholarly opinion on the other, logically secondary, questions; and, second, there is little point in hesitating to contaminate the theory with an ethical judgment at the first juncture since two more such judgments are required before any substantive results will follow.

CHAPTER 8

Designing the Control Structure

The task of designing a management control system is not easy. Considerable thought must be given to identification of the organization's goals and to their potential achievement through the motivation of employees. It will be recalled that management control is a process of identifying organizational goals and objectives, decomposing these objectives into subunit and individual performance criteria, and, finally, motivating through performance evaluation. The present chapter deals with the "technical" aspects of management control, that is, the process of identifying organizational goals and translating them into performance criteria. Later chapters review the motivational or "behavioral" segment of management control.

Through an examination of the organization's history, its past and current programs, and its management structure, one can infer what the organization seeks to accomplish. It is important that the statement of goals fully encompass the range of the organization's purposes.

By its very nature, a goal statement needs to be fairly broad rather than specific, since it attempts to express the general direction in which the organization is moving. For example, an agency for the physically handicapped might express one of its goals as being:

> To help the physically handicapped individual achieve his or her fullest potential.

Although the statement may describe what it is the agency is trying to accomplish, it is not so specific as to direct action. There are many directions that the organization could take in trying to accomplish that goal.

To provide operational guidance the goals need to be translated into objective statements, which represent intermediate targets the organization must meet if it is to accomplish its basic goals. An objective statement must be sufficiently specific so that it can be measured, that is, "Was it accomplished?", and dated, that is, "Was it accomplished on time?" Several objective statements may flow from one goal statement; care must be exercised that the statements fully encompass the content of the goal statement.

Examples of objective statements emanating from the goal statement cited above might be to:

Develop and implement within the next two years a public-awareness program.

Increase by 10 percent the target population participating in the agency's programs. This is to be accomplished by the end of the fiscal year.

Establish by the end of the current budget period an evaluation program in which the current academic level of each client is measured.

Except in the case of very small nonprofit agencies, responsibility for accomplishing the various objectives is assigned to subunits of the organization. The subunit or responsibility center, as it is often called, has as its aim the accomplishment of one or more of the objective statements. Its performance will be measured by the extent to which it is able to complete the specific objective by the assigned date.

If the quality of both goal translation into objective statements and of objective statements into responsibility center performance criteria is good, then total decomposition of agency goals has been successful. Moreover, the performance level of the organization as a whole can be viewed as an aggregate result of the individual responsibility centers' accomplishments.

While the effectiveness of responsibility centers is measured by the extent to which they have accomplished the centers' objectives (outcomes), efficiency is determined by examining the relationship between the resources utilized by the responsibility center (input) and the services it produced (output). It is important, therefore, that the organization's accounting system be capable of measuring units of input, output, and outcome.

Most likely a nonprofit agency will have different types of responsibility centers depending upon the various forms of input and output associated with a particular subunit of the organization. Some examples may help to illustrate the point.

1 In the case of a fund-raising department, there may be very little relationship between funds generated and expenses incurred by the department. Organizational performance is judged in terms of the amount of funds raised, which comprises the dominant measure of performance. This exemplifies a revenue center.

2 An organizational unit that is responsible for providing job skills training may exhibit a clear association between size of training staff and number of successful graduates of the job skills program. One measure of its success might be the ratio of total increase in lifetime earnings achieved by its graduates to the total expenses incurred by the responsibility center. The ratio represents the benefits divided by costs and hence the unit might be viewed as a "benefit–cost center."

3 The output of the agency's bookkeeping department is difficult to measure. This responsibility center is assumed to be an expense center and its performance is evaluated by what is considered to be a "reasonable" level of expenses.

Drucker in "What Results Should You Expect? A Users' Guide to MBO" discusses more specifically the issues involved in goal setting and objective determination. Several ideas put forth are essential to any discussion of goals and objectives. First is the notion that "there cannot be a single objective." Administrators must be willing to recognize the existence of multiple and at times mutually inconsistent objective statements. Second is recognition of the difficulty involved in communicating these multiple goals and their order or priority both to employees and to the public. A third point that deserves repeating here is that "It is not true that the activities of public service institutions cannot be measured."

In "University Goals: An Operative Approach," Conrad presents a discussion of goals that is useful to almost any social organization. A major contribution of the article is that it recognizes that, rather than being static, goals are continually being adapted to both internal and external pressures. Universities, like most complex organizations, depend upon the support of many constituencies. If this support is to continue, the organization must satisfy at least the minimum demands that each of these groups places upon the organization. These demands are thus constraints upon the organization, and satisfying them becomes part of the goal structure. The message to the manager of a nonprofit organization is to identify clearly organizational constituents. By determining the constraints that these groups place upon the organization, one can prepare for the eventual bargaining process when the constraints conflict with one another.

As stated earlier, an important part of the control process is identification of performance norms and targets for agency departments and individuals. The term *performance budgeting* describes this process. Of critical importance to the accomplishment of the organization's goals is that these performance measures capture fully the essence of the organization's objectives. If this is not the case, then individuals and departments tend to focus on one or two measures, and suboptimization is likely to take place. A classic though perhaps apocryphal example of this is the nail factory in the Soviet Union that had a performance goal specified in pounds of output. Its pound quota was easily met by simply concentrating production efforts on large spikes! Clearly this one measure does not encompass all of the goals that are expected of this organization.

A characteristic of social organizations is that it is difficult to quantify output and hence to translate goals and objectives into performance measures. The final article in this section, "Tailoring MBO to Hospitals" by Hand and Hollingsworth, discusses this problem at length. Their suggestions will no doubt give courage to managers in other types of social organizations. For example, the authors consider a nurse's performance to contain many intangible items not readily measurable. They recommend for jobs of this type that monthly performance ,reviews by the nurse's immediate supervisor be used in lieu of a quantifiable measure such as number of patient contact hours. Hand and Hollingsworth suggest that motivation be accomplished by "proper" measures of performance and that performance measures be linked to employee compensation.

WHAT RESULTS SHOULD YOU EXPECT? A USERS' GUIDE TO MBO

Peter F. Drucker

MBO has a longer history in governmental institutions than most of its present-day practitioners realize. The basic concepts are strongly advocated by Luther Gulick and his associates in the mid and late '30s, in their studies of the organization and administration of the federal government. Yet the concept of management by objectives and self-control originated with the private sector. It was first practiced by the DuPont Company after World War I. By the mid-'20s, Alfred P. Sloan, Jr., of General Motors used the term "Management by Objectives and Self-Control" systematically and with great conceptual clarity.

Yet today MBO seems to have become more popular in public service institutions than it is in the private sector; it is certainly more discussed as a tool of the public, especially the governmental administrator.

There is good reason for this popularity of MBO in the public sector. Public service institutions need it far more than any but the very biggest and most complex businesses. Public service institutions always have multiple objectives and often conflicting, if not incompatible objectives. While no institution, including business, has truly satisfactory measurements, the measurements generally available to government agencies and other public service institutions, especially in the budget area, rarely have anything to do with performance and goal attainment. Even a fairly small governmental agency, such as one of the smaller and less populous states or a medium-sized city, is a "conglomerate" of greater diversity and complexity than even ITT.

The resources of public service institutions are people, and the outputs are rarely "things." Therefore, direction toward meaningful results is not inherent in the work or in the process itself. Misdirection, whether by the individual employee or by the administrator, is at the same time both easy and hard to detect. Public service institutions are prone to the deadly disease of "bureaucracy"; that is toward mistaking rules, regulations, and the smooth functioning of the machinery for accomplishment, and the self-interest of the agency for public service.

Public service institutions, in other words, particularly need objectives and concentration of efforts on goals and results—that is, management. These are, of course, precisely the needs management by objectives and self-control (MBO) promises to satisfy. But the same reasons which make MBO potentially so productive for the public service institution also make it only too easy for the institution to mistake MBO procedures for the substance of both management and objectives. Indeed, they may encourage the fatal error of misusing MBO as a substitute for thinking and decision making.

Therefore, the administrator in the public service institution needs a "users' guide." He needs to know whether he uses MBO correctly or whether he misuses it. He needs to know, above all, the results MBO yields if used prop-

Source. Copyright © 1976 by the American Society for Public Administration. All rights reserved. Reprinted from *Public* Administration Review (January/February, 1976), pp. 12–19.

erly. That, I am afraid, is what few of the texts and manuals spell out. Yet only when these results have been achieved has MBO really been applied.

MBO is both management by *objectives* and *management* by objectives. What is needed, therefore, are two sets of specifications—one spelling out the results in terms of objectives and one spelling out the results in terms of management.

WHAT ARE OUR OBJECTIVES? WHAT SHOULD THEY BE?

The first result, and perhaps the most important one which the administrator needs to aim at in applying MBO, is the *clear realization that his agency actually has no objectives*. What passes for objectives are, as a rule, only good intentions.

The purpose of an objective is to make possible the organization of work for its attainment. This means that objectives must be operational: capable of being converted into specific performance, into work, and into work assignments. However, almost no public service agency has operational objectives. To say our objective is "the maintenance of law and order" or "health care" is operationally a meaningless statement. Nothing can be deduced from these statements with respect to the goals and the work needed. Yet these statements are already a good deal more operational, more nearly true objectives, than is commonly found in the objectives statements of public service agencies.

The first result to be expected from management by *objectives* is the realization that the traditional statement of objectives is inadequate, is indeed in most cases totally inappropriate. The first work to be done is to identify what the objectives should or could be.

The moment this question is raised, how-

ever, it will also be realized—and this is the second result to be obtained—that *objectives* in public service agencies are ambiguous, ambivalent, and multiple. This holds true in private business as well.

The hospital, while complex, is still a very small institution compared to most governmental agencies. Yet its objectives are by no means clear. "Health Care" sounds plausible; most hospitals have nothing to do with health care. They are concerned with the treatment and care of the sick. Clearly, the most intelligent and most effective way to produce health care is the prevention of sickness, rather than its treatment and cure. To the extent that we know how to provide health care it is not, bluntly, the task of the hospital at all. It is done by the public health measures such as vaccination, providing pure drinking water, and adequate treatment of sewage. Hospitals, in effect, are the result of the failure of health care, rather than agencies to provide it.

Yet even if the hospital defines its objectives very narrowly, as do the hospitals in the British Health Service, as the "treatment of the sick" (repair of damage already done), the objectives are still cloudy. Is the hospital, as in the traditional concept of the American community hospital, the private physician's plant facility and an extension of his office? Is it, in other words, the place where the physician takes care of those patients whom he cannot take care of in his own office or in his own private practice? Or should the hospital, as so many American hospitals have attempted, be the "health care center" for the community, through such activities as the well-baby clinic, counseling service for the emotionally disturbed, and so on? Should the hospital also become the substitute for the private physician and provide the physician's services to the poor—the objectives of the outpatient department in the American big city hospital today? If the hospital defines its function as care of the sick, what then is the role and function of the maternity service? Giving birth to a baby is, after all, no sickness, but a perfectly normal and indeed perfectly healthy occurrence.

Similarly, when the police department tries to make operational the vague term "maintenance of law and order" it will find immediately that there is a multiplicity of possible objectives—each of law and order" it will find immediately that there is a multiplicity of possible objectives—each of them, ambiguous. "Prevention of crime" sounds very specific. But what does it really mean, assuming that anyone knows how to do it? Is it, as many police departments have traditionally asserted, the enforcement of all the laws on the statute book? Or is it the protection of the innocent law-abiding citizen, with respect both to his person and to his property? Is it safety on the streets or safety in the home, or is it both? Is the primary task the eradication and prevention of corruption within the police force itself? The latter may sound quite peripheral, if not trivial. Yet in a recent major study of the job of chief of police, sponsored by one of the agencies of the federal government, the experienced police chiefs guiding the study maintained that to rid police forces of corruption was the first, and most important, objective in maintaining law and order.

In attempting to reduce pious intentions to genuine objectives, the administrator will invariably find that equally valid objectives are mutually incompatible or, at least, quite inconsistent.

The classic example is the American farm policy of the last 40 years. Strengthening the American farmer was the stated objective from the beginning, before New Deal days. Does this mean protecting the family farmer? Or does it mean making the American farmer efficient, productive, and capable of world market competition? Congress, in writing farm legislation,

has always used rhetoric indicating that the purpose of farm policy is to protect and preserve the small family farmer. However, the actual measures then enacted to achieve this purpose have primarily been aimed at making farming a more efficient, more productive, and more competitive industry, in which the small family farmer has practically no place and may indeed be an impediment to the attainment of the goal.

Thus the most important result of management by *objectives* is that it forces the administrator into the realization that there cannot be one single objective, notwithstanding the language of policy statements, whether acts of Congress or administrative declarations. To call realization of this fundamental problem a result of management by *objectives* may seem paradoxical. Yet it may be the most important result, precisely because it forces the administrator and his agency to a realization of the need to think and of the need to make highly risky balancing and trade-off decisions. This should be one of the results management by *objectives* strives for, which have to be attained if MBO is to be an effective tool which strengthens the performance of the institution.

The next area in which management by *objectives* has to attain results is that of *priorities* and *posteriorities*.

Public service institutions, almost without exception, have to strive to attain multiple objectives. At the same time each area of objectives will require a number of separate goals. Yet no institution, least of all a large one, is capable of doing many things, let alone of doing many things well. Institutions must concentrate and set priorities. By the same token, they must make risky decisions about what to postpone and what to abandon—to think through posteriorities.

One basic reason for this need to concentrate is the communications problem, both within the institution and among the various external publics. Institutions which try to attain simultaneously a great many different goals end up confusing their own members. The confusion is extended twofold to the outside public on whose support they depend.

Another cogent reason for concentration of goals is that no institution has an abundance of truly effective resources. We have all learned that money alone does not produce results. Results require the hard work and efforts of dedicated people; such people are always in short supply. Yet nothing destroys the effectiveness of competent individuals more than having their efforts splintered over a number of divergent concerns—a function of the frustration that results from giving part-time attention to a major task. To achieve results always requires thorough and consistent attention to the problem by at least one effective man or woman.

Finally, and this may be the most important factor, even a unitary or a simple goal often requires a choice between very different strategies which cannot be pursued at the same time; one of them has to be given priority, which means that the other one assumes secondary status or is abandoned for an unspecified time.

One example of this dilemma, which is familiar to every experienced administrator, is the educational policy in developing countries. That a trained and schooled population is desirable, and is indeed a prerequisite for social and economic development, would be accepted by practically all students of development. However, should primary emphasis be given to the education of a small, but exceedingly capable, elite? Or should the main drive be on "mass literacy"? Few countries can pursue both goals simultaneously—they must make a choice. If the first course is followed there is the risk of educating people to be highly skilled and at great expense to the country. The consequences are that the society cannot utilize the expertise it

has paid for and cannot provide meaningful jobs for those individuals. The result is then a "brain drain" in which the potentially most productive, most expensive resources of a poor country leave to find opportunities elsewhere for the application of their knowledge.

If the second alternative is being followed, there is the risk of educating large masses of people who are no longer satisfied with traditional employment and/or traditional subsistence standards of living. These people cannot find the jobs they have been trained for and have been led to expect, simply because institutions capable of employing them do not emerge, and the leadership is missing.

To set priorities is usually fairly simple, or at least seems policitally fairly simple. What is difficult and yet absolutely essential is the risk-taking and politically dangerous decision as to what the posteriorities should be. Every experienced administrator knows that what one postpones, one really abandons. In fact, it is a sound rule not to postpone but to make the decision not to do something altogether or to give up doing something. For in strategy, timing is of the essence. Nothing is usually less productive than to do ten years later what would have been an excellent and worthwhile program ten years earlier.

If an illustration is needed, the fate of so many of President Johnson's programs would supply it. What made so many of these programs fail is not that they were the wrong programs, or even that they were inadequately supported. They were, in large measure, five or ten years too late. These programs had been postponed, and when the time came to do them, that is when Congress was willing to consider them after long years of resistance, they were no longer the "right" programs.

In addition, public service institutions find "abandonment of yesterday" even more difficult than businesses. Business, of course, does not like to abandon. The product or service that no longer serves a purpose, no longer produces results, no longer fulfills a major need, is usually also the product or service which the people now at the top have spent the best part of their working lives to create and to make succeed. However, in business enterprise, the market eventually forces management to face up to reality and to abandon yesterday.

The Ford Motor Company held onto the Edsel as long as it could—far longer than economic reality justified. The American public had abandoned the Edsel long before Ford management was willing to accept the verdict. Eventually, however, even a very large, strong, and stubborn company had to accept reality.

No such pressure exists as a rule in the public service institution. Indeed, if we had had ministries of transportation around in 1850 or 1900 we might now have in every country major research projects, funded with billions of dollars, to reeducate the horse. In any public service institution, whether government agency, hospital, school, or university, any activity and any service almost immediately creates its own constituency: in the legislature, the press, or the public. Yet nothing is quite as difficult to do as to maintain the moribund. It requires greater energies, greater effort, and greater abilities to sustain an obsolete program than to make effective the responsive and productive program.

Thus, the public service agency is always in danger of frittering away its best people as well as a great deal of money on activities which no longer produce, no longer contribute, have proven to be incapable of producing, or are simply inappropriate.

Therefore, essential to management by *objectives* in the public service agency is the establishment of priorities, decisions concerning areas for concentration.

Equally essential is the systematic appraisal of all services and activities in order to find the *candidates for abandonment*. Indeed it is wisdom in a public service agency to put each service and activity on trial for its life every three or four years and to ask: if we had known what we now know at the time we established this service, would we have gotten into it? If the answer is no, one does not say, what do we have to do to make it viable again? One does not even say, should we consider getting out of it? One says, how fast can we get out?

Goals of abandonment and schedules to attain these goals are an essential part of management by *objectives*, however unpopular, disagreeable, or difficult to attain they might be. The great danger in large institutions, especially in public service institutions, is to confuse fat with muscle and motion with performance. The only way to prevent this degenerative disease is a systematic procedure for abandoning yesterday, setting specific and courageous goals for abandonment.

In this respect, the Budget Reform Act of 1974 may represent the biggest step forward in public administration in many decades, though it still remains to be seen, of course, whether the act will produce the desired results. This Act entrusted the General Accounting Office with the duty of appraising existing programs and projects in the federal service based on their suitability, stated objectives, and appropriateness.

But will the Congress that wrote the Act be willing to face up to its abandonment implications?

The next results are *specific goals*, with specific *targets*, specific *timetables*, and specific *strategies*. Implicit in this is the *clear definition of the resources* needed to attain these goals, the efforts needed, and primarily the *allocation* of available resources—especially of available manpower. A "plan" is not a plan unless the resources of competent, performing people needed for its attainment have been specifically allocated. Until then, the plan is only a good intention; in reality not even that.

Finally, management by *objectives* needs to bring out as a clear result of the thinking and analysis process how performance can be *measured,* or at least *judged.*

It is commonly argued that public service institutions aim at intangible results, which defy measurement. This would simply mean that public service institutions are incapable of producing results. Unless results can be appraised objectively, there will be no results. There will only be activity, that is, costs. To produce results it is necessary to know what results are desirable and be able to determine whether the desired results are actually being achieved.

It is also not true that the activities of public service institutions cannot be measured. "Missions" are always intangible, whether of business enterprise or of social service institutions.

Sears Roebuck and Company defined its mission in the '20s as being the "buyer for the American Family." This is totally intangible. But the objectives which Sears then set to accomplish this mission (e.g., to develop a range of appliances that most nearly satisfy the largest number of homeowners at the most economical price) was an operational objective from which clear and measurable goals with respect to product line, service, assortment, price, and market penetration could be derived. This in turn made possible both the allocation of efforts and the measurement of performance.

"Saving souls" as the mission of a church is totally intangible. At least the bookkeeping is not of this world. However, the goal of bringing at least two-thirds of the young people of the congregation into the church and its activities is easily measured.

Similarly, "health care" is intangible. But the goals for a maternity ward which state that the number of "surprises" in delivery must not be more than two or three out of every hundred deliveries; the number of post-partum infections of mothers must not exceed one-half of one percent of all deliveries; eight out of ten of all premature babies born live after the seventh month of conception must survive in good health are not intangible, but fairly easy to measure.

To think through the appropriate measurement is in itself a policy decision and therefore highly risky. Measurements, or at least criteria for judgment and appraisal, define what we mean by performance. They largely dictate where the efforts should be spent. They determine whether policy priorities are serious or are merely administrative doubletalk. For this reason it needs to be emphasized that measurements need to be measurements of performance rather than of efforts. It is not adequate, indeed it is misleading, to use measurements that focus on efficiency of operation, rather than on the services the agency delivers to somebody outside, whether another public service agency or the public. Measurement directs effort and vision. One of the central problems of public service agencies, indeed of all organizations, is the tendency to direct efforts and vision toward the inside, that is toward efficiencies, rather than toward the purposes on the outside for which every public service institution exists.

With measurements defined, it then becomes possible to organize the *feedback* from results to activities. What results should be expected by what time? In effect, measurements decide what phenomena are results. Identifying the appropriate measurements enables the administrator to move from diagnosis to prognosis. He can now lay down what he expects will happen and take proper action to see whether it actually does happen.

The actual results of action are not predictable. Indeed, if there is one rule for action, and especially for institutional action, it is that the expected results will not be attained. The unexpected is practically certain. But are the unexpected results deleterious? Are they actually more desirable than the results that were expected and planned? Do the deviations from the planned course of events demand a change in strategies, or perhaps a change in goals or priorities? Or are they such that they indicate opportunities that were not seen originally, opportunities that indicate the need to increase efforts and to run with success? These are questions the administrator in the public service agency rarely asks. Unless he builds into the structure of objectives and strategies the organized feedback that will force these questions to his attention, he is likely to disregard the unexpected and to persist in the wrong course of action or to miss major opportunities.

Organized feedback leading to systematic review and continuous revision of objectives, roles, priorities, and allocation of resources must therefore be built into the administrative process. To enable the administrator to do so is a result and an important result, of management by *objectives*. If it is not obtained, management by *objectives* has not been properly applied.

WHAT IS MANAGEMENT? WHAT SHOULD IT BE?

Management by objectives, similarly, has to attain a number of results to be properly applied.

The first result is *understanding*. *Management* by objectives is often described as a way to obtain agreement. But this is gross oversimplification. The decision which MBO identifies and brings into focus—the decisions on objectives and their balance; on goals and strategies; on priorities and abandonment; on efforts and resource allocation; on the appropriate measurements—are far too complex, risky, and uncertain to be made by acclamation. To make them intelligently requires *informed dissent*.

What MBO has to produce as the first *management* result is understanding of the diffi-

culty, complexity, and risk of these decisions. It is understanding that different people, all employed in a common task and familiar with it, define objectives and goals differently, see different priorities, and would prefer very different and incompatible strategies. Only then can the decision be made effectively.

The decisions to be made are also of such complexity and of such importance that the responsible administrator would not want to make them without understanding them. The full complexity of any issue can only be understood on the basis of informed dissent. "Adversary proceedings" are not the best way, as a rule, to make these decisions. Informed dissent is essential where people of good will and substantial knowledge find out how differently they view the same problem, the same mission, the same task, and the same reality. Otherwise, symptoms rather than the underlying problem will be attacked; trivia rather than results will be pursued.

It is almost 50 years since Mary Parker Follett applied the early insights of perception psychology to point out that people in an organization who seem to differ on the answers usually differ on what the right question is. The issues with which the administrator in the public service institution deals are of such complexity and have so many dimensions that any one person can be expected to see only one aspect and only one dimension rather than the total concept.

However, effective action requires an understanding of complexity. It requires an ability to see a problem in all its major dimensions. Otherwise, a maximum of effort will produce no results. but more commonly wrong and undesired results.

Management by *objectives* is an administrative process rather than a political process. This makes it all the more important to focus on understanding as the first management result—bringing out the basic views, the basic dissents, the different approaches to the same task and the same problem within the organization.

The major departments of the federal government that have been created in the last 20 years—the Department of Defense, the Department of Health, Education and Welfare (HEW), the Department of Transportation, and the Department of Housing and Urban Development (HUD)—are commonly criticized for being ineffectual as well as administrative labyrinths. They are often contrasted, to their detriment, with older agencies such as the Department of the Interior or the Department of Agriculture, which, it is alleged, are so much more effective. The reason usually given for the lack of effectiveness of these newer agencies is "lack of direction" or "internal division." What made these older agencies effective, especially in the New Deal days when they reached a peak of effectiveness, was, however, the intelligent use of informed dissent on the part of the men who led them. Harold Ickes in Interior or Henry Wallace in Agriculture took infinite care to produce informed dissent within the organization and thus to obtain understanding for themselves and to create understanding for their associates. Thus, when decisions on goals and priorities were made unilaterally by the top man himself, and by no means democratically, they were understood throughout the organization; the top man himself understood what alternatives were available as well as the position of his people on them.

Similarly, the Japanese system of "decision by consensus" is often cited these days as an example for the American decision maker. However, the Japanese do not make decisions by consensus, rather they deliberate by consensus. The seemingly long gestation period of a decision in Japanese organizations is devoted to bringing out the maximum understanding within the organization and to enabling those who are going to have to participate in the subsequent action to express their own views of the issues and their own definitions of the question. Consequently, they find out where their colleagues and associates stand, what they feel, and how they feel. Then a decision can be reached which the organization understands, even though large groups within it do not necessarily agree or would have preferred a different decision. Perhaps the greatest strength of the Japanese process is that priorities can actually be set and be made effective.

The second management result of management by objectives is to produce *responsibility* and *commitment* within the organization; to make possible *self-control* on the part of the managerial and professional people.

The advocate of MBO likes to talk about participation. This is a misleading term, or at least an inadequate term. The desired result is willingness of the individual within the organization to focus his or her own vision and efforts toward the attainment of the organization's goals. It is ability to have self-control; to know that the individual makes the right contribution and is able to appraise himself or herself rather than be appraised and controlled from the outside. The desired result is commitment, rather than participation.

For this reason the usual approach of MBO toward goal-setting for the individual or for the managerial component is inadequate and may even do damage. Usually MBO says to the individual manager, here are the goals of this institution. What efforts do you have to make to further them? The right question is, what do you, given our mission, think the goals should be, the priorities should be, the strategies should be? What, by way of contribution to these goals, priorities, and strategies, should this institution hold you and your department accountable for over the next year or two? What goals, priorities, and strategies do you and your department aim for, separate and distinct from those of the institution? What will you have to contribute and what results will you have to produce to attain these goals? Where do you see major opportunities of contribution and performance for this institution and for your component? Where do you see major problems?

Needless to say, it is then the task of the responsible administrator to decide. It is not necessarily true, as so many romantics in management seem to believe, that the subordinate always knows better. However, it is also not necessarily true that the boss always knows better. What is true is that the two, subordinate and boss, cannot communicate unless they realize that they differ in their views of what is to be done and what could be done. It is also true that there is no *management* by objectives unless the subordinate takes responsibility for performance, results, and, in the last analysis, for the organization itself.

The next results are *personnel decisions.* As stated earlier, MBO requires allocation of resources and concentration of effort. *Management* by objectives should always result in changing the allocation of effort, the assignment of people and the jobs they are doing. It should always lead to a restructuring of the human resources toward the attainment of objectives. It is not true, though administrative routine believes it, if only subconsciously, that every existing job is the right job and has something to contribute. On the contrary, the ruling postulate should be: every existing job is likely to be the wrong job and needs to be restructured, or at least redirected. Job titles may be sacred and in every large organization there is an unspoken but fervent belief that the Good Lord created section chiefs. In reality, job substance changes with the needs of the organization, and assignments, that is the specific commitment to results, change even more frequently.

Job descriptions may be semi-permanent. However, assignments should always be considered as short-lived. It is one of the basic purposes of managerial objectives to force the question, what are the specific assignments in this position which, given our goals, priorities, and strategies at this time, make the greatest contribution?

Unless this question is being brought to the surface, MBO has not been properly applied. It must be determined what the right concentration of effort is and what the manpower priorities are, and convert the answer into personnel action. Unless this is done there may be objectives but there is no management.

Similarly important and closely related are results in terms of *organization structure.* If the work in organizations over the last 40 years has taught us anything, it is that structure follows strategy. There are only a small number of organization designs available to the administrator.[1] How this limited number of organization designs is put together is largely determined by the strategies that an organization adopts, which in turn is determined by its goals. *Management* by objectives should enable the administrator to think through organization structure. Organization structure, while not in itself policy, is a tool of policy. Any decision on policy, that is, any decision on objectives, priorities, and strategies, has consequences for organization structure.

The ultimate result of *management* by objectives is *decision*, both with respect to the goals and performance standards of the organization and to the structure and behavior of the organization. Unless MBO leads to decision, it has no results at all; it has been a waste of time and effort. The test of MBO is not knowledge, but effective action. This means, above all, risk-taking decisions.

The literature talks about MBO often as a "tool for problem solving." However, its proper application is as a means of problem definition and problem recognition. Perhaps even more important, it is a means of problem prevention.

Thus, MBO is not a procedure to implement decision, a systematic attempt to define, to think through, and to decide. Filling out forms, no matter how well designed, is not management by objectives and self-control. The results are!

MBO is often called a tool of planning. It is not the same thing as planning, but it is the core of planning. MBO is usually called a management tool. Again, it is not all of management, but it is the core of management. It is not the way to *implement* decisions on policy, on goals, on strategies, on organization structure, or on staffing. It is the *process* in which decisions are made, goals are identified, priorities and posteriorities are set, and organization structure designed for the specific purposes of the institution.

It is also the process of people integrating themselves into the organization and directing themselves toward the organization's goals and purposes. The introduction of MBO into public service institutions, especially into governmental agencies during the last few years, may thus be the first step toward making public service institutions effective. So far it is only a first step. What has been introduced so far, by and large, is the procedure, and there is danger in procedure being mistaken for substance. Yet the great need of the public institution is not procedure. Most of them have all the procedures they need—the great need is performance. Indeed, performance of the public service institution may be the fundamental, the central, need of modern society. Management by objectives and self-control should help fill a good part of this need. However, its success depends upon the administrator: in applying MBO he or she must obtain the right results, with respect both to *objectives* and to *management*.

NOTE

1. Peter F. Drucker, *Management: Tasks; Responsibilities; Practices* (New York: Harper & Row, 1974), chapters 41–48.

UNIVERSITY GOALS: AN OPERATIVE APPROACH

Clifton Conrad*

Social scientists have produced a substantial body of knowledge about different aspects of organizational behavior. Yet there are relatively few studies of goals in complex organizations.

Source. Copyright © 1974 by the Ohio State University Press. Reprinted by permission from *Journal of Higher Education* (October, 1974), pp. 504–516.
*I am indebted to Charles Warriner, professor of sociology at the University of Kansas, who first stimulated my interest in the study of universities. Joseph Cosand and Marvin Peterson offered useful comments on a draft of this paper.

either the official statements of goals are taken at face value [16] or the goals are taken for granted, in which case the most effective ordering of resources and personnel is seen as the only problematical issue.

Given this lacuna, a number of reasons can be advanced as to why goals should be studied, particularly university goals: first, for a more complete understanding of organizational behavior. Identifying goals will allow social scientists to devote more attention to the function that goals play in an organization. In the case of universities, for example, is there a relationship between clarity of goals, number of goals, and other goal characteristics on the one hand and university performance on the other? Do university goals explain organizational behavior, or, as David Silverman [14] argues, are they chiefly legitimating symbols? In statistical parlance, to what extent are university goals powerful independent variables in explaining and predicting behavior and processes within the university?

Secondly, goals may serve a variety of purposes for the organization. They may (1) serve as standards by which to judge its success, (2) constitute a source of legitimacy, (3) define organizational needs and priorities, (4) define production units or "outputs" for the organization, (5) define its clientele, or (6) define the nature of the relationship between the organization and society. In most universities, goals are often implicit, residing in an extended body of collective understandings rather than in explicit statements. If university goals are to serve the purposes listed above, they must be identified more precisely.

Administrators, the most frequent interpreters of organizational goals, have a sizable stake in identifying the goals of their organizations. Given the rising demand for accountability in universities, the very legitimacy of institutions may hinge on their willingness and sincerity in providing specific goal statements for their various constituencies. As those formally entrusted with the reins of power, administrators must bear the burden of responsibility for clearly identifying the goals of their institutions.

The central purpose of this essay is to offer a new way of conceptualizing goals, especially those of the university. Several explanations will be offered as to why universities do not have formal goals. The concept of "operative goals" will be suggested as a more useful characterization, and this conceptualization

will be clarified through an illustration of how operative goals are defined in the university. The advantages of this conceptualization are discussed, and lastly, several ways of identifying university operative goals are suggested.

I

As used in most organizational theories, the concept of goals refers to a more or less explicit and consciously recognized value system that lists and ranks in value order the objects or conditions to be produced by the ongoing activities in the organization and serves as a criterion for decision-making [11]. Formal goals in the Parsonian sense are not characteristic of universities; we do not find a more or less conscious value system that is utilized in university decision-making processes. There appear to be several factors that militate against the existence of such formal goals: (1) Many decisions that affect the character and major activities of the university are directly influenced by a number of constraints from both inside and outside the organization which are more important than any a priori goal scheme, and which force upon the university a continual process of adaptation to the environment producing those constraints. (2) Control and authority in the university are diffuse and indirect. Faculty members are generally quite autonomous with regard to the content and orientation of their courses, tenure, and similar practices—which makes it difficult for any central officer in the university to exert pressure upon the allocation of faculty time or direction of effort. Similarly, students have considerable autonomy in selection of programs. (3) There is generally no central, single body of individuals that makes decisions on resource allocation, course and curricular programs, and university personnel. In some cases a particular decision involves the joint approval and support of a number of different individuals. (4) The various individuals and groups participating in the numerous university decisions often use quite different criteria and sources of criteria for judgments on important policy decisions.

If formal goals are not characteristic of universities, universities nevertheless appear to have a directionality and continuity of activities over time. The concept of "operative goals" can fruitfully be employed to refer to the ends sought through the recurring activities of the organization.[1] These operative goals of a university emerge out of the daily decisions, conscious and unconscious, as to what is to be done and how it is to be done that are made by a wide variety of individuals. Operative goals can be identified through what universities do, especially what they do in a systematically recurring fashion.

As alluded to earlier, the programmatic characteristics of what is done in organizations—the operative goals—are a function of a variety of constraints that define what is done, how it is done, and the expected consequences, and that are, furthermore, more important than any a priori goal scheme. Herbert Simon [15] uses the term *constraint* to analyze the parameters of the decision-making system in formal organizations. Simon contends that decisions are made by reference to a set of requirements or constraints rather than to formal goals, yet formal goals are included as one constraint on the decision-making process. Building upon Simon's framework, the operative goals of a university can be seen as a function of constraints—the category of factors that determine the direction of activities in the organization. These constraints are sometimes introduced deliberately by individuals, but they are often introduced unconsciously through choices, selections, and decisions of which no organizational participants are aware. For analytical purposes, "operative goals" will be defined as the totality of "constraints" on the ongoing activities of the organization.

We are particularly interested in accounting for stability in the activities of the organization. The stability of the operative goals, the fact that the university continues to perform "functions" in a particular direction, comes from two aspects of these constraints: (1) the continuity of each of the constraints—that is, each of the constraints may have continuity and directionality over time, imposing the same kind of directionality on action—and (2) the stability over time in the relative importance of particular constraints. It can be assumed that individual constraints generally direct action somewhat differently. Thus, if there is to be stability of functions performed, it is necessary that the different constraints maintain continuous importance. Therefore, we would expect that the organizational activities would remain stable over time as the constraints are, individually, continuous over time, and as their relative importance remains the same.

It is highly probable that we are dealing here with an equilibrium among the constraints that has continual potential for change as the individual constraints change in either direction or relative importance. Furthermore, it is likely that the character of this equilibrium differs from time to time. At certain times it appears that the equilibrium is unstable even though the resulting patterning of action may remain fairly constant.

In summary, central to this proposal is the concept of constraints as the category of factors

---

[1]The phrase *operative goals* is borrowed from Charled Perrow [12] but our definition is different: whereas Perrow distinguishes between official and operative goals, our definition does not preclude official goals. More important, our definition is made in terms of constraints, while Perrow particularly emphasizes unofficial goals, multiple goals, and alternate ways of achieving official goals. The concept of "operational goals" suggested by James March and Herbert Simon [8] is similar to this but is never defined systematically.

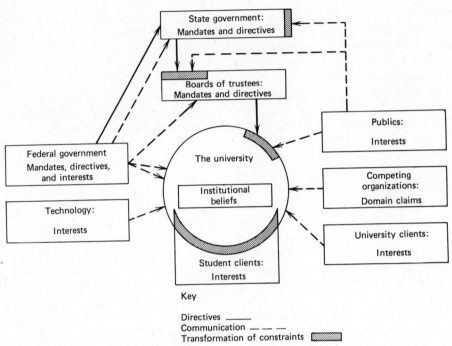

FIGURE 1   *Constraints on university operative goals*

that influence the directions of activities in the organization. Just as essential is some conception of the processes through which constraints perform this function. A tentative listing and discussion of the major constraints on activities in universities will be helpful in illustrating the concept and in identifying the processes of their operation. Figure 1 summarizes these constraints and the general nature of their impact on the university goals.

II

The major constraints on university operations include:

Institutional Beliefs

Within an institutional sphere, such as higher education, there are broad assumptions as to what are the "functions" of a university. These assumptions as to the appropriate, proper, and necessary "functions" may be implemented by laws which make distinctions between institutional types (e.g., tax laws distinguish educational, religious, and other nonprofit organizations from profit-making organizations); by licenses and other legal protections embedded in charters; and by the actions of outside organizations (industrial concerns act toward universities in different ways than they do toward other industrial concerns).

Most important, however, it is the conceptions of a university's functions by members of a university which determine the parameters of the institutional beliefs. The major work activities of a university are performed by the faculty. As members of the professional staff, they hold norms and values as to what they should do and how they should do it. The importance of these professional norms and values is expressed in the idea of faculty autonomy. Individually and collectively, faculty members resist any action that implies a violation of these norms and values. Similarly, as professional persons, the faculty have a variety of interests stemming from their professional training and identification with a professional establishment. Lastly, the faculty as a professional staff has a particular capacity for certain kinds of functions but not for others.

In summary, the institutional beliefs identify the range within which university operative goals may vary through the identification of the "functions" appropriate to universities. These assumptions of what are the functions of universities provide the major determinant of university operative goals. While the constraints hereafter discussed are variously important, the institutional beliefs provide the basic parameters of university operative goals.

State Government and Boards of Trustees

If an organization is primarily dependent upon the external environment for its resources, for its license to act, and for protection, then mandates and directives become important constraints on organizational operative goals. When an external body is superordinate and has some degree of power over the organization, its attempts at influencing operative goals are called mandating. Mandate statements may be rhetorical and directed toward some other public, may be criterion statements ineffectively implemented, or may be explicit and expressed only in control decisions. State universities, and many private institutions, are subject to mandates and directives from state legislatures and boards of trustees. Mandates and directives are often meant to have a coercive effect on university operative goals. Usually broad and vague, they are not always crucial to the functioning of the institutional goals and are almost always transformed as they pass into the organization; therefore, they are usually treated as an "opinion" to be taken into account, rather than as an absolute imperative. Increasingly, however, state governments and boards have exercised legal constraints over state universities which, coupled with the increased emphasis on state planning, may have important implications for future university operative goals.

Federal Government

Because the federal government and its various agencies are a major source of resources for the university and have numerous interests in the university, they exercise constraints in several ways, influencing operative goals through mandates and directives. Mandates have been used coercively by the federal government to insure the implementation of federal policies, e.g., the affirmative-action program. In the immediate future, new federal guidelines may take the form of directives.

Especially since World War II, government has influenced university operative goals through its multiplicity of interests, which are commonly manifest in enormous quantities of federally sponsored programs. While few perceive federal aid as a threat of governmental control over education, it nevertheless seems clear that many universities have adjusted their operative goals to federal interests in academe. Federal priorities in research, for example, have encouraged many upwardly mobile institutions to adjust their operative goals to include more emphasis on research-related activities. In light of its previous involvement, the mandates, directives, and interests of the federal government may continue to exert an important constraint on university operative goals.

Competing Organizations

External to organizations such as universities are other competing coordinate organizations which attempt to influence the operative goals by claiming domains of activity. These domain claims may be in terms of types of clients, geographical or social regions, types of activities, or types of consequences. Sometimes entire universities make domain claims in each of these areas. The University of Wisconsin at Green Bay, for example, with its emphasis on ecology, makes claims in terms of all the above.

Domain claims may be implemented by agreements among the organizations or by appeals to mandating bodies. In either case, the respective domain claims of competing organizations may directly (through mandates) or indirectly (by directives) affect the operative goals of universities.

University Clients

In addition to the federal government, the values produced in universities have other direct and indirect clients. Attempts by clients or customers to influence university operative goals are expressions of vested interests. They are often expressed by the purchase of or failure to purchase the university's product or service. Clients may organize as a special group to express their interest, appealing directly to the university or to its mandating bodies. Clients may also organize and gain status as quasi members of the university and attempt to influence operative goals from inside.

University clients might include: (1) industrial and financial organizations that use knowledge services; (2) other kinds of clients that might benefit from auxiliary services; and (3) the local community. While the impact of clients on university operative goals is unclear, they must be included in any listing of constraints.

Publics

Universities have a number of publics who have varied interests in the university. Interest may be expressed in some specific activity (such as

teaching methods), in the resources (taxes) required by the university, or in any number of organizational activities affecting the operative goals. The interests, opinions, and judgments of publics—such as alums, parents, and local communities—are transformed as they pass into the university; hence, though they are often taken into account, they seldom exercise a direct constraint. Interest expressions of publics are often implemented through mandating bodies (such as legislatures) or, more recently, through direct withholding of support for the university. In the latter case threat of such action provides a more direct constraint upon operative goals within the university.

Student Clients

Students are the major clients of universities. Their interests may become an important constraint on university activities either through their relationships with individual faculty members or through active participation in the decision-making processes of the university. Although there is almost a complete turnover of students every four or five years, the interests of students have historically tended to remain the same, as incoming students have usually been recruited from the same general population. However, many of the new students of the 1970s have differing population characteristics, e.g., unlike the students of the 1950s and 1960s, many of these students are "poor students academically" [2]. There is presently a scarcity of research on the potential impact of these new students on university activities and operative goals. At least a handful of observers has suggested that these new students—with their differing needs and motivational and ability characteristics—may provide a constraint of no mean proportion. But that prognostication must be tempered by the fact that student interests are seldom directly represented; rather the faculty, collectively and individually, transform expressed interests into needs. It is likely that these transformed statements of client interests change more slowly than do client interests themselves.

Technology

Although material technology has historically played a role in educational organizations, it has generally exerted a peripheral effect, either being developed to meet specific educational needs or only gradually being accepted from the external environment. However technology has been adapted, it is generally agreed that universities as organizations have probably affected more than they have been affected by emerging forms of technology; hence technology has not historically been a major constraint on university operative goals.

Recent innovations in material technology, coupled with corporations which are very adept at applying technology to the educational environment, have forced a reexamination of the impact of technology on universities. Major American companies, for example, the Control Data Corporation, have been promoting the possibilities of instructional computing. Moreover, since the technology employed in universities is relatively flexible, goals may be revised or adjusted quite easily to the technological resources available [17]. For these reasons, emerging forms of technology may increasingly serve as a major constraint on university operative goals.

To summarize, the operative goals of a university emerge out of the daily decisions, made by a wide variety of individuals, concerning what is to be done and how it is to be done. These decisions mark a continual adaptation to a variety of external and internal constraints. The stability of functions in a university comes from the relative stability of each of the constraints and the relative stability of the importance of each with respect to the others.

III

In this section, the advantages of our conceptualization of operative goals will be discussed. First, our definition does not preclude formal goals, yet it views the totality of constraints as more important than any a priori goal scheme. Put differently, our definition views constraints—which can include formal goals, but are not exclusively bound by them—as the major factors determining operative goals. Therefore, our use of operative goals avoids reification of organizational goals as synonymous with organizational behavior.[2] Furthermore, by viewing operative goals as problematic, dependent upon various constraints, we do not preclude looking at subgoals, multiple goals, and goal displacement—as does the usual use of "organizational goal." Indeed, our earlier illustration of constraints on university operative goals suggests the potential utility of our conceptual framework as a way of handling the shifting and complex nature of university goals.

There is a second and more compelling advantage of our concept of operative goals. In the past decade, several theoretical works on organizations have emphasized the interface between organizations and their environment [5,6,7]. When organizations must carry on transactions with their environment, they are viewed as open social systems, in which organizations are in turn influenced by their environment. Unfortunately, as Lawrence and Lorsch [6] point out, there has been a dearth of research on the organization—environment interface.

Unlike most definitions of organizational goals, which view goals as relatively static and

[2]Most of the literature assumes that goals explain organizational behavior. To avoid reification, however, we have used the term *operative goals* which, by definition, avoids this crude determinism.

uninfluenced by the environment, our definition of operative goals incorporates environmental inputs through the concept of constraints. Goals are viewed as continually being adapted not only to internal but also to external constraints.

Our earlier illustration suggests that external constraints are a potent factor in shaping the operative goals of universities. Inasmuch as most of its resources come from outside,[3] the university is subject to mandates, directives, and communications which influence its operative goals. By defining operative goals as a function of constraints, our concept includes the various external factors which may have an impact on the goals of the organization. In the case of universities, the impact of these constraints appears to be considerable.

IV

Thus far, our analysis implies that there is no single phenomenon that identifies the operative goals of a university at a particular time. It is necessary to seek indicators of goals and ultimately to construct an index of operative goals out of these several indicators. While a wide variety of phenomena might be used to assess operative goals in universities, we will offer two general approaches to the identification of university goals.

First, and following from our analysis, identification might involve the assessment of constraints on the organization. This would require identifying and measuring particular constraints as well as assessing their relative importance for the operative goals. The few studies of goal identification in universities have focused on organizational goals or "or-

ganizational climate" exclusively from inside the university and primarily from the standpoint of faculty and administrators. This focus is equivalent to the constraint we called "institutional beliefs."

There are a number of studies which identify and attempt to measure this constraint. The research of Gilbert [3] using administrators of a single large university and of Uhl [19] in five different types of institutions suggests the usefulness of a Q—sort technique with forced choice responses and of the Delphi approach. The college member's perception of his institution through the Institutional Functioning Inventory (IFI) [13] represents another attempt to measure this constraint. The Educational Testing Service has produced an Institutional Goals Inventory (IGI), which is a measure of how members of a college community (students, faculty, administrators, trustees) see the institution in terms of 90 goal statements. The most comprehensive attempt to measure university goals was the extensive survey by Edward Gross and Paul Grambsch [4] of faculty and administrators at 68 major universities. Their study conceptualized 47 output and support goals in five major categories and asked respondents to identify their perceived and preferred goals. While this instrument has generally been used to assess goal congruence among constituencies (faculty, students, and administrators) or congruence between perceived and preferred goals, it can also serve as a useful instrument for simply measuring the perceived goals as a measure of institutional beliefs. The IGI and the Gross and Grambsch instruments seem to be particularly good indices of the conceptions of a university's functions by members of the university—what we have called institutional beliefs.

While institutional beliefs identify the ranges through which operative goals may vary, they are only one constraint. Unfortunately, there are few, if any, available instru-

[3]In a suggestive article, James Thompson and William McEwen [18] argue that the university "competes as eagerly as any business firm, although perhaps more subtly." Also see Warren Bennis [1].

ments for measuring the other aforementioned constraints on university operative goals.[4] If we have correctly identified several key constraints, the immediate task is to construct valid instruments for measuring these various constraints. Only then can we broach the problem of determining the relative importance of constraints and offer judgments as to their functional import for the operative goals.

A second way of assessing operative goals is by inference through indirect indicators.[5] Captured in the institutional beliefs of universities are a number of beliefs about the connections between means and consequences. For example, it is assumed that for a university faculty to engage in scholarship it must have available a large and active library with professional librarians to provide access to the collections. These beliefs may give us clues to a number of indirect indices that can be used to assess operative goals.

If we are correct in thinking that the beliefs of institutions identify the ranges with which university operative goals may vary through the identification of the functions appropriate to universities, then it follows that the operative goals of a university are some mix of these functions. Therefore, universities will differ from each other in the relative importance given to certain functions and relative neglect of others. Therefore, our problem is (1) to identify these several functions and (2) to find reliable indices.

Because the institutional beliefs include

beliefs as to means for achieving these functions, beliefs that are used by universities, then the functional operative goals might be indicated by the relative presence of the means required for that function. For example: (1) scholarship and scientific research require access to the current work of other scholars and scientists; therefore, an organization oriented toward research and scholarship will have a higher number of journals and serials than an organization oriented toward teaching; (2) physical science research requires research laboratories and equipment; therefore, the research orientation will be shown by a high proportion of budget allocation for such supplies; (3) good undergraduate teaching requires the participation of senior faculty in that instruction; therefore, a teaching-oriented institution will have a high proportion of undergraduate instruction handled by full professionals. Once we have identified functions, agreed upon the means necessary to realize those functions, and developed valid instruments to measure the means, we can inferentially determine the operative goals of universities.

V

In conclusion, the basic purpose of this paper has been to offer a new way of conceptualizing goals, especially university goals. The lengthy illustration of constraints on university operative goals suggests the potential utility of such an approach. Although our conceptualization of operative goals is relatively complex, that complexity is necessary in light of the phenomena we are discussing. Finally, we have tentatively suggested two general methods of identifying university operative goals.

Because the theoretical understanding of organizations is dependent upon sound conceptualization, we must seek to further refine

[4]There have been attempts to measure students' perceptions of the general social and intellectual atmosphere of universities as reflected in Pace's College and University Environment Scales, CUES [10]. These "organizational climate" measures focus on student development and thus are an inadequate measure of the constraint we have titled "student clients."

[5]Miller and Rice [9] argue that the best method of determining "primary tasks" (goals) is for the observer to "infer" them through examining the behavior of the various parts of the organization.

our concepts. This paper is primarily an attempt to refine the concept of organizational goals within the context of the university.

REFERENCES

1. Bennis, Warren, "The Effect on Academic Goals of Their Market." *American Journal of Sociology,* 62 (July, 1956), 28–33.

2. Cross, K. Patricia. *Beyond the Open Door.* San Francisco: Jossey-Bass, Inc., 1971, p. 1.

3. Gilbert, C. C., III. *Identification of University Goal Structures Using Selected Research Methodologies.* (Doctoral dissertation, Southern Illinois University) Ann Arbor, Michigan: University Microfilms, 1971,. no. 72-16, 431.

4. Gross, Edward, and Paul V. Grambsch. *University Goals and Academic Power,* Washington, D.C.: American Council on Education, 1968.

5. Katz, Daniel, and Robert L. Kahn. *The Social Psychology of Organizations.* New York: John Wiley and Sons, Inc., 1966.

6. Lawrence, Paul R., and Jay W. Lorsch. *Developing Organizations: Diagnosis and Action.* Reading, Mass.: Addison-Wesley, 1969.

———, *Organization and Environment.* Cambridge, Massachusetts: Harvard Graduate School of Business Administration, 1967.

8. March, James G., and Herbert A. Simon. *Organizations.* New York: John Wiley and Sons, Inc., 1958.

9. Miller, Eric J., and Albert K. Rice, *Systems of Organizations; the Control of Task and Sentient Boundaries.* London: Tavistock, 1967.

10. Pace, Charles R. *College and University Environment Scales.* Princeton, New Jersey: Educational Testing Service, 1963.

11. Parsons, Talcott. "A Sociological Approach to the Theory of Formal Organizations." In *Structure and Process in Modern Societies.* Free Press of Glencoe, 1960.

12. Perrow, Charles. "The Analysis of Goals in Complex Organizations." *American Sociological Review,* 26 (December, 1961), 855.

13. Peterson, Richard, John Centra, Rodney Hartnett, and R. Linn. *Institutional Functioning Inventory: Preliminary Technical Manual.* Princeton, New Jersey: Educational Testing Service, 1970.

14. Silverman, David. *The Theory of Organizations.* New York: Basic Books, 1971, pp. 147.

15. Simon, Herbert. "On the Concept of Organizational Goal." *Administration Science Quarterly,* 9 (June, 1964), 1–22.

16. Stroup, Herbert. *Bureaucracy in Higher Education.* New York: The Free Press, 1966.

17. Thompson, James D., and Frederick Bates. "Technology, Organization, and Administration." *Administrative Science Quarterly,* 2 (December, 1957), 325–44.

18. Thompson, James D. and William J. McEwen. "Organizational Goals and Environment: Goal-Setting as an Interaction Process." *American Sociological Review,* 23 (February, 1958), 26.

19. Uhl, N. P. *Encouraging the Convergence of Opinion Through the Use of the Delphi Technique in the Process of Identifying an Institution's Goals.* Princeton, New Jersey: Educational Testing Service, 1971.

TAILORING MBO TO HOSPITALS

Herbert H. Hand and A. Thomas Hollingsworth

An increasingly difficult task faced by today's hospital administrators is the efficient utilization of employees and the retention of high performers. This article is concerned with the general problem of the administration of a hospital wage system and specifically concerned with the problems of employee productivity and turnover. Management by objectives (MBO) is suggested as a method by which administrators can best use their budgets to maximize utilization and retention of the hospital's human assets.

Hospital administrators report that hospitals have two major objectives: to provide quality patient care and to efficiently utilize financial resources. Inasmuch as salaries and wages are estimated to be 60—70 percent of the total operating costs of an average hospital, salary-wage expenditures are intimately related to the efficient utilization of financial resources. Total wage costs are, of course, a function of staff size, wage rates, employee benefits, and employee turnover. Therefore, as the effectiveness of individual employees decreases, either more staff is required (and wage costs subsequently increase) or the quality of patient care decreases and the hospital's objectives are unfulfilled.

The importance of employee turnover as a portion of total wage cost should be noted. Turnover costs contribute to both direct and indirect labor costs through inefficient job performance, improper supervision, and scheduling problems. Turnover rates for hospitals range from 36 to 72 percent annually.[1] Hospital administrators should be very much aware of how wages affect the vital areas of both employee productivity and employee turnover, because these areas appear to have a strong functional link to the two primary objectives of hospitals.

One could reasonably assume that hospital administrators have made a number of attempts to relate wages to productivity and turnover. This, however, is not the case. The majority of hospitals base wage increases primarily on tenure. The theory underlying this practice is that productivity improvement is primarily a function of time on the job and that rewards should be given to those who remain on the staff rather than keep high producers on the job.

This practice undermines any attempt to relate wages to productivity and therefore fails to utilize the motivational potential of wages. The succeeding paragraphs will deal with the effect of pay on employee turnover and productivity. In view of the large number of variables that are thought to affect productivity and turnover, the general recommendations which follow should be tailored to specific hospitals.

PAY AND PRODUCTIVITY

Measuring Employee Output

A hospital employee's output is a difficult quantity to determine. It is often confused through the use of macro-type measures, and it

Source. Copyright © 1975 by the Foundation for the School of Business at Indiana University. Reprinted by permission from *Business Horizons* (February, 1975), pp. 45—52.

[1]Training, Research, and Special Division, *Analyzing and Reducing Turnover in Hospitals* (New York: United Hospital Fund of New York, 1969), p. 2.

is often erroneously measured by the amount of cost reduction (or addition) attained over a period of time per employee. However, before pay can be related to productivity, a viable method of measuring individual performance must be utilized.

A number of traditional measures of productivity are used in hospitals. One is patient days, the unit of measure that represents facility utilization and services rendered between the census-taking time on two successive days. This measure does not consider ambulatory care, so adjusted patient days (APD) are often utilized to measure the total range of services provided per day by the hospital.

Another traditional measure is the full-time equivalent employee (FTE) to patient ratio. In 1970, the national average wsa 292 FTEs per 100 patients. This measure allows a macrocomparison among hospitals. Unfortunately, hospitals differ to a large extent, and such comparisons are poor at best.

The preceding macro-type measures must be supplemented by more precise measures if valid indicators of both departmental and individual effort are to be realized. Since hospitals provide so many functions, there is a need for a number of measurements particularized by functional or departmental area. Such a list is shown in the accompanying table.

These measures help evaluate a department's performance within the hospital, but they specify only labor input as an incremental average of total output. This may not measure an individual's effort. For instance, a single lab test may take five times as long to run as another. Therefore, weighting systems are needed. The table and corresponding weighting systems demonstrate the complexity of measuring individual performance across the numerous functional areas found in hospitals. Specific forms of performance measurement are needed if wages are to be successfully related to productivity.

Money as Motivator

Individual performance is thought to be a function of motivation and ability. Motivation to perform is determined by a number of variables. Specifically, how should the wage aspect of an administrator's budget affect the motivation of employees. Four conditions must be present for money to be a motivator.

First, a direct linkage must be perceived between pay and performance. *Second,* money must have some importance to the individual. *Third,* there must be a minimum of negative consequences associated with high performance. *Fourth,* conditions should provide intrinsic as well as extrinsic rewards.

Intrinsic rewards are those that are internal to an individual; they are provided through accomplishments. Extrinsic rewards are provided by the organization and are external to the individual (for example, a pay increase). Pay is a complex variable. Pay is importat not only in absolute amount, but also in perceived equity and in the administration of the pay system. When pay is treated as a quasi-fringe benefit by management, it cannot be an effective motivator; it must be directly related to performance to be effective.

Although money is a motivational tool, there is no well-defined theory that relates money to performance in organizations. However, a number of incentive programs have attempted to relate pay to productivity.

Incentive plans, no matter how well conceived, cannot compensate for deficiencies in other variables contributing to the total output of the organization. These plans can only attempt to improve the wage—performance relationship.

For example, one study compared the incentive systems of two hospitals. The sample consisted of 146 registered nurses (73 from each institution). The extrinsic reward policies in the two hospitals were highly differentiated. In

Measures of Performance in Hospitals

Department	Occasion of Service
Anesthesiology	Number of patients, hours of administration and use
Basal metabolism	Number of tests
Blood bank	Number of 500-cc. units prepared for transfusions
Central supply	Dollar value of processed requisitions
Delivery rooms	Number of deliveries
Dietary	Number of meals served
Electrocardiology	Number of examinations
Housekeeping	Hours of service rendered to various departments
Inhalation therapy	Number of hours that oxygen is administered
Laboratory	Number of tests
Laundry	Pounds or pieces processed
Nursing	Hours or days of service
Occupational therapy	Hours of teaching and supervision
Operation of plant	Thousands of pounds of steam produced, plus pounds of ice produced, plus kilowatt hours of electricity produced
Operating room	Number of operations, hours of use
Pharmacy	Dollar value of prescriptions and requisitions processed
Physical therapy	Number of treatments
Postoperative or post- anesthesia recovery rooms	Number of patient hours of service
Radiology/diagnostic	Number of films taken, plus number of fluoroscopic examinations
Radiology/therapeutic	Number of X-ray treatments, plus number of radium implementations, plus number of treatments by radioactive elements

Source. Nicole Williams, *The Management of Hospital Employee Productivity* (Chicago: American Hospital Association, 1973), p. 31.

one, rewards were based on effort; in the other, they were based almost strictly on tenure. The results of the study demonstrated that the nurses' performance was significantly greater in the hospital offering rewards based on effort. The authors feel that pay was a sufficient but not necessary cause for encouraging a high degree of effort on the part of the nurses.

Another study reported an incentive plan set up in a 205-bed hospital. A cost reduction program was based solely on cost savings (not performance). The program was deemed successful, and the success seemed to be the result of two variables. *First,* the hospital had an efficient cost system, which reported the monthly financial status of departments.

Second, the incentives were paid within the same time period as the cost reductions. This point is important, since it attempts to link wages directly with performance.

A third study compared hospitals with and without incentive systems. The individuals in the hospital without an incentive system tended to feel that pay is a function of a number of variables *other than performance.* The workers in the hospital with an incentive system tended to feel that pay is significantly related to their performance.

PAY AND ATTRITION

Turnover is a costly problem for any organization. Hospitals are no exception. Although there is no standard measure of turnover in hospitals, estimates range from 3 to 6 percent per month or 36 to 72 percent yearly. This figure appears to be substantially higher than that for most industrial concerns.

In 1969, it was estimated that the cost of replacing a low-skilled worker in a hospital was $300 and of replacing a staff nurse or department head, $500–$1,000. These costs include separation activities, advertising, interviewing, physical examination, payroll, orientation, training, and the initial job inefficiency caused by inexperience.[2] More recent figures are not available, but certainly costs have risen substantially.

In order to reduce turnover, the rate of turnover must be determined as well as where it is occurring in the hospital. Two methods of determining rate of turnover and whether it is localized or generalized follow:

1. $$\frac{\text{Total Separations for the Month}}{\text{Number on Payroll at Midmonth}} \times 100$$

   = Monthly Turnover Rate

2. $$\frac{\begin{array}{c}\text{Number of Employees Continuing}\\ \text{on Payroll for Full Year}\end{array}}{\begin{array}{c}\text{Number of Employees on Payroll}\\ \text{on First Day of the Year}\end{array}} \times 100$$

   = Annual Stability Rate

These two equations have three interpretations.

Turnover localized to specific jobs and positions—This occurs when both ratios are high. A high monthly turnover rate demonstrates that there is a turnover problem. However, when this is coupled with a high stability rate, turnover for the hospital in general is not high—a few departments are causing the high turnover rate, not the hospital in general.

General turnover problem—This occurs when the monthly turnover rate is high and the annual stability rate is low. This demonstrates that turnover is high and is occurring throughout the hospital.

Acceptable turnover rate—An acceptable turnover rate can be defined by a low turnover rate and high stability rate. This demonstrates that there are no specific problems, and, in general, the stability of the hospital's work force is high.

This approach indicates to an administrator the degree of his turnover problem and tells him whether it is a general problem or one confined to specific departments or jobs. By carefully utilizing the above information, an administrator can determine the extent of the difficulty and also where his efforts should be directed.

These measures define the problem of turnover but not its causes. James March and Herbert Simon, after a review of the literature, concluded that the major determinant in the decision to leave an organization is an individual's job satisfaction. As satisfaction increases, the probability of leaving decreases. The authors also postulated a number of variables affecting job satisfaction: conformity of job to self-image, predictability of job relationships, and conformity of job and other roles.[3] Based on the preceding variables, it is theorized that when an individual is inclined to leave an organization and perceives a number of attractive or equally attractive alternatives, he is not likely to remain. This indicates the complexity of the decision to leave a particular hospital.

[2]Training, Research, and Special Division, *Analyzing and Reducing Turnover in Hospitals* New York: United Hospital Fund of New York, 1968), p. 6.

[3]James March and Herbert Simon, *Organizations* (New York: John Wiley and Sons, Inc., 1958), p. 99.

A number of studies in hospitals and industry have illustrated the importance of job satisfaction to turnover. A study at the Mount Sinai Hospital in New York City found four major causes of employee separations: unsatisfactory interpersonal relationships, dissatisfaction with ratings, dissatisfaction with the pay systems, and general disappointment related to expectations (actual experiences did not match hospital advertising).

A second study concluded that turnover was inversely related to job satisfaction. Two other reviews of the literature concluded that there was a consistent negative relationsiip between job satisfaction and turnover. However, no simple relationship was found between job satisfaction and performance. Another study, after a review of the satisfaction literature, found that there was little evidence to support any relationship between job satisfaction and productivity, but there was a relationship between job satisfaction and turnover.

The above studies exemplify the fact that the decision to leave a job, while based on job satisfaction, is a complex decision confounded by a myriad of variables. The remainder of this section will examine job satisfaction with emphasis on how it can be affected by pay and how pay can aid in reducing turnover.

Job satisfaction is a multidimensional concept. Larry L. Cummings and Donald P. Schwab, after an extensive literature search, concluded that job satisfaction is a highly variable construct and must be measured in various ways.[4] Hence, total job satisfaction is the result of a number of causal variables. Pay distribution is only one of a number of reasons for job dissatisfaction. However, it is the primary one with which we are concerned. Its contribution to total job satisfaction may vary in different situations, but pay dissatisfaction is a probable major cause for attrition and may influence turnover even when it is a relatively unimportant determinant of total satisfaction.

A number of variables are related to pay satisfaction: importance of pay, job characteristics, and perceived equity in the pay system. Two notes of caution must be mentioned. *First*, no well-defined relationship between satisfaction and productivity has been shown. For instance, in a classic study, David L. Cherrington, Joseph H. Reitz and William E. Scott found that while pay did increase job satisfaction in all cases, it did not increase performance unless it was directly related to performance.[5]

Second, administrators should not rely on money to solve all their problems.

There is a tendency for hospital administrators to overemphasize the importance of economic rewards. While they rated wages as the primary determinants of employee satisfaction, employees did not. In a study of 83 nursing homes in Pennsylvania, Robert Percorchik and Borden H. Nelson found that while only 25 percent of those leaving cited pay as the cause of leaving, 40 percent of the administrators felt that pay was really the cause.[6] It might be generally concluded that all supervisors tend to overrate the importance of pay, relative to their subordinates.

These findings illustrate the complex relationship between pay and attrition. The problem for a budget director is to determine an optimum allocation of wages to minimize turnover. A variable budget approach is recommended to allow for specific differences of employees and to differentially reward superiors who are instrumental in decreasing

[4]Larry L. Cummings and Donald P. Schwab, "Theories of Performance and Satisfaction: A Review," *Industrial Relations* (October 1970), pp. 408–30.

[5]David L. Cherrington, Joseph H. Reitz, and William E. Scott, Jr., "Effects of Contingent and Noncontingent Reward on the Relationship Between Satisfaction and Task Performance," *Journal of Applied Psychology* (December 1971), pp. 531–36.

[6]Robert Pecorchik and Borden H. Nelson, "Employee Turnover in Nursing Homes," *American Journal of Nursing* (February 1973), pp. 289–90.

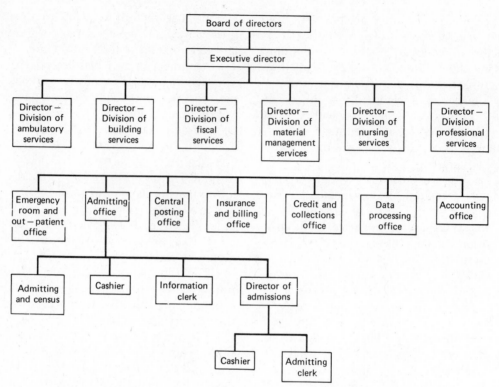

FIGURE 1 *Partial organization chart—example hospital*

attrition. These recommendations are covered fully in the final section regarding the implementation of an MBO program.

THE MBO PROGRAM

Management by objectives is recommended as a particularly effective method of relating salary and wages to productivity and attrition. Ideally, the program should be initiated when both the executive director and the board of directors not only establish positive support for the program, but also clearly define the overall mission of the hospital. Subsequently, the executive director should spend substantial blocks of time with the directors of the various services performed by the hospital (see Figure 1).

The purpose of these meetings is to have each director establish more specific objectives

that will support the hospital missions. Upon completion of the objectives-setting task, the director meets with his or her subordinates (see Director-Division of Fiscal Services portion of Figure 1) to establish goals that are compatible with the director's objectives. This process is continued through the hospital organization until all employees have taken part in the objectives-setting process. There are a number of suggested measures of activities in hospitals, and these measures should serve as a guide whenever possible.

William E. Reif and Gerald Bassford indicate that the crux of MBO is setting objectives, developing action plans, conducting periodic reviews, and appraising annual performance.[7]

[7]William E. Reif and Gerald Bassford, "What MBO Really Is," *Business Horizons* (June 1973), pp. 23–30.

It is incumbent upon the MBO program to take cost factors into consideration. Each supervisor should be provided financial performance records by which the performance efficiency of each individual can be ascertained. This is a very promising approach for gauging not only administrative performance in hospitals but also professional performance, such as nursing services, laboratory, EEG, EKG, inhalation therapy, pharmacy, and anesthesia.

For instance, while laundry can be measured by counting the output, a nurse's performance contains intangible items not readily measurable. An MBO program with monthly reviews is one of the best means of judging these intangible efforts. This program would require each supervisor to judge each subordinate's performance in relation to the overall objectives of the department and explicitly relate performance to objectives. Substantial evidence exists that MBO and employee compensation should be directly related.

The program recommended in Figure 2 is intended to decrease costs and improve patient care. However, quality is a major aspect of patient care and a measure of this is needed. More objective standards of quality should be utilized, such as average length of stay in terms of diagnoses, correlations between preoperative and postoperative diagnoses and between antemortem and postmortem diagnoses. Specific checklists have been established to measure various aspects of quality, such as patient welfare, patient comfort, patient charts, administering medication, and fulfilling doctors' orders.

These checklists should be established for each department so that quality does not de-

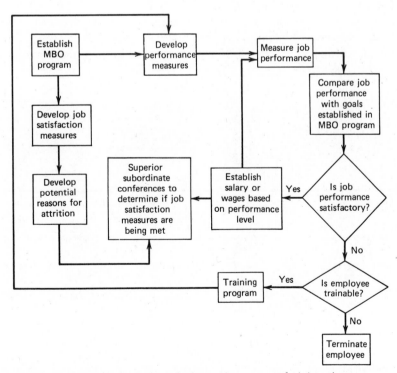

FIGURE 2   *A systematic program for improving a wage administration program*

teriorate while attempting to cut costs. This quality feedback could originate from a number of sources, and it could be used to develop a profile of a particular department of group. For example, a number of hospitals utilize patient feedback obtained on a follow-up questionnaire after the patient has been released for approximately ten days. In order to develop a profile, a number of sources would be used, including doctors, visitors, relatives, patients, and others utilizing the department's services. These measures could aid an administrator in determining trends of performance quality.

Figure 2 shows that the establishment of an MBO program can provide a springboard to develop not only performance measures but also job satisfaction measures. Following the job satisfaction track of Figure 2 indicates how administrators may work with the job attrition problem within the context of an MBO program. In a similar manner, the reader should concurrently follow the performance measure track to relate job performance to compensation. It should be specifically noted that both tracks merge at the superior—subordinate conferences where *all* job satisfaction measures (including salary or wage) and performance are openly discussed and evaluated.

While such a system appears to be initially simple, one should consider that a major problem in MBO is implementation of the program. Commitment to the precepts of management by objectives is perhaps the single most critical factor in improving a wage administration program in hospitals.

The above program is complex. However, hospitals are complex organizations, and oversimplified measures of performance will not suffice.

The recommended MBO program considers all of the aspects commonly associated with determining output in hospitals: individual effort, technology, supervisory skills, raw inputs, clarity of job specifications, ability, and motivation. Any system with a high degree of validity and reliability will have to be complex and will require a great deal of sophistication on the part of all managers involved.

CHAPTER 9

Organizing the Planning Process: Planning and Programming

The readings in this chapter explore the planning process of the nonprofit organization. The exact process of course varies with the mission of the organization, its size, and its method of funding. In spite of organization-specific differences, it is possible to establish a framework sufficiently general to fit virtually all nonprofit organizations and at the same time specific enough that it can be used as a reference point for the various readings. Many times the message of an otherwise good article is lost because the reader is unable to visualize at what point the proposed management technique fits into the general planning process. In the following discussion a framework encompassing the planning process is presented.

The terms *management by objectives, results-oriented management, planning-programming-budgeting systems (PPBS),* and *zero-base budgeting* appear often in the literature. While these terms and others similar to them frequently represent management techniques that are conceptually new, in other cases they represent an updated label for an old idea. Regardless of what labels are used to describe the activities, the four questions making up the organization's planning and control process are:

1 What should be accomplished?
2 How should it be accomplished?
3 Is it financially viable?
4 Is the agency achieving its plans?

The labels applied here, which correspond to the above questions, are (1) Planning; (2) Programming; (3) Budgeting; (4) Reporting. The exact label is unimportant. What is important is the process involved within each step and the sequence of the processes. Any attempt at structuring a process as complex as planning and control is to a certain extent artificial. The framework developed here is no exception, being artificial to the extent that the planning process cannot be broken down neatly into four separate activities. In practice, the activities overlap one another, and it may be necessary for the agency to begin activities contained within the programming process, for example, before the planning process is completed. In spite of this weakness, a framework is useful for organizing the conceptual steps that comprise what collectively is referred to as the planning and control process.

Planning is the process of identifying what it is the agency seeks to accomplish, its reasons for continuing in existence, its goals and strategies. It should be an interactive process among the top management of the agency, its professional employees, and its social constituents. Identification of goals and strategies must involve recognition of the community's needs and the capabilities of the agency. It is important for the success of the agency that the planning process result in a consensus of opinion on the part of the individuals involved in goal setting. This is not always easy to accomplish and will no doubt involve concessions and bargaining.

An open-door clinic that is to provide health care for drug abusers may be used by way of example. The clinic will not be viewed as successful by the community if the majority of the society expects it to provide total health care facilities whereas the staff sees its role as one of giving only emergency care and drug rehabilitation. If the conflict of views is not resolved, it may lead to withholding of support for the clinic by the community.

Once there exists a consensus regarding the basic goals and strategies of the social agency, the next question to be resolved is how those goals are to be achieved. What activities and programs can the agency employ to best meet the goals identified in the planning process? If the agency is already in existence, then it should go through a formal review process to determine how well the existing mix of activities is accomplishing goals. A difficult but important question for agencies to ask themselves is, "Is there a continuing demand for our program services in the community?"

It is during this programming process that new programs are evaluated along with the agency's current mix of services. The agency should attempt to identify whether new programs can accomplish the goals more efficiently than current ones or if changing community needs suggest that new programs should be added and old ones terminated.

Translating the agency's plans and programs into a financial plan is the next step. In the budgeting process the agency attempts to identify the adequacy of its financial resources for undertaking the program it wishes to implement. By forecasting the agency's financial position at the end of the present year, management may be able to anticipate and resolve financial problems before they arise.

A second part of the budgeting process is the establishment of performance norms and targets for agency departments and/or individuals. In effect, the agency's objectives are translated into performance targets for subelements of the agency. If this decomposition of agency objectives is properly done, the agency will accomplish its objectives, assuming that the subelements of the agency accomplish their performance targets. Examples of goal decomposition follow.

1   Given that the agency is to accomplish its social goals, each case worker will need to record 100 client contact hours per month.

2   Given the financial budget for the agency, Program A will have $10,000 available for the next year.

3   Given that the agency is to accomplish its social goals, each group of clients served by a case worker will need to score an average of 75 percent on the post-treatment examination.

The final stage in planning and control is the report process. In this process the actual performance of the agency is measured and compared with the performance norms and objectives established in the budgeting cycle. This information is made available to professionals within the agency so that corrective action can be taken if there are variances between what was planned and what was achieved. Information is made available additionally to outside funding agencies as a way of documenting the agency's accomplishments in comparison with its goals. Also of importance, of course, is financial data reflecting the stewardship activities of the agency.

Performance reports like the one described above can take many different forms depending upon the type of information the agency management needs to make its resource-allocation decisions. One example is provided by Beyer in "The Modern Management Approach to a Program of Social Improvement." Beyer describes a case study of a management-information system that was designed by a major national accounting firm for the city of Detroit.

A unique feature of the information system is that the human needs, for example, health status, education, training, income, and social stability, are measured and quantified. This information is utilized by the agency's management in two important ways. First, by aggregating the total needs of the client population the management information system employs a mathematical programming model to allocate the agency's resources (programs) in the most efficient manner. The objective of this model is to allocate the program's resources to fulfill the greatest needs in the shortest time.

The second major aspect of the management information system is that it provides a feedback reporting system designed to measure progress. It does this by taking random samples of the client population and determining the total contributions of each program by need characteristic and client type. Supplied with this periodic feedback information, management is able to identify how effective the programs are in meeting client needs.

A management-information model of the type described by Beyer is appropriate only for very large organizations involving the management of many separate programs. However, the approach taken by the city and the way it measures client needs may provide techniques that can be adapted for much smaller agencies.

Recognizing that the programming stage of the budget process is often compressed into a very short time frame, Lehan in "Programming—the Crucial Preliminary Work of Budgeting" offers practical suggestions of how programming can be turned into a year-long effort. He emphasizes the importance of a well-documented budget, made possible by sound programming techniques. Analytical procedures for identifying relationships between problems and underlying causal factors are discussed, with the author stressing the desirability of being able to predict the relationship between output and input. Once this is achieved, a budget can be justified with some objectivity, reducing the chance of arbitrary influences. This is the essence of good programming.

Up to this point, the focus has been the control of ongoing programs. Wacht in "A Long-range Financial Planning Technique for Nonprofit Organizations" develops a model for planning and control of cash resources associated with large-scale prospective capital-investment projects. The mathematical model developed in his essay employs adjustments for both the time value of money and inflation factors. Output produced from the model is used to determine total cash requirements for the project. In addition, by comparing actual cash collections, for example, donations, with planned collections the decision maker can assess potential problems of underfinancing.

THE MODERN MANAGEMENT APPROACH TO A PROGRAM OF SOCIAL IMPROVEMENT

Robert Beyer

America the beautiful has an ugly scar across her face.

Her cities are torn by violence and crime. Prejudice and racial hatred flare harshly. Her rivers and streams are polluted. Her hospitals are overcrowded and poorly staffed.

Despite much-publicized affluence, pockets of poverty throughout the nation swell with bitter and hopeless men and women in search of dignity, opportunity, and self-respect.

Something has gone wrong in our society and something must be done to correct it. Not next year. Not tomorrow. But now.

This is not to say that nothing has been done, or is being done. Billions of dollars are being poured into action programs designed to alleviate society's ills. The question is: How effectively is this money being used?

Are the programs reaching the right people? Are we properly defining the needs of the disadvantaged? Are we attending to the needs in their proper order of priority? Are we paying sufficient attention to alternative ways of helping the poor? Are we reversing the tides of deterioration in our nation?

It would be difficult for even the most talented administrator, program director, or sociologist to come up with precise answers to such questions if left to his own devices. But aided by the accountant's knowledge of handling data, he should be able to set up a system to measure these so-called unmeasurable aspects of human needs.[1]

Touche, Ross, Bailey & Smart pioneered such a project in 1965 for Detroit's war on poverty. The firm was asked to work with the Mayor's Committee for Human Resource De-

Source. Copyright © 1969 by the American Institute of Certified Public Accountants, Inc. Reprinted with permission from *The Journal of Accountancy* (March, 1969), pp. 37–46.

[1]David F. Linowes, "Socio-Economic Accounting," *JofA*, Nov. 68, p. 37.

velopment to structure a modern information and management system that would help the city with its vast and complex problems.

We thought the project challenging and agreed to try to design and develop such a system.

The preliminary survey took about a month. During this time the management services consultants, supervised by Jean-Paul Ruff, who had been working since 1960 on measuring nonmeasurables in terms of human needs, examined what information was currently being generated and how, and what further information would be needed to manage the program most effectively. The information requirement boiled down into two main categories: (1) data needed to justify the appropriations of the funding agencies involved, most notably the number of clients to be served (the hard practicality of the matter is that without proper justification, funding is not possible); (2) internal information needed to upgrade the effectiveness of management judgments and action.

Mr. Ruff and his management team studied objectives of the organizations participating in the program. They attended several meetings organized by program administrators and held in modern business offices. Other meetings called by loosely organized groups representing the city's poor were held in empty flats. Present at the meetings was a cross section of program administrators, educators, and sociologists; also counselor-aides and members of the hard-core poor and unemployed along with their leaders and representatives.

Based on the preliminary analysis, a set of basic conclusions was drawn up:

1 It is vital to the success of the program that maximum participation of the poor be achieved in defining client needs, determining corrective actions to be taken, and setting goals.

2 A definition of client needs must be clearly spelled out and agreed upon by all parties involved in the program, recipients as well as planners and administrators.

3 Prompt and decisive action must be taken to streamline paperwork and simplify business-type problems.

Two principal objectives were spelled out following the preliminary investigation. The first was short range. Its purpose was to design a system for keeping track of individual clients and services rendered. This would establish a foundation for analysis and it would generate the data required for funding and action. It would also establish a base for the overall system. As experience testifies, a system is no more effective than the input it receives.

Objective number two, the long-range goal, was to outline the total management system. This was designed to measure what had been done in the past in order to improve on a continuing basis the effectiveness of future planning and action. Subgoals of the total management system were:

1 Measure the relative urgency of various client needs.

2 Measure the resources—manpower, money, equipment, supplies, etc.—available to meet these needs.

3 Develop techniques to assess the alternative plans proposed for the allocation of available resources.

3 Provide the methodology for responding to changes in concept or procedure with regard to any aspect of the program when the measurement program indicates the desirability of such change.

5 Set up an information feedback network that would serve management in its continuing effort to optimize its planning and action.

After the preliminary analysis was completed, we were asked to continue working with the mayor's committee to design and develop the total management program.

THE MODERN MANAGEMENT APPROACH

The social accounting program which Mr. Ruff's team used is unique. For one thing, it quantifies and measures human needs and characteristics—long deemed incommensurable. For another, it utilizes concepts familiar to business systems and technology of modern management.

The basic differences between social and corporate management are well recognized. In social endeavors the chief "product" involved is the fulfillment of human needs. Thus no traditional market results are available to gauge the effectiveness of "product development"— in this case, the effectiveness of action programs that are instituted.

On the other hand, experience shows that important similarities exist between administering a large-scale social-improvement program and running a corporation. In each case substantial resources of manpower, money, and equipment must be allocated. Complex problems arise in both enterprises, and fact-based management decisions are required to solve them.

By using the strategies and technology of modern management, the social accounting program provides what is needed by the sociological community: a built-in system of evaluation and feedback which continuously assesses not only results, but the measurement system itself, thereby upgrading the organization, planning, and implementation of resource allocation.

The concept of the social accounting program is easy to understand and can be implemented by accounting firms of various sizes for projects that differ in size and complexity. But one thing should always be remembered: It is the accountant's job to handle the data, not to decide what data to handle. That task is turned

over to the sociologists, psychologists, and other staff of the program. A social accounting program is by its nature an interdisciplinary effort.

Objective number one is to point out and measure the individual's needs. This provides the input that is required to extend the measurement to groups of people. Once individual and group needs are determined, the program will work out the distribution of the means best suited to take care of the needs. After this, the results are measured.

The social accounting program then answers the questions that administrators, sociologists, program directors, and funding agencies need to have answered to get maximum value out of dollars invested: What has to be done? What resources do we have to do it with? What plans do we need to do it? How are we doing it? What do we do next?

How can this total picture be obtained readily? The system is highly computerized. It takes full advantage of sophisticated scientific management strategies such as operations research, simulation, and linear programming. It applies advanced managerial concepts and eliminates guesswork with proven professional controls.

Thus, with optimum flexibility assured, traditional limitations cannot scotch objectives.

But what about the measurement? Is it foolproof? Far from it. At the outset it will be full of flaws. But the important point—and one that planners increasingly are coming to recognize—is that even a relatively uncertain system of measurement is more desirable than no measurement at all. The trick is to structure the system so that it continuously evaluates and upgrades all aspects of the program so that it will be refined to a high degree of reliability.

THE BASE-LINE DATA SYSTEM

Information about individual clients—the term used by most social service agencies to designate recipients of aid—is recorded in the base-line data file. The BLD file consists of three main categories of information:

Client Information

This includes name and address, age, sex, etc., along with the identification number assigned to every client. The information is recorded only once and is normally located at the site of the first interview. An on-line identification center for the entire system is maintained at a point accessible by telephone from every service agency. The pooling of client identification data is handled by phone rather than computer for a number of reasons. For one thing, it is the easiest way for nontechnical people to operate.

Also, the effect of this arrangement is to eliminate client harassment. Traditionally, in a multiservice organization, the recipient is shunted from office to office and required to recite for interviewers the same information again and again.

Under the base-line data system, when a client appears at a service point a second time, a call is placed to determine whether he is a former client. If he is, his file is located, and repetitious questioning dispensed with.

The base-line data system also assures the confidentiality of the client file. The identification center is authorized to communicate only two kinds of information: the client's routine identification data, and the location of his BLD fle. The file is available only at the source location and at the discretion of the agency or program director. It is not available to clerical personnel and cannot be given to the unauthorized caller.

Objective Client Data

This portion of the BLD file records information required by the funding organization relating to the housing of clients, their employment, schooling, health, etc. It is not so much the purpose of the system to keep on hand all information about the individual as it is to locate the source of such information when it is needed. Thus the client's medical file, as an example, might be in his base-line data file.

The objective data is not a diagnostic tool. It is sometimes used by the social service agent to help with decisions regarding client eligibility to participate in certain programs. It is also used to prepare required statistical reports.

The amount of objective information used varies. This would depend on the needs and reporting requirements of the agency through which the client is processed. Often no more than 15 or 20 percent of the Objective Client Data is utilized. But if it is required, it is available.

Client's Service History

This section of the file records what happens to the client as he takes advantage of the services offered. It is used for reporting purposes and as a follow-up on the client's activity and progress. Each quarter the program generates a report showing the current status of each client. This encompasses all clients and all agencies. Thus an up-to-date record of client activity is available on a year-round basis.

Also, as will be seen later, the client's service history is used in combination with the identification portion of the base-line data file to generate samples needed for the measurement of client needs.

HOW THE BASE-LINE DATA SYSTEM WORKS

Identification, historical and service information is fed into the system at client entrance points and service agencies. Standard checks and controls of the type used in modern corporate accounting systems insure maximum accuracy. The problem of reliability was tackled early. Pitfalls and hazards were taken into account as carefully as they would be in setting up a corporate payroll or accounts receivable system. One such consideration was the large number of clerical personnel that would be needed to operate the system. Another was a predictably high rate of turnover. A third was the average person's lack of familiarity with accounting and numbering systems.

Thus one target agreed upon was maximum centralization and control. As a result, the program requires that base-line data be centrally edited by a small group of personnel trained by the agency with the help of the consultants. They are to be guided by a set of clear, simple, and carefully spelled-out rules. Control functions are designed to be further mechanized through a small third-generation computer programed in COBOL to generate exception reports which indicate clerical errors, incomplete information, missing documents, questionable logic, and the like.

Provisions are also made for the responsibility for accuracy to be channeled to a single control person whose job it will be to correct errors and see to it that data flows properly to and from the various input and output points of the computerized system.

Finally, the computer will be utilized on a monthly basis for the updating of all files and the production of reports. As is the case with any computerized system, reporting becomes an automatic by-product of the data fed into the system.

If the practitioner has no direct access to a computer installation, he can expect to use the system of the municipality or organization engaging his services, since most programs of this type are linked to a large organization.

Generally speaking the base-line data system has been designed to produce two kinds of reports. The first includes all of the documentation that is required for funding and statistical purposes.

The second are those necessary for better management of the service centers. Here typical examples would include: current status and completion results by service; number of clients referred to, and placed with, each major service according to referring service; services requested and services referred to for new clients by location of client intake; source of intake by intake location.

What's most important is that base-line data reports can be produced in time to allow prompt action on the conditions revealed. They can be produced in time to anticipate trouble before it erupts and to make changes and adjustments as required. Many other reports which formerly were not feasible because of time or cost factors involved can now be routinely generated at minimum cost because the required data is already available on punched cards or magnetic tape ready to be fed into the computer.

HOW THE INDIVIDUAL IS MEASURED

How does one determine and definitively state the needs of socially disadvantaged persons in a particular area? The idea is to start from the base of a single individual. If the needs of one person can be determined and quantitatively expressed, samples can be taken and aggregate population figures extrapolated in accordance with accepted statistical procedures.

In setting up a measurement system, the logical place to start is with the client population. The needs selected by the clients and social scientists in the program are those which, improved by the social action endeavors, will work to achieve the objectives of the program. Suppose, for example, we are dealing with a system designed to upgrade the level of public health. The needs would be defined to include such significant factors as speed of health care, accessibility of emergency services, availability of nursing care, pollution controls, etc.

Or take a poverty program. Here health, as a prime factor determining the employability of people, would be a characteristic in itself.

For each characteristic relating to the program's objective—in this case, the elimination of poverty—a numerical scale will be structured through consultation with the needy. What follows is an illustration of how a typical health scale might look:

HEALTH SCALE MODEL

Rating	Condition of Health
7	Excellent health
6	Generally good health with minor problems
5	Some health problems requiring doctor's care between two and four weeks
4	Continual poor health or periodical health lapses
3	Severe health problems requiring continuous doctor's care
2	Very severe health problems requiring periodic hospitalization
1	Failing health or continuous hospitalization

The poor should have a major role as well in the setting of needs priorities because the more accurately the needs set up by the program mirror the true feelings of the disadvantaged, the more successful the program will be.

It is also important in setting up a measurement system not to lose sight of what it is we are trying to measure. In a poverty program, for example, the goal is to identify all characteristics that contribute to poverty. In our health example, regardless of why the client's health is poor, measurement must be geared to reflect the amount of financial impairment imposed on the individual. Thus a client whose cancer is under control might rate higher on the scale than a person suffering from an ingrown toenail, since the former could function economically and the latter could not.

Finally, for each characteristic a target level is defined at which the client is in a position to stand on his own feet and, therefore, be terminated as a client. Thus the individual need is measured by the difference between a person's current rating and the level defined as acceptable.

What constitutes an acceptable level for a given characteristic? Experience has taught us that the actual level labeled as "acceptable" is not an all-important factor. As we shall see, the impact of this decision will be practically tempered by the varying weights assigned to the different population types.

RELATIVE IMPORTANCE OF CHARACTERISTICS

It's obvious that the work experience of a four-year-old child is unimportant regardless of how the work experience scale may read. There are thus two choices: to change the scale when considering a four-year-old child; or set up a series of weights to reflect the relative importance of work experience where a four-year-old child is concerned. Taking this latter and more practical course of action, the question now arises: In establishing weights, into how many different segments should the population be divided? And should other criteria besides age—i.e., sex, race, nationality—figure in the picture?

Working on this aspect of the program, the social scientists and administrators, the clients, and the accountants decided that age, sex, and race might all be valid criteria. The population was then broken down into 72 categories to reflect all significant combinations involved. When the results of this breakdown were analyzed, it was found that race was a totally indifferent criterion and that it had no effect on the weights. Though blacks may have more needs than whites, the conclusion was reached that in this situation the relative importance of needs is the same for people of all races.

As a result of these findings, the table of types was revised, reducing the original 72 categories to 11 basic types.

A set of weights was produced to reflect the importance of each need for each population type. The scale for each need will be tempered by the individual weights applied, and the acceptable level will be modified to meet the requirements of each population type.

THE INDIVIDUAL

The ultimate objective, in developing input data that properly reflects the client population, is to establish a profile for each individual with his current needs and his target levels spelled out. Source material can be obtained in either of two ways. It can be developed through depth analysis involving long questionnaires and the services of professional social scientists. This method has proved to be time-consuming, expensive, and not well received by the people being served. In addition, there is no proof that depth analysis produces more accurate results. The more practical method is for the sponsoring agency to train nonprofessional interviewers and equip them with decision tables, procedure manuals, and other aids.

In any case, after the necessary data is obtained, a profile for each client is drawn (see below). This ties in with the base-line data system. It enables statistical samples to be taken and extrapolations to be made to determine aggregate needs for the total population and for each segment of the population by client type and location category.

John Doe's total needs are 327, of which 80 derive from insufficient family income, 51 from inadequate education and training, etc. For the program to succeed, it must eliminate the needs specified and terminate him as a client.

This can also be used to measure any nonclient (a disadvantaged person not yet absorbed into the system)—at any time and at the completion of services. The measurement of nonclients as well as clients is significant, since it is the program's objective to serve all members of the community.

DEFINITION OF PROGRAMS

However well the program director is fortified with the ammunition of modern management, his work is still cut out for him. His main task is to use the resources available to him to fulfill the greatest number of needs in the shortest

Client Profile—John Doe

Characteristic	Condition	Rating	Acceptable Level	Non-weighted Need	Weight	Weighted Need
Health	Some health problems	5	6	1	20	20
Employment status	Part time, irregular	10	15	5	12	60
Work experience	Mechanic 2 years	4	7	3	13	39
Education and training	10th grade, no vocat'l	4	7	3	17	51
Housing	Sound, 1.6 pers. pr. rm.	9	14	5	7	35
Family income	$2,650	8	16	8	10	80
Public assistance income	None	0	0	0	4	0
Family stability	Nonsupportive, adequate	3	7	4	9	36
Social problems	No relevant problems	7	7	0	6	0
Urban adjustment	Moderate	4	7	3	2	6
					Total Needs	327

time. The system and the planning model he utilizes to distribute resources to the program will make all the difference.

Before resource distribution can be optimized, each program must be defined in terms of: (1) the number of needs it is capable of fulfilling for each type included in the client population, (2) the number of people of each type that might be helped under each of a variety of alternative programs, and (3) the number of resources required for operation under each of the alternatives specified.

Program alternatives are important. Most programs can be designed to operate with differing numbers of participants and a variety of client types. As long as the anticipated benefits per participant are the same, each level considered is a program alternative.

Evaluation of alternatives—before selection, while in progress, and after completion—is of key importance. To insure that dollar investment is sound, an answer to this question should be available at any time: To what degree is this program succeeding in the fulfillment of client needs?

This question has often been asked by social scientists, program administrators, funding agencies, and representatives of the poor. In most cases, straight and simple answers have been hard to come by.

In designing the social accounting program, our management services group made a special effort to provide these answers. A key objective was the simplification of the communications and intelligence-gathering effort. The voluminous documentation traditionally used to evaluate programs and decide on alternatives has been distilled to a single sheet of paper that the program director and other interested parties can easily absorb. Titled the program report, it provides a clear, simple, and total picture with regard to needs, resources, participants, and benefits, both anticipated and achieved.

The program report serves as both a guide

and a control. Unlike prior planning aids, it requires the program director to include alternatives for each program proposed and to specify the number and type of clients involved. Equipped with a total information picture one may easily find the most promising program alternatives and reveal planning weaknesses.

Perhaps the single phrase that plagues a program director most consistently is "What if . . .?"

Suppose that a particular need is not being adequately improved. What action should the program director take? Here again scientific planning generates valuable leads to conclusions. Perhaps the need is unfulfilled because no program exists to fulfill it. Perhaps it is unfulfilled because a program is not being implemented. Whatever the reason, planning, made simpler and more systematic by such tools as the program report, enables the program director to base his critical judgment on the evidence of proven results rather than on guesswork.

Another factor contributing to the replacement of instinct by scientific judgments is the program's use of the mathematical model and sophisticated simulation techniques to assist the decision-making process. The computer's ability to formulate program-by-program comparisons to analyze different alternatives, combinations of programs, and varieties of client mixes is virtually unlimited. Never before has management been better equipped to test the workability of a proposed effort before committing its resources to use. Guided by simulation we are able to superimpose any number of factors and probabilities on the model.

RESULTS EVALUATION

Evaluation after the fact is another consideration of importance to the program director and to all agencies involved in the social improvement effort. Program X, for example, has been in operation two years. How well is it doing in comparison with other programs? Is it living up to expectations? These questions involve difficult and complex aspects of social program management where multiservice operations are in force.

Many clients participate in more than one program. Assume, for example, that during the past 12 months client Jane Doe took advantage of a health program, an educational program, a social adjustment program. Today, gainfully employed, she is no longer a client. Where should credit for the fulfillment of her needs be applied? Obviously, an accurate evaluation of the existing plan is essential if we are to determine the best course of action to take for future Jane Does.

The social accounting program is geared to provide such assessment for single programs and for any combination of multiple programs through which a client might be processed. Consider, for example, the case of three clients. Client 1 goes through Program A, eliminating 10 of his needs. Client 2 goes through Program B, eliminating 90 of his needs. Client 3, taking advantage of both programs, A and B, has 130 of his needs eliminated. It is necessary in a system of results evaluation—the equivalent of profitability accounting in corporate management—to assign credit for achievements gained in order to evaluate the effectiveness of dollars invested. In our illustration, therefore, 10 percent of the credit where Client 3 was concerned might be applied to Program A and 90 percent to Program B on the basis of individual gains recorded. Though not necessarily accurate, it is one way of dealing with intangible elements and allocating credit in a practical and consistent manner.

ALLOCATION OF RESOURCES

Let us return briefly to the commercial enterprise analogy. Marketing research, we will assume, has told us what is needed and wanted. What next? At this point in a manufacturing operation, production would be consulted to determine what tools, materials, facilities, and manpower we would need to function at various levels of productivity. By matching the resources to the needs of the program, a production schedule would be developed. Next, the schedule would be reviewed, alternative strategies considered, and a final plan evolved. Later, when the plan went into effect, results would be reported and compared with expected production.

Resource allocation under the social-accounting program follows this same general concept. However, under a production setup dealing with human needs instead of widgets, unique problems and uncertainties arise. Program constraints relating to manpower availability, budget, equipment shortages, and other resource limitations complicate the planner's life to a greater degree than they do in industry.

For example, if earmarked funds enter the program as a constraint, to what degree will needs be fulfilled? On the other hand, if the constraint is removed, in what measure would the need fulfillment be altered? The difference between need fulfillment with and without the earmarking constraint is a measure of the constraint's cost.

The social-accounting program's mathematical model has been geared to answer such questions. It helps to identify the best theoretical allocation of resources to programs in order to reduce the inventory of needs to a minimum compatible with given constraints.

STRUCTURING OF POLICY CONSTRAINTS

This does not imply that allocation alternatives generated by the computer are always satisfactory. To illustrate, in one case analysis might indicate that not enough was done to reduce certain education needs. Perhaps 5 million needs exist, but the program calls for elimination of only 3 million. And analysis produces the conclusion that taking care of at least one million, or 50 percent of the remaining unfulfilled needs, is of prime importance to the program. The program director might therefore introduce a policy constraint which states that the additional one million needs must be eliminated within a given period. The question is how many other needs must be sacrificed to satisfy the constraint.

Needless to say, the structuring of such policy constraints will have an important bearing on the distribution of resources and the fulfillment of needs. Under the social accounting program, the policy constraints would be first introduced as input to the mathematical model. Each constraint will be tested by simulation and an analysis of its effect made, independently and in combination with other constraints. Aided by the analysis, the program director will be able to determine which constraints are feasible, where adjustments are needed, where new possible constraints are required.

When the simulation process is completed and all policies sharpened, refined, and agreed upon, the net result will be a listing of policy decisions designed to put available resources to use to fulfill the most needs in the least time. This listing would be available to the press, to funding agencies, to representatives of the poor, and to other interested parties. Most important, the program director would have at his fingertips the documentation required to explain why particular policies were selected and to relate policies to needs and accomplishments to policies.

The mathematical model, apart from its usefulness in supporting and justifying key decisions, functions primarily as a decision-making tool. It computes costs, explores innumerable alternatives, makes endless tests and comparisons at microsecond speeds. Quantification of the model's input is consistent with methods previously described.

The overriding objective, of course, is to whittle down to negotiable size the infinitely expandable number of "ifs" that crop up during the course of any social improvement program.

A key aim of the model is to produce a detailed operational plan for every program in force. This plan will include the number of participants expected by type and location, the needs expected to be fulfilled, and the resources that will be required for fulfillment. As a by-product of the plan, the budget will be prepared.

In another sense the planning model serves as special consultant to the program director. He might ask the computer: "What will be the effect on employment needs reduction if child day-care services are increased by 30 percent?"

Good, bad, or indifferent, the computer would take about ten seconds to come up with an answer.

SYSTEM REPORTING AND FLEXIBILITY

Although the measurement process begins with initial determination of the individual needs, the client profile is a starting point and no more. However scrupulously drawn, it is subject to the imperfections of human judgment, as are the programs designed to eliminate human needs. Thus, to work effectively, a measurement system must be designed with the goal of continuing improvement in mind.

Needs rarely remain static. They improve or intensify. They are influenced by many factors, some of them outside the program. The degree to which they are reduced, and the time it takes for reduction to occur, is the acid test of a program's success. Continuing measurement, reliably controlled in the best accounting tradition, provides a valuable instrument of continuing evaluation. The absence of this ingredient is responsible for the failure of more social improvement programs in the past than any other single factor.

The feedback reporting system of our social accounting program has been tailored to measure progress. It is achieved by selecting random samples from the base-line data file at given points of time. The sample data determines the total contribution of each program by need characteristic and client type. It also allocates specific contributions to specific programs where clients participate in two programs or more.

The beauty of a well-organized computer-based system is its great flexibility. Once data is gathered, checked for accuracy and validity, and fed into the program, it may be recalled at will, and at electronic speeds to provide feedback reporting in any form desired.

The social accounting program's feedback system has been geared to measure program results at different stages of development. Reports compare planned and actual results. They record contributions by program and location for specified periods of time. Changes in client need characteristics are reflected, not months later, but as the changes are taking place, so that corrective action can be taken as required. This is essential because social measurement and resource allocation are in a constant state of flux. It would be significant for a program director to know, for example, that, after 10 weeks of a 52-week program, 90 percent of all benefits expected were already obtained.

Feedback reporting helps police the entire endeavor. Where programs do not perform in line with expectations, variance reports are produced that point out problem areas in need of attention and revision.

Most men of conscience like to feel they are contributing to the betterment of society. One would be hard-pressed to find an undertaking more gratifying to the professional accountant than personal involvement in the social improvement effort described. We believe the main benefits of this modern management approach to social action accounting to be the following:

1 The program upgrades the efficiency of administration and processing at all levels.
2 It centralizes and consolidates client information, permitting better analysis while providing the utmost in the confidentiality of privileged client information.
3 It satisfies the management-information system reporting requirements of the funding agency, whether government or private.
4 Client needs and program resources are consistently quantified on an individual and aggregate basis. The system's input and output are scientifically controlled and reliably measured in the best traditions of management science and professional accounting.
5 Resources are allocated on a pre-planned and pre-tested basis.
6 Advanced and sophisticated techniques of operations research, simulation and linear programing are applied to refine the analysis of individual programs and program alternatives.
7 The social accounting program takes into account the constantly changing needs of a dynamic client population—influenced by factors both internal and external to the program. Measurement and evaluation are continuous.

The social accounting program, though initially designed for Detroit's war on poverty, is equally applicable to other areas of social improvement such as health, education, air and water pollution, housing, etc. Though programs vary substantially from area to area and problem to problem, the general concepts of scientific management, measurement, and control are broadly superimposable.

Does any of this imply that the system described is infallible? Far from it. Flaws most certainly exist. Certain aspects of the program are debatable.

But in attempting to improve the quality and effectiveness of social action programs, no guide serves so well as hard-won experience. "After the event," as Homer said, "even a fool is wise." But experience in the area of social improvement, however well conceived and formulated the research, diminishes in value as time passes. Conditions in the disadvantaged community change drastically from month to month and year to year. For research to be constructive, conclusions must be predicated on today's situation and tomorrow's needs as well as on yesterday's historical data.

With this in mind, we are of the "action now" school. The objective, we believe, is to get the best possible program under way as rapidly as possible. Gradually, as results are examined and expectations continuously compared against performance, improvements will be made and imperfections worked out of the system in a scientifically controlled debugging operation.

In the meantime progress, long overdue, will be made.

PROGRAMMING—THE CRUCIAL PRELIMINARY WORK OF BUDGETING GOVERNMENTAL FINANCE

Edward A. Lehan

All hands agree that budget appropriations are more or less based on certain representations and understandings of what is to be done, when, and how. That the representations and understandings are often confused and inaccurate should not obscure the fact that a budget is a contract of sorts between political authorities and program personnel, reflecting work plans (hopefully designed to pursue public goals).

Given this contractual nature of budgeting, the principal task (and highest duty) of administrators is to illuminate the relationship between work plans and associated expenditures and revenues. In budgeting, there is simply no substitute for a well thought-out work program, properly presented. Therefore, getting budgetary needs recognized and accepted most likely results from efforts to develop and share program knowledge.

In larger jurisdictions the task of program

analysis is often a duty shared by the program leadership (department and division heads, project managers, etc.) and specialized staff researchers and consultants. In the smaller jurisdictions, the analysis of programs is carried out by program leaders, if it is done at all, in a formal sense. This article is designed to help program leaders in the smaller jurisdictions improve the analysis and documentation of their programs—the crucial preliminary work of budgeting.

As indicated, the supreme importance of well thought-out work plans makes programming the heart of budgeting. Unfortunately, the customary division of the budgetary process into a so-called cycle of three phases (preparation, adoption, and execution) tends to squeeze programming into the preparation phase—a phase usually confined to a few hectic weeks of the third quarter of each fiscal year.

Let's face it: Most municipal governments do not encourage programming as a year round activity. Even more serious, the reflec-

Source. Copyright © 1976 by Municipal Finance Officers Association of the U.S. and Canada. Reproduced with permission from *Governmental Finance* (August, 1976), pp. 6–11.

tive, even playful nature of programming does not flourish in the "deadline" atmosphere which seems to accompany budget preparation everywhere. Then too, the very forms supplied for budget preparation will, more than likely, stress financial, rather than program data. This concentrates everyone's energy on pricing problems and the assembly of figures, rather than on the comparative value of goals and the relative worth of procedures.

This points up a serious problem: When budget preparation forms are on the desk, it is probably too late for any program leader or budget analyst to do a proper job, simply because deadlines and pressure discourage reflective work.

What's the answer? Obviously the heavy thinking about work goals and plans must be done months before budget preparation time rolls around. Ideally, such thinking goes on all year long. This requires administrative discipline—and procedures.

We have defined programming as a rather steady job. How then should the leaders of municipal programs organize for this job? The three-part discussion which follows may help to provide an answer:

Programming requires the collection of pertinent ideas and information. This collection, which we might call a *program evaluation and development file*, will help stir up memory and imagination. This file will also furnish the foundation for a "program memorandum," or "issue paper," which will sum up thinking. Building and maintaining this file represents an essential administrative procedure.

By keeping such a file, by encouraging others to contribute to it, by working it over from time to time, by writing up bits and pieces of experience, a program leader or budgetmaker can significantly expand the range and power of his programming effort. Don't trust to memory: Organize a file!

What is in a typical program evaluation and development file? Two examples follow:

A police chief would surely maintain sections dealing with type, timing, and volume of demands for police service, indexes of service quality, social trend and demographic data, manpower distribution in relation to demand, new technology, the linkage to other programs, such as education, recreation, health, etc.

A code administrator's file might include census materials, inspection and performance data, construction cost factors related to code provisions, notes on anticipated projects, new technological developments, etc.

Needless to say, comments from clientele groups and the public should find a special niche in a program evaluation and development file, especially complaints and criticism.

As noted above, a program evaluation and development file provides raw material for reflection on goals and procedures. Reflection by whom, we might ask? While final responsibility rests with the program leadership, programming by its very nature works best when a variety of viewpoints are put to work. It offers a solid opportunity to involve, not only subordinate personnel, but citizens and clientele groups as well. Don't try to work alone: Consult!

This consultive feature alone has important beneficial results. Because consultation promotes the development and sharing of program knowledge, it tends to enhance organizational vitality and effectiveness. We might say that an organization which programs together, stays together.

It is particularly important to develop and maintain contacts between program personnel and any nearby academic institutions, research organizations, and high-technology enterprises, all of which have key people who pioneer along the frontiers of social and technological change. Consultation with appropriate members of these organizations will pay rich dividends in ideas, evaluation, and orientation.

While programming need not involve a lot of paper work, it does require the production of "program memoranda." These memos, sometimes called "issue papers," sum up the information and ideas upon which the upcoming budget will be based.

Therefore, the composition of these documents is the most important event in the entire budget sequence.

A program memo consists of a multi-year projection and a five-part commentary covering the following topics: (1) Goal(s), (2) Target Population, (3) Performance Criteria, (4) Impacts and Benefits, and (5) Alternatives. This format is designed to help organize information and bring out the leading ideas behind a program.

The first step in the composition of a memo is a review of the program evaluation and development file. It should be a gold mine of information on significant issues and opportunities. Next, select a subject for in-depth analysis. Then, start a process of consultation by setting up meetings with people who can help with insight and advice.

Remember, a memo need not be prepared on all aspects of operations each year. Be selective—focus only on significant issues and opportunities. This strategy of selective programming not only conserves time but concentrates the mental energy of superiors, and perhaps, that of political authorities, thereby reducing the "intellectual" costs of budgeting by reducing the volume of information to be digested at any given time.

The next step in composing a program memo is the preparation of a goal statement. As a general rule, it is wise to avoid completely verbal goal statements, because they do not help much in relating expenditures to workload.

For example, a police chief might be tempted to identify "protection of life and property" as the end product of patrol activity. But that statement, although true, would not shed much light on police problems. Try this one instead: "The patrol program is designed to protect life and property by responding to (x) number of service calls, with (y) percent of these responses made within (z) minutes." This goal statement points the way for a discussion of manpower use, district size, communications, etc. In other words, the numerical goal statement helps relate expenditures to workload.

In addition, setting goals in a numerical way tends to ensure that a chosen goal is practical, and measurable. A goal, to be practical, must be attainable in a specific time. The accuracy of estimates (an important characteristic of budgetary craftsmanship) and a program leader's credibility are closely related to success in choosing goals which are practical, and attainable.

Furthermore, it is easier to set milestones, or the performance check points, which are an essential part of a work plan, if the chosen goal is measurable. Wherever possible unit costs should appear in a goal statement. Why? Because measures of output are divided into expenditures to get unit costs, the use of unit costs automatically serves to link expenditures to workload, input to output. The formula is as follows:

$$\text{unit cost} = \frac{\text{expenditures}}{\text{output}}$$

Because of the close connection between costs and goals, the composition of a goal statement goes hand-in-hand with construction of an important exhibit in a program memo: a multi-year projection of expenditures and revenues.

If the memo is to deal with an ongoing activity, the estimated expenditures and revenues for the present year become the base for future projections. Using the base year prices and pay rates (ignoring inflation and other cost advancing factors), not only lessens the burden of calculation, but ensures that the projection reflects only changes in workload. (Of course, if purely inflationary pressures appear substantial, their impact should be noted at a suitable point in the commentary, perhaps as a footnote.)

An important point to remember: Revenues available for financing the program over the multi-year period must equal, or exceed, the projected expenditures.

Because every public program has a clientele, willing or not, the second part of a program memo deals with the target population. Target groups comprise those individuals, organized or not, who are affected by the expenditures outlined in the projection.

Because the description of impacts and benefits, discussed in the fourth part of a commentary, depends on a description of program clientele, it pays to be as accurate as possible in identifying the target population. Nevertheless, we must not expect more precision than the situation allows. For example, will a public works director, charged with "keeping the public way passable and safe" find it easy to accurately specify the number or characteristics of the persons benefiting from expenditures for street maintenance, lighting, snow removal, etc.? Of course, the answer is no. Thus, approximations must suffice.

A public works director can also develop data which can stand as a substitute, or proxy, for direct data on the target population. For example, information on traffic, its volume, speed, and direction, might substitute very nicely for people, particularly if such data is classified by type of street (local, connector, arterial, etc.) and is linked to accident and street crime information.

More than in any other part of a program memo, the section on performance criteria provides an opportunity to outline the leading ideas, the causal relationships, or the standards which influence the size and shape of a program.

In one way or another, recognized or not, performance criteria are reflected in many municipal operations. One familiar example is the influence of insurance industry standards on fire services in every nook and cranny of the United States. Many street lighting programs are referenced to the criteria put out by the Illuminating Engineers Society, another good example of local acceptance of authoritative standards published by nationally active interests.

The national societies of municipal professionals (engineers, librarians, educators, social workers, recreation leaders, etc.) are also important sources of performance criteria which, if judicially adapted to local situations, can be of great help to program leaders interested in evaluating the effectiveness and efficiency of their work.

If causal relationships are involved in a program design, by all means, discuss them. For example, public works and health officials might well design a vermin control program around the correlation between available food and infestations, and thus justify expenditures for inspection and waste collection on a causal relationship, rather than a standard. By contrast, funds for extermination services could not be justified by this causal relationship because extermination has no impact on the causal variable, the vermin's food supply.

The point is this: If you can demonstrate that a change in X will produce a desired change in Y, and this change in X can be brought about by certain expenditures, you have hold of a very powerful programming tool. There is no doubt about it: Correlations or causal relationships provide the firmest foundation for program planning. To illuminate and evaluate programs, budgetmakers should search out correlations and use them at every opportunity!

One final note before we turn to a discussion of impacts and benefits: It may be advisable to introduce more than one criterion into the structure of a program. For example, a police chief might well not only select "response time" as a standard around which to build elements of a public safety budget, but also consider using "time lapse between crime and arrest" as a factor in budgeting for patrol and investigatory services.

Because each criterion becomes a focus for the study of alternatives, multiple standards tend to help production of a well-rounded, more defensible program.

The section on Impacts and Benefits may be organized around a matrix of "cross classification" which assigns estimates to various impact categories. The device of cross classification permits exploration of several sides of a program, highlighting and emphasing the linkages, or multiple values and goals, which are characteristic of most public programs.

For example, a recreation budget may be cross classified to show its impact on education, public safety, culture, health, social service, economic development, etc., depending on the type of problems facing the jurisdiction.

The matrix in Exhibit 1 shows how a recreation budget for a community of 30,000 might be cross classified.

As another example: The linkages of day care service to education, health, social service, or recreation might be usefully explored by means of a matrix. Also, many expenditure patterns can be allocated to area-oriented (districts, census tracts, schools, etc.) or time-oriented categories (shifts, seasons, peakload periods, etc.), other useful applications of the technique of "cross classification."

The matrix in a program memo may also include data on some benefits which seem to accrue to the target population served by the program. However, as the following discussion points up, benefits are not always easy to identify and measure. Because of this difficulty, some words of caution are in order:

Always be on the lookout for evidence of tangible program benefits. Use this data whenever possible in studies of alternatives. But do not waste time or risk credibility by using benefit data which might appear contrived or artificial. Be conservative—take a selective approach!

As a general rule, where people are willing to pay for a service as they use and enjoy it, and the service or user charge covers costs, the need to calculate benefits is sharply lessened.

Cost Centers	Health	Education	Public Safety	Unallocated	Total	EXHIBIT 1
Administration				$15,000	$15,000	
Playgrounds	$ 5,000	$ 5,000	$ 5,000		15,000	
Athletic Activities	5,000	5,000	25,000		35,000	
Cultural Activities		5,000			5,000	
Supporting Services	1,000	1,000	5,000	3,000	10,000	
	11,000	16,000	35,000	18,000	80,000	

In this situation, the willingness to pay, the market price, and the resulting revenues regulate the size and shape of the service.

However, the situation is considerably different with tax-supported programs because taxing and appropriation procedures tend to separate payment from use and enjoyment. Of course, this split between payment and use is what makes the whole appropriation process so vulnerable to pressure from organized interests seeking to use and enjoy services paid for by others.

In a real sense, then, a search for tangible program outputs is a way of reducing any undue influence of pressure groups, because the display of benefit data encourages the comparison of programs (or alternatives within a program) in terms of relative net returns to society. Therefore, as budgetary craftsmen, we embrace the notion that every public program should "pay off"—that is, its benefits to society (or part thereof) should at least equal or exceed costs.

Furthermore, we assert that the return on any particular program should compete with the potential returns which might be earned by investing the same funds in other opportunities. This leads us pretty quickly to the study of alternatives.

On the other hand, we recognize the great difficulty of placing dollar values on the output of public programs—many of which are tax-supported precisely because the people will not, or cannot, pay for them on a service charge basis. Use of the public way, for example, may be rationed by means of toll gates and parking meters, but normally its use is "free"—that is, paid for by taxes, not service charges.

Sad to say, despite the spread of community planning and capital budgeting, public investments do not get the analytical attention they deserve in the average municipality. To this subject we now turn. At one time or another, almost every budgetmaker will participate in decisions to invest in public property which have substantial program and financial implications.

In addition to program costs, such investments usually build up amortization, interest, maintenance, and, perhaps, depreciation charges for years to come. The fact that these commitments may amount to many times the original investment has led many economists to advocate extended cost–benefit schedules for proposed public investments, amplified by a reasonable interest rate (to reflect "opportunity costs"), and reduced to "present value" (to eliminate differences in the time value of money).

At the present stage of development of municipal practice, it is not likely that these rather sophisticated analytical tools will be widely used, or understood. Nevertheless, every budgetmaker should become acquainted with the terms "opportunity cost" and "present value" and arrange for training in their use. Developing accurate cost estimates for public investments in land and buildings are generally considered to be more difficult than estimating the costs of operating programs.

Budgets are built up, piece by piece, meaning that appropriations and subsidiary allotments usually summarize, or aggregate, estimates from a number of cost centers. There is an important implication for the accuracy of the overall budget in this tendency to aggregate. From an estimator's point of view, a budget is a forecast—a prediction about the future which has certain statistical chances of achieving absolute accuracy. From this point of view, the better budget is one in which the variation of actual experience from the original forecast is at a minimum.

Achieving accuracy in the total budget boils down to achieving accuracy in the detail. The tendency to aggregate the overall budget from a mass of subordinate cost centers is an important step toward an accurate total, because the inevitable plus and minus errors of a mass of estimates tend to cancel one another out. (We assume that each estimate is carefully and honestly developed.) The whole mass of estimates thus tends toward zero variation.

One of the secrets, then, of accurate overall estimation, is in the making of a large number of subsidiary estimates, each based on the best information, or sources, available.

Estimates for public projects requiring land acquisition and construction work often suffer from the inability of program personnel to build up a total budget from a series of subsidiary estimates. The ability to do accurate pricing of public projects is usually limited at the proposal stage, chiefly due to the sketchiness of preliminary plans. The lack of detailed specifications usually means that gross measures, such as square footage of space, will be multiplied by a "guesstimate" cost factor to help produce a project of low reliability.

This lack of estimate reliability is unfortunate because of the political administrative sensitivity of public projects. Ideally, a budget for public projects should be set only after technical studies have produced detailed specifications and these have been priced competently. Short of this it behooves a budgetmaker to break the estimating problem down into as many components as possible.

Before concluding our discussion of programming, we should briefly dwell on two factors which, because of their powerful conditioning effect on municipal services, deserve special attention from program leaders: technology and peak loads.

Because energy-saving and energy-using tools play such a big role in the delivery of municipal services, budgetmakers must aggressively seek information about the technological alternatives which might be available to them.

Keeping your door open for salesmen—a prime source of information about equipment and machines—is one way of keeping in touch with technological developments. However, because of the obvious bias of salesmen, municipal officials should search for sources of advice and assistance whihc are more objective. These include: professional contracts and literature, Federal and State agency people and publications, university staffers, and independent consultants.

Program personnel should not neglect sources within their own government, particularly central process agencies, such as budget, purchasing, personnel, engineering, equipment maintenance, and data processing. By all means, keep these specialists abreast of your research and ideas. Seek their help in the evaluation of technological alternatives.

In order to compare alternatives, the technology currently on hand must be carefully evaluated, preferably by (1) physical inspection, (2) review of service records, and (3) assessment of the contribution each device makes to goals. This survey has many of the characteristics of an audit. A purge of obsolete equipment, equipment of low or no utilization, and equipment with high maintenance charges and/or uncertain serviceability will be one likely result of a thorough technological audit.

This audit will also, in combination with accumulating information on alternatives, help point the way to special in-depth studies which might pay off either in equipment replacement or in reorganization around the potential of some new technology.

Thus, the key to an aggressive technological policy is a persistent search for information about alternatives, and the comparison of these alternatives with current equipment and machinery by means of a technological audit.

Technological factors loom ever larger in budgetary calculations, not only because of cost-effectiveness considerations, but because the employment of technology brings the budgetmaker up against one of the most significant interconnected problems of our age, and future ages as well: energy and its life-threatening by-product: pollution.

Indeed, one can foresee the necessity to allocate British Thermal Units (BTUs) among the various municipal services, thus requiring an energy budget in addition to expenditure estimates!

Despite the centrality of technological factors, the typical budget process ends up giving machinery and equipment proposals short shrift. Like maintenance budgets, allotments for technology "can be put off until next year"—and frequently are.

Many municipal services cope with peak loads, a vexing problem for budgetary craftsmen interested in relating expenditures to workload, a concept which we have identified as a fundamental element of good budgeting.

A fire suppression service is a good example of an organization built up to meet fire potentials which occur randomly.

Police manpower may be somewhat more closely correlated with everyday service demands, but significant peaks and troughs of activity may occur within shifts, by area and by time, and between shifts. In these cases, a stable manpower allotment tends to reflect an effort to cope with peak loads, meaning that periods of low productivity are inevitable—unless a flexible mix of resources can be devised which varies with workload fluctuations.

The difficulties of adjusting or modulating public works budgets to varying demands, seasonal and otherwise, are well known. But, in contrast to the relative rigidity of public safety resources in the face of workload fluctuations, public works leaders can employ a combination of contractual services, temporary help, and overtime payments to help meet demand with a flexible response.

Study Exhibit 2. It displays some interesting fluctuations in performance criteria due to a lack of correspondence between changes in manpower and workload. It is based on actual performance data drawn from a building inspection service in a city of about 160,000 population:

Please note that because the permit workload increased by only 4%, a 24% increase in manpower resulted in a 16% drop in inspections per man per year. Note also that the number of inspections per permit improved by a scant 2%.

Of course, it might be argued that fewer inspections result in inspections of longer duration, and thus enhance the quality, rather than the quantity of inspection. This might be a valid claim, if the manpower had been added with that goal in mind. Unfortunately, it wasn't.

Budget review officials and political authorities often show keen interest in correlations such as those listed in the above exhibit, particularly the relationship, or lack of one, between "regular" payroll expenditures and

---

EXHIBIT 2

Performance Data	1963–64	1964–65	+ / −
Permits	5,376	5,600	+ 4%
Inspections	31,494	33,268	+ 6%
Man years	11.3	14.0	+24%
Inspect/permits	5.8	5.9	+ 2%
Inspect/man years	2,760	2,380	−16%

fluctuating workloads. It is only prudent to anticipate these questions by making the study of peak loads a special focus of programming.

It is particularly important for budgetmakers to seize opportunities to speak on the budget before budget review officials and interested parties, stressing the underlying rationale of the expenditure and revenue estimates. In these oral presentations, the budget should be shown in as many progam/performance dimensions as possible. Exploit, where practical, the full technology of audiovisual aids in these presentations.

In reflecting work plans in the budget, it is also important to be as accurate in estimates and justifications as one can. Budget papers should be neat and well-laid out. Developing a reputation for accurate detail and prediction can be a valuable asset, resulting in a reservoir of good faith among political authorities.

Perhaps no essay on the technical aspects of budgeting should end on a note of unqualified optimism—given the ultimate political nature of the budget process. Yet we know that analytical procedures can count, and count heavily, in determining budgetary outcomes. The procedures recommended in this essay should help to reduce the free play of arbitrary political influences, and thus help place the use of public power on a more solid basis of evidence and logic.

A LONG-RANGE FINANCIAL PLANNING TECHNIQUE FOR NONPROFIT ORGANIZATIONS

Richard F. Wacht

Colleges, universities, hospitals, museums, and other nonprofit community organizations are finding it increasingly difficult to stretch interest and dividend income from endowments and cash donations from their wealthy benefactors to cover both the increasingly widening gap between current costs and revenues and their capital needs. These financial problems of recent years are the result of the combined effects of an increase in the demand for the organizations' services, inflation-related cost pressures, and the increasing reluctance of both lenders and donors to provide needed long-term capital for asset replacement and growth.

In a recent article, for example, Vincent Fulmer discussed the impact of today's higher interest rates on capital formation in nonprofit organizations.[1] He cited two deleterious effects. First, high interest rates simultaneously make debt financing prohibitively expensive for nonprofit organizations and cause corporate donors to become reluctant to part with surplus cash balances which are capable of returning over 10% annually on near-riskless investments. The organizations' critical need for funds forces fund raisers to become more persuasive, thereby escalating fund-raising costs along with everything else.

Second, large gifts to eleemosynary in-

Source. Reprinted with permission from *Atlanta Economic Review* (September/October, 1976), pp. 22–27.

stitutions normally take the form of pledges payable over three- to five-year periods, and sometimes even longer. The present value of such gifts diminishes as interest rates rise, and the lack of coincidence between the near-term cash outlays for construction and program implementation and the delayed cash receipts from pledges often force the institutions to liquidate fixed income securities at depressed prices to cover cash flow deficits. The net result is a continuing liquidity crisis as construction is completed and program operations begin.

Fulmer's primary solution to the dilemma is donor education as a means of shortening the pledge period and providing ways of compensating nonprofit institutions for the loss of endowment income in periods of cash flow deficit. Another approach, suggested by Charles Ellis[2] and a Ford Foundation report,[3] involves integrating endowment operations with the long-term purpose of the institution in order to achieve a balance between maintaining the capital growth of the endowment fund and enhancing the real capital base of the institution. That approach requires the endowment fund manager to actively support capital formation projects by supplementing external fund-raising campaigns out of total endowment income, including the heretofore inviolable capital gains income.

Although both solutions possess certain merit, neither provides the administrator of the nonprofit organization with the tools he needs to enable him to cope with the complex problem of integrating capital asset and program planning with the organization's overall liquidity needs and related fund-raising efforts. And neither approach has attempted to define the relevant variables (beyond the market interest rate) the administrator must deal with in order to plan complete financial viability for new (incremental) capital investment projects or other long-term programs. It is necessary, therefore, to extend the previous

work and develop a normative approach to integrating capital asset (program) planning and liquidity management for eleemosynary organizations.

It is important to note that this article is not concerned with the significant economic problem of capital investment *evaluation* in nonprofit contexts; rather, it deals with the financial problem of integrating charitable fund-raising campaigns involving pledges of cash gifts with the acquisition and operation of the capital assets or institutional programs they are intended to finance. Its ultimate objective is to assist administrators in planning institutional expansion, including the construction of new facilities and their subsequent operation, on a financially viable basis.

THE MODEL

Briefly, the model developed here permits the administrator of a nonprofit organization to achieve financial self-sufficiency for incremental capital-investment projects by coordinating the cash outflows of a planned capital expenditure (or other long-term project involving operating deficits) with the cash inflows of the related fund-raising campaign. The solution of the model is expressed in terms of the (nominal) dollar "target" amount of the funds requirements. This particular solution was selected for its operational merit: fund-raising goals, expressed in terms of nominal dollar amounts, are readily communicated between both the administrator and the fund raiser (e.g., the college president and the alumni office) and the fund raiser and donor.

Although the solution is stated in nominal terms, the model employs the concept of the time value of money in equating the present value of future cash expenditures (adjusted for the effects of inflation) with the present value of cash receipts from the fund-raising campaign. The nominal value of total cash receipts is derived from the present value of cash inflows, given the relevant discount rate and estimates of the division of receipts between immediate cash gifts and future collections of pledges.

In addition to establishing the target amount of the fund-raising goal, the model permits the administrator to perform sensitivity analyses to obtain information with which to evaluate policy alternatives and the effects of uncertainty on several critical decision variables. Finally, by replacing estimated data with actual data as the fund-raising campaign and project implementation proceed, the administrator can use the model as a control device to predict future effects of (and can subsequently adjust for) significant cash flow variations from those originally forecasted.

The Capital Expenditure Program

The first step in applying the model is to calculate F, the present value of the capital expenditure program's inflation-adjusted cash outflows, in accordance with equation (1).

$$F = PVC_c + PVC_e + PVC_f \tag{1}$$

where PVC_c is the present value of construction costs, PVC_e is the present value of equipment costs, and PVC_1 is the present value of the net annual shortfall of project operating revenues under operating costs, all adjusted for the individually applicable inflation rates and discounted at a rate, r, equal to the return on investment from the institution's managed endowment fund.

The present value of construction costs is defined as

$$PVC_c = \sum_{t=n}^{m} [C_{ct}(1 + r)^{-t}] \cdot$$

$$(1 + i_c)^{n-1}$$

$$(t = 1, 2, \ldots, n, n + 1, \ldots m) \tag{2}$$

where n is the year in which construction begins; m is the year in which the construction is completed; C_{ct} is the progress payment made at the end of year t, based on the contract price of constructing the facility beginning in $t = n = 1$; and i_c is the inflation rate applicable to construction costs. Since bids on construction projects usually include allowances for cost inflation over the contract period, the adjustment for inflation, $(1 + i_c)^{n-1}$, relates only to the year in which the project commences (n). In other words, if $n = 1$, $(1 + i_c)^{n-1} = 1$, and hence no adjustment is made for inflation. If construction is delayed and begins in $n = 2$, construction costs will increase by $(1 + i_c)^{2-1}$. The longer the delay, the more costly the facility will be to construct.

Equipment costs, including donor relations and dedicatory expenditures, C_e, are generally incurred at the end of the construction period or in year m. The present value of these costs is therefore

$$PVC_e = [C_e/(1 + r)^m] \cdot (1 + i_e)^m \tag{3}$$

where i_e is the inflation rate applicable to equipment purchases (e.g., the equipment element in the U.S. Department of Commerce's wholesale price index).

The shortfall of operating revenues under operating costs for the project, c_{ft}, is assumed to begin in the year after the completion of construction, j, and continue to the kth year. The present value of these flows is therefore

$$PVC_f = \sum_{t=j}^{k} [C_{ft}/(1 + r)^t] \cdot (1 + i_f)^t \tag{4}$$

where i_f is the applicable inflation rate, which in most cases would be the difference between the rate of inflation on project revenues and the rate of increase in institutional wages and salaries. It is imaginable that C_{ft} could be negative—that is, the project might produce an excess of revenues over costs in each or most operating periods. In such cases, the term PVC_f would become negative and hence reduce F.

The Fund Raising Campaign

Next, the administrator must calculate the nominal value (net of fund-raising costs) of cash receipts from cash gifts and pledges as a result of fund-raising activities. This dollar value, Q, is calculated by setting PVQ, the present value of these cash receipts, equal to F and solving for Q in equation (5).

$$F = PVQ = Q[b_g(1 + r)^{-1}$$
$$+ \sum_{t=1}^{2} \frac{b_2}{2} (1 + r)^{-t}$$
$$+ \sum_{t=1}^{3} \frac{b_3}{3} (1 + r)^{-t}$$
$$+ \ldots + \sum_{t=1}^{a} \frac{b_a}{a} (1 + r)^{-t}]$$
$$= Q\alpha \qquad (5)$$

where b_g is the percentage of Q received as one-time, first-year gifts, and $b_2, b_3, \ldots . b_a$ are the percentages of Q to be received in equal annual installments from pledges of 2.3, ... a years' duration, respectively. The terms within the brackets in equation (5) reduce to a present value factor, α, which when divided into F yields the nominal fund raising campaign goal, Q. Thus

$$Q = F/\alpha \qquad (6)$$

Financing Cash Deficits

When an institution's fund-raising campaign meets its quota largely through long-term pledges, projected cash outflows for the capital project are likely to exceed cash inflows from fund raising by substantial margins in early years, thus creating cash deficits. If cash transactions for the capital investment project are handled through the institution's endowment fund, a cash deficit in any year, t, will be paid out of the endowment fund's liquid assets at a cost to the project equal to r (the endowment fund's rate of return on investment) times D_t, the project's cash deficit in that year. In this case, since the earnings rate and the borrowing cost are identical, the model outlined previously compensates automatically for the endowment's loss of income as a result of the deficit. Hence no further adjustment is needed.

If, however, the institution has no endowment and must borrow funds to cover any cash deficit at a rate higher than it is able to earn on cash surpluses, an adjustment to F is required. The adjusted present value of cash outflows, F^*, replaces equation (1). It is

$$F^* = PVC_c + PVC_e + PVC_f$$
$$+ \sum_{t=1}^{k} [(r^* - r) D_t]/(1 + r)^t \qquad (7)$$

where r^* is the institution's borrowing rate ($r^* > r$). The nomimal values for D_t are derived from comparing the nomimal values of cash inflows with the inflation-adjusted outflows in each year of the project. This procedure is illustrated in the following section.

ILLUSTRATIVE CALCULATION

Exhibit 1 contains the list of variables for which estimates are required as inputs to the model, along with values that will be used in an illustrative calculation. We will initially assume that the institution is endowed (i.e., $r^* = r$), and later remove that assumption in order to illustrate the calculation of F^*.

Endowed Institutions

The initial step in the application of the model to a capital expenditure program in an endowed institution is the calculation of F, the

EXHIBIT 1

Input Variables

C_c = contact price of facilities construction, $6 million, payable in 3 equal installments

C_e = equipment costs, $2.5 million

C_{ft} = shortfall of operating revenues under operating costs, $200,000 per year for 10 years

r = ROI from the institution's endowment fund, 9%

i_c = construction inflation rate, 18%

i_e = equipment inflation rate, 8%

i_f = institutional wage inflation rate, 6%

b_g = percentage of Q expected in one-time, first-year gifts, 24%

b_3 = percentage of Q expected in 3-year pledges, 12%

b_5 = percentage of Q expected in 5-year pledges, 20%

b_8 = percentage of Q expected in 8-year pledges, 44%

present value of the inflation-adjusted cash outflows for $n = 1$. This calculation is shown in Exhibit 2.

As shown in Exhibit 3, the present value factor, α, is equal to .782. By substituting in equation (6), we find that the fund-raising goal, Q, is equal to ($9.076/.782) or $11.606 million when $n = 1$ (i.e., when construction of the facilities begins in year 1).

Unendowed Institutions

When an institution must borrow funds from outside sources to finance cash deficits, and the borrowing rate, r^*, is greater than the discount rate, r, equation (7) is used in place of equation (1) in calculating Q. The procedure also involves an additional step, illustrated in Exhibit 4. This step determines the size and timing of the cash deficit (if any) so that the present value of the interest cost in excess of the discount rate (r^*-r) can be calculated and

added to F to determine F^*, and hence the value of Q.

As Exhibit 4 indicates, cash deficits of $1,260,000 and $523,000 are incurred at the end of years 3 and 4 respectively and must be financed until the end of each of the following years. If the assumed borrowing rate, r^*, is 13%, the final element in equation (7) becomes

$$(.13 - .09)[\$1,260,000/(1 + .09)^4 \\ +(\$523,000)/(1 + .09)^5] \\ = .04[\$1,260,000 \times .708) \\ +(\$523,000 \times .650) \\ = \$49,281$$

When this is added to the value previously determined for F when n = 1 ($9,076 million), we find that $F^* = \$9,076,000 + 49.281 = \$9.125$ million. The fund-raising campaign goal, Q, then becomes ($9,125/.782) or $11.669 million, $63,000 greater than the endowed institution's goal. This additional amount must be raised to cover the marginal interest cost of $71,320 that will be incurred in financing the expected cash deficits in years 4 and 5.

PROJECT TIMING

Until now, Q has been calculated under the assumption of immediate project implementation—that is, $n = 1$. This is probably the correct assumption in most cases; however, situations may occur in which the administrator wishes to examine the effects on Q of a delay in project implementation of one or more years. A priori analysis would suggest that the wisdom of such a delay is dependent upon certain key variables, the most important of which are: i, the inflation rates; r, the endowment portfolio return; b, the distribution of cash donations over time; and C_c, the dollar amount of the construction costs.

Exhibits 5, 6, and 7 portray graphically the changes in the fund-raising goal, Q, resulting from delaying construction up to the tenth

EXHIBIT 2

Calculation of the Present Value of Cash Outflows

(1)	(2)	(3) Adjustment for Inflation[a]		(4) Present Value Factors[†] @ 9%	(5) Inflation-adjusted Present Value (2)×(3)×(4)
Year	Project Costs ($ millions)	Percent	Factor		
$n = 1$	2,000	18	1.000	.917	1.834
2	2,000	18	1.000	.842	1.684
$m = 3$	2,000	18	1.000	.772	1.544
	2,500	8	1.260	.772	2.432
$i = 4$	.200	6	1.263	.708	.179
5	.200	6	1.338	.650	.174
6	.200	6	1.419	.596	.169
7	.200	6	1.504	.547	.165
8	.200	6	1.594	.502	.160
9	.200	6	1.690	.460	.155
10	.200	6	1.791	.422	.151
11	.200	6	1.898	.388	.147
12	.200	6	2.012	.356	.143
$k = 13$	.200	6	2.113	.320	.139
Totals	10,500				9.076

[a]Factors are found in Appendix Table A, Compound Value of $1.00, in Clifton H. Kreps and Richard F. Wacht, *Financial Administration* (Hinsdale, Illinois, The Dryden Press, 1975).
[†]Factors are found in Appendix Table B, Present Value of $1.00, in Kreps and Wacht, *Financial Administration*.

year under three sets of conditions. Variations from the data given in Exhibit 1 for the illustrative calculation form the basis for these results. It is assumed in all three cases that the institution is unendowed and must borrow funds in cash deficit years.

Exhibit 5 presents what currently would be the most common situation; that is, one in which construction inflation rates are higher than the endowment portfolio returns. Again, all of the data used to calculate the successive iterations for $n = 1$ to $n = 10$ are presented in Exhibit 1. In addition, the borrowing rate is set

at 12%. Because of the 18% annual inflation rate for construction costs, it is not surprising to find that delays in project implementation will increase the fund-raising goal indefinitely at an increasing rate. Thus Q_{min} is achieved when $n = 1$.

The situation illustrated in Exhibit 6 is the reverse of that in Exhibit 5; the construction inflation rate is reduced to 2%, with all other data remaining constant. The effect of that change causes the present value of the project costs to approach zero with an indefinite postponement of project implementation. But in-

EXHIBIT 3

Calculation of the Present Value Factor, α

(1) Year	(2) b_8Q	(3) $\frac{b_3}{3}Q$	(4) $\frac{b_5}{5}Q$	(5) $\frac{b_8}{8}Q$	(6) α_t (2) + (3) + (4) + (5)	(7) Present Value Factors @ 9%	(8) $PV\alpha_t$ (6) × (7)
1	.24Q	.04Q	.04Q	.055Q	.375Q	.917	.344Q
2		.04Q	.04Q	.055Q	.135Q	.842	.114Q
3		.04Q	.04Q	.055Q	.135Q	.772	.104Q
4			.04Q	.055Q	.095Q	.708	.067Q
5			.04Q	.055Q	.095Q	.650	.062Q
6				.055Q	.055Q	.596	.033Q
7				.055Q	.055Q	.547	.030Q
8				.055Q	.055Q	.502	.028Q
Totals	.24Q	.12Q	.20Q	.440Q	1.000Q		.782Q

EXHIBIT 4

Calculation of Cash Deficit [Dollar Figures in Millions]

(1) Year	(2) Inflation-Adjusted Cash Outflow[a]	(3) Nominal Cash Inflow[b]	(4) Nominal Net Cash Flow (3) + (2)	(5) Beginning Cash Balance	(6) Ending Interest Earned (5) × .09	(7) Cash Balance (4) + (5) + (6)
1	$2.000	4.352	2.352	$ 0	$ 0	$2.352
2	2.000	1.567	(.433)[c]	2.352	.212	2.131
3	5.150	1.567	(3.583)	2.131	.192	(1.260)
4	.253	1.103	.850	(1.260)	(.113)	(.523)
5	.268	1.103	.835	(.523)	(.047)	.265
6	.284	.638	.354	.265	.024	.643
7	.301	.638	.337	.643	.058	1.038
8	.319	.638	.319	1.038	.093	1.450
9	.338		(.338)	1.450	.131	1.243
10	.358		(.358)	1.243	.112	.997
11	.380		(.380)	.997	.090	.707
12	.402		(.402)	.707	.064	.369
13	.427		(.427)	.369	.033	(.025)[d]

[a]Nominal cash outflow times the appropriate inflation factor from column (3) in Exhibit 2.
[b]$11.606 million times α_1 from column (6) in Exhibit 3.
[c]Figures in parentheses are cash deficits.
[d]This figure does not equal zero because of rounding errors.

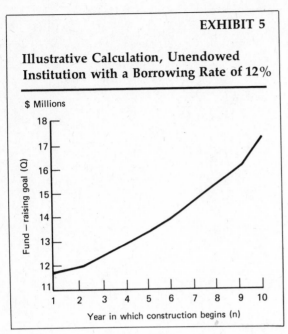

EXHIBIT 5

Illustrative Calculation, Unendowed Institution with a Borrowing Rate of 12%

$ Millions

Fund – raising goal (Q)

Year in which construction begins (n)

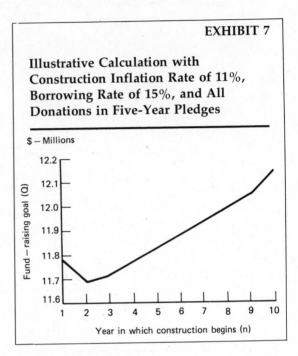

EXHIBIT 7

Illustrative Calculation with Construction Inflation Rate of 11%, Borrowing Rate of 15%, and All Donations in Five-Year Pledges

$ – Millions

Fund – raising goal (Q)

Year in which construction begins (n)

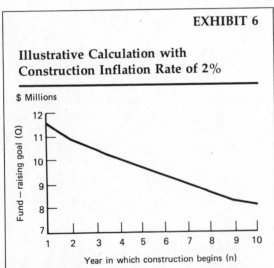

EXHIBIT 6

Illustrative Calculation with Construction Inflation Rate of 2%

$ Millions

Fund – raising goal (Q)

Year in which construction begins (n)

definite project postponement obviously is an unreasonable solution for an institution with urgent facilities requirements. Hence, the real benefit from calculating successive iterations is simply to determine the magnitudes of the incremental reductions in Q as n becomes larger. The application of the model in such

cases provides data that the administrator can employ in deciding the appropriate trade-off between delaying project implementation (and the institutional benefits produced therefrom) and increasing the nominal amount of funds to be raised. In this case, a delay of two years would result in a reduction of over $1 million in the fund-raising goal.

In some cases a true minimum exists for a given integer value of $n > 1$. Several combinations of variable values that will produce a U-shaped curve are imaginable, but the most likely is that which causes early large cash deficits with a high borrowing rate and a moderately high construction inflation rate. Exhibit 7 presents the values of Q for $n = 1$ to $n = 10$ when the fund-raising campaign produces all cash inflows in the form of five-year pledges, the borrowing rate is 15%, and the construction inflation rate is 11%. In this instance, Q is minimized at $n = 2$, with the resulting savings of about $85,000 over immediate project implementation.

SENSITIVITY ANALYSIS

As all managers and administrators know, the future cannot be predicted with absolute certainty. The model just described assumes that such predictions can be made accurately and produces "answers" based on that assumption. However, the model also provides a means of testing various assumptions about the future and allows the user to consider a range of forecasts for each variable listed in Exhibit 1. The difficulty, of course, is that the number of calculations required can be overwhelming. Again, computer assistance can be extremely helpful.

To demonstrate this capability, let us suppose that the aforementioned illustrative calculation represents the planning for a new university library. Suppose further that the alumni office feels that by spending an additional $400,000 for several gala fund-raising dinners, the timing of the gross cash inflows could be shortened considerably. Exhibit 8 compares the previous distribution of gifts and pledges with the new estimate. Following the procedure outlined earlier in Exhibit 3, we find that α now becomes 0.853, and Q equals

---

EXHIBIT 8

Comparison of Gift and Pledge Distributions

Gift Type	Previous	New
First-year gifts	24%	50%
Two-year pledges	—	—
Three-year pledges	12	15
Four-year pledges	—	10
Five-year pledges	20	—
Six-year pledges	—	25
Seven-year pledges	—	—
Eight-year pledges	44	—
	100%	100%

($9,076/0.853) or $10.64 million, nearly $1 million less than the previous goal. Of course, the $10.64 million is a net figure; therefore the $400,000 increase in fund-raising expenses would have to be raised along with the target amount.

Let's take another example, this time to illustrate the importance of planning for inflation. Assume in the illustrative calculation that all inflation rates are equal to zero. The effect is quite substantial. The present value of cash outflows drops from $9.076 million to $7.984 million, and the fund-raising goal, Q, drops by $1.396 million to $10.210 million, when construction begins in year 1.

Pretesting Decisions

Certain policy decisions can, and perhaps should, be pretested before committing the institution to implementing a particular capital expenditure program. For example, the administrator may wish to examine the implications of leasing, rather than purchasing, equipment. In the illustrative calculation, if equipment were leased, the cash outflow in year 3 for equipment purchases would be exchanged for greater cash operating deficits in years 4 through 13. These cash flows, however, would not be subject to the effects of inflation. Thus exchange could be examined separately by discounting the lease payments and comparing this figure with the present value of the inflation-adjusted equipment costs, both discounted at the rate r. The lower of the two figures would indicate the better choice from a fund-raising point of view. That figure would then be used to compute Q.

Other policy decisions, such as those suggested by Fulmer,[4] can also be pretested. Changes in project design, borrowing against pledges receivable to accelerate cash inflows, and undertaking a more expensive fund-raising campaign in order to reduce the proportion of the total campaign goal raised from long-term pledges were assumed feasible by Fulmer but should be subjected to analysis before such decisions are implemented.

CONTROLLING THE PROGRAM

A final benefit realizable from the application of the model is the production of data useful for controlling both the fund-raising and the project-implementation phases of the capital expenditure program. Exhibit 4, for example, can serve as a gross check on the project's cash inflows and outflows, variations of actual experience which would serve as signals that the desired results are not being achieved. For example, the failure to reach the desired fund-raising goal or a slowing of pledge payments in early years, if left unchecked, would result in a shortage of funds later in the project's implementation or operation phases. By replacing forecasted cash flows with actual experience, the administrator can perform the necessary computations to determine the extent of change required in the project as a result of the variations; that is, how much must be added to the campaign goal or cut from planned expenditures to reestablish equality between F and PVQ. Of course controls of this type would require a program accounting system in order to be effective.

Another important benefit from making explicit cash flow forecasts (such as provided by Exhibit 4) arises in connection with the endowment fund management. Knowledge of the timing of cash flows permits the endowment manager to schedule the maturities of fixed income securities to correspond with projected fund requirements or provides him with sufficient advance warning to permit the orderly liquidation of investment securities in advance of cash needs. Such information facilitates portfolio management by permitting the available funds to be more fully invested in higher yielding (longer maturity) investment

securities and minimizing the proportion of assets held in liquid form as a defense against uncertainty in cash outflows.

CONCLUDING COMMENT

The need to plan, coordinate, and control fund-raising and capital expenditure programs is obvious. Not so obvious or so simple as that statement implies is the specification of an appropriate methodology. This article has attempted to provide an approach that employs most of the relevant decision variables without becoming so complex in application as to destroy its usefulness in a large number of nonprofit institutions. Toward this end, some considerations have been omitted, such as the explicit treatment of uncertainty and the possibility of multipurpose fund-raising campaigns; however, sensitivity analysis can overcome the first of these deficiencies to some extent, and familiarity with the basic concepts underlying the model itself can permit the user to modify it to suit his purposes. Thus, despite its shortcomings, the model remains a potentially useful tool for planning and control. Finally, for those who may be interested in employing the model for their own use, a computer program written in Basic can be obtained from the author.

NOTES

1. Vincent A. Fulmer, "Cost/Benefit Analysis on Fund Raising," *Harvard Business Review*, March –April 1973, pp. 103–110.

2. Charles D. Ellis, "Let's Solve the Endowment Crises," *Harvard Business Review*, March–April 1970, pp. 92–102.

3. The Ford Foundation Advisory Committee on Endowment Management, *Managing Educational Endowments* (New York, The Ford Foundation, 1969).

4. Fulmer, "Cost/Benefit Analysis in Fund Raising," pp. 103–110.

CHAPTER 10

Organizing the Planning Process: Budgeting

The budget for the typical nonprofit organization has a central role in the existence of that body, being the basis upon which economic allocation decisions are made. Moreover, where public resources are involved, it frequently becomes a legal contract binding the organization to the plan. The discussion and readings in this chapter present additional insights into the budgeting process.

Probably the major reason historically that the budget has played such an important part in the existence of public agencies is the stewardship function it performs. The ability of the budget and accounting system to identify all funds appropriated as well as the purposes for which they were spent is of essence in the public sector.

Increasingly, the budget is being used in addition as a planning device for achieving efficiency and effectiveness. As a consequence, it becomes part of the arena in which the political bargaining process takes place. No one form of budget can accomplish all of these tasks to the satisfaction of all users. As a consequence, many suggestions for budgetary reform have surfaced in the last fifty years.

The defense of the traditional line-item budget made by Wildavsky in "A Budget for All Seasons? Why the Traditional Budget Lasts" provides an incisive and no doubt controversial examination of the budget process. The essay discusses the various budget reform movements and identifies the reasons why, in the author's view, the much maligned line-item budget continues to exist.

Wildavsky assumes a national budget setting, but many of the budgetary problems that he addresses are also identified with the smallest nonprofit organizations. For example, the role of the budget as a device for conflict resolution, control, and accountability are just as applicable for the local welfare agency as they are for the federal government. Therefore, many of the conclusions he draws at the federal level are equally valid at the local level.

Wildavsky concludes by attributing the line-item budget's success to its ability to avoid failing completely on any one budget criterion. While other forms of budgeting, for example, zero-base, planning-programming-budgeting, or stable-dollar budgeting, may be more successful in some areas, the author finds them wanting in others. In addition to the excellent discussion of budget types and behavior, another major contribution of the article is its identification of the wealth reallocation effects of various budget types.

The typical nonprofit organization may use several different budgets to manage various aspects of its activities. It may use a form of a performance budget that is capable of linking the input of resources with the output of programs. This budget format is very useful in the planning stages in that it allows the decision maker to assess the effects of budget changes on programs, facilitating the comparison of alternative programs. Thus, one can emphasize effectiveness in the decision-making process.

In the public sector an appropriations or expenditure budget is the usual document employed by the executive to request funds from the legislative branch. Typically, the format of this budget is line item in nature, that is, where the budget request is listed in order of line items with $X for supervisory personnel, $Y for clerical employees, $Z for supplies. More progressive organizations may list the expenditures by program and then by line item within separate programs.

Financial reports frequently compare actual results with budget data. In the case of the expenditure budget, this allows the reader to make judgments regarding control of expenditures; in the case of revenue statements, it permits assessment of management's ability to forecast revenues. The linking of revenue with expenditures is not commonly done for most nonprofit organizations since the cause-and-effect relationship between them is minimal. In addition, the reader usually finds the residual difference between the two of little interest.

In "From PPBS to Program Strategies," Woodie reflects the variety of budgets that a nonprofit organization may use, including performance budgeting, capital budgeting, and PPBS. The article gives an excellent description of how the city of Dayton modified PPBS budgeting to what the city terms "program strategies." Major advantages claimed for the method are its ability to incorporate categorical grants into the planning process and to communicate more effectively the usefulness of various city services.

Buttressing the article are particularly fine exhibits, exemplifying through the city "crime" report the entire budgeting and programming processes. The report links a descriptive status statement about Dayton's crime to the city's financial budget, as a means of communicating the relationship between the two to the city council. Objectives of the various programs and the quantitative measures for evaluating them are identified.

A budget process that has received much attention in recent years is zero-base budgeting. The article by Gordon and Heivilin, "Zero-Base Budgeting in the Federal Government: A Historical Perspective," provides not only an interesting historical view of federal government budgeting but also a concise description of zero-base budgeting (ZBB), its perceived advantages and disadvantages. Although specifically concerned with the federal government, the description of decision packages, the ranking process, and decision-making steps is sufficiently general to apply to many types of nonprofit organizations.

Gordon and Heivilin correctly point out that ZBB is not applicable to direct manufacturing costs but rather is "most appropriate for indirect service-oriented costs," a statement that could also be directed toward nonprofit organizations. If the major costs of a nonprofit organization vary directly with service output, then cost control through flexible budgets would be most appropriate. If, on the other hand, the major costs of the agency are indirect (i.e., do not vary directly with workload), then ZBB may be an effective budget method.

Anthony in "Zero-Base Budgeting: A Useful Fraud?" takes a closer look at some of the problems with ZBB and proceeds to explain why, in his view, the process does not work. A major criticism centers around the way ZBB combines the programming and budgeting process into a single decision-making process. Anthony contends that this ignores the political realities of resource allocation decision making as well as the amount of time available to the executive branch. The article concludes with the author's suggestions for controlling both ongoing and new programs.

Many welfare organizations that operate on a break-even basis may run a very close cash-flow balance. In such cases, the planning of cash resources is extremely important for the continued existence of the organization. In "How to Make Cash Forecasting Work for You," Gent outlines two effective ways for forecasting cash flows. The method chosen depends upon whether one is concerned with short-term or long-term requirements.

For example, if the financial manager is concerned with whether enough cash will be available at the end of the month to pay salary costs, then a short-term forecast is required. In this instance, the author suggests using a cash receipts and disbursement method. If, however, one is concerned with the cash-flow effects associated with the addition or deletion of a program, then a long-term cash forecast is most useful. For this, the method of adjusted provision for debt retirement is suggested.

The article by Nelson and Turk, "Financial Management for the Arts," is wide-ranging, including everything from personnel organization to the final reporting of results. Aimed specifically at managers of arts organizations, the article makes a more general and important contribution in exemplifying many different types of budgets and reports. Although the authors place primary emphasis on financial stewardship functions, a number of the featured reports illuminate management control. Of particular interest are the examples of the time budget, which is useful for determining staff size, and the program expenditure budget, which identifies expenditures with relevant programs.

A BUDGET FOR ALL SEASONS?
WHY THE TRADITIONAL BUDGET LASTS*

Aaron Wildavsky

Almost from the time the caterpillar of budgetary evolution became the butterfly of budgetary reform, the line-item budget has been condemned as a reactionary throwback to its primitive larva. Budgeting, its critics claim, has been metamorphized in reverse, an example of retrogression instead of progress. Over the last century, the traditional annual cash budget has been condemned as mindless, because its lines do not match programs, irrational, because they deal with inputs instead of outputs, short-sighted, because they cover one year instead of many, fragmented, because as a rule only changes are reviewed, conservative, because these changes tend to be small, and worse. Yet despite these faults, real and alleged, the traditional budget reigns supreme virtually everywhere, in practice if not in theory. Why?

The usual answer, if it can be dignified as such, is bureaucratic inertia. The forces of conservatism within government resist change. Presumably the same explanation fits all cases past and present. How, then, explain why countries like Britain departed from tradition in recent years only to return to it? It is hard to credit institutional inertia in virtually all countries for a century. Has nothing happened over time to entrench the line–item budget?

The line–item budget is a product of history, not of logic. It was not so much created as evolved. Its procedures and its purposes represent accretions over time rather than propositions postulated at a moment in time. Hence we should not expect to find them either consistent or complementary.

Control over public money and accountability to public authority were among the earliest purposes of budgeting. Predictability and planning—knowing what there will be to spend over time—were not far behind. From the beginning, relating expenditure to revenue was of prime importance. In our day we have added macro-economic management to moderate inflation and unemployment. Spending is varied to suit the economy. In time the need for money came to be used as a level to enhance the efficiency or effectiveness of policies. He who pays the piper hopes to call the tune. Here we have it: Budgeting is supposed to contribute to continuity (for planning), to change (for policy evaluation), to flexibility (for the economy), and to provide rigidity (for limiting spending).

These different and (to some extent) opposed purposes contain a clue to the perennial dissatisfaction with budgeting. Obviously, no process can simultaneously provide continuity and change, rigidity and flexibility. And no one should be surprised that those who concentrate on one purpose or the other should find budgeting unsatisfactory or that, as purposes change, these criticisms should become

Source. Copyright © 1978 by the American Society for Public Administration. All rights reserved. Reprinted from *Public Administration Review* (November/December, 1978), pp. 501–509.
*This paper grew out of my collaboration with Hugh Heclo on the second edition of *The Private Govercment of Public Money.* I wish to thank him, James Douglas, Robert Hartmen, and Carolyn Webber for critical comments.

constant. The real surprise is that traditional budgeting has not been replaced by any of its outstanding competitors in this century.

If traditional budgeting is so bad, why are there no better alternatives? Appropriate answers are unobtainable, I believe, so long as we proceed on this high level of aggregation. So far as I know, the traditional budget has never been compared systematically, characteristic for characteristic, with the leading alternatives.[1] By doing so we can see better which characteristics of budgetary processes suit different purposes under a variety of conditions. Why, again, if traditional budgeting does have defects, which I do not doubt, has it not been replaced? Perhaps the complaints are the clue: What is it that is inferior for most purposes and yet superior over all?

The ability of a process to score high on one criterion may increase the likelihood of its scoring low on another. Planning requires predictability and economic management requires reversibility. Thus, there may well be no ideal mode of budgeting. If so, this is the question: Do we choose a budgetary process that does splendidly on one criterion but terribly on others, or a process that satisfies all these demands even though it does not score brilliantly on any single one?

THE TRADITIONAL BUDGET

Traditional budgeting is annual (repeated yearly) and incremental (departing marginally from the year before). It is conducted on a cash basis (in current dollars). Its content comes in the form of line-items (such as personnel or maintenance). Alternatives to all these characteristics have been developed and tried, though never, so far as I know, with success. Why this should be so, despite the obvious and admitted defects of tradition, will emerge if we consider the criteria each type of budgetary process has to meet.

What purpose is a public-sector budget supposed to serve? Certainly one purpose is accountability. By associating government publicly with certain expenditures, opponents can ask questions or contribute criticisms. Here the clarity of the budget presentation in linking expenditures to activities and to responsible officials is crucial. Close to accountability is control: Are the funds which are authorized and appropriated being spent for the designated activities? Control (or its antonym "out of control") can be used in several senses. Are expenditures within the limits (1) stipulated or (2) desired. While a budget (or item) might be "out of control" to a critic who desires it to be different, in our terms "control" is lacking only when limits are stipulated and exceeded.

Budgets may be mechanisms of efficiency—doing whatever is done at least cost or getting the most out of a given level of expenditure—and/or of effectiveness—achieving certain results in public policy like improving the health of children or reducing crime.

In modern times, budgeting has also become an instrument of economic management and of planning. With the advent of Keynesian economics efforts have been made to vary the rate of spending so as to increase employment in slack times or to reduce inflation when prices are deemed to be rising too quickly. Here (leaving out alternative tax policies), the ability to increase and decrease spending in the short run is of paramount importance. For budgeting to serve planning, however, predictability (not variability) is critical. The ability to maintain a course of behavior over time is essential.

Now, as everyone knows, budgeting is not only an economic but a political instrument. Since inability to implement decisions nullifies them, the ability to mobilize support is as important as making the right choice. So is the capacity to figure out what to do—that is, to make choices. Thus, the effect of budgeting on conflict and calculation—the capacity to make and support decisions—has to be considered.

UNIT OF MEASUREMENT: CASH OR VOLUME

Budgeting can be done not only in cash but by volume. Instead of promising to pay so much in the next year or years, the commitment can be made in terms of operations performed or services provided. Why might anyone want to budget in volume (or constant currency) terms? One reason, obviously, is to aid planning. If public agencies know they can count not on variable currency but on what the currency can buy, that is, on a volume of activity, they can plan ahead as far as the budget runs. Indeed, if one wishes to make decisions now that could be made at future periods, so as to help assure consistency over time, stability in the unit of effort—so many applications processed or such a level of services provided—is the very consideration to be desired.

So long as purchasing power remains constant, budgeting in cash or by volume remains a distinction without a difference. However, should the value of money fluctuate (and, in our time, this means inflation), the public budget must absorb additional amounts so as to provide the designated volume of activity. Budgeters lose control of money because they have to supply whatever is needed. Evidently, given large and unexpected changes in prices, the size of the budget in cash terms would fluctuate wildly. Evidently, also, no government could permit itself to be so far out of control. Hence, the very stability budgeting by volume is designed to achieve turns out to be its major unarticulated premise.

Who pays the price for budgeting by volume? The private sector and the central con-

troller. Budgeting by volume is, first of all, an effort by elements of the public sector to invade the private sector. What budgeting by volume says, in effect, is that the public sector will be protected against inflation by getting its agreed level of services before other needs are met. The real resources necessary to make up the gap between projected and current prices must come from the private sector in the form of taxation or interest for borrowing. In other words, for the public sector volume budgeting is a form of indexing against inflation.

Given an irreducible amount of uncertainty in the system, not every element can be stabilized at one and the same time. Who, then, will be kept stable and who will bear the costs of change? Within the government the obvious answer is that spending by agencies will be kept whole. The central budget office (the Treasury, Ministry of Finance, or the Office of Management and Budget, as it is variously called) bears the brunt of covering larger expenditures and takes the blame when the budget goes out of control, i.e., rises faster and in different directions than predicted. In Britain, where budgeting by volume went under the name of the Public Expenditure Survey, the Treasury finally responded to years of severe inflation by imposing cash limits, otherwise known as the traditional cold-cash budget. Of course, departmental cash limits include an amount for price changes, but this is not necessarily what the Treasury expects but the amount it desires. The point is that the spending departments have to make up deficits caused by inflation. Instead of the Treasury forking over the money automatically, as in the volume budget, departments have to ask and may be denied. The local spenders, not the central controllers, have to pay the price of monetary instability.[2]

Inflation has become not only an evil to be avoided but a (perhaps *the*) major instrument of modern public policy. Taxes are hard to increase and benefits are virtually impossible to decrease. Similar results may be obtained through inflation, which artificially elevates the tax brackets in which people find themselves and decreases their purchasing power. Wage increases that cannot be directly contested may be indirectly nullified (and the real burden of the national debt reduced) without changing the ostensible amount, all by inflation. The sensitivity of budgetary forms to inflation is a crucial consideration.

From all this, it follows that budgeting by volume is counterproductive in fighting inflation because it accommodates price increases rather than struggling against them. Volume budgeting may maintain public sector employment at the expense of taking resources from the private sector, thus possibly reducing employment there. There can be no doubt, however, that volume budgeting is for counter-cyclical purposes because the whole point is that the amount and quality of service do not vary over time; if they go up or down to suit short-run economic needs they are bound to be out of kilter over the long run.

How does volume budgeting stack up as a source of policy information? It should enable departments to understand better what they are doing, since they are presumably doing the same thing over the period of the budget, but volume budgeting does poorly as a method of instigating change. For one thing, the money is guaranteed against price changes, so there is less need to please outsiders. For another, volume budgeting necessarily leads to interest in internal affairs—how to do what one wishes—not to external advice—whether there are better things one might be doing. British departments that are unwilling to let outsiders evaluate their activities are hardly going to be motivated by guarantees against price fluctuations.

TIME SPAN: MONTHS, ONE YEAR, MANY YEARS

Multi-year budgeting has long been proposed as a reform to enhance rational choice by viewing resource allocation in a long-term perspective. Considering one year, it has been argued, leads to short-sightedness—only the next year's expenditures are reviewed; overspending—because huge disbursements in future years are hidden; conservatism—incremental changes do not open up larger future vistas; and parochialism—programs tend to be viewed in isolation rather than in comparison to their future costs in relation to expected revenue. Extending the time span of budgeting to three or five years, it is argued, would enable long-range planning to overtake short-term reaction and substitute financial control for merely muddling through. Moreover, it is argued, the practice of rushing spending to use up resources by the end of the year would decline in frequency.

Much depends, to be sure, on how long budgetary commitments last. The seemingly arcane question of whether budgeting should be done on a cash or a volume basis will assume importance if a nation adopts multi-year budgeting. The longer the term of the budget, the more important inflation becomes. To the degree that price changes are automatically absorbed into budgets, a certain volume of activity is guaranteed. To the degree agencies have to absorb inflation, their real level of activity declines. Multi-year budgeting in cash terms diminishes the relative size of the public sector, leaving the private sector larger. Behind discussions of the span of the budget, the real debate is over the relative shares of the public and private sectors—which one will be asked to absorb inflation and which one will be allowed to expand into the other.

A similar issue of relative shares is created within government by proposals to budget in some sectors for several years, and, in others, for only one. Which sectors of policy will be free from the vicissitudes of life in the short term, the question becomes, and which will be protected from them? Like any other device, multi-year budgeting is not neutral but distributes indulgences differently among the affected interests.

Of course, multi-year budgeting has its positive parts. If control of expenditure is desired, for instance, a multi-year budget makes it necessary to estimate expenditures far into the future. The old tactic of the camel's nose—beginning with small expenditures while hiding larger ones later on—is rendered more difficult. Still, hard-in, as the British learned, often implies harder-out. Once an expenditure gets in a multi-year projection it is likely to stay in because it has become part of an interrelated set of proposals that could be expensive to disrupt. Besides, part of the bargain struck when agencies are persuaded to estimate as accurately as they can, is that they will gain stability. i.e., not be subject to sudden reductions according to the needs of the moment. Thus, control in a single year may have to be sacrificed to maintaining limits over the multi-year period; and, should the call come for cuts to meet a particular problem, British experience shows that reductions in future years (which are always "iffy") are easily traded for maintenance of spending in the all-important present. By making prices more prominent due to the larger time period involved, moreover, large sums may have to be supplied in order to meet commitments for a given volume of services in a volatile world.[3]

Suppose, however, that it were deemed desirable to reduce significantly some expenditures in order to increase others. Due to the built-in pressure of continuing commitments, what can be done in a single year is extremely limited. Making arrangements over a three to five year period (with constant prices, five percent a year for five years compounded would bring about a one-third change in the budget) would permit larger changes in amount in a more orderly way. This may be true, of course, but other things—prices, priorities, politicians—seldom remain equal. While the British were working under a five-year budget projection, prices and production could hardly be predicted for five months at a time.

As Robert Hartman put it, "there is no absolutely right way to devise a long-run budget strategy."[4] No one knows how the private economy will be doing or what the consequences will be of a fairly wide range of targets for budget totals. There is no political or economic agreement on whether budget targets should be expressed in terms of levels required for full employment, for price stability, or for budget balancing. Nor is it self-evidently desirable either to estimate where the economy is going and devise a governmental spending target to complement that estimate or to decide what the economy should be doing and get the government to encourage that direction.

In any event, given economic volatility and theoretical poverty, the ability to outguess the future is extremely limited. Responsiveness to changing economic conditions, therefore, if that were the main purpose of budgeting, would be facilitated best with a budget calculated in months or weeks rather than years. Such budgets do exist in poor and uncertain countries. Naomi Caiden and I have called the process "repetitive budgeting" to signify that the budget may be made and remade several times during the year.[5] Because finance ministries often do not know how much is actually in the nation's treasury or what they will have to spend, they hold off making decisions until the last possible moment. The repetitive budget is not a reliable guide to proposed expenditure, but an invitation to agencies to "get it if they can." When economic or political conditions change, which is often, the budget is renegotiated. Adaptiveness is maximized but predictability is minimized. Conflict increases because the same decision is remade several times each year. Agencies must be wary of each other because they do not know when next they will have to compete. Control declines, partly because frequent changes make the audit trail difficult to follow, and partly because departments seek to escape from control so as to reestablish a modicum of predictability. Hence, they obfuscate their activities, thus reducing accountability, and actively seek funds of their own in the form of earmarked revenues, thus diminishing control. Both efficiency and effectiveness suffer. The former is either unnecessary (if separate funds exist) or impossible (without continuity), and the latter is obscured by the lack of relationship between what is in the budget and what happens in the world. Drastically shortening the time-frame wreaks havoc with efficiency, effectiveness, conflict, and calculation. However, if it is immediate responsiveness that is desired, as in economic management, the shorter the span the better.

Just as the annual budget on a cash basis is integral to the traditional process, so is the budgetary base—the expectation that most expenditures will be continued. Normally, only increases or decreases to the existing base are considered in any one period. If budgetary practices may be described as incremental, the main alternative to the traditional budget is one that emphasizes comprehensive calculation. So it is not surprising that the main modern alternatives are planning, programming, and budgeting (PB) and zero-base budgeting (ZBB).

CALCULATION: INCREMENTAL OR COMPREHENSIVE

Let us think of PPB as embodying horizontal comprehensiveness—comparing alternative expenditure packages to decide which best contributes to larger programmatic objectives. ZBB, by contrast, might be thought of as manifesting vertical comprehensiveness—every year alternative expenditures from base zero are considered for all governmental activities or objectives treated as discrete entities. In a word, PPB compares programs and ZBB compares alternative funding.

The strength of PPB lies in its emphasis on policy analysis to increase effectiveness. Programs are evaluated, found wanting, and presumably replaced with alternatives designed to produce superior results. Unfortunately, PPB engenders a conflict between error recognition and error correction. There is little point in designing better policies so as to minimize their prospects of implementation. But why should a process devoted to policy evaluation end up stultifying policy execution? Because PPB's policy rationality is countered by its organizational irrationality.

If error is to be altered, it must be relatively easy to correct,[6] but PPB makes it hard. The "systems" in PPB are characterized by their proponents as highly differentiated and tightly linked. The rationale for program budgeting lies in its connectedness—like programs are grouped together. Program structures are meant to replace the confused concatenations of line-items with clearly differentiated, non-overlapping boundaries; only one set of programs to a structure. This means that a change in one element or structure must result in change reverberating throughout every element in the same system. Instead of alerting only neighboring units or central control units, which would make change feasible, all are, so to speak, wired together so the choice is effectively all or none.

Imagine one of us deciding whether to buy a tie or a kerchief. A simple task, one might think. Suppose, however, that organizational rules require us to keep our entire wardrobe as a unit. If everything must be rearranged when one item is altered, the probability we will do anything is low. The more tightly linked the elements and the more highly differentiated they are, the greater the probability of error (because the tolerances are so small), and the less the likelihood the error will be corrected (because with change, every element has to be recalibrated with every other one that was previously adjusted). Being caught between revolution (change in everything) and resignation (change in nothing) has little to recommend it.

Program budgeting increases rather than decreases the cost of correcting error. The great complaint about bureaucracies is their rigidity. As things stand, the object of organizational affection is the bureau as serviced by the usual line-item categories from which people, money, and facilities flow. Viewed from the standpoint of bureau interests, programs, to some extent, are negotiable; some can be increased and others decreased while keeping the agency on an even keel or, if necessary, adjusting it to less happy times without calling into question its very existence. Line-item budgeting, precisely because its categories (personnel, maintenance, supplies) do not relate directly to programs, is easier to change. Budgeting by programs, precisely because money flows to objectives, makes it difficult to abandon objectives without abandoning the organization that gets its money for them. It is better that non-programmatic rubrics be used as formal budget categories, thus permitting a diversity of analytical perspectives, than that a

temporary analytic insight be made the permanent perspective through which money is funneled.

The good organization is interested in discovering and correcting its own mistakes. The higher the cost of error—not only in terms of money but also in personnel, programs, and perogatives—the less the chance anything will be done about them. Organizations should be designed, therefore, to make errors visible and correctible—that is, noticeable and reversible—which, in turn, is to say, cheap and affordable.

The ideal, ahistorical information system is zero-base budgeting. The past, as reflected in the budgetary base (common expectations as to amounts and types of funding), is explicitly rejected. There is no yesterday. Nothing is to be taken for granted. Everything at every period is subject to searching scrutiny. As a result, calculations become unmanageable. The same is true of PPB, which requires comparisons of all or most programs that might contribute to common objectives. To say that a budgetary process is ahistorical is to conclude that it increases the sources of error while decreasing the changes of correcting mistakes. If history is abolished, nothing is settled. Old quarrels become new conflicts. Both calculation and conflict increase exponentially, the former worsening selection, and the latter, correction of error. As the number of independent variables grows, because the past is assumed not to limit the future, ability to control the future declines. As mistrust grows with conflict, willingness to admit and, hence, to correct error diminishes. Doing without history is a little like abolishing memory—momentarily convenient, perhaps, but ultimately embarrassing.

Only poor countries comes close to zero-base budgeting, not because they wish to do so but because their uncertain financial position continually causes them to go back on old commitments. Because past disputes are part of present conflicts, their budgets lack predictive value; little stated in them is likely to occur. Ahistorical practices, which are a dire consequence of extreme instability and form which all who experience them devoutly desire to escape, should not be considered normative.

ZBB and PPB share an emphasis on the virtue of objectives. Program budgeting is designed to relate larger to smaller objectives among different programs, and zero-base budgeting promises to do the same within a single program. The policy implications of these methods of budgeting, which distinguish them from existing approaches, derive from their overwhelming concern with ranking objectives. Thinking about objectives is one thing, however, and making budget categories out of them is quite another. Of course, if one wants the objectives of today to be the objectives of tomorrow, which is to say if one wants no change in objectives, then building the budget around objectives is a brilliant idea. However, if one wants flexibility in objectives (sometimes known as learning from experience) it must be possible to change them without simultaneously destroying the organization by withdrawing financial support.

Both PPB and ZBB are expressions of the prevailing paradigm of rationality in which reason is rendered equivalent to ranking objectives. Alas, an efficient mode of presenting results in research papers—find objectives, order them, choose the highest valued—has been confused with proper processes of social inquiry. For purposes of resource allocation, which is what budgeting is about, ranking objectives without consideration of resources is irrational. The question cannot be "what do you want?" as if there were no limits, but should be "what do you want compared to what you can get?" (Ignoring resources is as bad as neglecting objectives as if one were not interested in the question "what do I want to do this for?"). After all, an agency with a billion dollars would not only do more than it would with a million dollars but might well wish to do different things. Resources affect objectives as well as the other way around, and budgeting should not separate what reason tells us belongs together.

For purposes of economic management, comprehensive calculations stressing efficiency (ZBB) and effectiveness (PPB) leave much to be desired. For one thing, comprehensiveness takes time and this is no asset in responding to fast-moving events. For another, devices that stress the intrinsic merits of their methods—this is (in)efficient and that is (in)effective—rub raw when good cannot be done for external reasons, i.e., the state of the economy. Cooperation will be compromised when virtue in passing one test becomes vice in failing another.

I have already said that conflict is increased by ahistorical methods of budgeting. Here I wish to observe that efforts to reduce conflict only make things worse by vitiating the essential character of comprehensiveness. The cutting edge of competition among programs lies in postulating a range of policy objectives small enough to be encompassed and large enough to overlap so there are choices (trade-offs in the jargon of the trade) among them. Instead, PPB generated a tendency either to have only a few objectives, so anything and everything fit under them, or a multitude of objectives, so that each organizational unit had its own home and did not have to compete with any other.[7] ZBB worked it this way: Since a zero base was too threatening or too absurd, zero moved up until it reached, say, 80 percent of the base. To be sure, the burden of conflict and calculation declined, but so did any real difference with traditional incremental budgeting.

Insofar as financial control is concerned, ZBB and PBB raise the question of control over what? Is it control over the content of programs or the efficiency of a given program or the total costs of government or just the legality of expenditures? In theory, ZBB would be better for efficiency, PPB for effectiveness, and traditional budgeting for legality. Whether control extends to total costs, however, depends on the form of financing, a matter to which we now turn.

APPROPRIATIONS OR TREASURY BUDGETING

A traditional budget, without saying much about it, depends on traditional practice—authorization and appropriation followed by expenditure post-audited by external authorities. In many countries traditional budgeting is not, in fact, the main form of public spending. Close to half of public spending in the United States as well as in other countries does not take the form of appropriations budgeting, but what I shall call treasury budgeting. I find this nomenclature useful in avoiding the pejorative connotations of what would otherwise be called "backdoor" spending, because it avoids the appropriations committees in favor of automatic disbursement of funds through the treasury.

For present purposes, the two forms of treasury budgeting that constitute alternatives to traditional appropriations are tax expenditures and mandatory entitlements. When concessions are granted in the form of tax reductions for home ownership or college tuition or medical expenses, these are equivalent to budgetary expenditures except that the money is deflected at the source. In the United States, tax expenditures now amount to more than

$100 billion a year. In one sense this is a way of avoiding budgeting before there is a budget. Whether one accepts this view is a matter of philosophy. It is said, for instance, that the United States government has a progressive income tax. Is that the real tax system or is it a would-be progressive tax as modified by innumerable exceptions? The budgetary process is usually described as resource allocation by the president and Congress through its appropriations committees. Is that the real budgetary process or is it that process together with numerous provisions for "backdoor" spending, low interest loans, and other devices? From a behavioral or descriptive point-of-view actual practices constitute the real system. Then the exceptions are part of the rule. Indeed, since less than half of the budget passes through the appropriations committees, the exceptions must be greater than the rule, and some would say the same could be said about taxation. If the exceptions are part of the rule, however, tax expenditures stand in a better light. Then the government is not contributing or losing income but legitimately excluding certain private activities from being considered as income. There is no question of equity—people are just disposing of their own income as they see fit in a free society. Unless whatever is, is right, tax and budget reformers will object to sanctifying regrettable lapses as operating principles. To them the real systems are the ones which we ought to perfect—progressive tax on income whose revenues are allocated at the same time through the same public mechanism. Tax expenditures interfere with both these ideals.

Mandatory, open-ended entitlements, our second category of treasury budgeting, provide that anyone eligible for certain benefits must be paid regardless of the total. Until the legislation is changed or a "cap" limits total expenditure, entitlements constitute obligations of the state through direct drafts on the treasury. Were I asked to give an operational definition of the end of budgeting, I would say "indexed, open-ended entitlements." Budgeting would no longer involve allocation within limited resources but only addition of one entitlement to another, all guarded against fluctuation in prices.

Obviously, treasury budgeting leaves a great deal to be desired in controlling costs of programs, which depend on such variables as levels of benefits set in prior years, rate of application, and severity of administration. Legal control is possible but difficult because of the large number of individual cases and the innumerable provisions governing eligibility. If the guiding principle is that no one who is eligible should be denied even if some who are ineligible must be included, expenditures will rise. They will decline if the opposite principle—no ineligibles even if some eligibles suffer—prevails.

Whether or not entitlement programs are efficient or effective, the budgetary process will neither add to nor subtract from that result simply because it plays no part. To the extent that efficiency or effectiveness is spurred by the need to convince others to provide funds, such incentives are much weakened or altogether absent. The political difficulties of reducing benefits or eliminating beneficiaries speak eloquently on this subject. No doubt benefits may be eroded by inflation. Protecting against this possibility is the purpose of indexing benefits against inflation (thus doing for the individual what volume budgeting does for the bureaucracy).

Why, then, in view of its anti-budgetary character, is treasury budgeting so popular? Because of its value in coping with conflict, calculation, and economic management. After a number of entitlements and tax expenditures have been decided upon at different times, usually without full awareness of the others,

implicit priorities are produced *ipso-facto*, untouched as it were, by human hands. Conflict is reduced, for the time being at least, because no explicit decisions giving more to this group and less to another are necessary. Ultimately, to be sure, resource limits will have to be considered, but even then only a few rather than all expenditures will be directly involved, since the others go on, as it were, automatically. Similarly, calculation is contracted as treasury budgeting produces figures, allowing a large part of the budget to be taken for granted. Ultimately, of course, days of reckoning come in which there is a loss of flexibility due to the implicit pre-programming of so large a proportion of available funds. For the moment, however, the attitude appears to be "sufficient unto the day is the (financial) evil thereof."

For purposes of economic management, treasury budgeting is a mixed bag. It is useful in providing what are called automatic stabilizers. When it is deemed desirable not to make new decisions every time conditions change, as pertains to unemployment benefits, an entitlement enables funds to flow according to the size of the problem. The difficulty is that not all entitlements are counter-cyclical (child benefits, for example, may rise independently of economic conditions) and the loss in financial flexibility generated by entitlements may hurt when the time comes to do less.

Nevertheless, treasury budgeting has one significant advantage over appropriations budgeting, namely, time. Changes in policy are manifested quickly in changes in spending. In order to bring considerations of economic management to bear on budgeting, these factors must be introduced early in the process of shaping the appropriations budget. Otherwise, last-minute changes of large magnitude will cause chaos by unhinging all sorts of prior understandings. Then the money must be voted and preparations made for spending. In the United States under this process—from the spring previews in the Office of Management and Budget, to the president's budget in January, to congressional action by the following summer and fall, to spending, in the winter and spring—18 to 24 months have elapsed. This is not control but remote control.

"Fine-tuning expenditures," attempting to make small adjustments to speed up or slow down the economy, do not work well anywhere. Efforts to increase expenditure are as likely to decrease the expenditure in the short-run due to the effort required to expand operations. Efforts to reduce spending in the short run are as likely to increase spending due to severence pay, penalties for breaking contracts, and so on. Hence, even as efforts continue to make expenditures more responsive, the attractiveness of more immediate tax and entitlement increases is apparent.

The recalcitrance of all forms of budgeting to economic management is not so surprising; both spending programs and economic management cannot be made more predictable if one is to vary to serve the other. In an age profoundly influenced by Keynesian economic doctrines, with their emphasis on the power of government spending, however, continued efforts to link macro-economics with micro-spending are to be expected.

THE STRUCTURAL BUDGET MARGIN

One such effort is the "Structural Budget Margin" developed in the Netherlands. Due to dissatisfaction with the Keynesian approach to economic stabilization, as well as disillusionment with its short-term fine-tuning, the Dutch sought to develop a longer-term relationship between the growth of public spending and the size of the national economy. Economic management was to rely less on sudden starts and stops of taxation and expenditure, and greater effort was to be devoted to controlling public

spending. (The closest the United States has come is through the doctrine of balancing the budget at the level of full employment which almost always would mean a deficit). The Dutch were particularly interested in a control device because of the difficulty of getting agreement to hold down expenditures in coalition governments. Thus, spending was to be related not to actual growth but to desired growth, with only the designated margin available for new expenditure.

Needless to say there are differences in definition of the appropriate structural growth rate and it has been revised up and down. Since the year used as a base makes a difference, that has also been in dispute. As we would also expect, there are disagreements over calculation of cash or volume of services with rising inflation propelling a move toward cash. Moreover, since people learn to play any game, conservative governments used the structural budget margin to hold down spending and socialists used it to increase it, for then the margin became a mechanism for figuring out the necessary increases in taxation. Every way one turns, it appears, budgetary devices are good for some purposes and not for others.

WHY THE TRADITIONAL BUDGET LASTS

Every criticism of traditional budgeting is undoubtedly correct. It is incremental rather than comprehensive; it does fragment decisions, usually making them piecemeal; it is heavily historical looking backward more than forward; it is indifferent about objectives. Why, then, has traditional budgeting lasted so long? Because it has the virtue of its defects.

Traditional budgeting makes calculations easy precisely because it is not comprehensive. History provides a strong base on which to rest a case. The present is appropriated to the past which may be known, instead of the future, which cannot be comprehended. Choices that might cause conflict are fragmented so that not all difficulties need be faced at one time. Budgeters may have objectives, but the budget itself is organized around activities or functions. One can change objectives, then, without challenging organizational survival. Traditional budgeting does not demand analysis of policy but neither does it inhibit it. Because it is neutral in regard to policy, traditional budgeting is compatible with a variety of policies, all of which can be converted into line-items. Budgeting for one year at a time has no special virtue (two years, for instance might be as good or better) except in comparison to more extreme alternatives. Budgeting several times a year aids economic adjustment but also creates chaos in departments, disorders calculations, and worsens conflict. Multi-year budgeting enhances planning at the expense of adjustment, accountability, and possible price volatility. Budgeting by volume and entitlement also aid planning and efficiency in government at the cost of control and effectiveness. Budgeting becomes spending. Traditional budgeting lasts, then, because it is simpler, easier, more controllable, more flexible than modern alternatives like PPB, ZBB, and indexed entitlements.

A final criterion has not been mentioned because it is inherent in the multiplicity of others, namely, adaptability. To be useful a budgetary process should perform tolerably well under all conditions. It must perform under the unexpected—deficits and surpluses, inflation and deflation, economic growth and economic stagnation. Because budgets are contracts within governments signifying agreed understandings, and signals outside of government informing others of what government is likely to do so they can adapt to it, budgets must be good (though not necessarily great) for all seasons. It is not so much that traditional budgeting succeeds brilliantly on every criterion, but that it does not entirely fail on any one that is responsible for its longevity.

Needless to say, traditional budgeting also has the defects of its virtues. No instrument of policy is equally good for every purpose. Though budgets look back, they may not look back far enough to understand how (or why) they got where they are. Comparing this year with last year may not mean much if the past was a mistake and the future is likely to be a bigger one. Quick calculation may be worse than none if it is grossly in error. There is an incremental road to disaster as well as faster roads to perdition; simplicity may become simple-mindedness. Policy neutrality may degenerate into disinterest in programs. So why has it lasted? So far, no one has come up with another budgetary procedure that has the virtues of traditional budgeting but lacks its defects.

At once one is disposed to ask why it is necessary to settle for second or third best: Why not combine the best features of the various processes, specially selected to work under prevailing conditions? Why not multi-year volume entitlements for this and annual cash zero-base budgeting for that? The question answers itself; there can only be one budgetary process at a time: therefore, the luxury of picking different ones for different purposes is unobtainable. Again, the necessity of choosing the least worst, or the most widely applicable over the largest number of cases is made evident.

Yet almost a diametrically opposite conclusion also is obvious to students of budgeting. Observation reveals that a number of different processes do, in fact, coexist right now. Some programs are single year but others are multi-year, some have cash limits while others are open-ended or even indexed, some are investigated in increments but others (where repetitive operations are involved) receive, in effect, a zero-base review. Beneath the facade of unity, there is, in fact, diversity.

How, then, are we to choose among truths

that are self-evident (there can be only one form of budgeting at a time and there are many)? Both cannot be correct when applied to the same sphere but I think they are when applied to different spheres. The critical difference is between the financial form in which the budget is voted on in the legislature, and the different ways of thinking about budgeting. It is possible to analyze expenditures in terms of programs, over long periods of time, and in many other ways without requiring that the form of analysis be the same as the form of appropriation. Indeed, as we have seen, there are persuasive reasons for insisting that form and function be different. All this can be summarized: The more neutral the form of presenting appropriations, the easier to translate other changes—in program, direction, organizational structure—into the desired amount without making the categories into additional forms of rigidity, which will become barriers to future changes.

Nonetheless, traditional budgeting must be lacking in some respects or it would not be replaced so often by entitlements or multi-year accounts. Put another way, treasury budgeting must reflect strong social forces. These are not mechanisms to control spending but to increase it. "The Budget" may be annual, but tax expenditures and budget entitlements go on until changed. With a will to spend there is a way.

I write about auditing largely in terms of budgeting and budgeting largely in terms of public policy. The rise of big government has necessarily altered our administrative doctrines of first and last things. When government was small so was public spending. Affairs of state were treated as extensions of personal integrity, or the lack thereof. The question was whether spending was honest. If public spending posed a threat to society it was that private individuals would use government funds to accumulate fortunes as sources of power. State audit was about private avarice. As government grew larger, its manipulation meant more. Was it doing what it said it would do with public money? State audit became state compliance. However, when government became gigantic, the sheer size of the state became overwhelming. The issue was no longer control of the state—getting government to do what it was told—but the ability of the state to control society. Public policy, i.e., public measures to control private behavior, lept to the fore; and that is how auditing shifted from private corruption to governmental compliance to public policy.

Social forces ultimately get their way, but while there is a struggle for supremacy, the form of budgeting can make a modest difference. It is difficult to say, for instance, whether the concept of a balanced budget declined due to social pressure or whether the concept of a unified budget, including almost all transactions in and out of the economy, such as trust funds, makes it even less likely. In days of old when cash was cash, and perpetual deficits were not yet invested, a deficit meant more cash out than came in. Today, with a much larger total, estimating plays a much more important part, and it's anyone's guess within $50 billion as to the actual state of affairs. The lesson is that for purposes of accountability, and control, the simpler the budget the better.

Taking a large view as I know how, the suitability of a budgetary process under varied conditions depends on how well diverse concerns can be translated into its forms. For sheer transparency, traditional budgeting is hard to beat.

NOTES

1. But, for a beginning, see Allen Shick, "The Road to PPB: The Stages of Budget Reform," *Public Administration Review* (Dec. 1966), pp. 243–258.

2. Hugh Heclo, Aaron Wildavsky, *The Private Gov-*

ernment of Public Money: Community and Policy Inside British Political Administration, London, Macmillan; Berkeley and Los Angeles, University of California Press, (2nd edition forthcoming).

3. *Ibid.*

4. Robert A. Hartman, "Multiyear Budget Planning," in Joseph A. Pechman, ed. *Setting National Priorities: The 1979 Budget.* (The Brookings Institution, Washington, D.C. 1978) p. 312.

5. Naomi Caiden, Aaron Wildavsky, *Planning and Budgeting in Poor Countries*, New York, John Wiley and Sons, 1974.

6. This and the next eight paragraphs are taken from my "Policy Analysis Is What Information Systems Are Not," *New York Affairs*, Vol. 4, No. 2, Spring 1977.

7. See Jeanne Nienaber, A. Wildavsky, *The Budgeting and Evaluation of Federal Recreation Programs, or Money Doesn't Grow on Trees*, New York, Basic Books, 1973.

8. J. Diamond, "The New Orthodoxy in Budgetary Planning: A Critical Review of Dutch Experience," In *Public Finance*, Vol. XXXII, No. 1 (1977), pp. 56–76.

FROM PPBS TO PROGRAM STRATEGIES

Paul R. Woodie

Building upon the principles and techniques of a Planning-Programming-Budgeting System (PPBS) the City of Dayton has developed a unique approach to resource allocation which views budgeting as an integrated decision-making process. The development of the process was prompted on the one hand by the desire to make complex local government services comprehensible to our policymakers and on the other by the need to treat grant-supported programs as local government services.

In 1913, the first budget of the City of Dayton was published by the Bureau of Municipal Research announcing, "It is believed to be to the public advantage to have the annual appropriation ordinance in permanent form and available for distribution to all interested." In this 52-page document, the first 12 pages delineated such expense items as candles, graphite, and livestock. Dayton, like many other cities of the time, was small and its programs understandable. However, as the City grew, programs and services became more complex, making comprehension difficult and local government remote from the people. While adequate for a number of years, therefore, the budget which concentrated on what was purchased by the City rather than what services were provided to the community simply was not sufficient.

National solutions through categorical grants compounded the problem since conventional budgeting processes could not accommodate a myriad of differing application re-

Source. Copyright © by Municipal Finance Officers Association of the U.S. and Canada. Reproduced with permission from *Governmental Finance* (August, 1976), pp. 50–57.

quirements, guidelines, and grant periods. In Dayton, which became heavily involved with categorical grants during the late 1960s and early 1970s, financial planning and management by necessity was decentralized for grant supported projects. Our health projects, manpower projects, model cities projects, etc., all had their own project operators with a fiscal management capacity. Once a project was implemented, these operators were able to unilaterally report to sponsoring agencies at the Federal level and in effect became "governments within a government."

As a response to these problems, Dayton developed a budgeting process which, among other things, articulates municipal services in the language the community and the policymakers understand, while treating grant revenue as another resource at our disposal to support locally established priorities. Improvements in the fundamental system emerged gradually until 1968 when the City began an intensive effort to develop an operative PPBS system. The system as developed consists of five crucial components: (1) a program structure; (2) condition statements; (3) program policies; (4) multi-year financial forecast; and (5) management systems.

The program structure is a traditional element of PPBS. It provides the cornerstone of Dayton's budget, which we refer to as Program Strategies. The structure itself categorizes services and is merely a three-tiered hierarchy with each level serving a specific function in the design and execution of a program strategy. These three tiers and their respective functions are:

Levels	Function
Service Area	Mission Statement
Category	Condition Statement
	Policy Development
Program	Financial Forecast and
	Management Systems

The Service Area is the level at which the mission of the City is described. As a local government, we are charged with broad responsibilities which are prescribed in our City charter. Each of the 18 subcomponent categories in turn represent a major issue or concern of the City. This is the policy level around which community goals are expressed, long-range plans developed, and community priorities established for the allocation of resources. Finally, the program level is the plain at which resources are both forecasted and allocated and measurable objectives established for program evaluation.

In order to rationally set priorities it is essential that the community and the policymakers not only determine "what is" but also have the information needed to make a judgment concerning the critical nature of "what ought to be." Consequently, in our Program Strategies each category is preceded by a condition statement or a profile of the situations which exist in the community. The profiles themselves are composed using census information, R. L. Polk data, public opinion surveys, and a variety of other data sources. Excerpts from the crime category of our 1976 Program Strategies (partially displayed in the exhibits shown at the end of this article) illustrate our approach to assessing the conditions of the community. The exhibits represent only a partial illustration of the "Crime" report. As conditions in the community change, so do the condition statements change from one year to the next, adding or deleting items of relevance or monitoring critical variables to discern trends over time. More significant, however, is the philosophy which enables the profiles to serve a dual purpose both as background for the policymakers in setting priorities as well as a means of measuring the perceived and actual effectiveness of City services.

Following the condition statements, the

Program Strategies present the service programs recommended by the administration to the policymakers. Recommendations range from continuing or reducing selective service levels to proposals for new and expanded services. Each of the programs in turn is accompanied by program objectives and performance criteria by which those objectives will be measured (see exhibits).

With the condition statements preceding a discussion of the service programs, policy issues arise and consequently provide a mechanism for insuring that established policies are reviewed and evaluated and new ones formulated in response to changes in the community. The advantages to this approach are reflected in the fact that during the past several years, Dayton has developed a "strategic prospective" resulting in the design and implementation of a comprehensive Community Development strategy as well as a strategy for the delivery of human services. With rising costs and fixed or declining resources, we believe such strategies must emerge if cities are to survive as viable forms of local government in the future.

The fourth and perhaps the most traditional component of PPB takes its place in the system as techniques are developed to prepare a multi-year financial forecast. While the City of Dayton uses a number of techniques to develop a financial forecast, such as regression analysis and correlation matrices, the actual techniques employed are secondary to the results which permit us to consider current decisions in the context of long-range consequences.

Moreover, as a financial forecast is coupled with various service programs under a common structure, we are able to view the purpose for which an activity is performed and how it relates to other similar activities rather than focusing on a maze of isolated funds and separate organizational units. As a result, the continuation of current services in addition to proposals for new and expanded service levels can be deliberated with an understanding of the long-term resources available for program support.

This not only permits fiscally rational decision-making but also enables program trade-offs as priorities change or forecasts are modified. It is extremely important to notice that in the resource allocation exhibit, Dayton's crime programs have federal grant revenues as companions to general operating funds under the resource allocation. The most significant implication is that with integration it is no longer necessary to accept the contradictions imputed to local programs by the strings attached to cetegorical grants. On the contrary, grant revenues simply become another resource at the disposal of policymakers to support locally established priorities.

The final component needed to make Dayton's process truly systematic requires the development of management systems to ensure policy decisions are implemented. The City of Dayton has accomplished this through a management by objectives procedure which requires requesting departments and agencies to establish measurable objectives for each service program.

The Office of Management and Budget provides staff assistance in order to refine the objectives and performance criteria. The responsibility for monitoring performance also resides in the Office of Management and Budget which, through the use of an internal project-management procedure and a semi-annual performance review, enables the City administration to review and measure its success or failure in meeting expressed program objectives. Conceptually, Dayton's approach to management by objectives is similar to many others; however, three unique elements are worth mentioning.

First, the City Manager meets with his top

executive staff to negotiate mutually acceptable objectives for the ensuing period. Staff assistance is used only to the extent of ensuring all objectives are verifiable (not necessarily quantifiable) so subsequently a determination can be made as to whether or not a particular objective is achieved.

Second, once the policymakers make the final decision on service programs, the City Manager again meets with his top executive staff and negotiates a written performance contract binding the department or agency head to accomplish stated program objectives.

And finally, progress on the achievement of objectives is monitored and the results published quarterly.

These three elements in the process occur regardless of the funding source used to achieve a particular objective and are designed to ensure responsibility and authority for performance as properly delegated within the organization.

Although we have indeed advanced from the 1913 and conventional line-item budgeting through a brief interlude with PPBS and finally to Program Strategies, the mission has not yet been completed. Under recent federal legislation, particularly the Comprehensive Employment and Training Act and Community Development Block Grant programs, local governments have been given the opportunity to tailor strategies to deal with unique community problems.

To guarantee this opportunity, therefore, it is incumbent upon financial and program managers to employ methods which ensure policymakers the maximum flexibility in devising strategic approach. An axiom to the tenet of local self-government must be a belief in the ability of local policymakers to fashion the future. To fashion the future, policymakers must agree on what ought to be, must have knowledge of what is, and must bridge the path between them.

Excerpts From the City of Dayton, Ohio Program Strategies Report

CRIME

To Protect the Life and Property of All Citizens From Criminal Behavior By Preventing the Occurrence and Minimizing the Effects of Crime.

111   Crime Prevention & Control
112   Criminal Adjudication
113   Detention and Rehabilitation

Neighborhood Safety Remains Stable

The Dayton citizens feel as safe from crime in 1975 as they did in 1974 in spite of an increased crime rate (see chart below). On a neighborhood level, several significant shifts occurred in the residents' perception of security. In Southeast-South and Southwest, feelings of security increased 7% and 9% respectively. In Northwest the security level decreased 9% as citizens in that neighborhood continue to be concerned about the burglary rate. Greater police presence with the addition of officers and the

Percentage of Residents Feeling Safe in Their Neighborhoods:

resulting decrease in response time account for the stability.

Police Response Time Decreases

A primary factor in citizens' feelings of security is the amount of time it takes the police to respond to a request for service. The average time it takes police to respond to citizen calls for assistance has been reduced significantly between 1973 and 1975. As indicated on the chart, the decrease in response time has ranged from a 9-minute reduction (27%) in

EMERGENCY RESPONSE TIME

1973	1974	1975
9 min.	9 min.	8 min.

Police response time 1973, 1975 by priority board (all responses)

Average response time to all calls (in minutes)

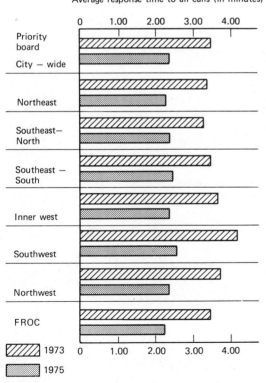

Southeast-North to a 16-minute reduction (37%) in Southwest. Response to emergency calls (such as serious crimes in progress and violent crimes) is much faster (8 min.). The average city-wide response time to all calls is 24 minutes. The primary reasons for the substantial reduction are: (1) an increase in the number of available crews and supervisors; and (2) improved dispatch and management procedures.

Comparative Crime Data: 1974—1975

The F.B.I. regularly collects and analyzes crime data from cities across the country. This information is used to determine national and local crime trends and enable the City to compare the local crime situation with that in other cities. The data presented here shows the percentage difference between the number of crimes committed for the first six months of 1974, and for the number committed in the same period in 1975. This data indicates that the percentage increase in crime in cities was less than in suburban and rural areas across the country.

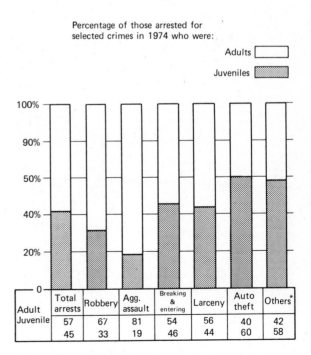

Percentage of those arrested for selected crimes in 1974 who were:

	Total arrests	Robbery	Agg. assault	Breaking & entering	Larceny	Auto theft	Others*
Adult	57	67	81	54	56	40	42
Juvenile	45	33	19	46	44	60	58

*Vandalism, malicious destruction of property

Among large Ohio cities, Dayton showed the second highest overall increase in the state behind Columbus (See Table 1).

Juvenile Crime

A large percentage of those arrested for crimes in Dayton are under 18 years of age. An especially high percentage of those arrested for breaking and entering, larceny, auto theft, vandalism, and malicious destruction of property are juveniles. In 1974, 5144 juveniles were referred to the Montgomery County Juvenile Court on delinquency complaints, an increase of 13% over 1973. Citizens' perceptions of juvenile crime are reflected on the map below, indicating that 43% of Dayton's citizens consider juvenile delinquency a neighborhood problem.

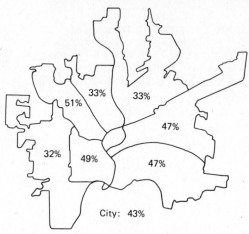

Percentage of residents identifying juvenile delinquency as a neighborhood problem: 1975

City: 43%

TABLE 1
Percentage Change in Crime (1974–1975)

| Area | NATIONAL TRENDS | | | | |
	Total Index Crimes	Violent Crimes	Property Crimes	Agg. Assault	Burglary
U.S.	+13%	+12%	+13%	+ 9%	+14%
Cities over 25,000	+12%	+11%	+12%	+ 8%	+12%
Suburban Areas	+14%	+16%	+14%	+11%	+17%
Rural Areas	+15%	+11%	+15%	+ 9%	+18%

| City | OHIO CITIES | | | |
	Total Index Crimes	Robbery	Agg. Assault	Burglary
Akron	+ 7%	− 5%	+33%	+ 1%
Canton	− 9%	+20%	−26%	−16%
Cincinnati	+ 9%	+ 9%	+30%	+ 1%
Cleveland	+17%	+30%	− 3%	+13%
Columbus	+34%	+38%	+21%	+43%
DAYTON	+27%	+52%	+15%	+18%
Toledo	+19%	− 6%	−13%	+22%
Youngstown	+ 5%	−10%	−16%	+ 5%

CRIME 110

PROGRAM

PPBS CODE 111	Crime Prevention and Control	1974 Actual	1975 Budget	1976 RESOURCE ALLOCATION				1977 Budget	1978 Budget
No.				General Operating Fund	Police Pension	Federal (C.E.T.A.) (L.E.A.A.)	Total		
1	Neighborhood patrol and criminal investigation	5,636,360	7,591,900	7,624,900	312,600	123,750	8,061,250	8,706,910	9,403,460
2	Residential street lighting	510,000	512,000	617,000	0	0	617,000	666,360	719,670
3	Gun control	0	72,250	16,440	0	0	16,440	17,760	19,180
4	Drug Abuse/Project Cure	22,160	90,100	0	0	76,500	76,500	70,200	75,820
5	Conflict management	76,670	49,500	0	0	40,230	40,230	0	0
6	Investigation of organized crime	64,460	37,920	0	0	51,430	51,430	0	0
7	Operation MACSI	25,000	50,000	0	0	61,270	61,270	0	0
8	Neighborhood assistance officers	166,580	100,000	18,880	0	55,560	74,440	80,400	86,840
9	Target hardening	16,970	0	0	0	0	0	0	0
10	Small business security	10,640	0	0	0	0	0	0	0
11	Personal crisis intervention	101,370	0	0	0	0	0	0	0
	Program Total	6,630,210	8,503,670	8,277,220	312,600	408,740	8,998,560	9,541,630	10,304,970

CRIME 110 (Continued)

PROGRAM

PPBS CODE 112	Criminal Adjudication	1974 Actual	1975 Budget	1976 RESOURCE ALLOCATION				1977 Budget	1978 Budget
				General Operating Fund	General Capital	Federal (L.E.A.A.)	Total		
No.									
1	Judicial review of criminal cases	238,070	271,050	339,810	0	0	339,810	366,990	396,350
2	Prosecution of criminal cases	67,130	79,680	87,660	0	0	87,660	94,680	102,260
	Program Total	305,200	350,730	427,470			427,470	461,670	498,610

PROGRAM

PPBS CODE 113	Detention and Rehabilitation	1974 Actual	1975 Budget	1976 RESOURCE ALLOCATION				1977 Budget	1978 Budget
				General Operating Fund	General Capital	Federal (L.E.A.A.)	Total		
No.									
1	Probation services	73,550	80,410	126,470	0	0	126,470	136,590	147,520
2	Operation of city jail	256,250	280,730	290,870	0	0	290,870	314,140	339,270
3	Operation of human rehabilitation center	776,280	1,107,600	1,188,170	0	0	1,188,170	1,286,210	1,389,110
4	Educational & vocational rehabilitation	103,530	123,960	0	0	73,570	73,570	0	0
5	Diagnostic services	26,970	54,190	0	0	18,520	18,520	0	0
6	Services for women	0	0	0	0	42,090	42,090	0	0
7	Capital improvements: therapeutic segregation quarters	0	0	0	36,330	109,600	145,930	0	0
	Ventilation—4th floor jail	0	0	0	14,000	0	14,000	0	0
8	Various capital improvements: human rehabilitation center	8,000	0	0	0	0	0	0	0
	Program Total	1,244,580	1,646,890	1,605,510	50,330	243,780	1,899,620	1,736,940	1,875,900
		1974	1975	1976				1977	1978
	CATEGORY TOTALS	8,179,990	10,501,290	10,310,200	362,930	652,520	11,325,650	11,740,240	12,679,480

PPBS CODE
111

PROGRAM
Crime Prevention and Control
PROGRAM DESCRIPTION
To prevent and control crime by eliminating the opportunity for criminal behavior and by the immediate intervention in potential criminal activity.

Key	Activity	Man-Year	Responsible Agency	1976 Budget
111-1	Neighborhood Patrol and Criminal Investigation	388	Police Department	$8,061,250

Objectives	Performance Criteria	Units			
		74 ACT.	75 EST.	75 Y.T.D.	76 EST.
1. To increase by 3% the level of perceived security among city residents, as measured by a public opinion survey.	1. Percent of public opinion survey respondents who classify neighborhood as "safe anytime", or "safe, if careful"	68%	71%	68%	71%
2. To limit the rate (crimes per 1,000 population) of increase in:	2. Crimes per/1000 population:				
a. Residential burglary to 7%	a. Residential burglary	26.8	32.0	27.1	34.3
b. Non-residential burglary to 3%	b. Non-residential burglary	10.4	11.6	10.9	11.9
c. Commercial robbery to 14%	c. Commercial robbery	2.9	4.5	3.8	5.3
d. Theft from auto to 14%	d. Theft from auto	24.5	35.8	29.9	40.8
e. Auto theft to 3%.	e. Auto theft	10.5	11.6	8.3	12.0
3. To reduce response time by one minute below the 1975 average.	3. Average response time for all dispatches (minutes)	31	23	23	22
4. To maintain "no crew available" responses for crime related dispatches to less than 1%.	4. Percent "no crew available" responses for crime related dispatches	3.5%	0%	1%	0%
5. To increase the clearance rate of felony offenses from 33 to 35%.	5. Clearance rate for felony offenses	28%	33%	32.9%	35%

CRIME 110 (Continued)

PPBS CODE	PROGRAM
111	Crime Prevention and Control

PROGRAM DESCRIPTION
To prevent and control crime by eliminating the opportunity for criminal behavior and by the immediate intervention in potential criminal activity.

Key	Activity	Man-Year	Responsible Agency	1976 Budget
111-1 (Continued)	Neighborhood Patrol and Criminal Investigation	388	Police Department	$8,061,250

		Units			
Objectives	*Performance Criteria*	74 ACT.	75 EST.	75 Y.T.D.	76 EST.
6. To perform an evaluation of all sworn positions within the Police Department and make recommendations for civilian replacement by 12/31/76.	6. Date evaluation report completed		12/75	In progress	12/76
7. To increase the Downtown Traffic and Security Squad from 7 to 14 officers.	7. Date completed				3/76

Key	Activity	Man-Year	Responsible Agency	1976 Budget
111-2	Residential Street Lighting	0	Urban Development	$617,000

		Units			
Objectives	*Performance Criteria*	74 ACT.	75 EST.	75 Y.T.D.	76 EST.
1. To install 300 residential street lights at a cost of approximately $17,000.	1. a. Number of lights installed	336	300	152	300
	b. Cost				$17,000

Key 111-3	Activity Gun Control	Man-Year 1	Responsible Agency Finance Department	1976 Budget $16,440

Objectives

1. To keep complaints to a minimum in the administration of the handgun owner I.D. program, to maintain program visibility through media coverage, and to issue approximately 5,000 additional cards in 1976.

2. To establish by February, 1976 a record keeping system that will provide prompt and accurate information on I.D. cards and permits issued.

Performance Criteria

		Units		
	74 ACT.	75 EST.	75 Y.T.D.	76 EST.
1 a. Number of I.D. cards issued		5000	3154	5000
b. Number of advertisements			7	7
c. Number of complaints filed (appeals)			56	40
2. Date record system established				2/76

Key 111-4	Activity Drug Abuse/Project CURE	Man-Year 0	Responsible Agency Human Resources	1976 Budget

Objectives

1. To provide detoxification services for 950 persons.

2. To maintain a monthly average of 230 clients receiving services.

3. To maintain an average of 30 clients per day in residential treatment.

4. To reduce the number of re-entries by 50% in 1976 below the total re-entries for 1975.

5. To insure that 35% of all persons discharged will be drug free for the period ending 2/29/76.

Performance Criteria

		Units		
	74 ACT.	75 EST.	75 Y.T.D.	76 EST.
1. Number of persons provided with detoxification services		475	164	950
2. Average number of clients per month		230	261	230
3. Average number of residential treatment clients per day		30	2	30
4 a. Percentage reduction of re-entries		50%	2%	50%
b. Number of re-entries				
5 a. Percent of drug free persons discharged		35%	25%	35%
b. Number of people discharged drug free			10	

CRIME 110 *(Continued)*

PPBS CODE	PROGRAM
111	Crime Prevention and Control

PROGRAM DESCRIPTION
To prevent and control crime by eliminating the opportunity for criminal behavior and by the immediate intervention in potential criminal activity.

Activity	*Responsible Agency*	*Man-Year*
Drug Abuse/Project CURE	Human Resources	0

Key 111-4 (Continued)

Objectives	Performance Criteria	74 ACT.	75 EST.	75 Y.T.D.	76 EST. 1976 Budget
			Units		
6. To provide urinalysis on a monthly basis for at least 230 clients.	6. Average number urinalysis provided monthly		230	231	230
7. To provide vocational and job development training that will result in 11% of the clients being given successful job placements.	7 a. Percent of clients given successful job placements		11%	0%	11%
	b. Number of clients placed in jobs				
8. To provide a minimum of 1,000 referral services.	8. Number of referrals provided		110	55	1,000
9. To insure that 75% of all clients are drug abuse clients	9 a. Percent of drug abuse clients		75%	94%	75%
	b. Number of clients			164	
	c. Number drug abuse clients			154	
	d. Number alcohol abuse clients			10	
10. To have 50% of the total clients be new clients for treatment	10 a. Percentage of new clients		50%	2%	50%
	b. Total number of clients			164	
	c. Number of new clients			3	

Key 111-5	Activity Conflict Management	Man-Year 11	Responsible Agency Police Department	1976 Budget $40,230			
Objectives	Performance Criteria		Units				
			74 ACT.	75 EST.	75 Y.T.D.	76 EST.	
1. To introduce a police/liaison program at Kiser High School beginning 1/76.	1. Number of police responses to Kiser High School			19	10	9	
2. To develop a family crisis intervention program to reduce police callback responses beginning 1/76.	2 a. Number of disturbances and family related responses		524	550	275	575	
	b. Number of repeat family disturbance responses over 3 per quarter			125	60	200	
	c. Number of families contacted under program		0	125	60	200	
3. To develop an informational and mediation service involving landlord/tenant disputes beginning 1/76.	3 a. Number of disputes mediated without further police involvement					25	
	b. Number of disputes diverted from police to adjudication					8	
4. To continue the police referral program increasing agency contact by 10% beginning 1/76.	4. Number of referrals			266	130	300	
5. To present 200 safety lectures for the Police Department.	5 a. Number of school traffic safety lectures presented		110	153	75	150	
	b. Number of home and personal safety lectures presented		N/A	50	25	50	

Key 113-7	Activity Capital Improvement/ Rehabilitation	Man-Year 0	Responsible Agency Human Resources	1976 Budget $159,930			
Objectives	Performance Criteria		Units				
			74 ACT.	75 EST.	75 Y.T.D.	76 EST.	
Therapeutic Segregation Quarters	$145,930						
Ventilation—4th Floor Jail	$ 14,000						

ZERO-BASE BUDGETING IN THE FEDERAL GOVERNMENT: AN HISTORICAL PERSPECTIVE

Lawrence A. Gordon and Donna M. Heivilin

Through a long chain of events, budgeting has evolved from a series of unrelated agency requests (made directly to the congressional appropriations committees) to an annual event composed of a series of interrelated legislative and executive actions.

A *budget*, in its broad sense, is a plan of action. More specifically, a budget is usually thought of as a financial plan stating the estimated revenues and expenditures required to accomplish specified tasks or programs.

HISTORICAL DEVELOPMENTS OF BUDGETING

Historically, budgeting in the Federal Government has gone through many changes. Prior to the Budget and Accounting Act of 1921, Congress dominated the spending and raising of Federal funds. Heads of executive departments and agencies presented their annual budget requests, emphasizing the object of expenditures, directly to specialized appropriation committees of Congress. These committees would allocate funds independently of one another, while the Senate Finance and House Ways and Means Committees were responsible for raising revenues. Thus, neither house had before it a comprehensive fiscal year budget. Furthermore, if an agency's request for funds were denied by one appropriations committee, the request could be submitted to another committee.

By the early 1900s it became evident that fiscal deficits, rather than surpluses, were be-

coming common. In response to this condition, Congress passed the Sundry Civil Expenses Appropriation Act in 1909 requiring the Secretary of the Treasury to inform Congress of anticipated fiscal deficits and recommended actions. President Taft, however, did not make use of this act. Instead, he requested, and was granted in 1910, funds to establish the Commission on Economy and Efficiency.

The Need for a National Budget Surfaced

Two years after the commission was established it recommended to President Taft that the executive branch prepare an annual comprehensive budget of anticipated revenues and expenditures. According to this proposal each department and agency would submit their budget request to the President, who would consolidate the individual requests into a total proposed budget, which would then be submitted to Congress. The recommendations of the Taft Commission represented a major potential shift in budgetary power in that the President would now play a leading role in the budgetary process.

It was not until 1920 that a budget and accounting bill was passed which included many of the recommendations of the Taft Commission. The bill did not, however, give the President the power to remove the head of what was to be the newly created accounting department, i.e., the Comptroller General, and thus President Woodrow Wilson vetoed it.

Eventually, under President Warren Harding, Congress passed the Budget and Account-

Source. Reprinted from *GAO Review* (Fall, 1978), pp. 57–64.

ing Act of 1921, which closely resembled the earlier bill. The major provisions of the 1921 act was concerned with (1) the establishment of a Bureau of the Budget, nominally within the Department of Treasury with a director to be appointed by the President, (2) the transmittal of a comprehensive budget by the President to Congress, and (3) the creation of the General Accounting Office, under the control and direction of the Comptroller General of the United States. The act, however, left departmental budgets and procedures for preparing them unchanged.

The Budget and Accounting Act of 1921 represented a major change in the budgetary process within the Federal Government. No longer would departments and agencies act as independent agents in search of congressional funding. Instead, through the centralizing effect of the new budget, the President would be able to exert budgetary power over subordinate departments and agencies. And although Congress maintained its ultimate authorizing and appropriating authority over the budget transmitted by the President, the executive branch began playing a more central role.

In 1939, as a result of the Reorganization Act, the Bureau of the Budget became an independent part of the newly created Executive Office of the President. This change was the direct outgrowth of the recommendations of the Brownlow Committee established in 1937 by President Franklin Roosevelt.

In 1949, a generation after the Taft Commission, the Hoover Commission recommended that the whole budgetary concept of the Federal Government be refashioned based on functions, activities, and projects—a performance budget. This was made a legislative requirement by the National Security Act Amendments of 1949 and the Budgeting and Accounting Procedures Act of 1950. The second Hoover Commission in 1955 recommended that the budget be classified in terms of programs or functions—a program budget. Thus, the move toward being able to compare program alternatives continued.

During President Richard Nixon's tenure in office, the Bureau of the Budget was renamed the Office of Management and Budget, which more accurately reflected the broad managerial scope of this office.

Planning, Programming, and Budgeting System

In 1961, under President John F. Kennedy, the Department of Defense installed the Planning, Programming, and Budgeting System (PPBS). Whereas traditional budgeting was input oriented, PPBS is a long-range output oriented approach to budgeting. The system places great emphasis on defining program objectives, with cost—benefit analysis an integral part of determining how a program is carried out. Therefore, PPBS requires the quantitative specification of the relationship between inputs and outputs. In sum, the introduction of PPBS was an extension of the scientific management, or rational economic way of thinking. Under President Lyndon Johnson, in 1965, PPBS was utilized across the entire executive branch of government.

Management by Objectives

Management by objectives (MBO) was yet another executive branch step toward viewing the budgeting process from a scientific management approach. MBO, which was introduced in 1973, emphasizes setting up decision points, or milestones, against which objectives are measured. Participative management, decentralization, and self-evaluation are concepts which are often associated with MBO. It must be noted, however, that MBO is more of a management philosophy, to be used in conjunction with a budget process, than a separate budgeting process.

The Institution of a Comprehensive Legislative Budget Process

In 1974 Congress passed Public Law 93–344, more commonly known as the Congressional Budget and Impoundment Control Act of 1974. It established, among other things, (1) a new congressional budget process, (2) Budget Committees in each House, (3) a Congressional Budget Office (CBO), and (4) a procedure providing congressional control over the impoundment of funds by the executive branch. These changes were indeed profound in terms of restoring the waning congressional control over the Federal budgetary process.

ZERO-BASE BUDGETING

The election of President Jimmy Carter in 1976 has set into motion the workings of yet one more budgetary reform concerned with controlling Federal expenditures. Upon election, President Carter promised to implement zero-base budgeting (ZBB) across the executive branch beginning with fiscal year 1979. According to Carter, ZBB can reduce Federal spending and more efficiently allocate resources utilized. Growth in government expenditures, combined with general public reluctance to accept further tax increases as evidenced by California's well publicized Proposition 13, has made such a stance popular.

ZBB COMPARED TO INCREMENTAL BUDGETING

Incremental budgeting assumes that current budget appropriations are the result of past appropriations adjusted for only small changes. Implicit in this budgeting process is the idea that existing programs are carried forward. Furthermore, incremental budgeting is usually assumed to be more political in nature than analytical. Thus, its critics usually claim that incremental budgeting leads to excessive total government spending and a misallocation of funds among programs.

Unlike incremental budgeting, ZBB does not assume that existing programs are automatically carried forward. Instead, all existing and proposed programs are considered on their future merits without regard to previous appropriations. Therefore, some old programs are expected to expire while new ones are expected to emerge. In sum, an analytical or rational economic approach, as opposed to a political process, is assumed to dominate the ZBB process.

ZBB APPLIED TO VARIOUS TYPES OF ORGANIZATIONS

The origin of ZBB has been traced back to at least 1924 and probably goes back much further. As early as 1962, the U.S. Department of Agriculture used a variant of ZBB to formulate their fiscal year 1964 budget estimates. However, the process was branded a failure and was not used again until the late 1960s, when Texas Instruments, Inc., developed and effectively utilized a modern version of ZBB. Their success with ZBB apparently prompted other corporations (including Xerox, Boeing, Eastern Airlines, Westinghouse Electric, and General Dynamics) and States (including Georgia, New Jersey, California, Texas, and Missouri) to adopt the concept.

The modern version of ZBB is usually considered as not being applicable to direct manufacturing costs since these expenditures are determined by market factors where cost–benefit analysis seems less appropriate. Instead, ZBB is seen as a budgeting process which is most appropriate for indirect, service oriented, costs. Of course, such costs are of prime importance in the Government sector and thus ZBB has apparently found a home in governmental budgeting.

THE BASICS OF ZBB

The modern version of zero-base budgeting consists of the following five basic steps: (1)

determining decision units, (2) developing decision packages for each decision unit, (3) ranking decision packages, (4) consolidating the rankings at higher organizational levels, and (5) allocating resources.

Decision units represent discrete organizational activities for which a separate budget, or budget line, is prepared. That is, since ZBB is output oriented, decision units represent any meaningful organizational element that requires individual attention, such as a program, project, or work plan. From a practical standpoint, decision units are often chosen based on cost centers, providing these centers are tied to the organization's objectives.

For each decision unit a set of decision packages is prepared. A decision package describes the activity under consideration as well as its objective(s). Alternative ways of performing the activity and alternative levels of effort (assuming various levels are feasible) for the course of action chosen would be noted in a decision package. Separate packages are prepared for incremental levels of spending for each activity. For example, a particular activity may have three associated packages often called "a set of packages," i.e., one of three, two of three, and three of three. The minimum level package might be 70 percent of last year's activity level and the second and third packages could be the activity level up to 90 percent and 110 percent, respectively. Decision packages also contain descriptions of the costs and benefits associated with performing the activity, as well as the consequences of not performing the activity.

The format, content, and usefulness of these decision packages seem to vary greatly among and within the organizations using ZBB. Yet, in some sense decision packages represent the "nuts and bolts" of ZBB. Therefore, if ZBB is to have any chance of inspiring more efficient resource allocations, it seems mandatory that decision packages be prepared with the utmost conscientiousness. The time and effort spent at

this stage of the process will most likely determine the success of ZBB.

Once the preparation of all the decision packages for an organizational unit is completed, they are ranked in descending order of importance. That is, the most important package would receive the highest ranking, the second most important package would receive the next highest, and so on. In ranking a set of packages relating to a given activity, the package relating to the minimum level of effort would have to be ranked higher than the other packages in that set. The same principle would hold for the incremental decision packages relating to an activity, i.e., the first increment would have to be ranked higher than the second increment, etc. However, the set of packages relating to one activity do not have to be ranked consecutively. Each package stands alone and must compete with the packages developed from other activities. Once this ranking process is completed, the packages are sent to the next organizational level manager, who continues the ZBB process.

As decision packages are sent up the organizational ladder, the manager of the next level is theoretically required to consolidate the rankings of the various subunits reporting to him/her. Ultimately, it is top management's task to establish the final priority rankings for the entire organization. In the case of the executive branch of the Federal Government, this means that the President and his staff have final responsibility for the way programs are ranked. In theory they should be able to compare programs across agencies. Thus, while many argue that ZBB encourages decentralization because decision packages are initiated at the lowest levels of the organization, an equal number argue that in the final analysis ZBB really encourages centralization.

The completion of the ZBB ranking process is followed by the allocation of the organization's resources. Theoretically, higher ranked projects would be funded before lower ranked projects up to the point that all resources are fully allocated. Operationally, this logical allocation procedure may break down, especially where the consolidation process is stopped at a middle level of the organization.

In sum, zero-base budgeting is an attempt at increasing the rational-comprehensive, or scientific management, approach to budgeting. It is means—end oriented, relying heavily on a clear statement of the objective(s) and value(s) of an activity. Quantitative economic analysis is given a prominent role in the process. In terms of the Federal Government, ZBB is a system by which the executive branch can gain tighter managerial control over the budgeting process, possibly at the expense of the legislative branch.

SOME ADVANTAGES AND DISADVANTAGES OF ZBB

Among those points commonly noted in favor of ZBB are: (1) it is a rational, optimizing approach to budgeting, (2) it forces objectives to be clearly stated, (3) it forces a clear statement on program priorities, (4) it encourages decentralization, (5) it opens up channels of communication between those involved, and (6) it allows existing programs to be terminated. The points often noted against ZBB include: (1) the results are no different than if incremental budgeting were used, (2) the paperwork generated is excessive, (3) the workload imposed upon managers is greatly increased, (4) the benefits from many programs cannot be quantified in the sense that is required for the ranking process, (5) the process really has a centralizing, rather than decentralizing organizational effect, and (6) it attempts to turn what is naturally a political process into a managerial process.

The above lists of advantages and disadvantages of ZBB can easily be extended. However, ZBB's real worth, or lack thereof, is an empirical question which requires experience to be answered. President Carter's introduction of ZBB will provide just such experience at the Federal budgeting level.

FEDERAL GOVERNMENT EXPERIENCE WITH ZBB

The Federal Government's implementation of ZBB began in October 1976. At that time the House Committee on Appropriations asked the National Aeronautics and Space Administration (NASA) and the Consumer Product Safety Commission (CPSC) to prepare appropriations justification materials for fiscal year 1978 along ZBB lines. The purpose of this request was for the House to have a pilot test on the applicability of ZBB to the Federal Government. This pilot test was restricted to three NASA centers: the Kennedy, Johnson, and Marshall Space Centers, and to CPSC.

Given the newness of the ZBB procedures as applied to the Federal Government, it seems unfair to judge the pilot test with NASA and CPSC. Yet, at least two points resulting from this test are worthy of mention. First, it became immediately apparent that the development of cost—benefit analyses or sophisticated performance measures was a problem that required solving if ZBB were to be successfully used in the Federal Government. In the case of the pilot test, neither NASA nor CPSC developed such measures. And, not surprisingly, given the relationship between the cost—benefit analyses and ranking procedure, neither NASA nor CPSC ranked the decision packages. Second, the budget execution, as opposed to its proposal, may be improved as a result of ZBB. That is, ZBB can help in implementing a budget due to its focus on priority choices and the increased communication among managers concerning those choices.

Upon taking office in January 1977, President Carter wasted little time in implementing ZBB throughout the Federal Government.

White House Bulletin No. 77−9, issued on February 14, 1977, requested the various departments and agencies to prepare the fiscal year 1979 budget under a ZBB system. As a result, the 1979 budget that Carter transmitted to the Congress in January 1978 was the first Federal budget prepared using ZBB principles and procedures. Given that this was the first wide-scale use of the technique, it is probably still premature to bring in a verdict on the process. However, a plethora of critics and supporters have already begun to surface.

ASSESSMENT OF ZBB IN THE FEDERAL GOVERNMENT

The White House, in their May 2, 1978, press release provided a balanced view on the experience of the first year with ZBB. Among the benefits attributed to ZBB were: (1) elimination of a few programs, (2) identification of program trade-offs, (3) greater involvement by top agency officials in the budget process, (4) improved communications among top, middle, and lower levels of management, and (5) greater clarity of program objectives. The problems noted included: (1) increased paperwork, (2) need to modify decision unit structures, (3) problems in defining program objectives, (4) difficulty in ranking programs, and (5) determining minimum levels of funding, which presented problems for most agencies.

The use of ZBB in fiscal year 1979 must be viewed as a trial run since it takes time to set in place any new system. Even the critics of ZBB generally concede this point. Thus, the real test will come with the fiscal year 1980 budget experience. In an effort to assure its success, OMB has addressed the first-year ZBB problems in its May 25, 1978, Circular No. A−11. Also, a pilot test to compare programs across agencies is being conducted by the Department of Energy and the Environmental Protection Agency. Only time, and empirical examination, will allow the rendering of the final judgment on the use of ZBB in the Federal Government.

ZERO-BASE BUDGETING: A USEFUL FRAUD?

Robert N. Anthony

By the standards of the Federal Trade Commission, the statements made about zero-base budgeting probably constitute false and misleading advertising. Zero-base budgeting is supposed to be a new way of preparing annual budgets, which contrasts with the current way, which is called incremental budgeting. Incremental budgeting, it is correctly said, takes a certain level of expenses as a starting point and focuses on the proposed increment above that level.

By contrast, if the word "zero" means anything, it signifies that the budgeting process starts at zero and that the agency preparing the budget request must justify every dollar that it requests.

There is only one recorded attempt to take such an approach to budgeting in a government organization of any size: this is in the State of

Source. Reproduced with permission from *The Government Accountants Journal* (Summer, 1977), pp. 7−10.

Georgia. In 1971, the governor hired a consultant to install such a system. He did so because of an article the consultant had written for *Harvard Business Review.* A casual reader of that article could easily get the impression that the author had successfully installed a zero-base budgeting system in a large industrial company. A more careful reader would learn that the author had installed a system in certain staff and research units of that company, comprising an unspecified fraction, but less than 25 percent, of the company's annual expenditures, and that the judgment that the system was a great success was entirely the author's and based on a single year's experience.

Anyway, the consultant started to work for the State of Georgia. He was a well-intentioned person, and he probably was sincere in his belief that it is possible to prepare and analyze a budget from scratch. This belief did not last long. Well before the end of the first budget cycle, it was agreed that expenditures equal to approximately 80 percent of the current level of spending would be given only a cursory examination and that attention would be focused on the increment.

Thus, even before one go around of the new system, the "zero" benchmark was replaced by 80 percent. Moreover, the amounts above this floor were in fact "increments," despite the claim that the process is the opposite of incremental budgeting.

In its judgment about false and misleading advertising, the Federal Trade Commission would, I believe, conclude that 80 percent is a long way from zero and that increments above 80 percent are just as much increments as increments above some other base. This would seem to make a prima facie case that the term *zero-base budgeting* is fraudulent.

The facts don't even support the glowing reports about what happened with respect to the amounts above the 80 percent. In 1974, 13 heads of Georgia departments were interviewed, and only two went so far as to say that zero-base budgeting "may" have led to a reallocation of resources. (The whole idea of budgeting is to allocate resources.) None of 32 budget analysts reported that the system involved a "large" shifting of financial resources, and only seven said it caused "some" shifting; 21 said there was no apparent shifting, and 4 were uncertain. (These data are taken from a study by Roger H. Hermanson and George S. Minnier, *Atlantic Economic Review,* Vol. 26, No. 4.) Zero-base budgeting had approximately zero impact.

If research on a commercial product resulted in data like the above, it is doubtful that the Federal Trade Commission would permit its manufacturer to advertise that it was "extremely valuable" or "great."

NOT WORKABLE

People experienced in budgeting know that zero-base budgeting, as it is described in a book and many articles and speeches, won't work. Basically, the idea is that the entire annual budget request is to be broken down into "decision packages," these packages are to be ranked in order of priority, and budget decisions are made for each package according to the justification contained therein and its relative priority ranking. There are several things wrong with this approach.

The first, and most important, is that a large number of decision packages is unmanageable. In Georgia, there were 11,000 of them. If the Governor set aside four hours every day for two months he could spend about a minute on each decision package, not enough time to read it, let alone make an analysis of the merits. If he delegated the job to others, the whole idea of comparing priorities is compromised. In the Defense Department, whose budget is 30 times as large as Georgia's, top management makes budget judgments on a few hundred items, certainly not as many as a thousand.

Even if the numbers of decision packages were reduced to a manageable size, it is not possible to make a thorough analysis during the time available in the annual budget process. In a good control system, basic decisions are made during the programming process, which precedes the budget process, and the annual budget process is essentially one of fine tuning the financial plan required to implement these decisions during the budget year; there is not time to do anything else. In zero-base budgeting, there is no mention of a programming process; the assumption evidently is that program decisions are made concurrently with budget decisions. This simply can't be done in an organization of any size; there isn't time.

Experience also shows that the idea of ranking decision packages according to priority doesn't work. Such rankings have been attempted from time to time in government agencies, as far back as 1960. They have been abandoned. If agency heads are honest, they will admit that program priority is influenced by the amount of funds likely to be available, rather than the other way around. If they are less than honest, they will deliberately structure the priorities so that essential or politically popular decision packages are given a low priority, knowing that these packages will probably be approved and that their approval will automatically constitute approval of packages listed as having a higher priority. Only quite naive people would not expect this to happen.

A PAPER MILL?

A tremendous amount of useless paperwork is involved in zero-base budgeting. The example that is most frequently used in describing the process is a decision package for an $80,000 increment to the budget of an air quality laboratory (3/100,000 of the Georgia budget). The form used to justify this, and all other, increments contains 15 items of information, including the answers to such questions as: What are the consequences of not approving the package? and What alternative ways are there of doing this work? Experienced budget analysts know that the answer to the first question, stated in various ways, invariably is that the consequences of not approving the package are too terrible to contemplate, and that the answer to the second question is that all alternatives cost more money, don't do the job as well, or both. It is a waste of time and paper to have such answers restated in 11,000 different ways. This is "information saturation" at its worst.

The budget process is not primarily a ranking process. It is primarily the fine tuning of an approved program. The worthwhileness of programs can't be determined by reading words on a two-page form. Judgments about new programs are based on discussions with the people involved, in which words on paper play some, but not a dominant, part. The budget analyst has a whole set of techniques for squeezing water out of budget requests for ongoing programs; reading "decision packages" is not one of them.

Compared with the antiquated budget process which Georgia had at the time, zero-base budgeting was probably an improvement—almost any change would have been an improvement. Compared with the procedures that already are used in the Federal Government, it has nothing of substance to offer. The new parts are not good, and the good parts are not new.

POSSIBLE USEFULNESS

Nevertheless, zero-base budgeting is rapidly becoming a highly prestigious term. Is there some way of capitalizing on this prestige so as to give impetus to improvements in the budget process that really do need to be made? I think there is. Few people really know what the term means. We can take advantage of this fact.

First, by a slight change in wording, the push behind the phrase might be transferred to a process called "zero-base review." This is an extremely valuable part of the control process. It is used by some agencies, but it is not widely used in a systematic way. It should be made systematic and extended throughout the government. In a zero-base review, outside experts go into an agency, or some part of it, and examine in great depth its reason for being, its methods of operation, and its costs. Reading words on a "decision package" form is no substitute for this. It is a time-consuming process, and it is a traumatic one for people in the agency whose current ways of doing things are being challenged, so it cannot conceivably be conducted annually. Instead, the timetable should insure that each agency is examined about once every five years. It is by far the best way of controlling ongoing programs, just as benefit—cost analysis is the best way of making decisions on proposed new programs.

There is no connection between zero-base review and zero-base budgeting except the frist two words, but so what? If the effort, and particularly the rhetoric, could be shifted slightly so that it resulted in widespread use of zero-base review techniques, great good would come about. (The term *sunset legislation* is another buzz word that gets at this problem, but this deals only with the legislative aspect. The thorough analysis of programs that need to be continued is a job for technical experts; Congressional staffs can't do it by themselves.)

Second, the "decision packages" which are talked about so glibly could be used to give renewed emphasis to program budgeting, as contrasted with the old-fashioned line-item budgeting which still persists in some agencies.

Decision packages actually are what are called program elements in a program budget system. Budgeting by programs was a central part of what was called the PPB system, installed by Robert S. McNamara and Charles Hitch in the Defense Department in the early 1960s. In 1965, an effort was made to extend this system to the whole government, but the extension was made without adequate preparatory work. Partly for this reason, and partly because it was developed in a Democrat administration, PPB fell into disrepute and was officially killed by the Republicans in 1969.

The basic idea of program budgeting remains sound, however. Indeed, in many agencies the basic idea continues to be used under other labels. The zero-base budgeting rhetoric could well be used to push for the complete installation of program budgeting throughout the government. As an example, an article extolling the virtues of zero-base budgeting in a New York school district actually describes a program budget, and even uses the same program structure that I gave in a report prepared in 1972. Let's not criticize such articles; let's applaud the good that can come from them.

Third, the emphasis on stating measurable results in the budget proposal, which is implied in the form used to describe the decision packages, is a good one, even though there is nothing new about it except the label. Under the term *management by objectives* this idea has been common in industry and in certain parts of the government for years. The zero-base budgeting movement could be used to strengthen it, and particularly to focus more serious attention on the development of better output measures.

One other feature is badly needed as part of the control process in government. This is the development of an accounting system that matches the budget system. Without such a system, there is no sound way of assuring that resources are used in the way that the approved budget intends. Zero-base budgeting is silent about this, and the only way that the term can be used to accomplish this is to pretend, contrary to fact, that it is part of what people mean by zero-base budgeting. We can assume that most zero-base budgeting advocates would be in favor of it once they knew about it because the need is obvious.

So, even though zero-base budgeting is a fraud, and even though the good parts of it are not new, experienced budget people should not let the phrase make them nauseated. They should disregard the rhetoric as the words of well-intentioned but naive people. They should latch onto the term as a way of accomplishing what really needs to be accomplished anyway. Maybe this goes against the grain of people who believe that the end never justifies the means, but improvement in financial controls in government is so badly needed that it may be desirable to make an exception in this instance.

HOW TO MAKE CASH FORECASTING WORK FOR YOU

Donald I. Gent

Health care writers generally approach a subject by observing that: (1) industry has developed management techniques which are applied infrequently in hospitals; (2) health care expenditures are increasing rapidly; (3) the public is becoming restive about the high cost of health services; (4) hospital administration has been slow in developing, and, finally, (5) progress is being made.

The comments and concerns may be valid. Many of these concerns are on the theoretical or ideal level. This level is necessary, but when problems exist, they must be dealt with on the realistic or practical level. One realistic or practical concern of every hospital financial manager is cash flow. The hospital financial manager recognizes the need for and benefit of

Source. Copyright © 1972 by the Hospital Financial Management Association. Reprinted with permission from *Hospital Financial Management* (July, 1972), pp. 27–28, 30, 32.

programs. At the same time, he watches the cash flow dwindle. He sees a future crisis in cash flow or lack of sufficient cash to operate his institution.

Cash management and forecasting is not a new concept. In fact, it is one of the oldest and simplest techniques available to management. Cash planning can be accomplished by almost anyone. One must recognize that, when prosperity exists, the need for cash planning seems to disappear. On the other hand, when a crisis is foreseen, the need for planning seems urgent. The dilemma is more complex when one thinks about the past decade in which there has been a highly stimulated economy. Even though declines have occurred, the economy is still highly stimulated for growth, yet a crisis in cash flow for the hospital seems to be on the horizon. It may be that when prosperity existed the hospital failed to utilize the oldest, simplest, and most useful technique—cash planning.

THE OBJECTIVE OF CASH PLANNING

The cash planning technique is simply an estimate of future cash receipts and disbursements. The technique is a supportive one: to provide for the adequate availability and safekeeping of funds under varied economic conditions in order to achieve desired objectives. Billing patients, collecting money, and paying bills have always been functions of cash planning. Note the term *safekeeping*. It means not only the ability to protect but also to draw a return in investment of funds.

FORECASTING OF CASH

Generally, cash planning is discussed within the framework of budgeting. We may have left the impression that cash planning is the result of an elaborate compehensive budget process. This is not necessarily true. Cash planning can be done without a budget, but it is more effective when the organization has a budget. It is possible to have elaborate budgets, well-negotiated reimbursement contracts, and a declining cash flow.

      Cash can usually be forecast with accuracy. Forecast of cash can be classified as short-term or long-term. This article will demonstrate both in a concise manner. Short-term forecasts are used to determine the cash requirements and the high and low points in the cash cycle, whether weekly, monthly, quarterly, or annually.

      In contrast to the short-term cash forecast, which goes into great detail, the long-term forecast attempts to show significant changes and the long-range financial growth of the hospital. Both types of forecast should indicate whether sufficient cash will be generated to support the operation and show when the hospital can expect to be low on funds or even run out of money.

      The strongest type of forecasting system is one which features both methods. A daily or monthly forecast of cash receipts and disbursements to maintain close control over the cash flow should be combined with a quarterly or annual forecast.

THE LENGTH OF THE FORECAST

The length of forecast will depend upon the nature of the hospital. The medical school or university hospital, the state hospital, the church-related hospital, the private hospital, and the community hospital each have unique cash needs. The operation that is subject to wide fluctuation is more likely to need a short-term cash forecast, while more stable operations may lean toward long-term forecasting. The purpose of the forecast may determine its length. The philosophy of operation may determine the type of forecast. For example, the hospital that operates on a break-even basis and depends upon donations for equipment and expansion may run a very close cash-flow situation, while the hospital that intentionally operates with a growth factor may have sufficient cash.

FORECASTING METHODS

The two methods demonstrated in this article may be called: (1) the cash receipts and disbursement method and (2) the adjusted provision for debt retirement method. The first may be classified as a short-term method, while the latter is a long-term method.

      Orville R. Keister in his article, "Cash Management in Hospitals," states there are basically four approaches in cash budgeting:

. . . the cash receipts and disbursement method; the balance sheet projection method; the adjusted net income method; and the working capital difference method.[1]

[1]*Hospital Financial Management* (Journal of the Hospital Financial Management Association) Vol. 23, No. 9, November 1969.

Realistically, there are only two methods—the short-term approach and the long-term approach. These may also be labeled the cash receipts and disbursements method and the adjusted provision for debt retirement method. The latter method has been given this name because we do not think in terms of net income but rather in terms of taking excesses to retire debt. The method labeled "adjusted net income method" by Keister is called adjusted provision for debt retirement in this article. The "balance sheet" method and the "working capital difference" method are part of the source and application of funds process and can really be expressed as the adjusted provision for debt retirement method. The adjusted provision for debt retirement method (source and application of funds) projects changes in the balance sheet, particularly in working capital items. This demonstrates the complexity of the theoretical or ideal approach because the concept can actually be expressed simply.

Each method has certain advantages and disadvantages. The cash receipts and disbursement method is more helpful in the day-to-day control of cash, while the adjusted provision for debt retirement method tends to produce a more accurate estimate of the cash position in forecasts for a quarter or longer.

THE CASH RECEIPTS AND DISBURSEMENT METHOD

Exhibit 1 reflects a typical forecast. This type of forecast is based on each source of cash as well

EXHIBIT 1

Cash Receipts and Disbursement Method
Memorial Hospital

	Last Year's Monthly Actual	This Year's Monthly Forecast	This Year's Monthly Actual	Increase or Decrease
Cash Receipts				
Collection on Receivables	$ 868,000	$960,000	$980,000	$ 112,000
Donations and Contributions	3,800	3,950	4,000	200
Interest Income	1,500	1,900	2,000	500
Sale of Assets	800	800	1,000	200
Other	200	210	250	50
Total Cash Receipts	$ 874,300	$966,860	$987,250	$ 112,950
Cash Disbursements				
Operating Expenses				
Payroll & Professional Fees	$ 550,000	$610,000	$609,000	$ 59,000
Other Related Salary Cost				
Retirement	1,600	11,800	11,750	10,150
Life Insurance	1,825	2,175	2,200	375
Health Insurance	7,600	8,150	8,200	600
Social Security	21,350	23,500	23,200	1,850
Workmen's Compensation	2,100	2,500	2,450	350
Total Salaries—Fees & Related Items	$ 584,475	$658,125	$656,800	$ 72,325

(Continued)

EXHIBIT 1 *(Continued)*

	Last Year's Monthly Actual	This Year's Monthly Forecast	This Year's Monthly Actual	Increase or Decrease
Cash Disbursements				
Contracted Laundry	11,300	11,950	12,000	700
Pharmaceuticals	21,800	23,600	23,500	1,700
Dues & Subscriptions	1,300	1,500	1,450	150
Electricity & Power	6,500	7,800	8,000	1,500
Film	8,000	8,600	8,500	500
Food	23,700	25,500	25,000	1,300
Fuel, Gas & Oil	1,000	1,275	1,250	250
Gases	1,000	1,150	1,100	100
Supplies	190,000	198,000	200,000	10,000
Total Other O/P Expenses	$ 264,600	$279,375	$280,800	$ 16,200
Other Needs				
Repayment of Loan	10,400	15,800	15,600	5,200
Acquisition of Equipment	30,700	10,800	10,500	(20,200)
Total Other Need	41,100	26,600	26,100	(15,000)
Total Need	$ 890,175	$964,100	$963,700	$ 73,525
Excess Cash Provided	(15,875)	2,760	23,550	39,425
Cash & Short-Term Securties at Beginning of Period	529,000	513,125	513,125	(15,875)
Increase (decrease) in Bank Loans	(15,875)	2,760	23,550	39,425
Cash & Short-Term Securities at End of Period	513,125	515,885	536,675	23,550

as each type of disbursement. It is only one variation of several kinds of forecasts which can be developed to meet the specific needs of a given institution. For example, the hospital may want to consider only major receipts and disbursements.

Exhibit 2 demonstrates another variation in the cash receipts and disbursement method. This variation performs the same function except that it is based on anticipated income rather than on collection. Anticipated disbursements and other needs are considered in the projection. Increases in accounts receivable and inventories may be planned into this type of forecast.

Either variation may be developed on a daily, weekly, or monthly basis. The reliability of this forecast will rest heavily on the accuracy of the data developed in the individual hospital.

This method had disadvantages and limitations. First, in daily projection, problems such as disruption of service caused by weather, strikes, etc., may cause temporary variance between actual and projected cash receipts and

EXHIBIT 2

**Income and Disbursements Forecast Memorial Hospital
Budget—October, 19_____ to September 30, 19_____**

Cash in Bank—General Fund—Oct. 1, 19__		$ 35,000
Plus: Anticipated Revenue		
Accounts Receivable	$4,478,300	
Other revenue	105,400	
Total Anticipated Revenue		4,583,700
		4,618,700
Less: Anticipated Cost		
Salaries and Wages	2,692,200	
Professional Fees	142,800	
Supplies & Other Expenses	990,000	
Total Anticipated Cost		3,825,000
		793,700
Less: Other Cost or Reduction in Revenue		
Interest Expense	80,000	
Discounts and Charity	62,200	
Bad Debts	61,400	
Contractual Loss	88,200	
Miscellaneous	2,500	
Total Other Cost		294,300
Possible Cash Flow Available for Other Needs		499,400
Less: Other Anticipated Needs		
Principal—Long Term	100,000	
Principal—Short Term	50,000	
Feasibility Study	35,000	
Budgeted Capital Equipment	140,600	
Remodeling of Building	100,000	
Parking Lot Resurfacing	15,000	
Total Other Anticipated Needs		440,600
		58,800
Less: Possible Increase in Accounts Receivable due		24,100
to Rate Increase		
Cash in Bank—General Fund—Sept. 30, 19__		$ 34,700

				EXHIBIT 3

Adjust Provision for Debt Retirement Method
Memorial Hospital

	Last Year's 1969–70 Actual	This Year's 1970–71 Forecast	This Year's 1970–71 Actual	Increase or Decrease
Sources of Cash				
Provision for Debt Retirement	$ 387,587	$353,500	$336,500	$ (51,087)
Depreciation	412,239	460,000	470,021	57,782
Gifts not Previously Pledged	93,244	75,000	51,180	(42,064)
Rental Income	18,000	22,000	22,500	4,500
Interest Income	1,000	20,000	24,000	23,000
Sale of Assets	9,600	9,000	8,806	(794)
Total Cash Provided	$ 921,670	$939,500	$913,007	$ (8,663)
Uses of Cash				
Increases in Accounts Receivable	$ 212,783	$100,000	$101,669	$ (111,114)
Increases in Inventories	8,615	10,000	15,504	6,889
Increases in Property, Plant & Equipment	368,026	130,000	125,906	(242,120)
Increase in Accounts Payable	(7,059)	20,000	46,049	53,108
Acquisition of Property	281,775	100,000	91,034	(190,741)
Reduction of Debt	125,000	190,000	187,327	62,327
Total Uses of Cash	$ 989,140	$550,000	$567,489	$ 421,651
EXCESS CASH PROVIDED	$ (67,470)	$389,500	$345,518	$ 412,988
Cash & Short-Term Securities at Beginning of Period	$ 529,000	$461,530	$461,530	$ (67,470)
Increase (decrease) in Bank Loans	$ (67,470)	$389,500	$345,518	$ 412,988
Cash & Short-Term Securities at End of Period	$ 461,530	$851,030	$807,048	$ 345,518

disbursements. Second, this method cannot show small but steady changes that may be taking place in the receivables or inventories.

THE LONG-TERM FORECAST

Exhibit 3 reflects the long-term cash forecast. This method projects changes in the balance sheet, particularly in working capital items, and is the result of a source and application of funds statement. The method reflects significant changes and growth or decline in the operation. The long-term method will assist management in determining what programs should be approved, deferred, or abandoned. It will show management financial capabilities and also will assist in the securing of funds. Lenders want to see a comprehensive cash forecast. The long-term perspective is preferred, even though it is less accurate and less detailed. Its intent is to indicate long-range cash needs and trends.

SUMMARY

The accompanying exhibits are for illustrative purpose and are oversimplified. They may be detailed by the administrator, assistant administrator, controller, business manager, accountant, secretary, or clerk.

Failure in cash planning is one of the more common causes of business failure, even though the process is a very simple one.

The biblical parable of the talents, describing the ultimate fate of the man who buried his talent in the ground, may be the first recorded failure of a short-term money manager. The primary objectives of short-term investments are two-fold in the area of cash management: safety of principal (the creditworthiness of the investment and its marketability) and yield (return). The poor soul in the parable achieved one effectively but failed to achieve the other, and in determining policy concerning the investment of excess cash both objectives must be accommodated.[2]

To be effective, both types of forecast must be utilized. In most hospitals it is essential to know current, as well as long-range, availability of cash. The hospital can plan its cash. Start now—cash planning may make the difference between success and failure.

[2]Hill, Roger W., Jr., *Cash Management Techniques,* American Management Association, Inc. 1970.

FINANCIAL MANAGEMENT FOR THE ARTS

Charles A. Nelson and Frederick J. Turk

It is unfortunate that arts councils, museums and galleries, dance companies, and theater groups cannot be sustained by enthusiasm and artistic flair alone. If they could, the prolific spawning of arts exhibits and performances in cities great and small—such as has happily characterized the American scene in the past two decades—would evoke unmixed celebration. But the experience of these recent years, in which the arts have freed themselves from the patronage of the very few, suggests that the patronage of many—not yet the masses, but more than the very few—carries with it special burdens of institution building.

An institution represents a brave attempt to extend the life of an inspiration. Extending

Source. Copyright © 1976 by Peat, Marwick, Mitchell & Company. All rights reserved. Reprinted with permission from *Management Controls* (October/November, 1976), pp. 166–177.

that life inevitably involves building a structure, with staff and governing board (organization), thinking ahead (planning), making financial plans (budgeting), maintaining financial records (accounting), and preparing the necessary reports (reporting). This article is in the nature of a primer dealing broadly with the nonartistic (that is, the financial management) aspects of the life of an arts organization—planning, budgeting, accounting, and reporting.

The range of size and complexity of arts organizations is enormous. Great opera companies and symphony orchestras of national reputation are multimillion-dollar operations. Small community theaters and dance companies, on the other hand, often subsist on budgets of barely five figures. Although the financial difficulties of arts organizations are not limited to those with small budgets—

several renowned organizations of great size have been forced to suspend or to terminate their activities during the past year—we have had to determine the target audience for this article and have deliberately selected the smaller organization with a budget in the range of, say, $20,000 to $200,000 in annual expenditures. There are several reasons for this choice. Such organizations are less likely to have personnel trained in all the complexities of management. They are less likely to have funds with which to engage expert management advice when they need it. And no primer designed specifically for managers of these organizations appears to be available.

At the same time, we have sought to emphasize the broader aspects of financial management, although on occasion, as in the case of the discussion on cash management, we have made narrower reference to specific procedures and controls. If large arts organizations find concepts and suggestions of value in these pages we shall naturally be pleased, but we disclaim any intention of treating here the more complex issues that arise from large-scale operations.

THE FINANCIAL FUNCTION

The financial and related activities of small arts institutions with annual budgets in the range of $20,000 to $200,000 are basically similar. Variations are related to the number of transactions and the complexities of the programs provided. Essentially, the role of the financial function is to assist managers of the institution in planning and budgeting and in operating, controlling, evaluating, and reporting activities.

Planning

In the planning process, it is necessary to anticipate the financial impact of various program alternatives being considered.

Budgeting

Once plans are formulated and financial results forecast, the plan serves as the framework for the annual budget. Here the financial function provides through its accounting system necessary detailed data and guidance for estimating the specific resources needed and available and the amount to be expended in the budget year.

Operating

The process of implementing the program activities described in the annual budget is the operating side of the financial function. Should actual experience vary from the expectations reflected in the budget, a change in plan may be required. For instance, if membership revenue is substantially less than originally predicted without a compensating decline in expenditures, management must take steps to increase revenues in some other way or to reduce expenditures in order to keep the budget in balance. The financial function must provide the information needed to assist those responsible in drawing appropriate conclusions.

Controlling

The fiduciary responsibility of safeguarding institutional assets is fundamental to the role of the financial function. In essence this responsibility involves controlling expenditures to ensure that funds are used in the manner intended. To carry out this responsibility, the organization must use appropriate internal controls and reports. These include effective systems and procedures for receiving and disbursing cash, investing unused cash according to the policies of the institution, and establishing effective internal controls in order to safeguard institutional assets.

Evaluating

An after-the-fact process of evaluation follows. This entails comparing actual performance with plans to determine the effectiveness of operations and to see what lessons can be learned by studying the successes and failures of the past year. The financial function should produce a significant amount of the information required for a perceptive review.

Reporting

The financial function must also help to meet external reporting requirements. Private contributors are interested in knowing how their funds are used. Foundations and public funding sources are also concerned that their support has been used for the purposes intended and may require financial reports as evidence of stewardship. Special reports must also be prepared annually for Federal and state agencies to meet their requirements.

ORGANIZATIONAL RELATIONSHIPS

Typically in a small arts organization a combination of volunteers and paid staff carries out the responsibilities of management. The board of trustees is formed to act as a policymaking body but, in many small organizations, designated members of the board also serve in an operating capacity by assisting in day-to-day activities. If the institution is large enough, a director, a business manager, and other staff may be employed full-time or part-time. If adequate professional staff is available, the trustees should confine their activities to policymaking and review.

In setting up the combination of volunteer and paid staff required by the size and resources of the organization, management should assign responsibilities so that all the financial functions metnioned earlier are per-

formed. Three organization structures may be envisaged.

Board, Director, and Business Manager

This structure is one in which the institution can employ a full-time or part-time business manager. In such a case, the business manager should perform all operating financial functions. He or she should report directly to the director who, in turn, reports on the financial performance of the institution to the board of trustees. For purposes of internal control, the director should review financial reports, sign checks according to institutional policy, review bank reconciliations at the end of each month, determine that all cash receipts are deposited, ensure that institutional assets are preserved, and perform other functions on a test basis to make certain that the financial functions are being carried out effectively.

Board and Director

In this case, the operating organization is composed of a full-time or part-time director and other staff. It is assumed that the staff does not act in the capacity of business manager, although certain bookkeeping functions such as receiving and depositing cash, paying bills, and maintaining the books of account may be performed by a combination secretary-bookkeeper. In this instance, the director or a designated staff person other than the bookkeeper should perform the planning and budgeting, investing, controlling, and reporting aspects of the financial function. A member of the board may be asked to supplement the efforts of the director in dealing with financial affairs. As in the first case, the director should be responsible for all operating activities and, in addition, should ensure that adequate internal controls exist.

Board

In the third situation, the organization is staffed by volunteers who are typically members of the board of trustees. In this case, the trustees should delegate operating responsibilities to specific individuals or committees of the board as appropriate. If a treasurer or finance committee is designated, these individuals should be given the responsibility for carrying out the financial function. As in the other cases, effective internal controls should be established to ensure that funds are used in the manner intended.

Certain organizations find it beneficial to obtain external assistance to record financial transactions in the books of account and to prepare monthly financial reports. In any event, an independent audit of their financial statements is often considered advisable by the board, the director, or other responsible parties, and may even be necessary to satisfy the requirements of governmental bodies, private contributors, foundations, or other funding sources.

PLANNING AND BUDGETING

As an overview of some key features of the planning and budgeting aspects of financial management for an arts company we present below a series of brief statements preliminary to considering some of the concepts in greater detail:

- Resources are scarce. The task of management is to allocate resources optimally among programs.
- As an essential precondition of any intelligent allocation of resources, programs should be identified and defined.
- Support programs, as well as primary programs, should be identified and defined. Primary programs are those for the sake of which the organization exists. Support programs are those without which the primary programs could not succeed.
- Personnel costs are the largest single item in the typical organization budget. Unless a manager knows how people spend their time, he cannot determine the cost of programs. The typical line-item budget is of little assistance. The first necessary step is the development of a program time budget of the type shown as Exhibit 1.
- A program expenditure budget can then be developed (see Exhibit 2) which reflects the translation of personnel time into dollars (as shown in Exhibit 3) and adds other expenditures in the appropriate program categories.
- Anticipated revenue should also be analyzed to distinguish funds for general purposes from those that are program related, as shown in Exhibit 4.
- The program expenditure and revenue budgets provide the basis for determining whether optimum allocation of resources is being achieved and, more specifically, for helping to answer such questions as: What is the full cost of this program? the net cost? the incremental cost? How much will a proposed new program actually cost? When the anticipated benefits of the new program are compared with those of old programs, does it appear that a major reallocation is warranted? If so, what must be sacrificed? How productive is each of the support programs when revenue generated is compared with cost? Should more or less of the total expenditures be allocated to support programs?

Many organizations look ahead only one year, but a longer time perspective can be useful even for a small organization. If a director plans to make program changes, his trustees should ask: What will be the effect of these changes on expenditures and revenue three

EXHIBIT 1

Time Budget
July 1, 1975, to June 30, 1976

| | Primary Programs | | | | Support Programs | | | |
| | Traveling Exhibits | Art Instruction | School Art Appreciation | Permanent Acquisitions | Membership Maintenance and Services | Fund Raising | Administrative Support | Total Man Days |
Position								
Full-time staff								
Director	80	35	55	30	5	15	15	235
Program associate	10	95	95	10	5	5	15	235
Membership secretary	5				215		15	235
Bookkeeper-secretary	70	25	45	10	25	10	50	235
Receptionist-typist	70	25	25	5	100	5	5	235
Handyman	40	50					145	235
								Total Man Hours
Part-time staff								
Publicity aide	120	80	60	12	98	98	12	480
Guards	775							775
Instructors		700						700

EXHIBIT 2

Program Expenditure Budget
July 1, 1975, to June 30, 1976

| | Primary Programs | | | | Support Programs | | | |
Expenditure Item	Traveling Exhibits	Art Instruction	School Art Appreciation	Permanent Acquisitions	Membership Maintenance and Services	Fund Raising	Administrative Support	Total
Salaries, wages and benefits	$15,100	17,800	11,700	3,400	11,800	2,300	7,300	$ 69,400
Prizes		700						700
Acquisitions				4,000				4,000
Professional fees		500					5,000	5,500
Office supplies					1,300	300	800	2,400
Telephone	400	200	100	50	900	200	150	2,000
Travel and subsistence	600			200		100		900
Printing/artwork, etc.	3,000	600	250		3,500	150		7,500
Subscriptions—reference publications	100	50	50	50	50	50	150	500
Equipment			500					500
Shipping charges	1,500	100						1,600
Art instruction materials		1,000						1,000
Utilities	1,800	900	200		1,400	200	2,100	6,600
Insurance	2,700			600			300	3,600
Grounds maintenance (contract)							3,800	3,800
Other							400	400
Totals	$25,200	21,850	12,800	8,300	18,950	3,300	20,000	$110,400
Contingency								3,700
Total estimated expenditures								$114,100

EXHIBIT 3

Personnel Cost by Program
July 1, 1975, to June 30, 1976

Position	Primary Programs				Support Programs			Total
	Traveling Exhibits	Art Instruction	School Art Appreciation	Permanent Acquisitions	Membership Maintenance and Services	Fund Raising	Administrative Support	
Full-time staff								
Director	$ 6,630	2,905	4,563	2,496	410	1,248	1,248	$19,500
Program associate	559	5,252	5,252	559	273	273	832	13,000
Membership secretary	178				7,778		544	8,500
Bookkeeper-secretary	1,563	557	1,003	226	557	226	1,118	5,250
Receptionist-typist	1,563	557	557	110	2,243	110	110	5,250
Handyman	918	1,150					3,332	5,400
Part-time staff								
Publicity aide	600	400	300	60	490	490	60	2,400
Guards	3,100							3,100
Instructors		7,000						7,000
Totals	$15,111	17,821	11,675	3,451	11,751	2,347	7,244	$69,400

EXHIBIT 4

Revenue Budget
July 1, 1975, to June 30, 1976

Source	General Purposes	Traveling Exhibits	Art Instruction	School Art Appreciation	Permanent Acquisitions	Total
				Program Related		
Membership contributions	$45,000					$45,000
Other contributions	8,000	1,000		400	600	10,000
Foundation grant	15,000					15,000
Government grant				7,500		7,500
Endowment income	2,900					2,900
Tuition			3,500			3,500
Exhibitions		4,200				4,200
Totals	$70,900	5,200	3,500	7,900	600	$88,100

years from now? The answer—even if it is hedged in uncertainties—can be the crucial factor in the decision to proceed with changes in the next year's program and budget. Then, too, in the arts, grants from foundations and governments are a significant source of revenue. To make an effective case, the director should usually display a program plan over at least a two- or three-year period, with accompanying estimates of expenditures and revenues. Given the uncomfortably long lag that typically characterizes decision-making processes of governments and large foundations, it is so much the more necessary to plan far ahead so that the timely flow of revenue from such sources can be ensured.

Such long-range planning also provides perspective for a review of the basic goal or mission of the organization. Frequently, organizations slip unawares into an untenable position relative to a long-held goal that is outmoded. An art museum, for example, may have been founded as a showcase for original paintings of top quality to be purchased by the museum. But the resources available to the museum—its own funds and the generosity of its friends—are now completely inadequate to support the purchase of such paintings in the current market. The museum must either revise its basic purpose or suffer ignominy in its decline. Such basic issues must be faced in the long-range plan. If fundamental redirection of the organization is necessary, a major function of the plan—perhaps even over a five-year period—is to provide for an orderly transition. It will also set forth from year to year the required program changes and at the same time identify new sources of revenue, current outlays that are no longer necessary, and estimated costs of the new programs.

ZERO-BASED VERSUS INCREMENTAL BUDGETING

In many organizations, the budgeting process begins with an estimate of revenue. The director or the business officer estimates that the total funds available next year will be, say, approximately 5 percent over the current level. Then the officer focuses all attention on how to spend the additional 5 percent, raising such questions as: If salaries rise 7 percent to keep pace with inflation, can expenditures remain level for certain other categories so that the overall increases lie within the estimated limit? This process is called *incremental budgeting* because attention is focused on the increment— the 5 percent—rather than on the total. (In a bad year, a 5 percent cut necessitates a similar though more painful process.) The basic underlying assumption of incremental budgeting is that nothing fundamental should be changed; that current funding levels for the various activities are equitable and necessary; and therefore that the budgeting process is limited to allocating the anticipated increment.

A more probing process than that of incremental budgeting is zero-based budgeting. Its basic assumption is that every activity must justify itself—its very existence as well as its level of support. In practice, it is not feasible for organizations to "start from zero" in budgeting every activity every year. The process is too diquieting, and if applied throughout it would threaten any plan that could not be fully achieved in one year. So in its complete application, zero-based budgeting must be employed less frequently for the organization as a whole or applied on a scheduled basis to specific program elements every few years. A scheduled application of zero-based budgeting is well suited to large, complex organizations such as a major national art museum, whereas a complete application is better suited to a small organization.

A serious effort at zero-based budgeting imposes disciplines that are healthy for any organization. For a given activity to justify its existence, it must contribute significantly to the goal of the organization. In turn, the goal may have to be clarified. Justifying the particular level of support sought for an activity inevitably leads to questions of program performance. How well is an art appreciation program doing? How does one assess whether it is going well or badly? How much of the association's resources is it entitled to, in view of its results to date and its prospects? Such questions can lead to the establishment of specific objectives for programs—objectives that are described in enough detail in advance so that when the year is over it is possible to judge whether or not, and to what degree, they were actually achieved. Any such improvements in the processes of review can make a substantial difference in the effectiveness of the organization.

CONTINGENCY PLANNING

The truism that life is uncertain and that the unexpected often occurs applies to organizations as well as to people. The actual results of a year's activity will never occur precisely as planned. When the variances are very small there is no problem, but when they are substantial, severe complications may arise. Even a small organization must do some contingency planning.

Two types of contingency plans can be made. The first is to include in the budget an estimated contingency item as a reserve. Every budget should have such an item, the size of which depends upon a variety of circumstances. Such a reserve can be a hedge against a decrease in revenue, a completely unexpected expense, or an unexpected rise in cost. The amount will depend upon a number of considerations such as predictability of levels and sources of income, relative stability of the organization, extent to which expenditures are fixed in advance, and experience of management.

Frequently, an officer or a trustee deletes a contingency reserve, especially when funds are tight and a deficit is looming (on the ground that, "We can't afford it"), but the reasoning is wrong. The purpose of the contingency reserve is to provide for an expense that cannot be avoided but also cannot be predicted. In the absence of the reserve, the expense may still occur. Some budgetmakers make up for the lack of a contingency reserve by "padding" each of the individual items, but this practice often prevents a superior officer or a trustee finance committee from conducting a good tough-minded budget review. Then there is the frequently heard argument against the use of the contingency reserve, that if it appears in the budget it will be spent, even unnecessarily. Such an objection is readily answered by a provision that the reserve can only be spent with the prior approval of the finance committe or the chairman of the board.

The second type of contingency planning provides for a shift to an alternative budget if a particular event occurs or fails to occur. For example, in their efforts to develop a balanced budget the trustees may decide on an increase in membership dues, say from $45,000 to $54,000, a 20 percent increase. They recognize that this one item is the major uncertainty in the budget and wonder whether the extra $9,000 will actually be achieved. Because the membership drive, let us say, takes place in October, they will have a good idea of the result by November 1. Therefore, they may ask that an alternative budget be prepared specifying how $9,000 can be eliminated from planned expenditures between November 1 and June 30.

Many organizations can be spared severe financial crises if they prepare such an alternative budget plan. The key to the successful application of this budget alternative is usually identifying the major source of uncertainty on the revenue side, estimating the magnitude of the possible shortfall, and then developing an expenditure plan that clearly identifies the specific items to be adjusted and the timing of the adjustments.

CASH MANAGEMENT

In this section of our article, we will limit our discussion of cash management to a series of statements designed to summarize some of the fundamental—perhaps elementary—principles of management and control.

- To manage cash most effectively, it is necessary first to determine cash position, and second to predict when cash may be received or disbursed in the future. For these purposes, cash status and cash projection reports should be prepared as required— weekly, monthly, etc.

- If excess cash is available, it should be invested, but investments should be of such a nature that the instituion can readily obtain the use of these monies in case an emergency should arise.

- An organization should establish effective controls over all cash assets, such as:

  - Requiring dual signatures (preferably including the signature of an officer of the institution) for all checks over a certain amount.

  - Limiting check-signing authority to as few responsible individuals as possible while still allowing for an efficient flow of work.

  - Separating the cashiering and cash-related functions from the accounting function.

  - Conducting a periodic count and examination of cash funds to ensure that all cash and cash items are accounted for.

  - Requiring a monthly reconciliation of all bank accounts to the accounting records of the organization. These reconciliations should be reviewed periodically to ascertain that they have been prepared properly and to ensure that all reconciling items are properly accounted for.

  - Establishing an imprest petty cash fund of limited amount.

  - Requiring that all employees performing cashiering functions be adequately bonded.

  - Establishing change funds in a fixed amount with custodianship responsibilities clearly fixed.

- Because of the complexity of box office activities, the arts organization should establish effective procedures to ensure appropriate controls. These procedures include the following:

  - Requiring that each person selling tickets in the box office operate with a single change fund for which he alone is responsible. If more than one person is selling tickets, a separate fund should be established for each person.

  - Specifying that appropriate change fund procedures be employed, and that a change fund report be prepared daily and submitted for review.

  - Utilizing preprinted tickets indicating the title of the performance date, seat number if reserved, ticket number, and price of each ticket. Tickets should provide a detachable stub, which then serves as a receipt for reconciling daily sales to the amounts collected in the change fund.

  - Requiring periodically (daily, weekly, or monthly, depending on need) a box office accountability statement reconciling assets held by the box office to all tickets assigned to the box office for sale.

  - Reviewing periodically (daily, weekly, or monthly, depending on the amount on hand) cash balances held by the box office for future performances to determine the amount and length of time "excess" monies can be invested.

• Requiring that all cash received be deposited daily and intact. Copies of all bank deposit slips stamped as received by the bank should be returned directly to appropriate personnel who are not themselves performing box office activities.

• Assigning responsibility for preparing a monthly bank reconciliation to appropriate personnel who are not performing box office activities.

• Performing periodic surprise examinations of box office activity during the performing arts season.

FUNDS AND FUND ACCOUNTING

Unlike business corporations, not-for-profit institutions receive gifts, grants, and legacies to support their activities. Often, these contributions are for specific purposes, and the institution must give assurance to donors or trustees that the funds are spent (or preserved) for the purposes for which they were given. The need to ensure that funds are used according to the intention of the donor gave rise to what is called *fund accounting*.

The fundamental principle in fund accounting is stewardship: accountability for the receipt and use of resources. In addition to contributions that are restricted to specific uses by the donor, unrestricted funds may be designated for specific use by action of the board of trustees of an organization. In either case, the institution's management has a fiduciary responsibility to utilize the funds according to the stipulated conditions. It is the objective of fund accounting to record, classify, summarize, and report financial transactions to reflect the purposes for which the funds were established.

In order to report on the contributions of other income received by the institution, separate accounts are established to recognize the unique characteristics of each fund but, unless required by the funding source, separate bank accounts are not necessary. As the number of funds can be many, it is common practice for reporting purposes to combine funds with like characteristics into fund groups, each fund group being treated as a separate entity with self-balancing assets, liabilities, and fund balances. Some of the fund groups that may be found in arts institutions are Current Funds, Endowment and Similar Funds, Annuity and Life Income Funds, Plant Funds and Agency Funds. Because circumstances differ, each institution must examine its resources to determine which fund groups are relevant. For instance, small institutions may find that their resources fall into the current funds group exclusively, while other institutions may have endowment funds, plant funds, and other resources. To assist in the classification process, we will describe briefly each fund group.

• *Current funds.* Most financial transactions of an arts institution reflect the conduct of everyday operations or activities. The fund group that accounts for these operating activities is the current funds group which can be separated into two subgroups:

• *Unrestricted current funds.* These funds contain resources available for general operations to be used at the discretion of the organization. Funds received for services rendered, such as tuition and exhibition revenues, are included in this category. Similarly, gifts, bequests, and other contributions to support the general purposes of the institution would be included here, including membership contributions and unrestricted foundation grants. The board of trustees may elect to set aside resources to be used for specific operating purposes. This designation of funds occurs as a result of formal board action indicating how and when management is to use them, and these funds may be expended for these purposes only. The board can, of course, reverse itself later, and the funds would then become available for general operations.

• *Restricted current funds.* These funds are received from sources external to the institution to be used for *specific* current operating purposes. The funds must be recognized as restricted because the source of the funds has identified how they are to be used. The restriction should be communicated to the institution in writing and signed by the donor. Funds received as a result of a campaign may also be restricted if the solicitation literature indicates an intention to use such funds for a specific purpose.

• *Endowment and similar funds.* These are funds the principal of which is held for purposes of investment. The income generated from investment may be used for unrestricted or restricted purposes. Such funds may be classified according to the following subgroups:

• *Endowment funds.* In this category are funds received from donors who have stipulated that the principal be held intact in perpetuity. The income derived from investment of these funds is used according to the wishes of the donor.

• *Term endowment funds.* These are funds received from donors who have stipulated that the principal may be expended on the occurrence of a particular event or after a period of time.

• *Quasi-endowment funds.* Here we have funds established as a result of board of trustees' action. Whatever their source, these funds have been set aside for the purposes of investment to produce revenue for the institution. The principal of these funds may be expended if the board of trustees so desires.

• *Annuity and life income funds.* An arts institution may receive contributions from external sources requiring that a certain amount of money be provided to persons designated by the donor. One such fund is called an annuity fund. In this case, the donor gives the institution money or securities with the understanding that a fixed amount is to be paid periodically to the donor or the donor's beneficiary. The life income fund, although comparable to the annuity fund in many ways, is somewhat different because it requires that a variable payment be made to the donor or a beneficiary for his or her lifetime. Typically, this periodic payment is equal to the revenue earned from the investment of funds received from the donor. Because annuity and life income funds are subject to provisions of state and Federal laws, institutions should carefully review and evaluate such gifts.

• *Plant funds.* Used to account for the land, buildings, and equipment owned by the arts institution, the plant fund group is composed of two basic subgroups:

• *Unexpended plant funds.* This group includes funds contributed to the institution or transferred from other fund groups for the purpose of acquiring land, buildings, and major equipment—all of which are used to carry on the activitites of the institution.

• *Investment in plant.* After the funds are

expended, the land, buildings, and equipment acquired are treated as a separate fund. These assets should be recorded at cost or, in the absence of original historical cost records, at the current appraised value. Subsequent additions would naturally be at cost. Plant assets donated to the institution are recorded at their fair market or appraised value on the date of the gift.

Agency funds. As funds held by the arts institution as a custodian for third parties, the institution has no legal right to these assets but merely acts as an agent that receives, holds, and finally disburses the funds in accordance with the wishes of the depositor. An example of agency funds might be ticket sales held for an independent producer or exhibitor renting the facilities of the arts institution. If these funds are small in size and infrequent, they may be included as accounts payable in the current funds group.

ACCRUAL ACCOUNTING

Fund accounting can be accomplished by using either the cash basis or the accrual basis of accounting. The cash basis method of accounting recognizes revenues when cash is received and expenditures when cash is paid. The accrual method of accounting recognizes revenues when earned and expenditures when materials are used and services are performed.

Whenever practical, arts organizations should adopt the accrual basis of accounting rather than the cash basis because the former provides a more accurate portrayal of the institution's financial position and operations. Thus, the cash basis system does not recognize as an expenditure liabilities incurred for materials received and used, but unpaid for, in conducting the activities of the organization. Accrual accounting recognizes this transaction as an expenditure because the materials were used and the liability incurred during the current period. A similar situation occurs when the organization receives cash or makes payments that benefit future periods. In a cash basis accounting system, both the cash received and the payments made are considered revenues and expenditures of the current period even if they pertain to future operations. Accrual accounting, on the other hand, relates expenditures and receipts to the period in which the activity actually occurs, regardless of when the bill is sent out or the payment is received.

Before formally embracing accrual accounting, however, a small organization should recognize that maintaining such a system on a continuous basis may be costly and therefore impractical. Another approach that will achieve the same result permits the accounting records to be maintained on a cash basis throughout the year, but periodically as financial statements are prepared, accruals may be introduced to adjust the statement for material items the omission of which would distort the financial presentation. At the end of the fiscal year, accruals are formally recorded in the books of account, permitting the year-end financial statements to be prepared on an accrual basis.

FINANCIAL REPORTING

Financial reports are prepared to assist trustees and management in meeting their responsibilities for controlling resources as well as for budgeting future organizational activities. Often such reports are also required by interested outside parties such as donors, foundations, and government agencies. Good financial reporting requires adherence to a whole complex of fundamental reporting principles of which the following are illustrative:

- *Summarization of information.* Reports should be prepared in a manner that permits the board and staff to review financial information without dwelling on unnecessary detail. To achieve the desired level of summarization, individual accounts may be combined into account groups. If necessary, detailed information can be maintained on worksheets in the books of account to answer specific questions concerning a particular category.

- *Exception reporting.* To facilitate understanding of financial reports, emphasis should be placed on highlighting specific situations requiring attention. For instance, where unfavorable financial results are being experienced, brackets may be placed around such figures. In addition, a short description of the situation may be advisable.

- *Whole-dollar reporting.* Amounts appearing on financial reports should be rounded to the nearest whole dollar or, where appropriate, to the nearest hundred dollars. This simplification focuses attention on the essential financial message without distracting the reader with immaterial amounts.

- *Timeliness.* To be of value, reported financial information must be made available soon after month-end so that staff and officers can examine conditions or matters of serious consequence as quickly as possible in order to consider alternatives and decide upon the appropriate course of action.

Ideally, certain financial reports should be prepared at least monthly. Others may be required only once a year. The timing and frequency should reflect the specific needs of the organization and the time available to those preparing the reports. The following are some of the more significant reports that arts institutions should render for the edification of

its board of trustees as well as for internal administrative purposes:

- *Budget status report.* Presents the status of financial operations for a specified period by comparing actual revenues and expenditures and their projections to year-end with the approved budget, along with expected variances. (See Exhibit 5.)

- *Balance sheet.* Presents the financial position of the institution and the funds for which it is responsible at a given time. (See Exhibit 6).

- *Statement of changes in fund balances.* Presents a summary of additions, deductions, and transfers among funds which represent the changes in fund balances for a specified period. (See Exhibit 7.)

- *Statement of current funds revenues, expenditures, and transfers.* Presents the results of current operations in terms of unrestricted and restricted revenues, expenditures, and other changes in current funds for a specified period, along with a comparison with the results of the prior year's operations. (See Exhibit 8).

- *Analysis of program expenditures by object.* Presents an analysis of current operating expenditures by the object of expenditures within the program. This report is in the same format as the Program Expenditure Budget illustrated in Exhibit 2.

These reports—in content, form, and the relationships of the information included therein—emphasize again how integrally related are programs and financial management. In an arts organization, a budget is in effect a plan that reflects the program commitments of the budgetmakers, while the reports that are subsequently rendered after these programs have been underway provide the information needed to evaluate the correspondence of ac-

EXHIBIT 5

Budget Status Report
Eight Months Ended February 28, 1976

Revenues/Expenditures	Approved Annual Budget	Actual to Date[a]	Projected to Year End	Expected Favorable or (Unfavorable) Variance
Revenue				
Membership contributions	$ 70,000	55,000	10,000	$ (5,000)
Other contributions	10,000	5,000	5,100	100
Foundation grant	15,000	7,500	7,500	—
Government grant	7,500	3,500	4,000	—
Endowment income	2,900	2,100	1,000	200
Tuition	3,500	3,000	700	200
Exhibitions	4,200	3,400	1,700	900
Total revenues	$ 113,100	79,500	30,000	$ (3,600)
Expenditures				
Primary programs				
Traveling exhibits	$ 25,200	7,000	9,000	$ 9,200
Art instruction	21,900	15,000	7,500	(600)
School art appreciation	12,800	6,800	5,500	500
Permanent acquisitions	8,300	4,300	3,000	1,000
Total	$ 68,200	33,100	25,000	$ 10,100
Support programs				
Membership maintenance and services	$ 19,000	11,000	7,500	$ 500
Fund raising	3,300	2,300	1,200	(200)
Administrative support	20,000	12,000	7,700	300
Contingency	3,700	—	—	3,700
Total	46,000	25,300	16,400	4,300
Total expenditures	$ 114,200	58,400	41,400	$ 14,400
Excess (deficiency) of revenue over expenditures	$ (1,100)	21,100	(11,400)	$ 10,800

[a]Obtained from books of account maintained during the year on a cash basis.

EXHIBIT 6

Balance Sheet
June 30, 1976, with Comparative Figures for 1975

Assets	Current Year	Prior Year	Liabilities and Fund Balance	Current Year	Prior Year
Current funds			**Current funds**		
Cash	$ 11,500	$ 28,000	Accounts payable	$ 2,500	$ 1,500
Receivables	2,700	1,500	Fund balances		
Other assets	500	500	Unrestricted	7,700	25,500
			Restricted	4,500	3,000
			Total fund balances	12,200	28,500
Total current funds	$ 14,700	$ 30,000	Total current funds	$ 14,700	$ 30,000
Endowment and similar funds			**Endowment and similar funds**		
Cash	5,000	5,000	Fund balances		
Investments (market value $54,000 and $51,000 respectively)	56,000	50,000	Endowment	25,000	25,000
			Term endowment	10,000	10,000
			Quasi-endowment—unrestricted	21,000	20,000
			Annuity and life income funds	5,000	—
			Total fund balances	61,000	55,000
Total endowment funds	$ 61,000	$ 55,000	Total endowment funds	$ 61,000	$ 55,000
Plant funds			**Plant funds**		
Cash	2,000	1,000	Accounts payable	500	—
Land, buildings, and equipment	303,000	300,000	Fund balances		
			Unexpended:		
			Unrestricted	1,000	1,000
			Restricted	500	—
			Total unexpended	1,500	1,000
			Investment in plant	303,000	300,000
Total plant funds	$305,000	$301,000	Total plant funds	$305,000	$301,000
Agency funds			**Agency funds**		
Cash	2,000	500	Funds held for others	2,000	500
Total agency funds	$ 2,000	$ 500	Total agency funds	$ 2,000	$ 500

EXHIBIT 7

Statement of Changes in Fund Balances:
Year Ended June 30, 1976

	Current Funds		Endowment and Similar Funds				Plant Funds		
				Term	Quasi-	Annuity and	Unexpended Plant Funds		Investment
	Unrestricted	Restricted	Endowment	Endowment	Endowment	Life Income	Unrestricted	Restricted	in Plant
Additions									
Unrestricted current fund revenues	$ 75,500								
Restricted contributions		1,500							
Government grant		7,500							
Expended for plant							3,000	500	3,000
Annuity fund —restricted						3,000			
Life income fund —restricted						2,000			
Total revenues and Other additions	75,500	9,000		—	—	5,000	3,000	500	3,000
Deductions									
Program expenditures	92,300	7,500							
Expended for plant							3,000		
Total expenditures and other deductions	92,300	7,500		—	—	—	3,000	—	—
Transfers among funds—									
Additions (deductions)	(1,000)								
To quasi-endowment					1,000				
Total transfers	(1,000)			—	1,000				
Net increase (decrease) for the year	(17,800)	1,500		—	1,000	5,000	—	500	3,000
Fund balance at beginning of year	25,500	3,000		10,000	20,000	—	1,000	—	300,000
Fund balance at end of year	$ 7,700	4,500		10,000	21,000	5,000	1,000	500	303,000

EXHIBIT 8

Statement of Current Funds, Revenues, Expenditures, and Transfers
Year Ended June 30, 1976

| | Current Year | | | Prior |
	Unrestricted	Restricted	Total	Year Total
Revenue				
Membership contributions	$ 40,000		40,000	$ 43,250
Other contributions	8,600		8,600	8,765
Foundation grant	15,000		15,000	30,000
Government grant		7,500	7,500	7,450
Endowment income	3,100		3,100	3,000
Tuition	3,700		3,700	3,520
Exhibitions	5,100		5,100	4,210
Total current revenues	75,500	7,500	83,000	100,195
Program expenditures				
Traveling exhibits	16,000		16,000	26,300
Art instruction	22,500		22,500	21,252
School art appreciation	4,800	7,500	12,300	12,230
Permanent acquisitions	7,300		7,300	7,900
Membership maintenance and services	18,500		18,500	17,500
Fund raising	3,500		3,500	2,900
Administrative support	19,700		19,700	14,300
Total program expenditures	92,300	7,500	99,800	102,382
Transfers and other additions (deductions)				
Excess of restricted receipts over transfers to revenues[a]		1,500	1,500	1,000
To quasi-endowment funds[b]	(1,000)		(1,000)	
Total transfers and other additions	(1,000)	1,500	500	1,000
Net increase (decrease) for the year	$ (17,800)	1,500	(16,300)	(1,187)

[a] This is the unused portion of restricted receipts received during the fiscal year. It is therefore an addition to current restricted fund revenues.
[b] This is a deduction from current unrestricted fund revenues.

tuality with plan, and the resources available for future operations. Anyone who wants to influence the program direction of an institution must know that he must make a strong impact at the time that resources are allocated—that is, when the budget is made up—and must participate in the evaluation process—that is, as the accounting reports are later reviewed.

Financial management is thus inextricably tied to the artistic efforts of an arts institution. The notion held by some that financial management can be carried on without implicit program judgments is simply not correct and can be harmful. In helping to sustain and nourish the arts organization, management itself is a creative endeavor and may even be looked upon as an art.

CHAPTER 11

Reporting and Evaluation of Performance

The report and evaluation cycle of the overall planning and control process involves the measurement of actual performance and its comparison with the plan. Differences between actuality and plan are referred to as variances; if these are significant, it indicates that the organization is not working toward its goals. Management action may be required to correct the situation so that the organization will be "put back on track." In other cases the environment in which the organization exists may have changed so drastically that revision of goals and objectives is necessitated.

An example drawn from personnel performance may help to illustrate some of the major concepts in reporting and evaluation. The board of directors of the Open Door Clinic estimated at the beginning of 1981 that the clinic would serve 5,000 clients during the years. Demand for the clinic's services is spaced evenly throughout the year, so that 420 clients are expected during January. From past experience the board estimates that about four hours of professional counselor time are required per client and about 160 hours of clerical time per month.

If at the end of January the actual performance is determined to be 1,800 professional hours and 200 clerical hours, the report to the board may appear in the following format.

Performance Report: Open Door Clinic, January 1981

	Actual Activity	Plan	Variance
Professional staff hours	1800	1680[a]	(120 hours)
Clerical staff hours	200	160	(40 hours)

[a]4 hours × 420 clients = 1680

In the case of both professional and clerical work, the actual hours exceeded those budgeted. Two questions immediately come to mind: Why did the unfavorable variances appear? Is corrective action by the board required? The answers to these questions are not apparent from the performance report as it appears; the report is not very useful in helping management determine the reasons for the variances. After exploring some of the major factors responsible for variances, suggestions for revising the report are made below.

The uncertainty of demand for the clinic's services constitutes an important reason for the variance in the example. Apart from making the clinic's services better known to the public, the clinic has little control over the demand for them. Demand most likely is tied to such exogenous variables as economic conditions in the community, changes in programs by other social agencies, and altered regulations.

A second factor that may account for variances between plan and actuality is the assumed input/output relationship between staff hours and clients counseled. Based on past experience the clinic's board estimated four hours of professional counselor time per client. This input/output relationship may change according to the complexity of cases dealt with by the clinic. More difficult cases may require additional professional staff time, hence requiring an adjustment in the input/ output ratio. It is also expected that in an activity dominated by human contact certain deviations from "normal" will occur from case to case. Variations outside an expected "normal" range, however, provide a signal to management that intervention may be required. Perhaps excessive hours are due to a failure to use standardized treatment procedure. Additional problems may be poor scheduling of activities, improper standards for client admissibility, or ineffective counseling methods. Investigation by management is needed to identify the precise reasons before corrective action can be initiated.

Individual performance is a third factor related to differences between plan and actuality. The amount of effort which both professional and clerical employees apply to the job task varies from day to day and from job to job. Once again, normal variations from the standard can be expected and do not call for corrective action by management.

An improved performance report would help management to identify the specific problems noted above, at the same time presenting additional information in a more easily interpreted format. An improved report for the Open Door Clinic appears below.

Performance Report: Open Door Clinic, January 1981

	Master Budget	Actual Activity	Performance Budget	Activity Variance	Other Variance
Number of clients served	420	445	445[a]	25[b]	
Professional staff hours	1,680	1,800	1,780[c]	100[d]	(20)[e]
Clerical staff hours	160	200	160[f]	—	(40)

[a]The performance budget column is based upon the actual activity of the clinic. Activity for the Open Door Clinic is measured in terms of number of clients served.

[b]The activity variance represents the difference between the original 420 clients expected and the 445 actually served.

[c]445 clients × the planned 4 hours per client input/output relationship. This represents the number of professional hours required given the actual work load.

[d]Original master budget 1,680 hours subtracted from 1,780 hours allowed by performance budget = 100 hours activity variance.

[e]1,780 hours performance budget minus 1,800 actual hours = 20 hour variance.

[f]Clerical hours are assumed to be unrelated to output. Therefore, performance budget = master budget.

This format of the report separates out the exogenous uncertainties over which management has little control and refers to them as activity variances. One sees that twenty-five more clients than expected were seen during January and that this greater work load accounted for 100 additional hours by the professional staff. The twenty hours of "other variances" may be a result of input/output uncertainties and/or individual performance variances. The amount is small in relation to total hours "allowed" by the performance budget (20 / 1780 $\sim$ 1%) and is probably not significant.

The forty hours of "other variances" associated with the clerical staff is also a combination of input/output uncertainties and/or individual performance variances. In this case the amount is quite large in relation to the hours "allowed" by the personnel performance budget (40/160 = 25%), calling for investigation by management.

Techniques similar to those exemplified through the case of the Open Door Clinic for evaluation of personnel performance can be utilized in financial performance evaluation as well. An important step in the evaluation of financial performance is usage of a management report that compares actual costs with planned costs. Such a comparison process is made difficult and potentially misleading if one does not recognize the ways in which costs can vary with activity level. Some costs are relatively stable despite fluctuations in the activity of the organizational unit, whereas other types of costs change in direct proportion to activity level. The former group is referred to as "fixed costs" and the latter as "variable costs." For example, the utility costs of electricity and water for a child welfare agency are "fixed" and do not vary with the number of cases handled, which comprises the measure of activity. On the other hand, costs of transportation and supplies are likely to vary in proportion to the number of cases handled per month.

Holder and Williams in "Better Cost Control with Flexible Budgets and Variance Analysis" describe an effective financial performance evaluation process, which deals specifically with the issue of fixed versus variable costs. The step-by-step approach taken by the authors and their extensive use of reporting illustrations enhance the value of the article. While taking as its reference point a hospital operating room, the authors suggest procedures of performance evaluation which can be used with very little modification by managers of many different activities.

Reporting and evaluating performance requires an accounting system capable of producing a reliable performance measure. Letzkus, in "Zero-Base Budgeting: Some Implications of Measuring Accomplishments," addresses the measurement issue. Although the discussion's purpose is to examine performance measurement problems associated with zero-base budgeting, the article is relevant to any budget type. Besides discussing the various kinds of measures, the author examines the equally important issue of behavioral results of performance measurement and the potential for dysfunctional consequences. An adequate reporting and evaluation system must start with clearly defined goals and objectives and proper measures. The latter must be judiciously applied and reported in a manner recognizing the motivational aspects of information. As the author suggests, this task becomes increasingly difficult as one moves from reporting the performance of the organization to performance of the subunit to performance of the individual.

The traditional application for zero-base budgeting is the budget cycle of the programming, budgeting, and review sequence. Brown in "Beyond Zero-Base Budgeting," however, illustrates ways of employing ZBB concepts in the perofrmance review cycle. These applications have advantages of making ZBB more amenable to smaller organizations, enabling small as well as larger organizations to apply ZBB techniques more effectively.

Brown discusses two additional performance review techniques: sunset legislation and performance auditing. Besides describing how these systems overlap in their intended purposes, Brown concludes with an effective checklist that management can use in helping to decide which review system should be used.

BETTER COST CONTROL WITH FLEXIBLE BUDGETS AND VARIANCE ANALYSIS

William W. Holder and Jan Williams

Cost analysis, understanding and control is one of the most important functions of hospital management. If costs are not regularly scrutinized and compared to predetermined standards, they may creep up unnoticed, presenting significant operational and cash flow problems. Although Public Law 92-603 requires formulation of a forecast one-year operating budget and current Social Security Administration regulations further require detailed cost finding and statistical cost allocation; the underlying causes of cost deviations from budgets may still go undetermined.

Cost *control* and *understanding* is especially important in an industry such as health care which has an unusually high fixed cost structure. Studies indicate that from 66 to 85 percent of all hospital costs are fixed costs.[1] Changes in volume of utilization and activity thus have dramatic effects upon the cost per unit of activity and the general financial well-being of hospitals. Therefore, full and complete understanding of cost variations is currently important for effective operations and is even more necessary when the implications of possible programs of prospective rate setting are considered.

This article attempts to demonstrate methods and techniques which might be usefully adopted in a program of cost analysis and control. The discussion does not cover a complete system of hospital cost analysis because of operational differences among hospitals and even among functional areas within a single institution. A general model for cost analysis

Source. Copyright © 1976 by the Hospital Financial Management Association. Reprinted with permission from *Hospital Financial Management* (January, 1976), pp. 12–20.

[1]Richard Houser, "Cost Variation with Volume in a Non-Federal, Short-Term General Hospital," unpublished Ph.D. dissertation, University of Wisconsin, 1971, p. 13.

and control is presented. It is both logical and relatively simple to apply and can substantially enhance the operational effectiveness of hospitals.

The first portion of this article develops in some detail hypothetical data for a typical operating room. Again, let us stress that the model has general applications to many hospital cost centers and can be adopted either partially or completely depending upon the needs of the institution in question.

AN OPERATING ROOM MODEL

This model not only will employ detailed variance analysis but will also incorporate the additional analytical powers of flexible or variable budgeting. The information needed and the steps employed in this analysis are:

1 The preparation of an expected budget based on cost estimates and a measure of activity.
2 The application of the flexible budget technique to the activity level achieved in a specific budget period.
3 The comparison of the actual costs with the flexible budget for the activity level achieved to identify cost variances.
4 The identification of variance causes and the incorporation of corrective action.

It should be noted throughout that this analysis is based on currently existing data and that no significant additional data are necessary.

FLEXIBLE BUDGETING

A flexible budget is a budget designed for various levels of activity rather than for a single level. The flexible budget allows one to determine the costs which should have existed, based on predetermined cost behavior patterns, for various levels of activity. Horngren, a leading writer in the general area of cost

control, describes the flexible budget approach:

. . . flexible budgets . . . have the following distinguishing features: (a) They are prepared for a range of activity instead of a single level. (b) They supply a dynamic basis for comparison because they are automatically geared to change in volume. The flexible-budget approach says, "You tell me what your activity level was during the past week or month, and I'll provide a budget that specifies what costs *should have been*. I'll tailor a budget to the particular volume—after the fact."[2]

Flexible budgeting is not a new idea in hospital cost control literature. Boer and Parris describe the general flexible budgeting approach in "Flexible Budgeting: A Cost Control Tool." They conclude: "Flexible budgeting won't solve all cost control problems, but it is a start in the right direction toward effective cost control."[3] The advantages of flexible budgeting as opposed to a static approach are further expanded by Seawell in *Hospital Financial Accounting Theory and Practice* in which he concludes that a fixed budget is useless and perhaps even misleading.[4]

Table 1 presents a flexible budget–cost comparison for the operating room. Key to the preparation of this analysis are the determination of the normal level of activity, the estimation of costs at this level of activity, and the application of these standards to the actual level of activity experienced in the example, it is estimated that 75 percent of maximum capacity is a reasonable level of activity which may be expected in the period under analysis (col-

[2]Charles Horngren, *Cost Accounting: A Managerial Emphasis* (Englewood Cliffs, N.J.: Prentice-Hall, Inc., 1972) p. 227.
[3]Germain Boer and Walter Parris, "Flexible Budgeting: A Cost Control Tool," *Planning the Hospital's Financial Operations* (Chicago: Hospital Financial Management Association, 1972) p. 92.
[4]L. Vann Seawell, *Hospital Financial Accounting Theory and Practice* (Chicago: Hospital Financial Management Association, 1975) p. 133.

TABLE 1
Operating Room Flexible Budget—Cost Comparison
100 Percent Capacity = 600,000 Minutes

	Column 1		Column 2		Column 3		Column 4	
	Normal Budget: *75% Capacity*[a]	%	*Budget for* *Actual Activity*[a]	%	*Actual* *Experience*	%	*Variance*	%
Major surgery	4,450		4,895		4,895			
Minor surgery	1,650		2,315		2,315			
OR minutes	450,000		510,000		534,000		24,000	4.9
Direct costs								
Variable:								
Salaries	$100,000	18.7	$113,333	18.7	$126,500	20.4	$ 13,167	11.6
Supplies	125,000	23.4	141,667	23.4	175,000	28.1	33,333	23.5
Total variable	$225,000	42.1	$255,000	42.1	$301,500	48.5	$ 46,500	18.2
Fixed:								
Salaries/supervision	$280,000	52.3	$317,333	52.3	$295,000	47.5	($22,333)	(7.0)
Space equipment	30,000	5.6	34,000	5.6	25,000	4.0	(9,000)	(26.5)
Total fixed	$310,000	57.9	$351,333	57.9	$320,000	51.5	($31,333)	(8.9)
Total costs	$535,000	100%	$606,333	100%	$621,500	100%	$15,167	2.5%

	Cost Application Rates	Budget Amount for Actual Experience
	(based on 450,000 minutes)	(applied to 510,000 minutes)
Variable costs:		
Salaries	$100,000/450,000 = .2222	.2222 × 510,000 = $113,333
Supplies	$125,000/450,000 = .2778	.2778 × 510,000 = 141,667
Total variable	.5000	.5000 × 510,000 = $255,000
Fixed costs:		
Salaries/supervision	$280,000/450,000 = .6222	.6222 × 510,000 = $317,333
Space/equipment	$ 30,000/450,000 = .0667	.0667 × 510,000 = $ 34,000
Total fixed	.6889	.6889 × 510,000 = $351,333
Total	1.1889	1.1889 × 510,000 = $606,333

[a]Budgeted time for actual level of experience:
  major surgery: 4895 × 90 minutes = 440,550
  minor surgery: 2315 × 30 minutes = 69,450
                                      510,000

umn 1). At this level of activity it is further estimated that 4,450 major and 1,650 minor surgeries will be performed. Major surgeries are expected to take 90 minutes; minor surgeries are expected to take 30 minutes. Thus, total operating room minutes at the normal level of activity would be 450,000:

Major surgeries: 4,450 × 90 minutes = 400,500
Minor surgeries: 1,650 × 30 minutes = 49,500

                                       450,000

Costs at this level of activity should be developed based on past experience and known or expected differences in cost behavior during the budget period. This allows the preparer to develop cost application rates for flexible budgeting purposes, based on the normal or expected level of activity (see note 1 of Table 1).

The actual budget used for cost analysis and control should be based on the actual level of performance achieved, not on the expected or normal level of performance. Such flexible budget figures are developed in column 2 of Table 1 in which the cost application rates based on the normal activity level are applied to the actual level of activity: 4,895 major surgeries and 2,315 minor surgeries or the budget level of 510,000 operating room minutes. The variable cost figures, which fluctuate with changes in activity level, are those expected to exist at the activity level experienced. The fixed costs are actually not expected to vary as one might conclude from the cost analysis. On the contrary, the purpose of the fixed cost budgeted figures at the 510,000 minute activity level is to demonstrate the cost advantage of spreading fixed costs over a greater volume of activity (i.e., more operations requiring more operating room time) than was originally expected.

Column 3 of Table 1 includes the actual costs experienced during the period. Column 4 demonstrates the variance from the budget by comparing columns 2 and 3, the actual experience with the flexible budget figures for that level of activity.

VARIANCE ANALYSIS

These flexible budgeting techniques significantly expand the ability of management to assess budget cost variances. However, the full meaning and underlying causes of these deviations are still hidden and require additional analysis. The variances presented in column 4 of the operating room flexible budget—cost comparison do not provide adequate information to allow management to make knowledgeable corrective action. Therefore, additional detailed variance analysis is necessary for adequate cost control. It should be noted that this concept of variance analysis applied to hospitals is not completely novel. Price has previously demonstrated somewhat similar variance analysis for revenue accounts in a selected ancillary department of a hospital.[5]

Actual total direct operating room expenses exceeded standard operating room costs (for the level of activity achieved) by $15,167. Although this total variance is "explained" in Table 1 by the line item variances isolated in column 4, no causal relationships can be established. Thus, superficial inspection of the original variances can result in the drawing of erroneous conclusions based on incomplete information. In Table 2, operating room cost analysis #1, the variances are divided into causal components, reflecting radical fluctuations and offsetting subvariances summing to the total variance of $15,167.

SPENDING VARIANCE

The first variance isolated is for price differences between actual and planned costs. Since fixed cost totals are not expected to change over a range of operating levels, only the original budgeted totals for fixed costs are included in the budget allowance computed for actual time consumed. Variable costs, however, are extended at the predetermined standard rate ($.5000/minute) by the actual minutes (534,000) used. The resulting total of $577,000 fixed and variable costs represents the expected cost level for the actual operating time used. Thus, an unfavorable variance of $44,500 emerges which is related exclusively to spend-

[5]James W. Price, "What's Really in a Budget Variance?" *Planning the Hospital's Financial Operations* (Chicago: Hospital Financial Management Association, 1971) p. 131.

TABLE 2
Operating Room Cost Analysis #1, Overall Variance Analysis

Computation			
A. Actual total expenses incurred		= $621,500	
			$44,500 U. spending variance
B. Budget allowance @ actual time fixed costs expected (budgeted):	= 310,000		
variable cost expected:			
534,000 (minutes) × .5000 (variable cost rate)	= 267,000	= $577,000	
			($57,870) F. Utilization variance
C. Budget allowance @ standard rate 534,000 (minutes) × 1.1889 (total cost rate)		= $634,870	
			$28,537 U. Time var.
D. Standard costs: 510,000 (minutes) × 1.889 (total cost rate)		= $606,333	
		Total variances	$15,167 U.

ing levels. This variance is further discussed in a later section of this article.

UTILIZATION VARIANCE

The second variance isolated is the effect of using the facility at a higher or lower utilization rate than previously budgeted. Obviously, as fixed csts are spread over additional levels of activity, each incremental unit added will allow all units to absorb smaller amounts of the same total fixed cost. Thus, the utilization variance depicts the dollar impact of this fixed cost spreading effect. The total standard cost rate of $1.1889/minute was determined at the original budgeted level of activity. The fixed portion of the total standard cost rate is $.6889/minute only at the standard level of activity (450,000 minutes). To the extent that actual utilization differs from 450,000 minutes a utilization, variance will emerge. The $57,870 variance represents the dollar impact of utilizing the operating room for 84,000 more minutes than was forecast initially. In essence, the variance represents the dollar amount of the favorable economy of scale achieved by using the facility more intensely than planned.

TIME VARIANCE

The final variance isolated is the cumulative amount of time required to perform the particular activity in question. In this instance it "should" have taken 510,000 minutes to perform the surgeries actually accomplished. Since it took 534,000 minutes to do so, one can conclude that additional time and costs were involved in rendering these services. The measure of the additional costs may be determined by extending the total cost rate of $1.1889/minute by the difference between the actual time required (534,000) and the standard time (510,000) that was anticipated. One must note that this variance should not necessarily be considered unfavorable. This statistic indicates that the procedures performed may have been more complicated or sophisticated and thus required time in excess of that budgeted. Of course, this may have resulted in additional revenues and thus have a net favorable effect on hospital operations. Additionally, the detection of such alterations in the mix and complexity of services rendered provides timely, relevant information for future planning and forecasting.

TABLE 3
Operating Room Cost Analysis #2, Line-item Variance Analysis

Item	Actual	Spending Variance	Budget @ Actual	Utilization Variance	Budget @ Std.	Time Variance	Standard
Variable costs:							
Salaries	$126,500	$ 7,883 U	$118,667[a]	0	$118,667[a]	$ 5,334 U	$113,333
Supplies	175,000	26,667 U	148,333[a]	0	148,333[a]	6,666 U	141,667
Total variable	$301,500	$34,500 U	$267,000	0	$267,000	$12,000 U	$255,000
Fixed costs:							
Salaries/super.	$295,000	$15,000 U	$280,000	$52,270 F	$332,270[a]	$14,937 U	$317,333
Space/equip.	25,000	5,000F	30,000	5,600 F	35,600[a]	1,600 U	34,000
Total fixed	$320,000	$10,000 U	$310,000	$57,870 F	$367,870	$16,537 U	$351,333
Total costs:	$621,500	$44,500 U	$577,000	$57,870 F	$634,870	$28,537 U	$606,333

[a]Budget at standard

Item	Cost rate	Minutes	$
Variable:			
Salaries	.2222	534,000	$118,667
Supplies	.2778	534,000	$148,333
Fixed:			
Salaries/super.	.6222	534,000	$332,270
Space/equip.	.0667	534,000	$ 35,600

360

LINE-ITEM COST VARIANCES

Throughout this analysis the total operating room cost variance has been divided into three causal components: spending, utilization, and time. However, managers still face difficulty in responding to these variances with proper action because specific individual cost variances have not been isolated and remain obscure. Table 3, operating room cost analysis #2, depicts the three aspects of cost deviation for each individual direct cost included in the operating room cost center.

The analysis contained in this presentation does not differ in principle from the preceding one. The variances are merely isolated for each line item classification of cost within the cost center as opposed to total cost figures as was done in the first analysis. It is of interest to note that variable costs do not contribute either favorably or unfavorably to the utilization variance. Since variable costs have been defined as those that are responsive to changes in utilization, it follows that utilization changes alone will not give rise to variances when compared with a properly developed flexible budget.

This illustrates the unique power of combining flexible budgeting and variance analysis. Attributes of specific cost performance as well as deviations from forecasts are approached more from economic reality, providing accurate, relevant, and timely information for decision making.

A summary of the variances developed in Table 3 is presented in Table 4. It can be seen that the total cost variance of $15,167 is broken into 10 variances, each helpful in identifying the cause of the original total variance.

Once variances have been analyzed in this manner, hospital administrators will be in a better position to take corrective action. This includes more realistic estimates and forecasts of the future as well as alterations in purchas-

TABLE 4
Restatement of Operating Room Cost Variances

Variance	Amount		Causal Factor
Spending variances			
Salaries	$ 7,883		Price of goods and service unit
Supplies	26,667		purchased greater or less than
Salaries/supervision	15,000		budgeted price/unit
Space/equipment	(5,000)	$ 44,500	
Utilization variances			
Salaries/supervision	$(52,270)		Activity levels achieved greater
Space/equipment	(5,600)	(57,870)	or less than activity levels budgeted; relates exclusively to performance attributes of fixed costs and changing levels of utilization
Time variances			
Salaries	$ 5,334		Operations performed required
Supplies	6,666		more time to perform and
Salaries/supervision	14,937		complete than budgeted
Space/equipment	1,600	28,537	
Total variance		$ 15,167	

ing, hiring, and operating policies. Similar analysis can be fruitfully applied to many if not all of the other cost and revenue centers in a hospital.

ADDITIONAL CONSIDERATIONS

In some instances a further breakdown of variances may be possible. In fact, such a breakdown may be mandatory to identify portions of variances which can be controlled and to identify responsibility for those variances.

As an example of a further analysis, the *supplies spending variance* in the above model ($26,667U) will be analyzed in light of the following assumed additional information: (1) in general, prices in the economy rose 10 percent during the year under analysis, (2) specific prices of operating room supplies rose at a 13 percent rate during the year due to rapidly increasing prices in the petroleum, textile, and other underlying industries, and (3) supplies were used approximately evenly throughout the year. This last item of information means that supplies used early in the year were acquired at prices approximating those in

effect when the budget was set. Those used at the end of the year, however, were acquired at significantly higher prices.

The expanded breakdown of the supplies spending variance is presented in Table 5.

This breakdown of the supplies spending variance serves to illustrate the point that a part of any spending variance may be uncontrollable, particularly if chanigng prices account for part of the difference between actual and standard. In this situation, of the $26,667 total variance, $9,642 ($7,417 + $2,225) is accounted for by price changes and the remaining $17,025 is due to possible controllable factors such as inefficient acquisition practices and excessive or inefficient use of supplies.

In cases where it is estimated that the costs of supplies or services have risen at approximately the same rate as general price level, the step which breaks out the variance due to price increases in excess of general may be omitted. In the example above, this further analysis simply serves to highlight the point that inflation has fallen harder on this aspect of operations than on other aspects of operations or on the economy in general. An alternate tech-

---

TABLE 5
Operating Room Cost Analysis #3, Breakdown of Supplies Spending Variance

Actual cost of supplies used $175,000

Standard cost of supplies used
(restated for all price changes:
$148.333 × 106.5%[a]) $157,975

> $17,025
> controllable spending
> variance

Standard cost of supplies used
(restated for general price changes:
$148,333 × 105%[a] $155,750

> $ 2,225
> variance due to price
> increases in excess of
> general

Standard cost of supplies used
(unadjusted for price changes) $148,333

> $ 7,417
> variance due to general
> price increases

Total supplies spending variance $26,667

[a]The "average" price level for the year is used as an approximation:

$$106.5\% = \frac{100.0 + 113.0}{2}$$

$$105.5\% = \frac{100.0 + 110.0}{2}$$

nique to this breakdown is to anticipate the impact of inflation when setting the standard. For example, with an expected 10 percent rate of inflation the standard would have beeen set at approximately $155,750 rater than $148,333.

It should be further noted that the spending variance is based on supplies used, not supplies acquired. To the extent that a supplies inventory exists, a supplies purchased spending variance may be isolated. Another approach would be to compute the spending variance on supplies based on acquisition, not use. Such variances, initially isolated in a central stores cost center, could then be traced to the consuming department in the same manner as supply items are currently charged. However, this would involve substantially increased record keeping requirements, while the variance analysis presented in the operating room model would not.

CONCLUSION

The operating room model developed here illustrates the use of two analytical tools; variable (flexible) budgeting and variance analysis. While these techniques are typically identified with manufacturing operations, they can be applied to most if not all areas of a hospital.

The prerequisites for development of a functional system of variance analysis are a budget which separates fixed and variable cost, a measure of output for the activity or cost center under analysis, and a record of the actual costs experienced during the analysis period. Functional areas and output measures which may be useful for similar analysis in various areas of hospitals are suggested in Table 6.

While this type of analysis is currently useful as a cost control device, it is also important to note that programs of prospective rate setting are a likely possibility in the near future. Sattler states, "Prospective rate setting would place hospitals at financial risk and

TABLE 6
Selected Functional Areas and Output Variables

Functional Area	Measurable Output Variable
Special service centers	
Operating room	minutes
Delivery room	deliveries
Anesthesia	occasions of service
X-ray	films
Laboratory	examinations
Blood bank	transfusions
Inpatient centers	
Inpatients	patient days
CCU, ICU	CCU and ICU patient days
Nursery	newborn days
Outpatient centers	
Outpatients	occasions of service
Emergency	occasions of service
Cost centers	
Laundry	inpatient days, pounds of laundry
Housekeeping	inpatient days, hours of service
Dietary	inpatient days, meals served
Admitting	admissions

should, according to theory, encourage hospitals to: put increased emphasis on the identification and surveillance of the costs associated with the mix and output of various services provided."[6] He further notes that calls for the adoption of prospectively determined rates have been strong and have come from a wide variety of governmental and professional organizations. It would seem that hospital administrators would be well advised to become as familiar as possible with cost performance characteristics and tendencies within their institutions. Flexible budgeting with related cost variance analysis provides powerful tools in understanding and controlling institutional costs.

[6]Fredric L. Sattler, "Hospital Prospective Rate Setting—Issues and Options," 55A/Interstudy, 1975, p. 3.

ZERO-BASE BUDGETING: SOME IMPLICATIONS OF MEASURING ACCOMPLISHMENTS

William C. Letzkus

Much of the literature as to public sector financial planning, budgeting, and management has over time addressed the need to measure performance. Performance measures are needed both to measure the accomplishment of stated objectives (effectiveness) and to assess these accomplishments in terms of resources used (efficiency).

The purpose of this study is to identify and briefly discuss certain of the problems associated with the identification and measurement of the accomplishments of public sector programs/organizations.[1] Also addressed are a number of behavioral implications inherent in any performance measurement system. For simplicity, the assumption is made that costs can be reasonably well identified to relevant public sector programs.

The need for some measure(s) of accomplishment was and is integral to the concept of PPB (planning-programming-budgeting) and cost–benefit analysis. More recently, Title VII of the Congressional Budget and Impoundment Control Act of 1974 has called for greater emphasis on review and evaluation of the results of government programs and activities. Similarly, the requirement for periodic assessments of the costs and benefits (accomplishments) of all Federal programs has surfaced with the proposed Government Economy and Spending Reform Act of 1976 (S.2925), the so-called sunset legislation.

Of immediate concern, however, is the zero-base budgeting (ZBB) concept which President Carter has directed be used in the preparation of the fiscal 1979 budget. In its most basic sense, a ZBB system requires the annual analysis, evaluation, and ranking of all existing and proposed discrete activities, functions, and operations (hereafter called programs) in terms of anticipated costs and benefits. These actions require that the following data be identified for each program:

- Purpose, goal(s), or objective(s) of the program
- Consequences of not continuing or implementing the program
- Performance measure(s)
- Alternative(s)
- Costs and benefits

The matching of costs and revenues is fundamental to the profit-oriented private sector and is ably discussed throughout the accounting literature. But what of the public sector? In the absence of profits, how is public sector performance (accomplishments) to be measured?

Given a ZBB environment, the very existence of a proposed or existing program may well depend on the identification and measurement of its accomplishments or benefits. The "reward" is program continuation or implementation, the "penalty" is . . .

THE NEED FOR CLEARLY STATED OBJECTIVES

Since the authorized activities of public sector programs and organizations are presumably established within the parameters of relevant objectives, it follows that an assessment of

Source. Reproduced with permission from *The Government Accountants Journal* (Summer, 1978), pp. 34–42.

efficiency and effectiveness will concomitantly provide some measure of assessment of the extent to which these objectives have been achieved. An explicit articulation of objectives is thus required.

Most authorities believe that it is impossible to evaluate the effectiveness of public sector management in the absence of a clear, unambiguous statement of objectives which identifies performance standards and expectations over the period of time in question. In this vein, the ZBB implementing instructions of the Office of Management and Budget state:

Program and organization objectives should be explicit statements of intended output, clearly related to the basic need for which the program or organization exists. The task of identifying objectives requires the participation by managers at all levels to determine the ultimate realistic outputs or accomplishments expected from a program or organization (major objectives) and the services or products to be provided for a given level of funding during the budget year (short-term objectives).

As objectives are identified, managers should simultaneously determine the key indicators by which performance and results are to be measured. Agencies should specify measures of effectiveness, efficiency, and workload for each decision unit. . . .[2]

The ZBB concept thus explicitly requires a clear statement of program objectives. While such statements can be made a prerequisite of new or proposed programs, what of existing programs? In particular, how does one now articulate the objectives and performance measures of those programs previously established through the legislative process?

Past efforts to evaluate public sector programs have frequently encountered difficulties due to a failure to clearly state program objectives. For example, one may well ask the objective(s) of the Federal food stamp program or of the various Federal programs which provide aid to education. Failure to specify objectives may be intentional in order to secure political agreement of divergent interests.

Such failure severely inhibits, however, the assessment of program/organizational performance.

The General Accounting Office (GAO) is among those encountering difficulties in the evaluation of social programs. No matter what program was reviewed, the GAO has encountered an absence of clear, specific program goals and objectives. A second, pervasive problem has been the lack of usable program performance data. For social programs, there are few standards by which to measure performance.[3]

Quite obviously, the basic requirement of any program evaluation is a clear, specific statement of objectives. Assuming, perhaps heroically, that these objectives have been clearly and specifically stated, one is next faced with the requirement to determine how best to assess program/organizational performance.

IDENTIFICATION OF BENEFITS

In order to justify its existence, every organization or program must accomplish something. It must provide either tangible goods or intangible services. If the output is in the form of intangible services—as is the case with most government programs/entities—it is often difficult, if not impossible, to identify this output.

There are two basic problems as to the identification of performance measures for government operations. One relates to the differentiation between measures of work accomplished and the effectiveness of goal accomplishment. The second problem is the determination as to whether single, multiple, or composite measures will provide a true measure of performance.

WORKLOAD VERSUS EFFECTIVENESS

How does one differentiate between the services provided and the results of these services? Anthony and Herzlinger differentiate performance measures as (1) results measures,

(2) process measures, and (3) social indicators.[4] The AAA Committee on Concepts of Accounting Applicable to the Public Sector (1970–71) discusses this differentiation in terms of (1) operations indicators, (2) program impact indicators, and (3) social indicators.[5] For the most part these (and other) classifications are essentially the same.

Operations Indicators.   Operations indicators are measures associated with the outputs of activities and are indicators in nonfinancial terms of what is produced for the money and effort expended. Largely workload and performance statistics, these measures provide little insight into how well needs or objectives are being met. Operations indicators are often selected on the basis of simplicity of understanding and data availability rather than on the basis of relevance and include the kind of data commonly used for the determination of unit costs.

Operations indicators would include such measures as hours or sorties flown, work orders processed, engines repaired, tickets issued, students graduated, hours or weeks of training, meals served, etc. These measures indicate work performed. They do not, however, indicate the quality of performance nor the results achieved.

Frequently there is a temptation to measure the resources applied to the attainment of program/organizational objectives rather than to measure attainment of these objectives. This misplaced emphasis is more likely to occur with the more intangible objectives and may lead to viewing resource utilization as an end in itself, to the neglect of the actual objectives. An example of such a situation would be the measurement of direct maintenance man-hours used to accomplish operational requirements rather than measurement of the attainment of the maintenance objectives, per se.

Program Impact Indicators.   Program impact indicators are directly related to a public need

or policy and (theoretically) are expressed in or implied by stated program objectives. Outputs of programs should be described in terms that provide a basis for evaluating actual against planned accomplishments. These indicators generally are relevant to levels above the operating level. Examples of program impact indicators are aircraft or vehicular accidents averted, wages earned and welfare costs avoided due to handicapped persons being made self-sufficient, the change in the amount of pollutants in the atmosphere or in water etc.

Social Indicators.   Social indicators reflect changes in social conditions. These changes may result from a single program, but more likely reflect the results of a combination of programs. National defense is a public good which influences the "quality of life." The problem is to find a social indicator(s) which measures national defense.

A Spectrum of Measures.   The three classes of performance indicators form a spectrum—a spectrum wherein the identification of benefits/accomplishments and their measurement become increasingly difficult as one moves from the concrete to the abstract. At one end of the spectrum are indicators which are easily understood and applied (quantified), but give little indication of accomplishment. As one moves along this spectrum, indicators of increasing relevance for program evaluation may be identified. However, they become increasingly difficult to quantify. At the opposite end, indicators are more closely related to the social objectives of the program than at any point along the spectrum. These indicators are, however, extremely difficult to identify and quantify.[6]

Single, Multiple, or Composite Measures

A single index measure may provide misleading information and the user thereof must recognize its limitations. Reliable measurements of programs thus frequently require the specification of various dimensions; i.e., multiple measures rather than single measures may be requisite. These multiple indicators may in turn be combined into a single overall index to measure all dimensions. Development of a single overall index requires weighting the relative importance of the various dimensions and indicators and choosing the statistical procedures to represent their relative value. One must avoid, however, over-reliance on the quantiative dimensions of performance measurement vis-à-vis the qualitative dimensions.

Single Measures. V. F. Ridgway discusses the issue of whether to use single, multiple, or composite measures on the basis of other studies in the field of performance measurement. With respect to a single criterion, he notes:

In all studies mentioned above, the inadequacy of a single measure of performance is evident. Whether this is a measure of an employee at the working level, or a measure of management, attention is directed away from the overall goal. The existence of a measure of performance motivates individuals to effort, but the effort may be wasted . . . or may be detrimental to the organization's goal. . . .[7]

One of the dangers of relying on a single quantitative measure is the very fact that such a measure cannot normally address all facets of an organization's or program's activity. There are dimensions of activity—"hidden outputs"—which cannot be included in a single performance criterion. Under such circumstances, when pressed by a higher authority to decrease its costs in relation to its output, an organization may simply divert resources from hidden or unreported outputs to the output being measured.

Multiple Measures. Multiple measurements offer somewhat greater promise as to an ade-

quate and fair measurement of performance. Here too, however, problems exist. Two basic and interrelated problems are (1) that action on one measure might adversely influence another measure(s) and (2) that there must be some explicit weighting or hierarchy of measures so as to direct management effort to the most important areas. Again referring to Ridgway's observations:

The use of multiple criteria assumes that the individual will commit his or the organization's efforts, attention, and resources in greater measure to those activities which promise to contribute the greatest improvement to overall performance. There must then exist a theoretical condition under which an additional unit of effort or resources would yield equally desirable results in overall performance, whether applied to production, quality, research, safety, public relations, or any of the other suggested areas. . . .

Without a single overall composite measure of performance, the individual is forced to rely upon his judgment as to whether increased effort on one criterion improves overall performance, or whether there may be a reduction in performance on some other criterion which will outweigh the increase in the first. This is quite possible, for in any immediate situation many of these objectives may be contradictory to each other.[8]

Composite Measures. Composite measures require an implicit or explicit weighting of the various (and sometimes conflicting) objectives and criteria by which performance is to be evaluated. Such measures are not, however, a panacea as to the problems of performance. Ridgway, in discussing the observations presented in several studies of composite performance measures, noted ". . . a clear indication that their use may have adverse consequences for the overall performance of the organization."[9]

These adverse consequences include tension, role and value conflicts, communications distortions and blockages, etc. A basic cause for these adverse consequences was found to be that whereas under a system of multiple measurement criteria an individual might relieve pressure by emphasizing one criterion vis-à-vis a second criterion, such relief is not normally possible with a composite criterion. Ridgway goes on to discuss the common situation wherein goals were raised without a concomitant increase in available resources—the "ratchet principle." Under such circumstances workers may tacitly agree to restrict their output so as to avoid future "quota" increases.[10]

Measurement of Benefits

Concomitant with and inseparable from the problem of identifying measures which adequately describe performance is the problem of measuring these measures. It serves no useful purpose to identify a performance measure which cannot itself be measured. In such instances one frequently encounters the use of operations indicators (workload statistics). Although these indicators shed little light on what is accomplished by the utilization of program resources, they do at least provide some measure of program magnitude.

Even the use of operations indicators is not assurance, however, that measurement problems will be resolved. These measures may themselves present some problems of quantification.

Indirect Measures.   Available data frequently do not provide a basis for adequately measuring stated mission objectives. Even if data on several performance indicators are available, it may not be feasible to combine them into a single index due to the fact that these various measures are not additive or comparable. Given either of these circumstances, one is faced with the necessity of selecting a performance indicator(s) which may only indirectly measure the accomplishment of stated mission objectives (or some dimension thereof).

An excellent example of a mission objective within the defense establishment which cannot be directly measured is the general objective of deterring aggression and the resultant mission requirement of defense organizations to maintain a capability to perform. The basic problem here is to distinguish between and measure actual operating performance vis-à-vis maintenance of a capability to perform. One might measure the operating performance of a B-52 squadron in terms of operations indicators such as the number of hours flown or the number of sorties flown. How does one measure, however, the maintenance of a capability to perform within parameters of time and effectiveness?

The basic difficulty under these circumstances is that whereas actual operating performance presumably can be measured in quantitative terms (assuming an appropriate measure has been identified), maintenance of a capability to perform is quite difficult to measure in quantiative terms alone—qualitative measures are required. But qualitative measures in turn present such additional problems as being subjective in nature and nonadditive in measurement.

Measurement of Collective Attributes.   Much of the data available for measuring the attainment of program objectives is based on the formal organizational structure rather than along lines relevant to the parameters of program objectives. In many instances a number of organizations and/or programs may contribute to the attainment of the same objective(s). A basic measurement problem thus is to determine the benefits (accomplishments) to be attributed to each of the various contributing programs and organizations.

A question also exists as to which costs are relevant at the operating level to the various program objectives. A program or organization may work toward the attainment of a number of objectives. The various benefits (however defined) accruing from these efforts should be matched to the costs of attaining them. But what are the costs? Should total costs be matched against each of these benefits? Should it be marginal costs? But if marginal costs, how does one determine what are marginal costs and to which of the several benefits these costs accrue? Where performance measures are nonadditive and multiple measures exist, the problem could be quite complex.

Nonstationarity. Objectives and requirements change over time. Given this change, not only do the programs and organizations responsible for accomplishing these objectives change, the measures of accomplishment change. In short, measures of effectiveness must be adaptive over time in order to be relevant in a dynamic environment.

For example, a military organization's output often changes with changes in mission assignment. Whether this change is temporary or permanent, some measure of mission accomplishment must be provided. The measure(s) of accomplishment of a national guard unit relative to a natural disaster is quite different from the measure(s) associated with the unit's normal missions of training and maintaining a capability to perform.

BEHAVIORAL IMPLICATIONS

The preceding sections have addressed some of the problems associated with the identification and measurement of "benefits" accruing from government activities. The basic purpose of these discussions is to emphasize the scope and complexity of this area and to establish a basis for discussion of certain of the behavioral implications of a performance measurement system. Indeed, the very scope and complexity of measuring performance in terms of both efficiency and effectiveness is itself a basic contributing factor to one's attitudes toward a performance measurement system and one's actions thereunder.

The Influence of Standards. Integral to an assessment of performance is the establishment of performance standards. One's opinions as to whether these standards and their enforcement are fair and realistic will influence not only attitudes toward the performance measurement system, but actions as well.

These standards and the associated performance measurement system may or may not, however, achieve the desired results. As Douglas McGregor observes, most managers probably agree that a performance measurement system works—but rather less well then they desire. He goes on to identify some of the possible unintended consequences of a performance measurement system, viz.:

1 Widespread antagonism to the controls and to those who administer them.
2 Successful resistance and noncompliance by many employees at all levels within an organization up to the top (and sometimes there also).
3 Unreliable performance information because of employee antagonism and resistance to the administrative controls.
4 The need for close surveillance of employees. This results in a dilution of delegation, which cuts into managerial time and impedes the development of workers.
5 High administrative costs. [11]

Whatever standard of good performance is adopted, it is likely to be effective as a means of control only if the person being judged agrees that it is a good standard. Most authorities thus agree that managers will be more receptive to performance evaluation if they play some role in the development of performance standards.

Perceived Threat. A number of authorities discuss the possibility that performance evaluation may be perceived as a potential threat by those operating managers being evaluated against stated performance standards. McGregor emphasizes that the "threat" need not actually exist—opeating managers need only perceive a threat (real or imagined).

One fundamental reason control systems often fail and sometimes boomerang is that those who design them fail to understand that an important aspect of human behavior in an organizational setting is that *noncompliance tends to appear in the presence of perceived threat.*

This noncompliance takes the form of defensive, protective, resistant, aggressive behavior. Note that I have used the words 'perceived threat.' Feelings are facts! The question is not whether management believes the control procedures are threatening; the question is whether those affected by them feel they are.[12]

McGregor goes on to identify three conditions under which a threat is likely to be perceived. The first condition is where punishment is emphasized rather than offering support and help in meeting standards and objectives. A second condition under which threat may be perceived is where trust is lacking in the relationships between higher authority and the operating manager and between line and staff personnel who administer the control program(s). The third condition cited by McGregor arises when the feedback of information negatively influences the individual's self-esteem, his career expectations, and his emotional security in the employment relationship.[13]

It is indeed unfortunate that many financial management systems are introduced into the public sector with little, if any, thought given as to the behavioral implications of these systems. For example, the DOD introduced a system for management of operating resources (PRIME-Priority Management Efforts) with such statements as:

. . . output measures must be developed so that at any level both the operating manager and his superior can obtain an accurate picture of the rela-

tionship between input and output. Ultimately, this should permit the superior to gauge the operating manager's performance and, if warranted, give him greater control over his resources and more decision-making authority.[14]

Although comparisons between budgets and actual are vital to any sound management control system, operating managers were concerned that differences would be ascribed to mismanagement without the careful analysis necessary to pinpoint the causes of difference. There were (and still are) few valid, quantitative measures that would permit comparison of work done with resources consumed. Operating managers had had some experience with other management control systems— experience which was not always pleasant. One could hardly expect the announcement of a new and as yet untested management control system (performance measurement system if one prefers) to be greeted with enthusiasm.

A more current, perceived "threat" might be the implementation of zero-based budgeting (ZBB) into the Federal budget process. Given the difficulties of measuring public sector performance and the potential impact of ZBB on a program's "life or death," it is not unlikely that Federal managers will perceive ZBB as a threat. These perceptions may in turn engender the behavior noted earlier by McGregor.

Side Effects. A number of authors discuss the condition wherein data provided by the accounting system determines the actions of the operating manager—actions that may or may not be compatible with mission objectives stated by higher authority. Even where performance measures are instituted purely for purposes of information, they may well be interpreted as definitions of the important aspects of that job or activity and hence have important implications for the motivation of behavior.[15]

Performance measurement systems must

be careful to avoid unwanted side effects— effects which may result from poorly formulated measures of mission effectiveness and efficiency. Such measures may be susceptible to manipulation at the operating level and thus may adversely affect the attainment of stated mission objectives.

A frequently cited example of unintended "side effects" is the situation wherein pressure to decrease the cost per flying hour could cause an increase in the number of flying hours in order to spread the fixed costs over a larger base. Such an action would waste resources in a way detrimental to the mission objectives for which they were obtained.

Schultze discusses a number of areas wherein the attainment of desired objectives could be thwarted by inadequate specification of objectives and measures of performance. For example, inadequate specification of the multiple objectives sought by a manpower training program might result in the letting of an incentive contract which in turn might focus on retaining trainees for long periods to the detriment of desired outputs (e.g., training in a useful skill).[16]

Some of the more interesting examples as to poorly formulated performance measures are those in the area of the early socialist production systems. Among the many authors addressing this area, Schultze cites the example of the manager of a nail factory whose quota was based on the number of nails produced and who was rewarded as he made or exceed his quota. Under these circumstances the manager was "encouraged" to produce large numbers of nails, regardless of the market demand. Changing the production quota to a stated total weight of nails produced, the manager was now "encouraged" to produce a smaller number of very heavy nails—again without reference to market demand.[17]

The basic purpose of providing these examples is twofold. First, the examples indicate the fact that undesired side effects can occur in a wide variety of situations. Second, these examples emphasize a point made earlier in this study, the necessity of an explicit, accurate statement of mission objectives and output. The requirement for a careful specification of objectives and output may be, however, both an advantage and a disadvantage. It is an advantage because it forces a specific statement of objectives and the relative weights to be attached to various aspects of output. It is a disadvantage, however, because we often are literally unable, given the present state of knowledge, to specify objectives and assign weights to various aspects of performance with sufficient confidence to warrant the introduction of incentive systems.[18]

Competing Systems. A manager's performance may be measured by a number of competing management control systems. The operating manager's performance as to quality control may be measured by one system, his performance as to cost control by a second system, and his performance as to volume by yet a third system. Given these competing systems, the operating manager will tend to attach relative weights of importance to these three aspects of his performance. The problem is that this hierarchy of relative weights may not be what higher authority intended.

The problem presented here is similar to that discussed above as to multiple measures of performance. The basic distinction to note, however, is that the situation noted here explicitly assumes multiple control systems, a condition which may or may not exist with multiple measures.

The situation of multiple control systems is not uncommon to the public sector manager. Again using the example of a flying organization, the commander may be placed in the position of both meeting mission flying-hour requirements and reducing the cost of fuel consumption. Under such circumstances a decision must be made as to which competing goal is the more important. In a similar vein, the author has encountered the situation wherein the responsible manager was faced with the choice of reducing costs or justifying the retention of assigned motor vehicles (with retention based on the number of miles driven).

SUMMARY

Within the public sector the need for performance evaluation which adressed the dual criteria of efficiency and effectiveness is well established. The requirements of zero-based budgeting (ZBB) serve only to further emphasize this need. Significant problems exist, however, as to the identification and measurement of services or results provided by public sector programs.

Assuming a clear, explicit statement of program objectives, one must next identify the output or results of program operations. There must be a differentiation between workload accomplished and results achieved. Workload indicators are relatively concrete and easy to identify and quantify. They do not, however, measure the quality of program accomplishment (performance) nor the results achieved. Effectiveness and efficiency are abstract concepts which are difficult to define and measure.

One must also ensure that all major facets of program accomplishment are identified and included in the measure of operating performance. Are single, multiple, or composite measures required? Each approach has its strong points, but also its weaknesses and behavioral implications.

Concomitant with and inseparable from the problem of identifying performance measures is the problem of measuring these measures. It frequently is difficult, if not impossible, to construct a measure (or measures) that fairly and adequately addresses all major aspects of the relevant program objective(s). Among the problems encountered are (1) whether designated measures should be quantitative or qualitative, (2) how to measure the various dimensions of program objectives, (3) whether the measures of these dimensions are comparable or additive, and (4) whether one is attempting to measure means rather than objectives. Measurement problems also exist when one attempts to determine the extent to which program objectives have been achieved by the various contributing activities.

Performance standards and the related performance measurement systems may actually inhibit efficient and effective operations rather than contribute to the achievement of stated program objectives. Managers may perceive these standards and performance measurement systems as a threat and react accordingly. Similarly, a manager may receive conflicting signals from competing performance measurement systems. If the stated measures of performance are poorly formulated, they may provide the manager with an opportunity to manipulate performance data so as to make himself appear good—but at the expense of efficient and effective program operations.

Summarizing the GAO experiences with evaluating the effectiveness of social programs, Staats concludes:

> Our concepts and our methods of accounting for the results of social programs are primitive at best. We need to develop methods of accounting that not only will clearly show what we invest in these programs but what is accomplished in relation to what was sought.

> We need accounting techniques to measure the differences in social conditions. We need to know what happens to people affected by certain programs as compared to people who are not affected. [19]

The need for greater information as to what is being accomplished by government is an unassailable requirement of public sector accounting systems. This need is not, however, a sudden revelation of the zero-based budgeting concept. The requirement to measure public sector accomplishments has existed for many years, and there have been many attempts to resolve this need.

One cannot discount the difficulties of assessing the costs and benefits/accomplishments of public sector programs and of evaluating their impact. Given the adventt of zero-based budgeting, however, resolution of these problems may now be a matter of program "life or death."

NOTES

[1]For a more thorough discussion of the problems associated with this subject, see: U.S. Department of Health, Education and Welfare, *Toward a Social Report* (Washington: 1969); "Report of the Committee on Concepts of Accounting Applicable to the Public Sector, 1970–71," *The Accounting Review*, Supplement to Vol. XLVII (1972), pp. 80–86 and 98–106; "Report of the Committee on Non-Financial Measures of Effectiveness," *The Accounting Review*, Supplement to Vol. XLVI (1971), pp. 165–211; "Report of the Committee on Measures of Effectiveness for Social Programs," *The Accounting Review*, Supplement to Vol. XLVII (1972), pp. 336–396; "Report of the Committee on Nonprofit Organizations, 1973–74," *The Accounting Review*, Supplement to Vol. XLX (1975), pp. 1–39; and Charles L. Schultze, *The Politics and Economics of Public Spending* (Washington: The Brookings Institution: 1968); et al.

[2]Office of Management and Budget, *Zero-Base Budgeting*, Bulletin No. 77-9 (Washington; April 19, 1977), pp. 4–5.

[3]Elmer B. Staats, "Evaluating the Effectiveness of Federal Social Programs," *The Federal Accountant*, (December 1974), p. 30.

[4]Robert N. Anthony and Regina Herzlinger, *Management Control in Nonprofit Organizations* (Homewood, Ill; Richard D. Irwin, Inc; 1975), pp. 141–144.

[5]State-Local Finances Project. *Output Measures for a Multi-Year Program and Financial Plan-PPB Note 7* (Washington: The George Washington University; 1968), pp. 9ff, as discussed in "Committee on Concepts Applicable to the Public Sector," pp. 103–104.

[6]"Committee on Concepts Applicable to the Public Sector," p. 104.

[7]V. F. Ridgway, "Dysfunctional Consequences of Performance Measurements," in Alfred Rappaport (ed.), *Information for Decision Making* (Englewood Cliffs, N.J.: Prentice-Hall, inc; 1975), p. 348.

[8]Ibid., p. 350.

[9]Ibid., p. 351.

[10]Ibid.

[11]Douglas McGregor, "Do Management Control Systems Achieve Their Purpose?" *Management review*, Vol. 56, No. 2 (February, 1967), pp. 5–6.

[12]Ibid., p. 8.

[13]Ibid.

[14]U.S. Department of Defense, *A Primer on Project PRIME* (Washington: April, 1967), pp. 66–67.

[15]Ridgway, p. 351.

[16]Charles L. Schultze, "The Role of Incentives, Penalties, and Rewards in Attaining Effective Policy," in *The Analysis and Evaluation of Public Expenditures: The PPB System*, Vol. I, 91st Congress, 1st Session, a compendium of papers submitted to the Subcommittee on Economy in Government (Washington, 1969), p. 222.

[17]Ibid., pp. 221–222.

[18]Ibid., p. 222.

[19]Staats, p. 35.

BEYOND ZERO-BASE BUDGETING

Ray L. Brown

Have you or one of your clients ever asked: "Can my organization use zero-base budgeting (ZBB)? If so, how should it be implemented?"

Questions about the practicality and implementation of ZBB seem to come most often from small and medium-sized businesses where the standard ZBB system doesn't seem clearly applicable. According to an American Management Association's survey, more than half the businesses using ZBB had sales over $500 million, and, in the nonprofit area, 59% had over one thousand employees.

Even though small and medium-sized CPA firms and businesses may find that using ZBB would not be cost-effective, there are some aspects of the system that can be adapted for organizations of every size—from the federal government to the family unit. CPAs in practice and in industry should not overlook its potential. The key is to find out which aspects can be applied productively in a particular situation.

Because every organization's budgeting needs are different, those who recommend or implement ZBB systems keep modifying the standard ZBB systems to meet those differences. As a result, we now have ZBB, modified ZBB, bracket budgeting, simplified ZBB, and incremental ZBB plus many other titles which indicate that the ZBB concept can be tailored to meet specific requirements. Even

the format and types of forms used for ZBB are usually modified to meet each user's needs. And it is not unusual to find that the forms change from year to year or that different forms are used in different parts of the organization.

This article discusses the basic concepts of ZBB and then gives some ideas on how to effectively apply some of its aspects to any size company or CPA firm.

WHY ZBB IS POPULAR TODAY

ZBB became popular in the early 1970s, at a time when many organizations were having financial problems. There were a recession, double-digit inflation, and supply difficulties; in the public sector, the growth of revenues was falling far below the demand for growth in expenditures. An additional issue in both the private and public sectors was the continued increase in staff and services whose cost-effectiveness was questionable but could not be measured.

The old tried-and-true budget techniques were not adequate to handle all these problems. ZBB became useful in some cases. Its objective is to allocate resources to those operations contributing the most to an organization's goals. Although this is the objective of all budget systems, ZBB applies a relatively unused but helpful systematic approach.

Theoretically, the ZBB approach consists of:

1   Assuming nothing of value about current operations and functions.

Source. Copyright © 1981 by the American Institute of Certified Public Accountants, Inc. Reprinted with permission from *The Journal of Accounting* (March, 1981), pp. 44–48, 50, 52.

2 Rejustifying each operation and function annually.

3 Showing the cost of every budget program (old and new).

4 Presenting the output of each program.

5 Reviewing and ranking each program according to its cost-effectiveness, i.e., cost vs. output.

6 Making final a budget based on the highest cost-effective programs. In nonprofit organizations, programs are funded to the extent of forecasted revenues.

Most of the collected data is entered in a document labeled a decision package. This document contains one or more pages describing the activity and its relation to the organization's goals, cost inputs, effectiveness and efficiency output measurements, the impact of not continuing the activity, and space for ranking information.

Some organizations can adopt ZBB without too much difficulty. Production organizations in particular find much of the process easy for those operations with engineered input—output ratios because they already have the information needed for steps 3 to 5 above.

ZBB can usually be the most beneficial in determining staff and service costs. For example, there is no accepted standard on how many secretaries a personnel department needs or a set ratio of personnel department employees to total employees. ZBB decision packages (i.e., budget documentations) listing the functions, costs, and output of the personnel department at least give management information about the types of activities and related costs it wants to authorize.

PROBLEM AREAS

Most accountants see problems with ZBB. It is difficult for some organizations to categorize costs by department, much less by function,

and meaningful output measurements are difficult to generate. Once the output measurements are derived, the problem then becomes one of comparing them with the inputs (costs) in order to create a cost-effectiveness ratio. This ratio is necessary to rank one function against another, a difficult task because an objective input is being compared with a subjective output. It can be done, but it requires a high level of managerial experience and judgment.

Also, ZBB requires a lot of management time and paperwork (or computer time) to make it work well. For example, a manager may have to prepare four or five decision packages for each separate operation—a basic package covering anywhere from 50% to 80% of the cost of present operations; a second package covering some specified increment of current operations, e.g., 80% to 90%; a third package covering 90% to 100%; an enhanced package covering new activities; and a package covering alternative methods of doing the activity.

Finally ZBB is criticized because the decision packages must be prepared and evaluated each year for every continuing function such as the president's salary.

Because ZBB requires a lot of paperwork and time, and because it doesn't always result in a better budget, some critics even question whether ZBB is cost-effective. It really can be, especially if the following conditions are present:

- Many staff or service functions that lack engineered input—output ratios.

- A good accounting system.

- Managers at all levels who will diligently prepare decision packages.

- Output measurements that exist or can be generated.

- Top management that actively supports the system.

One thing to remember, though, is that, even though ZBB may not be cost-effective or even practical in your situation, it usually results in a good budget and almost without exception provides a complete overview of the financial management system.

There are, however, several ways to get the benefits of ZBB without going through the entire process or without going through it every budget cycle.

SUNSET

For example, the biggest proponent of ZBB (the government) has two related programs in process or under consideration—sunset legislation and performance auditing. Sunset means that a program or function will cease on a given date unless the state legislature votes to give it new life.

The principles of the sunset concept can also be applied to organizations. For example, an analysis of a client's various functions should reveal some areas that might be questionable in terms of overall effectiveness, efficiency, or economy—areas that management should analyze. These should be listed in order of priority. Priorities can be established on the basis of the dollar volume involved, your judgment concerning the degree of need for an in-depth review, or some other criteria you deem appropriate.

After placing the potential problem areas in order, the next step is to set up a time schedule indicating the inception and termination dates for each activity chosen for review. However, you may not want to adopt the full sunset concept where these functions cease to exist on a given date. This concept seems unnecessary—even in the governmental sector—since the majority of functions are retained as is or in a modified form as a result of the review. But a termination date does tend to motivate those involved to get their reviews finished on time.

How can the review be accomplished? There are two general approaches one can use: ZBB or performance auditing.

ZBB

The ZBB approach is more appropriate when one wants the managers involved to do their own analyses. Often, an organization finds that it receives a personal commitment from its managers if they themselves recommend the changes to be made. When used in this manner, ZBB does not have to be part of the budget process. Instead, one can stop after step 5 (review and rank). Those functions which are not cost-effective can be discarded or revised. The effect of any changes should be included in the next budget cycle. Westinghouse used ZBB in this manner with good results but did not use it as a regular budget tool.

Performance Auditing

Performance auditing is most appropriate when there is an internal audit function for nonfinancial auditing, when organizations use CPA firms or consultants who perform this type of auditing for them, or when management personnel can be assigned to this type of activity.

Performance auditing is used here as a generic term to mean nonfinancial auditing, but it also has several related names, e.g., operational auditing or management auditing. Basically, performance auditing is used to determine whether an activity contributes to goal achievement and whether tasks are accomplished efficiently and economically.

The federal government always intended to use performance auditing to supplement its ZBB program. In 1977, the director of the U.S. Office of Management and Budget (OMB) stated that performance auditing would be used for an in-depth analysis of any activity that looked questionable during the review and ranking of ZBB documentation. He was aware that ZBB alone would probably not provide the type of analysis needed to judge fully the merits of a given operation because so many operations were being lumped together in one decision package and because the packages did not analyze each operation from zero expenditures.

ADVANTAGES AND DISADVANTAGES OF PERFORMANCE AUDITING

Performance auditing has several advantages over ZBB. It:

1 Provides a greater in-depth analysis.
2 Requires no change in the budgeting or accounting systems.
3 Looks only at the activities where questions concerning effectiveness, economy, and efficiency have arisen.
4 Need not coincide with the budget cycle.
5 Can usually overcome the bias or myopia a manager may have in filling out the ZBB documentation for his or her own operation.
6 Need not be done every year or even more than once.
7 Is relatively more cost-effective than a complete change in budgeting systems.

ZBB has a built-in discipline, i.e., the budget cycle, that provides at least a perfunctory analysis of all the various activities within an organization. With performance auditing, particularly, there is no pressure of meeting a budget deadline, and therefore an in-depth analysis could be postponed or might even be abandoned.

MODIFIED ZBB

There is another approach to an in-depth analysis of the activities of an organization that also results in a budget. I call it modified ZBB because it accomplishes as much as, if not

more than, the ZBB approach. And it does it more simply, yet more professionally, than ZBB.

In the typical ZBB system, the basic decision package (steps 2 to 4) includes some level of current activity, e.g., from 0% to 80% of the present operations. (The federal government generally used 90%.) What this means is that the analysis is not really made from a base of zero but from a base of 80% to 90% of current operations, which is why one prominent authority has labeled ZBB as misleading. By starting at a base as great as 90%, for example, management is accepting 90% of last year's budget as being absolutely essential. Consequently, a wide variety of functions are all being labeled equally valuable to the organization, a situation that probably isn't true.

Georgia began its ZBB at a base of zero activity and quickly found that the volume of effort and the time involved were prohibitive. It then changed to an 80% base. Even then, 11,000 decision packages, i.e., budget documentation for a given function or level of operation, were prepared. This still proved to be too much to evaluate in an analytical manner. Even the federal government, starting at a 90% base, generated 23,000 decision packages, 10,000 of which were sent to the OMB for analysis and further processing. Even at this level, each decision package covered an average of almost $50 million in budget activities. Obviously an in-depth analysis was impossible, but, without this analysis, ZBB can hardly live up to its title of analyzing every program and function from the ground up.

A smaller organization probably cannot afford this much time and effort, even at a proportionally reduced dollar level of activity. And if one really has financial problems, the ZBB system does not lend itself to the kind of analysis that will address most of them. Thus, a smaller, more flexible, and more analytical budget system than ZBB is necessary.

The modified ZBB system described below

provides the type of budget analysis many organizations need and can afford since it focuses on only that portion of the budget that management really wants to analyze.

For example, if management needs to reduce costs by $100,000 or wants to cut current costs by that amount in order to start a new program, modified ZBB could operate in the following manner.

The current budget would be analyzed to determine where cuts could be made. Perhaps management believes that administrative and selling cost center, program, or function will be asked to submit a ZBB decision package for the least essential 10% of their costs. That is, as with unmodified ZBB, management least essential 10% of their costs. That is, as with unmodified ZBB, management accepts—at least initially—90% of last year's budget. It will normally ask to analyze more costs than the budget cut desired because it knows that some if not all of those areas analyzed will be found to be essential to meet current goals. This approach is certainly more sane than making a 5% across-the-board budget cut, which typically punishes the efficient manager and fosters a behavioral reaction to pad the budget in order to survive future arbitrary cuts.

The budget analysis procedures for the modified ZBB system are also quite different.

Under ZBB, each budget decision package is evaluated and then ranked. Typically, the ranking is done consecutively at various levels of management, beginning at lower levels. After all of the packages are listed, those ranked the highest are funded with available revenues. Those packages ranked the lowest may not be included in the budget at all.

Under modified ZBB, each decision package is analyzed by a team of top managers in conference with the operating managers affected. Top management can accept, reject, or partially accept each decision package. Thus, the modified system can avoid the all-or-nothing proposition of ZBB.

If a decision package is accepted, no further budget analysis is made of that particular function or program. However, when management completely or partially rejects a decision package, it has several courses of action. First, it reduces the budget by the dollar amount rejected. Additionally, it can ask for more decision packages, particularly if it rejects all of the packages submitted by one department. One organization using this system ultimately reduced a department's budget by 70%—with the department's budget manager's concurrence. (Management should also ask for more decision packages if it believes there were more vulnerable areas not included in the initial set.)

Under modified ZBB, top management is involved in every budget decision. Lower levels of management need not be involved in evaluating and ranking decision packages. They only have to prepare them for their 5%, 10%, etc., most vulnerable areas and only if requested to do so. Thus, operating managers prepare detailed justifications for only those parts of the budget where real decisions are likely to be made. Under ZBB, every function and program must be documented, reviewed, and ranked even when there is no question about their appropriateness, e.g., the president's salary.

Another advantage of the modified ZBB system is that it provides for more substantive budget discussions than other systems. Operating managers must talk to the top management and convince the executives that they have properly presented the least cost-effective portion of their operating budgets. They also get a chance to discuss the merits, problems, and impact of their total operations with higher-level managers. These discussions should lead to two other topics, too—areas in which further cuts can be made and those where there are opportunities for profitable growth or change.

The benefits of a modified ZBB system can be summarized as follows:

- More top management involvement in budget decisions.
- More substantive budget decisions.
- Shared decision making by operating and top managers.
- A basis for follow-up studies.
- Elimination of arbitrary budget cuts.
- Less paperwork.
- A more efficient budget.
- Only used as needed.

WHICH SYSTEM TO USE

Given these alternative budgeting and analysis systems, how can you decide when to use them in your firm or your client's company?

The answer depends on the problems you believe exist. The following information can help you decide which system is more appropriate for a given situation:

Use ZBB when you and/or management:

1 Believe that there are widespread budget problems.
2 Want a budget that presents the costs of all activities from the ground up rather than one in which only new programs and expanded portions of old programs are presented, i.e., a budget that provides more detail than the typical incremental budget.
3 Want to involve all managers in the budget process.
4 Desires an overview of the entire organization from a financial point of view.

Note that ZBB works best when top management actively supports the system, the budget department is willing to take the time to train managers, there is already a basic budget system with good accounting support, a large number of the costs are programmed or discretionary (as opposed to operations where engineered input–output ratios exist), and

people at all levels of the organization can judge the relative cost-effectiveness of their own programs and can rank them accordingly.

Use performance auditing when you and/or management:

1 Primarily want to look at only part of the organization.
2 Want a broader or more in-depth analysis than a budget system will provide, e.g., also want to look at effectiveness or want to analyze every cost from a base of zero.
3 Don't want to incorporate the analysis into the budget cycle or only want a one-time analysis.
4 Do not desire the objectives of ZBB.
5 Want an outsider's view of the operation(s) in question.

Use modified ZBB when you and/or management:

1 Want to make an in-depth analysis of only part of the budget.
2 Want to have substantive discussions of costs and budget decisions with the managers involved.
3 Do not want to alter the basic budget system.

HOW TO IMPLEMENT THE SYSTEM CHOSEN

Ordinary experience with budgeting should provide you with much of the general knowledge needed to implement these anlaysis and budget systems.

This is especially true for performance auditing, which is currently being used to generate material for management reports that list information believed to be of value to the client. There are a number of books and articles on performance auditing which can be reviewed to refresh or extend your knowleddge in this area.

ZZB is more complex than the majority of the budget systems in use today. A good reference covering the basic details of the procedures, forms, and training changes required for ZBB is *Zero-Base Budgeting Comes of Age.*[1] The details in this book can be modified to meet your or your clients' needs. The modifications are commonsense procedures to produce a budget in the environment in which you must operate. There is no standard ZBB system any more than there is a standard budget system of any type.

Modified ZBB is basically a case of deciding which costs will be analyzed and the form in which you want them presented. The key to this system is the in-depth discussions between the top management team and the operating managers. A book which describes how this system has been used is *Zero-Base Budgeting and Program Evaluation.*[2]

SUMMARY

ZBB became popular at a time when a plethora of financial problems was striking organizations. Older budget techniques did not and still do not seem to handle these problems too well.

ZBB seems to work best in large organizations, but even in these organizations it does not always work as well as its advocates and ZBB theory suggest.

Most organizations can successfully and economically use techniques other than ZBB to analyze the viability of their current operations and related budgets. Probably the two best techniques are performance auditing and a modified form of ZBB. The first provides an analysis of the effectiveness, efficiency, and economy of selected operations and also provides a lot of flexibility in the timing and depth of this analysis.

Modified ZBB not only provides the tools for developing better budgets but also presents top management and operating managers with a forum in which they can work together. Also, it eliminates many of the disadvantages of the ZBB systems currently in use.

Both performance auditing and modified ZBB are quite useful in organizations of all sizes but schould be of considerable value to small and medium-sized organizations because they can be applied selectively as management's needs and resources dictate.

[1]Logan M. Cheek, *Zero-Base Budgeting Comes of Age* (New York: AMACOM, 1977).
[2]Joseph S. Wholey, *Zero-Base Budgeting and Program Evaluation* (Lexington, Mass.: Lexington Books, 1978).